Social Motivation

Purposive, goal-directed behavior is one of the defining characteristics of human beings. This volume surveys the most recent theories and research on the psychological mechanisms involved in the planning and execution of motivated social behavior. The contributors are all leading international researchers, and their chapters discuss exciting topics such as how goals influence thinking and behavior, how affect and social motivation interact, how unconscious motivation operates, and the relationship between habits and intentions as sources of social action. The applications of contemporary research on motivation to practical questions in clinical, organizational, educational, and counseling psychology receive special attention. The book is written in a readable yet scholarly style. The chapters take a highly comprehensive and integrative approach, and the book should be of interest to students, practitioners, and researchers interested in the psychology of motivation and should also be suitable as an advanced textbook in this field.

Joseph P. Forgas is Scientia Professor of Psychology at the University of New South Wales, Sydney, Australia.

Kipling D. Williams is Professor of Psychology at Macquarie University, Sydney, Australia.

Simon M. Laham is a researcher in the school of Psychology, University of New South Wales, Sydney, Australia.

The Sydney Symposium of Social Psychology series

This book is Volume 5 in the Sydney Symposium of Social Psychology series. The aim of the *Sydney Symposia of Social Psychology* is to provide new, integrative insights into key areas of contemporary research. Held every year at the University of New South Wales, Sydney, the symposia deal with important integrative themes in social psychology, and the invited participants are leading researchers from around the world. For further details see the Web site at www.sydneysymposium.unsw.edu.au.

Previous books in the Sydney Symposium of Social Psychology series:

SSSP 1. FEELING AND THINKING: THE ROLE OF AFFECT IN SOCIAL COGNITION (Edited by Joseph P. Forgas). Contributors: Robert Zajonc (*Stanford*), Jim Blascovich and Wendy Mendes (*UC Santa Barbara*), Craig Smith and Leslie Kirby (*Vanderbilt*), Eric Eich and Dawn Macauley (*UBC*), Len Berkowitz et al. (*Wisconsin*), Leonard Martin (*Georgia*), Dan Gilbert (*Harvard*), Herbert Bless (*Mannheim*), Klaus Fiedler (*Heidelberg*), Joseph P. Forgas (*UNSW*), Carolin Showers (*Wisconsin*), Tony Greenwald, Marzu Banaji et al. (*U. Washington/Yale*), Mark Leary (*Wake Forest*), Paula Niedenthal and Jamin Halberstadt (*Indiana*). Cambridge University Press, New York, 2000; ISBN 0-521-64223-X (hardback), 0-521-01189-2 (paperback).

SSSP 2. THE SOCIAL MIND: COGNITIVE AND MOTIVATIONAL ASPECTS OF INTERPERSONAL BEHAVIOR (Edited by Joseph P. Forgas, Kipling D. Williams, and Ladd Wheeler). Contributors: Bill and Claire McGuire (*Yale*), Susan Andersen (*NYU*), Roy Baumeister (*Case Western*), Joel Cooper (*Princeton*), Bill Crano (*Claremont*), Garth Fletcher (*Canterbury*), Joseph P. Forgas (*UNSW*), Pascal Huguet (*Clermont*), Mike Hogg (*Queensland*), Martin Kaplan (*N. Illinois*), Norb Kerr (*Michigan State*), John Nezlek (*William & Mary*), Fred Rhodewalt (*Utah*), Astrid Schuetz (*Chemnitz*), Constantine Sedikides (*Southampton*), Jeffrey Simpson (*Texas A&M*), Richard Sorrentino (*Western Ontario*), Dianne Tice (*Case Western*), Kip Williams and Ladd Wheeler (*UNSW*). Cambridge University Press, New York, 2001; ISBN 0-521-77092-0 (hardback).

Continued following the Subject Index.

Social Motivation

Conscious and Unconscious Processes

Edited by

JOSEPH P. FORGAS
University of New South Wales

KIPLING D. WILLIAMS
Macquarie University

SIMON M. LAHAM
University of New South Wales

 **CAMBRIDGE**
UNIVERSITY PRESS

PUBLISHED BY THE PRESS SYNDICATE OF THE UNIVERSITY OF CAMBRIDGE
The Pitt Building, Trumpington Street, Cambridge, United Kingdom

CAMBRIDGE UNIVERSITY PRESS
The Edinburgh Building, Cambridge CB2 2RU, UK
40 West 20th Street, New York, NY 10011-4211, USA
477 Williamstown Road, Port Melbourne, VIC 3207, Australia
Ruiz de Alarcón 13, 28014 Madrid, Spain
Dock House, The Waterfront, Cape Town 8001, South Africa

http://www.cambridge.org

First published 2005

Printed in the United States of America

Typeface Palatino 10/12 pt.   *System* LaTeX 2_ε [TB]

A catalog record for this book is available from the British Library.

Library of Congress Cataloging in Publication Data
Social motivation : conscious and unconscious processes / edited by Joseph P. Forgas,
Kipling D. Williams, Simon M. Laham.
    p.   cm.
Includes bibliographical references and index.
ISBN 0-521-83254-3
1. Motivation (Psychology) – Social aspects.   I. Forgas, Joseph P.   II. Williams, Kipling D.
III. Laham, Simon M.
BF503.S65   2004
153.8 – dc22   2004043509

ISBN 0 521 83254 3 hardback

Contents

About the Editors   *page* xi

List of Contributors   xiii

Preface   xvii

  1 Social Motivation: Introduction and Overview   1
     Joseph P. Forgas, Kipling D. Williams, and Simon M. Laham

PART I. CONSCIOUS AND UNCONSCIOUS SOCIAL MOTIVATION:
GENERAL ISSUES

  2 Multiple Goals, Optimal Motivation, and the Development
    of Interest   21
     Judith M. Harackiewicz, Amanda M. Durik, and Kenneth E. Barron

  3 The Machine in the Ghost: A Dual Process Model of
    Defense Against Conscious and Unconscious
    Death-Related Thought   40
     Tom Pyszczynski, Jeff Greenberg, and Sheldon Solomon

  4 Habits and the Structure of Motivation in Everyday Life   55
     Wendy Wood and Jeffrey M. Quinn

  5 Motivation in Social Settings: Studies of Effort-Related
    Cardiovascular Arousal   71
     Guido H. E. Gendolla and Rex A. Wright

  6 Reflection and Impulse as Determinants of Conscious and
    Unconscious Motivation   91
     Fritz Strack and Roland Deutsch

  7 The Role of Motivation in the Unconscious: How Our
    Motives Control the Activation of Our Thoughts and Shape
    Our Actions   113
     Steven J. Spencer, Steven Fein, Erin J. Strahan, and Mark P. Zanna

PART II. SOCIAL MOTIVATION: COGNITIVE AND AFFECTIVE
IMPLICATIONS

8 From Evolved Motives to Everyday Mentation: Evolution,
   Goals, and Cognition   133
   Steven L. Neuberg, Douglas T. Kenrick, Jon K. Maner,
   and Mark Schaller

9 Automatic Goal Inference and Contagion: On Pursuing
   Goals One Perceives in Other People's Behavior   153
   Henk Aarts and Ran R. Hassin

10 The Interaction Between Affect and Motivation in Social
    Judgments and Behavior   168
    Joseph P. Forgas and Simon M. Laham

11 Internal and External Encoding Style and Social
    Motivation   194
    Pawel Lewicki

12 Authenticity, Social Motivation, and Psychological
    Adjustment   210
    Michael H. Kernis and Brian M. Goldman

13 Motivation and Construct Accessibility   228
    Nira Liberman and Jens Förster

PART III. CONSCIOUS AND UNCONSCIOUS SOCIAL MOTIVATION:
SOME CONSEQUENCES AND APPLICATIONS

14 Self-Regulatory Processes in Interracial Interactions: The
    Role of Internal and External Motivation to Respond
    without Prejudice   249
    Patricia G. Devine, Amanda B. Brodish, and Stephanie L. Vance

15 Exploring the Discrepancy Between Implicit and Explicit
    Prejudice: A Test of Aversive Racism Theory   274
    Leanne S. Son Hing, Greg A. Chung-Yan, Robert Grunfeld,
    Lori K. Robichaud, and Mark P. Zanna

16 Ostracism: When Competing Motivations Collide   294
    Wayne A. Warburton and Kipling D. Williams

17 Attentional and Regulatory Mechanisms of Momentary
    Work Motivation and Performance   314
    Howard M. Weiss, Neal M. Ashkanasy, and Daniel J. Beal

18 Social Motivation and Object Relations: Narcissism and
    Interpersonal Self-Esteem Regulation   332
    Frederick Rhodewalt

19 To Know or Not to Know: Consciousness,
   Meta-consciousness, and Motivation 351
   Jonathan W. Schooler and Charles A. Schreiber

Author Index 373
Subject Index 383

About the Editors

Joseph P. Forgas received his DPhil and subsequently a DSc from the University of Oxford. He is currently Scientia Professor of Psychology at the University of New South Wales, Sydney, Australia. He has also spent various periods of time working at the Universities of Giessen, Heidelberg, Stanford, Mannheim, and Oxford. His enduring interest is in studying the role of cognitive and affective processes in interpersonal behavior. His current projects investigate how mood states can influence everyday social judgments and interaction strategies. He has published some 14 books and more than 130 articles and chapters in this area. He has been elected Fellow of the Academy of Social Science in Australia, the American Psychological Society, and the Society for Personality and Social Psychology. He is recipient of the Alexander von Humboldt Research Prize (Germany) and a Special Investigator Award from the Australian Research Council.

Kipling D. Williams received his BS at the University of Washington. He then received his MA and PhD in social psychology at The Ohio State University. There he began his collaboration with Bibb Latané and Stephen Harkins, working on the causes and consequences of social loafing. Before coming to Macquarie University, Professor Williams taught at Drake University, the University of Washington, Purdue University, the University of Toledo, and the University of New South Wales. His recent focus is on ostracism – being excluded and ignored – on which his book *Ostracism: The Power of Silence* was published in 2001. He also has interests in psychology and law, including research on the tactic of stealing thunder, eyewitness accuracy, and the impact of crime heinousness on jury verdicts.

Simon M. Laham received his BSc (Psychology) in 2000 and is currently undertaking his PhD at the University of New South Wales, Sydney, Australia. He is a recipient of the Australian Postgraduate Award.

Contributors

Henk Aarts Department of Psychology, Utrecht University

Neal M. Ashkanasy Business School, University of Queensland

Kenneth E. Barron School of Psychology, James Madison University

Daniel J. Beal Department of Psychological Sciences, Purdue University

Amanda B. Brodish Department of Psychology, University of Wisconsin–Madison

Greg A. Chung-Yan Department of Psychology, University of Guelph, Ontario, Canada

Roland Deutsch Department of Psychology, University of Würzburg, Germany

Patricia G. Devine Department of Psychology, University of Wisconsin–Madison

Amanda M. Durik Department of Psychology, University of Michigan

Steven Fein Department of Psychology, Williams College

Joseph P. Forgas School of Psychology, University of New South Wales, Sydney, Australia

Jens Förster Department of Psychology, International University, Bremen

Guido H. E. Gendolla Institute of Psychology, University of Erlangen, Germany

Brian M. Goldman Department of Psychology, University of Georgia

Jeff Greenberg Department of Psychology, University of Arizona

Robert Grunfeld Department of Psychology, University of Guelph, Ontario, Canada

Judith M. Harackiewicz Department of Psychology, University of Wisconsin–Madison

Ran R. Hassin Department of Psychology, The Hebrew University

Douglas T. Kenrick Department of Psychology, Arizona State University

Michael H. Kernis Department of Psychology, University of Georgia

Simon M. Laham School of Psychology, University of New South Wales, Sydney, Australia

Pawel Lewicki Department of Psychology, University of Tulsa

Nira Liberman Department of Psychology, Tel Aviv University

Jon K. Maner Department of Psychology, Florida State University

Steven L. Neuberg Department of Psychology, Arizona State University

Tom Pyszczynski Department of Psychology, University of Colorado at Colorado Springs

Jeffrey M. Quinn Department of Psychology, Duke University

Frederick Rhodewalt Department of Psychology, University of Utah

Lori K. Robichaud Department of Psychology, University of Guelph, Ontario, Canada

Mark Schaller Department of Psychology, University of British Columbia

Jonathan W. Schooler Department of Psychology, University of British Columbia

Charles A. Schreiber Department of Psychology, University of Pittsburgh

Sheldon Solomon Department of Psychology, Skidmore College

Leanne S. Son Hing Department of Psychology, University of Guelph, Ontario, Canada

Steven J. Spencer Department of Psychology, University of Waterloo

Fritz Strack Department of Psychology, University of Würzburg, Germany

Erin J. Strahan Department of Psychology, University of Waterloo

Stephanie L. Vance Department of Psychology, University of Wisconsin–Madison

Wayne A. Warburton Department of Psychology, Macquarie University, Sydney, Australia

Howard M. Weiss Department of Psychological Sciences, Purdue University

Kipling D. Williams Department of Psychology, Macquarie University, Sydney, Australia

Wendy Wood Department of Psychology, Duke University

Rex A. Wright Department of Psychology, University of Alabama at Birmingham

Mark P. Zanna Department of Psychology, University of Waterloo

Preface

One of the hallmarks of being human is to have an independent will to engage in directed, purposeful, and motivated activity. Yet our understanding of the nature of social motivation remains sketchy, and even a clear and universally accepted definition of the term remains somewhat elusive. This book seeks to provide an up-to-date integration of some of the most recent developments in research on social motivation, and in particular, to explore the relationship between conscious and unconscious motivational processes in social behavior. Arguably, one of the most intriguing recent developments in social psychology has been the growing focus on unconscious motivational processes. It now seems that many social behaviors are performed in an automatic and unaware fashion.

These two motivational systems – conscious, goal-directed action and spontaneous, unconscious behavior – may frequently interact in determining social behavior. One key objective of this book is to provide an informative, scholarly, yet readable overview of recent advances in research on social motivation and to offer a closer integration between what we now know about the operation of implicit, unconscious and explicit, conscious motivational mechanisms. The chapters included here will argue that a proper understanding of social motivation requires a dynamic, interactive conceptualization that simultaneously focuses both on the cognitive, information processing strategies used and on the more fundamental subconscious mechanisms responsible for social action.

The chapters offer important new insights into the way everyday motivational processes operate and address a variety of intriguing questions such as: Why do some people become involved and interested in their work or studies and why do they remain motivated, whereas others abandon their goals and fail to maintain their motivation? What are the fundamental motivational consequences of the universals of human existence such as awareness of our own mortality? How do unconscious, well-rehearsed habits and conscious, intentional goals interact in producing motivated social behavior? What is the influence of motivational states on early-stage cognitive processes such as selective attention to information? Can people sometimes unconsciously adopt the motivational goals of others? What are the motivational consequences of affective states, and in turn, how can motivation be used to control affect? What role does motivation play in such important domains as the expression or inhibition of prejudice, workplace motivation, and reactions to social exclusion and ostracism?

We do recognize, of course, that no single book could possibly include everything that is interesting and exciting in contemporary social motivation research. In selecting and inviting our contributors, we aimed to achieve comprehensive and representative coverage, but, of course, we cannot claim to have fully sampled all of the relevant areas. This book is divided into three parts. The first part deals with some of the fundamental questions about the nature and characteristics of conscious and unconscious social motivational states. The second part considers the relationship between social motivation and cognitive and affective processes. The third part surveys how conscious and unconscious motivational processes influence specific areas of social behavior, including self-regulation, prejudice, work motivation, and reactions to social exclusion and ostracism.

The chapters in Part I look at such issues as the role of intrinsic and extrinsic factors (Harackiewicz, Durik, & Barron), mortality salience (Pyszczynski, Greenberg, & Solomon), habits (Wood & Quinn), task engagement (Gendolla & Wright), and the interaction between conscious and unconscious processes (Strack & Deutsch; Spencer, Fein, Strahan, & Zanna) in motivation. Part II examines the links between motivation, cognition, and affect, including motivational influences on early-stage cognitive processing (Neuberg, Kenrick, Maner, & Schaller), unconscious goal contagion (Aarts & Hassin), affective priming (Forgas & Laham), internal versus external encoding styles (Lewicki), authenticity motives (Kernis & Goldman), and conscious and unconscious knowledge activation (priming) (Liberman & Förster). Part III deals with the applications of motivational processes in fields such as prejudice and discrimination (Devine, Brodish, & Vance), aversive racism (Son Hing, Chung-Yan, Grunfeld, Robichaud, & Zanna), reactions to exclusion and ostracism (Warburton & Williams), workplace motivation (Weiss, Ashkanasy, & Beal), and self-regulatory processes (Rhodewalt). The concluding chapter (Schooler & Schreiber) offers a conceptual integration and synthesis of the contributions to the volume.

THE ORIGINS OF THIS BOOK: THE SYDNEY SYMPOSIUM OF SOCIAL PSYCHOLOGY SERIES

This book is the sixth volume in the Sydney Symposium of Social Psychology series, held every year at the University of New South Wales,

Sydney. Perhaps a few words are in order about the origins of this volume and the Sydney Symposium of Social Psychology series in general. First, we should emphasize that this is not simply an edited book in the usual sense. The objective of the Sydney Symposia is to provide new, integrative understanding in important areas of social psychology by inviting leading researchers in a particular field to a 3-day residential symposium in Sydney. This symposium has received generous financial support from the University of New South Wales as well as Macquarie University, allowing the careful selection and funding of a small group of leading researchers as contributors. Draft papers by all contributors are prepared and circulated well in advance of the symposium and are placed on a dedicated Web site. Thus, participants had an opportunity to review and revise their papers in the light of everybody else's draft contribution even before they arrived in Sydney.

The critical part of the preparation of this book has been the intensive 3-day face-to-face meeting between all invited contributors. Sydney Symposia are characterized by open, free-ranging, intensive, and critical discussion between all participants, with the objective of exploring points of integration and contrast between the proposed papers. A further revision of each chapter was prepared soon after the symposium, incorporating many of the shared points that emerged in our discussions. Thanks to these collaborative procedures, the book does not simply consist of a set of chapters prepared in isolation. Rather, this Sydney Symposium volume represents a collaborative effort by a leading group of international researchers intent on producing a comprehensive and up-to-date review of research on the social self. We hope that the chapters will succeed in conveying some of the sense of fun and excitement we all shared during the symposium. For more information on the Sydney Symposium series and details of our past and future projects please see our Web site (www.sydneysymposium.unsw.edu.au). Five previous volumes of the Sydney Symposium series have been published. All Sydney Symposium books feature original contributions from leading international researchers on key issues in social psychology. Detailed information about our earlier volumes can be found on the series page in this book and on our Web site.

Given its comprehensive coverage, the present book should be useful both as a basic reference book and as an informative textbook to be used in advanced courses dealing with social motivation. The main target audience for this book comprises researchers, students, and professionals in all areas of the social and behavioral sciences, such as social, cognitive, clinical, counseling, personality, organizational, and applied psychology, as well as sociology, communication studies, and cognitive science. The book is written in a readable yet scholarly style, and students at both the undergraduate and graduate levels should find it an engaging overview of the field and thus useful as a textbook in courses dealing with the self.

The book should also be of particular interest to people working in applied areas where using and understanding motivational processes is important, such as clinical, counseling, educational, forensic, marketing, advertising and organizational psychology, and health psychology.

We want to express our thanks to people and organizations who helped to make the Sydney Symposium of Social Psychology series, and the sixth volume in particular, a reality. Producing a complex multiauthored book such as this is a lengthy and sometimes challenging task. We have been very fortunate to work with such an excellent and cooperative group of contributors. Our first thanks must go to them. Because of their help and professionalism, we were able to finish this project on schedule. Past friendships have not frayed, and we are all still on speaking terms; indeed, we hope that working together on this book has been as positive an experience for them as it has been for us.

The idea of organizing the Sydney Symposia owes much to discussions with and encouragement by Kevin McConkey and subsequent support by Chris Fell, Mark Wainwright, Sally Andrews, Peter Lovibond, and numerous others at the University of New South Wales. Our colleagues at the School of Psychology at UNSW, and at Macquarie University – Rebekah East, Norman Chan, Cassandra Govan, Carla Walton, Carol Yap, Vera Thomson, and others – have helped with advice, support, and sheer hard work to share the burden of preparing and organizing the symposium and the ensuing book. We also wish to acknowledge financial support from the Australian Research Council, the University of New South Wales, and Macquarie University, support that was, of course, essential to get this project off the ground. Most of all, we are grateful for the love and support of our families, who have put up with us during the many months of work that went into producing this book.

Joseph Forgas, Kipling Williams, and Simon Laham
Sydney, September 2003

1

Social Motivation

Introduction and Overview

Joseph P. Forgas, Kipling D. Williams,
and Simon M. Laham

INTRODUCTION

One of the most striking characteristics of human behavior that has fascinated philosophers and writers since antiquity is its purposive, intentional
quality. Nearly everything we do is done for a reason. In everyday social
life, people are constantly pursuing goals and trying to satisfy their desires
and wants. It could even be argued that all social behavior and judgment
is *motivated* behavior and judgment. The objective of this book is to review
and integrate some of the most recent developments in research on social
motivation. Specifically, our aim is to explore how various motivational
mechanisms can influence, and are in turn influenced by, cognitive and
affective variables as people pursue their various social goals in everyday
social life.

Of course, not all motivated social behavior is necessarily conscious.
Indeed, one of the most interesting recent developments in the social psychology of motivation has been the growing recognition that many kinds of
social behaviors are performed in an almost automatic, spontaneous fashion, without conscious awareness. Even more intriguing are a growing
number of findings suggesting not only that social actors are frequently
unaware of the real motivational reasons for their behaviors, but more
strikingly, that when questioned they often come up with clearly incor-
rect or mistaken causal explanations for their actions (Wegner & Gilbert,
2000). Does this mean that the whole notion of intentional, purposive, goal-
directed social behavior should be questioned, and imply a need to revise
our deepest philosophical assumptions about human beings as conscious,
rational, goal-pursuing creatures? What exactly is the relationship between motivation and cognition, and between conscious and unconscious

Address correspondence to Joseph P. Forgas, School of Psychology, University of New South
Wales, Sydney, 2052, Australia; e-mail: jp.forgas@unsw.edu.au.

motivational processes in particular? And how do intrinsic and extrinsic, and conscious and unconscious, motivational influences interact in producing social behaviors? These are some of the issues we intend to explore in this volume.

We have divided this volume into three parts. The first part of the book addresses some of the general issues about the nature and characteristics of conscious and unconscious social motivational states (chapters by Harackiewicz, Durik & Barron; Pyszczynski, Greenberg, & Solomon; Wood & Quinn; Gendolla & Wright, Strack & Deutsch; and Spencer, Fein, Strahan, & Zanna). In the second part, a number of contributors consider the cognitive and affective implications of various social motives (Neuberg, Kenrick, Maner, & Schaller; Aarts & Hassin; Forgas & Laham; Lewicki; Kernis & Goldman; and Liberman & Förster). The third part of the book presents research that explores some of the specific consequences and applications of conscious and unconscious social motivation for important areas of social behavior, such as prejudice, work motivation, social exclusion and ostracism, and self-regulatory processes (chapters by Devine, Brodish, & Vance; Son Hing, Chung-Yan, Grunfeld, Robichaud, & Zanna; Warburton & Williams; Weiss, Ashkanasy, & Beal; and Rhodewalt). Finally, in the concluding chapter, Schooler and Schreiber integrate the topics presented here, and identify some of the key themes of this volume. We will begin, however, with a brief theoretical and historical review of motivation research in social psychology.

MOTIVATION IN SOCIAL PSYCHOLOGY: THE BACKGROUND

The term *motivation* appears to have first crept into psychologists' vocabularies in the early 1880s. Prior to that date, the more amorphous concept of the *will* was used by philosophers and social theorists when they discussed the antecedents and features of effortful, directed, and motivated human behavior. Early functionalist philosophers and psychologists adopted the term motivation usually in reference to voluntary action – behaviors that show direction (Bindra & Stewart, 1966). Initially, motivation was considered an entity that compelled one to action. However, by the early twentieth century motivation became increasingly conceptualized in terms of instinct explanations, an approach that seemed to rule out or at least made it unnecessary to consider conscious deliberation, choice, and goal pursuit as part of motivational processes. But the domain was divided. Thinkers such as Darwin (1872), Freud (1915/1957), and McDougall (1908) all considered instincts, or innate motivational forces, to be the prime movers of all directed behavior. Others, however, took a more cognitive or rational approach to purposive behavior, proposing conscious, directed volition as a key motivational force (James, 1890/1950). In the light of contemporary debates about the nature and epistemological status of rational, directed human action, it is interesting to note that even in the beginning of social psychology there appeared a clear distinction between what could be considered unconscious and conscious motivational forces.

As with so many promising areas in early psychology, however, motivation research was stunted by behaviorism. The early behaviorists' doctrinaire refusal even to consider the mediating role that internal psychological processes may play in behavior eliminated motivation as a construct of serious concern. When motivation was considered at all by behaviorists, it was thought of in terms of the rise and fall in the intensity of fundamental drive states, such as hunger or thirst, almost always investigated in animals other than humans. In those terms, motivation could be readily manipulated by subjecting animals to various degrees of food or drink deprivation to produce motivational changes. There was simply no room for intentional goal pursuit in such simplistic studies of stimulus–response (S–R) relationships. It is interesting to note, however, that even S–R explanations were deeply influenced by ideas such as Thorndike's concept of habit (Bargh & Ferguson, 2000), a concept that is now considered to be much like an unconscious social motive (Wood & Quinn, this volume). Nevertheless, social motivation, whether conscious or not, was not of explicit concern for behaviorists and was largely left out of their explanations of social behavior.

It soon became clear that S–R explanations of human behavior were inadequate, and even neo-behaviorists like Hull and Tolman realized that any sensible account of human social behavior required a consideration of the motivated nature of action. The interactions that people have with their environments are largely influenced by their goals, desires, and wants – their motives. This realization was also reflected in the social psychology of the time. Influential thinkers like Heider, Lewin, and Festinger developed theories of social behavior that had clear motivational components. Their contributions represent a key and enduring influence on contemporary thinking about motivation. As historians of our field note, it is largely thanks to them that even in the darkest days of orthodox behaviorism, social psychology always remained rather cognitive and motivational, and so was spared some of the more damaging consequences of the behaviorist domination that afflicted other fields (Allport, 1968).

In their various ways, Heider, Lewin, and Festinger all placed significant emphasis on the importance of motivational forces, and both conscious and unconscious mental representations about the social world, as the key to human social behavior. Heider, in his balance theory, was among the first to emphasize the fundamental human need for coherent, meaningful mental representations as a force in motivating social thinking and behavior. He also developed a comprehensive phenomenological account of how the search for causal explanations can play a key role in social understanding, an idea that led to the contemporary focus on causality in accounting for interpersonal actions. Lewin, in turn, in his field theory, proposed an entirely new, dynamic, motivational account of all social behavior based on social actors' mental representations of their life space, the subjective field within which alternative courses of action can be selected. For Festinger, motivation was, of course, the focal construct in his theory of cognitive dissonance, and he was among the first to propose clearly motivational explanations for many kinds of puzzling, unexpected, and apparently irrational social behaviors. These three classic social psychologists can be credited with creating models that continued to emphasize the importance of motivational forces in every aspect of social behavior, even when much of the rest of psychology was dominated by the absurd restrictions imposed on it by behaviorism. As a result, motivation research in social psychology was never extinguished. By the 1970s, however, the advent of the *cognitive revolution* brought with it a shift in perspective, and for a while, interest in motivation took a backseat to interest in cognition.

In the 1970s and 1980s *cold* social cognition became the dominant approach to the study of social behavior and judgment, and many social cognitive theorists initially tried to explain away motivational accounts of behavior in terms of cognitive, information processing mechanisms (see Forgas, 1981, 1983, for a critique of early social cognitive approaches). For researchers like Bem (1967), Nisbett and Ross (1980), and others, what were previously considered clearly motivational explanations of judgments and behavior became reconceptualized as cognitive errors due to faulty information processing. Many examples of social behavior, such as attitude change, self-serving biases, achievement motivations, and the like were increasingly explained in terms of cold information processing variables (Nisbett & Ross, 1980; Trope, 1975). During this time, the study of social motivation was once again relegated to a secondary role in explanations of social behavior.

We are not, of course, arguing that purely motivational accounts of human behavior can ever tell the whole story – far from it. By themselves, so-called hot cognition accounts are often just as inadequate as cold, information processing accounts. We suggest, however, something of an integration of the cognitive and motivational traditions of earlier social psychology, as represented in the classic work of Lewin, Heider, and Festinger, focusing on the interaction of motivational and cognitive processes in the explanation of human social behavior. Thus, we hope that this volume will contribute to a timely reintegration of cognition and motivation in social psychology, developing further the important contributions made to this process by Sorrentino and Higgins (1986) and by Higgins and Kruglanski (2000).

Social Motives

We hope we have not painted too dim a picture of motivation research in social psychology. While there has been a general neglect of motivational processes in much social cognition research, there are a number of different fields where motivation did receive reasonable empirical and theoretical attention. Primary among these are studies of goal-directed behaviors that are aimed at, or crucial to, social interaction (e.g., Carver & Scheier, 1998). The importance of social motives in everyday life is not surprising given that successful social interaction is a cornerstone of our remarkable evolutionary success as a species (Buss, 1999). Our ability to cooperate and interact with others in complex and mutually advantageous ways is a defining characteristic of *Homo sapiens*, and this ability is driven largely by various social motives. The motivation or need to belong, for example, is certainly fundamental to humans' sociability and gregariousness (Baumeister & Leary, 1995). It is both intuitively obvious and empirically evidenced that humans need meaningful social contact, and the motivation for such contact is crucial to the maintenance of a healthy sense of adjustment and a sense of identity. Indeed, so fundamental is this motivation to affiliate that any threat to this basic human need to form and maintain interpersonal relationships can have serious negative psychological consequences, as several chapters here will show (e.g., Warburton & Williams, this volume).

Self-preservation is another important motivation central to the evolutionary success of *Homo sapiens*. The *survival instinct* may indeed be the most basic or fundamental motive that we possess. Some researchers place this particular motivation at the heart of many other social motives, behaviors, and judgments. The desire to keep conscious knowledge of our mortality at bay can lead to symbolic defensive behaviors like maintaining high self-esteem, creating strong social bonds, and embracing others who share our cultural norms and values (see Pyszczynski et al., this volume). Clearly, our motivations to stay alive and to cope with the knowledge of our mortality are a driving force in many of our social behaviors.

Other social motivations have formed the basis of numerous influential theories in social psychology. The need for cognitive consistency, for example, is central to dissonance theory (Festinger, 1957) and Heider's balance model (1958). Humans need a social world that makes sense to them, where beliefs, attitudes, and behaviors are coherent and consistent. In the absence of such consistency, people experience psychological discomfort and have trouble planning and engaging in effective interpersonal relations (Mead, 1934/1970). These motivational issues have a clear impact on the way people perceive and process the social world. In essence, the motive to create and maintain meaning and consistency recruits many cognitive and perceptual processes to its service and shapes our representations of the social world into a coherent and sensible whole. The need for accuracy is another motive that clearly influences cognition and is central to understanding how people effectively function in the social environment (Pittman, 1998). The desire to make sense out of chaos drives many theories of attribution and causal reasoning. Accurate (or relatively accurate) attribution is an important part of interacting successfully with others in a variety of social contexts (Heider, 1958).

Although these motives appear to be fairly universal to the social functioning of all humans, there are numerous other, more specific motivational influences that are more variable and context-dependent across individuals and across situations. Another important distinction that has been made in motivation research is that between intrinsic and extrinsic motivation (see Harackiewicz et al., this volume). When a person adopts an intrinsic motivation orientation, she finds rewards inherent in simply engaging in a task; the activity is an end in itself. When external motivation is present, on the other hand, rewards are mediated by the task. Here, the activity serves as a means to an end. These different orientations can have important consequences for social information processing and interpersonal interactions (Pittman, 1998; see also Devine et al., this volume, for a discussion of internal and external motivational orientations relating to expressed prejudice).

In addition to these motivational distinctions, there are more specific motivational orientations aimed at particular social ends that have been explored by researchers. Self-related motivational strategies, for example, are primary among these more specific social motives. Although some authors have tried to dismiss self-serving biases as merely faulty cognitions, others consider them fundamental motivational processes. Particularly strong among these motives is the need for self-esteem (Steele, 1988; Tesser, 1988). A positive self-concept is an important component of a healthy social life and effective social interaction. Self-evaluation processes, for example, rest at the heart of numerous theories of social interaction (Tesser, 1986). The motivation for authenticity (the operation of the core self) is another example of a specific motive central to self-esteem maintenance and subjective well-being (see Kernis & Goldman, this volume). Indeed, some people may even develop a pathological concern with self-image, as highlighted by Rhodewalt's discussion of the vagaries of the narcissistic self (this volume). Clearly, motivations to promote positive conceptions of the self are an important consideration in any review of social motivation.

Affect and Social Motivation

In a discussion of motivation and cognition, we would be remiss not to consider the critical role that affect plays in motivational processes. Along with motivation, affect was neglected in the early days of the cognitive revolution, and many "cold" accounts of social behavior and cognition have since been criticized for excluding emotion and feelings (Forgas, 1981; Zajonc, 2000). Recently, however, numerous researchers have turned their attention to this important domain, with interesting results. Several influential theorists see affective states as essentially feedback signals that indicate the progress of motivated, goal-directed behaviors (Carver & Scheier, 1998). Although affect clearly has such a signaling function, this view of the relationship between affect and motivation appears unnecessarily restrictive to us. Rather, much recent evidence suggests that affective states and moods, however caused, can often be a powerful source of motivated cognition and behavior. For example, even mild mood states influence how people perceive, interpret, respond to, and communicate in social situations (Forgas, 2002; see also Forgas & Laham, this volume).

The motivational consequences of affect are particularly evident in work on affect as an influence on motivated cognitive strategies. Throughout evolutionary history, affective states have come to signal particular environmental circumstances – positive moods and emotions imply benign environmental surroundings, whereas negative affective states suggest an aversive social context. These affective states have thus come to mobilize cognitive strategies adapted to dealing with these environments. Positive affect often facilitates assimilative, top-down, and creative processing, useful in dealing with familiar, threat-free environments. Negative states, on the other hand, seem to promote the use of systematic, detail-oriented, accommodative information processing, a cognitive style more suited to dealing with novel or aversive situations (Fiedler, 2001; see also Forgas & Laham, this volume). In addition to these general mood effects on information processing, specific emotions like fear and anger can have particular influences on perceptual and cognitive processes (see Neuberg et al. and Weiss et al., this volume).

Recent research thus clearly illustrates the importance of studying the interactive relations between motivation, affect, and cognition. Many motivational and affective strategies can only become effective by recruiting cognitive processes to their service (Kunda, 1999). As a consequence, neglecting these hot processes on cold cognition can result only in an incomplete account of social behavior. As we suggested earlier, however, recent developments in social psychological research, have added another layer of complexity to the study of social motivation. Students of social behavior now also need to ask another crucial question: When and why are social motivations sometimes conscious and sometimes unconscious?

Conscious and Unconscious Social Motivation

There has been a recent trend in social psychological research toward the study of implicit cognitive processes, and this trend has not left motivation research untouched (Bless & Forgas, 2001). It is becoming increasingly apparent that a full understanding of social life requires a careful consideration of the interacting effects between conscious and unconscious perceptual, cognitive, and motivational processes (Bargh & Ferguson, 2000). Whereas many theories have traditionally proposed that conscious awareness is a requirement for the initiation of purposive action, recent challenges to this view assert the importance of spontaneous and automatic cognitive and motivational processes that occur outside of awareness, as several chapters here suggest (see Aarts & Hassin; Liberman & Förster; Strack & Deutsch; Wood & Quinn, this volume).

The notion of unconscious motivation has its roots in the cybernetics of the 1950s and 1960s. This movement maintained that systems could govern their own behavior based on environmental feedback without conscious intervention (see Bargh & Ferguson, 2000, for a review). This meant that systems could exhibit apparently complex, purposive, goal-directed behaviors in the absence of any underlying conscious processes such as choice and reasoning. Recent research in social cognition provides further evidence for the workings of unconscious social motivations in numerous domains including impression formation (Chartrand & Bargh, 1996), task performance (Bargh & Gollwitzer, 1994), and the experience of affect (Chartrand & Bargh, 1999). So not only do these unconscious motives impact on various information processing strategies, they also influence clearly observable and apparently purposive and motivated social behaviors. Indeed, the importance of these findings for a comprehensive account of social motivation is echoed by many of the contributions to this volume (see Liberman & Förster; Strack & Deutsch, this volume, for example). Quite simply, the study of social motives is necessarily the study of both the conscious and unconscious worlds of social actors, as most of the chapters presented here will illustrate.

OVERVIEW OF THE VOLUME

The contributions to this volume have been divided into three parts dealing with (a) general issues about conscious and unconscious social motivation, (b) the cognitive and affective implications of social motives, and (c) the consequences and applications of social motivation.

Part I. Conscious and Unconscious Social Motivation: General Issues

In the first chapter of this part, Harackiewicz, Durik, and Barron consider one of the key issues in recent educational and social psychological research: Why do some people become involved and interested in their work or studies and why do they remain motivated, whereas others abandon their goals? The chapter examines the variables responsible for the development of interest and continuing motivation for various activities, explores the role of intrinsic and extrinsic factors that influence optimal motivation, and discusses the difference between performance and mastery goals in motivation promotion. Several experiments show that both intrinsic and extrinsic factors can play a positive role in promoting performance and intrinsic motivation, and the authors propose a multiple goals perspective for the study of optimal motivation. Harackiewicz and her colleagues present clear evidence for the operation of multiple goals in maintaining motivation in tasks ranging from playing pinball to performing well at college. These findings are consistent with a model of motivation that considers intrinsic and extrinsic factors to be complementary forces that can promote optimal motivation.

The next chapter addresses the question of how our fundamental awareness of mortality may motivate specific cognitive and behavioral strategies in humans. In this chapter, Pyszczynski, Greenberg, and Solomon present the most recent research and evidence on the motivational consequences of mortality salience, based on their Terror Management Theory (TMT; Pyszczynski, Greenberg, & Solomon, 1997). Human beings, alone among all living species, have the unique ability to recognize their own mortality, and as a result, they experience existential terror about their own deaths. Pyszczynski and his collaborators discuss the mechanisms involved in coping with these conscious and unconscious death-related threats, with a focus on the role of the accessibility of death-related ideation and the potential for affect that this produces. They provide extensive recent experimental evidence demonstrating the motivational consequences of mortality salience in areas such as norm formation and maintenance, group identification, and self processes.

Wood and Quinn discuss the conditions under which social behavior can be predicted from implicit, unconscious versus explicit, conscious motivational factors, and focus especially on the distinction between intentional and habitual influences on behavior. In a number of interesting studies, the authors demonstrate the nonconscious nature of habits and the important role that such implicit cognitive mechanisms play in self-regulatory behavior. The chapter also explores implications for behavior change, emphasizing the multiple processes of behavior generation. Past acts are likely to be maintained in the future when habits proceed relatively automatically in stable contexts. However, when contexts change, or when for other reasons people are encouraged to think about their behavior, behavior comes under conscious control. Given sufficient motivation and ability, people can bring their behavior in line with their explicit intentions, which may often differ from the implicit intentions directing established habits.

Wood and Quinn conclude by outlining a general framework for understanding how the multiple cognitive processes guiding behavior interact in the generation of action.

The construct of effort, or task engagement, figures prominently in explanations of social psychological phenomena. Surprisingly, social psychologists have devoted relatively little attention to understanding fundamental effort processes. In the fourth chapter of this part, Gendolla and Wright examine the question of how effort, or task engagement, can influence social behavior. Based on Jack Brehm's earlier theory on motivational intensity, this chapter challenges commonsense ideas that effort is necessarily proportional to success importance and perceived ability in a performance realm. Gendolla and Wright outline a new framework for predicting momentary task engagement and also propose an empirical means of measuring it in terms of cardiovascular reactions that are hypothesized to change with task engagement. For example, their studies show how social evaluation can impact on effort, reflected in cardiovascular (CV) arousal. They also demonstrate how sex differences in CV response, self-involvement, resource depletion, and challenge and threat appraisals can all influence effort. Many of these findings call into question our commonsense beliefs about effort in social contexts and suggest that people sometimes expend effort nonconsciously.

Strack and Deutsch continue the exploration of conscious and unconscious social motivation with their Reflective Impulsive Model (RIM). These authors suggest that what people do is controlled by two interacting systems that follow different operating principles. While the Reflective System generates behavioral decisions that are based on knowledge about facts and values, the Impulsive System elicits behavior through associative links and motivational orientations. Importantly, Strack and Deutsch focus on the interaction of these unconscious and conscious systems, and discuss how they operate at different processing stages and how their outputs may determine behavior in a synergistic or antagonistic fashion. The implications of the RIM extend beyond those of typical dual-process models. The authors apply this model to a number of domains of mental functioning and integrate cognitive, motivational, and behavioral mechanisms. They highlight the possible applications of the RIM to our understanding of sometimes puzzling social phenomena like mass behavior, vandalism, and aggression, and present new results from their laboratories in support of the conceptual claims of the model.

In the final chapter of the first part, Spencer, Fein, Strahan, and Zanna consider the ways in which social motives can influence cognition. This chapter reviews four lines of research that demonstrate how people's implicitly activated thoughts and their explicit motives can interact. This research shows that implicit thoughts are most likely to influence behavior when explicit motivations make the implicit thoughts applicable to the situation. In one interesting study, for example, Spencer and his colleagues show that subliminally priming people with the concept of thirst leads them to choose a thirst-quenching beverage only when they also happen to be thirsty (i.e., explicitly motivated to reduce their thirst). The authors then review further evidence for this important motivation–cognition link from studies looking at stereotyping and self-esteem threats. This chapter perfectly highlights the interaction between implicit and explicit cognitive and motivational processes in influencing social judgment and behavior.

Part II. Social Motivation: Cognitive and Affective Implications

The second part of the book begins with a chapter by Neuberg, Kenrick, Maner, and Schaller that examines the role of social motivation in early-stage cognitive processing. In this chapter the authors address the question: What determines selective attention and its consequences? People spend much of their social lives in complex social environments and by necessity direct their limited information processing resources to a restricted set of social stimuli. What determines what kinds of information we will be motivated to notice, remember, and act upon? Neuberg and his collaborators attempt to answer these questions from a functional, ecological/evolutionary foundation. They focus on the motives of self-protection and mating and consider how these fundamental social goals adaptively influence early-stage perceptual and cognitive processes. Special attention is paid to the inhibitory and facilitative effects of the activation of these goals on forming judgments about targets of varying ethnicity, gender, and physical attractiveness. Neuberg et al. provide supportive evidence for the operation of these motives in both the cognitive domain (from studies on functional projection) and the perceptual domain (from studies on visual attention).

Next, Aarts and Hassin discuss the mechanisms responsible for producing unconscious goal pursuit and unconscious goal contagion. Most theories of motivated action emphasize the role of conscious choice in the adoption of goals and in the guiding of goal-directed behaviors. Recently, however, this widespread view has been challenged. In this chapter the authors present a convincing argument in support of this challenge. Within a two-component framework, Aarts and Hassin suggest that (a) people can automatically infer others' goals from their behavior and (b) these inferred goals may then be spontaneously adopted and pursued by the perceiver. They provide evidence from a number of studies showing that participants automatically infer goals from others' everyday behaviors without conscious intent, and that such goals can be unconsciously put into motion by the mere perception of others' behavior. Interestingly, the pursuit of these nonconscious goals displays many of the same characteristics as conscious goal pursuit. The authors conclude with a discussion of the importance of goal pursuit, both conscious and unconscious, in everyday social functioning.

Forgas and Laham review historical and contemporary evidence for the role of affect in social motivation and present an integrative theory of these findings. The chapter describes complementary experimental evidence demonstrating (a) the motivational consequences of mild affective states on thinking and behavior and, in turn, (b) the role of motivational states in maintaining and managing affective influences. Evidence for the direct motivational consequences of mood comes from research showing distinct mood-induced changes in motivated social behaviors and judgments such as strategic negotiation, bargaining, requesting, and social influence processes. The authors argue that mild mood states exert a motivational influence on behavior through selectively facilitating retrieval of and access to mood-congruent information when ambiguous social situations are interpreted and behavioral responses are planned. Several experiments from the authors' laboratory and from elsewhere indicate that motivation to achieve a particular objective can, in turn, often interfere with, and even reverse, commonly observed mood congruence effects. Forgas and Laham end the chapter by considering the general implications of their research for understanding the interactive links between affect and social motivation in everyday judgments and behavior.

Next, Lewicki considers the role of different information encoding styles on social motivation and judgment. He argues that people vary along a continuum of internal-external encoding. Internal encoders rapidly apply internalized schemas to the environment, often at the risk of poor schema–environment fit. External encoders, on the other hand, take their time fitting appropriate schemas to stimuli. These differences in encoding style, Lewicki argues, can be stable across ages and replicable across cultures. Further, these basic differences in motivated information processing strategies have important implications for an individual's personality characteristics and social interaction and coping strategies.

In the next chapter, Kernis and Goldman discuss a particular type of social motivation: the motivation to achieve personal authenticity. Historically, authenticity has been conceptualized as the awareness and operation of one's core self, and has been considered important for psychological functioning and well-being. These authors present a new, multifaceted view of authenticity and discuss the implications of this construct for social motivation. In short, they suggest that the multiple components of authenticity are separable but interactive, each having motivational implications for the others. Kernis and Goldman also present a new scale of authenticity, the Authenticity Inventory, a measure that shows authenticity to be positively correlated with self-esteem and life satisfaction. The chapter includes some interesting data indicating the key motivational role of authenticity in explaining constructs such as collective self-esteem, self-monitoring, cultural estrangement, social comparison, and attachment phenomena.

In the last chapter of Part II, Liberman and Förster present some interesting work on motivational priming. These contributors investigate the bases of unconscious and conscious knowledge activation (priming) and introduce a comprehensive theory of goal-related accessibility. In a series of interesting studies, we see that (a) goal accessibility persists as long as a goal is active, (b) goal accessibility diminishes once a goal has been reached, and (c) accessibility of a goal increases with increasing motivation to achieve that goal. Liberman and Förster then proceed to apply these important principles to a number of social psychological phenomena including person perception, thought suppression, and the catharsis of aggression. Finally, the authors integrate their findings with classical priming accounts and question the extent to which motivational priming is a conscious phenomenon.

Part III. Conscious and Unconscious Social Motivation: Some Consequences and Applications

The third part of the book addresses some of the applications of conscious and unconscious motivational processes. In the first chapter in this part, Devine, Brodish, and Vance discuss the role that internal and external motivation plays in the expression of nonprejudiced behaviors and attitudes. A review of the prejudice literature suggests that given compelling external reasons for concealing prejudice, internal reasons for doing so are often discounted. Devine et al. argue, however, that to increase understanding of the expression and control of prejudice, we need to examine the roles that both internal and external motives play in the expression or inhibition of prejudice. This chapter outlines the development and validation of measures of internal and external motivation to avoid prejudice and then offers evidence of the role of these motivations in important social judgments. Devine and her colleagues highlight the importance of knowing not only *how* one is motivated to respond without prejudice (internally or externally), but also *why* one is so motivated. This chapter provides a new conceptualization of the motivational nature and consequences of prejudice that has important implications for intergroup relations and behavior.

In the next chapter, Son Hing, Chung-Yan, Grunfeld, Robichaud, and Zanna further explore the motivational aspects of implicit and explicit prejudice, and the issue of aversive racism in particular. These authors focus on the paradoxical pattern of low prejudice at the explicit level linked to high prejudice at the implicit level. In particular, they examine the discriminatory behavior of aversive racists: people who consciously claim to be nonprejudiced but are unconsciously prejudiced. These people typically avoid discriminatory behavior when they are made aware of their negative attitudes and rationalize their discriminatory behavior more than others. Son Hing and her colleagues show that aversive racists feel more guilty and discriminate less when they are reminded of past hypocrisies, but show more discrimination when presented with a non-race-related excuse to discriminate. The authors stress the importance of these findings for understanding motivational influences on implicit and explicit prejudice and emphasize the applied consequences of their results.

One of the most important motivations that all humans have is the need to belong. In the next chapter of the book, Warburton and Williams consider the motivational strategies people employ when they are deprived of this fundamental social need. They identify two primary strategies for dealing with social ostracism: (a) motivation to increase social attractiveness in order to be included and (b) motivation to engage in retaliation and aggression, either to the rejecting group or to innocent others. The authors argue that different contextual factors can prompt either one of these two motivated coping strategies. This chapter offers a theoretical integration of the antecedents and motivational consequences of social exclusion and ostracism, and presents empirical evidence that elucidates the conditions that will trigger either pro- or antisocial behaviors. The broader implications of this research for our understanding of the motivational mechanisms that regulate interpersonal behavior are also discussed.

In the next chapter, Weiss, Ashkanasy, and Beal examine the role that emotional states play in the motivation of workplace performance. Specifically, these authors focus on the potentially disruptive effects of affect on performance and argue that daily experienced emotional states can deplete self-regulatory resources. For example, Weiss and his colleagues suggest that higher organizational demands on employees to engage in emotional labor will deplete regulatory resources, and thus will often lead to lower employee motivation and performance. In addition, they show that employee motivation and productive work performance are likely to be adversely affected by a negative organizational climate that further depletes their regulatory resources.

In the final chapter of this part, Rhodewalt examines the motivational consequences of narcissism and its effects on interpersonal self-esteem. This chapter briefly reviews clinical perspectives on narcissism and describes a recently proposed interpersonal self-regulatory processing model of narcissism. The author's primary focus, however, is on the narcissist's chronic, motivated self-esteem regulation. Rhodewalt presents evidence of three components of this motivated self-regulatory process, including (a) factors that motivate interpersonal engagement, (b) interpersonal self-regulatory behaviors, and (c) the intra- and interpersonal consequences of such interpersonal exchanges. The chapter argues that enduring personality characteristics such as narcissism can play an important role in generating long-term motivational strategies that people employ in their social relationships.

SUMMARY AND CONCLUSIONS

In the final chapter, Schooler and Schreiber review and integrate the contributions to this volume. These authors identify three common underlying themes in the research presented here, dealing with three basic questions in social motivation research: (a) What is the relationship between conscious and unconscious processes in social motivation? (b) How does self-regulation mediate motivation? and (c) What role does evolution play in social motivation? Schooler and Schreiber then outline a tripartite model of consciousness as it applies to the evidence presented in the chapters here and, in particular, consider how conscious, unconscious, and meta-conscious aspects of social motivation are represented.

In this summary chapter, as well as in the other contributions to this volume, we can clearly see the benefits of integrating research on conscious and unconscious social motivation. Understanding how and why people adopt purposive action is one of the most interesting yet complex tasks in social psychology. Whereas the history of the discipline reveals a great deal of emphasis on the cognitive processes that underlie social behavior, recent work illustrated in this book suggests the need for the development of a more balanced approach and greater focus on the interaction of cognitive and motivational mechanisms. Our purpose here is to offer an up-to-date survey of the field and an integration of recent work on the unconscious and conscious processes involved in social motivation. We very much hope that the contributions to this volume will achieve their objective and generate further interest in this fascinating area of social psychology.

References

Allport, G. W. (1968). The historical background of modern social psychology. In G. Lindzey & E. Aronson (Eds.), *The handbook of social psychology* (Vol. 1, pp. 1–80). Reading, MA: Addison-Wesley.

Bargh, J. A., & Ferguson, M. J. (2000). Beyond behaviorism: On the automaticity of higher mental processes. *Psychological Bulletin, 126,* 925–945.

Bargh, J. A., & Gollwitzer, P. M. (1994). Environmental control of goal-directed action: Automatic and strategic contingencies between situations and behavior. In W. Spaulding (Ed.), *Integrations of motivation and cognition: The Nebraska symposium on motivation* (Vol. 41, pp. 71–124). Lincoln: University of Nebraska Press.

Baumeister, R. F., & Leary, M. R. (1995). The need to belong: Desire for interpersonal attachment as a fundamental human motivation. *Psychological Bulletin, 117,* 497–529.

Bem, D. J. (1967). Self-perception: An alternative interpretation of cognitive dissonance phenomena. *Psychological Review, 74,* 183–200.

Bindra, D., & Stewart, J. (1966). *Motivation*. Middlesex: Penguin.

Bless, H., & Forgas, J. P. (2001). *The message within: The role of subjective experience in social cognition and behavior*. Philadelphia: Psychology Press.

Buss, D. M. (1999). *Evolutionary psychology*. Boston: Allyn and Bacon.

Carver, C. S., & Scheier, M. F. (1998). *On the self-regulation of behavior*. New York: Cambridge University Press.

Chartrand, T. L., & Bargh, J. A. (1996). Automatic activation of impression formation and memorization goals: Nonconscious goal priming reproduces effects of explicit task instructions. *Journal of Personality and Social Psychology, 71*, 464–478.

Chartrand, T. L., & Bargh, J. A. (1999). The chameleon effect: The perception–behavior link and social interaction. *Journal of Personality and Social Psychology, 76*, 893–910.

Darwin, C. (1872). *The expression of emotions in man and animals*. New York: Appleton.

Festinger, L. (1957). *A theory of cognitive dissonance*. Palo Alto, CA: Stanford University Press.

Fiedler, K. (2001). Affective influences on social information processing. In J. P. Forgas (Ed.), *The handbook of affect and social cognition* (pp. 163–181). Mahwah, NJ: Erlbaum.

Forgas, J. P. (1981). *Social cognition: Perspectives on everyday understanding*. New York: Academic Press.

Forgas, J, P. (1983). What is social about social cognition? *British Journal of Social Psychology, 22*, 129–144.

Forgas, J. P. (2002). Feeling and doing: Affective influences on interpersonal behavior. *Psychological Inquiry, 13*, 1–28.

Freud, S. (1915/1957). Instincts and their vicissitudes. *Stanford Edition*, Vol. 14. London: Hogarth Press.

Heider, F. (1958). *The psychology of interpersonal relations*. New York: Wiley

Higgins, E. T., & Kruglanski, A. W. (2000). *Motivational science: Social and personality perspective*. Ann Arbor, MI: Taylor and Francis.

James, W. (1890/1950). *The principles of psychology* (Vol. 1). New York: Diver Books.

Kunda, Z. (1999). *Social cognition: Making sense of people*. Cambridge, MA: MIT Press.

McDougall, W. (1908). *An introduction to social psychology*. London: Methuen.

Mead, G. H. (1934/1970). *Mind, self and society*. Chicago: University of Chicago Press.

Nisbett, R., & Ross, L. (1980). *Human inference: Strategies and shortcomings in social judgment*. Englewood Cliffs, NJ: Prentice-Hall.

Pittman, T. S. (1998). Motivation. In D. T. Gilbert, S. T. Fiske, & G. Lindzey (Eds.), *The handbook of social psychology* (Vol. 1, pp. 1–38). Hillsdale, NJ: Erlbaum.

Pyszczynski, T., Greenberg, J., & Solomon, S. (1997). Why do we need what we need? A terror management perspective on the roots of human social motivation. *Psychological Inquiry, 8*, 1–21.

Sorrentino, R. M., & Higgins, E. T. (1986). *Handbook of motivation and cognition: Foundations of social behavior*. New York: Guilford Press.

Steele, C. M. (1988). The psychology of self-affirmation: Sustaining the integrity of the self. In L. Berkowitz (Ed.), *Advances in experimental social psychology* (Vol. 21, pp. 261–302). San Diego, CA: Academic Press.

Tesser, A. (1986). Some effects of self-evaluation maintenance on cognition and action. In R. M. Sorrentino & E. T. Higgins (Eds.), *Handbook of motivation and cognition* (Vol. 1, pp. 435–464). New York: Guilford Press.

Tesser, A. (1988). Toward a self-evaluation maintenance model of social behavior. In L. Berkowitz (Ed.), *Advances in experimental social psychology* (Vol. 21, pp. 181–227). San Diego, CA: Academic Press.

Trope, Y. (1975). Seeking information about one's own ability as a determinant of choice among tasks. *Journal of Personality and Social Psychology, 32,* 1004–1013.

Wegner, D. M., & Gilbert, D. T. (2000). Social psychology: The science of human experience. In H. Bless & J. P. Forgas (Eds.), *The message within: Subjective experience in social cognition and behavior* (pp. 1–9). Philadelphia: Psychology Press.

Zajonc, R. B. (2000). Feeling and thinking: Closing the debate over the independence of affect. In J. P. Forgas (Ed.), *Feeling and thinking: The role of affect in social cognition* (pp. 31–58). New York: Cambridge University Press.

PART I

CONSCIOUS AND UNCONSCIOUS SOCIAL MOTIVATION

General Issues

2

Multiple Goals, Optimal Motivation, and the Development of Interest

Judith M. Harackiewicz, Amanda M. Durik, and
Kenneth E. Barron

INTRODUCTION

Why do some students become involved and interested in their studies,
and why do they continue in a particular academic discipline? Why do
some athletes become engaged in their sport, persist at practice, and seek
competition against others? Answering these questions requires that we
consider the processes underlying intrinsic motivation, or the motivation
to engage in an activity for the value inherent in doing it (Deci & Ryan,
1985). As Wood and Quinn (this volume) note, behavior can be guided
through several processes that vary in the degree of attention required
(see also Schooler and Schreiber, this volume). We have focused on intentional determinants of achievement behavior. In particular, we have studied the factors that influence optimal motivation and believe that goals
play an important role in shaping intrinsic motivation and performance.
To study goals and motivation, we have examined the role of intrinsic factors such as self-set goals and personal values in promoting interest and
performance in academic contexts over time. We have also examined the
effects of extrinsic factors such as goal interventions and task characteristics on intrinsic motivation in laboratory studies. How do these intrinsic and extrinsic factors combine to influence performance and ongoing
motivation?

Our work has been guided by Harackiewicz and Sansone's (1991;
Sansone & Harackiewicz, 1996) process model of intrinsic motivation.
Harackiewicz and Sansone draw an important distinction between goals
that are suggested or implied externally and the goals that are actually
adopted by an individual in a particular situation (the perceived goal; see
Figure 2.1). Rather than assume a one-to-one correspondence between an
assigned goal and a personal goal, we suggest that the goals an individual

Address correspondence to Judith M. Harackiewicz at e-mail: jmharack@wisc.edu.

21

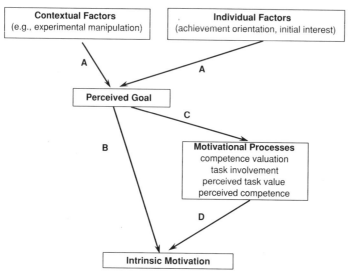

FIGURE 2.1 A process model of intrinsic motivation.

adopts in a given situation can have multiple determinants (see Aarts & Hassin, this volume, for a discussion of how goals can be automatically activated by situational cues). These effects are represented as A paths in Figure 2.1. One type of determinant involves contextual factors, such as an experimental manipulation in a laboratory setting or a particular characteristic of a task. A second important type of determinant involves individual factors, such as initial interest, personal values, or personality differences in achievement orientation.

In this model, we focus on two levels of goals: purpose and target goals. Purpose goals reflect the reason for engaging in a task and represent what an individual hopes to accomplish in a particular situation. Target goals, on the other hand, reflect more specific goals for how an individual might achieve an overarching purpose goal (Bandura, 1986; Locke & Latham, 1990). For example, athletes may set a target goal of practicing a particular skill three times each week. This specific standard serves as a more proximal mechanism to help them achieve their higher-level purpose, which might be to improve their skills. These goals are conscious intentions most relevant to the reflective system described by Strack and Deutch (this volume), and we would expect them to operate according to the dynamic principles discussed by Liberman and Förster (this volume).

To better understand *when* and *why* goals have particular effects, moderator and mediator variables have been incorporated into the model. First, we consider the possibility that goals may have different effects in different contexts and/or for different types of individuals. In other words, the effects of goals on intrinsic motivation can be moderated by personality and situational factors, such that the direct effect of goals on motivation (the B path in Figure 2.1) can vary as a function of individual factors and/or the situation. Second, Harackiewicz and Sansone (1991) argued that goals at different levels of specificity can also interact such that higher-order goals moderate the effects of lower-order goals. In other words, the direct effect of a target goal on intrinsic motivation can vary as a function of higher-order purpose goals.

The question of *why* goals have particular effects is addressed with mediator variables that allow us to examine the underlying process through which goals affect intrinsic motivation. When mediation is established, the direct effect of a predictor on an outcome (the B path of goals to intrinsic motivation) can be better understood through the predictor's effect on process variables (the C paths), which in turn influence the outcome (the D path). In particular, four key mediators of goals are shown in Figure 2.1: competence valuation, task involvement, perceived task value, and perceived competence. All four of these processes can promote intrinsic motivation. Specifically, individuals are more likely to experience intrinsic interest in an activity to the extent that they value doing well in the activity (competence valuation), become absorbed in the activity while engaged in it (task involvement), find meaning or value in the task (perceived task value), or feel competent at the activity (perceived competence). Including moderator and mediator variables has provided a richer understanding of when goals are likely to enhance intrinsic motivation and why they have these effects.

THE ROLE OF ACHIEVEMENT GOALS IN OPTIMAL MOTIVATION

We believe that intrinsic motivation is critical in any achievement endeavor and that an important indicator of success is whether individuals develop interest in their course material or sport and pursue further learning or continue to play their sport (Maehr, 1976; Nicholls, 1979). Indeed, most of our own research has focused on factors that increase or undermine intrinsic motivation. However, our competitive culture often defines success in terms of performance, measured in terms of how well a person performs relative to others. In a sports context, the criteria for success are clear – players win or lose. In an educational context, the most obvious indicator of success is academic performance, or grades, which may be based on normative curves. Of course, these may not be the only indicators of successful performance, but normative comparisons seem to underlie most conceptions of excellence in achievement situations. We therefore adopt a multifaceted definition of success and examine both performance and interest as indicators of optimal motivation.

In our first studies, we addressed the question of optimal motivation using an achievement goal approach. Achievement goals reflect the purpose or reason for an individual's achievement pursuits in a particular situation (Ames, 1992; Dweck & Leggett, 1988; Maehr, 1989), and theorists have identified two general types of achievement goals: mastery and performance goals. When pursuing mastery goals, an individual's reason for engaging in an achievement activity is to *develop* competence at an activity. In contrast, when pursuing performance goals, an individual's reason for engagement is to *demonstrate* competence relative to others. Dweck and Leggett (1988) argued that achievement goals create a framework for how individuals approach and experience achievement tasks, and that mastery goals are more likely to foster an adaptive pattern of motivation and performance goals a maladaptive pattern. For example, early research suggested that when students pursued mastery goals they selected more challenging tasks, persisted in the face of difficulty, and held more positive attitudes toward learning. Conversely, students pursuing performance goals chose easier tasks and withdrew effort when difficulty was encountered (Ames & Archer, 1988; Elliott & Dweck, 1988). The hypothesis that mastery goals are adaptive and performance goals are maladaptive will be referred to as the *mastery goal perspective* because it implies that only mastery goals can have positive consequences and that performance goals will have deleterious consequences.

Although there is little debate about the positive effects of mastery goals, others disagree with the second component of the mastery goal perspective. More recent reviews of the achievement goal literature suggest that strong conclusions about the negative effects of performance goals may be premature (Harackiewicz, Barron, & Elliot, 1998; Hidi & Harackiewicz, 2001), and we endorse a *multiple goal perspective* in which mastery and performance goals are both considered adaptive (Harackiewicz, Barron, Pintrich, Elliot, & Thrash, 2002). In particular, they argue that performance goals can have positive effects because they orient individuals to competence and can promote adaptive achievement behaviors in some situations and for certain individuals.

We will review experimental work that reveals some of the conditions under which performance goals promote intrinsic motivation, as well as correlational work that reveals a positive association between performance goals and academic performance. We will then demonstrate how our findings, whether experimental or correlational, support a multiple goals perspective rather than the mastery goal perspective. Finally, we will discuss research that begins to integrate goals and personal values. Values can influence the achievement goals an individual adopts in a particular situation, and goals can influence the value that individuals come to find in tasks. Moreover, task values may also play an important role in the development of interest.

EVIDENCE FOR POSITIVE EFFECTS OF BOTH GOALS FROM THE LABORATORY

In a series of experimental studies, Harackiewicz and Elliot (1993, 1998; Elliot & Harackiewicz, 1994) examined the effects of achievement goals on intrinsic motivation. The experimental activity in each of these studies involved playing an enjoyable pinball game. Before the start of the session, a mastery or performance goal was suggested to participants, who were all college students. Their mastery purpose goal manipulation highlighted development and improvement of pinball skills, and their performance purpose goal manipulation highlighted normative comparisons and demonstration of pinball ability. Participants played two games, and performance was controlled experimentally to ensure that all participants achieved a similar level of overall performance. After the second game, intrinsic motivation was measured with both self-report and behavioral measures.

Moderator Effects

The results revealed no main effects of achievement goals. Instead, the effects of assigned goals were moderated by achievement motivation (Jackson, 1974). Specifically, individuals low in achievement motivation (LAMs) showed higher levels of intrinsic motivation when assigned mastery goals, whereas individuals high in achievement motivation (HAMs) showed more interest when assigned performance goals. In explaining this pattern, Harackiewicz and Elliot noted that HAMs characteristically enter activities with a desire to increase their competence (Atkinson, 1974; McClelland, 1961). Assigning a mastery goal may not add much to how they typically approach achievement situations. A performance goal, however, provides the additional challenge of outperforming others and demonstrating competence, and thus may make the game more exciting and interesting for HAMs (Tauer & Harackiewicz, 1999). In contrast, LAMs typically avoid normative comparisons and experience performance anxiety in achievement settings (Atkinson, 1974). Assigning a performance goal can undermine interest for LAMs, but a mastery goal may help them appreciate their development of competence in the activity, increasing their interest in the game. In sum, neither achievement goal proved optimal for all participants.

Harackiewicz and Sansone (1991) argued that congruence between an individual's higher- and lower-order goals is another key determinant of intrinsic motivation. Goals are congruent (or match) when they orient an individual to the same end. This *matching hypothesis* is consistent with other theories suggesting that behavior is regulated optimally when lower-order standards facilitate the attainment of higher-level standards (see also Carver, Lawrence, & Scheier, 1996). Thus, target goals that help an individual achieve his or her purpose goal should optimize intrinsic motivation. Harackiewicz and Elliot (1998) tested the matching hypothesis with mastery and performance goal manipulations in another pinball study. Participants were assigned a mastery or performance target goal in the context of either a performance or neutral purpose goal. In this study, the effects of target goals on intrinsic motivation were moderated by purpose goals. Performance target goals enhanced intrinsic motivation more than mastery target goals when participants were given a performance purpose goal, whereas mastery goals enhanced intrinsic motivation more than performance target goals in the neutral control condition.

The findings from these pinball studies clearly suggest that performance goals can promote interest above baseline levels for some people (i.e., HAMs) and in some situations (i.e., when they match higher-order goals) and are *more* effective than mastery goals in these cases. These findings indicate that both mastery and performance goals can promote interest and that performance goals are sometimes superior to mastery goals. Inclusion of important personality and situational moderator variables revealed the conditions under which externally assigned mastery and performance goals can each enhance interest (see also Senko & Harackiewicz, 2002). Moreover, these effects highlight the complexity involved in influencing motivation with externally assigned goals. A given intervention may promote intrinsic motivation or not, depending on the individual and the context.

Mediator Effects

These findings raise the question of *why* both types of goals can increase interest in an activity. To address this question, we now turn to mediation analysis to help understand the motivational processes that were triggered in response to these goal manipulations. Mediators represent the more proximal mechanism underlying the relationship between a predictor and an outcome. For example, Gendolla and Wright (this volume) have examined the role of effort motivation, measured in terms of cardiovascular responses, in mediating the effect of social goals on performance. In our own work, we have identified four variables as mediators of intrinsic motivation: competence valuation, task involvement, perceived task value, and perceived competence. For example, students' intrinsic motivation would depend on whether they valued the skills and knowledge that they were learning, whether they became absorbed in class activities, whether they perceived the task as meaningful or important, and whether they developed a sense of competence in dealing with the material. However, in the research to be described, we will focus on the role of competence valuation and task involvement as mediators. Although we consider all four mediators important, our research has concentrated on the two processes initiated earlier in the motivational process (competence valuation and task involvement), because we have found these processes most relevant to goal effects. Specifically, goals can make individuals care more about doing well, and they can promote involvement in activities. For example, Harackiewicz and Elliot (1998) found that competence valuation and task involvement mediated the direct effects of goals on intrinsic motivation. Performance target goals were especially effective in promoting competence valuation and task involvement in the performance purpose goal condition, whereas mastery target goals had similar positive effects in the neutral purpose goal condition. In turn, higher levels of competence valuation and task involvement during the game promoted intrinsic interest in pinball and mediated the goal matching effect. These results revealed a process in which participants first became affectively committed to attaining competence and then became cognitively involved in the pinball game, resulting in increased intrinsic motivation. The process by which positive affect influences information processing and involvement has been discussed by Forgas and Laham (this volume).

In sum, the experimental work by Harackiewicz and Elliot revealed that both achievement goals could promote intrinsic motivation. Specifically, positive mastery and performance goal effects depended on personality differences (e.g., whether an individual was characteristically high or low in achievement motivation) or on characteristics of the situation (e.g., the match with other goals in the situation). Furthermore, by examining the underlying motivational process, Harackiewicz and Elliot found that mastery and performance goals facilitated interest through the same key mechanisms (competence valuation and task involvement). What proved more critical than the type of goal pursued was whether the goal fostered competence valuation and task involvement. These experimental results reveal that mastery and performance goals can both initiate positive motivational processes. Thus, this initial experimental work led us to consider a multiple goal perspective in which both goals could have positive consequences.

However, a limitation of these and other experimental studies is that participants have typically been asked to work on some activity under a mastery *or* a performance goal. Such designs force us into either-or inferences that compare one goal to the other, and tell us nothing about the additional benefits or disadvantages of pursuing a performance goal in conjunction with a mastery goal. Barron and Harackiewicz (2001) sought to test the effects of multiple goals by assigning both mastery and performance goals to participants in an experimental study, creating a multiple goal manipulation, which was compared to a mastery goal–only condition and a performance goal–only condition. They devised a laboratory version of an academic activity to simulate a classroom learning experience.

Students were taught new methods for solving math problems. These methods used simple strategies to add, subtract, multiply, and divide complex numbers mentally (as opposed to more traditional strategies of working out problems with paper and pencil). The self-report and behavioral measures of intrinsic motivation were the same as those used in the pinball studies.

No one type of goal (or combination of goals) proved optimal for all participants. Instead, the effects of assigned goals were again moderated by achievement orientation. For LAMs, mastery goals promoted the highest levels of interest in the math activity. In contrast, performance goals promoted the highest levels of interest for HAMs, replicating the experimental results reviewed earlier (Harackiewicz & Elliot, 1993). Interestingly, the multiple goal condition led to similar moderate levels of interest for both LAMs and HAMs. Although the multiple goal condition did not promote the highest levels of interest, it appeared to at least offer some buffer to low achievers who enjoyed learning the new technique the least when assigned only a performance goal, as well as to high achievers who enjoyed it the least when assigned only a mastery goal. These results once again suggest that both mastery and performance goals can promote intrinsic motivation. Moreover, a multiple goal manipulation may offer a compromise because it has elements that are effective for both HAMs and LAMs but may not be as effective as assigning the single preferred goal.

EVIDENCE FOR POSITIVE MASTERY AND PERFORMANCE GOAL EFFECTS IN COLLEGE CLASSES

We have conducted a series of survey studies in college classrooms to examine the joint effects of mastery and performance goals on optimal motivation. In these correlational studies, students are surveyed in actual classroom settings and asked to indicate the extent to which they pursue each type of goal in their coursework. Thus achievement goals are measured rather than manipulated. Survey studies consistently find that measures of mastery and performance goals are either uncorrelated (e.g., Ames & Archer, 1988; Harackiewicz, Barron, Carter, Lehto, & Elliot, 1997; Middleton & Midgley, 1997) or positively correlated (e.g., Archer, 1994; Midgley et al., 1998; Wolters, Yu, & Pintrich, 1996). Mastery and performance goals can therefore be construed as relatively independent motivational orientations, and it is important to test for the simultaneous effects of mastery and performance goals, as well as to test whether mastery and performance goals interact to predict important educational outcomes (Ames & Archer, 1988; Harackiewicz et al., 1997).

The basic paradigm for each of our studies involved measuring goals, interest, and performance in college classes at different points in a 15-week academic semester. First, we collected self-report measures of students' mastery and performance goals for the class at the outset of the semester (2–3 weeks into the term). We then collected self-report measures of students' interest in the course near the end of the term and finally obtained students' final course grades at the end of the term.

In our first study, we tracked college students enrolled in introductory psychology classes throughout the course of one semester (Harackiewicz et al., 1997). We evaluated both the independent and interactive effects of mastery and performance goals on interest and performance and found a simple pattern of main effects. Students who endorsed mastery goals at the beginning of the course were more likely to report interest in the course at the end of the semester, but performance goals were unrelated to interest. In contrast, students who endorsed performance goals at the beginning of the course were more likely to achieve higher grades in the course, but mastery goals were unrelated to students' final grades. Thus, mastery and performance goals each had independent, positive effects on interest and performance, respectively.

Although we documented a clear and important advantage of adopting mastery goals, our classroom findings also challenge the mastery goal perspective in two ways. First, we found no evidence that pursuing performance goals negatively affected students' interest. Second, we found a direct, positive effect of performance goals on grades. Because mastery and performance goals were each linked to a different educational outcome, adopting both goals would appear to be an optimal strategy. The student who adopts mastery goals is more likely to develop interest in the course, and the student who adopts performance goals is more likely to do well, but the student who adopts both goals is more likely to achieve both outcomes.

In a second classroom study (Harackiewicz, Barron, Tauer, & Elliot, 2002), we again tracked introductory psychology students over the course of a semester, but we also extended the study in time to examine longer-term consequences across students' entire undergraduate careers. Once again, students' achievement goals measured at the beginning of the semester predicted their interest and final grades in the course, replicating the pattern we found in our first study (Harackiewicz et al., 1997). To determine whether the consequences of mastery and performance goals observed in the short term (over the course of a semester) changed over the longer term, we tracked students' course choices and academic performance in the semesters following the semester in which they took introductory psychology, all the way through to their graduation or departure from the university. We computed two measures of continuing interest in psychology by counting the number of course credits taken in psychology over subsequent semesters and recording whether students chose psychology as their academic major. Our long-term measures of interest reflect continuing motivation in the field of psychology (Maehr, 1976), and the course credits measure is conceptually similar to behavioral measures of intrinsic motivation employed in laboratory research.

We found that the goals adopted in an introductory course continued to predict students' interest in psychology and academic performance, and that these effects were comparable to those observed in the short term. Specifically, mastery goals were positively related to continued interest in psychology and majoring in psychology, and performance goals were positively related to subsequent grades in psychology courses (for those students who actually enrolled in additional psychology courses) and subsequent academic performance (for all students in our sample). Thus, the same pattern of goal effects obtained in the short term was also observed on behavioral measures of continued interest and performance collected over additional semesters. These results suggest that *both* mastery and performance goals continue to have positive consequences on different indicators of academic success, and that the goals adopted by students in introductory classes may have far-ranging implications for their subsequent academic work.

One explanation for the positive performance goal effects found in our classroom research concerns the type of classroom environment that we studied. Introductory psychology classes at our university may represent a college environment in which performance goals are particularly adaptive. These classes are taught as large lecture courses (300–400 students), and instructors rely on multiple-choice exams to evaluate students' learning. Grades are based on normative curves, and students must therefore outperform others to obtain good grades. Competence is clearly defined in terms of relative ability and normative comparisons. Thus, a performance goal orientation may be well matched to this type of context. This idea is consistent with Harackiewicz and Sansone's (1991) matching hypothesis that goal effects depend on the general context in which they are pursued. In other words, students who are striving to outperform other students may be optimally motivated in a university context in which excellence is defined in terms of an individual's performance relative to others and in which grades are typically assigned on normative curves.

We recently tested this idea by studying the effects of goals in a different type of college classroom environment. Specifically, we surveyed psychology students taking advanced capstone courses in which the type of learning environment and assignments fostered mastery and deep-level processing of the material (through essay exams, projects, papers, etc.). A measure of perceived classroom climate revealed that students did indeed perceive these advanced courses as more mastery goal–oriented than performance goal–oriented. However, we found the same pattern of multiple goal effects as we did in our earlier classroom goal studies. Mastery goals predicted students' end-of-semester interest, and performance goals predicted students' final grades in these courses. Although this finding does not support the matching hypothesis at the classroom level, it does support it at the more general university context level. In other words, we suspect that the general context of university courses is performance-oriented. Thus it may still remain adaptive and optimal to pursue performance goals, regardless of specific classroom environments, because performance goals are well matched to the general university climate (Barron & Harackiewicz, in press).

In sum, when we examined the consequences of self-adopted mastery and performance goals in college classes, we continued to find that both types of achievement goals promote important educational outcomes. Across all of our classroom studies, students who adopted mastery goals reported more interest in the class. However, mastery goals had no effect on any measure of academic performance. Instead, we documented a clear advantage of performance goals on measures of academic performance. Success in college and university contexts depends on both performance and interest, and our results demonstrate the independent contributions of mastery and performance goals in promoting these two outcomes. Moreover, because neither type of goal promoted both outcomes, our results suggest that the optimal pattern of goal adoption would include both mastery and performance goals.

DEBATES AND BEYOND

Considered together, our experimental and classroom results pose a serious challenge to the mastery goal hypothesis, and we think they offer strong support for the multiple goal perspective. Additional evidence is beginning to accumulate from other labs as well (Church, Elliot, & Gable, 2001; Elliot & Church, 1997; Elliot & McGregor, 1999, 2001; Pintrich, 2000). Our results have proven to be controversial, especially in the field of educational psychology. We have engaged in heated debates about the theoretical significance of the performance goal effects reported in our papers at scientific meetings and in print (see Harackiewicz et al, 2002a; Hidi & Harackiewicz, 2001; Kaplan & Middleton, 2002; Midgley, Kaplan, & Middleton, 2001). We continue to examine the parameters of performance goal effects by extending our research to different educational settings (e.g., Barron & Harackiewicz, in press).

Somewhat ironically, however, it is the less controversial findings that have sparked our continued research attention. Although we were not surprised to learn that mastery goals predicted interest in the introductory college course and continued interest in the field, we wanted to explore this relationship in more depth. Some mediational findings from our longitudinal classroom studies were of particular interest. We had hypothesized that the long-term effects of mastery goals on continued interest and major choice would be mediated through their short-term effect on interest in psychology. We measured two components of short-term interest to distinguish specific reactions to the lectures (enjoyment) from more general reactions to the course content (interest). Although we found mastery goal effects on both enjoyment and interest, we hypothesized that interest in the subject matter of the introductory psychology course was most likely to promote continued interest in the topic, compared with enjoyment of the lectures (Harackiewicz et al., 2000a; Renninger, 1992). We found that interest partially mediated the direct effect of mastery goals on continued interest and academic major choice, but as hypothesized, enjoyment did not predict continued interest in psychology or academic major choice. The fact that students' self-reported interest during the introductory course was correlated with their actual course enrollment behavior and choice of academic major over the ensuing 4- to 7-year period is evidence of the crucial role that interest can play in college education.

FURTHER EXPLORATIONS OF INTEREST

A more detailed analysis of interest requires that we identify the basic components of interest and define the types of interest discussed in the literature. We will also need to integrate theory on interest with the model of intrinsic motivation described earlier (Harackiewicz & Sansone, 1991). Theorists have described interest as involving both a feeling component and a meaning component (Schiefele, 1991). The feeling component includes the positive affective experience that accompanies engagement and involvement in an activity. The meaning component connects the person to the topic at a deeper, more personal level (Krapp, Hidi, & Renninger, 1992). In addition to the two components of interest, feeling and meaning, two types of interest are recognized in the literature, distinguished on the basis of their source. Interest that resides within the individual over time has been distinguished from interest that emerges in response to situational cues. The former, *individual interest*, has a dispositional quality, and is deep and enduring. Individual interest may be related to authenticy, as discussed by Kernis and Goldman (this volume). Renninger (2000) argues that individual interest requires having substantial knowledge of a topic and valuing that knowledge. In other words, value is a core feature of individual interest. In contrast, *situational interest* emerges spontaneously as a result of features of the environment (Hidi, 1990). After situational interest is aroused, it may or may not last. If situational interest endures, it can eventually become a deep individual interest. Deep interest that endures over time corresponds to intrinsic motivation. This analysis highlights the importance of considering multiple determinants of motivation, as discussed in many of the chapters in this book (by Aarts & Hassin; Devine et al.; Schooler and Schreiber; Spencer et al.; Strack & Deutsch; and Wood & Quinn).

Given the importance of meaning and value in interest theory, perceived task value is likely to be a key determinant of whether deep interest develops. By *value*, we mean the extent to which a task or activity is important to an individual (Wigfield & Eccles, 1992). For example, a creative writing course might be very important to someone who hopes to become a novelist. In this case, the perceived value originates from within the individual and is likely to result from having initial interest in the topic. In contrast, a person who takes the class because friends are taking it may not be interested at the outset, but may come to value the course because of the way it is taught or because he or she discovers the relevance of the course material to his or her own life. This distinction between individual and contextual factors is reflected in Figure 2.1, indicating that both individual and contextual factors can ultimately influence perceived task value. We included value as both an individual factor (initial interest) and a motivational process (perceived task value). In this way, we recognize that individuals can enter situations with preexisting interest in the topic or not. This initial interest is likely to affect the goals individuals adopt and their subsequent motivation. Moreover, individuals who enter situations with low or nonexistent initial value must come to perceive the task as valuable in order to develop ongoing interest.

We explored the role of initial interest in goal adoption by testing whether the reasons students gave for enrolling in courses predicted the achievement goals they adopted (Harackiewicz & Durik, 2003). We asked introductory psychology students why they enrolled in the class. Coding the reasons yielded three distinct groups. One group cited interest as the sole reason they enrolled in the course (e.g., "I've always been fascinated by how the mind works"). A second group reported enrolling in the course in order to satisfy a requirement (e.g., "It's required for my business major"). Finally, a third group of students cited both interest and requirements as reasons for enrollment (e.g., "This class is required for my major, but I would have taken it anyway because I'm interested in why people do the things they do"). These classifications predicted the achievement goals students adopted at the beginning of the semester. Students who enrolled in the course because of pure interest adopted mastery goals but not performance goals. In contrast, students who enrolled in the course because it fulfilled a requirement endorsed performance goals but not mastery goals. Finally, students who enrolled in the course because it interested them *and* because it fulfilled a requirement were most likely to adopt both types of goals. Thus interest appears to predispose individuals to adopt mastery goals.

We next examined the causal direction of the observed relationship between mastery goals and interest at the end of the course. As reported earlier, mastery goals adopted at the outset of a college course positively predicted interest at the end of the semester. However, the results just described suggest the possibility that initial interest may account for the observed relationship between mastery goals and interest. To examine this, we measured initial interest in psychology during the first week of an introductory psychology course and then measured self-set mastery goals approximately 2 weeks later (Harackiewicz, Durik, Barron, Tauer, & Linnenbrink, in prep.). We tested both initial interest and mastery goals as predictors of interest at the end of the course. Replicating prior work, we found that mastery goals predicted interest in the course, and we also found that initial interest had an independent positive effect. Moreover, after controlling for initial interest in psychology, the relationship between mastery goals and interest in the class remained significant. In other words, although initial interest strongly predicted mastery goal adoption, as well as interest at the end of the semester, adopting mastery goals also predicted interest at the end of the semester. These data suggest that interest in introductory courses is multiply determined and can be facilitated by adopting mastery goals.

In addition to the initial interest individuals might bring to a situation, interest can also develop and change over time. In order for this to happen, individuals must come to perceive value in the task. This may happen because they find personal meaning or significance in the task. Perceived task value is represented in Figure 2.1 as a motivational process that is important for the development of intrinsic motivation. For example, a student might enroll in an introductory psychology course because it is required but may have very little knowledge about psychology as a scientific discipline. As this student gains knowledge about the topic, she may or may not find value in the class and the course material. Finding the material valuable is an important step in the development of interest because it can last over time and is a fundamental component of continued interest. We examined the role of perceived value in the development of interest in introductory psychology (Durik & Harackiewicz, 2003). Specifically, several weeks into the semester but before the first exam, we measured the extent to which students found the course material personally valuable or important (e.g., "What we are learning in this class is important for my career," "The material in the class is not relevant to my life" [reversed]). At that point in the semester, students had a sense of what they would learn in the course and whether it would be valuable to them. We found that meaning, measured in terms of perceiving personal value in the material, predicted interest in the topic at the end of the course, in addition to mastery goals, which independently predicted interest. These relationships remained even after controlling for initial interest, which had been measured at the beginning of the course. Thus perceived value contributed uniquely to the development of interest in the topic.

Using an experimental approach, it is possible to test whether contextual factors can also affect these processes. In other words, regardless of the prior experiences individuals bring with them to an achievement setting, features of the situation itself can affect the development of interest. John Dewey (1913) hypothesized two processes implicated in the development of interest. First, an individual's attention must be *caught* by the topic or activity. Then, because this initial phase is not anchored in the individual, interest must be *held* in order for it to last (Hidi & Baird, 1986; Mitchell, 1993). We conducted several studies in which we independently manipulated the presence of features hypothesized to catch and hold interest. In these studies, undergraduate students learned about a topic with a notebook and an accompanying audiotape (e.g., the mental math technique described earlier, the biology of fungi, or fundamentals of probability theory). The manipulations hypothesized to catch and hold interest were embedded in the notebook materials used to teach participants about each topic. Although there may be many ways to catch attention, we focused on superficial features of the learning context so that catch factors could be more cleanly distinguished from hold factors. Specifically, we manipulated catch by enhancing the aesthetic appeal of the learning materials with brightly colored text and pictures. For example, in our mental math paradigm, participants in catch conditions saw pictures of human brains illuminated so as to suggest mental activity. In our biology of fungi paradigm, the catch materials included colorful pictures of a wide variety of mushrooms, molds, and mildews. In contrast, the materials of participants in noncatch conditions were devoid of color and pictures. The notebook pages in noncatch conditions contained the same information as that in the catch conditions, but all of the text was black on a white background.

The catch manipulation in each study was crossed with a manipulation hypothesized to facilitate hold, or perceived task value. Although perceived value might develop in response to a number of factors (Eccles, 1983; Wigfield & Eccles, 1992), our manipulations centered on the personal relevance or utility of the material to be learned. For example, participants in hold conditions who learned fundamentals of probability theory learned how the material could be helpful when evaluating statistics in the media. In the fungi paradigm, we manipulated perceived value by pointing out ways fungi affect people (e.g., antibiotics, alcohol, and athlete's foot). In nonhold conditions, we did not mention how the topic could be personally relevant. At the end of each session, we measured enjoyment of the learning session, interest in the activity, and willingness to return for another session.

These studies are still in progress, but some preliminary results suggest an important distinction between interest in an activity and enjoyment of the situation in which the activity is learned. Catch and hold both had positive effects, but on different outcomes. Participants in hold rather than nonhold conditions reported greater interest in the activity. However, catch factors affected the level of enjoyment individuals evidenced during the learning part of the session. Consistent with this, when contacted 2 weeks after the initial session, participants in catch versus noncatch conditions reported greater willingness to return for another session. Thus both types of situational factors play a role in the development of interest, but they seem to do so by way of separate processes. Catch factors changed the initial experience of the task in such a way that it was more fun to learn about the topics presented, whereas hold factors seemed to affect individuals' evaluation of the topic. Continued interest may depend on both enjoying the learning experience and finding the material interesting and important. The enjoyment of learning a task will soon be forgotten if the task was not perceived as valuable. Our classroom results in which interest, but not enjoyment, predicted continued interest in psychology support this analysis. Deep individual interests are cultivated over time, and involve both feelings of involvement and enjoyment, as well as personal value. Although our work on this topic is just beginning, it is clear that a comprehensive understanding of interest requires an appreciation for the multiple determinants, both intrinsic and extrinsic, that influence motivational dynamics over time.

References

Ames, C. (1992). Classrooms: Goals, structures, and student motivation. *Journal of Educational Psychology, 84*, 261–271.

Ames, C., & Archer, J. (1988). Achievement goals in the classroom: Students' learning strategies and motivation processes. *Journal of Educational Psychology, 80*, 260–267.

Archer, J. (1994). Achievement goals as a measure of motivation in university students. *Contemporary Educational Psychology, 19*, 430–446.

Atkinson, J. W. (1974). The mainsprings of achievement oriented activity. In J. W. Atkinson & J. O. Raynor (Eds.), *Motivation and achievement* (pp. 11–39). Washington, DC: Winston.

Bandura, A. (1986). *Social foundations of thought and action: A social cognitive theory.* Englewood Cliffs, NJ: Prentice-Hall.

Barron, K. E., & Harackiewicz, J. M. (2001). Achievement goals and optimal motivation: A multiple goals approach. *Journal of Personality and Social Psychology, 80*, 706–722.

Barron, K. E., & Harackiewicz, J. M. (in press). Revisiting the benefits of performance-approach goals in the college classroom: Exploring the role of goals in advanced college courses. *International Journal of Educational Research.*

Carver, C. S., Lawrence, J. W., & Scheier, M. F. (1996). A control-process perspective on the origins of affect. In L. L. Martin, & A. Tesser (Eds.), *Striving and feeling: Interactions among goals, affect, and self-regulation* (pp. 11–52). Mahwah, NJ: Erlbaum.

Church, M. A., Elliot, A. J., & Gable, S. L. (2001). Perceptions of classroom environment, achievement goals, and achievement outcomes. *Journal of Educational Psychology, 93*, 43–54.

Deci, E. L., & Ryan, R. M. (1985). *Intrinsic motivation and self-determination in human behavior.* New York: Plenum Press.

Dewey, J. (1913). *Interest and effort in education*. Boston: Riverside Press.

Durik, A. M., & Harackiewicz, J. M. (2003). Achievement goals and intrinsic motivation: Coherence, concordance, and achievement orientation. *Journal of Experimental Social Psychology*, *39*, 378–385.

Dweck, C. S., & Leggett, E. L. (1988). A social-cognitive approach to motivation and personality. *Psychological Review*, *95*, 256–273.

Eccles, J. S. (1983). Expectancies, values and academic behaviors. In J. T. Spence (Ed.)., *Achievement and achievement motives: Psychological and sociological approaches* (pp. 75–146). San Francisco: W. H. Freeman.

Elliot, A. J., & Church, M. A. (1997). A hierarchical model of approach and avoidance achievement motivation. *Journal of Personality and Social Psychology*, *72*, 218–232.

Elliot, A. J., & Harackiewicz, J. M. (1994). Goal setting, achievement orientation, and intrinsic motivation: A mediational analysis. *Journal of Personality and Social Psychology*, *66*, 968–980.

Elliot, A. J., & McGregor, H. A. (1999). Test anxiety and the hierarchical model of approach and avoidance achievement motivation. *Journal of Personality and Social Psychology*, *76*, 549–563.

Elliot, A. J., & McGregor, H. A. (2001). A 2 × 2 achievement goal framework. *Journal of Personality and Social Psychology*, *80*, 501–519.

Elliott, E. S., & Dweck, C. S. (1988). Goals: An approach to motivation and achievement. *Journal of Personality and Social Psychology*, *54*, 5–12.

Harackiewicz, J. M., Barron, K. E., Carter, S. M., Lehto, A. T., & Elliot, A. J. (1997). Determinants and consequences of achievement goals in the college classroom: Maintaining interest and making the grade. *Journal of Personality and Social Psychology*, *73*, 1284–1295.

Harackiewicz, J. M., Barron, K. E., & Elliot, A. J. (1998). Rethinking achievement goals: When are they adaptive for college students and why? *Educational Psychologist*, *33*, 1–21.

Harackiewicz, J. M., Barron, K. E., Pintrich, P. R., Elliot, A. J., & Thrash, T. M. (2002). Revision of achievement goal theory: Necessary and illuminating. *Journal of Educational Psychology*, *94*, 638–645.

Harackiewicz, J. M., Barron, K. E., Tauer, J. M., Carter, S. M., & Elliot, A. J. (2000). Short-term and long-term consequences of achievement goals in college: Predicting continued interest and performance over time. *Journal of Educational Psychology*, *92*, 316–330.

Harackiewicz, J. M., & Durik, A. M. (2003). *Task value in the college classroom: Predicting goals, interest, and performance*. Presented at the meeting of the European Association for Research on Learning and Instruction, Padova, Italy.

Harackiewicz, J. M., Durik, A. M., Barron, K. E., Tauer, J. M., & Linnenbrink, L. (in preparation). *The development of interest in the college classroom: The role of individual difference factors and performance*. Manuscript.

Harackiewicz, J. M., & Elliot, A. J. (1993). Achievement goals and intrinsic motivation. *Journal of Personality and Social Psychology*, *65*, 904–915.

Harackiewicz, J. M., & Elliot, A. J. (1998). The joint effects of target and purpose goals on intrinsic motivation: A mediational analysis. *Personality and Social Psychology Bulletin*, *24*, 675–689.

Harackiewicz, J. M., & Sansone, C. (1991). Goals and intrinsic motivation: You can get there from here. In M. L. Maehr & P. R. Pintrich (Eds.), *Advances in motivation and achievement* (Vol. 7, pp. 21–49). Greenwich, CT: JAI Press.

Hidi, S., & Baird, W. (1986). Interestingness – a neglected variable in discourse processing. *Cognitive Science, 10*, 179–184.

Hidi, S., & Harackiewicz, J. M. (2001). Motivating the academically unmotivated: A critical issue for the 21st century. *Review of Educational Research, 70*, 151–179.

Jackson, D. N. (1974). *Personality research form manual.* Goshen, NY: Research Psychologists Press.

Judd, C. M., & Kenny, D. A. (1981). Process analysis: Estimating mediation in treatment evaluations. *Evaluation Review, 5*, 602–619.

Kaplan, A., & Middleton, M. J. (2002). Should childhood be a journey or a race? Response to Harackiewicz et al. (2002). *Journal of Educational Psychology, 94*, 646–648.

Krapp, A., Hidi, S., & Renninger, K. A. (1992). Interest, learning and development. In K. A. Renninger, S. Hidi, & A. Krapp (Eds.), *The role of interest in learning and development* (pp. 3–25), Hillsdale, NJ: Erlbaum.

Locke, E. A., & Latham, G. P. (1990). *A theory of goal setting and task performance.* Englewood Cliffs, NJ: Prentice-Hall.

Maehr, M. L. (1976). Continuing motivation: An analysis of a seldom considered educational outcome. *Review of Educational Research, 46*, 443–462.

Maehr, M. L. (1989). Thoughts about motivation. In C. Ames & R. Ames (Eds.), *Research on motivation in education: Goals and cognitions* (Vol. 3, pp. 299–315). New York: Academic Press.

Middleton, M., & Midgley, C. (1997). Avoiding the demonstration of lack of ability: An under-explored aspect of goal theory. *Journal of Educational Psychology, 89*, 710–718.

Midgley, C., Kaplan, A., & Middleton, M. (2001). Performance-approach goals: Good for what, for whom, under what circumstances and at what cost? *Journal of Educational Psychology, 93*, 77–86.

Midgley, C., Kaplan, A., Middleton, M., Maehr, M., Urdan, T., Anderman, L., Anderman, E., & Roeser, R. (1998). The development and validation of scales assessing students' achievement goal orientations. *Contemporary Educational Psychology, 23*, 113–131.

Mitchell, M. (1993). Situational interest: Its multifaceted structure in the secondary school mathematics classroom. *Journal of Educational Psychology, 85*, 424–436.

Nicholls, J. G. (1979). Quality and equality in intellectual development. *American Psychologist, 34*, 1071–1084.

Pintrich, P. R. (2000). Multiple goals, multiple pathways: The role of goal orientation in learning and achievement. *Journal of Educational Psychology, 92*, 544–555.

Pintrich, P. R., & Schunk, D. H. (1996). *Motivation in education: Theory, research and applications.* Englewood Cliffs, NJ: Merrill Prentice-Hall.

Renninger, K. A. (1992). Individual interest and development: Implications for theory and practice. In K. A. Renninger, S. Hidi, & A. Krapp. (Eds.), *The role of interest in learning and development* (pp. 361–395). Hillsdale, NJ: Erlbaum.

Sansone, C., & Harackiewicz, J. M. (1996). "I don't feel like it": The function of interest in self-regulation. In L. L. Martin & A. Tesser (Eds.), *Striving and feeling:*

Interactions among goals, affect, and self-regulation (pp. 203–228). Mahwah, NJ: Erlbaum.

Schiefele, U. (1991). Interest, learning and motivation. *Educational Psychologist, 26,* 299–323.

Senko, C. M., & Harackiewicz, J. M. (2002). Performance goals: The moderating roles of context and achievement orientation. *Journal of Experimental Social Psychology, 38,* 603–610.

Tauer, J. M., & Harackiewicz, J. M. (1999). Winning isn't everything: Competition, achievement orientation, and intrinsic motivation. *Journal of Experimental Social Psychology, 35,* 209–238.

Wigfield, A., & Eccles, J. S. (1992). The development of achievement task values: A theoretical analysis. *Developmental Review, 12,* 265–310.

Wolters, C. A., Yu, S. L., & Pintrich, P. R. (1996). The relation between goal orientation and students' motivational beliefs and self-regulated learning. *Learning and Individual Differences, 8,* 211–238.

3

The Machine in the Ghost

A Dual Process Model of Defense Against Conscious and Unconscious Death-Related Thought

Tom Pyszczynski, Jeff Greenberg, and Sheldon Solomon

INTRODUCTION

The proposition that people are often unaware of the forces that lead them to do the things they do is one of the oldest, most widely accepted, but at times most controversial ideas in the history of psychology. Since psychology's inception, the popularity of accounts of behavior that emphasize unconscious motivational forces has waxed and waned. Although virtually all psychologists probably agree that people are typically not aware of *all* the forces and processes that determine their behavior, the idea that people's thoughts, feelings, and actions are driven by powerful fears and needs of which they are unaware is considerably more contentious. Building on earlier theorizing in existential philosophy and psychoanalytic psychology, Terror Management Theory (TMT; Greenberg, Pyszczynski, & Solomon, 1986; Solomon, Greenberg, & Pyszczynski, 1991) posits that a very deeply rooted fear of death unique to our species motivates a great deal of human behavior. A substantial literature consisting of over 170 separate studies conducted in at least nine different countries has accumulated over the past 15 years, supporting a variety of hypotheses derived from TMT (for reviews, see Greenberg, Solomon, & Pyszczynski, 1997; Pyszczynski, Solomon, & Greenberg, 2003). This research demonstrates that thoughts of death affect a broad range of human behavior, but that these effects occur in the absence of consciously experienced affect and occur primarily when death-related thoughts are on the fringes of consciousness.

The purpose of this chapter is to provide a brief overview of TMT and research, explore the cognitive and motivational processes engendered by death-related thoughts, more clearly explicate the role that potential affect plays in these processes, and review the empirical evidence supporting our dual process model of conscious and unconscious defense.

Address correspondence to Tom Pyszczynski at e-mail: tpyszczy@uccs.edu.

TERROR MANAGEMENT THEORY AND RESEARCH: AN OVERVIEW

TMT posits that the juxtaposition of an instinctive desire or motive for continued life with awareness of the inevitability of death creates the potential for paralyzing terror, or death-related anxiety. According to the theory, this potential for anxiety is managed by a cultural anxiety buffer consisting of (a) a cultural worldview, which provides an explanation for existence, standards through which individuals can attain a sense of personal value, and the promise of literal or symbolic immortality to those who live up to these standards, and (b) self-esteem, which is acquired by believing in the worldview and living up to its standards.

Because these anxiety-buffering structures are fragile social constructions, they require ongoing consensual validation to function effectively. Given the vital role that self-esteem (see Kernis & Goldman, and Warburton & Williams, this volume) and cultural worldviews play in protecting people from deeply rooted fears, substantial social thought and behavior are thus oriented toward maintaining them and defending them against threats. Accordingly, from the perspective of TMT, a diverse array of human activity viewed by other theories as conceptually distinct can be profitably conceptualized as directed toward maintaining the functional integrity of this cultural anxiety buffer.

To date, over 170 separate experiments conducted in nine different countries have supported hypotheses derived from TMT. Most of this research has been guided by two primary hypotheses. The *anxiety-buffer hypothesis* states that, to the extent that a psychological structure provides protection against anxiety, strengthening that structure should make one less prone to anxiety in response to threats. Consistent with this proposition, tests of the anxiety-buffer hypothesis have shown that (a) increasing self-esteem reduces self-reported anxiety in response to graphic reminders of death, physiological arousal in response to the threat of electric shock, and death-denying defensive distortions (e.g., Greenberg et al., 1992, 1993) and (b) increasing self-esteem reduces the increased defense of the cultural worldview, self-esteem striving, and the delayed increase in the accessibility of death-related themes that normally occurs in response to death reminders (e.g., Harmon-Jones et al., 1997). Most recently, Arndt and Greenberg (1999) found that although a self-esteem boost generally reduces mortality salience–induced derogation of a worldview-threatening target, it does not do so if the target threatens the very values on which that self-esteem boost is based. This provides further evidence linking self-esteem to cultural values by showing that self-esteem loses its anxiety-buffering properties when the values from which it is derived are undermined.

The *mortality salience (MS) hypothesis* states that, to the extent that a psychological structure provides protection against anxiety, reminding people of the source of their anxiety should lead to increased need for that structure, and thus more positive reactions to entities that support it and more negative reactions to entities that threaten it. Tests of the MS hypothesis have shown that reminding people of their mortality (typically by having participants answer two brief open-ended questions about their feelings about their own death in the context of a study purporting to examine various personality traits and interpersonal judgments) leads to increased defense of the worldview in the form of more positive reactions to those who uphold it and more negative reactions to those who threaten it. Specifically, MS has been shown to lead to (a) harsher evaluations of moral transgressors and more favorable evaluations of those who uphold moral standards (e.g., Rosenblatt, Greenberg, Solomon, Pyszczynski, & Lyon, 1989); (b) more favorable evaluations of those who praise the culture and more negative evaluations of those who criticize it (e.g., Greenberg, Pyszczynski, Solomon, Simon, & Breus, 1994); (c) more favorable evaluations of ingroup members and more negative evaluations of outgroup members (Greenberg et al., 1990); (d) increased acceptance of others with worldviews different from one's own among those committed to the value of tolerance, especially when that value has recently been primed (Greenberg et al., 1992); (e) increased discomfort with and difficulty performing behavior counter to cultural norms (e.g., Greenberg et al., 1994); (f) avoidance of self-focusing stimuli (Arndt, Greenberg, Solomon, Pyszczynski, & Schimel, 1999); (g) increased perceptions of social consensus for one's attitudes (e.g. Pyszczynski et al., 1996); (h) increased aggression against attitudinally dissimilar others (e.g., McGregor et al., 1998); (i) increased pursuit of optimal distinctiveness in response to information that threatens one's uniqueness or normality (Simon et al., 1997a); (j) increased liking for stereotypic members of minority groups and decreased liking for counterstereotypic members of minority groups (e.g., Schimel et al., 1999); (k) increased imposition of cognitive structure in social information in the form of increased primacy, balance, and heuristic effects (Dechesne & Kruglanski, 2004; Landau et al., under review); (l) increased avoidance of pictures of spiders among spider phobics and more thorough hand-washing among obsessive-compulsives (Strachan et al., 2003); and a variety of other effects (see, e.g., Arndt et al., 1999).

Additional research has shown that MS increases self-esteem striving. Specifically, MS has been shown to (a) increase bold driving in Israeli soldiers who derive self-esteem from their driving ability (Taubman-Ben-Ari, Florian, & Mikulincer, 1999); (b) increase identification with one's body among those with high body self-esteem and decrease appearance monitoring among those with low body self-esteem (Goldenberg, McCoy, Pyszczynski, Greenberg, & Solomon, 2000); (c) increase white participants' sympathy for someone who expressed white pride (e.g., Greenberg, Schimel, Martens, Solomon, & Pyszczynski, 2001b); (d) increase positive attitudes and charitable contributions to valued charities (Jonas, Schimel,

Greenberg, & Pyszczynski, 2002); and (e) increase identification with valued ingroups but decrease identification with ingroups when they are framed negatively (Arndt et al., 2002a; Dechesne, Greenberg, Arndt, & Schimel, 2000). And Dechesne et al. recently demonstrated that although MS generally increases the self-serving tendency to perceive positive personality feedback as especially accurate, this effect is eliminated if participants are provided supposedly scientific evidence that there is life after death.

Other recent work has shown that mortality concerns affect attitudes toward sex, the body, and disgust. The core idea is that our physical animal nature is threatening because it reminds us that we are mortal, and that many cultures therefore separate humankind from the rest of nature and attempt to imbue our creaturely aspects with abstract symbolic meaning. In accord with this notion, (a) MS leads to negative reactions to an essay emphasizing our similarities with other animals (Goldenberg et al., 2001, Study 2); (b) MS leads to increased disgust reactions to reminders of animality (Goldenberg et al., 2001, Study 1); (c) MS leads to low rating of the appeal of physical aspects of sex among high neurotics and among people who have been reminded of our similarities to other animals (Goldenberg et al., 2002; Goldenberg, Pyszczynski, McCoy, Greenberg, & Solomon, 1999); (d) salience of physical aspects of sex leads to increased death-thought accessibility among high neurotics and people who have been reminded of our similarities to other animals; inducing subjects to think about romantic love eliminates these effects (Goldenberg et al., 1999, 2002); (e) MS intensifies sex-typical responses to thoughts of emotional and sexual infidelity (Goldenberg et al., 2003); and (f) MS leads to more positive evaluations of attractive women among men but more negative reactions to the same women if they are dressed in a sexually provocative way (Landau et al., under review).

Mikulincer, Florian, and Hirschberger (2003) have recently summarized compelling evidence for the notion that close personal relationships serve a particularly important terror management function. From the first statement of the theory (Greenberg et al., 1986; see also Becker, 1962/1971), we have argued that the anxiety-buffering properties of self-esteem and cultural worldviews develop from attachments to parents and primary caretakers forged early in life. We have argued that as love and protection become increasingly conditional during socialization, the security-providing properties of these attachments become transferred to investment in the worldview and self-worth. In contrast, Mikulincer et al. have proposed that attachments continue throughout life to serve a terror management function distinct from that provided by cultural worldviews and self-esteem. Their findings include evidence that (a) MS leads to more desire for intimacy, more initiation of, and optimism about, social interactions, inflated self-perception of social skills, reduced fear of rejection, increased social skills, and more relationship commitment, especially for securely attached individuals; (b) MS leads to more willingness among high-self-esteem individuals to compromise their ideal standards to establish a long-term relationship; (c) thinking about a romantic relationship and a secure attachment style reduces the effects of MS on worldview defense; and (d) for people high in attachment anxiety, thinking about relationship problems and separation from a loved one increases death-thought accessibility.

This impressive body of work clearly shows that close personal relationships play a central role in terror management processes. However, we believe that further research is needed to determine whether close relationships are best viewed as an additional third component of the terror management system, as Mikulincer et al. propose, or as a particularly vital source of worldview and self-worth validation.

Clearly, this wide-ranging body of research supports broad, robust effects of thoughts of one's own mortality. Research also supports the specificity of these effects to death-related ideation. Although MS has been typically operationalized by open-ended questions about one's own death, similar effects have been found with fear-of-death scales, physical proximity to funeral homes and cemeteries, and subliminal death primes. Parallel conditions in which subjects contemplate other aversive events, such as giving a speech, taking or failing an exam in an important class, intense physical pain, being paralyzed, social exclusion, worries after graduation from college, or actually experiencing a failure on a supposed IQ test do not produce parallel effects, even though these other conditions sometimes produce negative affect. Although McGregor, Zanna, Holmes, and Spencer (2001) have reported that manipulations of existential uncertainty, involving thoughts of major value clashes or how the world in which we live will be dramatically changed in future years, produce some effects similar to those of MS (see also van den Bos, 2001), Chaudhary, Tison, and Solomon (2002) have recently demonstrated that one of the uncertainty inductions used by McGregor et al. produces an increase in the accessibility of death-related thoughts. To the extent that existential uncertainty undermines one's anxiety buffer enough to increase the accessibility of death-related thoughts, it follows from TMT that such an induction would consequently produce increased worldview defense and/or self-esteem striving. In addition, Landau et al. (in press) recently reported very different effects of MS and the uncertainty induction used by van den Bos.

In summary, research findings converge in showing that thoughts of death influence a wide range of superficially unrelated human behaviors, and thus support the TMT assertion that many specific human motives, such as needs for self-esteem, faith in our conceptions of reality, and close personal relationships exist, at least in part, because they provide protection from a deeply rooted fear of death that is inherent in the human condition (Pyszczynski, Greenberg, & Solomon, 1997). Although most of us are sometimes aware of this fear, most of the time it lies beneath the surface of our consciousness. In William James's (1890/1918, p. 158) colorful words, death is ultimately the "worm at the core" of many of our more conscious needs and desires. But how does an unconscious fear that only occasionally impinges on our conscious experience influence such a broad range of attitudes and behaviors?

A DUAL COMPONENT MODEL OF DEFENSIVE RESPONSES TO CONSCIOUS AND UNCONSCIOUS THREAT

We suspect that some of the initial skepticism surrounding TMT resulted from two facts. The first is that people are not generally aware of engaging in a lot of death-related thought. The second is that people have trouble seeing how such thoughts could be related to judgments and actions that bear no obvious relation to the problem of death. Although recent work has certainly restored the credibility of positing influences from outside consciousness on thought and behavior (e.g., Bargh, 1996; Greenwald et al., 2002), TMT and related research takes this a step further than other work by positing a connection between nonconscious constructs and seemingly semantically unrelated thoughts and actions. We have proposed a dual process model of the cognitive and motivational processes underlying MS effects (Pyszczynski, Greenberg, & Solomon, 1999), which postulates that distinct defensive processes are activated by conscious and nonconscious death-related thoughts. Symbolic *distal* terror management defenses, involving self-esteem and faith in one's worldview, are activated when thoughts of death are highly accessible but not in current focal attention. These defenses bear no obvious logical or semantic relation to the problem of death and provide protection by enabling the individual to perceive him- or herself as a valuable contributor to a meaningful universe. Distal terror management defenses acquire their anxiety-buffering properties by virtue of early socialization experiences with one's parents or primary caregivers, in which the safety and security associated with parental attachment come to be associated with the sense of personal value that comes from living up to parental standards of value and accepting the version of reality (i.e., the version of the cultural worldview) that they teach us.

Defenses instigated by conscious thoughts of death are more direct and rational. These threat-focused *proximal* defenses entail denying one's vulnerability to death in a rational manner or simply distracting oneself in order to remove thoughts of death from conscious awareness. These defenses include (but are not necessarily limited to) vulnerability-denying distortions (e.g., "Really emotional people die young; thank God I'm so even-keeled"); pushing death into the distant future by exaggerating one's health, hardiness, and likely longevity (e.g., "I'm in great health, I don't smoke, and my grandfather lived to be 112"); making promises to do things that are believed to increase one's longevity and forestall death (e.g., "I'm going to quit smoking tomorrow, start getting more exercise, and quit my job at the nuclear power plant"); or simply suppressing thoughts of death by distracting oneself from the problem (e.g., turning up the music on the radio as one passes a fatal accident site; thinking of white bears while waiting for the results of diagnostic medical tests) or avoiding confrontation with reminders of one's mortality (e.g., refusing to attend funerals or get diagnostic medical tests). The defining features these proximal defenses share is that they tackle the unpleasantness of conscious contemplation of death either by rationally minimizing the problem of death or by distracting attention from it.

Distinct proximal and distal defenses are needed because although each is effective in its intended domain, neither is effective outside of it. Whereas denying one's vulnerability to disease, accident, and general mayhem is an effective way of banishing thoughts of death from consciousness, such cognitive distortions do nothing to deny the ultimate inevitability of death, nor are they effective in short-circuiting the potential for anxiety that high levels of accessibility of death-related thoughts portend. Similarly, whereas clinging to one's worldview or sense of personal value provides a sense of security and thereby serves to reduce the accessibility of death-related thoughts that are outside of conscious attention, once such thoughts enter consciousness, rational thought undermines their defensive effectiveness. It becomes apparent that no matter how correct one's worldview is or how much of a hero one is within the context of one's worldview, death is still an inevitable reality waiting for us all. To paraphrase Ecclesiastes, Shakespeare, and many others, death is a fate we all share, whether great or humble, good or evil, right or wrong in our beliefs.

Empirical Evidence

Consistent with this analysis (a detailed review of the empirical evidence supporting this dual process model would be beyond the scope of this chapter; for a more thorough review, see Pyszczynski et al., 1999), studies have shown that (a) subtle reminders of mortality produce stronger effects than more blatant ones (Greenberg et al., 1994, Study 1); (b) MS effects occur when subjects are distracted from the problem of death prior to assessment of dependent variables but not when they are forced to keep death-related themes in focal attention (Greenberg et al., 1994, Studies 2 and 3); (c) whereas worldview defense occurs only after distraction from death-related thoughts, a bias to reduce perceived vulnerability to a short life expectancy occurs only immediately after MS (Greenberg, Arndt, Simon, Pyszczynski, & Solomon, 2000); (d) the accessibility of death themes does not increase immediately after a MS induction but does increase when subjects are distracted after MS (Greenberg et al., 1994, Study 4); however, putting subjects under high cognitive load produces an immediate increase in death theme accessibility in response to MS (Arndt, Greenberg, Solomon, Pyszczynski, & Simon, 1997); this suggests that subjects actively suppress death-related thoughts in response to MS (cf. Wegner, 1994), which leads to a delayed increase in accessibility; (e) whereas our typical supraliminal MS induction does not produce effects on worldview defense until after a delay and distraction, subliminally presented death reminders produce immediate effects on worldview defense (Arndt, Greenberg, Pyszczynski, & Solomon, 1997a); (f) following MS, and a delayed increase in death theme accessibility, worldview defense reduces death theme accessibility to baseline (Arndt et al., 1997b); (g) worldview defense causes a dissipation of death-related thought rather than a renewed active suppression (Greenberg, Arndt, Schimel, Pyszczynski, & Solomon, 2001a); (h) whereas MS leads to increased worldview defense and a delayed increase in death thought accessibility when subjects are in an experiential mode of processing (cf. Epstein, 1994), this does not occur when subjects are in a rational mode of processing (Simon et al., 1997a); and (i) MS immediately increases intentions to improve one's physical fitness (proximal defense) but, after a delay, increases fitness intentions only in individuals who derived self-esteem from their fitness level (distal defense; Arndt, Schimel, & Goldenberg, 2003). Taken together, these results provide converging support for our contention that proximal defenses, which deal with the problem of death in a head-on and relatively rational manner are activated when thoughts of death are in current consciousness, and distal terror management defenses, which deal with the problem of death by embedding the individual as a valuable contributor to a meaningful world, are activated when death-related thoughts are on the fringes of consciousness.

The Role of Affect in Terror Management Processes

An extremely consistent finding across the TMT literature that has been surprising to some observers is that the inductions used to remind participants of death that consistently produce worldview defense in MS studies almost never produce any signs of affect, anxiety, or arousal in participants. In the few studies where MS has been found to influence affective responses, no evidence of mediation by consciously experienced affect or physiological arousal has been found (Arndt, Allen, & Greenberg, 2001; Greenberg et al., 1997; Pyszczynski et al., 1999). This has been viewed as a problem for the theory by some observers, and prompted Muraven and Baumeister (1997) to ask, "where is the terror?"

From early on (Solomon et al., 1991), we argued that it is not consciously experienced affect that activates increased clinging to one's worldview or self-esteem striving and defense, but rather the *potential* for "paralyzing terror" that awareness of death produces. We use the term *terror* to link it explicitly to the problem of death and to denote the intensity of the affective experience that we believe awareness of death would produce in the absence of an effectively functioning cultural anxiety buffer provided by one's worldview and self-esteem. Reminders of mortality signal the potential for anxiety, which people avert by affirming or defending their worldviews, self-esteem, or close relationships (see also Warburton & Williams, this volume). TMT thus posits that one's worldview, self-esteem, and close personal attachments enable one to avoid the experience of existential terror, just as well-learned avoidance responses enable animals to avert the experience of fear or anxiety portended by the presence of stimuli associated with aversive stimulation (Solomon & Wynne, 1954).

This potential for affect that we argue mediates defensive responses to thoughts of death can be thought of as *implicit affect*, similar in some ways to the various types of implicit attitudes investigated by Greenwald and colleagues (e.g., Greenwald et al., 2002; Greenwald, McGhee, & Schwartz, 1998). When thoughts of death are activated, the potential for affect that is tied up in such thoughts may produce preconscious precursors to the experience of affect. Exactly what these preconscious precursors to affect entail is a difficult question that will require a more thorough understanding of preconscious processes to answer. However, it is clear, from both common experience and empirical research (e.g., Greenberg et al., 1992, 1993), that thoughts of death sometimes produce strong affective responses. Just think of the last time a car swerved in front of you as you were driving or a doctor said that a lump, mole, or other symptom "looks suspicious" and that he or she would like to perform some diagnostic tests. From a TMT perspective, if there were no potential for affective experience associated with thoughts of death, there would be no need to activate the various defensive strategies that consistently emerge after reminders of one's mortality in the literature and in life.

Although this analysis is highly consistent with the available evidence, we have only recently conducted research to assess the role that a potential for anxiety is posited to play in these processes. Greenberg, Martens, Jonas, Eisenstadt, Pyszczynski, and Solomon (2003) demonstrated that the potential for affect does indeed play a central mediating role in the defensive responses that MS activates. We reasoned that if the potential to experience affect mediates defensive responses to MS, then no such defensive responses should emerge among individuals who are led to believe that their potential to experience anxiety has been temporarily blocked. To test this hypothesis, participants were told that they were participating in a study on the effect of herbal medicines and were induced to drink a glass of tea purported to contain a highly effective herbal mixture that is known to either block one's potential to experience fear and anxiety or enhance one's memory. Both of these concoctions were in fact placebos. After consuming the tea, half of the participants were exposed to a typical

MS induction and half to a parallel induction focused on other aversive events, after which their evaluations of authors and essays that praised or criticized the United States were assessed. As in many previous studies, the difference between participants' evaluation of the pro- and anti-U.S. essays served as our measure of worldview defense. Whereas participants in the memory-enhancing placebo condition exhibited a pattern of increased worldview defense after MS similar to that found in previous research, participants in the anxiety-blocking placebo condition were unaffected by MS.

These findings provide additional evidence that it is the potential rather than the actual experience of affect that activates defensive processes when one contrasts them with what would be expected if actual affective or arousal states were, in fact, involved in the process. The misattribution of arousal literature suggests that if participants are experiencing affect or arousal, then giving them a placebo that they believe will block their potential for such experience would augment the subjective experience of emotion (e.g., Zanna & Cooper, 1974). This prior research has shown that placebos that are presented as producing relaxation produce an increase in dissonance reduction or self-serving attributional biases rather than the decrease in defensive responses observed in the present study. The contrast between the present findings and those of these classic studies reinforces our contention that it is the potential for affect rather than the actual experience of affect that instigates terror management processes. Research is currently underway to further explore the nature of this implicit affect that awareness of death produces and how it mediates the relationship between death thought accessibility and the activation of terror management defenses.

THE ACTIVATION OF WORLDVIEW DEFENSE

Given the multifaceted nature of individuals' cultural worldviews and the standards they use to attain self-esteem, an important question emerges: Which of the many possible ways of affirming meaning and personal value will they resort to in order to defend against the threat that thoughts of death pose? In other words, how does death thought accessibility lead to the shoring up of particular aspects of the individual's terror management system?

To examine this question, Arndt et al. (2002a) conducted some initial studies of the effect of MS on the spontaneous accessibility of cultural worldview (CWV)–relevant concepts. TMT posits that over the course of development, children learn to ward off the fear of death by clinging to the CWV in which they are embedded. This suggests that reminders of death might spontaneously increase the accessibility of central CWV-related constructs. In the first study, MS led to a delayed increase in the accessibility of nationalistic constructs, as indicated by an increase in the frequency of word completions like *flag* and *anthem*, but only for male participants. A second study found that MS increased the accessibility of nationalistic constructs for men but relationship constructs for women. A third study replicated this effect with women and showed that, consistent with previous findings on the time course of the accessibility of death-related thoughts after MS, this increased CWV accessibility occurs after a delay but not immediately. A fourth study using men showed that subliminal death primes lead to an immediate increase in the accessibility of nationalistic thoughts. A fifth study using women showed that subliminal death primes lead to an immediate increase in relationship accessibility, using reaction times on a lexical decision task rather than word-stem completions as the accessibility measure. A sixth study showed, within the same design, that conscious contemplation of mortality only increased CWV accessibility after a delay, whereas a subliminal death prime did so immediately. Finally, a seventh study showed that if America is first primed, MS increases the accessibility of nationalistic rather than relationship constructs among women.

These studies suggest that death-related ideation is closely associated with CWV-related thought, but that the type of CWV-related constructs made spontaneously accessible differs systematically by gender (at least in American culture). For men, national identity appears particularly central for terror management, whereas for women, romantic relationships seem more important. This is consistent with research on sex differences that suggests that, whether due to genetic correlates of gender or sex role socialization practices, men are more focused on nationalism and women are more focused on relationships (e.g., Moskowitz, Suh, & Desaulniers, 1994; Norrander, 1999). However, these findings seem superficially inconsistent with the general absence of sex differences in previous MS studies. However, prior MS research always presented participants with stimuli and questions that made particular aspects of their CWV salient (e.g., the pro-U.S. bias studies confront participants with pro- and anti-U.S. essays). In contrast, these studies assessed spontaneous accessibility without making particular aspects of the CWV salient – except for Study 7, which showed that reminding women of America did lead to an MS-induced increase in nationalism accessibility. Recent research has also shown that situational primes of values such as kindness, fairness, and competitiveness seem to direct responses to MS toward behavior supporting these primed values (Jonas, Martens, & Greenberg, 2003). Understanding the relationship between death-related thoughts and the individual and situational factors that influence the accessibility of thoughts related to different aspects of the individual's worldview helps explain which of the many possible directions for defense particular individuals will take.

CONCLUSION

The problem of knowledge of the inevitability of death is a daunting one that we all must face. TMT asserts that this uniquely human problem lies at the core of some fundamental human motives. Research testing hypotheses derived from the theory has documented the very wide range of human behavior that is affected by this awareness. This research has also led to more detailed theoretical analyses of the underlying psychological processes through which the problem of death exerts its effect that we hope will ultimately also inform other areas of inquiry concerning the interplay of conscious and unconscious processes and the role they play in human thought, emotion, and behavior.

References

Arndt, J., Allen, J., & Greenberg, J. (2001). Traces of terror: Subliminal death primes and facial electromyographic indices of affect. *Motivation and Emotion, 25,* 253–277.

Arndt, J., & Greenberg, J. (1999). The effects of a self-esteem boost and mortality salience on responses to boost relevant and irrelevant worldview threats. *Personality and Social Psychological Bulletin, 25,* 1331–1341.

Arndt, J., Greenberg, J., & Cook, A. (2002a). Mortality salience and the spreading activation of worldview-relevant constructs: Exploring the cognitive architecture of terror management. *Journal of Experimental Psychology: General, 131,* 307–324.

Arndt, J., Greenberg, J., Pyszczynski, T., & Solomon, S. (1997). Subliminal exposure to death-related stimuli increases defense of the cultural worldview. *Psychological Science, 8,* 379–385.

Arndt, J., Greenberg, J., Solomon, S., Pyszczynski, T., & Schimel, J. (1999). Creativity and terror management: The effects of creative activity on guilt and social projection following mortality salience. *Journal of Personality and Social Psychology, 77,* 19–32.

Arndt, J., Greenberg, J., Solomon, S., Pyszczynski, T., & Simon, L. (1997b). Suppression, accessibility of death-related thoughts, and cultural worldview defense: Exploring the psychodynamics of terror management. *Journal of Personality and Social Psychology, 73,* 5–18.

Arndt, J., Schimel, J., & Goldenberg, J. L. (2003). Death can be good for your health: Fitness intentions as a proximal and distal defense against mortality salience. *Journal of Applied Social Psychology, 33,* 1726–1746.

Bargh, J. (1996). Automaticity in social psychology. In E. T. Higgins & A. W. Kruglanski (Eds.), *Social psychology: Handbook of basic principles* (pp. 169–183). New York: Guilford Press.

Becker, E. (1962/1971). *The birth and death of meaning.* New York: Free Press.

Chaudhary, N., Tison, J., & Solomon, S. (2002, June). *What's death got to do with it? The role of psychological uncertainty on implicit death accessibility.* Presented at the annual meeting of the American Psychological Society, New Orleans.

Dechesne, M., Greenberg, J., Arndt, J., & Schimel, J. (2000). Terror management and sports fan affiliation: The effects of mortality salience on fan identification and optimism. *European Journal of Social Psychology, 30*, 813–835.

Dechesne, M., & Kruglanski, A. W. (2004). Terror's epistemic consequences. In J. Greenberg, S., Koole, & T. Pyszczynski (Eds.), *Handbook of experimental existential psychology*. New York: Guilford Press.

Epstein, S. (1994). Integration of the cognitive and the psychodynamic unconscious. *American Psychologist, 49*, 709–724.

Goldenberg, J. L., Cox, C. R., Pyszczynski, T., Greenberg, J., & Solomon, S. (2002). Understanding human ambivalence about sex: The effects of stripping sex of meaning. *Journal of Sex Research, 39*, 310–320.

Goldenberg, J. L., Landau, M., Pyszczynski, T., Cox, C., Greenberg, J., Solomon, S. et al. (2003). Gender-typical responses to sexual and emotional infidelity as a function of mortality salience induced self-esteem striving. *Personality and Social Psychology Bulletin, 29*, 1585–1595.

Goldenberg, J. L., McCoy, S. K., Pyszczynski, T., Greenberg, J., & Solomon, S. (2000). The body as a source of self-esteem: The effects of mortality salience on identification with one's body, interest in sex, and appearance monitoring. *Journal of Personality and Social Psychology, 79*, 118–130.

Goldenberg, J. L., Pyszczynski, T., Greenberg, J., Solomon, S., Kluck, B., & Cornwell, R. (2001). I am not an animal: Mortality salience, disgust, and the denial of human creatureliness. *Journal of Experimental Psychology: General, 130*, 427–435.

Goldenberg, J. L., Pyszczynski, T., McCoy, S. K., Greenberg, J., & Solomon, S. (1999). Death, sex, love, and neuroticism: Why is sex such a problem? *Journal of Personality and Social Psychology, 77*, 1173–1187.

Greenberg, J., Arndt, J., Schimel, J., Pyszczynski, T., & Solomon, S. (2001a). Clarifying the function of mortality-salience induced worldview defense: Renewed suppression or reduced accessibility of death-related thoughts? *Journal of Experimental Social Psychology, 37*, 70–76.

Greenberg, J., Arndt, J., Simon, L., Pyszczynski, T., & Solomon, S. (2000). Proximal and distal defenses in response to reminders of one's mortality: Evidence of a temporal sequence. *Personality and Social Psychology Bulletin, 26*, 91–99.

Greenberg, J., Martens, A., Jonas, E., Eisenstadt, D., Pyszczynski, T., & Solomon, S. (2003). Psychological defense in anticipation of anxiety: Eliminating the potential for anxiety eliminates the effect of mortality salience on worldview defense. *Psychological Science, 14*, 516–519.

Greenberg, J., Pyszczynski, T., & Solomon, S. (1986). The causes and consequences of a need or self-esteem: A terror management theory. In R. F. Baumeister (Ed.), *Public self and private self* (pp. 189–212). New York: Springer-Verlag.

Greenberg, J., Pyszczynski, T., Solomon, S., Pinel, E., Simon, L., & Jordan, K. (1993). Effects of self-esteem on vulnerability-denying defensive distortions: Further evidence of an anxiety-buffering function of self-esteem. *Journal of Experimental Social Psychology, 29*, 229–251.

Greenberg, J., Pyszczynski, T., Solomon, S., Rosenblatt, A., Veeder, M., Kirkland, S., & Lyon, D. (1990). Evidence for terror management II: The effects of mortality salience on reactions to those who threaten or bolster the cultural worldview. *Journal of Personality and Social Psychology, 58*, 308–318.

Greenberg, J., Pyszczynski, T., Solomon, S., Simon, L., & Breus, M. (1994). Role of consciousness and accessibility of death-related thoughts in mortality salience effects. *Journal of Personality and Social Psychology, 67,* 627–637.

Greenberg, J., Schimel, J., Martens, A., Solomon, S., & Pyszczynski, T. (2001b). Sympathy for the devil: Evidence that reminding Whites of their mortality promotes more favorable reactions to White racists. *Motivation and Emotion, 25,* 113–133.

Greenberg, J., Solomon, S., & Pyszczynski, T. (1997). Terror management theory on self-esteem and cultural worldviews: Empirical assessments and conceptual refinements. In M. P. Zanna (Ed.), *Advances in Experimental Social Psychology* (Vol. 29, pp. 61–136). New York: Academic Press.

Greenberg, J., Solomon, S., Pyszczynski, T., Rosenblatt, A., Burling, J., Lyon, D., Simon, L., & Pinel, E. (1992). Why do people need self-esteem? Converging evidence of an anxiety-buffering function. *Journal of Personality and Social Psychology, 63,* 913–922.

Greenwald, A. G., Banaji, M. R., Rudman, L. A., Farnham, S. D., Nosek, B. A., & Mellott, D. S. (2002). A unified theory of implicit attitudes, stereotypes, self-esteem, and self-concept. *Psychological Review, 109,* 3–25.

Greenwald, A. G., McGhee, D. E., & Schwartz, J. L. K. (1998). Measuring individual differences in implicit cognition: The implicit association test. *Journal of Personality and Social Psychology, 74,* 1464–1480.

Harmon-Jones, E., Simon, L., Greenberg, J., Pyszczynski, T., Solomon, S., & McGregor, H. (1997). Terror management theory and self-esteem: Evidence that increased self-esteem reduces mortality salience effects. *Journal of Personality and Social Psychology, 72,* 24–36.

James, W. (1890/1918). *Principles of psychology.* Toronto, Ontario: General Publishing.

Jonas, E., Schimel, J., Greenberg, J., & Pyszczynski, T. (2002). The Scrooge effect: Evidence that mortality salience increases prosocial attitudes and behavior. *Personality and Social Psychology Bulletin, 28,* 1342–1353.

Landau, M. J., Goldenberg, J. L., Greenberg, J., Gillath, O., Solomon, S., & Cox, C., Martens, A., & Pyszczynski, T. (under review). *The siren's call: Terror management and the threat of sexual attraction.* University of Arizona, Tucson.

Landau, M. J., Johns, M., Greenberg, J., Pyszczynski, T., Martens, A., Goldenberg, J., & Solomon, S. (in press). A function of form: Terror management and structuring the social world. *Journal of Personality and Social Psychology.*

McGregor, H., Lieberman, J. D, Solomon, S., Greenberg, J., Arndt, J., Simon, L., & Pyszczynski, T. (1998). Terror management and aggression: Evidence that mortality salience motivates aggression against worldview threatening others. *Journal of Personality and Social Psychology, 74,* 590–605.

McGregor, I., Zanna, M. P., Holmes, J. G., & Spencer, S. J. (2001). Compensatory conviction in the face of personal uncertainty: Going to extremes and being oneself. *Journal of Personality and Social Psychology, 80,* 472–488.

Mikulincer, M., Florian, V., & Hirschberger, G. (2003). The existential function of close relationships: Introducing death into the science of love. *Personality and Social Psychology Review, 7,* 20–40.

Moskowitz, D. S., Suh, E., & Desaulniers, J. (1994). Situational influences on gender differences in agency and communion. *Journal of Personality and Social Psychology, 66*, 753–761.

Muraven, M., & Baumeister, R. F. (1997). Suicide, sex, terror, paralysis, and other pitfalls of reductionist self-preservation theory. *Psychological Inquiry, 8*, 36–40.

Norrander, B. (1999). The evolution of the gender gap. *Public Opinion Quarterly, 63*, 566–576.

Pyszczynski, T., Greenberg, J., & Solomon, S. (1997). Why do we need what we need? A terror management perspective on the roots of human social motivation. *Psychological Inquiry, 8*, 1–21.

Pyszczynski, T., Greenberg, J., & Solomon, S. (1999). A dual-process model of defense against conscious and unconscious death-related thoughts: An extension of terror management theory. *Psychological Review, 106*, 835–845.

Pyszczynski, T., Solomon, S., & Greenberg, J. (2003). *In the wake of 9/11: The psychology of terror.* Washington, DC: American Psychological Association.

Pyszczynski, T., Wicklund, R. A., Floresky, S., Gauch, G., Koch, S., Solomon, S., & Arndt, J. (1996). Whistling in the dark: Exaggerated estimates of social consensus in response to incidental reminders of mortality. *Psychological Science, 7*, 332–336.

Rosenblatt, A., Greenberg, J., Solomon, S., Pyszczynski, T., & Lyon, D. (1989). Evidence for terror management theory I: The effects of mortality salience on reactions to those who violate or uphold cultural values. *Journal of Personality and Social Psychology, 57*, 681–690.

Schimel, J., Simon, L., Greenberg, J., Pyszczynski, T., Solomon, S., Waxmonsky, J., & Arndt, J. (1999). Stereotypes and terror management: Evidence that mortality salience enhances stereotypic thinking and preferences. *Journal of Personality and Social Psychology, 77*, 905–926.

Simon, L., Greenberg, J., Arndt, J., Pyszczynski, T., Clement, R., & Solomon, S. (1997a). Perceived consensus, uniqueness, and terror management: Compensatory responses to threats to inclusion and distinctiveness following mortality salience. *Personality and Social Psychology Bulletin, 23*, 1055–1065.

Solomon, S., Greenberg, J., & Pyszczynski, T. (1991). A terror management theory of social behavior: The psychological functions of self-esteem and cultural worldviews. In M. P. Zanna (Ed.), *Advances in experimental social psychology:* Vol. 24, (pp. 93–159). New York: Academic Press.

Solomon, R. L., & Wynne, L. C. (1954). Traumatic avoidance learning: The principles of anxiety conservation and partial irreversibility. *Psychological Review, 61*, 353–385.

Taubman Ben-Ari, O., Florian, V., & Mikulincer, M. (1999). The impact of mortality salience on reckless driving – A test of terror management mechanisms. *Journal of Personality and Social Psychology, 76*, 35–45.

van den Bos, K. (2001). Uncertainty management: The influence of uncertainty salience on reactions to perceived procedural fairness. *Journal of Personality and Social Psychology, 80*, 931–941.

Wegner, D. M. (1994). Ironic processes of mental control. *Psychological Review, 101*, 34–52.

Zanna, M. P., & Cooper, J. (1974). Dissonance and the pill: An attribution approach to studying the arousal properties of dissonance. *Journal of Personality and Social Psychology, 29*, 703–709.

4

Habits and the Structure of Motivation in Everyday Life

Wendy Wood and Jeffrey M. Quinn

INTRODUCTION

Many of the motivational challenges in daily life recur at routine intervals. For example, most appetitive drives (e.g., hunger, sleep) are cyclic, and people act to address them at certain times of the day in certain circumstances. Many other goals, such as getting to work or achieving physical fitness, also involve periodic activities that occur in specific, recurring times and places. This regularity in motivated behavior organizes everyday experience into repeated patterns of goal-directed activities in particular circumstances. With repetition of behavior in stable contexts, actions become automatic in the sense that deliberation about behavior becomes unnecessary. These well-practiced behaviors represent habits, and in this chapter we consider the role of habitual behavior in motivational processes.

A role for habits in motivated behavior was outlined early in classic learning theories, which specified how habits emerge from previous motivated responding and how they structure subsequent motivated responding. For example, Hull (1943, 1950) believed that habits are stimulus–response (S–R) linkages that develop when a given response is reinforcing because it successfully reduces a drive state such as hunger or thirst. This reinforcement increases the association between the stimulus and the response and thereby increases habit strength. Thus, habits orient people to repeat activities that have in the past successfully met motivational needs.

In this present chapter, we build on the idea that habits can structure motivated responding (see Bargh & Gollwitzer, 1994). Repetition in stable contexts changes the motivation for action. Actions that initially were goal

Preparation of this chapter was supported by National Institute of Mental Health Award 1R01MH619000-01. Correspondence should be addressed to Wendy Wood, Department of Psychology: Social and Health Sciences, Duke University, Box 90085, 9 Flowers Drive, Durham, NC 27708. E-mail: wendy.wood@duke.edu.

directed come to be cued by the antecedents of action (Thorndike, 1898). Habits are cognitively represented and guided by an associative system that is based on regularities in past experience, especially on similarity and on spatial and temporal contiguity. Actions that have been performed frequently in particular circumstances are activated in memory and tend to be repeated when these circumstances recur.

Habitual repetition of well-learned responses is not the only system through which action is generated. In the chapter, we compare habitual responding to expectancy-value models of motivation in which behavior is oriented toward expected, valued outcomes and away from expected, devalued ones (e.g., Carver & Scheier, 2001; Eccles & Wigfield, 2002; Higgins, 1997). In particular, we compare habits to expectancy-value models of attitudes that specify how action is generated through intentions and conscious decisions to act (e.g., Ajzen, 2002; Fishbein & Ajzen, 1975). In contrast to habits, intentions direct action through a variety of thought processes as people reason deliberatively about their intentions or invoke them spontaneously.

After describing the associative processing system that underlies habits and the symbolic, verbal system that underlies intentions, we will consider the motivational implications of each system. Acting habitually is an efficient mode of performance that is triggered by temporal and contextual cues that have been associated with the response in the past. In contrast, acting intentionally requires a conscious decision, and sometimes effort and ability. Although habits and intentions represent separate systems, they interact in guiding behavior, and this is most evident when they conflict. The conflicting guides to action pose unique motivational challenges. Not only can habits interfere with the best-laid plans, but also, given sufficient effort and opportunity, the intentional system can control well-practiced behavior. The remainder of the chapter illustrates the role of habits in important aspects of motivation involving emotions and the self.

REPRESENTATION AND PROCESSING OF HABITS AND INTENTIONS

Habits and Associative Processing

Habits are behavioral tendencies to repeat well-practiced acts given stable circumstances (Ouellette & Wood, 1998). They develop as people repetitively perform actions in recurring contexts. Repetition of a behavior in stable circumstances promotes automaticity in responding as actions come to be performed quickly, in parallel with other activities, and with the allocation of minimal focal attention (Posner & Snyder, 1975). With practice, associations develop in memory among aspects of circumstances, behaviors, and goals that co-occur in time and space and possess similar features (Aarts & Dijksterhuis, 2000a, 2000b).

Connectionist network models provide a plausible way of thinking about how associative systems operate (Lieberman, Gaunt, Gilbert, & Trope, 2002; McClelland, 2000; Smolensky, 1988). In these accounts, whole patterns of co-occurring events, such as behaviors and supporting circumstances, can be represented in memory in terms of connection weights between units of processing (e.g., neurons). These processing units are subsymbolic, meaning that they do not by themselves represent any particular thing or experience. Instead, learning is represented in the activation patterns across multiple units in a network. Specifically, with repetition, behaviors and typical performance circumstances become linked in broad patterns in memory through joint activation of the respective connection weights (McClelland, 2000). Subsequent presentations of aspects of the learned pattern promote reconstruction of other aspects, as the pattern is filled in on the other processing units. Thus, the experience of being in the kitchen in early morning can prompt practiced actions such as making coffee. In this way, connectionist mechanisms explain how people smoothly and quickly enact well-practiced actions when their current circumstances are similar to those that have repeatedly co-occurred with the action in the past.

Associative processes provide a plausible account of how habits are triggered by external factors without conscious intentions. The factors guiding habits occur largely outside of awareness. Learned patterns associating circumstances and actions can be activated without conscious recognition or any decision to do so. Thus, people can simultaneously perform habits and think about unrelated things, including yesterday's lunch and their summer plans. Evidence of the minimal thought about habits in daily life was provided by a series of diary investigations in which college student and community samples reported hourly on their thoughts, actions, and feelings (Quinn & Wood, under review; Wood, Quinn, & Kashy, 2002). Participants' thoughts often were unrelated to what they were doing when they were performing habits. Specifically, about 60% of participants' diary entries involving habits indicated that participants were not thinking about their actions. In contrast, participants' thoughts when performing nonhabits typically concerned their behavior and were focused elsewhere only about 35% of the time. Given that participants thought about habits during performance about 40% of the time, it seems that habits are guided by minimal or sporadic cognitive monitoring rather than by a complete absence of thought.

The evidence that people sometimes think about habits during performance is consistent with the idea that intentions and goals play a role in some aspects of habit development and performance. It makes sense that intentions are important initially to repeat actions and develop habits (e.g., practice an athletic skill). Habits most likely develop as people intentionally repeat behaviors in order to achieve some explicit goal. However, with continued practice, intentions change in a number of ways. In part, intentions become abstract so that they refer to broad goals and action sequences rather than to specific actions (Vallacher & Wegner, 1987). Thus, answering the phone might initially be instigated by decisions about which hand to use or how to hold the receiver. With practice, the same actions are instigated by decisions about how to stop the annoying ringing and find out who is calling. Even more fundamental changes can occur if intentions and goals themselves become automated and implicit in habit performance (e.g., Aarts & Dijksterhuis, 2000a). That is, practice can forge associative links between goals and external cues, with the result that exposure to the cues automatically activates the relevant goal and directs action outside of awareness (Bargh & Barndollar, 1996; Bargh & Chartrand, 1999). In short, habit development is associated with a motivational shift from the outcomes to the antecedents of action.

In sum, habits emerge from associative systems that promote repetition of practiced actions given recurring circumstances. In this way, behaviors that were motivated in the past, perhaps to achieve a goal or attain some outcome, can be cued directly by stable features of supporting circumstances without involving intentions or other decision-making processes. Habits thus can automate behavior and channel it in directions pursued in the past.

Intentions and Symbolic Rule-Based Processing

In addition to habitual repetition via associative processing, actions can be generated through expectancy-value mechanisms as people pursue desired outcomes and avoid unwanted ones (e.g., Eccles & Wigfield, 2002). Many expectancy-value theories of motivation do not specify any particular cognitive process that generates action. An exception is Ajzen's (2002) theory of planned behavior, a well-known expectancy-value approach to attitudes. In this analysis, expected outcomes form the basis for behavioral intentions, and these motivated decisions to act then generate action. In terms of cognitive processing, intentions are likely to be organized in memory according to linguistic and logical rules that concern anticipated outcomes and the expected likelihood of these outcomes (see Brewer, 2003; Lieberman et al., 2002; Strack & Deutsch, this volume).

Behavioral intentions can emerge from thoughtful or more spontaneous assessments of behavioral outcomes (Ajzen, 2002). People can reason explicitly to identify intentions that yield desirable outcomes and avoid undesirable ones, and then carefully implement these plans through action. For example, someone wishing to lose weight can decide whether to do so by increasing exercise or decreasing food intake, and then implement the relevant intentions. This explicit reasoning differs from the associative mechanisms that underlie habitual action in that it is deliberative, it follows linguistic and logical rules, and it is symbolically represented.

People also can form and implement intentions in a less thoughtful manner. In this mode, decisions to act derive from heuristics and other simple rules. For example, impulse buying occurs when people seeking to elevate their mood or enhance their self-esteem spontaneously apply a simple heuristic that links purchase intentions with emotions (e.g., "I'll buy it, I'm worth it;" see Verplanken & Herabadi, 2001). As Brewer (2003) noted, this mode is a hybrid of associative and symbolic processing. It is built on implicit processes, but the resulting intentions are consciously represented and applied to direct action. Thus, spontaneous intentions guide behavior through a separate mechanism from relatively direct, habitual responses to the environment that are not mediated by thought.

The intentional and associative systems do not exist in isolation. Instead, they proceed simultaneously, and information can be transferred between them (Lieberman et al., 2002; Smith & DeCoster, 2000; Strack & Deutsch, this volume). For example, the outcomes of associative processing can be interpreted in rule-based logic so that people can report on their own habits. Thus, people's understanding of their habits involves re-representing this behavior in symbolic terms, and does not necessarily reflect any direct access to the associative mechanisms guiding behavior (Schooler, 2002). Behaviors guided by the symbolic system also can come to be represented in associative networks. For example, behaviors that were originally intended can become habitual with practice and guided by associations separately from intentions. As we explained in the section on habits and associative processing, with repetition, intentional thought becomes unnecessary to direct actions because the actions are cued by recurring circumstances that are linked to them in associative networks. In this way, behaviors that originally were intended can be performed without even fleeting awareness of intentions.

In sum, motivated behavior can emerge through a variety of cognitive processes. Habits tend to be repeated through associative mechanisms without conscious decisions to act. Habits automatically channel future actions in the directions pursued in the past. It is reasonable to assume that people repeated actions in the past that yielded desired outcomes and avoided unwanted ones. In this sense, habits are part of the *wise unconscious* (Bargh & Barndollar, 1996) that guides behavior in situations in which people chronically engaged in certain actions in the past. In contrast, intentions reflect conscious decisions to act and are symbolically represented and organized according to verbal logic systems. Intentions are motivated in the sense that they reflect people's understanding of the value and likelihood of various behavioral outcomes. Intentions can be generated through a careful analysis of outcomes or through relatively automatic processes, and they can be implemented deliberatively or more spontaneously.

INTENTIONS AND HABITS DIRECT BEHAVIOR THROUGH SEPARATE BUT INTERACTING SYSTEMS

The separate systems that guide action pose specific challenges for understanding motivated behavior. That is, actions that achieve goals or other desired outcomes can emerge from people's intentional decisions or from habitual dispositions to repeat past behavior. The multiple systems guiding behavior are not apparent when they correspond, and people intend to do what comes habitually. Then, similar behaviors are enacted regardless of whether people follow habits or intentions. The differences between the systems become apparent when they conflict and, for example, people intend to eat healthy foods but do not do so. These seeming motivational failures in daily life can be explained in terms of conflict between the multiple systems guiding behavior.

Given that habits and intentions can both guide behavior, readers might wonder about the typical outcome when these guides conflict. The typical outcome of the interaction between habits and intentions in everyday life is illustrated in the findings from behavior prediction studies. In a typical prediction study, people report on their intentions to perform some behavior and their past performance habits, and these two measures are used to predict subsequent behavior. Meta-analytic syntheses of existing behavior prediction research along with primary investigations have found that intentions direct action primarily when habits have not been formed (e.g., Albarracin, Kumkale, & Johnson, unpublished; Ferguson & Bibby, 2002; Ouellette & Wood, 1998; Verplanken, Aarts, van Knippenberg, & Moonen, 1998). That is, intentions predict subsequent behavior primarily when the behaviors are not well practiced or the supporting contexts are unstable. In contrast, when habits have been formed, they guide behavior in stable contexts regardless of whether people intend to engage in the habitual response. This overall interaction pattern indicates that habits predominate in guiding action when they conflict with intentions.

The hegemony of habits in guiding behavior is understandable given that intentional control requires effort and ability, especially when it involves overriding conflicting habits (Fazio & Olson, 2003). Self-control is a limited resource that is easily depleted by small acts of self-regulation (Baumeister, Bratslavsky, Muraven, & Tice, 1998; Baumeister, Muraven, & Tice, 2000). Apparently, in the everyday settings tapped in behavior prediction research, people typically do not have sufficient self-regulatory resources to carry out intentions that conflict with established habits. Habits are highly efficient and do not tax effort or ability. Thus, even when they conflict with explicit intentions, they often runoff uninterrupted.

In addition to effort, intentional control requires processing capacity. The importance of capacity is suggested by research on *action slips* in which habits intrude on intentional action (Hay & Jacoby, 1996; Heckhausen & Beckmann, 1990; Reason, 1979). Habit intrusions represent well-practiced action sequences that belong to some activity other than the one intended, and include unintentionally repeating actions (e.g., taking an extra vitamin pill) and following old plans instead of new ones (e.g., dialing an old phone number instead of the new, correct one). Habit intrusions, like other action slips, are especially likely to occur when people are distracted or preoccupied by something other than their immediate behavior (Aarts & Dijksterhuis, 2000b; Reason, 1984; Reason & Lucas, 1984). When cognitive ability is impaired in this way, people are not able to act on their intentions; instead, behavior is guided by habitual associative mechanisms that require minimal thought. Thus, they find themselves engaging in well-practiced but unwanted habits.

Even more direct evidence that limits in processing ability affect controlled but not habitual responding comes from Jacoby and colleagues' work on errors in memory tasks in laboratory settings (summarized in Kelley & Jacoby, 2000). In this research, intentional recollection of learned material (but not practiced, habitual responding) was impaired by (a) aging and associated reductions in cognitive ability, (b) distractions that divided people's attention from their response, and (c) time limits that reduced the opportunity to respond. Thus, a variety of cognitive deficits impair intentional but not habitual responding.

The apparent strength of habits in behavior prediction research, studies of action slips, and laboratory memory research emerges in part from the efficiency with which habits are performed. In contrast to intentional action, habits minimally drain effort and cognitive capacity. In addition, habits have a timing advantage. They are likely to be immediately available as guides to action, given the characteristic speed of associative processing (Sloman, 1996). Intentions may take longer to form and implement, especially when they are generated in an explicit, thoughtful manner. For these reasons, habits that conflict with intentions often predominate in guiding action. That is, motivated behavior is often channeled in past directions even when these do not coincide with people's currently reported wishes and desires.

Habits do not always win out in conflicts with intentions and, given certain conditions, intentions can guide behavior despite conflicting habits. For example, most people can implement New Year's resolutions for at least a few days following the holiday. However, because implementing the resolutions can drain self-regulatory resources, and thereby reduce motivation and the ability to act in line with intentions, people may have difficultly maintaining the desired behavior over longer periods. Another instance in which intentions predominate over habits occurs when changes in circumstances block the smooth repetition of habits. In contrast, changes in circumstances do not necessarily disrupt the effects of intentions on behavior (i.e., unless they change the value or likelihood of behavioral outcomes). Empirical evidence that habits but not intentions are disrupted by changes in supporting circumstances was provided in Wood, Tam, and Guerrero-Witt's (under review) study of college students transferring to a new university. When the cues supporting their habitual everyday activities (e.g., reading the newspaper, exercising) changed with the transfer, students were apparently unable to smoothly repeat past actions. Presumably, the changed circumstances disrupted automatic habit performance and caused students to think about their behavior. For example, for reading the newspaper, whether students' roommates read the paper proved to be an important aspect of the supporting circumstances. For some students in the study, their roommates' behavior changed with the transfer so that the roommates began to read the paper or did so no longer. When this change occurred, students' habits were disrupted and their behavior at the new university was directed by their intentions. In contrast, students who did not have habits for these behaviors were minimally affected by changes in supporting cues; at the old as well as the new universities, their actions were guided by intentions. Thus, habits were uniquely vulnerable to shifts in supporting circumstances, so that when these changed, students were apparently forced to deliberate about their behavior and bring it in line with their intentions.

In sum, motivated action emerges from the interplay between intentions and established habits. In general, habits are likely to predominate in everyday life, given the effort and ability required to carry out intentions and the immediacy with which habitual guides are generated. However, intentions predominate when sufficient self-control and ability are available to override habits and when changes in supporting circumstances disrupt the smooth performance of habits.

HABITS AND OTHER FORMS OF AUTOMATICITY

Habits represent a specific form of processing that differs from the variety of other forms of automaticity that have been noted in the literature. In contrast to our definition, Aarts and his colleagues (Aarts & Dijksterhuis, 2000a, 2000b; Verplanken & Aarts, 1999) defined habits as mental associations between goals and behaviors that are represented as elements of schemas or personal scripts. Such a definition is congruent with our own to the extent that these schemas or scripts correspond to associative network patterns that enable relatively immediate response to practiced cues. However, given that scripts are sometimes defined as knowledge structures that represent people's *understanding* or symbolic representation of stereotyped sequences of action (Abelson, 1981), they do not correspond to our current perspective on habits.

Habits also can be contrasted with implementation intentions that link performance of a desired action with contextual features that signify an opportunity for performance (i.e., "when *x* occurs, I will do *y*"; Brandstätter, Lengfelder, & Gollwitzer, 2001, p. 947; see also Gollwitzer, 1999). Although in some accounts, implementation intentions elicit behavior automatically (Gollwitzer, 1999), performance of behaviors triggered by implementation intentions may require conscious monitoring of the environment to detect cues for action initiation (McDaniel & Einstein, 2000).

Additionally, habits are more specific patterns of response than the primed responses that are elicited by automatically accessible goals and constructs. For example, activation of stereotypes of the elderly has been found to induce behavior consistent with those stereotypes, such as walking slowly (Bargh, Chen, & Burrows, 1996; Dijksterhuis, Bargh, & Miedema, 2000). Unlike habits, priming of abstract goals and constructs affects a variety of relevant behaviors (e.g., walking speed, memory performance). In addition, priming sometimes has relatively long-term behavioral effects that continue independently of the initial context (e.g., if primed goals are not satisfied; Bargh & Chartrand, 1999).

In sum, we propose that the mechanisms guiding habits are the repeated circumstances and goals that directly and automatically trigger well-practiced action sequences. Research on cognitive schemata, on implementation intentions, and on priming effects all provide important insight into facets of automatic responses, but the relevant processes do not map directly onto the operation of habits.

HABITS AND THE SELF

The different features of habitual and intentional guides to action have implications for behavior in a variety of motivational domains. To illustrate some of these implications, we apply our two-system model of behavior generation to the domains of self-regulation, emotion, and understanding of the self.

Self-Regulation

The efficiency that emerges from acting with minimal thinking has important self-regulatory benefits. Habits provide a mechanism to generate action without depleting self-control resources. In support of this idea, participants in Wood et al.'s (2002) diary study of everyday behavior reported feeling less overwhelmed and stressed when engaged in habitual compared with nonhabitual behaviors.

The self-regulatory benefits of acting habitually with minimal thought should be especially evident when people are engaged in effort-intensive goal pursuit. That is, people are most likely to succeed at a difficult task when they don't try to do other demanding things at the same time. In support of this prediction, Guerrero-Witt and Wood (in progress) found that people engaged in a 14-week exercise program to improve their physical fitness were more likely to achieve their fitness goals by the end of the program if they reported that their other top goals during that period required minimal thought to accomplish. Apparently, when other important goals did not drain self-regulatory resources, participants were able to focus their thought and energy on achieving their fitness goals. In general, people are likely to facilitate their success at challenging activities in chosen domains by limiting other demands on deliberative processes. For this reason, structuring life around a core of habits is beneficial to goal pursuit because people then have the self-regulatory resources to accomplish additional effortful goals. This strategy likely works in conjunction with other, often nonconscious strategies of goal pursuit (e.g., goal shielding; Shah & Kruglanski, 2002) to help people to focus their resources on desired goals and to avoid distraction from competing or less important goals.

Emotion

Habit performance also has implications for people's emotional experiences. Specifically, Wood et al.'s (2002) diary assessments of everyday behavior revealed that people experienced less intense emotions when performing habits than nonhabits. This pattern, apparent with both positive and negative emotions, was anticipated by Frijda's (1988) laws of emotion, in which "continued pleasures wear off; continued hardships lose their poignancy" (p. 353). From this perspective, people adapt psychologically and physiologically to the emotion-inducing aspects of repeated actions in stable contexts in a way that reduces emotional intensity. In addition, the less intense emotions associated with habits can be explained by Mandler's (1975) theory of mind and emotion. In this view, emotions arise when the interruption of one's plans and organized behavior sequences generates arousal and initiates an interpretation of the interruption that implicates particular emotions. Because infrequently performed behaviors and behaviors in unstable contexts are plausibly more likely than habits to encounter difficulties and interference, nonhabitual behaviors are more likely to be associated with emotions. Finally, from the perspective of Carver and Scheier's (1998, 2001) cybernetic model of self-regulation, emotions emerge from discrepancies between people's behavior or related outcomes and their goals and self-standards. Specifically, emotions emerge from changes in the rate at which behaviors and outcomes meet or fail to meet self-goals. Although Carver and Scheier offer few speculations about the factors that might lead people to recognize such discrepancies and thus to experience emotion, it seems plausible that people will attend more to discrepancies when deliberating about behavior than when acting habitually. In sum, a variety of theoretical perspectives can account for people's less intense emotions when engaged in habitual than nonhabitual behavior.

One implication of the limited emotional responses associated with habits is that when people do experience emotions during performance, the emotions are likely to be linked to their thoughts rather than their behavior. Because habits require minimal explicit thought, people are able to entertain unrelated concerns, and the intruding thoughts may themselves be highly emotionally charged. Thus, when performing behaviors habitually, Wood et al.'s (2002) participants reported that their emotions sometimes were associated with their actions and sometimes with their unrelated thoughts. In contrast, the emotions associated with nonhabitual behaviors emerged primarily from action.

This general pattern in which habit-related emotions are low in intensity and elicited by thoughts as well as behavior could have implications for broader lifestyle patterns. We speculate that people whose lives are structured by habits and who therefore devote little thought to action may find that their emotional experiences become dull and subdued over time. Much like Thurber's (1942) character Walter Mitty, they may find that their own ruminations and fantasies are the primary source of their emotions rather than their immediate behavioral experiences.

Understanding of the Self

Habits do not seem to play an important role in people's self-concepts. In Wood et al.'s (2002) diary investigation of everyday behavior, participants judged their habits as relatively uninformative to others about the self and as relatively unimportant to attaining personal goals. Furthermore, participants seemed uncertain as to the causes of their habits. Habits were rated as less likely than nonhabits to arise from either internal causes or external causes such as the situation or the circumstance. Habits also were less likely to generate a feeling of pride. The one exception to this pattern of habits being dissociated from the self was that people reported feeling worse about themselves when they engaged in habitual than nonhabitual behavior. Thus, habitual behaviors proved to be, at best, unrelated to participants' self-concepts and, at worst, associated with negative feelings.

People's negative spin on habitual behavior can be understood as part of the dissociation between explicit intentions and implicit associational guides (see Fazio & Olson, 2003; Liberman et al., 2002). This dissociation is easy to understand if habits were not originally intended. Yet, even given that habits were initially intended, implicit behavioral dispositions can differ from explicit intentions because of the phenomenology of habit and intention systems. As Lieberman et al. (2002) note, responses that are produced through the associative system feel involuntary, uncontrollable, and easy, whereas responses that are intended feel voluntary, controllable, and somewhat effortful. Because we decide to produce intentional acts, they feel as if they are closely associated with our identities. Thus, regardless of whether habits were initially intended, the generation of behavior through the associative system generates the feeling that the action is not a highly authentic indicator of the self.

In daily life, the disconnection between habitual behavior and the self has a number of implications. For example, if people do not see themselves as especially responsible for their habits, they may not believe that they have sufficient efficacy to change such acts. Also, goals achieved through routinized activity may not be a strong source of pride. Thus, for example, healthy lifestyle decisions that become routinized as part of one's daily behavior may not yield a sense of personal accomplishment because the behavior does not appear to reflect personal choice.

CONCLUSION

In this chapter we argued that behavior can be guided through relatively separate habitual and intentional systems. For frequently performed behaviors in stable contexts, recurring circumstances can activate practiced behavioral routines in a nonintentional process that occurs largely outside of people's awareness. We contrasted this habitual, association-based system with intentional guides to behavior that are implemented in a relatively thoughtful or a more spontaneous fashion.

Despite the separate nature of habitual and intentional guides, it would be a mistake to conclude that most behavior is a product of strictly habitual tendencies or of intentional thought. Any given behavior likely involves multiple aspects of memory and motor performance systems, and some of these aspects may be well practiced and proceed automatically, whereas others may be more novel and require intentional guidance. Presumably, it is because some components of habitual actions require monitoring that people sometimes think about their habits during performance (Quinn & Wood, under review; Wood et al., 2002). Intentional guidance may be especially useful at the beginning and end of well-practiced sequences of actions to initiate and terminate the series. In a parallel manner, well-practiced aspects of more thoughtful behaviors can proceed with minimal awareness, as indicated by the phenomenon of one's mind wandering while reading (Schooler, 2002).

In everyday life, people are likely to be aware of multiple guides to action when they are trying to change their habits and perform behaviors that are more desirable, perhaps because they are healthier. People's heightened awareness of the habit-intention conflict at such times is understandable given that habits are so difficult to override. Even people who successfully get fit or lose weight may have many false starts before establishing the desired habits. Although the typical outcome of a conflict between habits and intentions seems to be one in which habits win out, habits can be undermined by changes in the supporting circumstances. Changes in supporting cues that disrupt the smooth performance of habits can compel people to think about their behavior and can bring action under intentional control (Wood et al., under review). Thus, the typical outcome of habits guiding behavior is not the only outcome when habits and intentions interact in guiding performance.

References

Aarts, H., & Dijksterhuis, A. (2000a). Habits as knowledge structures: Automaticity in goal-directed behavior. *Journal of Personality and Social Psychology, 78*, 53–63.

Aarts, H., & Dijksterhuis, A. (2000b). The automatic activation of goal-directed behaviour: The case of travel habit. *Journal of Environmental Psychology, 20*, 75–82.

Abelson, R. P. (1981). Psychological status of the script concept. *American Psychologist, 36*, 715–729.

Ajzen, I. (2002). Residual effects of past on later behavior: Habituation and reasoned action perspectives. *Personality and Social Psychology Review, 6*, 107–122.

Albarracin, D., Kumkale, G. T., & Johnson, B. T. (unpublished). *Influences of population and methodological factors on reasoning in condom use: A meta-analysis.*

Bargh, J. A., & Barndollar, K. (1996). Automaticity in action: The unconscious as repository of chronic goals and motives. In P. M. Gollwitzer & J. A. Bargh (Eds.), *The psychology of action: Linking cognition and motivation to behavior* (pp. 457–481). New York: Guilford Press.

Bargh, J. A., & Chartrand, T. L. (1999). The unbearable automaticity of being. *American Psychologist, 54*, 462–479.

Bargh, J. A., Chen, M., & Burrows, L. (1996). Automaticity of social behavior: Direct effects of trait construct and stereotype activation on action. *Journal of Personality and Social Psychology, 71*, 230–244.

Bargh, J. A., & Gollwitzer, P. M. (1994). Environmental control of goal-directed action: Automatic and strategic contingencies between situations and behavior. In W. D. Spaulding (Ed.), *Integrative views of motivation, cognition, and emotion: Nebraska Symposium on Motivation* (Vol. 41, pp. 71–124). Lincoln: University of Nebraska Press.

Baumeister, R. F., Bratslavsky, E., Muraven, M., & Tice, D. M. (1998). Ego depletion: Is the active self a limited resource? *Journal of Personality and Social Psychology, 74*, 1252–1265.

Baumeister, R. F., Muraven, M., & Tice, D. M. (2000). Ego depletion: A resource model of volition, self-regulation, and controlled processing. *Social Cognition, 18*, 130–150.

Brandstätter, V., Lengfelder, A., & Gollwitzer, P. M. (2001). Implementations intentions and efficient action. *Journal of Personality and Social Psychology, 81*, 946–960.

Brewer, M. B. (2003). Implicit and explicit process in social judgment: Deep and high. In J. P. Forgas, K. D. Williams, & W. von Hippel (Eds.), *Social judgments: Implicit and explicit processes* (pp. 387–396). New York: Psychology Press.

Carver, C. S., & Scheier, M. F. (1998). *On the self-regulation of behavior*. New York: Cambridge University Press.

Carver, C. S., & Scheier, M. F. (2001). Optimism, pessimism, and self-regulation. In E. C. Chang (Ed.), *Optimism and pessimism: Implications for theory, research, and practice* (pp. 31–51). Washington, DC: American Psychological Association.

Chartrand, T. L., & Bargh, J. A. (1999). The chameleon effect: The perception–behavior link and social interaction. *Journal of Personality and Social Psychology, 76*, 893–910.

Dijksterhuis, A., Bargh, J. A., & Miedema, J. (2000). Of men and mackerels: Attention and automatic behavior. In H. Bless & J. P. Forgas (Eds.), *Subjective experience in social cognition and behavior* (pp. 36–51). Philadelphia: Psychology Press.

Eccles, J. S., & Wigfield, A. (2002). Motivational beliefs, values, and goals. *Annual Review of Psychology, 53*, 109–132.

Fazio, R. H., & Olson, R. H. (2003). Implicit measures in social cognition research: Their meaning and use. *Annual Review of Psychology, 54*, 297–327.

Ferguson, E., & Bibby, P. A. (2002). Predicting future blood donor returns: Past behavior, intentions, and observer effects. *Health Psychology, 21*, 513–518.

Fishbein, M., & Ajzen, I. (1975). *Belief, attitude, intention and behavior: An introduction to theory and research*. Reading, MA: Addison-Wesley.

Frijda, N. H. (1988). The laws of emotion. *American Psychologist, 43*, 349–358.

Guerrero-Witt, M., & Wood, W. (in progress). *Thinking limits on goal success*. Research.

Gollwitzer, P. M. (1999). Implementation intentions: Strong effects of simple plans. *American Psychologist, 54*, 493–503.

Hay, J. F., & Jacoby, L. L. (1996). Separating habit and recollection: Memory slips, process dissociations, and probability matching. *Journal of Experimental Psychology: Learning, Memory, and Cognition, 22*, 1323–1335.

Heckhausen, H., & Beckmann, J. (1990). Intentional action and action slips. *Psychological Review, 97*, 36–48.

Higgins, E. T. (1997). Beyond pleasure and pain. *American Psychologist, 52*, 1280–1300.

Hull, C. L. (1943). *Principles of behavior: An introduction to behavior theory*. New York: Appleton-Century-Crofts.

Hull, C. L. (1950). Behavior postulates and corrolaries – 1949. *Psychological Review, 57*, 173–180.

Kelley, C. M., & Jacoby, L. L. (2000). Recollection and familiarity: Process-dissociation. In E. Tulving & F. I. M. Craik (Eds.), *The Oxford handbook of memory* (pp. 215–228). New York: Oxford University Press.

Lieberman, M. D., Gaunt, R., Gilbert, D. T., & Trope, Y. (2002). Reflexion and reflection: A social cognitive neuroscience approach to attributional inference. In M. P. Zanna (Ed.), *Advances in experimental social psychology* (Vol. 34, pp. 199–249). New York: Academic Press.

Mandler, G. (1975). *Mind and emotion*. New York: Wiley.

McClelland, J. L. (2000). Connectionist models of memory. In E. Tulving & C. I. M. Fergus (Eds.), *The Oxford handbook of memory* (pp. 583–596). London: Oxford University Press.

McDaniel, M. A., & Einstein, G. O. (2000). Strategic and automatic processes in prospective memory retrieval: A multiprocess framework. *Applied Cognitive Psychology, 14*, S127–S144.

Ouellette, J. A., & Wood, W. (1998). Habit and intention in everyday life: The multiple processes by which past behavior predicts future behavior. *Psychological Bulletin, 124*, 54–74.

Posner, M. I., & Snyder, C. R. R. (1975). Attention and cognitive control. In R. L. Solso (Ed.), *Information processing and cognition: The Loyola symposium* (pp. 55–85). Hillsdale, NJ: Erlbaum.

Quinn, J. M., & Wood, W. (under review). *Habits across the lifespan*. Manuscript.

Reason, J. (1979). Actions not as planned: The price of automatisation. In G. Underwood & R. Stevens (Eds.), *Aspects of consciousness, Vol. 1: Psychological Issues* (pp. 67–89). London: Academic Press.

Reason, J. (1984). Absent-mindedness and cognitive control. In J. E. Harris & P. E. Morris (Eds.), *Everyday memory: Actions and absent-mindedness* (pp. 113–132). London: Academic Press.

Reason, J., & Lucas, D. (1984). Using cognitive diaries to investigate naturally occurring memory blocks. In J. E. Harris & P. E. Morris (Eds.), *Everyday memory: Actions and absent-mindedness* (pp. 53–70). London: Academic Press.

Schooler, J. W. (2002). Re-representing consciousness: Dissociations between experience and meta-consciousness. *Trends in Cognitive Sciences, 6*, 339–344.

Shah, J. Y., & Kruglanski, A. W. (2002). Priming against your will: How accessible alternatives affect goal pursuit. *Journal of Experimental Social Psychology, 38*, 368–383.

Sloman, S. A. (1996). The empirical case for two systems of reasoning. *Psychological Bulletin, 119*, 3–22.

Smith, E. R., & DeCoster, J. (2000). Dual-process models in social and cognitive psychology: Integration and links to underlying memory systems. *Personality and Social Psychology Review, 4*, 108–131.

Smolensky, P. (1988). On the proper treatment of connectionism. *Behavioral and Brain Sciences, 11*, 1–74.

Thorndike, E. L. (1898). Animal intelligence: An experimental study of the association processes in animals. *Psychological Review Monograph, 2* (Whole No. 8).

Thurber, J. (1942). *My world – and welcome to it*. New York: Harcourt, Brace.

Vallacher, R. R., & Wegner, D. M. (1987). What do people think they're doing? Action identification and human behavior. *Psychological Review, 94*, 3–15.

Verplanken, B., & Aarts, H. (1999). Habit, attitude, and planned behavior: Is habit an empty construct or an interesting case of goal-directed automaticity? In W. Stroebe & M. Hewstone (Eds.), *European review of social psychology* (Vol. 10, pp. 101–134). Chichester, England: Wiley.

Verplanken, B., Aarts, H., van Knippenberg, A., & Moonen, A. (1998). Habit versus planned behaviour: A field experiment. *British Journal of Social Psychology, 37*, 111–128.

Verplanken, B., & Herabadi, A. (2001). Individual differences in impulse buying tendency: Feeling and no thinking. *European Journal of Personality, 15,* S71–S83.

Wood, W., Quinn, J. M., & Kashy, D. (2002). Habits in everyday life: Thought, emotion, and action. *Journal of Personality and Social Psychology, 83,* 1281–1297.

Wood, W., Tam, L., & Guerrero-Witt, M. (under review). *Changing contexts, disrupting habits.* Manuscript.

5

Motivation in Social Settings

Studies of Effort-Related Cardiovascular Arousal

Guido H. E. Gendolla and Rex A. Wright

INTRODUCTION

The construct of effort, or task engagement, figures prominently in contemporary explanations of a number of social psychological phenomena. However, social psychologists have often based their analyses on intuitive effort assumptions, with two being especially prominent: (a) that effort increases with the perceived importance of success (Eisenberger, 1992; Fowles, 1983) and (b) that effort is greater in people who view themselves as capable with respect to a task than in people who view themselves as incapable with respect to a task (Bandura, 1986).

In this chapter, we discuss programs of research from our laboratories that have sought to improve understanding of fundamental effort processes and explore implications of those processes for responses in social settings. The programs rely heavily on Jack Brehm's theory of motivational intensity (e.g., Brehm & Self, 1989). The programs also take as a working hypothesis the proposition advanced by the late Paul Obrist (1981) that sympathetic nervous system influence on the heart varies with task engagement (what Obrist termed *active coping*), being greater when engagement is high than when it is low. Together, Brehm's theory and Obrist's proposition provide a framework for predicting engagement and a means of measuring it.

Order of authorship was determined alphabetically. The authors contributed equally to this work. The research reported in this chapter was facilitated by grants from the Deutsche Forschungsgemeinschaft (Ge 987/1-1, Ge 987/3-1, Ge 987/5-1) awarded to Guido Gendolla and by National Science Foundation Grant SBR97-27707 awarded to Rex Wright. Correspondence should be addressed either to Guido Gendolla, University of Geneva, FPSE Section of Psychology, 40 Bd. du Pont d'Arve, 1211 Geneva 4, Switzerland (e-mail: guido.gendolla@pse.unige.ch) or to Rex Wright, Department of Psychology, 415 Campbell Hall, University of Alabama at Birmingham, Birmingham, AL, USA 35294; e-mail: rwright@uab.edu.

MOTIVATIONAL INTENSITY THEORY

Fundamental Arguments

Brehm's motivational intensity theory is concerned with the determinants of momentary effort, that is, effort expended at a point in time. Drawing from the classic *difficulty law of motivation* (see Ach, 1935), it argues that such effort is determined by appraisals of task difficulty. However, it does not hold that effort rises indefinitely with difficulty. Rather, it asserts that effort should rise with difficulty up to one of two points. One point is the difficulty level at which success is viewed as impossible. The other point is the difficulty level at which success is believed to require more effort than is warranted by its importance. Beyond these difficulty levels, effort should be low because it would either yield no benefit (impossible case) or yield benefit but result in a net loss of resources ("requires too much effort" case).

To illustrate, consider a woman challenged to lift an amount of weight. According to the preceding theory, the woman's effort should be proportional to the difficulty of the lift so long as she views the lift as possible and worthwhile. If the woman believes the lift is impossible or calls for more effort than she is willing to muster, her effort should be low.

Brehm's motivational intensity theory identifies the upper limit of what a person would be willing to do to succeed as the level of *potential motivation* and proposes that it should be a function of success importance. Success importance, in turn, should be a function of at least three variables:

1. The value of the benefit associated with success.
2. The performer's need for the associated benefit.
3. The strength of the association between success and benefit attainment.

Thus, one would expect potential motivation to be greater in the lifter if she believed she could earn a lot of money by meeting the lift challenge than if she believed she could earn only a little money by doing so. Similarly, one would expect potential motivation to be greater in the lifter if she were poor than if she were wealthy, and greater if she were sure she would be paid after meeting the lift challenge than if she were not sure.

Implications

There are several noteworthy implications of Brehm's motivational intensity reasoning. One is that performance challenges should tend to elicit greater engagement when they are moderate (difficult) than when they are mild or extreme. This is because effort should correspond to difficulty when success is possible and worthwhile, but be low when success is impossible or excessively difficult, given the perceived importance of success. A second implication is that the relationship between engagement, on the one hand, and the difficulty of a possible challenge, on the other, should be moderated by success importance. If importance is high enough to justify the effort that is required to meet the challenge, engagement should be proportional to challenge difficulty, that is, high if the challenge is substantial and low if the challenge is mild. However, if importance falls short of this level, engagement should be minimal irrespective of challenge difficulty. A third implication is that success importance should have no impact on effort when a challenge is impossible to meet. If nothing can be done to succeed, then engagement should be low no matter how important success is perceived to be.

The preceding implications are straightforward and significant; however, it is important to note that they apply only to performance challenges that Brehm and Self (1989) have characterized as *fixed*. Brehm and Self identify such challenges as ones that call for a particular level of performance. Brehm and Self assume that people presented with an *unfixed* challenge – that is, a challenge without a clear performance standard – will strive for the highest possible performance level that they are willing to attain. Consequently, they argue that when performance is unconstrained, effort should correspond to success importance until maximum effort has been achieved.

ABILITY PERCEPTION EXTENSION

Ability and Difficulty Appraisals

Ability perception is a key construct in many areas of psychology, including social psychology. Although the construct was not discussed in early articulations of Brehm's motivational intensity theory, it is not difficult to incorporate. All that is required is the assumption that performers judge tasks to be increasingly difficult the less capable they view themselves to be within relevant performance domains (e.g., Kukla, 1972). If this assumption is accepted, it is a simple matter to map separate effort-to-difficulty functions for people with lower ability appraisals (low-ability people) and people with higher ability appraisals (high-ability people). As seen in Figure 5.1, effort should increase with difficulty up to a point, and then drop precipitously, for both low- and high-ability groups. The difference between the functions for the groups is that the one for low-ability people starts at a higher point on the y-(effort) axis than does the one for high-ability people (Figure 5.1) because of the difference in difficulty perception.

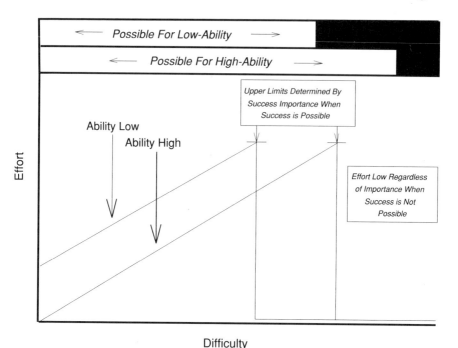

FIGURE 5.1 Effort as a function of challenge difficulty for people low and high in ability perception. (Source: Wright & Franklin, in press, Figure 1. Used by permission.)

Implications

Inspection of the separate functions for low- and high-ability people makes apparent a number of ability perception implications, including the following:

1. Low-ability people should strive harder to meet performance challenges than should high-ability people so long as they view success as possible and worthwhile. The reason is that effort should be proportional to the perceived challenge difficulty when challenges can be met and are worth meeting. In theory, difficulty appraisals should be higher for low-ability people than for high-ability people. Therefore, effort should be greater for low-ability people.
2. Low-ability people should sometimes exert less effort than high-ability people. The reason is that low-ability people should withhold effort at a lower level of challenge difficulty than should high-ability people. To be precise, low-ability people should exert less effort than high-ability people when success appears impossible or excessively difficult to them but possible and worthwhile to the high-ability group.

3. Effort should sometimes be minimal regardless of ability perception. The reason is that even high-ability people should withhold effort if the challenge difficulty is great enough. Once this difficulty level has been reached, effort should be low and equivalent for low- and high-ability groups.

It should be clear that all of these implications pertain to situations involving fixed challenges. To date, there has been limited consideration of how ability perception should impact effort in people presented with unfixed challenges. An idea advanced by Wright and Kirby (2001) is that unfixed challenges may lead both low- and high-ability groups to strive for the highest performance level that is both possible and justified for them, resulting in no effort differences between the groups. A different idea, discussed by Gendolla and his colleagues (e.g., Gendolla, Abele, & Krüsken, 2001a), is that unfixed challenges may lead low-ability people to strive harder than high-ability people because low-ability people should view all performance levels as more difficult to attain than should high-ability people. Underlying this latter idea is the assumption (elaborated later in this chapter) that people use their ability beliefs as information in making difficulty assessments.

COMPARISON WITH INTUITIVE VIEWS

Brehm's motivational intensity theory and the ability perception extension from it present a view of effort that is markedly different from intuitive views that are commonly seen in social psychology. Recall that two intuitive ideas are especially prominent in contemporary analyses of social phenomena: (a) that effort rises with perceived success importance and (b) that effort is greater in high-ability people than in low-ability people. The first of these conflicts with Brehm's idea that success importance does not determine effort directly, but rather sets the upper limit of what people would be willing to do (i.e., sets the level of potential motivation). Granted, in situations involving unfixed challenges, importance should predict effort upto a point by determining the performance standard that people set for themselves. However, even in those situations, importance should lose its predictive power once a maximum effort has been justified.

The second intuitive idea discussed earlier, pertaining to ability perception, conflicts with the extension idea that ability perception effects should depend on the nature of a performance challenge (fixed versus unfixed) and, in the fixed challenge case, on the difficulty of a performance challenge. When a challenge is unfixed, effort should either be equivalent for low- and high-ability people (Wright & Kirby, 2001) or greater for the former group than for the latter (e.g., Gendolla et al., 2001a). When a challenge is fixed, ability should be negatively associated with effort under some difficulty conditions (lower ones), positively associated with effort under other difficulty conditions (higher ones), and dissociated from effort under still other difficulty conditions (even higher ones).

STUDIES OF CARDIOVASCULAR RESPONSE

Recent literature reviews indicate that there is considerable evidence supporting the effort view presented by Brehm's motivational intensity theory and its ability perception extension (e.g., Brehm & Self, 1989). The best of this evidence comes from studies that have measured cardiovascular (CV) responses in people confronted with performance challenges, accepting the proposition by Obrist (1981) that sympathetic CV influence increases with engagement. Therefore, those studies will be our focus here.

Typical studies supporting the basic intensity theory found that (a) performance challenges elicit greater task engagement when they are moderate than when they are mild or extreme (e.g., Wright, Contrada, & Patane, 1986) and that (b) the relationship between task engagement and the difficulty of a possible challenge is moderated by perceived success importance (e.g., Wright, Williams, & Dill, 1992). These studies used systolic blood pressure (SBP) responsiveness as primary index of task engagement because SBP is partially determined by how forcefully the heart contracts, and this is determined chiefly (if not solely) by sympathetic nervous system arousal (Papillo & Shapiro, 1990).

A typical study supporting the ability perception extension from Brehm's theory is an experiment by Wright and Dill (1993). This investigation addressed the extension implications that low-ability people should (a) strive harder to meet performance challenges than high-ability people, so long as they view success as possible and worthwhile, but (b) exert less effort than high-ability people when success appears impossible or excessively difficult to them but possible and worthwhile to the high-ability group. After induction of low- versus high-ability beliefs with regard to a scanning task, participants performed a second scanning task with instructions that they could earn a prize by attaining either a high or a low performance standard. Systolic responses assessed just before and during the second performance period were in the expected crossover pattern, reflecting relatively greater responsiveness for low-ability participants than for high-ability participants when the standard was low but the reverse when the standard was high. Analysis of diastolic blood pressure (DBP) responses yielded the same interaction.

EFFORT IN SOCIAL SETTINGS

Studies such as those just described provide important data relevant to Brehm's motivational intensity theory and its ability perception extension. However, more telling with respect to social motivation are CV effort studies that have included stronger social components and, indeed, have been designed to address particular questions in social psychology.

One set of CV effort studies with stronger social components comes from Tim Smith's laboratory at the University of Utah. Smith and his associates have repeatedly examined CV responses in people engaged in persuasive communication. Findings generally have accorded with the motivational intensity theory and the ability perception extension. Consider, for example, results of an experiment that provided participants with the chance to earn a monetary reward by making a speech that was mildly, moderately, or extremely convincing to an audience (Smith, Baldwin, & Christenson, 1990). As expected, blood pressure and heart rate (HR) responses measured just before and during the speech were greater when the performance standard was moderate than when the standard was low and extreme. Other CV effort studies with stronger social components have been conducted in our laboratories.

Empathy and Social Evaluation

Two types of studies with stronger social components are concerned with effort effects of empathy and social evaluation. Effort effects of empathy were examined in an experiment that gave participants the chance to benefit another person by meeting an easy or a moderately difficult performance challenge (Wright, Shaw, & Jones, 1990, Experiment 2). Specifically, the participants were assigned an easy (2-trigram) or moderately difficult (10-trigram) memorization task and told that if they succeeded they would earn a monetary donation for a woman with various personal problems. Half had listened earlier to an audiotape describing the woman's situation, with instructions to imagine how she must feel. The rest had listened to the audiotape with instructions to attend to technical aspects of the presentation.

Based on research and theory implicating empathy in the activation of altruistic motives (Batson, 1987), it was assumed that the need to help (and, hence, success importance) would be greater in participants who took the victim's perspective than in participants who took the technical perspective. Consequently, it was predicted that effort would increase with helping difficulty among victim-perspective (high-importance) participants but not among technical-perspective (low-importance) participants. Systolic responses assessed just prior to performance supported the prediction. For victim-perspective participants, responsiveness was greater in the moderately difficult condition than in the easy condition. By contrast, for technical-perspective participants, responsiveness was low regardless of the task assigned.

Effort effects of social evaluation have been examined in several studies. All have assumed that social evaluation manipulations frequently

constitute manipulations of incentive value because people who are evaluated often have greater reason to try than people who are not evaluated
(Geen & Bushman, 1989). To the degree that evaluation increases the incentive value, it should increase success importance but not determine effort
directly. What should determine effort is the difficulty of the performance
challenge with which performers are confronted. More specifically, people confronted with fixed challenges should evince effort in proportion
to challenge difficulty if they view success as possible and worthwhile,
and should demonstrate low effort if they view success as impossible or
excessively difficult. People confronted with unfixed challenges should
evince effort in proportion to potential motivation up to the point where
the maximum effort has been achieved.

One social evaluation study examined evaluation effects across five levels of performance challenge difficulty (Wright, Dill, Geen, & Anderson,
1998). Participants were presented with five versions of a recognition memory task ranging in difficulty from very low to very high. Specifically, in
different work periods, they were presented with memory challenges involving 2, 4, 6, 8, and 10 characters. Half were led to believe that their
responses would be known to a senior graduate student, and half were
led to believe that their responses would be private. The expectation was
that the relation between effort and difficulty would depend on whether
responses were or were not evaluated. Where there was evaluation, effort
was expected to rise with difficulty to a point and then fall. Where there
was not evaluation, effort was expected to either rise to a more modest
difficulty level before falling or remain low in all difficulty conditions.

Results revealed the expected Difficulty $\times$ Evaluation interaction for
SBP measured during the work (Figure 5.2). When performance was public, SBP responses increased with difficulty to a point and then dropped to a
low level. By contrast, when performance was private, the responses were
relatively low at all difficulty levels. HR and DBP responses were comparable to the SBP responses; however, analysis of the DBP data produced
only a marginally reliable ($p < .06$) difficulty effect.

The other social evaluation studies compared responses obtained under
easy fixed challenge conditions to responses obtained under unfixed challenge conditions. For example, Wright, Killebrew, and Pimpalapure (2002,
Experiment 1) directed participants either to press a computer mouse key
once each time they heard a tone sound at 10-second intervals (challenge
fixed) or to press the key repeatedly for as long as each tone continued to
sound, with the aim of pressing as many times as possible (challenge unfixed). Some participants (no-observer, NO) were told that their responses
would be private; the rest were told that their responses would be observed by an undergraduate (low-status-observer, LSO) or by a medical
school professor (high-status-observer, HSO). The investigators assumed
(a) that the benefit derived from success in an evaluator's presence depends

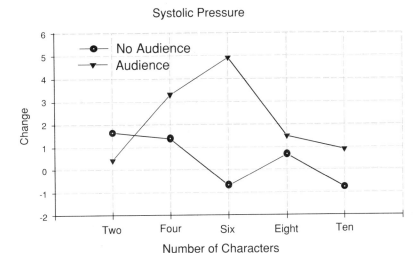

FIGURE 5.2 SBP response (i.e., change) as a function of challenge difficulty for participants whose performance could and could not be observed. Change is measured in millimeters of mercury. (Source: Wright et al., 1998, Figure 2. Used by permission.)

in part on the significance of the evaluator's opinion and (b) that low-status evaluators' opinions are likely to be regarded as less significant than high-status evaluators' opinions (Seta & Seta, 1992). Accordingly, they predicted that evaluation would increase effort insofar as the depicted evaluator had status when the challenge was unfixed, and would be low regardless of the presence or status of the evaluator when the challenge was fixed.

Again, work-related CV responses confirmed expectations (Figure 5.3). Participants in the unfixed/HSO condition had higher SBP elevations than did participants in the remaining conditions. Participants' HR and DBP responses were in the same pattern, although an analysis of variance (ANOVA) on the DBP data yielded only a main effect for type of challenge.

Ego Involvement and Personal Identity

Additional studies with stronger social components examined effort effects of ego involvement and personal identity. One ego involvement study led some participants (ego-involved) to believe that a memory task was diagnostic of an important ability – learning under time pressure – and other participants (ego-uninvolved) to believe that the task had no diagnostic value with respect to this or any other ability (Gendolla & Richter, 2003). We reasoned that ego-involved participants would consider success to be relatively important because it would allow them to display to others their

Systolic Pressure

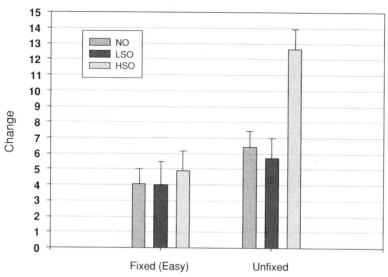

FIGURE 5.3 SBP change scores and associated standard errors at each level of the observer factor for fixed-challenge and unfixed-challenge participants. NO = no observer; LSO = low-status observer; HSO = high-status observer. Change is measured in millimeters of mercury. (Source: Wright et al., 2002, Figure 1. Used by permission.)

high ability on an important performance dimension (Klein & Schoenfeld, 1941). By contrast, ego-uninvolved participants should have viewed success as relatively unimportant because it afforded no opportunity to display or confirm an important ability and was not associated with any other notable benefit.

The study included four challenge conditions. In an unfixed condition, participants were presented with 15 nonsense letter series and instructed to memorize as many as they could in 5 minutes. In three fixed conditions, participants were presented with 2 (easy), 6 (moderately difficult), or 15 (very difficult) nonsense letter series and instructed to memorize them in the same amount of time. A key feature of the study was that it directed all participants to report to the experimenter what they had memorized once the memory session was completed. What was considered to be important from an ego-involvement perspective is that some participants could display a *valued* ability, whereas others could not.

Analysis of SBP data collected during performance produced a Challenge × Involvement interaction. As can be seen in Figure 5.4, values were higher for ego-involved participants than for ego-uninvolved participants

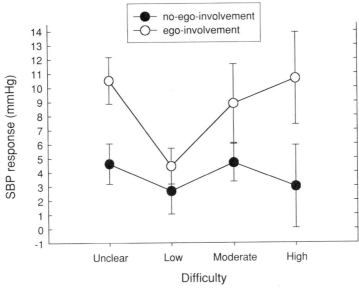

FIGURE 5.4 SBP change scores and associated standard errors as a function of ego in-volvement for fixed-challenge and unfixed-challenge participants. Change is measured in millimeters of mercury. (Source: Gendolla & Richter, 2003, Experiment 1).

when the challenge was unfixed. Figure 5.4 also shows that the relation between difficulty and SBP responsiveness in the fixed challenge conditions depended on ego involvement. When involvement was high, SBP responses rose steadily with difficulty. By contrast, when involvement was low, SBP responses were relatively low irrespective of difficulty.

A reasonable conclusion with respect to data in the unfixed condition is that ego-involved participants set a higher performance goal than did ego-uninvolved participants. Reasonable conclusions with respect to data in the fixed conditions are (a) that ego-involved participants considered success to be possible and worthwhile in all difficulty conditions and (b) that ego-uninvolved participants placed so little value on success that they viewed task requirements as excessive even when success was easy. Most interestingly, the ego-involvement studies demonstrate that the *difficulty law of motivation* applies to ego involvement – which had been denied previously (Dweck, 1986; Nicholls, 1984). In a broader context, these studies contribute to the evidence that ego involvement can have positive and enhancing effects on performance (Harackiewicz & Elliot, 1993).

Investigation of personal identity effects was inspired in part by an analysis by Baumeister (1986). The analysis observed that whereas in previous times people's place in society was automatically determined by factors like gender, social status, and the profession of the father, today people generally establish social identities on their own. Specifically, people first *decide* which identity they want to pursue (e.g., doctor, lawyer, priest) and then invest *effort* to acquire that identity. All else being equal, people should consider it more important to succeed on tasks instrumental to acquiring a desired identity than to succeed on tasks not instrumental to doing so; thus, one would expect the difficulty of a task to combine with the identity character of the task to determine effort.

The preceding reasoning was evaluated by studying CV responses in university freshmen who had set for themselves the goal of becoming professional psychologists (Gendolla, 1998). Participants were challenged to memorize a relatively brief (8-item) or lengthy (40-item) list of names in 5 minutes, being provided with either no information about the list (identity-irrelevant conditions) or instructions indicating that the list consisted of prominent psychologists whose names must be memorized in order to earn a degree in psychology (identity-relevant conditions). Analysis revealed Difficulty × Identity-Relevance interactions for SBP and HR responses measured during work. Both CV responses were stronger in the identity-relevant/40-item condition than in all other conditions.

CV Influence of Mood

Some final studies with stronger social components than the studies described previously looked at effort effects of mood. Central to these studies is the idea that mood impacts effort not directly, but rather indirectly by influencing appraisals of ability and difficulty, and thus ultimately engagement in the response to performance challenge. Drawing from Gendolla's *mood-behavior model* (Gendolla, 2000), investigators assumed that ability appraisals should tend to be lower in negative moods than in positive moods (see also Forgas, 1995; Forgas & Laham, this volume; Wyer, Clore, & Isbell, 1999). This implies that subjective difficulty appraisals should tend to be higher in negative moods than in positive moods and that mood–effort relations should be the same as the perceived-ability–effort relations depicted in Figure 5.1.

With the preceding analysis in mind, investigators assessed CV mood effects during two periods, one in which participants had a positive or negative mood induced and another in which participants were presented with a task. The general expectation was that mood would not affect effort during the first period but would affect it during the second period. However, precise predictions with respect to effort during performance depended on the nature of the assigned task and on task-relevant instructions.

Some studies presented a single task of unfixed difficulty in the performance period, assuming that the task would appear more difficult to negative-mood participants than to positive-mood participants. Typical of these is a study by Gendolla et al. (2001), which induced mood by having participants listen to (elating or depressing) music or recall (happy or sad) life events and involved a letter-cancellation task in which participants were instructed to perform as well as they could. During the mood induction, CV responses were unaffected by mood. By contrast, during performance, SBP responses were inversely proportional to mood valence.

Other studies administered tasks with fixed performance standards and varied the difficulty of the task presented in the performance period. Typical in this case is another experiment that induced mood with (elating or depressing) music and involved a letter-cancellation task (Gendolla & Krüsken, 2001b). Difficulty was manipulated by telling participants that they would have to attain a performance standard 20% slower (easy condition) or 20% faster (difficult condition) than one they had attained in practice. As in the previous study, there were no CV mood effects during the induction period. However, during performance there were Mood × Difficulty interaction patterns for SBP and DBP responsiveness. When difficulty was low, pressure elevations were relatively greater for the negative-mood group than for the positive-mood group. By contrast, when difficulty was high, pressure elevations were relatively greater among the positive-mood participants, presumably because the negative mood-participants viewed the difficult task as impossible or excessively difficult.

Still other mood studies examined a very complex implication of the preceding mood analysis: When success appears possible to both negative- and positive-mood groups, success importance should determine the difficulty level at which each group withholds effort (Gendolla & Krüsken, 2002, Experiments 1 and 2). CV assessments were made while participants went through a mood induction procedure and then again later while participants performed an easy or a difficult memory task. The induction technique involved watching an excerpt from a (funny or sad) film; the task was to memorize either four or seven groups of four randomized letters in 5 minutes. Success importance was manipulated by telling some participants (importance low) that a pleasant relaxation period would follow the performance period and telling other participants (importance high) that a relaxation period would follow the performance period *only* if they did well, making the relaxation period performance-contingent. The latter participants were told that if they did poorly, they would have to perform the memory task again.

The main findings for these studies were virtually identical and are reflected in the values displayed in Figure 5.5. When success importance was low ("non-contingent" values shown in the left panel of the figure), SBP responses were consistent with the view that negative-mood participants tried harder than positive-mood participants under easy conditions but withheld effort under difficult conditions. By contrast, when success

Task Performance

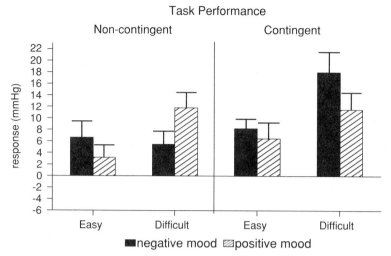

FIGURE 5.5 SBP change scores and associated standard errors during the task performance (lower panel) period for participants assigned easy and difficult tasks under conditions of low success importance (non-contingent) and high success importance (contingent). Change is measured in millimeters of mercury. (Source: Gendolla & Krüsken, 2002, Experiment 1, Figure 2. Used by permission.)

importance was high ("contingent" values shown in the right panel of the figure), responses were consistent with the view that negative-mood participants tried harder than positive-mood participants at *both* levels of difficulty, because the very high effort that was necessary in the negative-mood/difficult condition was here justified.

COMMENTARY

Studies such as those just presented bear out the validity and social applicability of Brehm's motivational intensity theory and its ability perception extension. At the same time, they cast doubt on the intuitive notions discussed earlier that effort (a) rises with success importance and (b) is greater in high-ability people than in low-ability people. Numerous findings are at variance with these notions. Consider, for example, results from the social evaluation study by Wright et al. (1998). Presumably, success was more important when responses could be evaluated than when responses could not be evaluated. Yet, the social evaluation factor did not produce main effects on the CV response measures, as would be predicted by the first notion presented. Rather, it interacted with challenge difficulty to determine CV responsiveness.

Also consider results from the Wright and Dill (1993) experiment and the mood investigations by Gendolla and his associates. Wright and Dill manipulated ability perception and found it to be *positively* associated with BP responsiveness at one level of difficulty (difficult) but *negatively* associated with BP responsiveness at another level (easy). The mood studies examined ability perception by proxy. They both conceptually replicated the CV effects observed by Wright and Dill and extended those effects, demonstrating that ability perception is *dissociated* from CV responsiveness under some difficulty and success importance conditions. Findings from these studies conflict with the second intuitive notion presented because this notion implies ability perception main effects, reflecting stronger sympathetic CV responses under high-ability conditions than under low-ability conditions.

Alternative CV Analyses

Significantly, the present CV findings cannot be explained easily in terms of two popular CV hypotheses: that CV response varies with (1) the value of available incentives, and (2) with subjective threat (Wright & Kirby, 2001). The incentive hypothesis has difficulty with the data because it implies that CV responses should have been stronger under high-importance conditions than under low-importance conditions, irrespective of difficulty. The threat hypothesis has difficulty with the data because it applies only to studies that involved aversive performance contingencies and because it implies that CV responses in those studies should have been (a) proportional to danger and (b) inversely associated with control. Empirical limitations of the threat hypothesis are illustrated by results of the Wright et al. (1992) study mentioned earlier. This study measured CV responses in participants led to believe they could earn a low or high chance of avoiding noise by succeeding on an easy or difficult memory task. Subjective threat should have been greatest in the difficult/low-probability condition, where the risk of noise exposure was greatest. Yet, CV responses in that condition were minimal, substantially lower than those in the difficult/high-probability condition, where high effort was expected and strong SBP and HR responses were found.

The CV findings also cannot be easily explained in terms of the idea advanced recently that people display *challenge* CV responses when perceived resources meet, moderately exceed, or fall just short of perceived demand and display *threat* CV responses when perceived resources fall moderately short of perceived demand (Blascovich & Mendes, 2000; Blascovich, Mendes, Hunter, & Lickel, 2000). Challenge responses are proposed to consist of powerful increases in heart contraction force and cardiac output (blood volume produced on a heartbeat × HR), paired with a decline in peripheral resistance (resistance to flow in the vascular network). Contrasting threat responses are proposed to consist of modest heart contraction increases, no change or a decrease in cardiac output, a modest increase or no change in peripheral resistance, and a relatively large increase in BP. Investigators in this research area contend that HR does not vary with challenge and threat, but rather varies with effort, which in turn varies with goal relevance, defined roughly as success importance.

One reason the challenge versus threat idea has difficulty with the present data is that it is based on an analysis that is problematic in important respects (Wright & Kirby, 2003). For example, the analysis defines *demand* as an evaluation resulting from a calculus involving appraisals of required effort, uncertainty, and danger, which means that resources cannot in fact be compared to it. A further reason the idea has difficulty with these data is that it anticipates CV effects contrary to those that have been obtained. Consider, for example, results of studies discussed here that showed greater BP responsiveness under moderately difficult task conditions than under easy and very difficult task conditions (e.g., Smith et al., 1990). These results conflict with the prediction that people should have challenge appraisals and, consequently, weak BP responses when perceived resources moderately exceed or fall just short of perceived demand. Consider as well the interaction effects obtained for HR in studies that have crossed importance factors with difficulty factors (e.g., Gendolla, 1998). These conflict with the notion that HR should vary with goal relevance (success importance).

Future Directions

There would seem to be no limit to the directions that new effort research along these lines might take. One goal for future research might be to address the question of whether people are always cognizant of the effort they expend. Our guess is that they are not. That is, we suspect that even complex effort modulation can occur nonconsciously, based on implicit appraisals of challenge fixedness, challenge difficulty, and benefit. Relevant evidence comes from CV effort studies that have asked participants to report their effort levels. Results have shown a correspondence between effort reports and CV responsiveness in some instances and no relation between these outcomes in others. The inconsistency of results in these studies accords with the view that effort awareness is possible but not necessary.

Related to this issue is a distinction that has been made between habitual behavior and intentional behavior (e.g., Aarts & Dijksterhuis, 2000; Aarts & Hassin, this volume; Dewey, 1897; Strack & Deutsch, this volume; Wood & Quinn, this volume; Wood, Quinn, & Kashy, 2002). Whereas intentional behavior is believed to be deliberate and effortful, habitual behavior is believed to be automatic and effortless. We would suggest that habits are not effort free, but rather largely free from the *experience* of effort. Habitual behaviors vary in difficulty, just as nonhabitual behaviors do. And difficult behaviors require more effort than do easy behaviors irrespective of how the behaviors are engendered (i.e., automatically versus nonautomatically). Thus, although we may be relatively unaware of how much effort we expend when we behave out of habit, effort is likely to be involved in both habitual and nonhabitual activities.

A second goal for future research might be to explore linkages between Brehm's view of effort and major alternative effort views. One alternative view of special interest is Locke and Latham's (1990) theory of goal setting and performance. Another alternative view of special interest is Atkinson's (1957) classic achievement motivation theory. These views appear contrary to Brehm's reasoning in certain respects but might be reconciled with the reasoning upon careful review.

Yet another goal for future research might be to expand social applications of the motivational intensity theory and its ability perception extension. One can easily imagine additional studies related to social topics, including studies related to aggression, conformity, interpersonal attraction, ostracism, persuasion, self-regulation, and encoding style. Consider, for example, an experiment on ostracism (Warburton & Williams, this volume). CV responses could be measured in participants who have the opportunity to earn entry into a group by performing some activity. Presumably, the participants' responses would depend on the nature of the performance challenge, the difficulty of the challenge, the participants' ability perception with respect to the challenge, and the importance of the group.

Summary and Conclusions

We have outlined and discussed CV evidence relevant to a set of ideas concerned with the determinants of momentary effort. The core assertion embodied in these ideas is that effort is a function of what can, will, and must be done to achieve outcomes. Studies of effort-related CV response bear out the validity and social applicability of this assertion. At the same time, they call into question certain popular effort assumptions and raise doubts about several CV response hypotheses. The effort ideas discussed here have potential for shedding light on innumerable social motivational processes.

References

Aarts, H., & Dijksterhuis, A. (2000). Habits as knowledge structures: Automaticity in goal-directed behavior. *Journal of Personality and Social Psychology, 78*, 53–63.

Ach, N. (1935). *Analyse des Willens [Analysis of the will]*. Berlin: Urban & Schwarzenberg.

Atkinson, J. W. (1957). Motivational determinants of risk-taking behavior. *Psychological Review, 64*, 359–372.

Bandura, A. (1986). *Social foundations of thought and action.* Englewood Cliffs, NJ: Prentice-Hall.

Batson, C. D. (1987). Prosocial motivation: Is it ever truly altruistic? In L. Berkowitz (Ed.), *Advances in experimental social psychology* (pp. 65–122). New York: Academic Press.

Baumeister, R. F. (1986). *Identity: Cultural change and the struggle for self.* New York: Oxford University Press.

Blascovich, J., & Mendes, W. B. (2000). Challenge and threat appraisals: The role of affective cues. In J. Forgas (Ed.), *Feeling and thinking: The role of affect in social cognition* (pp. 59–82). Cambridge: Cambridge University Press.

Blascovich, J., Mendes, W. B., Hunter, S. B., & Lickel, B. (2000). Stigma, threat, and social interactions. In T. F. Heatherton, R. E. Kleck, M. R. Hebl, & J. G. Hull (Eds.), *The social psychology of stigma* (pp. 307–333). New York: Guilford Press.

Brehm, J. W., & Self, E. A. (1989). The intensity of motivation. *Annual Review of Psychology, 40,* 109–131.

Dewey, J. (1897). The psychology of effort. *Psychological Review, 6,* 43–56.

Dweck, C. S. (1986). Motivational processes affecting learning. *American Psychologist, 41,* 1040–1048.

Eisenberger, R. (1992). Learned industriousness. *Psychological Review, 99,* 248–267.

Forgas, J. P. (1995). Mood and judgment: The affect infusion model (AIM). *Psychological Bulletin, 117,* 36–66.

Fowles, D. C. (1983). Motivational effects on heart rate and electrodermal activity: Implications for research on personality and psychopathology. *Journal of Research in Personality, 17,* 48–71.

Geen, R. G., & Bushman, B. J. (1989). The arousing effects of social presence. In H. Wagner & A. Manstead (Eds.), *Handbook of social psychophysiology* (pp. 261–281). London: Wiley.

Gendolla, G. H. E. (1998). Effort as assessed by motivational arousal in identity relevant tasks. *Basic and Applied Social Psychology, 20,* 111–121.

Gendolla, G. H. E. (2000). On the impact of mood on behavior: An integrative theory and a review. *Review of General Psychology, 4,* 378–408.

Gendolla, G. H. E., Abele, A. E., & Krüsken, J. (2001a). The informational impact of mood on effort mobilization: A study of cardiovascular and electrodermal responses. *Emotion, 1,* 12–24.

Gendolla, G. H. E., & Krüsken, J. (2001b). The joint impact of mood state and task difficulty on cardiovascular and electrodermal reactivity in active coping. *Psychophysiology, 38,* 548–556.

Gendolla, G. H. E., & Krüsken, J. (2002). The joint effect of informational mood impact and performance-contingent incentive on effort-related cardiovascular response. *Journal of Personality and Social Psychology, 83,* 271–285.

Gendolla, G. H. E., & Richter, M. (2003). *Ego-involvement, mental task demand, and the intensity of motivation: Effects on effort-related cardiovascular response.* Unpublished manuscript, University of Erlangen.

Harackiewicz, J. M., & Elliot, A. J. (1993). Achievement goals and intrinsic motivation. *Journal of Personality and Social Psychology, 65,* 904–915.

Klein, G. S., & Schoenfeld, N. (1941). The influence of ego-involvement on confidence. *Journal of Abnormal and Social Psychology, 36,* 249–258.

Kukla, A. (1972). Foundations of an attributional theory of performance. *Psychological Review*, *79*, 454–470.

Locke, E. A., & Latham, G. P. (1990). *A theory of goal setting and performance.* Englewood Cliffs, NJ: Prentice-Hall.

Nicholls, J. G. (1984). Achievement motivation: Conceptions of ability, subjective experience, task choice, and performance. *Psychological Review*, *91*, 328–346.

Obrist, P. A. (1981). *Cardiovascular psychophysiology.* New York: Plenum Press.

Papillo, J. F., & Shapiro, D. (1990). The cardiovascular system. In J. T. Cacioppo & L. G. Tassinary (Eds.), *Principles of psychophysiology: Physical, social, and inferential elements* (pp. 456–512). New York: Cambridge University Press.

Seta, C. E., & Seta, J. J. (1992). Increments and decrements in mean arterial pressure as a function of audience composition: An averaging and summation analysis. *Personality and Social Psychology Bulletin*, *18*, 173–181.

Smith, T. W., Baldwin, M., & Christenson, A. J. (1990). Interpersonal influence as active coping: Effects of task difficulty on cardiovascular reactivity. *Psychophysiology*, *27*, 429–437.

Wood, W., Quinn, J. M., & Kashy, D. (2002). Habits in everyday life: The thought and feel of action. *Journal of Personality and Social Psychology*, *83*, 1281–1297.

Wright, R. A., Contrada, R. J., & Patane, M. J. (1986). Task difficulty, cardiovascular response, and the magnitude of goal valence. *Journal of Personality and Social Psychology*, *51*, 837–843.

Wright, R. A., & Dill, J. C. (1993). Blood pressure responses and incentive appraisals as a function of perceived ability and objective task demand. *Psychophysiology*, *30*, 152–160.

Wright, R. A., Dill, J. C., Geen, R. G., & Anderson, C. A. (1998). Social evaluation influence on cardiovascular response to a fixed behavioral challenge: Effects across a range of difficulty levels. *Annals of Behavioral Medicine*, *20*, 277–285.

Wright, R. A., & Franklin, J. (in press). Ability perception determinants of effort-related cardiovascular response: Mood, optimism, and performance resources. In R. A. Wright, J. Greenberg, & S. S. Brehm (Eds), *Motivational analyses of social behavior: Building on Jack Brehm's contributions to psychology.* Hillsdale, NJ: Erlbaum.

Wright, R. A., Killebrew, K., & Pimpalapure, D. (2002). Cardiovascular incentive effects where a challenge is unfixed: Demonstrations involving social evaluation, evaluator status, and monetary reward. *Psychophysiology*, *39*, 188–197.

Wright, R. A., & Kirby, L. D. (2001). Effort determination of cardiovascular response: An integrative analysis with applications in social psychology. In M. P. Zanna (Ed.), *Advances in experimental social psychology* (Vol. 33, pp. 255–307). New York: Academic Press.

Wright, R. A., & Kirby, L. D. (2003). Cardiovascular correlates of challenge and threat appraisals: A critical examination of the psychobiosocial analysis. *Personality and Social Psychology Review*, *7*, 216–233.

Wright, R. A., Shaw, L. L., & Jones, C. R. (1990). Task demand and cardiovascular response magnitude: Further evidence of the mediating role of success importance. *Journal of Personality and Social Psychology*, *59*, 1250–1260.

Wright, R. A., Williams, B. J., & Dill, J. C. (1992). Interactive effects of difficulty and instrumentality of avoidant behavior on cardiovascular reactivity. *Psychophysiology, 29,* 677–689.

Wyer, R. S., Clore, G. L., & Isbell, L. M. (1999). Affect and information processing. In M. P. Zanna (Ed.), *Advances in experimental social psychology* (Vol. 31, pp. 1–77). New York: Academic Press.

6

Reflection and Impulse as Determinants of Conscious and Unconscious Motivation

Fritz Strack and Roland Deutsch

INTRODUCTION

Social behavior may be determined by both conscious and unconscious forces. Indeed, a first look at the dominant theories of motivation (Higgins & Kruglanski, 2000) suggests that this distinction lends itself to a meaningful classification of motivational mechanisms. Conscious accounts are based on the assumption that humans (and to some degree other primates) are endowed with reason and insight. What they do can therefore be construed as deliberate action, the mental precursor of which is a decision or a choice. As Ajzen (1996, p. 298) has put it, acting "involves a choice even if the alternative is no action." It is therefore useful to study people's reflective judgments as precursors to their choices. Specifically, decisions are based on the perceived value of the outcomes of an action and the subjective probability that they can be achieved. This expectancy-value perspective has influenced many theoretical approaches (for a review, see Feather, 1982). Most prominently, perhaps, Fishbein and Ajzen's theories of reasoned action (Ajzen & Fishbein, 1980) and of planned behavior (Ajzen, 1991) have invoked this model to specify the influence of attitudinal judgments on human behavior. Also, Bandura's (1977) theory of social learning has adopted central elements of the expectancy-value paradigm.

Another variant of the conscious approach to motivation invokes people's intentions in the context of goal pursuit (see also Aarts & Hassin, this volume). Specifically, actors are assumed to intentionally control and regulate their behavior in order to reach a specific end state. While this general idea has deep roots in the history of psychology (e.g., Ach, 1905,

Address for correspondence: Fritz Strack or Roland Deutsch, LS Psy
sität Würzburg, Röntgenring 10, 97070 Würzburg, Germany; e-mail: stra
wuerzburg.de, deutsch@psychologie.uni-wuerzburg.de.

1910; see also Lewin, 1926), many motivational implications have recently been identified and tested by Gollwitzer (e.g., Gollwitzer & Moskowitz, 1996).

According to these classic accounts, decisions and goal-directed intentions require a sufficient degree of consciousness. However, other accounts of social behavior do without this assumption. One example is models that focus on habits as a central determinant of behavior. According to Wood and Quinn (this volume), habits are "behavioral tendencies to repeat well-practiced acts given stable cues." Some researchers, borrowing from their precursors in the behaviorist tradition (e.g., Hull, 1943), have recently reintroduced habits into social psychology (e.g., Verplanken & Aarts, 1999), with a focus on their automaticity and situational constancy. Although people may be aware of habitual behaviors, such awareness is not crucial for their execution. Mere repetition under stable conditions is sufficient for habits to be formed and elicited given the appropriate situational cues.

Another principle of human motivation represents two fundamental reactions toward the environment: approach and avoidance. In particular, motivational orientations toward approach or avoidance are assumed to direct behavior toward positive aspects and away from negative aspects of a given situation. These mechanisms have been found to correspond to specific neural systems in the brain and seem to be related to hemispheric asymmetries (Gray, 1982; Lang, 1995; Sutton & Davidson, 1997).

While each of these processes has received considerable attention, it has become obvious that none is able, by itself, to account for the entire range of behavioral determinants. Under the theme of *automaticity* (Bargh, 1997), researchers have recognized that both conscious and unconscious mechanisms may play an important role. One widespread strategy for integrating the two types of processing is the duplication of the mental universe. For example, explicit attitudes are assumed to have implicit counterparts that direct people's behavior under suboptimal circumstances (e.g., Wilson, Lindsey, & Schooler, 2000). Similarly, goals are believed to operate in an unconscious fashion (Chartrand & Bargh, 2002). This idea of transposing the same procedure from one psychological mode to another is compelling, parsimonious, and goes back to Helmholtz's (1867) notion of *unconscious inferences*.

However, it remains open to question whether the operational principles stay the same. Although experiments have successfully elicited goal-consistent behavior subliminally (Chartrand & Bargh, 2002), the question arises as to whether other characteristics of conscious goal pursuit can be equally transposed to an unconscious mode of operation (see also Liberman & Förster, this volume). One example is the possibility that goals can be construed in a hierarchical fashion, which allows people to circumvent obstacles. That is, if a particular goal is blocked, people may check the instrumentality of the obstructed goal vis-à-vis a superordinate objective and choose a different means to the same end. It has yet to be demonstrated that this important characteristic of goal-directed action operates in an unconscious fashion. To be sure, unconscious behaviors may often enfold *as if* they were the result of reasoning and planning when in fact they are produced by a different mechanism.

There is no doubt that consciousness is an important psychological dimension and is defined by the phenomenal experience of the actor. However, there is doubt as to whether it is the most suitable dimension for studying the duality of motivational processes. One reason is that consciousness is still poorly understood. We simply do not know precisely how it arises from psychological or neural processes. Consequently, consciousness is often seen as an *epiphenomenon* rather than an integral part – let alone a causal force – of cognition (Libet, Gleason, Wright, & Pearl, 1983; Wegner, 2002). Categorizing a process as conscious or unconscious therefore provides little information about its computational nature.

In an effort to focus more directly on the operating mechanisms, the model of social behavior we propose is not based on the conscious–unconscious distinction. Instead, it specifies different types of motivation that are rooted in distinct mechanisms of processing. Specifically, it assumes that humans possess two regulatory systems that contribute jointly to a behavioral outcome. To understand how human behavior is elicited jointly by mostly conscious reflection and by spontaneous and often unconscious impulse, we have developed a more general model that describes the different processes that influence behavior by means of cognitive and affective mechanisms (Strack & Deutsch, in press).

Although there are numerous approaches that draw on different psychological mechanisms (see Chaiken & Trope, 1999), none provides a general account of human behavior. Specifically, existing models are either general but have little to say about motivation and the specific mechanisms of behavior (e.g., Chen & Chaiken, 1999; Sloman, 1996) or they are tailor-made to explain a specific aspect of motivation and behavior but lack generality (e.g., Metcalfe & Mischel, 1999). We have therefore proposed a model that may account for both decision-based and automatic aspects of behavior while trying to maintain the explanatory power of previous dual-process accounts. In this sense the current model may be seen as a motivational "update" of the existing state of theorizing.

BASIC PROPERTIES OF THE MODEL

Although the *Reflective-Impulsive Model* (RIM) attempts ultimately to explain social behavior, its behavioral mechanisms are strongly tied to cognitive processes. For that reason, we will briefly describe the model with respect to its nonbehavioral features. We will then turn to a characteristic that is more directly tied to behavioral outcomes, namely, its *final common pathway that* translates *behavioral schemata* into overt behavior. The remainder of the chapter will describe how various forces resulting from reflective and impulsive mechanisms exert influence on the activation and execution of behavioral schemata and thereby direct overt behavior.

The Reflective and the Impulsive System

The *Impulsive System* is conceptualized as a simple network in which information is processed automatically through a fast and parallel spread of activation between associated contents. Processes of symbol manipulation and rule-based reasoning, on the other hand, are assumed to be carried out in a *Reflective System*. While this ensures great flexibility, the Reflective System operates slowly and is more easily disrupted by other processes, and its processes are dependent on intention.

Specifically, the Impulsive System represents environmental regularities as patterns of activation in an associative network. In this network, links are created or strengthened if stimuli are presented in close temporal or spatial proximity. Additionally, behaviors in response to stimuli as well as affective reactions can become integrated into such associative clusters. These associative clusters are assumed to represent simple concepts (Barsalou, 1999). In essence, we assume that the Impulsive System works like a simple memory system (see Johnson & Hirst, 1991), which slowly forms enduring, nonpropositional representations of the typical properties of the environment over many learning trials (see McClelland, McNaughton, & O'Reilly, 1995; Smith & DeCoster, 2000). An important divergence from some other network models (e.g., Collins & Quillian, 1969) is that links in the Impulsive System have no semantic meaning by themselves. The only relationship between elements is that of mutual activation. Consequently, propositions cannot be represented in the Impulsive System, since they presuppose that an abstract relationship (e.g., *is a, is not*) is applied to two or more elements. Processes in the Impulsive System may be accompanied by an experiential mode of awareness. Without necessarily knowing its origin, a person may experience a feeling with its distinct phenomenal quality, such as a perception of sweetness, a pleasant feeling, or the experience or familiarity without knowledge about related concepts.

Take as an example a person repeatedly seeing, smelling, and finally eating a pie. According to the outlined principles, all sensory and motor representations that occur during the episodes will be linked, and an associative cluster relating to pie will emerge. When the individual encounters a similar situation, this cluster will be activated, leading to anticipatory sensations of taste and smell, as well as of affective consequences such as the pleasure of a sweet taste. Likewise, behavioral schemata related to eating will undergo activation. However, this activation does not represent knowledge that the percept is a pie, elicits pleasure, or is usually eaten with a fork.

Abstract relations (such as *is a*) rely on symbolic representation and can be applied flexibly to varying information. According to the RIM, this can only be accomplished in the Reflective System. If a proposition is generated or processed, concepts and the relationship applied to them are retrieved from the Impulsive System and are then combined to form the proposition. Because the Reflective System only serves the function of a short-term memory, representations cannot be stored in a propositional format over extended periods of time. Instead, through frequent pairing, the constituents of the proposition (i.e., the concepts and relationships) can become associatively stored in the long-term memory of the Impulsive System.

Once knowledge has been generated, syllogistic rules guide inferences that go beyond the information given (Bruner, 1973). Take again the example of a person exposed to a pie. Through reflection, the percept may be linked to an appropriate category (i.e., pie, cake), and the relation of class membership (i.e., *is a*) may be assigned to it. At the same time, further elements associated with the category (e.g., sweet) may receive activation and be used for additional reasoning. For instance, a high calorie content may be inferred from the property of sweetness.

There is a basic difference to the mere activation of the concept, which facilitates the inference but does not generate knowledge about pies being high in calories. This knowledge, in turn, may be used for behavioral decisions (e.g., not to eat the pie). The phenomenal awareness that something is or is not the case accompanies operations of the Reflective System. Such *noetic* states of awareness may go along with *experiential* states of awareness. For example, trying to answer an almanac question may be accompanied by a *feeling of knowing* (Koriat, 1993) that is distinct from knowing that something is the case (see Schooler & Schreiber, this volume).

Final Common Pathway to Behavior

An important feature of the RIM is that it does not stop with representation, feeling, and judgment. Instead, mechanisms adapted to optimize behavior are integrated into cognitive and affective structures. The core mechanism that serves this function is a final common pathway to overt behavior, consisting of *behavioral schemata* of different abstractness. Behavioral schemata are assumed to connect frequently co-occurring motor representations with both their antecedent conditions and their consequences. Behavioral schemata and their links to other contents in the Impulsive System can be understood as habits (see also Aarts & Dijksterhuis, 2000;

Wood & Quinn, this volume). They are parts of the Impulsive System and are strongly interconnected with perceptual and conceptual structures.

Like other contents of this system, behavioral schemata are subject to spreading activation and differ in their activation potential. If one part of a behavioral schema is activated, excitation will spread to the remaining elements of the cluster. At a given point in time, impulsive and reflective sources such as goals, perceptions, or actual behaviors may activate a schema. Which of these schemata is executed depends on the relative strength of its activation. Although both impulsive and reflective processes can lead to the activation of a behavioral schema (see also Norman & Shallice, 1986), they differ in how this activation is carried out.

DIFFERENT FORCES DIRECTING BEHAVIOR

The two systems use different operations to elicit behavior. In the Reflective System, behavior is the result of a decision that is based on the assessment of a future state in terms of its value and the likelihood that it can be attained through this behavior. The Impulsive System, in contrast, elicits behavior through the mere spread of activation to behavioral schemata, modulated by motivational orientations and homeostatic dysregulations.

Reflective Determinants

In the Reflective System, behavior is the outcome of reasoning that leads to a noetic decision about the desirability and feasibility of a particular action (cf. Ajzen, 1991; Bandura, 1977). Of course, actual or anticipated feelings may enter this decision, along with factual knowledge about actions and outcomes. If the execution of the behavior is judged to be feasible and its outcome positive, a behavioral decision will create a relation between the self and the behavioral outcome. If, for instance, a person deliberates about eating a slice of pie, the delicious taste of the pie may enter the computation along with the positive social consequence of not refusing the pie offered by a friend who has prepared it for the occasion. Also, fragmentary anticipatory feelings of its taste may be perceived and used to infer a positive attitude. The decision to eat it is expected to come with a link between *eating the pie* and the self, resulting in the propositional representation *I want to eat the pie*.

It is important to note that a goal-directed behavior may not be elicited immediately by a behavioral decision, because behavioral schemata that are incompatible with the behavioral decision might be activated. We will discuss this possibility later. Additionally, the behavioral decision may refer to a remote point in time. This problem will be addressed in the following section.

Intending

Often an action cannot be carried out at the time the behavioral decision is made. In fact, the execution of many decisions depends on conditions that have not yet been fulfilled. As a result, there can be a temporal gap between a behavioral decision and an action. This gap may be bridged by the constant activation of the relevant behavioral schemata. However, such a permanent rehearsal of behavioral programs by the Reflective System would absorb a great amount of cognitive capacity. We therefore include a process of *intending* (e.g., Gollwitzer, 1999), which is assumed to bridge temporal gaps by automatically reactivating the behavioral decision and thus the behavioral schemata that are appropriate in the situation. Through intending, the Impulsive System is monitored for information that enables the behavioral implementation of the decision. If the behavior is executed or if the goal of the preceding behavioral decision has already been fulfilled, the mechanism of intending is terminated.

Impulsive Determinants

From a subjective perspective, a decision is most likely seen as the precursor to behavior. However, other mechanisms that are less open to introspection may contribute to overt behavior.

The simplest source of activation for behavioral elements in the Impulsive System is its perceptual input. Although not in the form of simple reflexes, perception may be linked to behavior in a direct fashion. Describing his ideo-motor principle, James (1890) assumed that "every representation of a movement awakens in some degree the actual movement which is its object" (p. 396). Consistent with James's notion, the RIM assumes that in the Impulsive System, conceptual content and behavioral schemata are linked (for a review of supporting research see Dijksterhuis & Bargh, 2001). For instance, the act of seeing a cake activates behavioral schemata associated with cakes, as well as other relevant concepts. In this case, schemata related to using a fork as well as the concept *fork* might become activated.

This setup depicts the Impulsive System as more rigid than the Reflective System when it comes to behavioral control. Specifically, changing evaluations in the Reflective System may immediately result in new behavioral decisions and actions. In contrast, changes of perception–behavior links in the Impulsive System are assumed to develop through mechanisms of slow learning.

However, the RIM specifies ways in which the Impulsive System can also react more flexibly, taking external and internal conditions into consideration. To account for external conditions, the Impulsive System is believed to alternate between two distinct motivational orientations that guide further processing and behavior. For internal conditions, we propose a specific way in which homeostatic dysregulations may influence impulsive processing. Both motivational aspects will now be outlined in more detail.

Homeostatic Dysregulations

The deprivation of a basic need calls for a rapid reversal of the situation and thus for a more specific disposition to act. The RIM accounts for the influence of deprivation by a mechanism that is similar to assumptions in early drive theory (Hull, 1943). If a state of deprivation is ended, the satisfying behaviors and their situational circumstances become strongly linked to the experience of this deprivation. Thus, if the same state of deprivation occurs again, the behavioral schemata and conceptual contents that were previously satisfying will be activated. This will establish a *behavioral preparedness* and a *perceptual readiness* for the processing of relevant information in the environment (Bruner, 1957). For example, the deprivation of food will activate behavioral schemata related to eating as well as conceptual representations of food. As a consequence, food stimuli should be recognized more easily under conditions of food deprivation (see also Liberman & Förster, and Spencer, Fein, Strahan, & Zanna, this volume).

This was found in an experiment conducted by Wispe and Drambarean (1953), who asked hungry or satiated participants to recognize words that were presented very briefly on a computer screen. Specifically, the words were either food-related or not. As a main result, hungry participants were faster at detecting food-related words than neutral words. However, no such difference was observed in participants who were not hungry. Similar results were recently obtained by Aarts, Dijksterhuis, and De Vries (2001) for thirst and thirst-related words.

Motivational Orientation

Whereas homeostatic dysregulations direct behavior in a very specific manner, the Impulsive System is also endowed with a more global behavioral orientation. As we have pointed out, the principal benefit of the Impulsive System is its capacity to act quickly under suboptimal conditions. In particular, we suggest that this is achieved by the system's being preset toward approach or avoidance (Cacioppo, Priester, & Berntson, 1993). This motivational orientation may be triggered by

- the perception of approach or avoidance
- the processing of positive or negative information
- the experience of positive or negative affect
- the execution of approach or avoidance behaviors

Like other theorists (e.g., Gray, 1982; Lang, 1995; Sutton & Davidson, 1997), we assume that these functional orientations serve to prepare the organism for two fundamental reactions toward the environment. Approach orientation is understood as a preparedness to *decrease* the distance between the person and an aspect of the environment. This can be achieved by physical locomotion, instrumental action, and consumption, real or imagined. Avoidance orientation, in contrast, can be conceived as a preparedness to *increase* the distance between the person and the environment. This can be accomplished either by moving away from a target (*flight*) or by causing it to be removed (*fight*).

The prevailing motivational orientation facilitates the processing of information, the experience of affect, and the execution of behavior under conditions of compatibility. Under approach, the processing of positive information, the experience of positive affect, and the execution of approach behavior are facilitated. Under avoidance, the processing of negative information, the experience of negative affect, and the execution of avoidance behavior are facilitated. Moreover, we propose a *principle of bidirectionality*, that is, a reverse causal influence. That is to say, a motivational orientation may be elicited by the valence of the processed information, the valence of affect, or the orientation of a behavior (approach versus avoidance).

Most important, the principle of bidirectionality implies that behavior may exert a causal influence on evaluative judgments and experiences. In the Reflective System, people may use their behavior to draw inferences about their internal states (e.g., attitudes; see Bem, 1967). Such inferences, however, require that the behavior is propositionally categorized. In contrast, the principle of bidirectionality in the Impulsive System allows a behavior to influence processing without being assigned to a propositional category. In other words, people are influenced by what they are doing even if they do not recognize its meaning.

We will now review evidence supporting the idea that behavior may have a direct effect on the processing of information that occurs in the Impulsive System and is therefore not mediated by syllogistic inferences. At the same time, this evidence supports the compatibility principle of the Impulsive System. Subsequently, we will concentrate on the reversed direction of influence and describe studies that illustrate the impact of evaluative information on behavior.

THE COMPATIBILITY PRINCIPLE I: THE DIRECT IMPACT OF BEHAVIOR ON MENTAL PROCESSES

One important illustration of the direct impact of behavior on mental processes is facial feedback. It has long been argued (e.g., Darwin, 1872/1965) that bodily expressions may increase or diminish the intensity of an affective experience. Applied to the face, Darwin's *facial-feedback hypothesis* has been studied from the vantage point of self-perception theory (Bem, 1967). For example, Laird (e.g., 1974) found that experimental participants who had been asked to adopt a smiling expression judged themselves (e.g., their own well-being) and affective stimuli (e.g., cartoons) more positively. According to self-perception theory, these participants inferred their affective state from their facial expression. As mentioned before, such an inference requires the behavior to be interpreted as the expression of a particular affective state. Concretely, a person can infer that she must be happy (or amused) only if she knows that she is smiling.

The RIM implies that this is not the only way in which an overt behavior may influence mental processes. While the inferences described by self-perception theory operate in line with the principles of the Reflective System, in the Impulsive System behavior may directly influence information processing. Specifically, the behavioral schemata that activate an emotional expression are assumed to be linked to evaluatively compatible thought contents and perhaps to affective experiences, and this facilitates the processing of the affective information.

Evidence for such a mechanism comes from a set of studies in which participants' facial expressions were elicited by task requirements that were unrelated to emotional contents. For example, Strack, Martin, and Stepper (1988) asked experimental participants to hold a pen either between their teeth or between their puckered lips while rating several cartoons that were interspersed among other tasks. In the teeth condition (where the task activated the zygomaticus muscle, which is used in smiling), cartoons were rated as funnier than in the lips condition (where the task prevented a smiling expression) or in a no-treatment control condition.

Although the teeth-holding position activated the zygomaticus muscle, the cover story prevented participants from interpreting their facial action as a smile. Nevertheless, people assigned to this experimental condition reported feeling more amused and rated the cartoons as funnier than people who held the pen with their puckered lips.

The same logic was subsequently applied to postural expressions. Stepper and Strack (1993) found that participants who were induced to adopt an upright posture while learning about their above-average performance in a previous task felt prouder than participants induced to assume a slumped posture.

While these studies demonstrate the phenomenon, they are not sufficiently explicit about the exact mechanisms that afford such a direct behavioral influence on mental processes. Subsequent studies shed more light on the underlying processes. In a series of experiments that explored the effect of head movements on the recognition of words, Förster and Strack (1996) asked participants to nod or shake their head while reading positive and negative words. To prevent participants from interpreting the head movements as expression of agreement or disagreement, they were asked to "test head phones to be used while dancing" (Wells & Petty, 1980) and to perform either horizontal or vertical head movements while the words were played on a cassette recorder.

As expected, the head movements affected performance in a surprise recognition task. Specifically, participants who had been induced to nod were superior at recognizing positive words, whereas participants who had been induced to shake their head were better at recognizing negative words. Moreover, this was not a response bias that affected the threshold for words of a particular valence. Instead, it was the compatibility between the head movement and the valence of the word that improved participants' discrimination of whether or not the word had been presented. This suggests that the behavior influenced the processing of the words at the time of encoding.

These findings show motor influences on mental processing when the behavior has no immediate evaluative implications. However, these implications are mediated by a motivational subsystem to which the behavior belongs. Because nodding is a nonverbal signal for agreement in most cultures and shaking one's head is a signal for disagreement, these head movements are linked to an orientation toward approach or avoidance, which influences the impulsive regulation of behavior.

Similar results were obtained for a behavior that had previously been found to influence positive and negative affect. Specifically, Cacioppo and his collaborators (e.g., Cacioppo et al., 1993) discovered that pressing one's hand from the bottom against the surface of a table, thereby contracting the flexor muscle of the arm, led to positive attitudinal judgments, whereas pressing from the top against a table, thereby contracting the extensor muscle, led to negative attitudinal judgments. Cacioppo et al. argued that flexor and extensor contractions, through previous associations, elicit a motivational orientation of approach versus avoidance.

Cacioppo et al.'s (1993) notion of a motivational orientation that can be activated by any behavior compatible with approach or avoidance is integrated into and extended by the RIM. It should therefore be possible to apply the described influence of head movements to reproduction memory (Förster & Strack, 1996) using the flexor-extensor paradigm. This was in fact achieved by Förster and Strack (1997) for the reproduction of famous names. That is, contracting the flexor muscle facilitated the recall of positively connotated names, whereas contracting the extensor muscle improved the recall of negatively connotated names.

Finally, the postulated principle of compatibility and bidirectionality found support in a study by Neumann and Strack (2000) that used a different dependent variable. In particular, participants who were presented with words on a computer screen had to decide whether these words were positive or negative in valence. As predicted by the RIM, positive words were categorized more rapidly when participants had to flex their arm, whereas negative words were categorized more rapidly when participants had to extend their arm.

THE COMPATIBILITY PRINCIPLE II: THE IMPACT OF EVALUATIVE INFORMATION ON THE EXECUTION OF BEHAVIOR

Bidirectionality as a central characteristic of the Impulsive System implies not only that a behavior may activate a compatible motivational orientation, but also that the valence of information may exert a facilitating influence on compatible behaviors. Specifically, it follows that the behaviors that served as independent variables in the studies described in the preceding section should also operate as dependent variables. There is evidence to support this assumption.

Facial Expression

As previously described, unobtrusively manipulated facial expressions may influence evaluative judgments (Strack et al., 1988). The principle of bidirectionality entails that facial actions will be facilitated if compatible information is processed. This prediction was confirmed in an unpublished set of studies by Neumann and Hess (2001), in which participants had to respond by contracting either the corrugator or the zygomaticus muscle. While participants assessed the valence of words presented on a computer screen, surface electrodes recorded the electromyographic (EMG) activity of both muscles. As predicted, the positivity of words was indicated faster if the zygomaticus (smiling) muscle had to be activated, whereas the negativity of words was assessed faster if participants were using the corrugator (frowning) muscle. As in previous studies, it was important to determine whether the effect depended on the evaluative nature of the task. To that end, Neumann and Hess conducted a second study in which participants were simply asked to indicate when a positive or negative word appeared on a computer screen. Once again, the reactions had to be provided by contracting either the corrugator or the zygomaticus muscle. As in the previous experiment, the compatibility between the valence of the stimuli and the nature of the motor action determined the response latencies. Participants were faster at indicating the appearance of positive words when using the zygomaticus muscle and faster at indicating the appearance of negative words when using the corrugator muscle (see also Dimberg, Thunberg, & Grunedal, 2002).

Approach and Avoidance Through Isotonic Movements

Earlier studies using a procedure by Cacioppo and associates (e.g., Cacioppo et al., 1993) showed that the processing of positive versus negative information was facilitated depending on whether the arm was moved toward or away from the person (Förster & Strack, 1997, 1998; Neumann & Strack, 2000). The postulate of bidirectionality allows for the opposite causal direction. In particular, movements that are directed toward the person should be facilitated if positive information is processed, whereas movements away from the person should be easier if the information is negative.

Initial evidence for this influence came from a study by Solarz (1960), who presented his test subjects cards with words that were either positive or negative. Depending on the valence of the words, participants had to either push these cards away from themselves (avoidance) or pull them toward themselves (approach). The results showed that participants were faster if the valence of the word and the movement were compatible. That is, faster reactions were obtained if positive words had to be pulled toward the person and negative words had to be pushed away.

Recently, this finding was replicated by Chen and Bargh (1999), who had participants categorize words on a computer screen as "good" or "bad" by either pushing or pulling a lever. In agreement with Solarz's (1960) findings, shorter response latencies were obtained if the valence of positive words had to be indicated by pulling the lever or the valence of negative words indicated by pushing it away. Chen and Bargh (1999) demonstrated in a second study that this compatibility effect did not depend on the evaluative nature of the task. Specifically, the predicted effect was also obtained if the task was simply to indicate whether a word (either positive or negative) appeared on the screen.

Head Movements

Vertical or horizontal movements of the head were found to influence the encoding of negative or positive information (Förster & Strack, 1996). However, the reverse is also the case. Whereas Wells and Petty (1980) found that people nodded more often if they agreed with the content of the message they heard through headphones, Förster and Strack found that participants nodded more often while encoding positive words and shook their head more frequently while encoding negative words.

Affect as a Determinant of Motivational Orientation

Lang and his associates (for a review see Lang, Bradley, & Cuthbert, 1990) proposed a model that is closely related to the distinction between two motivational orientations. In particular, they postulated appetitive and aversive *motivational systems* that facilitate behavioral responses. Based on evidence from biology and neuropsychology, these researchers assume that "associations, representations, and action programs that are linked to the engaged motivational system have a higher probability of success" (Lang,

1995, p. 377). Moreover, these motivational systems can be activated by the emotional or affective state of an organism. An extensive program of research with both animals and humans found that startle responses were intensified when negative affect had been elicited. At the same time, the startle response was found to be inhibited if the organism was in the state of positive affect. These findings support the assumption of a motivational orientation that links mental and behavioral processes (see Forgas & Laham, and Neuberg, Kenrick, Maner & Schaller, this volume, for other work on the links between affect and motivation).

THE INTERPLAY OF DECISIONS AND IMPULSES

Although the two systems are assumed to be governed by distinctive principles of operation, they operate in parallel most of the time and interact at various stages of processing. Such interactions can occur in both directions and are predicted to influence cognition, affect, and behavior.

Impulsive Processes Influence Reflection

How can decisions and antecedent reflection be influenced by impulsive processes? The principles set up in the RIM predict several ways in which influence can be exerted, the most important being the *accessibility* of elements in the Impulsive System. Because the Reflective System uses contents from the Impulsive System to generate knowledge and noetic, evaluative, and behavioral decisions, it can be strongly influenced by the accessibility of conceptual contents. Factors determining altered accessibility are recent and frequent activation (Higgins, 1996), motivational orientations, and deprivation. For instance, increased accessibility of need-relevant concepts may also guide the *interpretation* of ambiguous stimuli. This was demonstrated in a classic study by McClelland and Atkinson (1948), where hungry participants were more likely than satiated participants to identify ambiguous stimuli as food-related objects. This influence may not only affect the interpretation of objects. Reflective processing may also be directed by the differential accessibility of information about behavioral options or about relevant aspects of the alternatives. Thus, although a procedure may be rational with respect to a normative model, it may be influenced by contents whose accessibility is influenced by factors that are unrelated to rational considerations (e.g., Gregory, Cialdini, & Carpenter, 1982).

The second influence rests on the assumption that propositional representations can refer to many kinds of states. Those might be objects from the outside world, but also experiences that serve as messages "from within" (Bless & Forgas, 2000), such as motivational orientations, hunger, thirst, or affective feelings (e.g., Spencer et al., this volume). In particular, feelings of different qualities may be propositionally categorized and contextually qualified, and thus enter into reflective processes (e.g., Schwarz & Clore, 1983). How feelings that emerge from impulsive processes can enter into reflection and determine choice is demonstrated in a study by Bechara, Damasio, Tranel, and Damasio (1997). Participants had to choose cards from four decks, two of which offered high gains at the risk of an occasional high loss, and two that offered lower gains but with a smaller risk of loss. In essence, the less risky decks generated a higher total payoff. While selecting cards, participants reported having a feeling about which of the decks were good and which were bad long before they could name the payoff matrix of the game. This impulsive reaction to the playing situation was also mirrored by changes in skin conductance before participants chose a risky card, and participants frequently based their choice on these feelings.

Knowledge about the self may also be inferred from one's own behavior or from impulsively activated behavioral schemata, as described by attribution and self-perception theory (Bem, 1967; Kelley, 1967). For instance, if the perception of a cake activates schemata associated with eating such that the individual feels an urge to grab or eat it, a positive attitude toward eating the cake may be inferred.

In sum, at least three influences are predicted from the present framework: (a) the accessibility of concepts and behavioral schemata is assumed to affect thinking and decision making in a direct manner; (b) affective and nonaffective feelings generated by the Impulsive System may be interpreted and enter into decisions; and (c) self-perceived behavioral tendencies may enter into the decision process.

Reflective Processes Influence Impulses

One of the most important influences the Reflective System exerts on the Impulsive System is manifested in the process of intending. As outlined earlier, intending activates behavioral schemata after a behavioral decision has been made. However, other influences of reflection on impulses can be predicted from the operational principles of the RIM.

Because the Reflective System uses contents from the Impulsive System, reflective operations alter the accessibility of these contents. As a result, operations in the Reflective System will be affected by preceding operations. This becomes apparent in the so-called anchoring bias (Tversky & Kahneman, 1974). In a series of experiments, Mussweiler and Strack (see Strack & Mussweiler, 1997; for a review see Mussweiler & Strack, 1999) demonstrated that this judgmental distortion is due to the use of information that has been activated through selective hypothesis testing before the judgment.

Because conceptual and behavioral contents are interconnected in the Impulsive System, the same mechanism may also activate behavioral schemata. Evidence supporting this idea originates from research on the relationship between perception, concepts in memory, and overt behavior (for a review see Dijksterhuis & Bargh, 2001). Results from this area indicate a strong interconnection of *conceptual* and *motor* representations (Jeannerod & Frak, 1999). For instance, a functional magnetic resonance imaging (fMRI) study conducted by Roth et al. (1996) demonstrated that the same brain regions that are activated when a muscle is contracted are activated when the movement is merely imagined. The same thing happens if the movement is observed while it is enacted by another person (Rizzolatti & Arbib, 1998). Most important, studies have demonstrated automatic influences on behavior by the mere activation of traits (e.g., Carver, Ganellen, Froming, & Chambers, 1983), stereotypes (e.g., Kawakami, Young, & Dovidio, 2002), or concepts associated with a specific behavior (e.g., Epley & Gilovich, 1999). Consequently, the act of reflectively considering behavioral options is predicted to inevitably preactivate the behavioral schemata in the Impulsive System, thereby making the related behaviors more likely, even when the decision is ultimately against performing the behavior.

Whereas the influences described so far have dealt primarily with "cool" cognitive interactions, research on the interplay of appraisal and affect has revealed that thinking sometimes causes feeling (Lazarus, 1991). In a recent experiment (Deutsch, Gawronski, & Strack, submitted), we studied how motivational orientations are affected by reflective processes. Specifically, participants were asked to respond to affirmed and negated words of positive and negative valence such as *no money, no disease,* or *a party.* We chose these stimuli because processing negations presupposes propositional representations, and hence reflection. To enhance or prevent reflection, we had participants respond to affirmed and negated words by focusing either on the *color* or on the *overall valence* of the stimulus. Participants' motivational orientations were assessed by having them either push a joystick (a movement associated with avoidance) or pull a joystick (a movement associated with approach) (Chen & Bargh, 1999). When participants responded according to the overall valence, negated positive words facilitated avoidance motivation, whereas negated negative words facilitated approach motivation. In contrast, when participants responded to the color of the words, negated positive words facilitated approach motivation, whereas negated negative words facilitated immediate avoidance motivation. This pattern of results indicates that the *inferred* valence of stimuli (inferred through application of the negation) can override the *perceived* valence of the words, irrespective of negations and the connected motivational orientation. However, if inferences are undermined, the *perceived* valence determines the motivational orientation.

Another influence the Reflective System exerts on impulses originates from the contents of perceptions and imaginations. Research on the ability to delay gratification demonstrates that distraction from tempting stimuli is a very effective self-regulatory strategy (Metcalfe & Mischel, 1999), whereas actively searching or imagining the gratification that is to be delayed hampers self-control. In other words, reflective regulation of the perceptive or imaginative conditions that stimulate the Impulsive System is a strong source of variance in motivated behavior.

Taken together, the Reflective System is predicted to influence impulsive processes in at least three ways: (a) passively, because merely thinking of or considering a behavior or its outcome activates the related behavioral schemata; (b) actively, through the process of intending; and (c) actively, through regulation of perceptual or imaginative input.

Antagonistic Influences

Up to now, we have described joint influences of impulsive and reflective processes on behavioral schemata. However, the two systems may also stand in competition if they activate incompatible schemata or if the Reflective System inhibits a behavior that is impulsively activated. Such antagonistic activation may be accompanied by feelings of conflict and temptation. Imagine a person on a diet who is offered a delicious apple pie with whipped cream. On the one hand, this percept will activate an approach orientation, together with behavioral schemata of eating, as well as fragmentary anticipatory feelings of the taste and pleasure associated with eating the pie. On the other hand, knowledge about the dietary consequences of eating the pie may be generated and integrated into a behavioral decision not to eat it.

Thus, a conflict may arise between the reflective knowledge about what is good and an impulse to act in a way that is incompatible with this knowledge. This conflict has been captured in research on *delay of gratification* (Mischel, 1996; see also Metcalfe and Mischel, 1999) with children. Using adults as experimental participants, we tried to create a functionally equivalent situation (Deutsch & Strack, 2002) and established a setting in which people were led to emit impulsive reactions that were opposed to their reflective knowledge. In a learning phase, participants opened red and blue "doors to a photo gallery" on a computer screen. Depending on the color of the door, opening the door was immediately followed by presentation of a photo of either an extremely negative or positive valence. Four seconds later, a picture of the opposite valence appeared for a much longer time, and these images were therefore assumed to be hedonically more relevant.

Asked which photo gallery they would prefer, people more frequently chose the contingency consisting of the immediate but short exposure to the unpleasant photo, followed by the delayed but much longer exposure to the pleasant photo. However, the delayed utility did not determine participants' reaction if a response was given without much reflection. Specifically, the immediate impulse to open (as measured with the Stop

Paradigm; Logan, Schachar, & Tannock, 1997) was stronger for contingencies with immediate positive but delayed negative pictures. This suggests that the stimuli may have acquired "hot" features (see Metcalfe & Mischel, 1999) through learning, which influenced impulsive reactions and conflicted with the "cool" knowledge about reward contingencies.

SUMMARY AND CONCLUSION

In this chapter, we have argued that to account for the entire range of social behavior, it is useful to invoke two motivational systems. However, to understand how behavior is controlled under different circumstances, it is not sufficient to define these systems by phenomenal experience that accompanies their operation. Instead, we believe that it is necessary to use the operational principles as the primary distinction. Although a partition of the motivating determinants into conscious and unconscious varieties may be consistent with our intuitive understanding, it does not cut mental nature at its operational joints. Moreover, the direct transfer of phenomena defined by their consciousness experience into an unconscious mode of processing may further obscure their operational characteristics.

The model we have described stands in the tradition of dual-process models (cf. Sloman, 1996; Smith and DeCoster, 2000) and connects social behavior with different mental mechanisms. In particular, we have described a Reflective System that is specialized to generate and transform knowledge using mechanisms of categorization and syllogistic inference. At the same time, we have postulated an Impulsive System that creates, strengthens, and activates associative links. Most important, the Impulsive System has a motivational orientation with a facilitating and an inhibiting function, depending on the compatibility between valence and approach versus avoidance. Both systems are assumed to operate in parallel and to interact at various stages of processing. As part of a common pathway to behavior, both systems contribute jointly to the activation of behavioral schemata. This may result in synergistic or antagonistic consequences.

We presented evidence supporting the proposed RIM. In addition, we are convinced that this conceptualization will be able to shed new light on some motivational phenomena that are central to social psychology and beyond. Specifically, we believe that the model may be profitably applied in studying the delay of gratification, regulatory focus, aggression, and health behavior.

References

Aarts, H., & Dijksterhuis, A. (2000). Habits as knowledge structures: Automaticity in goal-directed behavior. *Journal of Personality and Social Psychology, 78*, 53–63.

Aarts, H., Dijksterhuis, A., & De Vries, P. (2001). On the psychology of drinking: Being thirsty and perceptually ready. *British Journal of Psychology, 92*, 631–642.

Ach, N. (1905). *Über die Willenstätigkeit und das Denken.* Göttingen: Vandenhoek und Ruprecht.

Ach, N. (1910). *Über den Willensakt und das Temperament.* Leipzig: Quelle und Mayer.

Ajzen, I. (1991). The theory of planned behavior. *Organizational Behavior and Human Decision Processes, 50,* 179–211.

Ajzen, I. (1996). The social psychology of decision making. In E. T. Higgins & A. W. Kruglanski (Eds.), *Social psychology: Handbook of basic principles* (pp. 297–325). New York: Guilford Press.

Ajzen, I., & Fishbein, M. (1980). *Understanding attitudes and predicting social behavior.* Englewood Cliffs, NJ: Prentice-Hall.

Bandura, A. (1977). *Social learning theory.* Englewood Cliffs, NJ: Prentice-Hall.

Bargh, J. A. (1997). The automaticity of everyday life. In R. S. Wyer, Jr. (Ed.), *The automaticity of everyday life: Advances in social cognition* (Vol. 10, pp. 1–61). Mahwah, NJ: Erlbaum.

Barsalou, L. W. (1999). Perceptual symbol systems. *Behavioral and Brain Sciences, 22,* 577–660.

Bechara, A., Damasio, H., Tranel, D., & Damasio, A. R. (1997). Deciding advantageously before knowing the advantageous strategy. *Science, 275,* 1293–1295.

Bem, D. J. (1967). An alternative interpretation of cognitive dissonance phenomena. *Psychological Review, 73,* 185–200.

Bless, H., & Forgas, J. P. (Eds.). (2000). *The message within: The role of subjective experience in social cognition and behavior.* Philadelphia: Psychology Press.

Bruner, J. S. (1957). On perceptual readiness. *Psychological Review, 64,* 123–152.

Bruner, J. S. (1973). *Beyond the information given: Studies in the psychology of knowing.* New York: W. W. Norton.

Cacioppo, J. T., Priester, J. R., & Berntson, G. G. (1993). Rudimentary determinants of attitudes: II. Arm flexion and extension have differential effects on attitudes. *Journal of Personality and Social Psychology, 65,* 5–17.

Carver, C. S., Ganellen, R. J., Froming, W. J., & Chambers, W. (1983). Modeling: An analysis in terms of category accessibility. *Journal of Experimental Social Psychology, 19,* 403–421.

Chaiken, S., & Trope, Y. (Eds.). (1999). *Dual-process theories in social psychology.* New York: Guilford Press.

Chartrand, T. L., & Bargh, J. A. (2002). Nonconscious motivations: Their activation, operation, and consequences. In A. Tesser, D. A. Stapel, & J. V. Wood (Eds.), *Self and motivation: Emerging psychological perspectives* (pp. 13–41). Washington, DC: American Psychological Association Press.

Chen, M., & Bargh, J. A. (1999). Consequences of automatic evaluation: Immediate behavioral predispositions to approach or avoid the stimulus. *Personality and Social Psychology Bulletin, 25,* 215–224.

Chen, S., & Chaiken, S. (1999). The Heuristic-Systematic Model in its broader context. In S. Chaiken & Y. Trope (Eds.), *Dual-process theories in social psychology* (pp. 73–96). New York: Guilford Press.

Collins, A. M., & Quillian, M. R. (1969). Retrieval time from semantic memory. *Journal of Verbal Learning and Verbal Behavior, 8,* 240–247.

Darwin, C. R. (1872/1965). *The expression of emotions in man and animals.* Chicago: University of Chicago Press.

Deutsch, R., Gawronski, B., & Strack, F. (submitted for publication). *"Not good" may feel quite positive! Affective and behavioral consequences of processing negated information.* Manuscript.

Deutsch, R., & Strack, F. (2002). *Evaluative learning with delayed gratification. Impulsive and reflective processes.* Unpublished manuscript, University of Würzburg, Germany.

Dijksterhuis, A., & Bargh, J. A. (2001). The perception–behavior expressway: Automatic effects of social perception on social behavior. In M. P. Zanna (Ed.), *Advances in experimental social psychology* (Vol. 33, pp. 1–40). San Diego: Academic Press.

Dimberg, U., Thunberg, M., & Grunedal, S. (2002). Facial reactions to emotional stimuli: Automatically controlled emotional responses. *Cognition and Emotion, 16*, 449–472.

Epley, N., & Gilovich, T. (1999). Just going along: Nonconscious priming and conformity to social pressure. *Journal of Experimental Social Psychology, 35*, 578–589.

Feather, N. T. (1982). *Expectations and actions. Expectancy-value models in psychology.* Hillsdale, NJ: Erlbaum.

Förster, J., & Strack, F. (1996). The influence of overt head movements on memory for valenced words: A case of conceptual-motor compatibility. *Journal of Personality and Social Psychology, 71*, 421–430.

Förster, J., & Strack, F. (1997). Motor actions in retrieval of valenced information: A motor congruence effect. *Perceptual and Motor Skills, 85*, 1419–1427.

Förster, J., & Strack, F. (1998). Motor actions in retrieval of valenced information: II. Boundary conditions for motor congruence effects. *Perceptual and Motor Skills, 86*, 1423–1426.

Gollwitzer, P. M. (1999). Implementation intentions. Strong effects of simple plans. *American Psychologist, 54*, 493–503.

Gollwitzer, P. M., & Moskowitz, G. B. (1996). Goal effects on action and cognition. In E. T. Higgins & A. W. Kruglanski (Eds.), *Social psychology: Handbook of basic principles* (pp. 361–399). New York: Guilford Press.

Gray, J. A. (1982). *The neuropsychology of anxiety: An enquiry into the functions of the septo-hippocampal system.* New York: Clarendon Press/Oxford University Press.

Gregory, W. L., Cialdini, R. B., & Carpenter, K. M. (1982). Self-relevant scenarios as mediators of likelihood estimates and compliance: Does imagining make it so? *Journal of Personality and Social Psychology, 43*, 89–99.

Helmholtz, H. (1867). *Handbuch der physiologischen Optik.* Leipzig: Voss.

Higgins, E. T. (1996). Knowledge activation: Accessibility, applicability, and salience. In E. T. Higgins & A. W. Kruglanski (Eds.), *Social psychology: Handbook of basic principles* (pp. 133–168). New York: Guilford Press.

Higgins, E. T., & Kruglanski, A. W. (Eds.) (2000). *Motivational science.* Philadelphia: Psychology Press.

Hull, C. L. (1943). *Principles of behavior.* New York: Appleton-Century-Crofts.

James, W. (1890). *The principles of psychology.* New York: Holt.

Jeannerod, M., & Frak, V. (1999). Mental imaging of motor activity in humans. *Current Opinion in Neurobiology, 9*, 735–739.

Johnson, M. K., & Hirst, W. (1991). MEM: Memory subsystems as processes. In A. Collins, S. Gathercole, M. Conway, & P. Morris (Eds.), *Theories of memory* (pp. 241–286). Hillsdale, NJ: Erlbaum.

Kawakami, K., Young, H., & Dovidio, J. F. (2002). Automatic stereotyping: Category, trait, and behavioral activations. *Personality and Social Psychology Bulletin, 28*, 3–15.

Kelley, H. (1967). Attribution theory in social psychology. In D. Levine (Ed.), *Nebraska symposium on motivation* (Vol. 15). Lincoln: University of Nebraska Press.

Koriat, A. (1993). How do we know what we know? The accessibility model of the feeling of knowing. *Psychological Review, 100*, 609–639.

Laird, J. D. (1974). Self-attribution of emotion: The effects of expressive behavior on the quality of emotional experience. *Journal of Personality and Social Psychology, 29*, 475–486.

Lang, P. J. (1995). The emotion probe – studies of motivation and attention. *American Psychologist, 50*(5), 372–385.

Lang, P. J., Bradley, M. M., & Cuthbert, B. N. (1990). Emotion, attention, and the startle reflex. *Psychological Review, 97*, 377–395.

Lazarus, R. S. (1991). *Emotion and adaptation.* New York: Oxford University Press.

Lewin, K. (1926). Untersuchungen zur Handlungs- und Affektpsychologie. II.: Vorsatz, Wille und Bedürfnis. *Psychologische Forschung, 7*, 330–385.

Libet, B., Gleason, C. A.,Wright, E. W., & Pearl, D. K. (1983). Time of conscious intention to act in relation to onset of cerebral activity (readiness-potential). *Brain, 106*, 623–642.

Logan, G. D., Schachar, R. J., & Tannock, R. (1997). Impulsivity and inhibitory control. *Psychological Science, 8*, 60–64.

McClelland, D. C., & Atkinson, J. W. (1948). The projective expression of needs: I. The effect of different intensities of the hunger drive on perception. *Journal of Psychology, 25*, 205–222.

McClelland, J. L., McNaughton, B. L., & O'Reilly, R. C. (1995). Why there are complementary learning systems in the hippocampus and neocortex: Insights from the successes and failures of connectionist models of learning and memory. *Psychological Review, 102*, 419–457.

Metcalfe, J., & Mischel, W. (1999). A hot/cool-system analysis of delay of gratification: Dynamics of willpower. *Psychological Review, 106*, 3–19.

Mischel, W. (1996). From good intentions to willpower. In P. M. Gollwitzer & J. R. Bargh (Eds.), *The psychology of action: Linking cognition and motivation to behavior* (pp. 197–218). New York: Guilford Press.

Mussweiler, T., & Strack, F. (1999). Comparing is believing: A selective accessibility model of judgmental anchoring. *European Review of Social Psychology, 10*, 135–167.

Neumann, R., & Hess, M. (2001). *The latency of facial action differentiates the valence of processed information: Evidence that facial action is activated by evaluative processing.* Unpublished manuscript, University of Würzburg.

Neumann, R., & Strack, F. (2000). "Approach and avoidance": The influence of proprioceptive and exteroceptive cues on encoding of affective information. *Journal of Personality Social Psychology, 79*, 39–48.

Norman, D. A., & Shallice, T. (1986). Attention to action. Willed and automatic control of behavior. In R. J. Davidson, G. E. Schwartz, & D. Shapiro (Eds.), *Consciousness and self regulation: Advances in research* (pp. 1–18). New York: Plenum Press.

Rizzolatti, G., & Arbib, M. A. (1998). Language within our grasp. *Trends in Neurosciences, 21*, 188–194.

Roth, M., Decety, J., Raybaudi, M., Massarelli, R., Delon-Martin, C., Segebarth, C., Morand, S., Gemignani, A., Decorps, M., & Jeannerod, M. (1996). Possible involvement of primary motor cortex in mentally simulated movement. A functional magnetic resonance imaging study. *NeuroReport, 7*, 1280–1284.

Schwarz, N., & Clore, G. L. (1983). Mood, misattribution, and judgments of well-being: Informative and directive functions of affective states. *Journal of Personality and Social Psychology, 45*, 513–523.

Sloman, S. A. (1996). The empirical case for two systems of reasoning. *Psychological Bulletin, 119*, 3–22.

Smith, E. R., & DeCoster, J. (2000). Dual process models in social and cognitive psychology: Conceptual integration and links to underlying memory systems. *Personality and Social Psychology Review, 4*, 108–131.

Solarz, A. K. (1960). Latency of instrumental responses as a function of compatibility with the meaning of eliciting verbal signs. *Journal of Experimental Psychology, 59*, 239–245.

Stepper, S., & Strack, F. (1993). Proprioceptive determinants of emotional and nonemotional feelings. *Journal of Personality and Social Psychology, 64*, 211–220.

Strack, F., & Deutsch, R. (in press). Reflective and impulsive determinants of social behavior. *Personality and Social Psychology Review.*

Strack, F., Martin, L. L., & Stepper, S. (1988). Inhibiting and facilitating conditions of the human smile: A nonobtrusive test of the facial feedback hypothesis. *Journal of Personality and Social Psychology, 54*, 768–777.

Strack, F., & Mussweiler, T. (1997). Explaining the enigmatic anchoring effect: Mechanisms of selective accessibility. *Journal of Personality and Social Psychology, 73*, 437–446.

Sutton, S. K., & Davidson, R. J. (1997). Prefrontal brain asymmetry: A biological substrate of the behavioral approach and inhibition systems. *Psychological Science, 8*, 204–210.

Tversky, A., & Kahneman, D. (1974). Judgment under uncertainty: Heuristics and biases. *Science, 185*, 1124–1131.

Verplanken, B., & Aarts, H. (1999). Habit, attitude, and planned behaviour: Is habit an empty construct or an interesting case of automaticity? *European Review of Social Psychology, 10*, 101–134.

Wegner, D. M. (2002). *The illusion of conscious will.* Cambridge, MA: MIT Press.

Wells, G. L., & Petty, R. E. (1980). The effects of overt head movements on persuasion: Compatibility and incompatibility of responses. *Basic and Applied Social Psychology, 1*(3), 219–230.

Wilson, T. D., Lindsey, S., & Schooler, T. Y. (2000). A model of dual attitudes. *Psychological Review, 107*, 101–126.

Wispe, L. G., & Drambarean, N. C. (1953). Physiological need, word frequency, and visual duration thresholds. *Journal of Experimental Psychology, 46*, 25–31.

7

The Role of Motivation in the Unconscious

How Our Motives Control the Activation of Our Thoughts and Shape Our Actions

Steven J. Spencer, Steven Fein, Erin J. Strahan, and Mark P. Zanna

INTRODUCTION

Research over the past two decades has demonstrated the importance of unconscious thoughts in shaping our behavior (Epstein, 1994; Kihlstrom, 1987; Westen, 1998). More recently, a number of researchers have highlighted the importance of motivation in these unconscious processes (Bargh & Chartrand, 1999; Gollwitzer & Moskowitz, 1996; Higgins, 1996; Shah, Kruglanski, & Friedman, 2002). This symposium is timely in bringing together much of that research. For example Neuberg, Kenrick, Maner, and Schaller (this volume) describe how evolutionary motives, and Pyszczynski, Greenberg, and Solomon (this volume) describe how the fear of death, shape unconscious processing. Indeed, a number of the chapters in this book (by Aarts & Hassin; Liberman & Förster; Son Hing, Chung-Yan, Grunfeld, Robichaud, & Zanna, this volume; Strack & Deutsch; Wood & Quinn) have provided important insights about how our motives and our implicit thoughts interact. We are very pleased to be included in this effort.

From the fairly grandiose title of this chapter, it might appear that we are trying to delineate a grand theory of how motivation operates in the unconscious, but our aims are much more circumspect. Rather than a grand theory, we believe that the research we report in this chapter – on stereotype activation and application and on subliminal priming and persuasion – has demonstrated two important ways that motivation interacts with unconscious thoughts: (a) motivation can trigger the activation of thoughts concerning the satisfaction of the relevant motive, and (b) motivation can

This research was supported by grants from the Social Sciences and Humanities Research Council of Canada to the first and fourth authors. Correspondence regarding this chapter can be directed to Steven J. Spencer, Department of Psychology, University of Waterloo, Waterloo, ON, Canada, N2L 3G1; e-mail: sspencer@watarts.uwaterloo.ca.

affect the link between thought (including nonconscious thought) and action to facilitate the satisfaction of the motive. Without the motivation, these thoughts either would not be activated or would not lead to action.

THE ROLE OF MOTIVATION IN THE ACTIVATION OF CONCEPTS

The idea that motivation can affect the nature of concepts that are activated when people are exposed to a stimulus is not entirely new. Bruner and his colleagues (Bruner, 1957; Bruner, Postman, & McGinnies, 1947) in the New Look perspective in perception certainly believed that motivation could determine what people perceived when exposed to a given stimulus. More recently, Bargh's (1990) auto-motive model of cognition has also proposed that motives, when combined with cues in the environment, can lead to the automatic activation of particular thoughts. We believe that our own research has emphasized that motivation can lead to the activation of thoughts that work to fulfill the desires contained in these motives, and in this way motivation leads to the activation of thoughts that would not be activated in the absence of the motivational state.

Stereotype Activation

In one line of research, we have examined how the motive to maintain a positive self-image can affect the activation of stereotypes. Previously we had hypothesized that stereotyping others may often result from the motive to restore a threatened self-image. We demonstrated that when people's self-images are threatened, they became more likely to stereotype others, and these stereotypic evaluations, in turn, help restore their self-esteem (Fein & Spencer, 1997). In a subsequent series of studies, we reasoned further that this motivation might affect not only conscious evaluation of stereotyped targets but unconscious stereotype activation as well (Spencer, Fein, Wolfe, Fong, & Dunn, 1998).

In the first of these studies, for example, we manipulated the threat to White participants' self-esteem by providing them with either positive or negative feedback on an intelligence test. Subsequently they saw either an Asian or a White woman holding a series of cards that contained word fragments that they needed to complete to form words. Some of these word fragments could be completed stereotypically (e.g., S__Y could be completed as *SHY* or *SLY*), and others were fillers. Previous research by Gilbert and Hixon (1991) had demonstrated that when participants were not under cognitive load, they activated the stereotype (i.e., they completed more of the stereotypic word fragments with stereotypic words) when they were exposed to the Asian woman, but under cognitive load they did not. In our study, we placed all participants under cognitive load to make stereotype activation more difficult. As we predicted, we found that despite cognitive load, participants activated the stereotype when exposed to the Asian woman – if they had received the self-image-threatening feedback.

In the second study, we examined whether even a subliminal exposure to a stereotypic target would trigger activation of the stereotype. Participants were exposed to either Black or White faces subliminally (for 16 ms) while under high or low cognitive load. They subsequently completed a series of word stems. Some of these word stems could be completed with words consistent with stereotypes about Blacks (e.g., *DAN__*could be completed as *DANGER* or *DANGEROUS*), and others were fillers. We found that when people were not under cognitive load they activated the stereotype after exposure to the Black faces, but under cognitive load they did not.

In the third study, we examined whether self-image threat would lead to the activation of the Black stereotype in this paradigm even when people were under cognitive load. Participants received either positive or negative feedback on an intelligence test and then completed the word stems under cognitive load after being subliminally exposed to either Black or White faces. As can be seen in Figure 7.1, when people's self-image had been

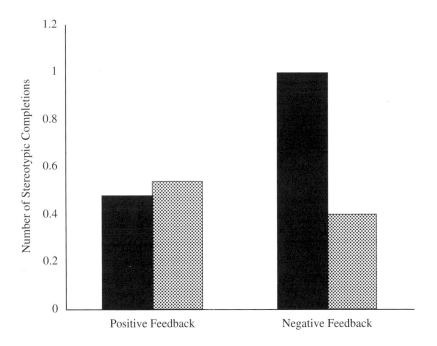

FIGURE 7.1 Stereotype activation as a function of self-image threat and ethnicity of the subliminal prime.

threatened and they were exposed to the Black face, they activated the stereotype, but when their self-image had not been threatened (or when they were exposed to the White face), they did not.

Recently, we have replicated this effect (in a study described in more detail later; Fein & Spencer, 2004) with the stereotype of gay men. In this study, men received either positive or neutral feedback on an intelligence test and then were subliminally primed with the word *gay* or the word *hat*. They subsequently completed a number of word stems under cognitive load. Some of these word stems could be completed with words associated with stereotypes about gay men (e.g., *FAI__*could be completed as *FAIRY*). We found that men who received negative feedback and who were exposed to the *gay* prime were significantly more likely to complete the word stems stereotypically than were men who received neutral feedback or who were exposed to the *hat* prime.

These sets of results suggest that the motivation to maintain one's self-image can lead people to activate stereotypes that bolster their self-image even when their cognitive resources are taxed and the exposure to stereotypic stimuli is minimal. Thus, the motivation to maintain one's self-image leads to the activation of thoughts (i.e., stereotypes) that function to maintain one's self-image – thoughts that would not be activated in the absence of this motivational state. But what would happen if people were motivated to avoid stereotyping others?

Stereotype Inhibition

Stereotyping others can function as a self-image maintenance strategy, but there are also times when people are motivated to *avoid* stereotyping others. Indeed, this motive to avoid being, or appearing to be, prejudiced has played a crucial role in contemporary theories of prejudice and discrimination (e.g., Devine, Brodish, & Vance, this volume; Dovidio, Kawakami, & Gaertner, 2000; Kunda & Spencer, 2003; Monteith, Sherman, & Devine, 1998). In a new set of studies (Spencer, Fein, Davies, & Hoshino-Browne, 2004) we extended our research on the role of motivation in automatic stereotype activation by testing the hypothesis that the motivation to avoid stereotyping can lead to the inhibition of stereotypes.

In the first of these studies, we gave students one of two types of (bogus) feedback that was allegedly based on a questionnaire they had completed earlier in the term. The feedback indicated how they scored relative to their peers on 10 scales. Each of the participants received feedback indicating that he or she scored exceptionally high on one scale and exceptionally low on another scale. For half of the participants, the feedback indicated that they scored high on a "contemporary racism" scale and low on a "racial tolerance" scale. The remaining participants were given relatively neutral feedback and served as a control group. They learned that they scored

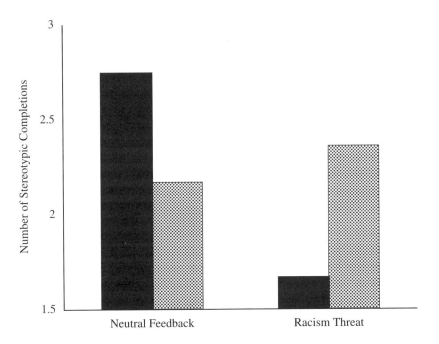

FIGURE 7.2 Stereotype activation as a function of racism threat and ethnicity of the subliminal prime.

high on a "sensing versus feeling" scale and low on a "cognitive versus perceptual orientation" scale. The explanations of these particular scales were written in a way that made it clear that there were no positive or negative associations with either pole of either scale.

After receiving the feedback, participants were primed with either Black male faces or White male faces and then they completed word stems.[1] Some of the word stems could be completed with words related to the Black stereotype. The results of this study are illustrated in Figure 7.2. As in our previous research, participants activated the Black stereotype after being exposed to the Black faces in the control condition when they received

---

[1] In this study we primed participants with both a subtle prime and a subliminal prime. The subtle prime occurred when participants read a newspaper story (one of four stories they read) about a lottery winner. The photograph that accompanied this story was either of a Black man or a White man. In addition to this subtle prime, before each word stem that participants completed we subliminally flashed a drawing of a Black face or a White face. The subtle prime and the subliminal prime were matched for race. In follow-up studies we used only a subtle prime or only a subliminal prime. We found no evidence that the type of prime (subtle vs. subliminal) mattered.

neutral feedback. When participants were threatened with being high in racism, however, they showed inhibition of the Black stereotype after being exposed to the Black faces.

We have replicated this stereotype inhibition effect in subsequent studies using other measures of stereotype activation. In one of these studies, participants received either neutral feedback or feedback suggesting that they had scored high in racism, and then they were exposed to subtle primes of either a Black or a White male face. Participants then completed a Stroop task in which they named the color of the font in which each of a series of words was printed. Some of these words were consistent with the Black stereotype, whereas others were not. The logic of the Stroop task is that when people activate a concept, this facilitates reading words associated with the concept, but this readiness to read the word interferes with naming the color of the font in which the word is printed. Therefore, when a concept is activated, people take longer to name the color of the words associated with the concept.

We found that after neutral feedback, participants who were primed with Black faces activated the Black stereotype (i.e., they were slower to name the color of words associated with the Black stereotype than were people who were primed with White faces). In contrast, among the participants who had received feedback suggesting that they scored high in racism, participants primed with the Black faces inhibited the stereotype (i.e., they were faster to name the color of words associated with the Black stereotype than were participants who were primed with White faces).

In a third study of stereotype inhibition, we again provided participants with either neutral feedback or feedback indicating that they scored high in racism. Participants were exposed to subliminal primes of either White or Black male faces and then completed a lexical decision task (LDT) in which they were presented with various strings of letters and had to decide whether each letter string was a real word or not. Some of the letter strings were real words and some were not. Among the real words, some were consistent with the Black stereotype, whereas others were not. The logic behind the LDT is that the activation of a concept facilitates the identification of words related to that concept, and therefore participants will make the appropriate lexical decision faster for these words (but not for other items) than if the concept was not activated.

Among the participants in this study who received neutral feedback, those who were primed with Black male faces were faster in identifying Black-stereotypic words than were participants primed with White male faces, thereby exhibiting stereotype activation. In contrast, among participants who received feedback indicating that they scored high in racism, those primed with Black faces were *slower* in identifying stereotype-relevant words than were participants primed with White faces, thereby exhibiting inhibition of the stereotype.

In this set of three studies, we find that when people are motivated to avoid stereotyping, they inhibit stereotypes in situations in which they otherwise would activate the stereotypes in the absence of this motivation. These results, together with the results reported earlier on the effect of self-image maintenance goals on stereotype activation, demonstrate that stereotype activation can be dramatically affected by people's motivations. On one hand, when people are motivated to maintain a threatened self-image, they activate stereotypes even in situations that typically do not foster such activation – such as when their cognitive resources are taxed and the exposure to the stereotypic target is minimal. On the other hand, when people are motivated to avoid prejudice, they inhibit the activation of stereotypes even in situations that otherwise promote stereotype activation.

Given these results, we believe that any complete model of stereotyping must account for the role of motivation in even the earliest stages of processing. Fortunately, several recent studies in addition to those reported here have begun to document this important aspect of stereotyping. For example, Moskowitz and his colleagues (Moskowitz, Gollwitzer, Wasel, & Schaal, 1999) have shown that chronic egalitarian goals can inhibit stereotype activation, and Sinclair and Kunda (1999) have shown that impression formation goals can lead to both activation and inhibition of stereotypes. The results of these programs of research converge with our own in highlighting the important role of motivation in stereotype activation (see Kunda & Spencer, 2003, for a review).

Subliminal Priming and Persuasion

In our research on subliminal priming and persuasion (Strahan, Spencer, & Zanna, 2002), we also noticed the important role that motivation can play in the activation of unconscious thoughts. In this research, we asked people to come to the lab after not eating or drinking anything for 3 hours. They believed that they would be participating in a study in which they would evaluate a number of products. We had participants taste a dry cookie and then either gave them some water to drink to "cleanse their palate" or not. Thus, half of the people were thirsty and half were not. After this cookie taste test, we told participants that they would take a break from the evaluation of products and that they would complete a computer task. In this task we subliminally primed people with the words *thirst* and *dry* or neutral words as they were completing an LDT.

In scrutinizing the data from the LDT, we noticed that motivation and the subliminal prime interacted to affect people's responses to some of the words on the LDT. As can be seen in Figure 7.3, when people were thirsty and were subliminally primed with the thirst-related words, they activated

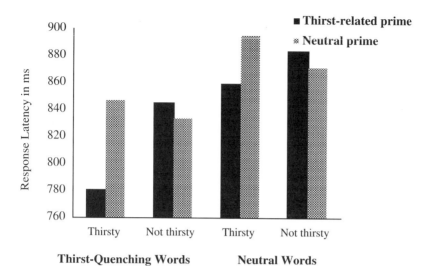

FIGURE 7.3 Activation of thirst-quenching and neutral words as a function of motivation and subliminal prime.

words related to quenching thirst (i.e., *liquid, moist,* and *rain*). When people weren't thirsty or when they weren't primed with thirst-related words, they did not activate these concepts. In addition, motivation and the subliminal prime had no effect on the activation of neutral words.

In a conceptual replication of this study, we had people come to the lab believing that they were going to complete a number of tasks. In the last task, they expected either to be alone or to interact with another person. Erber and his colleagues (Erber, Wegner, & Therriault, 1996) have shown that such a manipulation affects people's motivation to repair their mood. When they expect to interact with another person they engage in mood-repairing activities, but when they expect to be alone they do not. After explaining the nature of the tasks in which participants would be participating, we then had them complete an LDT in which we subliminally primed them with either a sad face or a neutral stimulus.

In examining the results, we again found that motivation and the subliminal prime interacted to affect participants' responses to some of the words on the LDT. In particular, only when people expected to interact with another person (i.e., when they were motivated to repair their mood) and were primed with the sad face did they activate words related to a positive mood (i.e., *happy, cheerful, joyous*). In contrast, people showed no activation of these concepts when they were primed with a sad face and expected to be alone – and thus were presumably less motivated to repair their mood – or when they were primed with the neutral stimulus, regardless of their expectation about interacting with someone else.

Thus, in both of these studies, when people were motivated and subliminally primed with stimuli that were motivationally relevant, they activated concepts that were related to satisfying their motives even though these concepts were semantic opposites of the concepts that were primed. In contrast, when people were not motivated, they showed no such activation. These intriguing results led us to conduct two carefully designed studies to test these ideas more fully.

The first study was exactly the same as the thirst study described earlier (participants were either thirsty or not and were primed with thirst-related words or not) except that we included a longer list of words in the LDT. In particular, we had participants identify six words related to thirst per se and six words related to quenching thirst while completing the LDT. We found that, when primed with the thirst-related words, all participants activated words related to thirst (e.g., *desert, hot*), but only participants who were thirsty activated words related to quenching thirst (e.g., *beverage, quench*). Participants primed with the neutral words did not activate either concept.

The second study was exactly the same as the mood study described earlier (participants were either motivated to repair their mood or not and were primed with a sad face or a neutral stimulus) except that we again included a longer list of words in the LDT. In particular, we had participants identify 10 words related to sadness and 10 words related to happiness. We found that when primed with the sad face, all participants activated words related to sadness (e.g., *sad, gloomy*), but only participants who were motivated to repair their mood activated words related to happiness (e.g., *happy, joyous*). Participants primed with the neutral stimulus did not activate either concept.

Together these studies demonstrate that motivation can lead to the activation of functional concepts – concepts that prepare people to fulfill their motives – when they are presented with minimal stimuli that are semantically the opposite of their desires, and that these functional concepts are not activated in the absence of motivation. Thus, these studies provide strong evidence that our motives can lead to the activation of concepts that would not be activated in the absence of motivation. But does motivation affect whether these activated concepts lead to behavior? We turn to this question in the next section.

THE ROLE OF MOTIVATION IN SHAPING OUR ACTIONS

Moderating the Link Between Stereotype Activation and Application

Our research has shown not only the important role of motivation in activating thoughts, but also how motivation can determine whether thoughts that are activated lead to behavior. For example, in one study, briefly described earlier, male participants who received either positive or negative feedback were subliminally primed with either the word *gay* or the word *hat* and then completed word stems – some of which could be completed stereotypically – under cognitive load. After completing the word stems they went on to evaluate a target that was described either as gay or as straight. In particular, participants rated how much they would like this person to be their friend and how similar they thought they were to this person.

As reported, participants activated the stereotype only when they had received a self-image threat and had been subliminally primed with the concept *gay*. An additional finding, however, was that the degree to which participants exhibited automatic activation of the gay stereotype was associated with their tendency to apply the stereotype (i.e., distancing themselves psychologically from the gay target in their overt judgments) only if their self-esteem had been threatened ($r = .51$). Among participants whose self-image had not been threatened, there was no evidence of an association between stereotype activation and stereotype application ($r = .07$). Thus, implicit activation of a concept served to shape explicit evaluations only when participants were motivated to carry out this behavior.

We examined this idea more fully in a second study. Male students watched a video of a panel discussion on gay rights that had occurred on campus a couple of years earlier. We manipulated the apparent reaction of the audience during the discussion so that it appeared in one condition that the audience clearly favored gay rights, and that it appeared in the other condition that the audience clearly opposed gay rights. We created this manipulation by systematically inserting either silence (a cue to opposition) or applause (a cue to support) after points made by the various speakers. After watching the video of the panel discussion, all participants received negative feedback on an intelligence test and completed word stems under cognitive load. Finally, the participants learned about a target that was described as either gay or straight, and then evaluated him by indicating how much they wanted to be his friend and how similar they thought they were to him.

Perhaps not surprisingly, after watching the panel discussion on gay rights, participants across conditions activated the gay stereotype. However, the evaluation of the stereotypic target, and the relation between stereotype activation and evaluation of the target, were dramatically affected by the perceived local norm. Participants exposed to the version of the video suggesting that the local norm opposed gay rights distanced themselves from the target more when he was portrayed as gay than when he was not, but participants exposed to the version of the video suggesting that the local norm supported gay rights evaluated the target about the same regardless of the portrayal of his sexual orientation.

What is more important for the point we are making here, however, is that the relation between stereotype activation and evaluation of the target

TABLE 7.1 *The Relation Between Activation of the Stereotype and Distancing Oneself from the Target as a Function of the Perceived Local Norm and the Sexual Orientation of the Target*

	Sexual Orientation of the Target	
Perceived local norm	Gay	Straight
Opposition to gay rights	.40*	−.01
Support for gay rights	−.70*	.33

*$p < .05$.

was affected by the manipulation of the perceived local norm. As can be seen in Table 7.1, among participants exposed to the anti-gay-rights norm, the more they activated the stereotype the *more* they distanced themselves from the target when he was portrayed as gay. Among the participants exposed to the pro-gay-rights norm, however, the more they activated the stereotype the *less* they distanced themselves from the target when he was portrayed as gay. When the target was not described as gay, there was no reliable relation between stereotype activation and evaluation of the target.

Why did this simple manipulation of the apparent norm of participants' peer group have these effects? We believe that perceptions of such norms can motivate individuals toward or away from particular attitudes or behaviors. Believing that the majority of one's peers support gay rights can motivate an individual to put aside negative stereotypes and exhibit positive attitudes and behaviors toward gays. Believing that one's peers clearly are opposed to gay rights, on the other hand, can remove such inhibitions and possibly promote motives to derogate gays and their cause. More generally, we propose that people's motivations may determine how activated thoughts shape actions. When people are motivated to distance themselves from a stereotypic target, activation of the stereotype leads to application of the stereotype. When people are motivated to accept a stereotypic target, however, stereotype activation may lead to more positive reactions toward the target. The relation between stereotype activation and stereotype application, therefore, may be moderated by people's motives.

Moderating the Link Between Subliminal Priming and Persuasion

Our research on subliminal priming and persuasion also highlights the important role that motivation plays in shaping our activated thoughts into actions. Recall that in the thirst study described earlier, we had people who were thirsty or not thirsty and who were subliminally primed with thirst-related words or neutral words complete an LDT in which they responded to thirst-quenching words (e.g., *liquid, moist, rain*). We found that people activated these thirst-quenching words more when they were thirsty and primed with thirst-related words than in the other conditions; but does this activation affect behavior?

After completing the LDT, participants completed a supposed taste test of two beverages (which were actually supersweet Kool-Aid) and measured how much participants drank. When participants were thirsty and primed with the thirst-related words they drank more, but more important for our point here, activation of the thirst-quenching words predicted how much people drank only when they were thirsty and primed with thirst-related words. In the other conditions, there was no relation between activation of the thirst-quenching words and the amount that people drank.

In a second study, after completing the LDT participants rated ads for two supposedly new sports drinks and decided how many coupons they wanted for each drink. The ad for one drink, called SuperQuencher, claimed that studies had found that it "quenches your thirst 25% better than any other sports drink on the market." It also included the tag line "When you are super thirsty drink SuperQuencher." The ad for the other drink, called PowerPro, claimed that studies found that it "replaces your electrolytes 45% better than any other sports drink" and included the tag line "Do your body a favor: Drink PowerPro!"

All participants were thirsty in this study, and half were primed with thirst-related words and half were primed with neutral words. The subliminal prime did affect people's preference for the ads and their choice of coupons. When people were primed with thirst-related words they preferred SuperQuencher, but when they were primed with the neutral words they showed no preference. More important for our point here, however, activation of the thirst-related words showed a significantly stronger relation to people's preferences for the products when they were subliminally primed with the thirst-related words ($r = .59, p < .05$) than when they were primed with neutral words ($r = .29, p > .20$).

We also found a similar pattern of effects in the mood study described earlier. Recall that we subliminally primed people with either a sad face or a neutral object when people expected to interact with another person – and thus were motivated to repair their mood – or expected to be alone – and thus were not motivated to repair their mood. As reported, people who were primed with the sad face and expected to interact with another person showed increased activation of happiness-related words (i.e., *happy, cheerful, joyous*), whereas those who were not motivated to repair their mood and those who were not primed with the sad face showed no such activation.

TABLE 7.2 *The Relation Between Activation of Happy Words and Preference for the Upbeat Tweed Monkeys CD*

	Subliminal Priming Condition	
Future Task Expectation	**Sad-Face Prime**	**Neutral Prime**
Expect to interact with another person	.51*	−.11
Expect to be alone	.21	.35

*$p < .05$

After the LDT that measured this activation, we had participants rate ads for CDs from two new bands and decide the number of songs that they wanted to listen to from each CD. One band, called Tweed Monkeys, was described as playing upbeat music, and the tag line for the ad said, "If you are looking for a CD that will put you in a good mood, this is the CD for you." The other band, called Crystal Hammer, was described as musically talented, and the tag line for the ad said, "If you like music with a strong sound, you will love this CD."

When people were primed with the sad face and were motivated to repair their mood, they preferred the ad for the upbeat Tweed Monkeys CD and wanted to listen to more songs from this band. When people were not motivated to repair their mood or were not primed with the sad face, they showed no preference for either ad and chose about the same number of songs from each band. More important for the point being made here, however, when people were primed with the sad face and were motivated to repair their mood, their activation of happy words was correlated with their preference for the upbeat band (see Table 7.2). In the other conditions, however, the activation of happy words was not reliably related to preferences for either band.

Together these results provide evidence that people's motivations can affect the way activated concepts shape behavior even when the activation of the concepts occurs outside of conscious awareness. When thirst and sadness were activated by subliminal primes, people's motivations channeled this activation into actions that could satisfy the motivation: when primed with thirst, thirsty people preferred a thirst-quenching beverage and drank more; when primed with a sad face, people motivated to repair their mood preferred an upbeat band and wanted to listen to upbeat music. These results, together with the results described earlier on how motivation affects the relation between stereotype activation and application, provide compelling evidence that our motives can channel our activated thoughts into actions that are functional – actions that facilitate the satisfaction of our motives.

GENERAL DISCUSSION

We have reviewed evidence from our research on stereotype activation and application and subliminal priming and persuasion that suggests two important ways that motivation influences unconscious thought. Motivation can lead to the activation of thoughts that would not be activated in the absence of the motivational state, and motivation can shape activated thoughts into actions that fulfill people's goals. In our research on stereotype application, we have found that when people are motivated to restore their self-image, they activate negative stereotypes about group members even when their cognitive resources are taxed and exposure to stimuli related to the stereotyped group is so minimal that they would not activate the stereotype in the absence of the motivated state. We also find, however, that when people are motivated to avoid being prejudiced, they inhibit stereotypes even in situations in which these stereotypes would normally be activated.

In our research on subliminal priming and persuasion, we find that when people are motivated to quench their thirst, they activate concepts related to quenching thirst (e.g., *liquid*) even when they are presented with minimal stimuli that are related to the semantic opposite (e.g., *dryness*). Likewise, when people are motivated to repair their mood, they activate concepts related to mood repair (e.g., *cheerfulness*) even when they are presented with minimal stimuli related to the semantic opposite (e.g., *sadness*). This sort of activation does not occur in the absence of motivation.

Together these studies suggest that motivation plays an important role in determining what concepts get activated when people are exposed to a given stimulus, and that the concepts that get activated are functionally relevant. They are concepts that prepare people to engage in actions that will fulfill their goals.

We also find that motivation affects the relation between the activation of concepts and the actions that people take, and here too we see a functional relation. When people are motivated, the activation of functionally relevant concepts is strongly associated with the actions that fulfill people's goals. In our research on stereotype activation and application, we find not only that people's motivation to restore their self-image leads to the activation of stereotypes, but also that the activation of these stereotypes is associated with negative evaluation of a stereotyped target. If, however, people are motivated to avoid stereotyping (due to a local norm that condemns such evaluations), then activation of the stereotype is associated with positive evaluation of the stereotyped target.

In our research on subliminal priming and persuasion, we find that when people are motivated to quench their thirst, subliminal thirst primes not only activate concepts related to quenching thirst, but the activation of these concepts is associated with increased drinking of a beverage and with the preference for a thirst-quenching beverage over an electrolyte-replacing beverage. Likewise, when people are motivated to repair their mood, we find that subliminal sadness primes not only activate concepts related to repairing their mood but also that the activation of these concepts is related to their preference for music that will repair their mood.

One issue that we have not addressed in this research is whether the motivations that drive the activation of people's thoughts and shape their actions operate at the conscious level or at the unconscious level. On the one hand, it is clear that at least in some of our studies the whole process that we have described – in which motivation leads to the activation of motivationally relevant thoughts, which in turn are shaped by motivation into actions that satisfy people's goals – is not fully conscious. In most instances we have described, it is fairly clear that people are not aware of the concepts that have become activated. Nevertheless, these concepts can still lead to motivationally relevant behaviors that satisfy people's motives and of which they are presumably aware. On the other hand, we do not want to claim that people in our studies are unaware of the motives that are driving their behavior. The people who experienced a self-image threat reported lower self-esteem; the people who were thirsty reported being thirsty; the people who were threatened with being racist would presumably report being motivated to avoid prejudice. Thus, our research seems to suggest that although people are not aware of the processes through which motivation affects their thoughts and actions, they are often aware of the motives.

But could the same processes operate even if the motives were unconscious? We suspect they could. In one of our studies, it is unclear whether people were fully aware of their motivation. When people expect to interact with another person and are subliminally primed with a sad face, are they consciously motivated to repair their mood? It seems that to be consciously aware that they want to repair their mood, people must be aware that they are in a bad mood and that they will be in a situation in which they want to get out of this mood. In our study, when people expected to interact with another person, they were presumably aware that they would be in a situation in which they would like to be in a positive mood. But were they aware that they were in a negative mood?

We suspect that they were aware on one level but were not fully aware of their negative mood. This state could be described as one of experiential awareness (see Schooler and Schreiber, this volume): Participants are aware of their mood at the moment, but not meta-aware, or aware that they are aware. The evidence for this conclusion is that when we directly asked people about their mood, they did not report being sadder after the sad face prime than after the neutral prime. On the other hand, when we asked people to evaluate a sad and gloomy piece of music (Prokofiev's *Russia Under the Mongolian Yoke*), they reported that the music was more sad and gloomy after the sad face prime than after the neutral prime. Given that this state had a strong effect on the activation of people's thoughts and the way these thoughts were related to actions, we suspect that when people are less aware of their motives, these motives will likely operate in much the same way as the more conscious motives that we have described.

One question that remains is: How often does motivation affect the activation of our thoughts and shape our actions? Such a question is, of course, difficult to answer, and the research we have reviewed provides us with little basis to claim how often these processes occur. Nevertheless, we suspect they are quite common. In everyday life, people often experience stronger motivations than are common in the lab. In our experiments, people are threatened by a poor score on an intelligence test. In everyday life, people are taunted and rejected by others. In our experiments, people avoid eating and drinking for 3 hours. In everyday life, people often go much longer without food or drink. In many lab studies, the situation is carefully contrived to limit people's motivations. These observations lead us to believe that the motivational effects that we describe here are likely to be both ubiquitous and powerful in everyday life. We welcome this symposium as an opportunity to examine these issues more fully.

References

Bargh, J. A. (1990). Auto-motives: Preconscious determinants of thought and behavior. In E. T. Higgins & R. M. Sorrentino (Eds.), *Handbook of motivation and cognition* (Vol. 2, pp. 93–130). New York: Guilford Press.

Bargh, J. A., & Chartrand, T. L. (1999). The unbearable automaticity of being. *American Psychologist, 54,* 462–479.

Bruner, J. S. (1957). On perceptual readiness. *Psychological Review, 64,* 340–358.

Bruner, J. S., Postman, L., & McGinnies, E. (1947). Personal values as determinants of perceptual selection. *American Psychologist, 2,* 285–286.

Dovidio, J. F., Kawakami, K., & Gaertner, S. L. (2000). Reducing contemporary prejudice: Combating explicit and implicit bias at the individual and intergroup level. In S. Oskamp (Ed.), *Reducing prejudice and discrimination. The Claremont symposium on applied social psychology* (pp. 137–163). Mahwah, NJ: Erlbaum.

Epstein, S. (1994). Integration of the cognitive and the psychodynamic unconscious. *American Psychologist, 49,* 709–724.

Erber, R., Wegner, D. M., & Therriault, N. (1996). On being cool and collected: Mood regulation in anticipation of social interaction. *Journal of Personality and Social Psychology, 70,* 757–766.

Fein, S., & Spencer, S. J. (1997). Prejudice as self-image maintenance: Affirming the self through negative evaluations of others. *Journal of Personality and Social Psychology, 73,* 31–44.

Fein, S., & Spencer, S. J. (2004). *Norms, threat, and prejudice: How local norms shape self-image processes in prejudicial evaluations.* Unpublished manuscript, Williams College.

Gilbert, D. T., & Hixon, J. G. (1991). The trouble of thinking: Activation and application of stereotypic beliefs. *Journal of Personality and Social Psychology, 60*, 509–517.

Gollwitzer, P. M., & Moskowitz, G. B. (1996). Goal effects on action and cognition. In E. T. Higgins & A. W. Kruglanski (Eds.), *Social psychology: Handbook of basic principles* (pp. 361–399), New York: Guilford Press.

Higgins, E. T. (1996). Knowledge activation: Accessibility applicability, and salience. In E. T. Higgins & A. W. Kruglanski (Eds.), *Social psychology: Handbook of basic principles* (pp. 133–168). New York: Guilford Press.

Kihlstrom, J. F. (1987). The cognitive unconscious. *Science, 237*, 1445–1452.

Kunda, Z., & Spencer, S. J. (2003). When do stereotypes come to mind and when do they color judgment? A goal-based theoretical framework for understanding stereotype activation and application. *Psychological Bulletin, 129*, 522–544.

Monteith, M. J., Sherman, J., & Devine, P. G. (1998). Suppression as a stereotype control strategy. *Personality and Social Psychology Review, 2*, 63–82.

Moskowitz, G. B., Gollwitzer, P. M., Wasel, W., & Schaal, B. (1999). Preconscious control of stereotype activation through chronic egalitarian goals. *Journal of Personality and Social Psychology, 77*, 167–184.

Shah, J. Y., Kruglansk, A. W., & Friedman, R. (2002). Goals systems theory: Integrating the cognitive and motivational aspects of self-regulation. In S. J. Spencer, S. Fein, J. M. Olson, & M. P. Zanna (Eds.), *Motivated social perception: The Ontario symposium* (Vol. 9, pp. 247–276) Mahwah, NJ: Erlbaum.

Sinclair, L., & Kunda, Z. (1999). Reactions to a Black professional: Motivated inhibition and activation of conflicting stereotypes. *Journal of Personality and Social Psychology, 77*, 885–904.

Spencer, S. J., Fein, S., Davies, P. G., & Hoshino-Browne, E. (2004). *How the threat of being racist leads to the automatic inhibition of stereotypes.* Unpublished manuscript, University of Waterloo.

Spencer, S. J., Fein, S., Wolfe, C., Fong, C., & Dunn, M. (1998). Stereotype activation under cognitive load: The moderating role of self-image threat. *Personality and Social Psychology Bulletin, 24*, 1139–1152.

Strahan, E., Spencer, S. J., & Zanna, M. P. (2002). Subliminal priming and persuasion: Striking while the iron is hot. *Journal of Experimental Social Psychology, 38*, 556–568.

Westen, D. (1998). The scientific legacy of Sigmund Freud: Toward a psychodynamically informed psychological science. *Psychological Bulletin, 124*, 333–371.

PART II

SOCIAL MOTIVATION

Cognitive and Affective Implications

8

From Evolved Motives to Everyday Mentation

Evolution, Goals, and Cognition

Steven L. Neuberg, Douglas T. Kenrick, Jon K. Maner, and Mark Schaller

INTRODUCTION

Walking across a crowding shopping mall, you may see a group of people who vary in their race, gender, attractiveness, clothing style, and demeanor. A similarly complex array of social stimuli confronts us at conferences, airports, farmer's markets, and college campuses. Rarely do we attend equally to all individuals in such complex social environments or to all characteristics of any given individual. Rather, we selectively direct our attention toward a smaller subset of individuals and characteristics. This selective direction of attention often occurs automatically, without conscious intent, and can have important consequences for subsequent thoughts and actions.

Who do we attend to, think about, and later remember? And how are the answers to this question linked to our goals at the moment? We recently embarked on a program of research to explore the processes that influence the selective and automatic direction of perceptual and cognitive resources. In this chapter, we present a conceptual framework that begins to articulate the role that fundamental social goals play in governing these processes. We focus, in particular, on the ways in which self-protection and mating goals selectively facilitate attention toward people who have characteristics relevant to those goals. Integrating theory and research on selective attention processes, the influence of goals on social cognition and behavior, and ecological theories of motivation and social cognition, our

Work on this chapter was supported by a grant from the U.S. National Institute of Mental Health to the first, second, and fourth authors. The ideas described here have benefited greatly from conversations with Vaughn Becker, Andy Delton, Brian Hofer, Jon Butner, and Chris Wilbur, and we thank Bill von Hippel for his helpful comments on a previous draft of this chapter. Correspondence can be directed to Steven L. Neuberg or Douglas T. Kenrick, Department of Psychology, Arizona State University, Tempe, AZ 85287-1104; e-mail: steven.neuberg@asu.edu or douglas.kenrick@asu.edu.

133

framework yields some novel hypotheses about how self-protection and mating goals influence attention to, perceptions of, and cognitions about individuals who differ in gender, physical attractiveness, and ethnicity.

THEORETICAL FOUNDATIONS

Selective Attention and Information Processing

Attention – and subsequent information processing – is *selective*. Because information processing capacities are inherently limited, individuals cannot simultaneously allocate attentional resources to all information in the environment (e.g., Kahneman, 1973; Norman & Bobrow, 1975; Pashler, 1994). Psychologists have long studied the processes involved in selective attention and information processing (Fiske & Taylor, 1991; Todd & Gigerenzer, 2000) and have inquired as to whether and why attention may be drawn more to certain types of stimuli rather than others (Funder, 1987; McArthur & Baron, 1983).

Attentional processes seem especially sensitive to *social* stimuli. For instance, people occupying the periphery of a visual field draw attention away from more visually prominent nonsocial stimuli in the center of that field (Rensink, 2000; Rensink, O'Regan, & Clark, 1997). Even simple geometric shapes have a more powerful impact on attention when those shapes are interpreted as social stimuli (e.g., as eyes rather than mere circles; Friesen & Kingstone, 1998). It appears, then, that information processing is *selectively selective*: Some categories of information are more intrinsically interesting and relevant than others. But what particular kinds of information are people likely to notice, remember, and act upon? What circumstances influence this selection and its consequences? A strategy for developing answers to these questions is suggested by a consideration of how goals affect social cognition.

Goals and Social Cognition

How people perceive the events in their lives, and how they organize and remember those events, are profoundly influenced by their goals (e.g., Bargh, 1990; Fiske & Neuberg, 1990; Kruglanski, 1989; Kunda, 1990). For example, people who have chronically higher needs for simple structure are especially likely to make quick judgments, to base those judgments on relatively little information, to make judgments compatible with existing beliefs, and to cling to those judgments more tenaciously in the face of contradictory evidence (e.g., Kruglanski & Webster, 1996; Moskowitz, 1993; Neuberg & Newsom, 1993; Schaller, Boyd, Yohannes, & O'Brien, 1995). Acutely activated goals have similar consequences: Circumstances that temporarily introduce a high need for structure (e.g., time pressure) lead to effects mirroring those of chronic needs for structure (e.g., Kruglanski & Freund, 1983), whereas circumstances that introduce accuracy goals (e.g., personal accountability, severe personal consequences for inaccuracy, outcome dependency) lead people to attend to and consider more carefully a wider variety of relevant information (e.g., Neuberg & Fiske, 1987; Tetlock & Kim, 1987).

Although much of the extant research has examined the effects of goals on inference processes and other aspects of higher-order cognition, it also appears that goals and need-states can influence lower-level perceptual and cognitive processes (e.g., Di Lollo, Kawahara, Zuvic, & Visser, 2001; Liberman & Förster, this volume; von Hippel, Hawkins, & Narayan, 1994). Bruner and Goodman's (1947) research, in which poor children were especially likely to overestimate the sizes of coins, is a classic illustration of this. Similar conclusions can be drawn from recent research by Spencer, Fein, Strahan, and Zanna (this volume) demonstrating that people who are thirsty are particularly sensitive to the presence of words related to the quenching of that thirst, such as *beverage* and *quench* (cf. Aarts, Dijksterhuis, & De Vries, 2001).

In some cases, goals influence perception and cognition in a fairly explicit, conscious way, as when people with a high need for accuracy deliberately expend extra effort in an attempt to reach more fully informed judgments. But goal-directed perception and cognition may also proceed less deliberately. Like other knowledge structures, goals and need-states can be activated automatically and may influence perception and thought without explicit conscious awareness (e.g., Bargh, 1990; Bargh & Chartrand, 1999).

Given the abundant evidence that goals influence how people perceive and cognitively organize their world, it seems reasonable that goals would also influence which specific stimuli people attend to. Perhaps because of its focus on explicating general psychological *processes*, however, cognitive psychology – even social-cognitive psychology – has largely ignored issues of domain-specific *content*. Fortunately, questions of how particular goals might relate to particular contents in the social environment have been considered by ecologically oriented theorists, and so we turn to this literature now.

Ecological/Evolutionary Approaches to Motivation and Cognition

Ecologically informed theory and research on motivation imply that the goals having the most immediate impact on the perception of social environments should be those that, over the course of human evolutionary history, have been most closely linked to adaptive outcomes (e.g., Bugental, 2000; McArthur & Baron, 1983; Plutchik, 1980; Scott, 1980; Stevens & Fiske, 1995). Given the central roles of survival and sexual reproduction in evolutionary processes, it follows that attention in social situations would be directed chronically by motivational states linked to survival and reproduction.

For example, Plutchik (1980) suggested that cues indicating the presence of a possible enemy activate a self-protective motive and its associated emotional responses (e.g., fear or anger, depending on the presence of related cues). This motivational-emotional system subsequently directs attention and alters the availability of behavioral response options (e.g., avoidance, attack) in such a way as to increase the likelihood of action that would have been associated with greater survival success in ancestral environments (Öhman & Mineka, 2001). Similarly, perceptual cues indicating the potential for reproductive success or failure may activate acutely a mating goal and its associated affective responses (Scott, 1980). This will, in turn, direct attention and alter the availability of behavioral responses in such a way as to increase the likelihood of responses that would have been associated with greater reproductive success in ancestral environments.

Empirical evidence is consistent with this general framework and reveals various ways in which specific contextual cues relevant to problems of survival appear to trigger content-specific adaptive cognitive mechanisms (Todd & Gigerenzer, 2000). For example, certain types of logical reasoning are facilitated under conditions in which the reasoning problem has content specific to the detection of cheaters on social contracts – who pose a particular type of social danger – and this effect occurs most strongly when individuals are in a context that connotes greater vulnerability to this danger (Cosmides & Tooby, 1992; Cummins, 1998). As another example, when people are literally in the dark – an ecological circumstance that heuristically connotes a greater vulnerability to harm – they are especially likely to perceive ethnic outgroup members to be hostile and threatening (e.g., Schaller, Park, & Faulkner, 2003; Schaller, Park, & Mueller, 2003).

Similarly, contextual cues pertaining to reproduction appear to trigger specific cognitive mechanisms associated heuristically with reproductive success (Buss, 1999; Kenrick, Li, & Butner, 2003; Kenrick, Sadalla, & Keefe, 1998). For instance, men and women exhibit different evaluative contrast effects on self-assessments of romantic desirability: Men judge themselves to be less desirable mates after being exposed to other men high in social dominance but not after being exposed to other physically attractive men. Women in contrast, judge themselves to be less desirable mates after being exposed to highly attractive women but not after being exposed to women high in social dominance. This pattern is consistent with sex differences in criteria for mate selection that would have been adaptive in ancestral environments (Gutierres, Kenrick, & Partch, 1999; Kenrick, Neuberg, Zierk, & Krones, 1994).

These lines of research (which we expand upon later) are consistent with an ecological approach to social cognition: Specific perceptual cues activate specific evolutionarily designed goals – goals linked to problems of survival or reproduction – which, in turn, direct cognitive processes to proceed in a manner that was adaptive throughout ancestral times. An important implication of this *adaptive motivational system* approach is the assumption, often implicit, that only one of these fundamental systems will predominate at any given moment in time. This assumption is consistent with research and theory on neural networks, and with research indicating that goal states may inhibit the activation of other goals (Tipper, 1992). For instance, Martindale (1980, 1991) reviewed evidence suggesting that inhibitory processes contribute to selective processing at every level of perception. Hierarchical processes of lateral inhibition and vertical activation lead to something like a winner-take-all psychological state. This is essential to functioning, as it allows the central nervous system to set priorities rather than being pulled every which way by millions of neural inputs. Martindale argued that these processes occur up to the highest level of cognition, so that only one executive system (or *subself*, in Martindale's terminology) predominates psychologically at any given time, facilitating attention to and processing of certain types of information and inhibiting attention to and processing of other types of information. Thus, for example, if a mating goal is activated, information relevant to mating will increase in salience, whereas information irrelevant to mating will recede into the perceptual background. Or, if a self-protective goal is activated, perceptual information relevant to threat and self-defense will increase in salience, whereas functionally irrelevant information will recede into the background.

Ecological approaches to social cognition are rich in explanatory power, and in conceptual and practical implications. However, as with any new line of inquiry in the psychological sciences, much of the theoretical speculation has yet to be substantiated by empirical data. Of the extant empirical investigations testing these theoretical speculations, most have addressed hypotheses pertaining to behavior or to conscious and deliberate higher-order social cognitive processes – logical reasoning, overt judgment, and behavioral decision making. There has been very little empirical research examining the impact of survival- and reproduction-relevant need-states on lower-order (and largely nonconscious) perceptual processing of complex social environments. One of our aims is to focus on these lower-level perceptual and attentional processes.

Transitional Summary

Considered separately, the three lines of inquiry just summarized suggest specific questions that remain unanswered and empirical gaps that remain to be filled. Considered jointly, they suggest an integrative line of theory and research that may help address those questions and fill those gaps.

Toward this end, we outline a general conceptual framework that yields
a number of novel and previously untested hypotheses about the effects
of ecologically important interpersonal goals and need-states on attention, encoding, retrieval, and judgment when people are presented with
complex social environments. Our conceptual model focuses on the ecologically important goals of *self-protection* and *mating*. Before summarizing
the model and hypotheses, therefore, we briefly discuss previous research
linking these two goals to social cognition.

IMPACT OF SELF-PROTECTION AND MATING GOALS
ON SOCIAL COGNITION

Because both self-protective and mating behaviors are presumed to have
played fundamental roles in human evolution, it follows that most people
are, to some extent, chronically sensitive to environmental cues bearing on
the satisfaction of these goals.

For instance, based on an extensive literature review, Öhman and
Mineka (2001) concluded that cues associated with potential physical threat
invoke rapid and automatic activation of dedicated neural circuits in the
amygdala. This circuitry has dense efferent connections with the cortex,
thereby suggesting, in combination with a number of experimental findings they review, that activating the self-protection/fear system has powerful directive implications for cognitive processes. Indeed, people are especially quick to notice, and are adept at encoding, information that implies
danger or threat, whether that information is conveyed by truly social cues
such as facial expressions (Hansen & Hansen, 1988; Öhman, Lundqvist,
& Esteves, 2001) or semantic cues such as words (Pratto & John, 1991).
Regarding mating goals, men and women – who are presumed to have
required different behavioral strategies as a means of satisfying reproductive goals – differentially appraise potential mates in ways consistent with
their different strategies of goal attainment (Buss, 1999; Buss & Kenrick,
1998; Gangestad & Simpson, 2000; Kenrick, 1994). In the absence of any
measure or manipulation of goals or need-states, however, results such as
these provide only indirect evidence of the impact of goals.

Somewhat more useful are studies that reveal correlations between
individual differences in variables that indirectly implicate need-states
and consequent cognitions about others. For instance, people who chronically feel highly vulnerable to danger (and so may have chronically activated self-protection goals) are more prejudiced against ethnic outgroups
and are especially likely to exaggerate threats posed by outgroup members (Altemeyer, 1988). Similarly, individuals who are chronically inclined
to seek short-term mating opportunities, or who are not currently involved in a committed relationship, are more attentive to mating-relevant
features of the opposite sex, such as physical attractiveness and social

dominance (Simpson & Gangestad, 1992; Simpson, Gangestad, & Lerma, 1990). At best, however, the correlational nature of these results offers indirect, imperfect, and incomplete evidence of the impact of goals on social cognition.

A more compelling inquiry into the impact of self-protection and mating goals demands the manipulation of goal activation. Some recent studies on intergroup cognition have taken such an approach, with results revealing that a variety of contextual manipulations connoting danger (and thus presumably activating self-protection goals) lead to exaggerated stereotypes and prejudices (e.g., Judd & Park, 1988; Mullen, Brown, & Smith, 1992; Rothgerber, 1997; Schaller et al., 2003). More directly relevant to the present inquiry, there is also evidence that a danger-connoting context (intergroup competition) can lead to enhanced recall of the personal characteristics of outgroup members (Judd & Park, 1988); this latter phenomenon also implies some impact of the goal state on attention processes.

Nonetheless, little evidence directly addresses the implications of the ecological approach to goal-directed social cognition. In particular, almost no evidence bears on the impact of temporarily activated self-protection goals on selective attention and other low-level processes of person perception, and there is little or no analogous evidence bearing on the impact of mating goals. Because lower-level processes such as attention and initial encoding constrain subsequent processing, these processes are likely to be especially influential. Furthermore, such processes are often outside voluntary control and hence are less subject to impression management. If you ask people whether they would find a particular target a potentially desirable mate, it is possible they will tell you what they think you want to hear. However, if their eyes are spontaneously and immediately drawn to some individuals rather than others, or if they are unable to report reliably whether particular individuals were even present in a social array, this provides a potentially nonreactive measure of basic social cognitive processes.

CONCEPTUAL MODEL AND HYPOTHESES

Integrating the lines of reasoning reviewed here leads to a straightforward model articulating the impact of self-protection and mating goals on attention and perception in complex social environments.

First, particular classes of stimuli in the social environment are likely to activate relevant goal systems. Some of these cues will be fairly explicit and obvious (eye contact from a smiling, attractive member of the opposite sex), whereas others will be more implicit and nonobvious (incidental perception of semantic information connoting sexual desire).

Once a goal is activated, it directs attention selectively to people who have characteristics heuristically relevant to successful goal attainment.

Features relevant to self-protection goal attainment are those related to the probability that another reason is potentially dangerous and should be avoided; these include gender (i.e., maleness), ethnic outgroup status, and angry facial expressions. Features relevant to mating goal attainment are those related to the probability that another would make a good mate; these include gender, physical attractiveness, and social dominance.

In addition to facilitating attention to individuals who possess goal-relevant features, the activated goal inhibits attention to and processing of other, goal-irrelevant categories of information. If self-protection goals are active, for instance, attention to and processing of physically attractive opposite-sex others are likely to be suppressed. If mating goals are active, attention to and processing of outgroup others are likely to be suppressed (but not as strongly, as discussed later).

Active self-protection and mating goals should also influence early-stage perception/interpretation processes in ways heuristically biased toward the successful implementation of the goal. For instance, individuals concerned for their safety should not only be particularly attuned to potential physical threats in their environment, but their threshold for perceiving individuals and events as threatening should be relatively low: Indeed, because the costs of failing to identify an authentic threat are high (Kurzban & Leary, 2001), such individuals may initially perceive threats where they objectively do not exist. Similarly, individuals interested in sex and romance may have a relatively low threshold for perceiving mating opportunities, and thus may "see" mating opportunities that objectively do not exist (Haselton & Buss, 2000).

Finally, the hypothesized effects of goal activation on attention and perception are expected to influence "downstream" processes. Thus, because of their proposed effects on attention and perception, self-protection and mating goals are each expected to influence memory differentially for different individuals in complex social environments, judgments about those individuals (such as changes in perceived frequency of individuals in salient categories), and evaluations of the social environments containing those differentially salient individuals.

The predictions generated by this functional framework are subtly, but importantly, different from those predicted by a traditional associative model. Although we must assume the operation of associative links between different features of cognition (e.g., between known cues, goals, and subsequent expectations), the current model does not merely assert that the activation of emotion or semantic information leads to the activation of associatively linked cognitions. Rather, the model generates more finely articulated predictions about the effects of specific types of emotion or semantic information on the activation – and inhibition – of specific aspects of attention and cognition. These predictions go beyond mere affective or semantic similarities.

For example, a strictly associative model leads one to expect the greatest amount of noticing and remembering of stimuli that are most closely linked, semantically or affectively, to an active goal or emotional state. Thus, when self-protection/fear or mating/romantic interest is primed, participants should be most likely to detect identical emotions in others (e.g., to detect fear when fear is primed) as well as emotions that are similarly valenced (e.g., anger, disgust, sadness, guilt). Our functional model compels a different set of predictions: When fear is primed, participants may indeed be more likely to detect fear cues in others, but they should be even more likely to detect threatening cues (e.g., anger) in others.

Another interesting implication follows from the ecological approach: A functional analysis implies intrinsic prioritization of goals. We have chosen as our exemplars two goals with clear functional significance. Yet, functional logic suggests a priority of self-protection goals over mating goals in circumstances involving the simultaneous presence of threats of physical harm and mating opportunities. Although a simplistic application of an evolutionary model might lead one to expect that mating goals will trump all others, given the central importance of reproduction to natural selection, this is unlikely to be the case in any given situation. Why? The individual who fails to respond to physical threats may suffer immediate harm and even loss of life, whereas the individual who misses an opportunity to mate will live to see other mating opportunities. Thus, there are very different functional implications of (a) attending to mating cues while failing to attend to threat cues versus (b) attending to threat cues while failing to attend to mating cues. This implication yields the hypothesis that attention to danger-relevant stimuli will be less easily inhibited than attention to mating-relevant stimuli.

EARLY EMPIRICAL INVESTIGATIONS

Although our research program is still quite young, we can briefly describe here two sets of studies that lend empirical support for several of the ideas just presented. The first explores how the physical attractiveness of same- and other-sex targets may capture attention within complex social contexts; the second explores how self-protection and mating goals influence the perception of emotion in the faces of others.[1]

---

[1] Our predictions are derived from adaptationist models of functional links between motivational states and attentional processes. It is important to note, however, that they represent heuristic implications several steps down the epistemological ladder from tests of underlying assumptions of the theory of natural selection (see Öhman & Mineka, 2001, for a discussion of these issues); our studies should not be viewed as tests of fundamental evolutionary theory. We should also note that, although some stimuli associated with motivational states such as fear may be represented innately (e.g., angry facial expressions;

Physical Attractiveness and the Eye of the Beholder

Because mating is a fundamental social goal, humans ought to be, in general, chronically attuned to features of others that heuristically bear on their desirability as mating partners. Much evidence indicates that physical attractiveness often plays a major role in romantic relationships (e.g., Feingold, 1990, 1992; Shackelford, 2001; Simpson et al., 1990), and so we might expect people to direct their attention selectively to individuals who are physically attractive; this tendency should be exaggerated among those perceivers currently interested in romance. We explored this general idea in a series of five experiments, focusing specifically on several alternative hypotheses derived from evolutionary considerations (Maner et al., 2003).

- The *opposite-sex beauty captures the eye* hypothesis states that both men and women will selectively focus on highly attractive members of the other sex. This hypothesis is consistent with theory and evidence that men tend to value highly the physical attractiveness of potential romantic partners (e.g., Buss & Schmitt, 1993; Kenrick, Sadalla, Groth, & Trost, 1990) and that women value the physical attractiveness of short-term (Buss & Schmitt, 1993; Gangestad & Simpson, 2000) and extra-pair partners (Scheib, 2001).
- Alternatively, the *one-sided gender bias hypothesis* states that men, more than women, selectively attend to attractive members of the other sex. This hypothesis is consistent with research suggesting that men value physical attractiveness in potential mates relatively more than females do (Buss, 1989; Feingold, 1990, 1992; Kenrick et al., 1990). For example, women shown photos of physically attractive men did not alter their commitment to their partners, as men did when exposed to physically attractive women (Kenrick et al., 1994). Also, whereas men invite mating opportunities with strangers, women tend to be somewhat less drawn to physically attractive strangers (e.g., Clark & Hatfield, 1989).
- Finally, the *female beauty captures the eye* hypothesis states that both men and women focus selectively on attractive female faces. Attractive women might be salient for female observers because such females represent potential intrasexual competitors (c.f. Gutierres et al., 1999). Consistent with this, Hassebrauck (1998) found that, when provided the opportunity, both male and female observers look at female stimulus features typically associated with judgments of female physical attractiveness (i.e., eyes, lips, waist, and hips) sooner and more often than for these same features on male targets. Also, both men and women show enhanced recognition for attractive female faces (Shepard & Ellis, 1973).

Darwin, 1857), most social stimuli that trigger fundamental motivational states are likely to be learned (albeit very efficiently) through experience (Öhman & Mineka, 2001).

In the first three studies, we presented participants with arrays of male and female faces of varying attractiveness under conditions of either unlimited or limited ability to attend to the arrays. Participants subsequently estimated the frequency of attractive faces they saw in the arrays. We reasoned that if physically attractive targets capture attention at an early stage of visual processing, observers would initially fixate on the most attractive people in an array of faces. Then, if the array of faces disappears after only a very short period of time, observers will not have had the opportunity to fully process the remainder of the faces (i.e., less attractive faces). Therefore, if observers are subsequently asked to estimate the proportion of physically attractive targets in the array, participants in the limited attention conditions should estimate higher numbers of attractive targets than should those in the full-attention conditions.

Results from these studies were consistent: Both male and female participants estimated relatively high proportions of attractive women under conditions of limited attentional opportunity. In contrast, when participants were provided the opportunity to attend to all the faces, they estimated equivalent proportions of attractive men and women. These studies thus suggest that, at an early stage of visual processing, female attractiveness captures the attention of both male and female observers. These results support neither the *one-sided gender bias* nor the *opposite-sexed beauty captures the eye* hypothesis: Women also estimated relatively high proportions of attractive women and did not show a bias toward attractive men in their estimation of men.

These studies employed only an indirect indicator of attention – frequency estimates under circumstances of constrained attentional ability. To measure attention more directly, we employed eye-tracker technology in a fourth study: We measured participants' eye fixations as they scanned the arrays of faces. In this study, we also measured chronic interest in sexual relationships so that we might assess the extent to which this motive might increase the focus on mating-relevant targets.

Replicating the previous results, both male and female observers in Study 4 were biased toward paying greater attention to physically attractive, as compared to average-looking, female targets. The data thus further support the *female beauty captures the eye* hypothesis.

However, unlike the results from the previous studies, women additionally exhibited a bias toward attending to attractive, as compared to average-looking, men, thereby lending support to the *opposite-sexed beauty captures the eye* hypothesis. Moreover, sexually unrestricted participants – who possess relatively greater mate-search goals – were particularly biased toward attending to attractive opposite-sexed targets. This was the case for both men attending to women and women attending to men, strongly suggesting that the motivation to seek mates plays a role in guiding attention toward attractive opposite-sex people.

Finally, there was a strong positive relationship between women's attention to attractive men and their attention to attractive women; no such relationship was found for male observers. Those women most visually interested in the attractive men – and who, if you recall, were dispositionally most interested in seeking new romantic partners – were the ones who spent the most time looking at the attractive women. These findings are consistent with the idea that heterosexual women with active mate-search goals may have an interest in assessing their competition.

Why did the more direct measure of attention – eye fixations – reveal directed female attention toward attractive men, whereas the other studies consistently revealed that women did not overestimate the proportion of attractive men in the arrays to which they had been exposed? Data from a fifth experiment suggests that women's memory for attractive men is relatively poor. One plausible explanation for the lack of frequency estimation bias, then, is that even though women's attention is initially drawn to attractive men, their cognitive processing of those attractive men subsequently begins to diminish: Because women are not as interested in male strangers as potential mates, and because physical attractiveness is not as important a determinant of female mating choices (Buss, 1989; Feingold, 1990, 1992; Kenrick et al., 1990), attractive men may not be cognitively benefited by their attractiveness (i.e., may not be increasingly likely to be encoded and remembered), and thus may not be especially likely to come to mind when one attempts to estimate their frequency in the social environment.

In sum, these data provide some early support for our framework by demonstrating that social motives can, in a predictable manner, direct attention toward mating-relevant stimuli.

Perceiving Emotions

As suggested earlier, people concerned about self-protection and mating should be biased toward perceiving others to be potential threats or mates, respectively. We explored this hypothesis in an experiment investigating how both chronic and manipulated goals would influence people's perceptions of others' facial expressions (Maner et al., 2003).

First, we hypothesized that individuals concerned with self-protection should be particularly sensitive to the presence of anger in others' faces, as angry expressions signal an increased possibility of aggression (e.g., Ekman, 1982; Scherer & Wallbott, 1994). Indeed, people selectively attend preconsciously to angry faces (Öhman & Mineka, 2001) and are able to detect them quickly (Hansen & Hansen, 1988; Öhman et al., 2001; Van Honk, Tuiten, de Haan, van den Hout, & Stam, 2001). And because failing to identify a physical threat is generally a more costly error than is perceiving a threat where one does not exist (Haselton & Buss, 2000), individuals concerned with physical safety should be biased toward seeing anger, at least initially, in even neutrally expressive faces.

This bias is likely to be especially strong when perceiving outgroup faces – particularly outgroup male faces – as outgroup men tend to be heuristically associated with physical threat. This bias might also be especially strong among male perceivers, as throughout our evolutionary history men have been the ones most likely to confront outgroup men (Daly & Wilson, 1988; Sidanius, Pratto, & Bobo, 1994; Wilson & Daly, 1992). Male intergroup contact, and hostility, predominate among primate species closely related to humans (Carpenter, 1974; Cheney, 1986; Goodall, 1986; Wrangham, 1987). Moreover, negative outgroup stereotypes tend to be more strongly associated with male outgroup members than with female outgroup members (Eagly & Kite, 1987).

This line of reasoning led us to predict that (a) activating a self-protective state by eliciting fear will lead white undergraduates, particularly white men, to perceive black male faces (but not white male faces or female faces) as exhibiting anger to a greater extent than when such a state has not been activated; (b) participants for whom self-protective goals are chronically active, compared to those with less active self-protective goals, should demonstrate a similar bias.

We followed a similar line of reasoning when considering the effects that active mating goals might have on the perception of sexual arousal in neutrally expressive faces. Because individuals interested in mating should process mating-relevant social information so as to facilitate behaviors aimed at procuring potential mates, we anticipated that romantic goals might increase the likelihood that one would perceive desirable others as romantically aroused themselves; such a bias would increase the likelihood that one might approach them (Haselton & Buss, 2000). In particular, because physically attractive others tend to be desired as mates, individuals with chronically or acutely active romantic goals should see physically attractive individuals as being romantically aroused. As we reviewed earlier, however, because women are somewhat less interested in unknown physically attractive men, we might expect this perceptual bias to be stronger for male perceivers than female perceivers. Indeed, whereas men tend to overestimate the amount of sexual intent in female behavior, women do not exhibit a similar bias (Abbey, 1982; Haselton & Buss, 2000).

Thus, we predicted that (a) activating a romantic goal would lead men to perceive attractive female targets as more sexually aroused than when such a goal has not been activated; (b) activating a romantic goal may not lead women to perceive attractive male targets as sexually aroused to the same extent that it will for men; (c) participants for whom mate-search goals are chronically active (i.e., sexually unrestricted individuals; Simpson & Gangestad, 1991, 1992), compared to those with less active mate-search goals, should demonstrate a bias toward perceiving attractive opposite-sexed targets as being sexually aroused. Finally, because pretesting indicated that participants in our population focus on own-race members as potential mates – and do not view members of other races as sexually desirable – we suspected that the motivational bias would be limited to perceiving sexual arousal in opposite-sexed members of one's own race.

We activated self-protective, romantic, or neutral motivational states via film clips: To activate the goal of self-protection, participants viewed scenes from *The Silence of the Lambs*, in which a white male serial killer stalks a white female FBI agent officer through a dark basement; to activate the mating goal, participants viewed scenes from *Things to Do in Denver When You're Dead*, in which an attractive white man and woman meet and have a romantic first date; in the neutral control clip, participants viewed scenes from the film *Koyaanisqatsi*, which included time-lapse videography of urban living (e.g., people going up and down on an escalator, people working on an assembly line). Participants then briefly viewed (1 second) male and female white and black faces of varying attractiveness and judged the emotions they believed were expressed in each target's face; all targets actually had neutral facial expressions. After viewing each face, participants rated the extent to which they believed the target was sexually aroused, angry, frightened, and happy. Finally, to assess effects associated with chronically active social goals, we obtained measures linked to chronic self-protective and romantic motivation.

Results strongly supported our predictions. First, both acute and chronic self-protective motives were associated with increased perceptions of anger in black male faces. After viewing a film clip designed to elicit self-protective motivation (as opposed to the control film), male (but not female) participants perceive a greater amount of anger in black male faces. Only black males were targeted by this bias. Moreover, male participants perceived only more anger, and not other emotions, in those black male faces. Finally, in the control condition in which no motivation was acutely activated, participants (both men and women) possessing chronic self-protective motives also perceived greater amounts of anger specifically in black male faces.

Second, romantic goals also led to the predicted social-perceptual bias. After viewing a film clip designed to elicit romantic motivation (as opposed to the control film), male participants perceived a greater amount of sexual arousal in attractive white female faces. These men did not perceive attractive white women to be experiencing the other emotions, nor did they view any other targets as sexually aroused. No parallel effects were exhibited by female participants. Finally, in the control condition in which no goal was explicitly activated, sexually unrestricted participants (both male and female) perceived greater amounts of sexual arousal in attractive opposite-sexed faces.

The specificity of these effects provides strong support for the functional motives perspective over a simple associative priming perspective. Our functional approach led to focused predictions about which emotions would be perceived in which targets as a function of the activated goal – and these predictions were often in conflict with those generated by traditional semantic or affective priming perspectives. For instance, activating fear did not lead participants to perceive more fear in target faces but rather more anger – an emotion more functionally relevant to one's own self-protective state. Moreover, whereas a simple associative perspective possesses little ability to generate specific predictions about which targets should elicit greater perceptions of anger, the functional motives perspective led us to predict, and confirm, that participants perceived more anger only in men of an outgroup that is heuristically viewed as physically threatening. These findings thus impressively demonstrate the utility of the functional motives perspective: Activating particular emotion/motivation systems leads to social-cognitive consequences that may facilitate potentially adaptive behavioral responses.

IN CLOSING

We suspect that most psychologists readily accept the premise that perception and cognition are for doing (e.g., Gibson, 1979; James, 1890/1981) – that, at some level, we perceive and think in order to act in ways that better serve our goals. Indeed, one could reasonably argue that some of the most significant advances in social psychological theorizing and research during the 1980s and 1990s were those related to explicating motivational influences on cognition (e.g., Bargh, 1990; Fiske & Neuberg, 1990; Kruglanski, 1989; Kunda, 1990; Petty & Cacioppo, 1986). In retrospect, it's not surprising that much of that effort focused on the effects of epistemic goals – on the desire for accuracy, on the needs for cognition, simplicity and structure, decisiveness, consistency, and the like. After all, these goals are explicitly *about* perception and cognition. As important as much of that work was, especially in the aggregate, one could reasonably suggest that its focus on epistemic goals failed to capture the more fundamental and ubiquitous set of concerns we have each day as social creatures. Don't we want to protect ourselves and those we care about? Don't we seek romance, friendships, and status? Motives such as these failed to find a place within the social-cognitive revolution.

Ironically, the 1980s and 1990s also hosted, albeit more controversially, the ascent of the evolutionary perspective as a theoretical player within social psychology. Whereas the social cognitive framework tended to focus its interest in motivation primarily on epistemic goals, constrained as it was from the beginning by the metaphor of the human as a computer-like information processor, the evolutionary perspective was from the beginning rich in theorizing about human social goals but somewhat impoverished in its weak focus on basic cognitive processing. Far from being incompatible, then, we view these two approaches as highly complementary: The contributions of each will be greatly strengthened by their integration.

Our empirical findings begin to illustrate this: Early-in-the-stream perceptual and cognitive processes are directed in functional ways by the fundamental social goals of self-protection and romance-seeking. Our future work will elaborate on these findings, reveal their implications for "downstream" cognition, judgments, and behaviors, test other features of the framework (e.g., hypotheses about asymmetrical influences of the self-protection and romance-seeking goals), and move to explore additional fundamental social goals.

We believe that the promise of our integrative perspective is great. By integrating theory from ecological and evolutionary psychology with a contemporary understanding of fundamental cognitive processes, and by empirically exploring this integration with modern methods and technologies, we believe that one can arrive at both a broader and deeper understanding of how and what people think about those around them.

References

Aarts, H., Dijksterhuis, A., & De Vries, P. (2001). On the psychology of drinking: Being thirsty and perceptually ready. *British Journal of Psychology, 92,* 631–642.

Abbey, A. (1982). Sex differences in attributions for friendly behavior: Do males misperceive females' friendliness? *Journal of Personality and Social Psychology, 42,* 830–838.

Altemeyer, B. (1988). *Enemies of freedom.* San Francisco: Jossey-Bass.

Bargh, J. A. (1990). Auto-motives: Preconscious determinants of social interaction. In E. T. Higgins & R. M. Sorrentino (Eds.), *Handbook of motivation and cognition: Foundations of social behavior* (Vol. 2, pp. 93–130). New York: Guilford Press.

Bargh, J. A., & Chartrand, T. L. (1999). The unbearable automaticity of being. *American Psychologist, 54,* 464–479.

Bruner, J. S., & Goodman, C. C. (1947). Value and need as organizing factors in perception. *Journal of Abnormal and Social Psychology, 42,* 33–44.

Bugental, D. B. (2000). Acquisition of the algorithms of social life: A domain-based approach. *Psychological Bulletin, 126,* 187–219.

Buss, D. M. (1989). Sex differences in human mate preferences: Evolutionary hypotheses tested in 37 cultures. *Behavioral and Brain Sciences, 12,* 1–49.

Buss, D. M. (1999). *Evolutionary psychology.* Boston: Allyn & Bacon.

Buss, D. M., & Kenrick, D. T. (1998). Evolutionary social psychology. In D. T. Gilbert, S. T. Fiske, & G. Lindzey (Eds.), *Handbook of evolutionary psychology* (4th ed., Vol. II, pp. 982–1026). Boston: MA: McGraw-Hill.

Buss, D. M., & Schmitt, D. P. (1993). Sexual strategies theory: An evolutionary perspective on human mating. *Psychological Review, 100,* 204–232.

Carpenter, C. (1974). Aggressive behavioral systems. In R. L. Holloway (Ed.), *Primate aggression, territoriality, and xenophobia* (pp. 459–496). New York: Academic Press.

Cheney, D. (1986). Interactions and relationships between groups. In B. B. Smuts, D. L. Cheney, R. M. Seyfarth, R. W. Wrangham, & T. T. Struhsaker (Eds.), *Primate societies* (pp. 267–281). Chicago: University of Chicago Press.

Clarke, R. D., & Hatfield, E. (1989). Gender differences in receptivity to sexual offers. *Journal of Psychology and Human Sexuality, 2*, 39–55.

Cosmides, L., & Tooby, J. (1992). Cognitive adaptations for social exchange. In J. H. Barkow, L. Cosmides, & J. Tooby (Eds.), *The adapted mind* (pp. 163–228). New York: Oxford University Press.

Cummins, D. D. (1998). Social norms and other minds: The evolutionary roots of higher cognition. In D. D. Cummins & C. Allen (Eds.), *The evolution of mind* (pp. 30–50). New York: Oxford University Press.

Daly, M., & Wilson, M. (1988). *Homicide*. Hawthorne, NY: Aldine de Gruyter.

Darwin, C. (1872/1998). *The expression of the emotions in man and animals*. New York: Oxford University Press.

Di Lollo, V., Kawahara, J., Zuvic, S. M., & Visser, T. A. W. (2001) The preattentive emperor has no clothes: A dynamic redressing. *Journal of Experimental Psychology: General, 130*, 479–492.

Eagly, A. H., & Kite, M. E. (1987). Are stereotypes of nationalities applied to both women and men? *Journal of Personality and Social Psychology, 53*, 451–462.

Ekman, P. (Ed.). (1982). *Emotion in the human face* (2nd ed.). Cambridge: Cambridge University Press.

Feingold, A. (1990). Gender differences in effects of physical attractiveness on romantic attraction: A comparison across five research paradigms. *Journal of Personality and Social Psychology, 59*, 981–993.

Feingold, A. (1992). Gender differences in mate selection preferences: A test of the parental investment model. *Psychological Bulletin, 112*, 125–139.

Fiske, S. T., & Neuberg, S. L. (1990). A continuum of impression formation, from category-based to individuating processes: Influences of information and motivation on attention and interpretation. In M. P. Zanna (Ed.), *Advances in experimental social psychology* (Vol. 23, pp. 1–74). New York: Academic Press.

Fiske, S. T., & Taylor, S. E. (1991). *Social cognition* (2nd ed.). New York: McGraw-Hill.

Friesen, C. K., & Kingstone, A. (1998). The eyes have it! Reflexive orienting is triggered by nonpredictive gaze. *Psychonomic Bulletin and Review, 5*, 490–495.

Funder, D. C. (1987). Errors and mistakes: Evaluating the accuracy of social judgment. *Psychological Bulletin, 101*, 75–90. Kahneman, D. (1973). *Attention and effort.* Englewood Cliffs, NJ: Prentice-Hall.

Gangestad, S. W., & Simpson, J. A. (2000). The evolution of human mating: Trade-offs and strategic pluralism. *Behavioral and Brain Sciences, 23*, 573–644.

Gibson, J. J. (1979). *The ecological approach to visual perception*. Boston: Houghton Mifflin.

Goodall, J. (1986). Social rejection, exclusion, and shunning among the Gombe chimpanzees. *Ethology and Sociobiology, 7*, 227–236.

Gutierres, S. E., Kenrick, D. T., & Partch, J. (1999). Contrast effects in self-assessment reflect gender differences in mate selection criteria. *Personality and Social Psychology Bulletin, 25*, 1126–1134.

Hansen, C. H., & Hansen, R. D. (1988). Finding the face in the crowd: An anger superiority effect. *Journal of Personality and Social Psychology, 54*, 917–924.

Haselton, M., & Buss, D. (2000). Error management theory: A new perspective on biases in cross-sex mind reading. *Journal of Personality and Social Psychology, 78*, 81–91.

Hassebrauck, M. (1998). The visual process method: A new method to study physical attractiveness. *Evolution and Human Behavior, 19*, 111–123.

James, W. (1890/1981). *The principles of psychology*. Cambridge, MA: Harvard University Press.

Judd, C. M., & Park, B. (1988). Out-group homogeneity: Judgments of variability at the individual and group levels. *Journal of Personality and Social Psychology, 54*, 778–788.

Kahneman, D. (1973). *Attention and effort*. Englewood Cliffs, NJ: Prentice Hall.

Kenrick, D. T. (1994). Evolutionary social psychology: From sexual selection to social cognition. In M. P. Zanna (Ed.), *Advances in experimental social psychology* (Vol. 26, pp. 75–121). San Diego, CA: Academic Press.

Kenrick, D. T., Li, N. P., & Butner, J. (2003). Dynamical evolutionary psychology: Individual decision-rules and emergent social norms. *Psychological Review, 110*, 3–28.

Kenrick, D. T., Neuberg, S. L., Zierk, K. L., & Krones, J. M. (1994). Evolution and social cognition: Contrast effects as a function of sex, dominance, and physical attractiveness. *Personality and Social Psychology Bulletin, 20*, 210–217.

Kenrick, D. T., Sadalla, E. K., Groth, G., & Trost, M. R. (1990). Evolution, traits, and the stages of human courtship: Qualifying the parental investment model. *Journal of Personality, 53*, 97–116.

Kenrick, D. T., Sadalla, E. K., & Keefe, R. C. (1998). Evolutionary cognitive psychology: The missing heart of modern cognitive science. In C. Crawford & D. L. Krebs (Eds.), *Handbook of evolutionary psychology* (pp. 485–514). Hillsdale, NJ: Erlbaum.

Kruglanski, A. W. (1989). *Lay epistemics and human knowledge*. New York: Plenum Press.

Kruglanski, A. W., & Freund, T. (1983). The freezing and unfreezing of lay-inferences: Effects on impressional primacy, ethnic stereotyping, and numerical anchoring. *Journal of Experimental Social Psychology, 19*, 448–468.

Kruglanski, A. W., & Webster, D. M. (1996). Motivated closing of the mind: "Seizing" and "freezing." *Psychological Review, 103*, 263–283.

Kunda, Z. (1990). The case for motivated reasoning. *Psychological Bulletin, 108*, 480–498.

Kurzban, R., & Leary, M. R. (2001). Evolutionary origins of stigmatization: The functions of social exclusion. *Psychological Bulletin, 127*, 187–208.

Maner, J. K., Kenrick, D. T., Becker, D. V., Delton, A. W., Hofer, B., Wilbur, C., & Neuberg, S. L. (2003). Sexually selective cognition: Beauty captures the mind of the beholder. *Journal of Personality and Social Psychology, 85*, 1107–1120.

Martindale, C. (1980). Subselves. In L. Wheeler (Ed.), *Review of personality and social psychology* (Vol. 1, pp. 193–218). Beverly Hills, CA: Sage.

Martindale, C. (1991). *Cognitive psychology: A neural-network approach*. Pacific Grove, CA: Brooks/Cole.

McArthur, L. Z., & Baron, R. (1983). Toward an ecological theory of social perception. *Psychological Review, 90*, 215–238.

Moskowitz, G. B. (1993). Individual differences in social categorization: The influence of personal need for structure on spontaneous trait inference. *Journal of Personality and Social Psychology, 65*, 132–142.

Mullen, B., Brown, R., & Smith, C. (1992). Ingroup bias as a function of salience, relevance, and status: An integration. *European Journal of Social Psychology, 22*, 103–122.

Neuberg, S. L., & Fiske, S. T. (1987). Motivational influences on impression formation: Outcome dependency, accuracy-driven attention, and individuating processes. *Journal of Personality and Social Psychology, 53*, 431–444.

Neuberg, S. L., & Newsom, J. T. (1993). Personal need for structure: Individual differences in chronic motivation to simplify. *Journal of Personality and Social Psychology, 65*, 113–131.

Norman, D. A., & Bobrow, D. G. (1975). On data-limited and resource-limited processes. *Cognitive Psychology, 7*, 44–64.

Öhman, A., Lundqvist, D., & Esteves, F. (2001). The face in the crowd revisited: A threat advantage with schematic stimuli. *Journal of Personality and Social Psychology, 80*, 381–396.

Öhman, A., & Mineka, S. (2001). Fears, phobias, and preparedness: Toward an evolved module of fear and fear learning. *Psychological Review, 108*, 483–522.

Pashler, H. (1994). Dual-task interference in simple tasks: Data and theory. *Psychological Bulletin, 116*, 220–244.

Petty, R. E., & Cacioppo, J. T. (1986). The elaboration likelihood model of persuasion. In L. Berkowitz (Ed.), *Advances in experimental social psychology* (Vol. 19, pp. 123–205). New York: Academic Press.

Plutchik, R. (1980). A general psychoevolutionary theory of emotion. In R. Plutchik, & H. Kellerman (Eds.), *Emotion: Theory, research, and experience.* (Vol. 1, pp. 3–33). New York: Academic Press.

Pratto, F., & John, O. P. (1991). Automatic vigilance: The attention-grabbing power of negative social information. *Journal of Personality and Social Psychology, 61*, 380–391.

Rensink, R. A. (2000). Seeing, sensing, and scrutinizing. *Vision Research, 40*, 1469–1487.

Rensink, R. A., O'Regan, J. K., & Clark, J. J. (1997). To see or not to see: The need for attention to perceive changes in scenes. *Psychological Science, 8*, 368–373.

Rothgerber, H. (1997). External intergroup threat as an antecedent to perceptions of in-group and out-group homogeneity. *Journal of Personality and Social Psychology, 73*, 1206–1212.

Schaller, M., Boyd, C., Yohannes, J., & O'Brien, M. (1995). The prejudiced personality revisited: Personal need for structure and formation of erroneous group stereotypes. *Journal of Personality and Social Psychology, 68*, 544–555.

Schaller, M., Park, J. H., & Faulkner, J. (2003). Prehistoric dangers and contemporary prejudices. *European Review of Social Psychology, 14*, 105–137.

Schaller, M., Park, J. H., & Mueller, A. (2003). Fear of the dark: Interactive effects of beliefs about danger and ambient darkness on ethnic stereotypes. *Personality and Social Psychology Bulletin, 29*, 637–649.

Scherer, K. R., & Wallbott, H. G. (1994). Evidence for universality and cultural variation of differential emotion response patterning. *Journal of Personality and Social Psychology, 66,* 310–328.

Scott, J. P. (1980). The function of emotions in behavioral systems: A systems theory analysis. In R. Plutchik & H. Kellerman (Eds.), *Emotion: Theory, research, and experience.* (Vol. 1, pp. 35–56). New York: Academic Press.

Shackelford, T. K. (2001). Self-esteem in marriage. *Personality and Individual Differences, 30,* 371–390.

Shepard, J. W., & Ellis, H. D. (1973). The effect of attractiveness on recognition memory for faces. *American Journal of Psychology, 86,* 627–633.

Sidanius, J., Pratto, F., & Bobo, L. (1994). Social dominance orientation and the political psychology of gender: A case of invariance? *Journal of Personality and Social Psychology, 67,* 998–1011.

Simpson, J. A., & Gangestad, S. W. (1991). Individual differences in sociosexuality: Evidence for convergent and discriminant validity. *Journal of Personality and Social Psychology, 60,* 870–883.

Simpson, J. A., & Gangestad, S. W. (1992). Sociosexuality and romantic partner choice. *Journal of Personality, 60,* 31–51.

Simpson, J. A., Gangestad, S. W., & Lerma, M. (1990). Perception of physical attractiveness: Mechanisms involved in the maintenance of romantic relationships. *Journal of Personality and Social Psychology, 59,* 1192–1201.

Stevens, L. E., & Fiske, S. T. (1995). Motivation and cognition in social life: A social survival perspective. *Social Cognition, 13,* 189–214.

Tetlock, P. E., & Kim, J. I. (1987). Accountability and judgment processes in a personality prediction task. *Journal of Personality and Social Psychology, 52,* 700–709.

Tipper, S. P. (1992). Selection for action: The role of inhibitory mechanisms. *Current Directions in Psychological Science, 1,* 105–109.

Todd, P. M., & Gigerenzer, G. (2000). Precis of "Simple Heuristics that Make Us Smart." *Behavioral and Brain Sciences, 23,* 727–780.

Van Honk, J., Tuiten, A., de Haan, E., van den Hout, M., & Stam, H. (2001). Attentional biases for angry faces: Relationships to trait anger and anxiety. *Cognition and Emotion, 15,* 279–297.

Von Hippel, W., Hawkins, C., & Narayan, S. (1994). Personality and perceptual expertise: Individual differences in perceptual identification. *Psychological Science, 5,* 401–406.

Wilson, M., & Daly, M. (1992). Competitiveness, risk-taking, and violence: The young male syndrome. *Ethology and Sociobiology, 6,* 59–73.

Wrangham, R. (1987). The significance of African apes for reconstructing human social evolution. In W. G. Kinzey (Ed.), *The evolution of human behavior: Primate models* (pp. 51–71). Albany, NY: SUNY Press.

9

Automatic Goal Inference and Contagion

*On Pursuing Goals One Perceives in Other
People's Behavior*

Henk Aarts and Ran R. Hassin

INTRODUCTION

The well-being and survival of social animals depends, among other things,
on grasping – and sometimes adopting – other people's goals. For example, to better prepare oneself for the future, one may need to be able to
successfully predict others' behaviors. Predictions of this sort must take
into account others' goals, as goals are important determinants of human
behavior. Furthermore, in everyday social interactions, an understanding
of the goals motivating others allows one to entertain similar goals and
to try to attain them oneself – for the sake of personal as well as social
needs.

A necessary prerequisite for processes of this sort is an ability to encode
others' behaviors in terms of the goals they desire and aim to attain. Sometimes these goals are readily available to the perceiver, as they are commu-
nicated explicitly. More often than not, however, goals are not explicitly
conveyed, due either to resource constraints that limit communication or
because they are nonconsciously pursued (and hence are not consciously
available even to the person who pursues them). Similar constraints may
thwart the adoption of others' goals even when such an adoption is warranted. Thus, limited resources, or lack of awareness, may hinder one's
capacity to consider and adopt the goals of other people.

Our well-being, then, may depend on processes that allow us to infer goals and adopt them effortlessly and nonconsciously. In this chapter

Henk Aarts is at Utrecht University, Psychology Department, P.O. Box 80140, 3508 TC,
Utrecht, the Netherlands; Ran Hassin is at The Hebrew University, Psychology Department, Mount Scopus, Jerusalem, Israel 91905. Correspondence may be sent to either author
at h.aarts@fss.uu.nl or ran.hassin@huji.ac.il The preparation of this chapter was supported
by a VIDI grant from the Netherlands Organization for Scientific Research (452-02-047) to the
first author.

we develop a framework for the comprehension and examination of automatic goal inference and pursuit. The framework consists of two key components. First, we propose that people can automatically infer other people's goals from behavioral information. Second, we suggest that these inferred goals can be automatically adopted and pursued by the perceiver. This way, people take on the goals of each other and thus become more similar in what they desire and strive for – without much conscious thought or intent. Before we present this framework in more detail, however, we will briefly address some general issues pertaining to the conceptualization of goals.

THE CONCEPT OF GOALS

Goals are desired states, where states are broadly construed as outcomes or behaviors an individual knows how to produce. States are desired if attaining them yields pleasure, provides incentives, or satisfies needs (Bindra, 1974; Cabanac, 1971; Geen, 1995; Nuttin, 1980; Pervin, 1989). That human behavior is propelled by efforts to attain desired states is emphasized, to take just one example, in the expectancy-value approach to motivation (Atkinson, 1974; Dickinson & Balleine, 2002; Tolman, 1932). This view holds that goal-directed activity is expected to arise if a person attaches positive valence or affect to a state, and thus desires or is motivated to reach it. This hedonistic view of goals as desired states is reminiscent of Damasio's (1994) somatic marker hypothesis that stresses the (often preconscious) function of affect attached to a state in motivating action ("It will feel good; let's go for it"). Goals, then, are mentally represented desired states that guide organisms to select and persist in activities that are instrumental for goal achievement.

Most theories of goals emphasize the role of conscious choice in the adoption of goals and in guiding goal-directed behaviors (Ajzen, 1991; Bandura, 1986; Deci & Ryan, 1985; Harackiewicz, Durik, & Barron, this volume; Locke & Latham, 1990; for a review, see Gollwitzer & Moskowitz, 1996). Thus, for example, it is assumed that people consciously focus on goal-relevant information and reflect on pros and cons when they decide whether or not they want to pursue a certain goal. Furthermore, people ponder on the means that aid goal attainment and formulate plans of action to ensure that goal-directed behavior will occur. It is clear, then, that according to these views the mere activation of goals does not directly put the body in motion. Instead, goal adoption needs to be accompanied by a conscious decision, and goal pursuit needs some form of *expressed mandate* to be initiated. In short, it is conscious awareness that allows people to adopt goals and start acting on them.

Recently, this common view of goals as conscious regulators of behavior has been challenged. Goals, it is argued, can be automatically put in place by situational cues, and they can guide behavior without a person's awareness of them (Aarts & Dijksterhuis, 2000a; Bargh, 1997; Bargh & Gollwitzer, 1994; Bargh, Gollwitzer, LeeChai, Barndollar, & Trötschel, 2001). This view is supported by numerous laboratory and field studies in which we have shown that the activation of goals automatically causes attention to and processing of goal-relevant information. Furthermore, activation of goals allows individuals to adopt and act on goals without the need to consciously consider pros and cons or to consciously make a plan of action (Aarts & Dijksterhuis, 2000a, 2000b, 2003; Aarts, Dijksterhuis, & De Vries, 2001; Aarts, Verplanken, & Van Knippenberg, 1997, 1998; Custers & Aarts, 2003; Sheeran, Aarts, Custers, Webb, Cooke, & Rivis, in press). In other words, we have shown that human beings are capable of engaging in automatic goal pursuit.

Automatic Goal Pursuit

Central to the idea of automatic goal pursuit is the assumption that goals are mentally represented in hierarchically ordered knowledge structures, along with other schema-relevant materials (Aarts & Dijksterhuis, 2000a; Bargh & Gollwitzer, 1994; Kruglanski et al., 2002). These representations include the context, the goal, and possible actions and means that may aid goal pursuit.

Given these mental representations, there are two steps to the process by which automatic goal pursuit emerges. First, recurrent activation of a certain goal A, upon perception of a certain (social) situation, strengthens the link between the situation and the goal. Second, repeated execution of actions $a_1 \ldots a_n$, when attempting to achieve goal A, strengthens the goal–action association and thus facilitates the effectuation of actions on goal activation. Because the representations of the situation, goal, and respective goal-directed actions are interconnected, perception of the situation may then directly and automatically activate the representation of the related goal and actions. This activation may lead individuals to engage in goal-directed behavior – without awareness of that goal.

Recent empirical work used conceptual priming procedures to test whether goals can be pursued automatically (e.g., Bargh et al., 2001; Chartrand & Bargh, 1996; Liberman & Förster, this volume). This research has established that the activation of goals (e.g., high performance) via exposure to words that are closely related to them (e.g., *succeed*, *strive*), exerts an unconscious influence on action in a subsequent goal-relevant situation, such as a word puzzle task. (Recently it has been shown that goals may also be primed by exposure to names of significant others; Fitzsimons & Bargh, 2003; Shah, 2003). Moreover, it has been demonstrated that primed goals persist over time and cause resumption of goal-related activities after task interruption, indicating that it is indeed a desired state that is primed.

In the work we report here, we extend the investigation of automatic goal pursuit in two major ways. First, we show that perceivers can automatically encode behaviors of others in terms of the goals that they serve. Second, we show that goal-driven behaviors of one actor may make another actor pursue that same goal. Thus, goals do not need to be directly primed via related concepts (or names) in order to be automatically pursued; the mere perception of others' behavior suffices.

In the next section, we describe work on automatic causal (social) inferences in general. Then we present novel evidence from our labs suggesting that goals can be automatically inferred upon observing another's behavior. In the following section, we describe new research that tested whether people can automatically adopt and pursue inferred goals, and we close the chapter with a general conclusion.

AUTOMATIC CAUSAL INFERENCES

Originally, automatic processes were thought of as unintentional, nonconscious, ballistic, and effortless. This monolithic approach, however, gave way to a more flexible view, according to which these characteristics do not always co-occur, and some automatic processes may exhibit only a subset of them (see, e.g., Bargh, 1994; Gilbert, 1989). A large body of social psychological research on the automaticity of inferences has focused on a specific collection of these features, namely, spontaneity (e.g., Winter & Uleman, 1984). An inference is said to be spontaneous if (a) it does not require explicit instructions, (b) people are usually unaware of their intentions to make it, and (c) people are usually unaware of the inference itself. Basically this means that inferences can occur without conscious intent (cf. Uleman, Newman, & Moskowitz, 1996).

The social psychological work on spontaneous inferences has focused on examining the automaticity of trait inferences. In almost two decades of research, Uleman and his colleagues (e.g., Todorov & Uleman, 2002; Uleman et al., 1996; Winter & Uleman, 1984) have taught us a lot about the automaticity of trait inferences. For example, upon reading the sentence "Peter interrupted the invited guest speaker about every 30 seconds," readers may spontaneously infer the trait *rude*. Trait inferences do not require conscious intent. They occur when participants are instructed to memorize sentences, as well as when they are just asked to familiarize themselves with them or judge how interesting they are.

Recently, it has been suggested that various types of spontaneous inferences described in the literature may be included under the same conceptual umbrella, that of automatic causal inferences (the ACI framework; Hassin, Bargh, & Uleman, 2002; see also Hassin, Aarts, & Ferguson, under review). That is, spontaneous inferences of traits (Winter & Uleman, 1984) and predictable events (Mckoon & Ratcliff, 1986) can be conceived of as instances of causal inferences – the former in terms of possible *reasons* for behavior and the latter in terms of its expected *results*.

An interesting implication of the ACI framework suggested by Hassin and colleagues is that people should be able to infer automatically other social categories that serve a prominent role in the causal chain of behaviors.[1] One such category is goals: the representations of desired states that we expect to attain by choosing certain actions over others. Unlike traits, which are relatively fixed mental characteristics, goals are more flexible and context-dependent. Thus, goals may help us understand why a person performs a variety of behaviors that seem inexplicable in terms of traits (e.g., when we see someone racing on a bicycle through the streets of Amsterdam, it is usually not because she is athletic). In addition, thinking about behaviors in terms of the goals they serve allows an appreciation of how the same behavior (e.g., a student who bicycles to a college campus), conducted in different contexts (e.g., in the morning or in the evening), may serve extremely divergent objectives (e.g., to attend mathematics or aerobics classes).

Goals range from mundane desired states such as drinking a glass of beer or riding a bicycle, through medium-level goals such as going to a bar or attending lectures, to more life-span goals such a becoming a good scientist. Knowing other people's goals at each of these levels provides information on the possible reasons and expected results of their observable actions. Inferring these goals, then, is important for understanding the people we interact with and the successful pursuit of our own goals (Byrne & Russon, 1998; Tomasello, Kruger, & Ratner, 1993).

AUTOMATIC GOAL INFERENCES

The idea that behaviors may be perceived in terms of goals has fascinated researchers in several areas in psychology. Classic work on causal perception in adults, as well as more recent research on infants and monkeys, suggests that primates, humans included, can encode animated behavior and self-propelled motion of objects in terms of goals (Gergely, Nadasdy, Csibra, & Biro, 1995; Hauser, 1999; Heider, 1958; Heider & Simmel, 1944; Michotte, 1963; Premack, 1990; Uller & Nichols, 2000). For example, Heider and Simmel (1944) showed that adults attribute causal mental properties (such as goals) to geometric shapes as long as they move in a particular interactive "social" way. Most research in this area seems to assume that goal

[1] Our focus here is not on the actual causal role but on the perceived one. That is, what people perceive – with or without conscious intent – as a potential cause is of more importance to our discussion than whether this event actually plays a causal role.

attributions are the *natural default* of our cognitive system. Whether these attributions can occur automatically, however, is an empirical question that has heretofore not been explicitly addressed.

Research on goal-based explanations of actions further shows that people perceive others' behaviors as goal-directed and understand the underlying goals that are implied by actions (see McClure, 2002, for a review). A commonly used paradigm in this research is to present participants with everyday scripted behaviors and ask them to rate how likely certain goals are to explain the described actions. For example, it has been demonstrated that actions that are not too extreme or too difficult (e.g., Wolfgang enters the kitchen to see how Maggie is doing) are readily explained in terms of goals (e.g., he wants to eat), rather than other social categories that may serve as explanatory causes of the actions, such as ability or traits (e.g., curious). It should be noted, though, that participants in these kinds of studies are explicitly asked to provide goal ratings, and hence their inferences are intentional. Evidence gathered in these paradigms is thus not conclusive with regard to the automaticity of goal inferences upon ·exposure to behavior.

In a recent set of studies, we (Hassin et al., under review) systematically examined whether people automatically infer the goals that motivate other persons' everyday actions. In a first study, we employed a surprise cued-recall paradigm to demonstrate the occurrence of automatic goal inferences. Participants read short sentences under instructions to rate "how interesting they are." These pilot-tested sentences described either a behavior performed to attain a certain goal (e.g., "The student is riding his bicycle to the campus as fast as he can" implies the goal of attending a lecture) or a similar behavior that did not imply this goal (e.g., "The student is riding his bicycle away from the campus as fast as he can"). The behaviors described in the goal-implying and control sentences were as similar as possible, and so were the words used in both kinds of sentences. After reading the behavioral information, participants engaged in a filler task for 5 minutes. The purpose of the filler task was to remove all contents of the sentences from working memory. Upon finishing the filler task, they were presented with a surprise cued-recall task for the sentences presented in the first part. The cues were either the implied goals (goal-cue condition) or a word taken from the sentences (repetition condition). A thorough debriefing revealed that only a couple of participants intentionally inferred goals or were aware of inferring them, and these participants were discarded from the analysis. Results showed that goal cues helped in retrieving goal-implying sentences more than control sentences, even though the two shared all the words that were semantically related to the cue. Importantly, no such effects were found with repetition cues. These results suggest, then, that people may nonconsciously infer other people's goals from descriptions of behaviors.

It has been argued that the relative benefit created by the cues in surprise cued-recall paradigms may result from retrieval processes and not from inferences at encoding (e.g., McKoon & Ratcliff, 1986). One way to deal with this critique is to examine whether goal inferences occur online at encoding. Hassin et al. (under review) took on this challenge and designed a second study in which they used a probe recognition task to measure online inferences of goals. In this task, devised after Mckoon and Ratcliff (1986), participants read short sentences, after which they saw a probe word. The time allotted for reading each sentence was very short (2.5 s), and the probe word appeared shortly thereafter. Participants' task was to decide whether the word had appeared in the previous sentence or not. As in the previous study, there were two kinds of sentences: goal-implying sentences and control sentences that used similar behaviors and wordings. The probe word, in both cases, was the goal that was implied in the goal-implying sentence. To disguise the critical trials, the goal-implying and control trials (i.e., sentence and corresponding probe word) were embedded in a large number of fillers. If goals are automatically encoded, we hypothesized, then their accessibility should increase after reading goal-implying sentences, thus rendering the judgment task more difficult. Hence, performance after goal implying sentences should be worse than performance after control sentences. This was exactly what we found: Responses to the probe (goal) words were slower when preceded by the goal-implying sentences than when preceded by the control sentences.

In a third study, Hassin et al. (under review) tried to raise the bar for automatic goal inferences at encoding by using a lexical decision paradigm. The structure of this study, and its target sentences, were identical to those in the probe recognition study. Instead of judging whether a test word had appeared in a previous sentence, however, participants in this study were asked to make a lexical decision: They were asked to decide whether a string of letters that appeared after a sentence comprised an actual word. Participants were instructed merely to read the sentence; the critical trials were embedded in a large number of fillers. Using this lexical decision task obscured even further the relation between the experimental sentences and the probes that followed them. (Indeed, in a thorough debriefing, participants indicated no intention to infer goals or awareness of any such inferences; cf. Zarate, Uleman, & Voils, 2001.) Still, if goals are automatically encoded, then the accessibility of the goal representation should increase after reading goal-implying sentences, thus speeding up the lexical decision. This was indeed the case: Responses to the test (goal) words were faster when preceded by the goal-implying sentences than when preceded by the control sentences. Errors were rare and were evenly distributed across conditions.

Taken together, our studies indicate that goals that motivate others' actions are inferred very rapidly and without conscious intent. This strongly supports the contention for automatic goal inferences upon perceiving others' behavior.

GOAL CONTAGION: FROM AUTOMATIC GOAL INFERENCES TO AUTOMATIC GOAL PURSUIT

Earlier we proposed that behaviors of others may activate goals, as well as means appropriate for their pursuit, in one's own mind, and that these activated mental representations may lead to goal-directed behavior. The interconnected nature of goals and means should allow this process to go on automatically. This chain of events, we argued, need not be consciously controlled. Thus, we suggest that automatic processes that begin with the perception of another's behavior may lead to what we call *goal contagion* – the automatic adoption of others' goals.

Recent advances in developmental psychology provide initial support for our thesis (e.g., Gattis, Bekkering, & Wohlschaleger, 2002; Meltzoff, 1995). For instance, in a series of studies on the adoption of simple goal-directed action patterns, Meltzoff examined whether preverbal infants would reenact what an adult actually did or what she tried to do. So, for example, an adult demonstrated an act with a test object (e.g., she tried to put a ring over a stick but never actually succeeded), and the 18-month-old participants were then given these objects. The toddlers were as likely to complete the target action after seeing the adult trying as they were after seeing a full demonstration that included the end state itself. In other words, infants in the goal group directly produced the target action, just like those who observed the full target action. These adoption effects of simple target actions are suggestive in regard to goal contagion: The babies seemed to handle the objects in a way that adults tried to do.

Circumstantial evidence supporting the suggestion that social goals that one is currently perceiving in another person may be taken on was obtained by Chen, Schechter, and Chaiken (1996). In their research program on heuristic and systematic processing, Chaiken and colleagues examined whether goals that result from thinking about concrete behaviors can alter the expression of attitudes. Participants in their study engaged, for 12 min, in imagining themselves as being in a certain situation. In one condition, the scenarios described behaviors related to accuracy goals (e.g., a reporter seeking the objective facts about a certain issue), whereas behaviors in the other condition were associated with the goal of providing a favorable impression of oneself (e.g., being on a blind date with a close friend's cousin). Next, participants were asked to engage in a discussion of a particular issue with another person. As predicted, participants who had been exposed to ingratiation goal scenarios were more likely to express attitudes that were evaluatively consistent with the partner's opinion than were those exposed to the impression goal scenarios. Suspicion probes showed that participants were not aware of these effects.

Although indicative, these results, like those of the developmental studies alluded to earlier, are not conclusive in regard to goal contagion. They provide no unequivocal evidence supporting the contention that the effects were produced by activated goals – that is, desired states. Furthermore, given the explicit nature of the perspective-taking instructions, as well as the relatively large amount of time devoted to imagining oneself in another's position, it is unclear whether these goal contagion effects occur on the mere exposure to behavioral information or whether they require a much more effortful process (see also Albrecht, O'Brien, Mason, & Myers, 1995).

Aarts and his colleagues (Aarts, Gollwitzer, & Hassin, in press; Aarts, Hassin, & Golwitzer, in prep.) conducted a series of studies to examine goal contagion directly.[2] In a first study, they investigated the effect of an implied money-making goal on subsequent goal-directed activity. In this study, Aarts et al. used a short behavioral script in which a student plans a vacation with friends. After planning the vacation the student either (a) goes to a farm to work as an assistant for a month (money-goal condition) or (b) goes to a community center to do volunteer work for a month (control condition). These scripts were briefly (30 s) presented on a computer screen just long enough for participants to read it. Participants were then instructed that the study was almost completed but that they had to perform another short mouse-click task. Crucially, participants were told that if enough time was left at the end of the session, they would be able to engage in a task in which they could earn money. Participants' quickness in removing this message from the computer screen served as a measure of goal-directed activity: The faster they erased the message, the stronger was their motivation to get to the last part of the session, where they could earn money.

Results showed that participants who were exposed to the goal-implying behavior were faster than those in the control condition. However, these behavioral differences emerged only when participants had a high need or desire to earn additional income (students who often lack income to run their daily lives). This latter effect thus strongly suggests that it is indeed goals that were primed (cf. Spencer and colleagues' work in this volume on the idea that goal-directed activity can be primed only if the goal is present as a desire state). Importantly, thorough debriefing indicated that participants were unaware of these effects; thus goal contagion effects seem to occur without conscious intent.

---

[2] In the experiments reported here, we do not examine whether our participants are able to actually reach the inferred goal in our lab. We wish only to demonstrate that priming of the implied goal is capable of automatically activating ways of behaving that are known to be instrumental in attaining the goal, thereby revealing goal contagion.

Another experiment replicated these effects in a different domain: that of seeking intimate (casual) relationships. Subjects (heterosexual men) in all conditions read a story about a man who meets a former female friend at a bar and spends a few hours with her. In the intimate goal-implying condition – but not in the control condition – the man asks the woman whether he can come up to her apartment.[3]

After having been exposed to the actor's behaviors, participants learned that the study was almost completed. This time, however, a message on the screen let them know that they would participate in a short interview with a (unknown) female undergraduate student if there was sufficient time left after the filler task. Again, we measured the time it took participants to erase this message from the screen and to move to the goal-relevant task (i.e., meeting the female student). Results showed that participants in the intimacy goal condition reacted faster than control participants. As in the previous study, debriefing revealed that none of the participants were aware of these behavioral effects.

It could be argued that the results of these studies demonstrate an automatic approach response to goal-relevant stimuli (e.g., money, women). According to the present perspective on automatic goal pursuit, however, primed goals do not only render goal-relevant stimuli more approachable or attractive; they also activate means appropriate for their pursuit. Hence, stronger evidence for goal contagion would consist of increased goal-relevant activity as a result of goal contagion.

In order to test this prediction, male participants were exposed to the script used in the previous study. To assess the effects on subsequent goal-directed activity, they were requested to provide feedback on a task they had performed earlier. In order to examine whether primed goals elicit goal-directed activity only when the target stimulus is applicable or relevant to the goal (Aarts et al., 2001; Hardin & Rothman, 1997; Higgins, 1996), participants were told that the task was developed by either a female or a male student and were then asked to help the experimenter by providing feedback. The amount of help was indexed as the number of words and seconds devoted by participants to feedback. Previous findings show that heterosexual men know that offering help is instrumental in attaining (casual) intimate relationships with women and that men behave accordingly (Buss, 1988; Canary & Emmers-Sommer, 1997; Downey & Damhave, 1991). Thus, goal contagion should lead participants to be more helpful. The results replicated and extended those of the previous studies. Male participants exerted more effort in helping a woman in the goal contagion

---

[3] Additional research, using an explicit judgment task and the probe recognition task to establish intentional and automatic goal inferences, showed that male students encode this behavior in terms of the goal of seeking casual intimacy (Aarts et al., in press, Studies 2 and 5; see also Clark & Hatfield, 1989).

condition than in the control condition. These behavioral changes did not occur if participants were asked to provide feedback to a male student, indicating the applicability or relevance of the target stimulus to the intimate goal (cf. Neuberg, Kenrick, Maner, & Schaller, this volume).

An alternative explanation of these results may suggest that the intimate goal pursuit script activated thoughts about how one should "be nice to women." These thoughts may have caused participants to construe the experimental situation in these terms and to behave accordingly. If, indeed, the contagion effects described were due to differential construal they should be rather short-lived, as effects of mere cognitive activation on subsequent judgment and behavior have been shown to decline rapidly (Higgins, 1996; see also Wilson & Capitman, 1982). Goals, in contrast, have been shown to possess a large and constant amount of activation that do not need rehearsal to sustain accessibility. That is, the mental representation of goal-related material remains accessible until the goal is completed or expressed (Anderson, 1983; Bargh et al., 2001; Goschke & Kuhl; 1993; Marsh, Hicks, & Bink, 1998; see also Liberman & Förster, this volume). Accordingly, the previous findings of the emergence of goal contagion would be even further bolstered if one could establish this important property of goals.

To determine this, Aarts et al. (in press, Study 3) asked another group of male participants to read the intimacy-goal behavioral script and to provide feedback about an earlier-performed task designed by a female undergraduate. However, in addition to participants for whom immediate measurement of the dependent variable – that is, help – was performed, other participants engaged in a 5-min filler task that was unrelated to the intimacy goal. If the previous effects on helping behavior are caused by differences in construal, then, according to the line of argument presented earlier, contagion effects should decrease after a delay. If the perception of the behaviors indeed activated the respective goal, however, the time at which the effects are measured is expected to have no effect. It was indeed the latter pattern that fitted the data. Male participants put more effort into helping a female experimenter irrespective of the time at which help was requested. These observations indicate that the effect persisted over time, and thus strongly support our contention that goal contagion effects result from activation of mental representations of goals. Further experiments revealed that these effects are not conditional on whether one is effortfully imagining oneself in another's position, thus suggesting that goal contagion is not an effortful process (Aarts et al., in press, Study 4).

CONCLUSION

Social animals are equipped with a highly sophisticated perceptual-cognitive system that renders others' behaviors very informative. Upon observing others' movements, gestures, ways of talking, and utilization of objects, we spontaneously perceive or infer a variety of causes that may account for these behaviors. These causal inferences may directly affect our own behaviors.

In this chapter we proposed and demonstrated that individuals are capable of automatically inferring goals from others' behaviors, and that these inferred goals may be automatically adopted by the perceiver if they are represented as desired states. Thus, our own goal pursuit – using one's knowledge and skills to reach desired states – can result directly from perceiving another's goal pursuit, a phenomenon we termed goal contagion. Goal contagion should be conceived of as an event that occurs when people encode the behavior of others in terms of states they know how to produce *and* desire to attain. Human motivated behavior, then, can emanate from the mere perception of other people's actions without much conscious thought or intent.

References

Aarts, H., & Dijksterhuis, A. (2000a). Habits as knowledge structures: Automaticity in goal-directed behavior. *Journal of Personality and Social Psychology, 78*, 53–63.

Aarts, H., & Dijksterhuis, A. (2000b). On the automatic activation of goal-directed behavior: The case of travel habit. *Journal of Environmental Psychology, 20*, 75–82.

Aarts, H., & Dijksterhuis, A. (2003). The silence of the library: Environment, situational norm and social behavior. *Journal of Personality and Social Psychology, 84*, 18–28.

Aarts, H., Dijksterhuis, A., & De Vries, P. (2001). The psychology of drinking: Being thirsty and perceptually ready. *British Journal of Psychology, 92*, 631–642.

Aarts, H., Gollwitzer, P. M., & Hassin, R. R. (in press). *Goal contagion: perceiving is for pursuing. Journal of Personality and Social Psychology.*

Aarts, H., Hassin, R. R., & Gollwitzer, P. M. (in preparation). *Being keen on implied goals: Automatic goal pursuit upon perceiving another person's behavior.* Manuscript.

Aarts, H., Verplanken, B., & Van Knippenberg, A. (1997). Habit and information use in travel mode choices. *Acta Psychologica, 96*, 1–14.

Aarts, H., Verplanken, B., & Van Knippenberg, A. (1998). Predicting behavior from actions in the past: Repeated decision making or a matter of habit? *Journal of Applied Social Psychology, 28*, 1356–1375.

Ajzen, I. (1991). The theory of planned behavior. *Organizational Behavior and Human Decision Processes, 50*, 179–211.

Albrecht, J. E., O'Brien, E. J., Mason, R. A., & Myers, J. L. (1995). The role of perspective in the accessibility of goals during reading. *Journal of Experimental Psychology: Learning, Memory, and Cognition, 21*, 364–372.

Anderson, J. R. (1983). *On the architecture of cognition.* Cambridge, MA: Harvard University Press.

Atkinson, J. W. (1974). Strength of motivation and efficiency of performance. In J. W. Atkinson & J. O. Raynor (Eds.), *Motivation and achievement* (pp. 193–218). Washington, DC: Winston.

Bandura, A. (1986). *Social foundations of thought and action: A social-cognitive theory.* Englewood Cliffs, NJ: Prentice-Hall.

Bargh, J. A. (1994). The four horsemen of automaticity: Awareness, intention, efficiency and control in social cognition. In R. S Wyer, Jr., and T. K. Srull (Eds.), *Handbook of social cognition* (2nd ed., pp. 1–40). Hillsdale, NJ: Erlbaum.

Bargh, J. A. (1997). The automaticity of everyday life. In R. S. Wyer (Ed.), *Advances in social cognition* (Vol. 10, pp. 1–61). Mahwah, NJ: Erlbaum.

Bargh, J. A., & Gollwitzer, P. M. (1994). Environmental control of goal-directed action: Automatic and strategic contingencies between situations and behavior. *Nebraska Symposium on Motivation, 41,* 71–124.

Bargh, J. A., Gollwitzer, P. M., LeeChai, A., Barndollar, K., & Trötschel, R. (2001). The automated will: Nonconscious activation and pursuit of behavioral goals. *Journal of Personality and Social Psychology, 81,* 1014–1027.

Bindra, D. (1974). Motivational view of learning, performance, and behavior modification. *Psychological Review, 81,* 199–213.

Buss, D. M. (1988). The evolution of human intra sexual competition: Tactics of mate attraction. *Journal of Personality and Social Psychology, 54,* 616–628.

Byrne, R. W., & Russon, A. E. (1998). Learning by imitation: A hierarchical approach. *Behavioral and Brain Science, 21,* 667–721.

Cabanac, M. (1971). Physiological role of pleasure. *Science, 173,* 1103–1107.

Canary, D. J., & Emmers-Sommer, T. M. (1997). *Sex and gender differences in personal relationships.* New York: Guilford Press.

Chartrand, T. L., & Bargh, J. A. (1996). Automatic activation of impression formation and memorization goals. Nonconscious goal priming reproduces effects of explicit task instructions. *Journal of Personality and Social Psychology, 71,* 464–478.

Chen, S., Schechter, D., & Chaiken, S. (1996). Getting at the truth or getting along: Accuracy- versus impression-motivated heuristic and systematic processing. *Journal of Personality and Social Psychology, 71,* 262–275.

Custers, R., & Aarts, H. (2003). On the role of processing goals in evaluative judgments of virtual environments: Effects on memory-judgment relations. *Journal of Environmental Psychology, 23,* 189–299.

Damasio, A. R. (1994). *Descartes' error: Emotion, reason and the human brain.* New York: Avon Books.

Deci, E. L., & Ryan, R. M. (1985). *Intrinsic motivation and self-determination in human behavior.* New York: Plenum Press.

Dickinson, A., & Balleine, B. (2002). The role of learning in the operation of motivational systems. In H. Pashler & R. Gallistel (Eds.), *Steven's handbook of experimental psychology: Vol. 3: Learning, motivation, and emotion* (pp. 497–533). New York: J. Wiley.

Downey, J. L., & Damhave, K. W. (1991). The effects of place, type of comment, and effort expanded on the perception of flirtation. *Journal of Social Behavior and Personality, 6,* 35–43.

Fitzsimons, G. M., & Bargh, J. A. (2003). Thinking of you: Pursuit of interpersonal goals associated with relational partners. *Journal of Personality and Social Psychology, 84,* 148–164.

Gattis, M., Bekkering, H., & Wohlschaleger, A. (2002). Goal-directed imitation. In A. Meltzoff & W. Prinz (Eds.), *The imitative mind: Development, evolution, and brain bases* (pp. 183–205). Berlin: Springer-Verlag.

Geen, R. G. (1995). *Human motivation: A social psychological approach*. Pacific Grove, CA: Brooks/Cole.

Gergely, G., Nadasdy, Z., Csibra, G., & Biro, S. (1995). Taking the intentional stance at 12 months of age. *Cognition, 56*, 165–193.

Gilbert, D. T. (1989). Thinking lightly about others: Automatic components of the social inference process. In J. S. Uleman & J. A. Bargh (Eds.), *Unintended thought* (pp. 189–211). New York: Guilford Press.

Gollwitzer, P. M., & Moskowitz, G. B. (1996). Goal effects on action and cognition. In E. T. Higgins & A. W. Kruglanski (Eds.), *Social psychology: Handbook of basic principles* (pp. 241–274). New York: Guilford Press.

Goschke, T., & Kuhl, J. (1993). Representation of intentions: Persisting activation in memory. *Journal of Experimental Psychology: Learning, Memory, and Cognition, 19*, 1211–1226.

Hardin, C. D., & Rothman, A. J. (1997). Rendering accessible information relevant: The applicability of everyday life. In R. S. Wyer (Ed.), *Advances in social cognition* (Vol. 10, pp. 143–156). Mahwah, NJ: Erlbaum.

Hassin, R. R., Aarts, H., & Ferguson, M. (under review). *Automatic causal inferences: The case of goals*. Manuscript.

Hassin, R., Bargh, J. A., & Uleman, J. S. (2002). Spontaneous causal inferences. *Journal of Experimental Social Psychology, 38*, 515–522.

Hauser, M. D. (1999). Primate representations and expectations: Mental tools for navigating in a social world. In P. D. Zelazo, J. W. Astington, & D. R. Olson (Eds.), *Developing theories of intention: Social understanding and self-control* (pp. 169–194). Mahwah, NJ: Erlbaum.

Heider, F. (1958). *The psychology of interpersonal relations*. New York: Wiley.

Heider, F., & Simmel, M. (1944). An experimental study of apparent behavior. *American Journal of Psychology, 57*, 243–259.

Higgins, E. T. (1996). Knowledge activation: Accessibility, applicability, and salience. In E. T. Higgins & A. W. Kruglanski (Eds.), *Social psychology; Handbook of basic principles* (pp. 133–168). New York: Guilford Press.

Kruglanski, A. W., Shah, J. Y., Fishbach, A., Friedman, R., Chun, W. Y., & Sleeth-Keppler, D. (2002). A theory of goal systems. In M. Zanna (Ed.), *Advances in experimental social psychology* (pp. 331–378). San Diego, CA: Academic Press.

Locke, E. A., & Latham, G. P. (1990). *A theory of goal-setting and task performance*. Englewood Cliffs, NJ: Prentice-Hall.

Marsh, R. L., Hicks, J. L., & Bink, M. L. (1998). Activation of completed, uncompleted and partially completed intentions. *Journal of Experimental Psychology: Learning, Memory, and Cognition, 24*, 350–361.

McClure, J. L. (2002). Goal-based explanations of actions and outcomes. *European Review of Social Psychology, 12*, 201–236.

McKoon, G., & Ratcliff, R. (1986). Inferences about predictable events. *Journal of Experimental Psychology: Learning, Memory and Cognition, 12*, 82–91.

Meltzoff, A. N. (1995). Understanding the intentions of others: Re-enactment of intended acts by 18-month-old children. *Developmental Psychology, 31*, 838–850.

Michotte, A. (1963). *The perception of causality* (T. R. Miles & E. Miles, Trans.). New York: Basic Books.

Nuttin, J. (1980). *Motivation, planning, and action*. Leuven, Belgium: Leuven University Press.

Pervin, L. A. (1989). *Goal concepts in personality and social psychology*. Hillsdale, NJ: Erlbaum.

Premack, D. (1990). The infant's theory of self-propelled objects. *Cognition, 36*, 1–16.

Shah, J. Y. (2003). Automatic for the people: How representations of significant others implicitly affect goal pursuit, *Journal of Personality and Social Psychology, 84*, 661–681.

Sheeran, P., Aarts, H., Custers, R., Webb, T. L., Cooke, R., & Rivis, A. J. (in press). *The goal-dependent automaticity of drinking habits. British Journal of Social Psychology.*

Todorov, A., & Uleman, J. S. (2002). Spontaneous trait inferences are bound to actors' faces: Evidence from a false recognition paradigm. *Journal of Personality and Social Psychology, 83*, 1051–1065.

Tolman, E. C. (1932). *Purposive behavior in animals and men*. New York: Appleton-Century-Crofts.

Tomasello, M., Kruger, A. C., & Ratner, H. H. (1993). Cultural learning. *Behavioral and Brain Sciences, 16*, 495–552.

Uleman, J. S., Newman, L. S., & Moskowitz, G. B. (1996). People as flexible interpreters: Evidence from spontaneous trait inferences. In M. P. Zanna (Ed.), *Advances in experimental social psychology* (Vol. 28, pp. 211–279). San Diego: Academic Press.

Uller, C., & Nichols, S. (2000). Goal attribution in chimpanzees. *Cognition, 76*, 27–34.

Wilson, T. D., & Capitman, J. A. (1982). Effects of script availability on social behavior. *Personality and Social Psychology Bulletin, 8*, 11–19.

Winter, L., & Uleman, J. S. (1984). When are social judgments made? Evidence from the spontaneousness of trait inferences. *Journal of Personality and Social Psychology, 47*, 237–252.

Zarate, M. A., Uleman, J. S., & Voils, C. I. (2001). Effects of culture and processing goals on the activation and binding of trait concepts. *Social Cognition, 19*, 295–323.

10

The Interaction Between Affect and Motivation in Social Judgments and Behavior

Joseph P. Forgas and Simon M. Laham

INTRODUCTION

The influence of affective states on motivated action has long been supported by anecdotal evidence as well as in literature. A well-known short story on chess by Thomas Mann describes how upbeat or downbeat background music can produce sudden shifts in mood, motivating chess players to shift their strategies from aggressive to defensive and back again in line with the changing affective tone of the melody. Just as in chess, social interaction demands complex and elaborate planning, as actors need to interpret ambiguous social situations and plan their interpersonal strategies accordingly (Forgas, 1998a). There is convergent recent evidence from evolutionary social psychology, neuropsychology, and psychophysiology supporting the view that affect is an essential component of motivated social thinking and behavior (Adolphs & Damasio, 2001; Blascovich & Mendes, 2000; Haselton & Buss, 2003).

This chapter will review recent empirical evidence, including several studies from our laboratory, showing that fleeting, superficial mood states can have highly predictable and significant motivational influences on how people behave in strategic social situations. Generally, participants in a good mood behave in a much more confident and even assertive way, while participants in a bad mood act in a pessimistic and cautious manner (Forgas, 1999a, 1999b, 2002). The chapter will also consider the psychological mechanisms that allow mild mood states to influence strategic social behaviors. Affective states have a particularly strong influence on thoughts and behaviors when social actors use open and elaborate cognitive processing when considering strategic options in social situations. As

This work was supported by the Australian Research Council and by the Alexander von Humboldt Foundation. Please address all correspondence in connection with this chapter to Joseph P. Forgas at the School of Psychology, University of New South Wales, Sydney 2052, Australia; e-mail: jp.forgas@unsw.edu.au

168

people search constructively for the next strategic move, mood-induced differences in the thoughts and associations they rely on inevitably influence their motivational objectives, the plans they make, and the behaviors they perform (Bower & Forgas, 2001; Forgas, 1998a–1998c, 1999a, 1999b). Based on recent theories and research, this chapter will review empirical evidence demonstrating such affective influences on goal-oriented behavior and will discuss how and why these effects occur.

The chapter will begin with a brief review of some key theoretical issues. Next, we will discuss recent evidence for affective influences on motivation, including a number of experiments carried out in our laboratory. Although affective states can often influence motivated behaviors, the reverse is also frequently the case: Motivational states can influence, magnify, or reduce the influence of affective states on thinking and action (Forgas, 1991). Importantly, motivational processes seem to play a role in the management and maintenance of our affective states (Erber & Erber, 2001; Forgas & Ciarrochi, 2002). The final section of the chapter will review evidence of such motivated strategies in affect control and affect management.

Some Theoretical Questions

Affect and Goals. The notions of goals and of purposive goal pursuit are central to many theories of social motivation (see Harackiewicz, Durick & Barron, Liberman and Förster, this volume, for example). However, the role of affective states in the generation of goals has not received much attention (see Neuberg et al., Weiss et al., this volume, for exceptions). Theories such as Carver and Scheier's (1998) model suggest that affect functions merely as a feedback signal indicating the presence or absence of progress toward goal attainment. In other words, feelings arise as a result of actors monitoring discrepancies between their goals and actual states. In this theory, affect is considered merely to regulate the *intensity* of motivation, with no direct influence on the *content and direction* of goal setting. This appears to be a restrictive conceptualization of the role of affect in motivated action. We shall review empirical evidence suggesting that affective states also have a significant directional function, exerting a marked influence on the motivations that guide people's thoughts, judgments, and strategic social behaviors.

The Links Between Affect, Cognition, and Motivation. It is now also clear that many affective states arise prior to elaborate cognitive processing, and that such *precognitive* affective reactions may in turn function as directional input to motivated behavior (Blascovich & Tomaka, 1996; Forgas, 1995; Zajonc, 1980, 2000). Some influential theorists have even argued that affect represents a distinct, separate mental faculty that operates independently of cognition, serving as input to cognitive and behavioral processes

(Clore, Schwarz, & Conway, 1994; Damasio, 1994; De Sousa, 1987). This chapter, however, emphasizes the mediating role of cognition in the affect–motivation relationship. Affect and cognition represent closely related and interacting systems allowing affective states to infuse and inform people's thoughts and in turn influence subsequent motivated behavior. Indeed, the same affective state can have a congruent, incongruent, or no effect on subsequent motivated action, depending on subtle shifts in people's preferred information processing strategies (Berkowitz, Jaffee, Jo, & Troccoli, 2000; Forgas, 1991, 1995; Sedikides, 1994).

Affect, Mood, and Emotion. There is still little general agreement in the literature as to how best to define terms such as *affect, feelings, emotions,* or *mood* (Fiedler & Forgas, 1988; Forgas, 1992, 1995, 2002) and how to distinguish their motivational consequences. We have argued elsewhere that affect may be used as a generic label to refer to both moods and emotions. Moods, in turn, could be described as "low-intensity, diffuse and relatively enduring affective states without a salient antecedent cause and therefore little cognitive content (e.g., feeling good or feeling bad)," whereas emotions "are more intense, short-lived and usually have a definite cause and clear cognitive content" (e.g., anger or fear) (Forgas, 1992, p. 230). Such a distinction may be highly relevant to understanding the motivational functions of affect. Not surprisingly, much research has shown the motivational consequences of specific emotions in social action. Anger, shame, guilt, and embarrassment are all emotions with strong motivational implications (Parrott, 2001). There is also considerable research, however, suggesting that subtle, nonspecific moods may often have a potentially more enduring, subtle, and insidious motivational influence on social cognition and social behaviors than distinct and intense emotions (Fiedler, 1991; Forgas, 1992a, 1995, 2002; Sedikides, 1992a, 1995). Accordingly, our primary concern here is the motivational effects of low-intensity moods on social behaviors.

Affect Infusion

Experiences of mildly positive or negative affect accompany us throughout our daily lives, and such transient moods do seem to have a significant influence on the content of cognition and behavior (*what* people think and do), as well as on the processes of thought and behavior production (*how* people think and act) (Bower, 1981, 1991; Forgas, 1995, 1998a, 1998b, 1999a, 1999b; Forgas & Fiedler, 1996; Sedikides, 1992a, 1995). Affect, once elicited, can have a dynamic influence on how social information is selected, interpreted, processed, and remembered (Forgas, 2001a). Such *affect infusion* effects were initially explained in terms of either psychodynamic (e.g., Feshbach & Singer, 1957) or associationist principles (Byrne & Clore, 1970; Clore & Byrne, 1974). Psychoanalytic theories assumed that affect has a dynamic, invasive quality and can "take over" judgments unless adequate psychological resources are deployed to control these impulses. Conditioning and associationist theories suggested that affective reactions are the products of a cumulative pattern of associations. Byrne and Clore (1970) and Clore and Byrne (1974) argued that affective states triggered by unrelated events can become *attached* to previously neutral stimuli and motivate people's responses to them. For example, an aversive environment can produce a negative affective reaction (and related motivational consequences) and influence reactions to a previously neutral stimulus, such as a person encountered in that setting (Clore & Byrne, 1974). While both psychodynamic and conditioning accounts did address the relationship between affect and social motivation, they ignored the important mediating role of cognition.

Unlike earlier psychoanalytic or associationist explanations, contemporary cognitive theories focus on the information processing mechanisms that allow affective states to influence both the content and processes of cognition and motivation. Bower's associative network model (1981) proposed that affect and cognition are integrally linked within an associative network of mental representations. An affective state should thus selectively and automatically prime related thoughts and ideas that are more likely to be used in constructive cognitive tasks – for example, tasks that involve motivated action. Clearly, these affective biases will have significant motivational consequences for the way people plan and execute social behaviors, as we shall see. Such affect congruity is more likely when the affective state is strong, salient, and self-relevant (although still lacking in clear cognitive content) and when the task involves the constructive generation and elaboration of information rather than the simple reproduction of stored details.

There is mounting evidence that affect infusion is most likely to occur in the course of *constructive processing* that requires the substantial transformation, rather than mere reproduction, of information (see Forgas, 1995, 2002, for a review). As Fiedler (1990) argued, affect "will influence cognitive processes to the extent that the . . . task involves the active generation of new information as opposed to the passive conservation of information given" (pp. 2–3). However, we also need to recognize that affect infusion is not an invariable phenomenon. Sometimes, a person's affective state appears to have no influence on the content of cognition and action, and may even have an inconsistent, mood-incongruent influence (Forgas & Ciarrochi, 2002; Sedikides, 1994). These diverse findings were recently integrated into the comprehensive Affect Infusion Model (Forgas, 1995, 2002).

An Integrative Model of Affect Infusion

Theories such as the *Affect Infusion Model* (AIM) proposed by Forgas (1995, 2002) maintain that the nature and extent of affect infusion will depend largely on what kind of processing strategy is adopted in a particular task. This is in marked contrast to the single-process assumptions of many social cognition theories. The AIM predicts that some social tasks such as setting and performing routine, recurrent actions may require little constructive thinking (Fiedler, 1991) and should be impervious to the infusion of affect. In contrast, interpersonal tasks that require the monitoring of ambiguous or indeterminate information and the production of complex responses may require highly constructive and generative cognitive processing that can be readily influenced by affect (Forgas, Bower, & Krantz, 1984).

The AIM identified four alternative processing strategies people might use in social situations, each characterized by different affect infusion potentials. (a) The *direct access* of a preexisting response or (b) *motivated processing* in the service of a preexisting goal both involve highly predetermined and directed information search and behavior patterns that require little generative, constructive processing, limiting the scope of affect infusion. In contrast, when an interpersonal task requires a degree of constructive processing, people may use either (c) a *heuristic*, simplified or (d) a *substantive*, generative processing strategy to plan their actions and produce a response. These are high-infusion strategies that require a degree of open, constructive thinking, where affect may either directly (Clore et al., 1994) or indirectly, through primed associations (Forgas & Bower, 1987), inform the response. The choice between these different processing styles should be determined by three categories of variables associated with the *task*, the *person*, and the *situation*, respectively. A detailed description of this model and the evidence supporting it has already been presented elsewhere (Forgas, 1992, 1995, 2002) and need not be repeated in detail here.

The major relevance of the AIM is that it offers a framework within which the presence or absence of affect infusion into social action and motivation can be explained. The distinction between different processing strategies as mediators of affect infusion should have considerable benefits for understanding mood effects on motivated interpersonal behaviors. For example, the *direct access* strategy recognizes that people possess a rich repertoire of routine, preexisting social moves requiring little on-line constructive processing and thus precluding affect infusion. *Motivated processing* represents a highly selective, guided, and targeted information processing strategy that is also impervious to affect infusion. Indeed, motivated processing seems to be the major mechanism involved in mood maintenance as well as mood repair in social encounters, as we will see (Forgas & Ciarrochi, 2002).

In contrast, *heuristic processing* tends to be adopted when people have no stored action plan or a strong preexisting motivation to guide their actions. Here, they use whatever shortcuts or simplifications are readily available to produce a response. Heuristic processing can lead to affect infusion in situations where actors directly rely on their affective state as an inferential cue to produce a reaction (cf. Clore et al., 1994). It is *substantive processing* that requires the most constructive and elaborate strategy for producing a response, as people need to select, learn, and interpret new information about a social situation and need to rely on their associative ideas and memories to accomplish this. Affect infusion is common during substantive processing, as "activation of an emotion node also spreads activation throughout the memory structures to which it is connected" (Bower, 1981, p. 135). Indeed, affect infusion may be greater when more extensive and constructive processing is required. This paradoxical effect has been repeatedly observed (Fiedler, 1991; Forgas, 1992, 1995, 1999a, 1999b; Sedikides, 1995).

Affective Influences on Processing Strategies

The AIM also recognizes the influence of affect on *how* people think. In addition to influencing the content and valence of memory representations and motivations, affect may influence the *process* of thinking (Clark & Isen, 1982; Forgas, 2000, 2001a). Early evidence suggested that positive affect motivates people to engage in less effortful and more superficial processing strategies, whereas negative affect seems to motivate more effortful, systematic, analytic, and vigilant processing (Clark & Isen, 1982). More recent studies have shown, however, that positive affect may produce some processing advantages, facilitating more creative, open, flexible, and inclusive thinking styles (Bless, 2000; Fiedler, 2000). The main consequence of positive and negative affect is thus not simply an increase or a decrease in processing effort. Rather, positive affect seems to promote a more assimilative, schema-based processing style, whereas negative affect produces a more accommodative, externally focused thinking strategy (Bless, 2000; Fiedler, 2000; Higgins, 2001).

An important implication of these findings is that different social motivations may be elicited by these mood-induced processing differences. One explanation of these differences in thinking styles is the cognitive tuning account, which suggests that affective states both inform the individual about the environment and elicit appropriate motivations to deal with that environment (Bless, 2000; Schwarz, 1990). The more open and flexible processing styles associated with positive affect allow individuals to deal appropriately with benign environmental conditions, whereas aversive conditions are better dealt with by the accommodative, detail-oriented cognition induced by negative affect. This account seems broadly consistent with evolutionary accounts that focus on the adaptive rele-vance of positive and negative affect triggering promotion-oriented or prevention-oriented processing styles (Frijda, 1986; Higgins; 2001).

The AIM can thus provide answers to a variety of intriguing questions about affect and motivation, such as: How can we account for the apparent context sensitivity of many mood effects on motivated behaviors? What sorts of motivated actions are most likely to be influenced by affect? What is the role of affect in the processing and evaluation of complex or ambiguous information about goal performance? Does more prolonged and extensive processing increase the incidence of affect infusion? In the next section, we shall briefly consider some of the empirical literature indicating affective influences on motivated cognition and behavior.

AFFECTIVE INFLUENCES ON MOTIVATION

As we have seen, affective states can play a complex and interactive role in strategic social behaviors. The AIM suggests that affect may influence both the *content* of people's actions and the *processes* of how they think and respond to social situations. Thus, a full understanding of how affect impacts on motivated behavior requires careful attention to the kinds of information processing strategies people adopt in particular social situa-tions. Empirical evidence supporting this mediational role of cognition in affect infusion, including research from our lab, will be considered next.

Affective Influences on Motivation in Strategic Encounters

Affective states can influence people's motivations to behave in particu-lar ways. In one series of experiments we investigated affective influences on people's motivations and actual performance in strategic negotiating encounters (Forgas, 1998a). Positive, control, or negative, mood was in-duced by giving participants positive, negative, or neutral feedback about their performance on a verbal test. Next, they engaged in an informal, in-terpersonal and a formal, intergroup negotiating task with another team in what they believed was a separate experiment. We were interested in how temporary moods might influence people's motivations, goal-setting strategies, and behaviors. Results showed that participants who were in a positive mood set themselves higher and more ambitious goals, formed higher expectations about the forthcoming encounter, and formulated spe-cific action plans that were more optimistic, cooperative, and integrative than did control or negative-mood participants. Furthermore, individu-als who formulated cooperative goals as a result of feeling good actually behaved more cooperatively, and were more willing to make and recip-rocate deals than were those in a negative mood (Figure 10.1). Perhaps the most interesting finding was that these mood-induced differences in

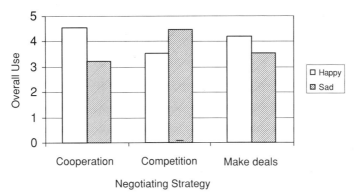

FIGURE 10.1 Mood-congruent influences on motivation and strategic behavior in negotiating encounters: Happy persons plan, and use, more cooperative and less competitive bargaining strategies, and are more likely to make and honor deals than are negotiators experiencing negative affect. (Data based on Forgas, 1998a.)

motivation and goal setting actually resulted in more successful performance. People who felt good did significantly better in this bargaining task than did those who felt bad. These results provide relatively clear-cut evidence that even slight changes in mood due to an unrelated prior event can significantly influence motivation, the goals that people set for themselves, the action plans they formulate, and their subsequent interpersonal behaviors.

In terms of information processing models such as the AIM, mood effects on motivation and interpersonal behavior can be explained by the operation of affect-priming mechanisms. Thinking about and planning a bargaining encounter is by definition a complex, indeterminate, and personally involving cognitive task where substantive processing should be the dominant strategy adopted. Positive mood should selectively prime more positive thoughts and associations, and should ultimately lead to the formulation of more optimistic expectations and the use of more cooperative bargaining strategies. In contrast, negative mood should produce more pessimistic, negative thoughts and associations, leading to less ambitious goals and less cooperative, less successful bargaining strategies.

Interestingly, the second experiment in this series showed that these mood effects were much less marked for individuals who scored high on individual difference measures such as machiavellism and need for approval. In terms of the AIM, these individuals should have approached the bargaining task from a strongly predetermined, motivated perspective, which would have limited their use of open, constructive processing and thus reduced affect infusion into their behaviors. In a way, their minds were made up about what to do before they started, reducing the likelihood of incidental affect infusion. Such individual differences in tendencies to use open, constructive or guided, motivated processing strategies may significantly influence the extent to which affective states are likely to infuse motivation and subsequent social behavior (Rusting, 2001).

Affective Influences on Motivated Self-Disclosure

Affective states may also influence people's motivations to communicate and disclose information about themselves. Self-disclosure is one of the most important communicative tasks undertaken in everyday life. Our ability to disclose intimate information is an essential skill in the maintenance and development of rewarding intimate relationships, and is also critical to mental health and social adjustment (Forgas, 1985). Inappropriate self-disclosure can lead to adverse evaluations by others and, ultimately, to relationship breakdown and social isolation. Do temporary mood states influence people's motivated self-disclosure strategies? Several lines of evidence suggest that the answer is "yes."

In a series of recent experiments, we explored the effects of induced mood on motivated self-disclosure strategies (Forgas, 2001b). Mood was induced by exposing people to positively or negatively valenced videotapes. Subsequently, in an allegedly unrelated experiment, they were asked to indicate the order in which they would feel comfortable disclosing a list of increasingly intimate information about themselves to a person they had just met. Results indicated a small but significant tendency for happy people to select more intimate disclosure topics than people in a negative mood. This pattern is consistent with positive mood inducing a more confident, assertive, and interactive communication style.

Of course, these effects occurred in a highly artificial, simulated context. In order to extend the ecological validity of the results, in a subsequent experiment participants were asked to interact with another person in a neighboring room via a computer link as if exchanging e-mail messages. In fact, there was no interlocutor; the computer was preprogrammed to respond with either consistently high or low levels of self-disclosure or a gradually increasing pattern of self-disclosure intimacy. This procedure allowed us to investigate not only the overall intimacy of self-disclosure as a function of mood, but also the effects of various partner disclosure patterns. Results again showed that mood motivated different levels of self-disclosure intimacy, but these effects were also dependent on the behavior of the partner (Figure 10.2). Individuals induced to feel good generally responded with more intimate disclosure, but only when their partner was also disclosing either consistently or increasingly intimate information. Positive mood did not increase the intimacy of self-disclosure when the partner was not disclosing. People in a positive mood also disclosed significantly more positive rather than negative information about themselves, and formed more positive impressions of the

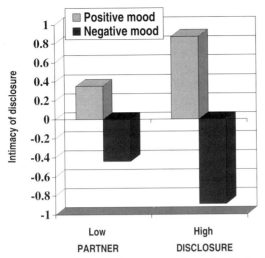

FIGURE 10.2 Mood effects on motivated self-disclosure: Positive mood motivates people to disclose more intimate information about themselves, and negative mood reduces motivation to disclose. These mood effects are amplified when the partner adopts a high-disclosure rather than a low-disclosure strategy (unpublished data).

"partner," than did people in a negative mood, consistent with the overall mood-congruent pattern found in other interpersonal tasks (Forgas, 2001b).

Why do these effects occur? When people face an uncertain and unpredictable social encounter, such as a task involving self-disclosure, they need to rely on open, constructive processing in order to formulate their plans and goals and to guide their behaviors. In other words, they must go beyond the information given, and rely on their available thoughts and memories to construct a response. Happy persons seem to disclose more because they selectively access positive thoughts and associations and assess the likelihood of a positive, accepting response and reciprocal disclosure more optimistically. However, these mood effects rapidly disappear when the interaction partner does not appear to match disclosure intimacy. Self-disclosure is a risky interpersonal strategy, because revealing too much about oneself may give away intimate information at too early a stage, which may be seen as socially inappropriate. Whether we undertake such a risky move depends on a constructive assessment of the situation; it is at this stage that affect may play a role, influencing the way intrinsically ambiguous social situations are interpreted as either benign or dangerous. The same mechanisms also seem to influence the way people formulate risky interpersonal requests, the way they respond to approaches by others, and the way they plan and execute negotiations (Forgas, 1998b, 1998c, 1999a, 1999b).

Mood Effects on Motivated Strategic Verbal Behaviors:
The Case of Requesting

If affective states can influence motivation in complex interactions such as bargaining, negotiation, and self-disclosure episodes, it should also be possible to demonstrate mood effects on motivation when performing specific identifiable social behaviors. In several experiments, we explored the effects of mood on one such example of strategic goal-oriented behavior: the way people formulate requests. Requesting is an intrinsically complex behavioral task characterized by goal pursuit and psychological ambiguity. Requests must be formulated with just the right degree of politeness so as to maximize compliance without risking giving offense. We expected that incidental mood should significantly influence the social mindset of requesters and their requesting strategies. We expected that people would adopt a more confident, direct requesting style when in a positive mood due to the greater availability of positively valenced thoughts and associations (Forgas, 1998b, 1999a, 1999b). Further, in the terms of the AIM, these mood effects would be particularly strong when the situation was more complex and demanding, and required more substantive and elaborate processing.

Mood was induced in an allegedly separate experiment by asking people to recall and think about happy or sad autobiographical episodes (Forgas, 1999a, Exp. 1). In a subsequent task, participants selected a more or less polite request formulation that they would use in an easy and a difficult request situation. Results showed that induced mood had a significant influence on request strategies. Happy participants preferred more direct, impolite requests, whereas sad persons used indirect, polite request alternatives. Further, these mood effects on requesting were significantly greater in the more difficult, demanding request situation, where more extensive, substantive processing was required (Figure 10.3).

Very similar procedures were used in a follow-up experiment, but participants now formulated their own open-ended requests, which were subsequently rated for politeness and elaboration by two independent raters (Forgas, 1999a, Exp. 2). Results again showed that mood had a significant influence on these strategic behaviors. Happy persons produced significantly more impolite and less elaborate requests than did sad individuals, and these effects were again greater in the more problematic and difficult situational context (Figure 10.3). These results confirm that moods can influence how people perceive and interpret social situations, and how they formulate and execute subsequent interpersonal behaviors such as requests. But why should mood effects be greater on requests in a more difficult and demanding social situation? More difficult interpersonal tasks require more elaborate processing, and according to the AIM, affect infusion should increase proportionally when more substantive processing is required to produce a social response.

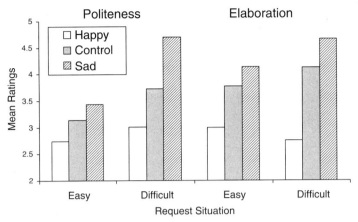

FIGURE 10.3 Mood effects on producing strategic messages: Negative mood increases and positive mood decreases request politeness and elaboration, and these mood effects are significantly greater in more difficult, demanding social situations that require more extensive processing. (After Forgas, 1999a.)

This pattern was again confirmed in a third experiment where participants were asked to select more or less polite request alternatives in a variety of different realistic situations (Forgas, 1999b, Exp. 1). Following an audiovisual mood induction (watching happy or sad films), participants selected more or less polite request forms they would use in each of 16 different request situations. Results confirmed that mood effects were greatest for the most direct, unconventional requests, those that are most likely to violate cultural conventions of politeness and recruit the most substantive, elaborate processing strategies. These findings indicate that mood effects on request motivations are indeed process-dependent, with affect infusion enhanced or reduced depending on just how much open, constructive processing is required to deal with more or less demanding interpersonal tasks (Fiedler, 1991; Forgas, 1995).

These effects are not restricted to controlled, laboratory tasks. Similar effects were obtained in a fourth, unobtrusive experiment looking at naturally produced requests (Forgas, 1999b, Exp. 2). After an audiovisual mood induction, the experimenter casually asked participants to get a file from a neighboring office. Their actual words in requesting the file were recorded by a concealed tape recorder, and subsequently were analyzed for politeness and other qualities. Results showed a significant mood effect on these natural, unobtrusively elicited social behaviors. Sad people used more polite, friendly, and elaborate request forms, whereas happy people used more direct and less polite forms. Negative mood also increased the latency of requests. Sad persons delayed their requests significantly longer than did control or happy persons and were more polite, elaborate, and hedging, consistent with their more cautious, defensive behavioral strategies

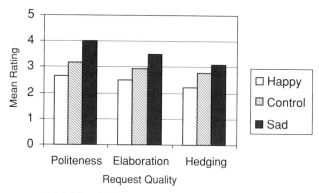

FIGURE 10.4 Mood effects on naturally produced requests: Positive mood increases and negative mood decreases the degree of politeness, elaboration, and hedging in goal-oriented strategic communications. (After Forgas, 1999b.)

and the more extensive processing these unconventional behaviors presumably required (Figure 10.4). An analysis of the subsequent recall of the requests confirmed that unconventional requests were also recalled significantly better. This confirms the predicted more elaborate, in-depth processing of these messages, and supports the core prediction of processing models such as the AIM that the greatest mood effects on motivated behavior occur when more elaborate, substantive processing is used by a communicator.

Mood Effects on Motivation When Responding to Strategic Situations

We have seen that mild mood states can have a profound influence on how people approach complex interpersonal tasks and behave in specific interpersonal episodes. Other experiments have found that mood states also influence motivation in how people respond spontaneously to unexpected situations, such as being confronted by a request from a stranger. Responding to an unexpected request by a stranger represents one of the simplest kinds of interpersonal tasks where an online reaction involving constructive cognitive processing is required. In a series of recent field experiments (Forgas, 1998b), we looked at the role of temporary affective states in how people evaluate and respond behaviorally to more or less polite requests directed at them in a public place. In order to increase the external validity of the design, an unobtrusive strategy was used. Students entering a library found pictures or text placed on their desks designed to induce good or bad moods. A few minutes later, they were approached by another student (in fact, a confederate) and received an unexpected polite or impolite request for several sheets of paper. A short time after the requesting incident, a second confederate explained to participants

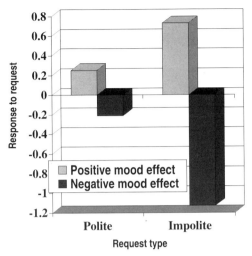

FIGURE 10.5 Mood effects on motivated reactions to an unexpected request in a public place (the library): Those in a positive mood are motivated to respond more positively, whereas those in a negative mood are motivated to respond more negatively (higher values indicate more positive evaluations). Positive mood produced more positive judgments. These mood effects on motivated reactions were greater when the request was impolite and atypical, and thus required more substantive processing. (Data based on Forgas, 1998b.)

that the request was staged, and asked them to complete a brief questionnaire evaluating their perceptions and their recall of the request and the requester. Results showed that there was a clear mood-congruent pattern in how students behaved in this situation. People in an induced negative mood were more likely to form a critical, negative view of requests and were less inclined to comply than were positive mood participants. In a particularly interesting result, we found a significant interaction between mood state and the level of politeness of the request (Figure 10.5). Overall, mood effects were significantly greater on the evaluation of, and responses to impolite, unconventional requests that required more substantive processing, as confirmed by better recall memory for these messages later on. Conventional, polite requests were apparently processed less substantively, were less influenced by mood, and were recalled in less detail later on.

This experiment shows that unrelated temporary mood states have a significant mood-congruent influence on the way people interpret and respond to unexpected social situations. These mood effects can be understood in terms of the motivational consequences of mood states. Further, consistent with the AIM, these results indicate that affect infusion into the planning and execution of impromptu social behaviors is significantly mediated by the kind of processing strategy people employ. Of course, it is not always a simple case of mood states influencing motivation and subsequent behavior. Sometimes, the situation is reversed: Preexisting motivational states can mediate the influence of affective states on thinking and behavior. Theoretical models such as the AIM explicitly predict such a link. Motivated processing, one of the four processing strategies identified within the AIM, is specifically predicted to serve the purpose of affect management and affect control. Several experiments have produced evidence supporting such a link.

MOTIVATIONAL INFLUENCES ON AFFECT

The evidence so far suggests that even short-term and relatively low-intensity moods may have a strong influence on social motivation in situations in which some degree of open, constructive processing is required. However, the relationship between affect, cognition, and behavior is not unidirectional. Just as affect can influence social thinking and behavior, changes in motivational states and information processing strategies can produce corresponding changes in prevailing affective states.

Motivated Processing and Affect Control

How do people go about controlling and managing their own affective states? Arguably, one of the most common and important goals people have in everyday life is the maintenance of a reasonably positive, optimistic affective balance despite the manifold challenges they face. The objectives of mood maintenance and mood regulation (Clark & Isen, 1982) probably play a disproportionately important role in the way many everyday behavioral and cognitive strategies are performed. Indeed some researchers suggest that such *emotional evanescence* is adaptive: It may simply be more advantageous not to be dysphoric or euphoric for too long (Wilson, Gilbert, & Centerbar, in press).

Accumulating evidence suggests that people may use a number of motivated strategies to control their affective states. These include selective exposure to mood-incongruent information (Erber & Erber, 2001; Forgas, 1992), recall of mood-incongruent memories (Sedikides, 1994), engaging in mood-incongruent behaviors (Cialdini & Kenrick, 1976), interacting with rewarding partners (Forgas, 1991), generating self-serving future predictions (Ross & Buehler, 2001), or distracting themselves from the source of their moods (Rusting, 2001). Within the AIM framework, the ongoing task of affect management and control can be best understood in terms of a routine and automatic switching between two complementary information processing strategies. Substantive processing typically results in affect infusion and the accentuation of the existing affective state. In contrast, motivated processing inhibits affect infusion and may produce targeted,

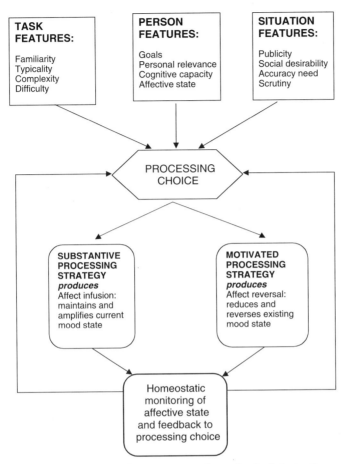

FIGURE 10.6 The mood management hypothesis: Substantive processing accentuates and motivated processing attenuates the valence of the existing affective state, and automatic switching due to a feedback loop between these two processing modes produces a homeostatic mood management system. (After Forgas, Johnson, & Ciarrochi, 1998.)

affect-incongruent outcomes. We recently proposed such a preliminary affect management model (Forgas, Johnson, & Ciarrochi, 1998) based on relevant aspects of the AIM (Forgas, 1995). A schematic outline of the affect management hypothesis is presented in Figure 10.6.

As this figure shows, the choice of either a substantive (affect infusion) or motivated (affect control) processing strategy is determined by a combination of personal, situational, and task-related input variables and the extremity of the prevailing affective state. So far, research suggests that a switch to motivated rather than substantive processing is more likely when (a) the task is of direct personal relevance (Forgas, 1991), (b) people are aware of the cause or consequences of their moods (Berkowitz et al., 2000; Clore et al., 1994), (c) they score high on individual differences measures that indicate motivated processing tendencies (such as machiavellism or need for control) (Forgas, 1998a), and/or (d) they experience an extreme or aversive affective state (Ciarrochi & Forgas, 1999; Forgas & Fiedler, 1996). Situational variables may also impact on processing and behavioral choices (Forgas, 1995). For example, persons who expect to engage in a demanding interaction with a stranger may in fact prefer to tone down their mood by reading articles that are the opposite in affective tone to their own mood (Erber & Erber, 2001).

A critical feature of the homeostatic affect management model is that it incorporates a feedback loop between the valenced outcome of the existing processing strategy and behavior and subsequent processing choices. As a consequence, the model provides for the possibility of continuous changes in processing strategies as a function of the prevailing mood state, a suggestion that is also supported by empirical evidence (Clark & Isen, 1982; Forgas, 1995; Sedikides, 1994). In practical terms, this means that if, as a result of an existing substantive processing strategy and ongoing affect infusion, the level of negativity in a person's thinking and behavior reaches a threshold, an automatic correction should take place that consists of a switch to motivated processing and a preference for mood-inconsistent thoughts and behaviors (Erber & Erber, 2001). We should note that some researchers suggest a similar regulatory system for positive affect, in which threshold levels of positivity instigate automatic correction measures serving to reduce euphoria (Wilson et al., in press). Although this does make sense from an adaptive viewpoint, no clear evidence of positive affect regulation was found in our studies.

The mood management model predicts that negative mood initially leads to affect infusion and mood-congruent thoughts until a threshold level of negativity is reached, at which point people should switch to motivated mood control and mood-incongruent associations. Sedikides (1994) found some initial support for such a hypothesis. In this study, participants were induced to feel good, neutral, or bad using guided imagery procedures, and were then asked to write an extended series of self-descriptive statements. Early responses showed a clear mood-congruence effect. However, with the passage of time, the negative self-judgments of sad participants were spontaneously reversed, suggesting something like an automatic mood management strategy.

Recently, we (Forgas & Ciarrochi, 2000) conducted several additional studies to test the hypothesis that negative affect leads first to affect infusion, followed by a spontaneous switch to a motivated affect control strategy. In Experiment 1, participants who were feeling good or bad after recalling happy or sad events from their past generated a series of trait adjectives. Negative mood initially produced mood-congruent adjectives, but over time, subjects spontaneously switched to generating mood-incongruent (positive) adjectives. In Experiment 2, a different, word completion task was used to measure mood effects on associations. A time-series regression analysis revealed that sad subjects again changed from affect-congruent to affect-incongruent recall. It appears that once a threshold level of negativity is reached due to affect infusion processes, sad people spontaneously change their cognitive and behavioral strategies and switch to motivated, incongruent recall as if seeking to control and eliminate their aversive moods.

In a further study, we explored the role of individual difference variables such as self-esteem (SE) in affect control strategies. Previous work shows that people low in SE are less likely than others to engage in conscious affect control (Smith & Petty, 1995). To examine this further, we induced mood by giving participants positive or negative feedback about their performance on a spatial abilities task. Next, they completed a series of sentences asking for self-descriptive adjectives. Results again indicated a clear first congruent, then incongruent pattern, but this result was particularly marked for high-SE people. Those scoring high on SE were rapidly able to eliminate a mood-congruent bias in their responses by producing mood-incongruent, positive descriptions after initially negative responses. In contrast, low-SE people persevered with mood-congruent responses throughout the entire task. This finding suggests that traits such as SE may moderate people's ability to adopt motivated behavioral strategies to control their affective states.

These studies (Forgas & Ciarrochi, 2000; Sedikides, 1994) support the notion of a homeostatic feedback loop model of affect management, suggesting that fluctuating affective states can play an important role in controlling processing strategies. Changes in processing style will in turn influence the degree of affect infusion and thus control the extremity of the mood state. In other words, affective states can be seen as integral components of social motivation, influencing our thoughts and actions but also being regulated by subtle shifts in processing strategies and behaviors.

Mood and Motivated Decisions. Affect itself may act as a trigger for motivated processing in self-relevant tasks. Several studies suggest that people will often engage in targeted information search and retrieval strategies in order to alleviate dysphoria (Forgas & Ciarrochi, 2002). Affect-related motivated processing may also influence tasks that have direct personal consequences. Schachter (1959) was among the first to show that anxious or frightened people are motivated to seek out the company of others, and particularly those in a predicament similar to theirs. This motivated strategy is adopted in an apparent effort to control negative affect by seeking self-relevant comparisons about an impending noxious event. Other evidence also suggests that people are generally motivated to interact with partners who are in a matching rather than a different mood (Locke & Horowitz, 1990).

In a series of experiments extending these ideas, we investigated mood effects on motivated partner choices. Happy or sad people were asked to select a partner either for themselves, or for another person. As expected, the combination of sad mood and a self-relevant task led to a highly motivated processing strategy: These people selectively looked for and found a rewarding companion, whereas in all other conditions task-competent partners were chosen (Forgas, 1989). Consistent with motivated, targeted processing, sad people performing a personally relevant task also selectively recalled more diagnostic information about rewarding partners later on (Forgas, 1991, Exp. 1). In later work, we analyzed the actual information search strategies used by judges motivated to achieve a particular outcome. Descriptions about potential partners were provided on a series of information cards (Forgas, 1991, Exp. 2) or on a computer file, allowing the step-by-step recording of each person's decision path and reaction latencies (Forgas, 1991, Exp. 3). Sad persons making a self-relevant choice were again motivated to find rewarding partners. They reached their decisions faster, but studied motivation-relevant details at greater length and remembered them better later on. As predicted by the AIM, motivated processing eliminated affect infusion in these judgments. Instead of selectively accessing affect-related information, judges motivated to achieve a predetermined outcome (to find a rewarding partner to improve their mood) looked for and used information most relevant to servicing their motivational objective in this instance, mood repair.

Interestingly, it seems that self-focused attention alone can also induce motivated thinking and reduce mood effects. In several ingenious experiments, Berkowitz et al. (2000) found that judgments were affectively congruent when subjects' attention was directed away from themselves, presumably because of the relatively automatic influence of the affective state. However, when people's attention was directed at themselves, they displayed affective incongruence, as self-directed attention apparently induced a controlled, motivated processing strategy.

Self-Esteem and Trait Anxiety as Motivational Influences on Affect Infusion. A number of individual difference variables such as SE also appear to moderate the effects of mood on social judgments and behaviors (Baumeister, 1998; Rusting, 2001). Low-SE persons generally have less certain and stable self-conceptions, and may thus be more influenced by situational judgment factors, than high-SE people. In the absence of a strong motivational influence provided by SE, affect may thus have a greater influence on judgments by low-rather than high-SE individuals. Such a link was demonstrated by Brown and Mankowski (1993), who used the Velten (1968) procedure or music to induce good or bad moods and subsequently asked participants to rate themselves on a number of adjectives. Induced mood had a significant mood-congruent influence on the self-judgments of low-SE persons but had a much less clear-cut effect on ratings by high-SE individuals.

A series of studies by Smith and Petty (1995) also confirmed this pattern. These authors induced happy and sad moods in high- and low-SE participants, who were then asked to report on three memories from their school years. Mood had a significant influence on both the quantity and quality of responses by the low- but not by the high-SE group. It appears that people with high SE have a more stable and certain self-concept and seem to respond to self-related questions using a more motivated processing strategy, a process that does not allow the incidental infusion of affect into judgments. Low-SE people, in contrast, seem to be motivated to engage in more open and elaborate processing when thinking about themselves, providing greater scope for current affect to influence their outcomes (Sedikides, 1995). Trait anxiety also seems to have a moderating motivational influence on affect infusion. In a study on intergroup judgments, sad White participants who were high or low on trait anxiety made judgments and recalled information about a threatening Black empowerment group (Ciarrochi & Forgas, 1999). A negative affect infusion effect was found, but only for low trait-anxious people. High trait anxious people produced more positive judgments and recall, consistent with a motivated processing strategy. It seems that negative affect served as a warning signal for high trait-anxious participants, indicating the need for a motivated reassessment of potentially prejudiced responses.

Positive Affect as a Motivational Resource

Positive affect may also serve motivational functions by allowing people to deal more effectively with potentially threatening self-relevant information (Trope, Ferguson, & Ragunanthan, 2001). The prospect of accepting negative feedback about ourselves often elicits powerful motivational conflicts, as we need to assess the immediate emotional cost of damaging information against the long-term benefits of gaining useful diagnostic feedback. Studies by Trope at al. (2001) confirmed that temporary mood influences the relative weight people assign to the emotional costs versus the informational benefits of receiving negative feedback. People in a positive mood were more likely to expose themselves voluntarily to threatening but diagnostic information. It seems that positive affect functions as a buffer, enabling people to better handle the emotional costs of negative self-related information. However, this effect is not unconditional. The negative feedback must be seen as diagnostic and useful before people will willingly undergo the emotional cost of acquiring it (Trope et al., 2001). These effects may also have important real-life consequences. Trope and his colleagues also found that people in positive moods not only selectively sought, but also processed in greater detail and remembered better negatively valenced arguments about health risks than did people sad people.

SUMMARY AND CONCLUSIONS

There is no doubt that affective states play an important role in shaping social motivation. While past theories have assigned affect a restricted, feedback-related role in goal-directed behavior, we hope that this review promotes a broader consideration of the influence of affect on social motives and intentions. We have provided substantial evidence for the role of affect in guiding people's interpersonal behaviors and have shown that cognitive processes mediate these relationships. Theories such as the AIM (Forgas, 1992, 1995) can offer a simple and parsimonious explanation of when and how affective states infuse purposive behaviors such as interpersonal decisions, bargaining and negotiation, self-disclosure, and the formulation of and responses to requests (Forgas, 1998a, 1998b, 1999a, 1999b). In addition to the influence of affect on social motivation, we have seen the constraints that various motives place upon affect infusion. The motivation for mood repair, as part of an affect management system, restricts the amount of affect infusion that occurs in people's social judgments and behaviors and even influences partner choices in interaction episodes. Further, the experiments described here show that dispositional motivations that accompany self-esteem and trait anxiety moderate this already complex relationship. The affect management model described earlier predicts that people may switch between two complementary processing strategies, substantive processing (producing affect infusion) and motivated processing (producing affect control), in order to achieve an automatic, homeostatic system of mood management (Forgas & Ciarrochi, 2000).

These findings tell us something interesting about the nature of social motivation. As also shown by several other contributors to this volume, our results suggest that affective, cognitive, and motivational processes are inextricably linked in the way people respond to social situations. Psychology has probably suffered from the long-standing tradition of attempting to separate and study in isolation fundamental mental faculties such as motivation, cognition, and affect (Hilgard, 1980). This chapter documents the highly significant influence that emotions and moods can have on the way people perceive and interpret social situations, the kinds of goals and plans they formulate, and the way they execute and regulate their social behaviors. Motivated changes in thinking, in turn, can be an important mechanism for managing affective states.

In conclusion, affect infusion into motivated judgments and behaviors is most likely in the course of open, constructive processing. It also appears that affect priming is the most likely mechanism to lead to mood congruence in motivated interpersonal tasks. Paradoxically, more extensive, substantive processing enhances mood congruity, as predicted by the AIM (Forgas, 1992, 1995, 1998a, 1998b, 1999a, 1999b, 2002). Conversely, other experiments demonstrated the absence of affect infusion whenever people approach a cognitive task from a highly directed or motivated perspective (Forgas, 1991; Forgas & Fiedler, 1996; Sedikides, 1995). The kinds of mood effects on motivated behaviors demonstrated here might be particularly important in everyday situations, including intimate relationships, organizational behaviors, and clinical situations (Baron, 1987; Forgas & Moylan, 1987; Mayer, Gaschke, Braverman, & Evans, 1992; Salovey, O' Leary, Stretton, Fishkin, & Drake, 1991; Sedikides, 1992a). Our intention in this chapter was to highlight the complexity of the relationship between affect and social motivation. We believe that affect plays a number of important roles in shaping our intentions and motives in everyday social encounters beyond that of a mere feedback signal. In highlighting this complexity, though, we can clearly see the need for future research in this interesting and important domain.

References

Adolphs, R., & Damasio, A. (2001). The interaction of affect and cognition: A neurobiological perspective. In J. P. Forgas (Ed.), *The handbook of affect and social cognition* (pp. 27–49). Mahwah, NJ: Erlbaum.

Baron, R. (1987). Interviewers' moods and reactions to job applicants: The influence of affective states on applied social judgments. *Journal of Applied Social Psychology, 16,* 16–28.

Baumeister, R. F. (1998). The self. In D. T. Gilbert, S. T. Fiske, & G. Lindzey (Eds.), *The handbook of social psychology* (pp. 680–740). New York: Oxford University Press.

Berkowitz, L., Jaffee, S., Jo, E., & Troccoli, B. T. (2000). On the correction of feeling-induced judgmental biases. In J. P. Forgas (Ed.), *Feeling and thinking: The role of affect in social cognition* (pp. 131–152). New York: Cambridge University Press.

Blascovich, J., & Mendes, W. B. (2000). Challenge and threat appraisals: The role of affective cues. In J. P. Forgas (Ed.), *Feeling and thinking: The role of affect in social cognition* (pp. 59–82). New York: Cambridge University Press.

Blascovich, J., & Tomaka, J. (1996). The biopsychosocial model of arousal regulation. *Advances in Experimental Social Psychology, 28,* 1–51.

Bless, H. (2000). The interplay of affect and cognition: The mediating role of general knowledge structures. In J. P. Forgas (Ed.), *Feeling and thinking: The role of affect in social cognition* (pp. 201–222). New York: Cambridge University Press.

Bower, G. H. (1981). Mood and memory. *American Psychologist, 36,* 129–148.

Bower, G. H. (1991). Mood congruity of social judgments. In J. P. Forgas (Ed.), *Emotion and social judgments* (pp. 31–53). New York: Pergamon Press.

Bower, G. H., & Forgas, J. P. (2001). Mood and social memory. In J. P. Forgas (Ed.), *The handbook of affect and social cognition* (pp. 95–120). Mahwah, NJ: Erlbaum.

Brown, J. D., & Mankowski, T. A. (1993). Self-esteem, mood, and self-evaluation: Changes in the mood and the way you see you. *Journal of Personality and Social Psychology, 64*, 421–430.

Buss, D. (1999). *Evolutionary psychology: The new science of the mind.* Needham Heights, MA: Allyn & Bacon.

Byrne, D., & Clore, G. L. (1970). A reinforcement model of evaluation responses. *Personality: An International Journal, 1*, 103–128.

Carver, C., & Scheier, C. (1998). The self-regulation of behavior. In R. Wyer & T. Srull (Eds.), *Advances in social cognition* (Vol. 12, pp. 1–106). Mahwah, NJ: Erlbaum.

Cialdini, R. B., & Kenrick, D. T. (1976). Altruism as hedonism: A social development perspective on the relationship of negative mood state and helping. *Journal of Personality and Social Psychology, 34*, 907–914.

Ciarrochi, J. V., & Forgas, J. P. (1999). On being tense yet tolerant: The paradoxical effects of trait anxiety and aversive mood on intergroup judgments. *Group Dynamics: Theory, Research and Practice, 3*, 227–238.

Clark, M. S., & Isen, A. M. (1982). Towards understanding the relationship between feeling states and social behavior. In A. H. Hastorf & A. M. Isen (Eds.), *Cognitive social psychology* (pp. 73–108). Amsterdam: Elsevier/North-Holland.

Clore, G. L., & Byrne, D. (1974). The reinforcement affect model of attraction. In T. L. Huston (Ed.), *Foundations of interpersonal attraction* (pp. 143–170). New York: Academic Press.

Clore, G. L., Schwarz, N., & Conway, M. (1994). Affective causes and consequences of social information processing. In R. S. Wyer & T. K. Srull (Eds.), *Handbook of social cognition* (2nd ed., Vol. 1, pp. 323–419). Hillsdale, NJ: Erlbaum.

Damasio, A. R. (1994). *Descartes' error.* New York: Grosste/Putnam.

De Sousa, R. D. (1987). *The rationality of emotion.* Cambridge, MA: MIT Press.

Erber, R., & Erber, M. (2001). The role of motivated social cognition in the regulation of affective states. In J. P. Forgas (Ed.), *The handbook of affect and social cognition* (pp. 275–292). Mahwah, NJ: Erlbaum.

Feshbach, S., & Singer, R. D. (1957). The effects of fear arousal and suppression of fear upon social perception. *Journal of Abnormal and Social Psychology, 55*, 283–288.

Fiedler, K. (1990). Mood-dependent selectivity in social cognition. In W. Stroebe & M. Hewstone (Eds.), *European review of social psychology* (Vol. 1, pp. 1–32). New York: Wiley.

Fiedler, K. (1991). On the task, the measures and the mood in research on affect and social cognition. In J. P. Forgas (Ed.), *Emotion and social judgments* (pp. 83–104). Elmsford, NY: Pergamon Press.

Fiedler, K. (2000). Towards an integrative account of affect and cognition phenomena using the BIAS computer algorithm. In J. P. Forgas (Ed.), *Feeling and thinking: The Role of affect in social cognition* (pp. 223–252). New York: Cambridge University Press.

Fiedler, K., & Forgas, J. P. (Eds.). (1988). *Affect, cognition, and social behavior: New evidence and integrative attempts* (pp. 44–62). Toronto: Hogrefe.

Forgas, J. P. (1985). *Interpersonal behaviour: The psychology of social interaction.* Oxford and Sydney: Pergamon Press.

Forgas, J. P. (1989). Mood effects on decision-making strategies. *Australian Journal of Psychology, 41,* 197–214.

Forgas, J. P. (1991). Mood effects on partner choice: Role of affect in social decisions. *Journal of Personality and Social Psychology, 61,* 708–720.

Forgas, J. P. (1992). Affect in social judgments and decisions: A multi-process model. In M. Zanna (Ed.), *Advances in experimental social psychology* (Vol. 25, pp. 227–275). San Diego, CA: Academic Press.

Forgas, J. P. (1995). Mood and judgment: The affect infusion model (AIM). *Psychological Bulletin, 117*(1), 39–66.

Forgas, J. P. (1998a). On feeling good and getting your way: Mood effects on negotiation strategies and outcomes. *Journal of Personality and Social Psychology, 74,* 565–577.

Forgas, J. P. (1998b). Asking nicely? Mood effects on responding to more or less polite requests. *Personality and Social Psychology Bulletin, 24,* 173–185.

Forgas, J. P. (1998c). Happy and mistaken? Mood effects on the fundamental attribution error. *Journal of Personality and Social Psychology, 75,* 318–331.

Forgas, J. P. (1999a). On feeling good and being rude: Affective influences on language use and request formulations. *Journal of Personality and Social Psychology, 76,* 928–939.

Forgas, J. P. (1999b). Feeling and speaking: Mood effects on verbal communication strategies. *Personality and Social Psychology Bulletin, 25,* 850–863.

Forgas, J. P. (Ed.). (2000). *Feeling and thinking: The role of affect in social cognition.* New York: Cambridge University Press.

Forgas, J. P. (Ed.). (2001a). *The handbook of affect and social cognition.* Mahwah, NJ: Erlbaum.

Forgas, J. P. (2001b). *Mood effects on self-disclosure.* Unpublished manuscript.

Forgas, J. P. (2002). Feeling and doing: Affective influences on interpersonal behavior. *Psychological Inquiry, 13,* 1–28.

Forgas, J. P., & Bower, G. H. (1987). Mood effects on person-perception judgments. *Journal of Personality and Social Psychology, 53*(1), 53–60.

Forgas, J. P., Bower, G. H., & Krantz, S. (1984). The influence of mood on perceptions of social interactions. *Journal of Experimental Social Psychology, 20,* 497–413.

Forgas, J. P., & Ciarocchi, J. (2000). Affect infusion and affect control: The interactive role of conscious and unconscious processing strategies in mood management. In Y. Rossetti & A. Revonsuo (Eds.), *Beyond dissociation: Interaction between dissociated implicit and explicit processing* (pp. 243–271). Amsterdam: John Benjamins.

Forgas, J. P., & Ciarocchi, J. (2002). On managing moods: Evidence for the role of homeostatic cognitive strategies in affect regulation. *Personality and Social Psychology Bulletin, 28,* 336–345.

Forgas, J. P., & Fiedler, K. (1996). Us and them: Mood effects on intergroup discrimination. *Journal of Personality and Social Psychology, 70,* 36–52.

Forgas, J. P. Johnson, R., & Ciarrochi, J. (1998). Affect control and affect infusion: A multi-process account of mood management and personal control. In M. Kofta, G. Weary, & G. Sedek (Eds.), *Personal control in action: Cognitive and motivational mechanisms* (pp. 155–189). New York: Plenum Press.

Forgas, J. P., & Moylan, S. J. (1987). After the movies: The effects of transient mood states on social judgments. *Personality and Social Psychology Bulletin, 13,* 478–489.

Frijda, N. (1986). *The emotions.* Cambridge: Cambridge University Press.

Haselton, M., & Buss, D. (2003). Errors in design or by design? An evolutionary perspective on biases in social judgment and decision making. In J. P. Forgas, K. D. Williams, & W. von Hippel (Eds.), *Responding to the social world: Implicit and explicit processes in social judgments and decisions* (pp. 23–43). Philadelphia: Psychology Press.

Higgins, E. T. (2001). Promotion and prevention experiences: Relating emotions to non-emotional motivational states. In J. P. Forgas (Ed.), *The handbook of affect and social cognition* (pp. 186–211). Mahwah, NJ: Erlbaum.

Hilgard, E. R. (1980). The trilogy of mind: Cognition, affection and conation. *Journal of the History of the Behavioral Sciences, 16,* 107–117.

Locke, K. D., & Horowitz, L. M. (1990). Satisfaction in interpersonal interactions as a function of similarity in level of dysphoria. *Journal of Personality and Social Psychology, 58,* 823–831.

Mayer, J. D., Gaschke, Y. N., Braverman, D. L., & Evans, T. W. (1992). Mood congruent judgment is a general effect. *Journal of Personality and Social Psychology, 63,* 119–132.

Parrott, W. G. (2001). The nature of emotion. In A. Tesser & N. Schwarz (Eds.), *Intraindividual processes* (pp. 375–390). Oxford: Blackwell.

Ross, M., & Buehler, R. (2001). Identity through time: Constructing personal pasts and futures. In A. Tesser & N. Schwarz (Eds.), *Intraindividual processes* (pp. 518–544). Oxford: Blackwell.

Rusting, C. (2001). Personality as a mediator of affective influences on social cognition. In J. P. Forgas (Ed.), *The handbook of affect and social cognition* (pp. 371–391). Mahwah, NJ: Erlbaum.

Salovey, P., O'Leary, A., Stretton, M., Fishkin, S., & Drake, C. A. (1991). Influence of mood on judgments about health and illness. In J. P. Forgas (Ed.), *Emotion and social judgments* (pp. 241–262). Oxford: Pergamon Press.

Schachter, S. (1959). *The psychology of affiliation.* Stanford, CA: Stanford University Press.

Schwarz, N. (1990). Feelings as information: Informational and motivational functions of affective states. In E. T. Higgins & R. Sorrentino (Eds.), *Handbook of motivation and cognition: Foundations of social behaviour* (Vol. 2, pp. 527–561). New York: Guilford Press.

Sedikides, C. (1992a). Changes in the valence of self as a function of mood. *Review of Personality and Social Psychology, 14,* 271–311.

Sedikides, C. (1992b). Mood as a determinant of attentional focus. *Cognition and Emotion, 6,* 129–148.

Sedikides, C. (1994). Incongruent effects of sad mood on self-conception valence: It's a matter of time. *European Journal of Social Psychology, 24,* 161–172.

Sedikides, C. (1995). Central and peripheral self-conceptions are differentially influenced by mood: Tests of the differential sensitivity hypothesis. *Journal of Personality and Social Psychology, 69*(4), 759–777.

Smith, S. M., & Petty, R. E. (1995). Personality moderators of mood congruency effects on cognition: The role of self-esteem and negative mood regulation. *Journal of Personality and Social Psychology, 68,* 1092–1107.

Trope, Y., Ferguson, M., & Raghunanthan, R. (2001). Mood as a resource in processing self-revalant information. In J. P. Forgas (Ed.), *The handbook of affect and social cognition* (pp. 256–274). Mahwah, NJ: Erlbaum.

Velten, E. (1968). A laboratory task for induction of mood states. *Advances in Behavior Research and Therapy, 6*, 473–482.

Wilson, T. D., Gilbert, D. T., & Centerbar, D. B. (in press). Making sense: The causes of emotional evanescence. In J. Carrillo & I. Brocas (Eds.), *Economics and psychology.* New York: Oxford University Press.

Zajonc, R. B. (1980). Feeling and thinking: Preferences need no inferences. *American Psychologist, 35*, 151–175.

Zajonc, R. B. (2000). Feeling and thinking: Closing the debate over the independence of affect. In J. P. Forgas (Ed.), *Feeling and thinking: The role of affect in social cognition* (pp. 31–58). New York: Cambridge University Press.

11

Internal and External Encoding Style and Social Motivation

Pawel Lewicki

INTRODUCTION

It is probably trivial to state that the main reason for the wide variety of social motives we encounter daily is that the people we observe simply differ from each other. If so, then it is surprising to find that research on social motivation usually deals with explanatory processes that are assumed to work similarly across individuals, and that very little research attention is devoted to individual differences (for some notable exceptions, see Kernis & Goldman, and Rhodewalt, this volume).

One of the possible reasons for this paradox is the lack of success of traditional research on individual differences to offer sufficiently *deep* explanations (i.e., explanations in terms of underlying processes) and a preoccupation with relatively simple taxonomies that have typically been descriptive (as opposed to explanatory) in nature. Traditional research on individual differences has been of more benefit to applied areas (e.g., personnel selection in industrial-organizational psychology) than for understanding the general determinants of social motivation.

One of the potential sources of new relevant evidence that could help us understand the nature of social motivation is research on implicit cognition and knowledge acquisition. As summarized by Greenwald and Banaji (1995):

Much social cognition occurs in an implicit mode. . . . The missing ingredient is now available, as cognitive psychologists have succeeded in producing several varieties of unconscious cognition reliably in the laboratory (see overviews by Greenwald, 1992; Kihlstrom, 1987 . . .), and investigations of implicit social cognition are well

Research reviewed in this chapter was partially supported by the National Institute of Mental Health Grant MH42715. Address for correspondence: Pawel Lewicki, Department of Psychology, University of Tulsa, Tulsa, OK 74104; e-mail: pawel-lewicki@utulsa.edu.

194

underway.... Perhaps the most significant remaining challenge is to adapt these methods for efficient assessment of *individual differences* in implicit social cognition. (p. 20)

Substantial progress has been made in understanding implicit cognition and some of the processes of nonconscious knowledge acquisition. Also, there are reasons to believe that these processes are a major driving force creating differences between individuals, especially differences in their schemata – which act as crucial filters limiting what a person can notice (encode) and determining the subsequent dynamics and further development of implicitly acquired knowledge.

This chapter summarizes a line of research that resulted from studies on the nonconscious acquisition of knowledge, which has produced consistent findings of individual differences that can explain differences in social motivation.

The starting point of this research was an unexpected observation of the results of some experiments on self-perpetuation conducted almost 10 years ago. We need to start with some background information on this research.

COGNITIVE SELF-PERPETUATION IN ENCODING

The phenomenon of self-perpetuation explains how individuals may sometimes acquire cognitive (encoding/interpretive) dispositions that are based on relations between variables that are not (statistically) interrelated in the real world and relations that do not reflect what these individuals have been encountering. It can also explain how such dispositions can gradually strengthen and grow over time in the apparent absence of any supportive evidence.

The Specific Mechanism

If an individual exhibits even a very weak (and not articulated) encoding bias implying a relation between two variables, A and B [e.g., "people with dark eyes (A) are arrogant (B)"], then any subsequent encounters with A (dark eyes) in the absence of unambiguous information about B (arrogance) may bias the encoding of the (objectively ambiguous) level of B in the direction that is consistent with the initial A–B relation. This may artificially generate experience that is functionally equivalent of encountering real instances supportive of the A–B relation, and as a result of this simple process of "filling in the blanks," the strength of the schema assuming the A–B relation can gradually grow over time despite the absence of any objectively supportive evidence.

Generality

This phenomenon appears to be quite ubiquitous. It has been demonstrated with a wide variety of stimulus materials and experimental conditions in over 50 experiments, and it may be responsible for the development of a wide variety of those individual differences that cannot be explained by more straightforward forms of explicit and implicit learning about the environment or by the genetic factors (Gill, 2000; Hill, Lewicki, Czyzewska, & Boss, 1989, Hill, Lewicki, Czyzewska, & Schuller, 1990; Hill, Lewicki, & Neubauer, 1991; Lewicki, Hill, & Czyzewska 1992, 1994, 1997; Lewicki, Hill, & Sasaki, 1989; Stamov-Rossnagel, 2001; Vequist, 2001). Previous research has also demonstrated that the starting point for that self-perpetuation process (i.e., the initial slight encoding bias to be subject to the further *perpetuation* process) can be triggered by entirely accidental and limited in scope experience, such as a single instance experience that does not need to be particularly salient or even meaningful (Lewicki, 1985). Self-perpetuation can contribute to the development of a wide variety of personality dispositions ranging from simple preferences for colors, music, art, landscapes, interest in specific subjects, activities, and attraction, to specific types of people, to the development of serious psychological disorders. Specifically, there are reasons to believe that cognitive self-perpetuation-like mechanisms may play a significant role in the gradual deepening of interpretive biases so often observed in a variety of disorders, from paranoia (Combs, in press) to anxiety disorders and depression (Hill et al., 1991).

At the same time, both theoretical reasoning and empirical data suggest that self-perpetuation may act as a catalyst, accelerating the process of development of new interpretive schemata and facilitating the acquisition of skills (Gill, 2000; Lewicki, Hill, & Czyzewska, 1992; Sailer & Grubb, 1999; Vequist, 2001).

Individual Differences

A qualitative analysis of these laboratory experiments on self-perpetuation revealed clear individual differences. That is, whereas self-perpetuation appears to be a general phenomenon that can be observed to some extent in most or all individuals, its dynamics turned out to vary significantly across individuals: In some, the encoding indicative of self-perpetuation represents only a slight bias in perception, whereas in others, it is strong and it progresses more rapidly. Moreover, these differences are not related to the ease of the initial acquisition of the covariation (A–B) to be self-perpetuated in the experiment, or to other potential indices of attention or the motivation to participate in the study. Also, these individual differences appeared to be stable across experiments when the same individuals participated in more than one experimental procedure.

It also appears that participants differ in their ability to abandon an encoding disposition when it appears to be inadequate and to switch to a new one. For example, the analysis of changes in participants' performance across segments of a task that requires switching of encoding algorithms (and the qualitative analysis of the false-alarm errors) has revealed that whereas some participants easily accept the inappropriateness of the current encoding algorithm, stop applying it, and start developing a new one, other participants appear less sensitive to the changing conditions and continue to – almost compulsively – act on the previously developed encoding algorithm despite its lack of fit to the new segment of the material.

STYLES OF COGNITIVE ENCODING

Because these systematic differences in behavior may pertain to some, potentially very general, low-level aspects or styles of encoding, we realized that understanding the cause (or the mechanism) of these differences could bring significant insights about the mechanisms of human cognition.

Explanation of Individual Differences in Self-Perpetuation: The Threshold of Instantiation of Schemata Hypothesis

We hypothesized that the observed individual differences in the tendency to self-perpetuate may result from individual differences in more elementary processes of encoding. Specifically, as it is widely accepted in cognitive psychology, encoding processes impose on stimuli preexisting categories (i.e., interpretive schemata) even if the stimuli do not match the categories very well. This process of imposing such imperfectly fitting interpretive schemata has been shown in a number of studies on pattern recognition and prototype abstraction (e.g., Posner, Goldsmith, & Welton, 1967; Reed, 1972), person perception (e.g., Cantor & Mischel, 1979; Higgins & King, 1981), and, more recently, in research on the nonconscious acquisition of information about covariations and its influence on subsequent encoding processes (Lewicki, 1986a, 1986b; Lewicki, Czyzewska, & Hoffman, 1987; Lewicki, Hill, & Bizot, 1988).

Even though, in order for an interpretive schema to be imposed on the stimulus, the match between the stimulus and the schema does not have to be perfect, there always needs to be a particular minimum amount of direct or indirect evidence (supportive of selecting the particular interpretive schema) available to the perceiver before the schema can be instantiated. Theoretically, the required threshold amount of such evidence (necessary to instantiate an interpretive schema) can represent a trade-off between speed and accuracy: The lower the threshold (i.e., the minimum amount of evidence) necessary to trigger the use of an encoding schema, the faster the encoding (at the expense of accuracy – because the hastily selected schema may not be the most appropriate one). On the other hand, the higher the threshold necessary to trigger the instantiation of an encoding schema, the more accurate the selection of the schema (at the expense of speed).

Internal versus External Encoding Style

In summary, the hypothesis that led to the development of this line of research states that observed individual differences in the tendency to self-perpetuate are at least partially due to the differences between participants in terms of how hasty (or *Internal* – i.e., based on internal encoding schemata) versus conservative (or *External* – based on data from external stimuli) their encoding processes are. Put another way, the hypothesized dimension of encoding style determines how much supportive evidence a perceiver needs to collect before imposing an interpretive schema on a stimulus (i.e., perceiving the stimulus as an instantiation of the schema).

The more Internal the style of encoding, the greater the probability that the environmental cues would be interpreted in terms of pre-existing (Internal) encoding schemata, thus providing support for those schemata and contributing to their reinforcement through the process of self-perpetuation, as discussed in previous sections.

Note that the distinction between such Internal and External perceptual styles has been used before in the context of situational factors affecting perception, for example in the context of the influence of affect on judgment. For example, Forgas and East (2003) stated, "As feeling good seems to produce a thinking style that relies more heavily on *internal* thoughts, dispositions and ideas than on the *external* stimulus information, in this mode of thinking individuals tend to pay less attention to *external* information" (p. 206, see also Forgas & Laham, this volume). However, the evidence presented here supports the notion that these styles may also represent stable individual differences caused by low-level mechanisms of encoding identified using laboratory cognitive methods such as patterns of reaction times.

EMPIRICAL EVIDENCE FOR COGNITIVE ENCODING STYLES

In a series of preliminary studies, we constructed a questionnaire to identify the hypothesized behavioral "symptoms" of the Internal encoding style and then correlated participants' responses to that questionnaire first with:

   a.   patterns of response times and responses in the cognitive (computer-controlled) tasks used to identify and measure self-perpetuation

and then with

   b.   other tasks designed to test the expected behavior of Internal and External encoders.

Experiencing Split-Second Illusions and the Encoding Style Questionnaire (ESQ)

Following the reasoning presented previously, we hypothesized that persons with the Internal encoding style – who in the process of encoding are more likely to impose imperfect or even wrong encoding schemata – would be more likely to experience *split-second illusions* when identifying certain known objects or phenomena. Pilot studies revealed that people differ sharply in terms of how often they experience such split-second encoding errors.

For example, we asked college students if, while driving, they have ever experienced split-second illusions of recognizing (erroneously) an animal moving on or off the road, only to find out a moment later that it was a piece of paper moved by the wind or a piece of an old tire.

We found marked differences in participants' responses. In a typical undergraduate class, approximately 30% of students reported having this experience very often, while approximately 40% of students reported having it sometimes. Interestingly, the remaining 30% of the students in a typical class deny ever having had this experience (some of them even expressed surprise that a normal person might have such a strange experiences and "see things that are not there").

Based on pilot studies and interviews with respondents, we identified several types of real-life situations in which the split-second illusion (or encoding error) occurs. Nine items asking about the relative frequency of these experiences were mixed with 22 filler items (also asking about the relative frequency of specific experiences), and they formed the ESQ (labeled for participants "NISROE Questionnaire"). Example items are as follows:

2. **When waiting on someone in the airport do you sometimes think that other people coming off the plane are the person you are waiting for?**
   1 . . 2 . . 3 . . 4 . . 5 . . 6

15. **Sometimes when driving down the road do you see a piece of paper blowing in the wind, and for a split second think it might be an animal?**
   1 . . 2 . . 3 . . 4 . . 5 . . 6

26. **Have you ever tried calling someone and thought for a split second that you heard their voice when someone else answers?**
   1 . . 2 . . 3 . . 4 . . 5 . . 6

28. **Have you ever seen a piece of rubber tire on the road while you were driving and for a split second thought it was an animal or something?**
   1 . . 2 . . 3 . . 4 . . 5 . . 6

The analysis of data from over 200 participants who completed the questionnaire indicates that the nine items have relatively homogeneous psychometric characteristics.

The score for the Internal encoding style was calculated as the average rating on the nine crucial items divided by the average rating on the remaining items (asking also about the frequency of relatively unusual experiences); the higher the score, the higher the reported (relative) frequency of having experiences indicative of the hasty application of encoding schemata.

A series of exploratory studies using a variety of tools did not reveal any reliable correlations between the measure of encoding style derived from the ESQ and the personality dimensions measured by the Myers-Briggs Type Indicator or any of the "big five" factors of personality. No correlations were found between the test score and the Social Desirability scale (Marlowe-Crowne) and lie scores from various tools, or a standard set of biographical data (including gender, socioeconomic status, and family structure). No correlations were found with IQ or any of the scales of intelligence, as measured by the Wechsler test (except for scales that involve visual information processing, where the scores of Internal encoders were higher). Also, no correlations were found with field dependence (Witkin & Goodenough, 1981), need for cognitive closure (Kruglanski, Atash, De Grada, Mannetti, & Pierro, 1997), or several other dimensions that might be speculated to be related to the style of encoding.

The Use of the Terms *Internal* and *External Encoding Style* (in This Chapter)

In this chapter, we use the terms Internal and External encoding style. However, this does not mean that we assume any dichotomous typologies of encoding styles. At this point, it is safe to assume that the two styles represent ranges on a continuum (from extremely internal to extremely external encoding style). The distributions of both the scores from the ESQ and the related cognitive/experimental methods (that will be mentioned later) appear to be normal or flattened normal.

The Relation Between Encoding Style and Laboratory Measures of Self-Perpetuation

Several experiments using cognitive research methods tested in the previous research on self-perpetuation have confirmed the expectation that those individuals who exhibit a relatively high level of self-perpetuation in laboratory conditions also experience split-second illusions in everyday life more often.

In one study, the ESQ was filled out by a group of college students who then took part in a computer-controlled experiment (*Bamboo task*) designed to measure self-perpetuation of newly acquired encoding algorithms (Gill, 2000). Consistent with expectations, the self-perpetuating increase in consistency of participants' responses with the newly acquired encoding algorithm was reliably related to participants' scores in the ESQ. Specifically, participants who reported relatively higher frequencies of split-second illusions also showed more self-perpetuation as measured in the computer-controlled cognitive task. This pattern was replicated in a follow-up study. In another study (using the *Brain scans procedure*: Lewicki et al., 1989, 1994; Stamov-Rossnagel, 2001 to measure self-perpetuation), the rate of self-perpetuation again correlated reliably with the Internality index from the ESQ. The same result was replicated in a study using the matrix scanning procedure (Lewicki et al., 1989; Stadler, 1989), where the correlation between self-perpetuation and Internality was again in the expected direction and was reliable.

Tachistoscope and Partial Displays Studies

In order to test the crucial hypothesis that Internal encoders exhibit a lower threshold of instantiation of interpretive schemata in the process of encoding, two studies were conducted. In the first one, 24 graduate students were exposed to tachistoscopic (and borderline subliminal) presentations of slides of everyday objects and asked to recognize them. As expected, Internal encoders were more accurate than external encoders (Gill, 2000). In the second study (Gill, 2000), slides of objects were replaced with incomplete displays of letters made of fuzzy dots (and also displayed borderline subliminally). As expected, the accuracy of encoding (recognition of letters) was found to correlate with participants' encoding style, with the Internal encoders being more accurate. This task also allowed us to register response times in which there was a clear trend suggesting that the Internal encoders might have taken less time to identify the letters.

Replication with 7-Year-Old Children

These studies were conceptually replicated with a sample of 52 7-year-old children (Brown, 1999). A version of the ESQ adjusted for this age group (e.g., "Have you ever thought that you saw an animal in the sky when it was really just a cloud?" "Have you ever been waiting for someone to pick you up from school (or a friend's house, etc.) and thought that you saw their car, but then it turned out to be someone else?"), was used and the index computed as before [i.e., the frequency of reporting split-second illusions relative to reporting other (unusual but irrelevant) experiences]. The tachistoscopic images were changed to pictures of cartoons for children (e.g., Roadrunner, a rabbit, an owl). Again, those children who were more Internal, as measured by the modified ESQ, were also better at accurate encoding of the tachistoscopically presented images (Brown, 1999). Obviously, true longitudinal data would be necessary to support a claim about the stability of the cognitive style over the individual's life, but this preliminary result is at least consistent with that notion.

Cross-Cultural Replication

Another conceptual replication of this study was obtained with a sample of inhabitants of a small, isolated island in a remote part of the Lau archipelago in the South Pacific, using a version of the ESQ adjusted for this group (e.g., "Have you ever thought for a moment that you saw a coconut crab when it turned out to be a piece of dark rock?" "Have you ever thought for a moment that you saw a Nuqua [a black square-shaped fish, commonly caught with a spear], only to realize it was just a weed or a shadow of something?"), with the tachistoscopic images changed to pictures of objects they were most familiar with (e.g., a bure, an octopus, a tabua, copra). Again, clear individual differences were found, and those who were more Internal, as measured by the modified ESQ, were also better at accurate encoding of the tachistoscopically presented images.

Specific Skills as Measured By Real-Life Performance (Sport Studies)

The hypothesized differences in the execution of encoding processes be-tween Internal and External encoders can produce testable hypotheses about the types of specific performance where the task requirements would benefit one encoding style over another.

Measures of specific aspects of performance in various disciplines of sport appear to provide good conditions to verify hypotheses about the theoretically expected advantages of Internal versus External encoders across types of performance, and we have collected supportive evidence in studies that focused on specific aspects of athletic skill acquisition and performance in tennis, soccer, and rowing. As expected, both External and Internal encoders were found to have specific advantages – different for each style – across different measures of their performance.

In one of these studies, Sandra Sailor (who was a psychology student and a professional tennis instructor and player; Sailor & Grubb, 1999) hypothesized that a particular skill that can be identified as a component of successful tennis playing can be facilitated by the Internal encoding style. Specifically, she noticed that one component of being a good tennis player is the ability to anticipate the subsequent move of the opponent based on relatively ambiguous (and "probabilistic only") evidence such as the extremely subtle and usually impossible to articulate cues potentially gen-erated by the opponent's body language. While this skill is not sufficient to be a winning player, this *anticipatory skill* is important and can be identified by experienced observers.

Sailor had hypothesized that External encoders would be relatively less capable of responding quickly to such potentially useful cues – because their threshold of instantiation of schemata is higher – and thus this as-pect of their game would be inferior to that of Internals. She recruited as

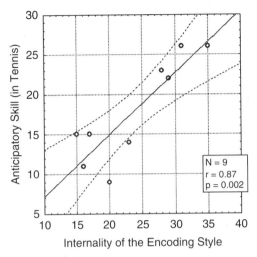

FIGURE 11.1

participants for this study all nine members of the University of Tulsa's top women's tennis team – a group of serious players, who treated tennis as an important part of their lives (most were supported by tennis scholarships), who trained together daily, played often against each other, and had reliable experience with each other's strengths and weaknesses as tennis players. Sailor had all of the them (a) fill out the ESQ and, at a different time, (b) rate each other on the dimension of the anticipatory skill (as explained earlier), using a forced choice method in which each player had to be qualified as belonging to the top (rating 3), middle (2), or bottom (1) group and the N in each of the three groups was supposed to be at least 2. The sums of ratings obtained by each player were found to be very highly correlated with the Internality of their encoding style ($r(7) = .87$, $p = .002$). The anticipatory skill of virtually all four players who were Internal encoders was rated high, and that of all five External encoders was rated low.

Evidence from the In-Depth Case Studies

Gill and Phillips (Gill, 2000), conducted in-depth cases studies of the personalities of 16 people selected (based on the results of the ESQ and other measures) as extremely Internal ($N = 8$) and extremely External ($N = 8$). The case study methodology involved three 1.5-hour structured interview sessions (for a total of 4.5 hours, where participants' responses to 131 open-ended questions were recorded and later rated independently to produce quantitative scores), questionnaires, and experimental tasks. The extensive results of this study (see Gill, 2000) can be fairly summarized as revealing

significant global (and also many specific) differences between the personalities of these two extreme groups.

Among others, the results of the interviews provided further support
for the notion that the Internal encoding style may unspecifically facilitate
(through self-perpetuation) the development of biases contributing to (or
associated with) symptoms of disorders (as confirmed before in the study
by Hill et al., 1991), and this was further confirmed by the results of the
NEO PI-R Inventory filled by the participants, where Internality of the
encoding style correlated not only with *Fantasy* [$r(14) = .75, p < .001$],
Feelings [$r(14) = .67, p < .004$], and the *Openness Domain* [$r(14) = .80, p < .0002$], but also with *Anxiety* [$r(14) = .52, p < .04$], *Depression* [$r(14) = .57, p < .02$], *Impulsiveness* [$r(14) = .71, p < .002$], and the *Neuroticism Domain*
[$r(14) = .58, p < .02$]. (Note that the values of these correlation coefficients
may have been artificially inflated by the fact that the sample was not
homogeneous but consisted of two extreme groups; however, they still
indicate clearly different scores for Internal and External encoders on the
respective scales of the NEO Inventory.)

These case studies produced a large number of testable hypotheses
about the personalities of Internal and External encoders, but among the
most easy to test (and perhaps interpret) is convergent evidence (from
both in-depth interviews and other measures) that across a spectrum of
dimensions (personal life, work and vocational preferences, aesthetic preferences), External encoders prefer structured environments with clearly
identifiable rules, whereas Internal encoders prefer less structured environments and do well in conditions of relative ambiguity that require reliance
on intuition and rapid decision making based on insufficient data.

This latter conclusion from the in-depth case studies, which also appears
consistent with the hypothesized core difference in the cognitive styles of
Internal and External encoders, was tested in several studies where the
actual preferences exhibited by participants in real-life conditions and their
satisfaction with the relevant social arrangements were tested.

Preference for Less Constrained Environments/Activities

The predicted preference of Internal encoders for less constrained environments was tested directly in a study conducted at the University of Tulsa
Management Assessment Center (MAC), a unit that conducts research and
provides services in the area of management training and assessment. Thir-
teen participants watched a training video tape of four persons (*assessees*)
taking part in a so-called leaderless group discussion in an assessment
center setting, and they were asked to rate the communication skill of the
assessees (McCord, 2002).

Roughly half of the participants first conducted the rating task by using
the Coding Rules method, which was based on a set of detailed, strictly

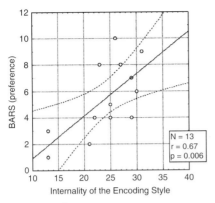
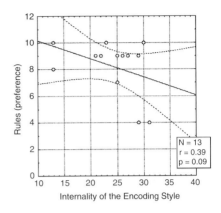

FIGURE 11.2

defined rating rules, leaving very little freedom or interpretive ambiguity. The other half of the participants conducted the first rating task by using the so-called Behaviorally Anchored Rating Scales (BARS). The BARS method is much less algorithmic and restrictive and gave participants more choice as to how to evaluate the performance of the assessees. In general, this method calls for a more global approach to the rating task. After a short break, the video was viewed again and the participants switched the rating methods. When the task was completed, the participants were asked to rate the ease of use of each tool on a scale of 1 to 10 (1 most difficult, 10 easiest).

The results were consistent with the expectation that Internal encoders would prefer the less constrained (BARS) method over the rule-bound Coding Rules method. The participants' scores of Internality correlated strongly with the preference for the BARS method [$r(11) = .679, p = .006$]; they also correlated negatively with the participants' preference for the Rules-based method [$r(11) = -39, p = .09$].

Tolerance for New, Unstructured Environments

Following the reasoning just presented, concerning the relatively higher tolerance (if not real preference) of Internal encoders for less structured environments, we hypothesized that Internal encoders would adapt relatively better to new social environments (such as living in a foreign country).

We tested a large group of foreign students attending a school in the United States, who have thus experienced a transition to a new and more ambiguous (because less well known) environment. Ascalon (2001) designed a comprehensive International Students Survey of satisfaction (with different aspects of their lives) and invited to participate in this survey

250 foreign students who were attending the University of Tulsa. The survey was relatively comprehensive and covered a wide variety of aspects of university, social, cultural, and personal life. Most questions were based on 6-point rating scales and covered such topics as the quality of the curriculum, the respondents' perceived personal safety, attitudes toward America, and possible frustrations with any aspects of their lives. As many as 80% of invited students (199 out of 250) participated in the survey (which was conducted over the campus Intranet) and, as expected, Internal encoders turned out to be overwhelmingly better adjusted to life in the new environment. Although no similar patterns of correlation were found when the same questions were asked of American students, foreign students who were Internal encoders turned out to be significantly more satisfied with virtually all aspects of their lives, perceiving themselves as more successful in the new environment and more self-confident. For example, foreign students who were Internal encoders felt more "comfortable about asking questions in class" [$r(197) = .55$], "accepted by American society" (.43), had more friends (.42), felt safer (.36), and felt better served by the school (.45). (All correlations significant at the $p < .0001$ level.)

This study was also the first, other than the in-depth case studies summarized earlier, to provide support for the hypothesis that the style of encoding would determine vocational preferences by facilitating both (a) different sets of specific cognitive skills and (b) preferences for dealing with specific types of environments. Based on the theoretical reasoning discussed at the beginning of this chapter and confirmed by the in-depth case study data, it was hypothesized that External encoders would make real-life vocational choices in favor of jobs that involve more strictly rule-bound activities (e.g., programming, engineering), whereas Internal encoders would choose jobs that are less rule-bound (e.g., the arts, the humanities).

Despite the very uneven distribution of majors chosen by members of this unusual sample (in which the majority of students who reported their majors specialized in engineering or computer science – specifically, 149 out of 183), the hypothesis was fully supported. Specifically, the average Internality score of 35 participants who majored in nonengineering or computer-related disciplines (such as art, the humanities, or psychology) was 4.13, which was significantly higher than the mean of 3.23 achieved in the group of 149 engineering and computer science students [$t(181) = 2.78, p = .003$].

We found this result to be important because it demonstrated how the consequences of encoding style may translate into real choices and motivation (measured in an ecologically valid manner) to devote one's professional life to very different types of activities. Therefore, we decided to test this result in a series of two designated studies with more representative samples of participants and more even distributions of vocational choices made.

Vocational Preferences of Internal and External Encoders

The study was conducted by Osicki (2002), who tested the hypothesis that External encoders would make real-life vocational choices in favor of jobs that involve dealing with strictly rule-bound and conforming types of reality or environment [such as computer programming, engineering (electrical, civil), or accounting], whereas Internal encoders would chose jobs that are less rule-bound and conforming (the arts, the humanities, business management). These expectations received consistent and strong support in two studies with large, highly representative samples of college graduates ($N = 146$ and $N = 345$). Moreover, the data collected by Osicki (2002) demonstrate that even when the analysis was restricted from the broad spectrum of majors (e.g., from math to the arts) to a much narrower range such as "Business School graduates only," the encoding style score (as measured by the ESQ) could still reliably predict the specialization of the student – with External encoders choosing accounting or management information systems and Internal encoders choosing business administration or international business.

SUMMARY AND CONCLUSIONS

The results of these studies demonstrate the role of cognitively interpretable individual differences as the determinants of motivations that people demonstrate in their real lives. The data provide consistent evidence for the existence of a dimension of encoding style that can be described in relatively specific terms of underlying cognitive mechanisms. These findings come from data collected using such indices as patterns of reaction times or rates of recognition of tachistoscopically presented stimuli and appear to determine a variety of interpretable behavioral consequences in important areas ranging from social adjustment (e.g., perpetuation of symptoms of mental disorders) to specific cognitive skills and vocational preferences.

As suggested by the presented data, research on encoding styles can explain crucial, easily observable (and subjectively experienced) aspects of human behavior with low-level mechanisms identified using objective measures of cognitive performance in well-controlled laboratory conditions. The mere fact that something as concrete, observable, and "experiential" as the frequency of experiencing split-second illusions was found to be predictably correlated with objective measures (selected a priori) of low-level cognitive processes (such as patterns of reaction time or tachistoscopic indices) is encouraging and suggests that this phenomenon is worth further research attention.

In short, this phenomenon appears to be relatively unique in research on basic cognitive processes in that it not only deals with individual differences (an area of psychology that offers so far relatively few low-level, cognitive explanations or root causes of its subject matter), but also offers explanations of more than abstract personality traits, because it can help us understand specific, observable behavioral choices made by people in their real lives (e.g., choices of careers).

References

Ascalon, E. (2001). *Encoding style and the satisfaction of international students (international student survey)*. Technical Report, University of Tulsa.

Brown, C. (1999). *Internal and external encoding styles in seven year old children*. Technical Report, University of Tulsa.

Cantor, N., & Mischel, W. (1979). Prototypes in person perception. In L. Berkowitz (Ed.), *Advances in experimental social psychology* (Vol. 12, pp. 3–52). New York: Academic Press.

Combs, D. (in press). Implicit Learning and non-clinical paranoia: Does content matter? *Personality and Individual Differences*.

Gill, T. (2000). *Individual differences in schema activation, as measured by the Revised Nisroe (The Encoding Style Questionnaire)*. Unpublished doctoral dissertation, University of Tulsa.

Greenwald, A. G. (1992). Unconscious cognition reclaimed. *American Psychologist*, 47, 766–779.

Greenwald, A. G., & Banaji, M. R. (1995). Implicit social cognition: Attitudes, self-esteem, and stereotypes. *Psychological Review*, 102, 4–27.

Forgas, J. P., & East, R. (2003). Affective influences on social judgments and decisions: The role of information processing strategies. In J. P. Forgas, K. D. Williams, & W. von Hippel (Eds.), *Responding to the social world: Implicit and explicit processes in social judgments and decisions.* (pp. 198–226). New York: Psychology Press.

Higgins, E. T., & King, G. A. (1981). Accessibility of social constructs: Information processing consequences of individual and contextual variability. In N. Cantor & J. Kihlstrom (Eds.), *Personality, cognition and social interaction* (pp. 69–121). Hillsdale, NJ: Erlbaum.

Hill, T., Lewicki, P., Czyzewska, M., & Boss, A. (1989). Self-perpetuating development of encoding biases in person perception. *Journal of Personality and Social Psychology*, 57, 373–387.

Hill, T., Lewicki, P., Czyzewska, M., & Schuller, G. (1990). The role of learned inferential encoding rules in the perception of faces: Effects of nonconscious self-perpetuation of a bias. *Journal of Experimental Social Psychology*, 26, 350–371.

Hill, T., Lewicki, P., & Neubauer, R. M. (1991). The development of depressive dispositions: A case of self-perpetuation of encoding biases. *Journal of Experimental Social Psychology*, 27, 392–409.

Kihlstrom, J. (1987). The cognitive unconscious. *Science*, 237, 1445–1452.

Kruglanski, A. W., Atash, M. N., De Grada, E., Mannetti, L., & Pierro, A. (1997). Psychological theory testing versus psychometric nay saying: Need for closure scale and the Neuberg et al. critique. *Journal of Personality and Social Psychology*, 73, 1005–1016.

Lewicki, P. (1985). Nonconscious biasing effects of single instances on subsequent judgments. *Journal of Personality and Social Psychology, 48*, 563–574.

Lewicki, P. (1986a). *Nonconscious social information processing.* New York: Academic Press.

Lewicki, P. (1986b). Processing information about covariations that cannot be articulated. *Journal of Experimental Psychology: Learning, Memory, and Cognition, 12*, 135–146.

Lewicki, P., Czyzewska, M., & Hoffman, H. (1987). Unconscious acquisition of complex procedural knowledge. *Journal of Experimental Psychology: Learning, Memory, and Cognition, 13*, 523–530.

Lewicki, P., & Hill, T. (1989). On the status of nonconscious processes in human cognition. *Journal of Experimental Psychology: General, 118*, 239–241.

Lewicki, P., Hill, T., & Bizot, E. (1988). Acquisition of procedural knowledge about a pattern of stimuli that cannot be articulated. *Cognitive Psychology, 20*, 24–37.

Lewicki, P., Hill, T., & Czyzewska, M. (1992). Nonconscious acquisition of information. *American Psychologist, 47*, 796–801.

Lewicki, P., Hill, T., & Czyzewska, M. (1994). Nonconscious indirect inference in encoding. *Journal of Experimental Psychology: General, 123*, 257–263.

Lewicki, P., Hill, T., & Czyzewska, M. (1997). Hidden covariation detection: A robust and ubiquitous phenomenon. *Journal of Experimental Psychology: Learning, Memory, and Cognition, 23*, 221–118.

Lewicki, P., Hill, T., & Sasaki, I. (1989). Self-perpetuating development of encoding biases. *Journal of Experimental Psychology: General, 118*, 323–337.

McCord, M. (2002). *Encoding style and perceived difficulty of rating systems: "BARS" vs. "coding rules" for the assessment center.* Technical Report, University of Tulsa.

Osicki, M. A. (2002). *Cognitive determinants of vocational preference: The internal/external encoding styles and choice of major.* Unpublished doctoral dissertation, University of Tulsa.

Posner, M. I., Goldsmith, R., & Welton, K. E., Jr. (1967). Perceived distance and the classification of distorted patterns. *Journal of Experimental Psychology, 73*, 28–38.

Reed, S. K. (1972). Pattern recognition and categorization. *Cognitive Psychology, 3*, 382–407.

Sailor, S., & Grubb, M. (1999). *The encoding style and the development of anticipatory skills in professional tennis players.* Technical Report, University of Tulsa.

Stadler, M. (1989). On learning complex procedural knowledge. *Journal of Experimental Psychology: Learning, Memory, and Cognition, 15*, 1061–1069.

Stamov-Rossnagel, C. (2001). Revealing hidden covariation detection: Evidence for implicit abstraction at study. *Journal of Experimental Psychology: Learning, Memory, and Cognition, 27*(4), 1276–1288.

Vequist, D. (2001). *Acquisition and self-perpetuating development of encoding dispositions: A flight simulator application.* Unpublished doctoral dissertation, University of Tulsa.

Witkin, H. A., & Goodenough, D. R. (1981). *Cognitive styles: Essence and origins: Field dependence and independence.* New York: International Universities Press.

12

Authenticity, Social Motivation, and Psychological Adjustment

Michael H. Kernis and Brian M. Goldman

INTRODUCTION

> To be or not to be, that is the question.
> To thine own self be true.
> 　　　　　　　　　　–Shakespeare

Playwrights, musicians, philosophers, and psychologists have long concerned themselves with notions of authenticity. Shakespeare, for example, wrote often of themes related to being "true" to oneself and presenting a "false" self to others. Philosophers such as Lacan, Nietzsche, and Rorty take aim at the construct of authenticity by denying the existence of a coherent, unified self. The Grateful Dead, purveyors of "psychedelic" enlightenment, exhort their diehard fans to "wake up to find out that you are the eyes of the world." The Electric Kool-Aid Acid Tests that they participated in were said to promote "higher states of consciousness" that elevated participants' understanding of their roles in the material and "cosmic" universes. What all these conceptions of authenticity have in common is that authenticity is rooted in subjective internal experiences that have implications for one's self-knowledge, understanding, and their relationship to behavior. In this chapter, we present a new multicomponent conceptualization of psychological authenticity and discuss its implications for a wide range of psychological and interpersonal functioning. We begin with a brief historical overview of the authenticity construct. Of necessity, this review is highly selective, focusing entirely on the psychological literature. Following this overview, we present our conceptualization of authenticity. We then report findings from our research that bears on this conceptualization.

Address correspondence to Michael Kernis, Department of Psychology, University of Georgia, Athens, GA 30602; e-mail: mkernis@uga.edu.

HISTORICAL OVERVIEW

Within psychology, those of the humanist tradition have been the main carriers of the authenticity torch. Maslow (1968), for example, suggested that authenticity comes when individuals discover their true inner nature. This discovery emerges as individuals satisfy their psychological needs for belonging and esteem and turn toward self-actualization strivings. According to Maslow, individuals turn toward satisfying these *being* or growth-oriented needs after satisfying their other physiological and psychological needs. Focusing on growth-oriented needs provides fuller self-knowledge and increased acceptance of one's true or intrinsic nature, furthering one's movement toward self-actualization (Maslow, 1968). Rogers (1961) asserted that authenticity reflects congruence between one's self-concept and immediate experience. He observed that maladjustment often stems from the lack of congruence between one's immediate experiences (or behaviors) and one's self-concept (see Rhodewalt, this volume). In such instances, people may deny, distort, or ignore immediate experiences to preserve their existing self-concepts. What happens, ironically, is that individuals' self-concepts no longer adequately reflect working self-concepts (Markus & Nurius, 1986) into which their immediate experience may be incorporated online or *in the moment*. Instead, they are replaced by rigid, defensive self-concepts that assimilate only what is acceptable according to standards directly imposed by significant others or *introjected* to be self-administered. We return to introjected regulation later in the chapter. For now, we note that discrepancies between individuals' experiences and their self-concepts are fostered by *conditions of worth* that involve withholding love and acceptance except when externally based standards or expectations are satisfied. Authenticity from this perspective reflects the interplay of immediate experiences and self-concepts that permit a richness and openness in self-knowledge and self-understanding.

More recently, scholars have emphasized the importance of self-regulatory processes to authenticity (e.g., Deci & Ryan, 1995, 2000; Sheldon & Kasser, 1995). Self-determination theory (Deci & Ryan, 1995, 2000) holds that authenticity is a by-product of self-regulation that reflects high levels of self-determination (i.e., intrinsic or identified regulation). In contrast, self-regulation based on meeting other people's (external regulation) or one's own (introjected regulation) expectations or demands promotes inauthentic functioning (see Sheldon & Kasser, 1995, for an empirical example). Considerable research confirms the benefits of self-determined regulation in many different domains, including academic achievement (Ryan, Stiller, & Lynch, 1994), compliance with medical regimens (Williams, Rodin, Ryan, Grolnick, & Deci, 1998), religiosity (Ryan, Rigby, & King, 1993), and political involvement (Koestner, Losier, Vallerand, & Carducci, 1996).

Our own research (Goldman, Kernis, Piasecki, Hermann, & Foster, in prep.) in addition to documenting the importance of these self-regulatory processes, demonstrates that the extent to which people frame their goals as "congruent with their true selves" also has important implications for psychological health and well-being. Participants in this study selected a set of eight strivings they were currently undertaking from a broad list of achievement strivings developed by Elliot and Sheldon (1997). To assess self-regulatory styles, participants rated the extent to which each of eight factors reflected their reasons for engaging in each striving. The factors comprise four categories that according to self-determination theory reflect varying degrees of self-determination (Ryan & Connell, 1989). Reflecting the most self-determination, *intrinsic regulation* involves engaging in activities purely for the fun and enjoyment they provide. *Identified regulation* involves a moderate degree of self-determination. Here, people freely engage in activities because of their consistency with personal values and/or their positive contribution to growth and development. *Introjected regulation* involves minimal self-determination as activities are undertaken to avoid guilt and anxiety, because one "should," or because one's self-esteem depends upon them. Finally, *external regulation* reflects the least amount of self-determination because it involves doing things merely to satisfy an external force or to obtain a tangible reward or avoid punishment. For purposes of analyses, we combined participants' responses into an overall self-determination index by adding introjected and external scores and subtracting this sum from the total of identified and intrinsic scores. Therefore, higher scores indicate greater self-determined regulation.

In addition to obtaining ratings of self-regulatory styles, we obtained goal construal ratings after all participants engaged in the following *true-self induction*:

Take a few minutes and think of whom you really are as a person.

Think about those qualities you possess, your wants and desires, your hopes and fears, your feelings and thoughts that characterize who you really are as a person. Not whom your parents, family, boyfriend or girlfriend, and friends think you are, but whom you think you are when you are answering only to yourself.

Following this induction, participants rated each striving on how much it reflected who they "really are as a person" (1 = not at all, 7 = very much) (Time 1). We computed a total true-self goal score by adding responses to this item for each of the eight strivings. Finally, all participants completed Ryff's (1989) multidimensional measure of psychological adjustment, as well as measures of global life satisfaction and daily positive and negative affect. Approximately 4 weeks later, participants again completed the adjustment and well-being measures (Time 2).

Our first goal was to replicate previous findings indicating that self-regulatory styles predict a wide range of positive outcomes. Our second goal, more importantly, was to demonstrate that our true-self goal measure predicted these outcomes even when the impact of self-regulatory styles was controlled. As expected, scores on the Self-Determination Index positively correlated with scores on the True-Self Goal Index ($r = .32$). To examine their unique contributions to predicting well-being, we conducted separate analyses for each of the six Ryff subscales (Self-Acceptance, Environmental Mastery, Positive Relationships, Autonomy, Purpose in Life, Personal Growth), life satisfaction, and affect. In each instance, Time 2 scores were regressed simultaneously onto the overall self-determination and true-self goal indexes. Higher self-determination index scores related to higher life satisfaction, self-acceptance, positive relations, growth, and autonomy, and to marginally greater positive affect and environmental mastery. More important, the true-self goals index predicted greater life satisfaction, positive affect, self-acceptance, purpose in life, positive relations, and environmental mastery and marginally greater growth. These findings demonstrate the unique contribution to psychological health and well-being of our true-self goal index over and above the contribution of the well-established index of self-regulatory styles.

Next, we conducted analyses to determine whether the self-determination and true-self goal measures predicted *change* in the health and well-being measures across a 4-week time-period. These analyses are more stringent because less variance is available (after controlling for Time 1 scores) to be accounted for. Not surprisingly, then, the unique contributions of both the self-determination and true-self goal indexes were somewhat less pervasive, though they consistently were in the same direction as before. The Self-Determination Index uniquely predicted increases in life satisfaction, self-acceptance, positive relations, and autonomy. In addition, the True-Self Goal Index uniquely predicted increases in life satisfaction, positive affect, self-acceptance, purpose in life (marginally so), positive relations, and environmental mastery. Thus, we were able to predict positive change in all but one of the psychological health and well-being measures with either the self-determination or the true-self goal index (and sometimes both).

In other research, Kernis, Paradise, Whitaker, Wheatman, and Goldman (2000) reported that self-determined regulation (i.e., intrinsic and identified self-regulation) related to higher levels of, and more stable, feelings of self-worth, whereas the reverse was true for non-self-determined regulation (introjected and external regulation). Clearly, the extent to which people experience authenticity in their goal pursuits, as expressed through self-regulatory styles or goal representations, confers positive benefits on a variety of psychological health and subjective well-being measures.

Two other recent studies focus on variables related to authenticity. Sheldon, Ryan, Rawsthorne, and Ilardi (1997) examined two aspects of self-integration with respect to various social roles including student,

employee, child, friend, and romantic partner. Specifically, they operationalized self-integration in terms of subjective authenticity across social
roles and as the consistency of trait profiles across roles. Participants rated
the extent to which they enacted each of a series of Big Five trait markers
when in each of the five aforementioned roles. Consistent with the idea
that authenticity/integration confers positive benefits on the individual,
their findings indicated that greater subjective authenticity and cross-role
consistency each related to lower anxiety, depression, and stress, fewer
physical symptoms, and higher self-esteem. McGregor and Little (1998)
examined the extent to which people displayed a sense of integrity in
their everyday personal projects and the relation of *project integrity* to psychological heath. As predicted, greater project integrity related to greater
psychological health.

   The research reviewed in this section indicates that personal consistency,
self-determined regulatory styles, and integrity in one's goal pursuits are
integral to psychological health and well-being. Each of these constructs
is also relevant to the construct of psychological authenticity in that they
highlight the importance of self-integration and inclinations toward a full
sense of choice and expression of one's true self. We now present our multicomponent conceptualization of authenticity.

A MULTICOMPONENT CONCEPTUALIZATION OF
PSYCHOLOGICAL AUTHENTICITY

Goldman and Kernis (2002; see also Kernis, 2003) define authenticity as
the unobstructed operation of one's true, or core, self in one's daily enterprise. More specifically, we suggest that authenticity has four discrim-
inable components: *awareness, unbiased processing, behavior,* and *relational
orientation*. The awareness component refers to having awareness of, and
trust in, one's motives, feelings, desires, and self-relevant cognitions. It includes, but is not limited to, being aware of one's strengths and weaknesses,
trait characteristics, and emotions and their roles in behavior. An important aspect of this component is being aware of one's inherent polarities
or, as Perls (Perls, Hefferline, & Goodman, 1951) characterized it, being
aware of both *figure* and *ground* in one's personality aspects. In Perls's
view, people are not exclusively masculine *or* feminine, extroverted *or* introverted, dominant *or* submissive, and so on. Rather, although one aspect of these dualities generally predominates over the other, both aspects
exist. As individuals function with greater authenticity, they are aware that
they possess these multifaceted self-aspects, and they utilize this awareness in their interchanges with others and with their environments. In
short, the awareness component of authenticity involves knowledge of
one's needs, values, feelings, figure–ground personality aspects, and their
roles in behavior.

Note that our perspective on the awareness component of authenticity differs from other recent social psychological perspectives of self-concept structure, most notably the construct of self-concept *clarity* (Campbell, 1990; Campbell et al., 1996). According to Campbell, self-concepts characterized by high clarity are internally consistent, held with confidence, and temporally stable. From this perspective, an individual who endorses as self-descriptive both introverted and extroverted is low in self-concept clarity. Although we agree that some degree of internal consistency in self-judgments is healthy (see also Sheldon et al., 1997), we disagree with the prima facie use of mutual exclusivity of trait characteristics as a benchmark for assessing clarity.

In some self-concept clarity research, respondents make yes/no self-judgments of presumably polar opposite trait adjectives. One of the major problems with such judgments is that respondents make them without reference to situational contexts. Mischel and Shoda (1995) have shown that personality consistency (or coherence) is best thought of in relation to specific situational contexts. Consistent with this view, Sande, Goethals, and Radloff (1988) have shown that people prefer to think of themselves in ways that are complex and multifaceted rather than simplistic. In short, decontextualized yes/no self-judgments are unnecessarily constraining, as they do not permit individuals to indicate that whether they enact specific personality characteristics often depends on the situation. Another shortcoming of yes/no judgments is that they do not permit respondents to endorse possessing trait characteristics to varying degrees. As previously stated, the notion of figure–ground in personality that Perls promotes is that although one aspect of a trait duality predominates, the other, although weaker, is not absent. From Perls's perspective, to deny the existence of the weaker aspect reflects self-concept fragmentation, not clarity. So as not to digress further, we close by suggesting that more complex assessment techniques are needed to differentiate between the views espoused by Campbell versus Perls (and us), and we urge researchers to develop such techniques.[1]

A second component of authenticity involves the *unbiased processing of self-relevant information*. Stated differently, this component involves not denying, distorting, exaggerating, or ignoring private knowledge, internal experiences, and externally based evaluative information. Instead, it involves objectivity and acceptance of one's positive and negative aspects, attributes, and qualities. Some people, for instance, have great difficulty

---

[1] In fairness to Campbell, we acknowledge that research on self-concept clarity does not rely exclusively on yes/no judgments, but includes measures of subjective confidence and graduated Likert scale ratings. Nonetheless, the underlying conceptual focus is on the mutual exclusivity of trait dualities, which we take exception to in our conceptualization of the awareness component of authenticity.

acknowledging that they may not be very skillful at a particular activity. Rather than accept their poor performance, they may rationalize its implications, belittle its importance, or completely fabricate a "new" score. Others may have difficulty accepting and incorporating into the self the various ground aspects of personal qualities, as if some "alien," and not they, possesses these qualities, though at some level they may be aware of their existence. Still others have difficulty acknowledging certain unpleasant emotions in themselves, such as anger or anxiety, and instead misrepresent them as sadness or boredom, respectively.

These defensive processes are motivated, at least in part, by self-esteem concerns, and we would expect to find them for both negative and positive information. For example, people may delude themselves into believing that a triumph over a clearly inferior opponent validates their own extremely high level of ability, or they may take it for what it is – the one-time defeat of an inferior opponent.

Our view of the unbiased processing component of authenticity is consistent with recent conceptualizations of ego defense mechanisms. The recent upsurge of interest in defense mechanisms has been fortified by findings linking individual differences in defense styles to a wide range of physical and psychological outcomes. Notable in this regard is Vaillant's longitudinal work showing that adaptive defense styles that involve minimal reality distortion predict greater psychological and physical well-being many years into the future (e.g., Vaillant, 1992). In contrast, maladaptive or immature defenses that involve greater reality distortion and/or failure to acknowledge and resolve distressing emotions relate to numerous psychological and interpersonal difficulties, including poor marital adjustment (Ungerer, Waters, Barnett, & Dolby, 1997).

A third component of authenticity involves *behavior*, specifically whether people act in accord with their true selves. In our view, behaving authentically means acting in accord with one's values, preferences, and needs as opposed to acting merely to please others or to attain rewards or avoid punishments through acting "falsely" (see also Deci & Ryan, 1995; 2000; Sheldon & Kasser, 1995). Harter (1997) identified three distinct motives that underlie the display of false-self behavior among adolescents. The first motive involves devaluation of the self by self and/or others. The second motive involves wanting to please or be liked by others. The third motive involves wanting to experiment with different selves as a form of social role playing. "Those citing motives emphasizing devaluation of the self report the worst outcomes in that they (1) engage in the highest levels of false self behavior, (2) are more likely not to know who their true self really is, and (3) report the lowest self-esteem coupled with depressed affect. Those endorsing role experimentation report the most positive outcomes (least false behavior, most knowledge of true self, highest self-esteem and cheerful affect), with the approval seekers concerned with impression management falling in between" (p. 90).

We believe that, at times, role experimentation may reflect authenticity striving in that it may reflect an extension of one's true self in action. Adolescents are constantly experiencing new situations, meeting new people, and so forth. Identities may feel new or experimental in these novel contexts. They can reflect authenticity, however, to the extent that they are informed by what one knows to be true of the self. Moreover, role experimentation may be a catalyst for self-improvement and growth as individuals respond to the complex of normative changes across the life span. Role experimentation may help foster the process of experiencing life transitions as freely chosen and personally endorsed. In addition, role experimentation may enrich the breadth of possibilities included in one's reservoir of behavioral options by elaborating one's multifaceted self-concept (see Kernis & Goldman, 2002, for discussion). In other words, self-relevant information acquired during role experimentation may be integrated into one's self-concept and facilitate personally expressive choices that foster growth and self-improvement. In contrast, in those instances where one deliberately enacts an identity opposed to one's true self, role experimentation is likely to be inauthentic. As an example, recall the Seinfield episode in which George Costanza thinks about how he would normally react and deliberately does exactly the opposite.

Admittedly, instances exist in which the unadulterated expression of one's true self may result in severe social sanctions (see Rhodewalt, this volume). Here, we would expect authenticity to reflect sensitivity to the fit (or lack of) between one's true self and the dictates of the environment and an awareness of the potential implications of one's behavioral choices. Authenticity does not reflect a *compulsion* to be one's true self, but rather the free and natural expression of core feelings, motives, and inclinations (cf. Deci & Ryan, 2000). When this expression stands at odds with immediate environmental contingencies, we expect that authenticity will be reflected in short-term intrapsychic conflict. How this conflict is resolved can have considerable implications for one's felt integrity and authenticity. Rather than focusing exclusively on whether authenticity is or is not reflected in one's actions per se, focusing on the manner in which processes associated with the awareness and unbiased processing components inform one's behavioral selection is likely to be useful. For example, when a person reacts to pressure by behaving in accord with prevailing social norms that stand in contrast with his or her true self, authenticity may still be operative at the awareness and processing levels. In such instances, although authenticity is compromised at the behavioral level, it can be preserved at the awareness and unbiased processing levels. As this example indicates, sometimes the needs and values of the self are incompatible with those of society. In these instances, authenticity may be reflected in awareness of one's needs and motives and an unbiased assessment of relevant evaluative information. In some instances the resulting behavior may also reflect authenticity, but in others it may not. It follows, then, that although the awareness, unbiased processing, and behavior components of authenticity are related to each other, they remain separable.

A fourth component of authenticity involves one's *relational orientation toward others*, in other words, the extent to which one values and achieves openness and truthfulness in one's close relationships. Relational authenticity also entails valuing close others seeing one's real self, both good and bad. Toward that end, an authentic relational orientation involves a selective process of self-disclosure that fosters the development of mutual intimacy and trust. In short, relational authenticity means being genuine, and not *fake*, in one's relationships with close others.

EMPIRICAL INVESTIGATIONS USING THE AUTHENTICITY INVENTORY

Goldman and Kernis (2001) developed the Authenticity Inventory (AI) to measure these four components of authenticity. Table 12.1 includes a summary description of each authenticity component and sample items from the first version of the AI (Version I; Goldman & Kernis, 2001). The inventory contains a 15-item *Awareness* subscale ($\alpha = .74$), a 10-item *Unbiased Processing* subscale ($\alpha = .51$), a 13-item *Behavior* subscale ($\alpha = .73$), and a 6-item *Relational Orientation* subscale ($\alpha = .32$). The total scale thus contained 44 items ($\alpha = .83$). Subsequent revisions of the scale have produced different subscale compositions and accompanying changes in psychometric properties. We discuss these as warranted later in the chapter.

Authenticity, Psychological Health, and Well-Being

In our first empirical venture using the AI, we (Goldman & Kernis, 2002) examined the relations between authenticity and well-being. More specifically, we examined the relationships between authenticity and self-esteem level, contingent self-esteem (feelings of self-worth that are dependent upon the achievement of specific outcomes or evaluations, a form of fragile self-esteem; Deci & Ryan, 1995; Kernis, 2003; Kernis & Paradise, 2002), daily positive and negative affect, and life satisfaction. We expected that greater authenticity would relate to more favorable psychological health and subjective well-being.

Our participants were approximately 80 male and female introductory psychology students. They completed the following measures:

TABLE 12.1 *Authenticity Inventory Components and Sample Items*

Awareness
- Awareness of, and trust in, one's motives, feelings, desires, and self-relevant cognitions
- Includes awareness of one's strengths and weaknesses, figure-ground personality aspects, and emotions, and their roles in behavior
- Items
  1. I would like to better understand those aspects of my personality that I generally do not focus on.
  2. I am aware of when I am not being my true self.

Unbiased Processing
- Not denying, distorting, exaggerating, nor ignoring private knowledge, internal experiences, and externally based self-evaluative information
- Objectivity and acceptance of one's positive and negative aspects
- Items
  1. I tend to find it easy to pretend that I do not have faults.[a]
  2. I generally am capable of objectively considering my limitations and shortcomings.

Behavior
- Acting in accord with one's values, preferences, and needs
- Not acting merely to please others or to attain rewards or avoid punishments
- Items
  1. When I am nervous, I smile a lot.[a]
  2. I am willing to wear the right social mask for the right social occasion if it will get me what I want.[a]

Relational Orientation
- Valuing and achieving openness and truthfulness in one's close relationships
- Important for close others to see the real you, good and bad
- Relational authenticity means being genuine and not "fake" in one's relationships with others
- Items
  1. I place a great deal of importance on close others understanding who I truly am.
  2. People I am close to would be shocked and surprised if they discovered what I keep inside me.[a]

[a] These items are reverse scored.

(a) Rosenberg's (1965) Self-esteem Scale, a well-validated measure of global self-esteem level; (b) the Contingent Self-Esteem Scale (CSS; Kernis & Paradise, in prep.), a 15-item scale that assesses the extent to which individuals' self-worth depends upon meeting expectations, matching standards, or achieving specific outcomes or evaluations; (c) Life Satisfaction (Diener, Emmons, Larsen, & Griffin, 1985), a 7-item measure that assesses how satisfied individuals feel about their lives in general over the past few days; and (d) the Positive Affect/Negative Affect Scale (Brunstein, 1993), a 20-item measure that assesses experiences of positive and negative affect over the past few days. We computed a net negative affect index for the last measure by summing positive affect scores and subtracting that sum from the sum of negative affect scores.

We computed zero-order correlations between each of the measures of well-being, total AI scores, and subscale AI scores. Importantly, total AI scores significantly related to each of the psychological well-being measures. Specifically, greater self-reported authenticity related to higher levels of self-esteem and life satisfaction, and to lower self-esteem contingency and net negative affect.

In terms of the individual subscales, the Awareness subscale related to three of the four well-being measures. Specifically, greater self-reported awareness related to higher life satisfaction and self-esteem but to lower net negative affect. The Unbiased Processing subscale related only to life satisfaction such that more unbiased processing related to greater life satisfaction. The Behavior subscale related to two well-being measures. Specifically, greater behavioral authenticity related to higher levels of self-esteem and to less contingent self-esteem. Finally, the Relational Orientation subscale related to two well-being measures. Specifically, greater relational authenticity related to higher life satisfaction and to less net negative affect.

The findings from this study offer initial support for our conceptualization and assessment of multiple components of authenticity. Total Authenticity Scale scores were positively related to self-esteem level and life satisfaction, and negatively related to self-esteem contingency and net negative affect. Importantly, these findings suggest that authenticity is related to feelings of self-worth that are not only more positive, but that are more secure as well (i.e., less contingent on specific outcomes). Our findings also indicated that greater self-reported authenticity was related to the frequency of experiencing negative emotions (i.e., less net negative affect), as well as more global appraisals of individuals' perceived satisfaction in life (i.e., more life satisfaction). Taken as a whole, these findings provide initial empirical support for the contention that authenticity relates to healthy psychological functioning and positive subjective well-being.

Two findings stand out with respect to the scale itself, namely, the unacceptably low internal reliabilities obtained for the Unbiased Processing and Relational Orientation subscales. We are currently attempting to rectify these shortcomings through item revisions. In the next scale version (AI Version 2), items pertaining to relational orientation were rewritten so that they explicitly refer to relationships with close others rather than to others in general. This change alone produced over a 100% increase in the obtained alpha coefficient ($\alpha = .66$). Item revisions to the Unbiased Processing subscale yielded an alpha coefficient of .60. Although these values are improvements, they can still be improved further.

Authenticity, Goal Strivings, Psychological and Interpersonal Adjustment

In our next study (Goldman, Kernis, Piasecki, Herrmann, & Foster, in prep.), we sought to flesh out the implications of authenticity for a variety of realms of psychological and social functioning. Authenticity as an individual difference construct may be particularly important in delineating the adaptive features of optimal self-esteem. Optimal self-esteem reflects favorable conscious and nonconscious feelings of self-worth that are relatively nondefensive, stable, and not dependent upon specific outcomes or evaluations (Kernis, 2003). As Kernis describes, the favorable feelings of self-worth that characterize optimal self-esteem arise naturally from dealing successfully with life challenges, the operation of one's core, true, authentic self as a source of input to behavioral choices, and relationships in which one is valued for who one is and not for what one achieves. At least two major implications follow from the assertion that authenticity promotes optimal self-esteem. First, individuals' goal pursuits should provide opportunities for competence, self-determination, expressing one's true self, and positive self-feelings, especially for individuals who are high in authenticity. Second, high levels of authenticity should relate positively to global measures of psychological and interpersonal adjustment that assess these same qualities in the person rather than in goal pursuits.

To examine these issues, Goldman et al. (in prep.) examined how authenticity relates to the meanings with which people imbue their personal projects. After generating a list of personal projects, participants selected the eight projects that "together provide the most complete and informative overview of your life." They next rated each striving on 31 project-meaning dimensions. Many of these were selected from McGregor and Little (1998), although a few were generated specifically for this study. We combined items tapping into the same meaning dimension to form categories that we deemed relevant to authenticity (i.e., the operation of one's core or true self). The categories along with sample items are displayed in Table 12.2. We therefore anticipated that higher authenticity scores would be related to goals providing opportunities for efficacy, autonomy, positive self-feelings, and the operation of the true or core self (e.g., fun and absorption).

The findings we report here were obtained from a sample of 111 male and female undergraduate students. We limit our discussion primarily to findings that emerged with the awareness component because awareness represents a particularly fundamental aspect of authenticity that provides the initial elements of self-knowledge and understanding that are incorporated into the other components. For example, for individuals to match their actions with their values (i.e., behavioral authenticity), they must first have an understanding of the values they accept as their own. Given this knowledge component, awareness should play a particularly central role

TABLE 12.2 *Project Meaning Dimensions and Sample Items*

Self-Worth Benefit (3 items)
- To what extend do you feel that being engaged in this project contributes to your sense of self-worth?
- How important or significant does this project make you feel when engaged in it?

Efficacy (6 items)
- How competent are you to complete this project?
- How much do you feel that you are in control of this project?

Fun (3 items)
- Some projects are intrinsically fun, whimsical, or delightful. How much fun is this project for you?

Authenticity (4 items)
- Most of us have some projects that are "really us" and some others that we don't really feel "ourselves" when doing. To what extent does this project reflect who you really are?
- How much do you feel that it was your decision to take on this project?

Absorbed (1 item)
- To what extent do you become engrossed or deeply involved in this project?

---

in the meanings that participants ascribe to their goal pursuits. All findings were significant at $p < .05$ or lower.

First, scores on the Awareness subscale correlated positively with the index of project *authenticity*. This correlation indicates that the higher individuals' scores on the Awareness subscale, the more they viewed their goal pursuits as reflecting their true selves, the more autonomy they experienced with respect to goal initiation, the more they viewed their goals as personally meaningful, and the more they viewed their goals to be consistent with their broad values. This suggests that authentic individuals engage in strivings that provide them opportunities to express who they really are and that are representative of their core values. Second, Awareness scores correlated positively with an index of striving efficacy. That is, the higher individuals' Awareness scores, the greater their felt competence and control, and the less stress and project difficultly they reported. Third, the higher individuals' awareness, the more they perceived their strivings as conferring them self-worth benefit. This last finding suggests that high-awareness individuals' personal projects provide opportunities for positive self-feelings to arise naturally from their goal pursuits. Finally, high awareness scores related to higher ratings of project fun and absorption.

The relations just reported are consistent with the view that goal pursuits are one way to link processes associated with authenticity to those associated with optimal self-esteem (Kernis, 2003). That is, engaging in goal-oriented behaviors that provide opportunities to express one's true self fosters self-esteem that is secure as opposed to fragile (see Kernis & Paradise, 2002). This may be especially true when these goal-oriented behaviors also promote feelings of efficacy and self-worth.

A second aspect of this study focused on the relation of authenticity to global measures of psychological adjustment. As discussed earlier, Ryff (1989) argued cogently for a multifaceted conceptualization of psychological well-being that has six core components: (a) self-acceptance, characterized by holding positive attitudes toward oneself; (b) positive relations with others, characterized by the capacity for love, friendship, and identification with others; (c) autonomy, characterized by qualities such as self-determination, independence, and regulation of behavior from within; (d) environmental mastery, characterized by the ability to choose or create environments suitable to one's psychic conditions; (e) purpose in life, characterized by beliefs that give one the feeling that there is purpose and meaning to life; and (f) personal growth, characterized by continued development of one's potential and self-realization. Scores on the Awareness subscale correlated positively with scores on each of the other subscales, substantiating the pervasive benefits associated with the motivation and capacity for self-understanding. In addition, scores on the Unbiased Processing subscale correlated positively with autonomy and positive relations with others. Furthermore, the Behavioral and Relational Orientation subscales correlated with each of Ryff's subscales, with the exception of self-acceptance for behavioral authenticity. Thus, higher authenticity scores across subscales generally are linked with greater psychological well-being.

We also measured the hedonic aspects of psychological well-being, specifically depression experienced over the past few weeks, positive and negative affectivity, and general life satisfaction. Authenticity (awareness) correlated positively with positive affectivity and life satisfaction and negatively with negative affectivity and depression. In addition, we replicated several findings from Goldman and Kernis (2002). For example, the Awareness, Behavioral, and Relational Orientation subscales correlated positively with self-esteem level, and all the authenticity subscales were negatively correlated with self-esteem contingency, again suggesting that optimal self-esteem may be intimately linked with authenticity.

To examine how authenticity relates to healthy interpersonal functioning, we asked participants to complete the Bartholomew and Horowitz (1991) attachment measure, consisting of 30 items that assess four distinct types of attachment styles: secure, fearful, dismissive, and preoccupied. We expected that authenticity would relate positively to secure attachment styles and negatively to insecure attachment styles. Overall, the findings that emerged were supportive. Scores on the Awareness and Relational Orientation subscales correlated positively with the secure attachment style and negatively with both the fearful and preoccupied attachment style, but were unrelated to the dismissive attachment style. Why no relationship emerged for the dismissive style is unclear. However, the significant findings that did emerge have important implications for our conceptualization of authenticity and its relation to interpersonal functioning.

Taken as a whole, these findings indicate that authenticity generally relates to a wide range of measures tapping into psychological health, well-being, and interpersonal functioning, and, we would argue, to optimal self-esteem. They also provide initial support for conceptualizing authenticity as a multicomponent construct. Certainly, more research is needed to address the conditions under which each component contributes to specific aspects of functioning and well-being.

FUTURE DIRECTIONS

The findings reported in this chapter provide initial validation for our conceptualization of authenticity. We recognize that our work is just beginning and that many questions remain to be addressed. One important avenue for future research is to validate our measure of authenticity. A good deal of this validation will necessarily rely on data other than those that are obtained from self-reports. Our self-report measure of authenticity has the same inherent difficulties as the majority of self-report measures. Specifically, some people may deliberately misrepresent themselves or have limited access to the information upon which valid responses to the authenticity measure depend. Obtaining validity data that cannot easily be explained in terms of response biases is one way to deal with these difficulties. In this regard, we presented data showing that scores on one self-esteem fragility measure (contingent SE) related to lower authenticity scores, including awareness scores. Likewise, we presented data demonstrating that higher authenticity scores (in particular, awareness) related to a variety of subsequently measured aspects of healthy goal pursuits. What might be more convincing, however, are validity data that involve behaviors or reactions to manipulated circumstances. A number of interesting questions can be asked regarding each of the subscales in our AI. We present some of these in the following subsections.

Awareness Subscale

First, do high awareness scores relate to lower susceptibility to misattribution of arousal effects? Second, do high scores relate to individuals' understanding of their emotions, motives, and so on when they are asked to describe a meaningful past experience in detail? Third, if individuals are given an opportunity to gain knowledge about self-aspects (positive or negative), are high awareness scores related to greater interest and investment?

Unbiased Processing

First, does unbiased processing relate to the relative absence of the self-serving bias? Second, does unbiased processing relate to more mature or adaptive defense mechanisms that involve little reality distortion? Third, does unbiased processing relate to less self-enhancing retrospective memories pertaining to one's performances (e.g., on standardized tests) or personal qualities? Relatedly, are childhood memories less idealized?

Behavior

First, if individuals are made uncomfortable or anxious, do high behavioral authenticity scores relate to fewer instances of smiling and laughter (behaviors incongruent with one's internal state)? Second, do high behavioral scores relate to less susceptibility to *symbolic self-completion manipulations* in which actual goal completion efforts are thwarted and people tend to symbolize completion instead? Third, do high behavioral scores relate to greater behavioral consistency across audiences and contexts? Relatedly, do high behavioral scores relate to greater attitude–behavior consistency?

Relational Orientation

First, do self and partners' relational orientation ratings converge? Second, do relational orientation scores relate positively to valuing and engaging in intimate self-disclosures with partners and with self–other overlap? Third, do relational orientation scores relate negatively to gameplaying (ludus) and manipulativeness in close relationships?

To the extent that our future research yields theoretically predicted findings to questions such as those just posed, we suspect that concerns regarding the validity of our authenticity measure will be reduced. Until such time, it is especially important that we remain vigilant in our sensitivity to its limitations. The research and theory reported in this chapter are in their infancy. Nonetheless, they point to the viability of a multicomponent conceptualization of authenticity. This is no small feat, given the extreme difficulty of capturing authenticity within a scientific framework. Despite its elusiveness, authenticity deserves its place alongside other critical aspects of the human condition that define who we are and what we are able to become. Our hope is that our work stimulates other scholars to join in our quest to understand authenticity.

References

Bartholomew, K., & Horowitz, L. M. (1991). Attachment styles among young adults: A test of a four-category model. *Journal of Personality and Social Psychology, 61*(2), 226–244.

Brunstein, J. (1993). Personal goals and subjective well-being: A longitudinal study. *Journal of Personality and Social Psychology, 65*, 1061–1070.

Campbell, J. D. (1990). Self-esteem and clarity of the self-concept. *Journal of Personality and Social Psychology, 59*, 538–549.

Campbell, J. D., Trapnell, P. D., Heine, S. J., Katz, I. M., Covollee, L. F., & Lehman, D. R. (1996). Self-concept clarity: Measurement, personality correlates, and cultural boundaries. *Journal of Personality and Social Psychology, 70*, 141–156.

Deci, E. L., & Ryan, R. M. (1995). Human agency: The basis for true self-esteem. In M. H. Kernis (Ed.), *Efficacy, agency, and self-esteem* (pp. 31–50). New York: Plenum Press.

Deci, E. L., & Ryan, R. M. (2000). The "what" and "why" of goal pursuits: Human needs and the self-determination of behavior. *Psychology Inquiry, 11*, 227–269.

Diener, E., Emmons, R., Larsen, R., & Griffin, S. (1985). The Satisfaction with Life Scale. *Journal of Personality and Social Psychology, 49*, 71–75.

Goldman, B. M., & Kernis, M. H. (2001). *Development of the authenticity inventory, version 1.* Unpublished data, University of Georgia.

Goldman, B. M., & Kernis, M. H. (2002). The role of authenticity in healthy psychological functioning and subjective well-being. *Annals of the American Psychotherapy Association, 5*(6), 18–20.

Goldman, B. M., Kernis, M. H., Piasecki, R., Hermann, A., & Foster, J. D. (in preparation). *Authenticity, goal construal, and well-being.* Manuscript.

Harter, S. (1997). The personal self in social context: Barriers to authenticity. In R. D. Ashmore & L. J. Jussim (Eds.), *Self* and *identity. Fundamental Issues* (pp. 81–105). New York: Oxford University Press.

Kernis, M. H. (2003). Toward a conceptualization of optimal self-esteem. *Psychological Inquiry 14*, 1–26.

Kernis, M. H., & Goldman, B. M. (2002). Stability and malleability in self-concept and self-esteem. In M. R. Leary & J. P. Tangey (Eds.), *Handbook of self and identity* (pp. 106–127). New York: Guilford Press.

Kernis, M. H., & Paradise, A. W. (2002). Distinguishing between secure and fragile forms of high self-esteem. In E. L. Deci & R. M. Ryan (Eds.), *Handbook of self-determination research* (pp. 330–360). Rochester, NY: University of Rochester Press.

Kernis, M. H., & Paradise, A. W. (in preparation). *Contingent self-esteem: Scale development and relation to anger arousal.* Manuscript.

Kernis, M. H., Paradise, A. W., Whitaker, D., Wheatman, S., & Goldman, B. (2000). Master of one's psychological domain? Not likely if one's self-esteem is unstable. *Personality and Social Psychology Bulletin, 26*, 1297–1305.

Koestner, R., Losier, G. F., Vallerand, R. J., & Carducci, D. (1996). Identified and introjected forms of political internalization: Extending self-determination theory. *Journal of Personality and Social Psychology, 70*, 1025–1036.

Markus, H., & Nurius, P. (1986). Possible selves. *American Psychologist, 41*(9), 954–969.

Maslow, A. H. (1968). *Toward a psychology of being* (2nd Ed.). Princeton, NJ: Van Nostrand.

McGregor, I., & Little, B. R. (1998). Personal projects, happiness, and meaning: On doing well and being yourself. *Journal of Personality and Social Psychology, 74,* 494–512.

Mischel, W., & Shoda, Y. (1995). A cognitive-affective system theory of personality: Reconceptualizing situations, dispositions, dynamics, and invariance in personality structure. *Psychological Review, 102*(2), 246–268.

Perls, F., Hefferline, R. F., & Goodman, P. (1951). *Gestalt therapy.* New York: Julian Press (reprinted 1965, Dell Press).

Rogers, C. R. (1961). *On becoming a person: A therapist's view of psychotherapy.* Boston: Houghton Mifflin.

Rosenberg, M. (1965). *Society and the adolescent self-image.* Princeton, NJ: Princeton University Press.

Ryan, R. M., & Connell, J. P. (1989). Perceived locus of causality and internalization: Examining reasons for acting in two domains. *Journal of Personality and Social Psychology, 57,* 749–761.

Ryan, R. M., Rigby, S., & King, K. (1993). Two types of religious internalization and their relations to religious orientations and mental health. *Journal of Personality and Social Psychology, 65,* 586–596.

Ryan, R. M., Stiller, J., & Lynch, J. H. (1994). Representations of relationships to teachers, parents, and friends as predictors of academic motivation and self-esteem. *Journal of Early Adolescence, 14,* 226–229.

Ryff, C. (1989). Happiness is everything, or is it? Explorations on the meaning of psychological well-being. *Journal of Personality and Social Psychology, 57,* 1069–1081.

Sande, G. N., Goethals, G. R., & Radloff, C. E. (1988). Perceiving one's own traits and others': The multifaceted self. *Journal of Personality and Social Psychology, 54*(1), 13–20.

Sheldon, K. M., & Kasser, T. (1995). Coherence and congruence: Two aspects of personality and integration. *Journal of Personality and Social Psychology, 68,* 531–543.

Sheldon, K. M., Ryan, R. M., Rawsthorne, L. J., & Ilardi, B. (1997). Trait self and true self: Cross-role variation in the Big-Five personality traits and its relations with psychological authenticity and subjective well-being. *Journal of Personality and Social Psychology, 73,* 1380–1393.

Unger, J. A., Waters, B., Barnett, B., & Dolby, R. (1997). Defense style and adjustment in interpersonal relationships. *Journal of Research in Personality, 31,* 375–385.

Vaillant, G. (1992). *Ego mechanisms of defense: A guide for clinicians and researchers.* Washington, DC: American Psychiatric Press.

Williams, G. C., Rodin, G. C., Ryan, R. M., Grolnick, W. S., & Deci, E. L. (1998). Autonomous regulation and long-term medication adherence in adult outpatients. *Health Psychology, 17,* 269–276.

13

Motivation and Construct Accessibility

Nira Liberman and Jens Förster

INTRODUCTION

Given the recent trend toward distinguishing between implicit and explicit processes in a number of areas in social psychology, the present volume can make a timely contribution to applying this distinction to motivational processes. In this chapter, we will focus mainly on implicit motivational mechanisms and, in particular, on the role of goal-related accessibility in motivated thinking and behavior. Theories in both cognitive and social psychology propose that motivational states such as needs, goals, intentions, and concerns are characterized by enhanced accessibility of motivation-related constructs (Anderson, 1983; Bruner, 1957; Higgins & King, 1981; Wyer and Srull, 1986, 1989). Similar ideas came from theories of motivation and volition (Ach, 1935; Gollwitzer 1996; Gollwitzer & Moskowitz, 1996; Goschke & Kuhl, 1993; Kuhl, 1983; 1987; Kuhl & Kazén-Saad, 1988). In this chapter, we summarize some general principles of accessibility from motivational sources, and briefly review extant and novel empirical evidence for these principles. We then discuss a possible theoretical account for these principles within a general functional approach to accessibility. Finally, we examine some implications of the outlined theory for person perception, postsuppressional rebound, and catharsis of aggression.

This research was supported by a grant from the Deutsche Forschungsgemeinschaft to Jens Förster (FO244/8-1) and by a Heisenberg award from the Deutsche Forschungsgemeinschaft to Jens Förster. We would like to thank the Sydney Conference and Tory Higgins for invaluable discussions. Correspondence concerning this chapter should be addressed to Nira Liberman, Department of Psychology, Tel Aviv University, P.O. Box 39040, Tel Aviv, 69978, Israel; e-mail: niralib@post.tau.ac.il.

ACCESSIBILITY FROM MOTIVATIONAL SOURCES:
GENERAL PRINCIPLES

We propose the following principles to characterize accessibility from motivational sources such as goals, needs, or concerns: (a) Motivation enhances the accessibility of motivation-related constructs; (b) accessibility from motivational sources persists until the motivation is fulfilled or becomes irrelevant; (c) fulfillment of the motivation inhibits the accessibility of motivation-related constructs; and (d) accessibility of motivation-related constructs and postfulfillment inhibition are proportional to the strength of the motivation. We now examine the empirical evidence for these four principles. In the following section, we offer a broader theoretical explanation for these principles within a functional view of accessibility.

The first two principles – that motivation enhances accessibility and that accessibility persists as long as the motivation is active – are well supported in the psychological literature. For example, Goschke and Kuhl (1993) made participants rehearse a series of actions and then informed them that they would either perform the actions (a goal) or observe another person performing them (nongoal). Using a recognition test, they found a higher accessibility of the actions in the goal condition than in the nogoal condition even when rehearsal of the actions was not possible in the intervening time. These results were interpreted as supporting the notion of persisting activation due to the formation of an intention. In a related study, Bargh and Barndollar (1996) showed that activation of an achievement goal by priming constructs related to achievement increased performance on an anagram task. Moreover, they found the performance facilitation to be more pronounced after a delay than immediately, a finding that was interpreted as evidence for the operation of a motivational system (see also Aarts, Hassin, & Gollwitzer, under review). Interestingly, the relatively slow decay of accessibility from motivational sources distinguishes it from accessibility from recent semantic priming, which is known to produce decay over relatively short periods of time (Higgins, Bargh, & Lombardi, 1985; Srull & Wyer, 1979). Recently, research on stereotype activation and use (Spencer, Fein, Strahan, & Zanna, this volume) has also conceptualized accessibility of stereotypes in motivational terms as related to goals.

Persistence of accessibility from unfulfilled goals was also theorized to underlie rumination and intrusive thoughts (Martin & Tesser, 1996), and unresolved (i.e., current) concerns were theorized to underlie occurrence in dreams of concepts related to these concerns (Klinger, 1977, 1987, 1996). Such activation, it was theorized, remains until the individual either reaches the goal or disengages from it (Lewin, 1951; Martin & Tesser, 1996). These real-life phenomena of rumination, intrusive thoughts, and dreams demonstrate that unfulfilled goals may maintain the accessibility of goal-related constructs over extended periods (months and even years).

The third principle, postfulfillment inhibition, is illustrated by the Zeigarnik effect, whereby people remembered interrupted tasks better than completed tasks (Zeigarnik, 1927; for reviews see Butterfield, 1964; Heckhausen, 1991; Wicklund & Gollwitzer, 1982). According to Lewin's field theory (1951), the Zeigarnik effect occurs because interruption preserved the goal to complete the task and kept intact the goal-related tension, whereas task completion released the tension and reduced the memory of the task. Although Lewin and Zeigarnik did not formulate their findings in terms of accessibility, the free recall measure they applied could be interpreted in those terms (Tulving & Patterson, 1968). The Zeigarnik effect could suggest, then, that goals enhance the accessibility of goal-related constructs, and goal fulfillment then reduces this accessibility.

Marsh and colleagues (1998, 1999) extended the paradigm of Goschke and Kuhl (1993), mentioned earlier, and used a lexical decision task to examine the accessibility of intended actions both prior to and after completion. Replicating the study of Goschke and Kuhl, they found that before completion, accessibility of intended actions was enhanced relative to nonintended (i.e., to-be-observed) actions. They also found that after performance, the accessibility of the performed action was inhibited and became lower than that of observed actions, a result that is in line with the notion of postfulfillment inhibition.

Finally, the fourth principle states that accessibility from motivation and postfulfillment inhibition should be proportional to the strength of the motivation. For example, classic theories of motivation state that a motivation to attain a goal increases with the expectancy of reaching the goal and with the goal's value (e.g., Atkinson, 1964; Fishbein & Ajzen, 1974). According to this principle, therefore, accessibility of goal-related constructs and postfulfillment inhibition would increase with the goal's expectancy and value. To our knowledge, no research in social psychology has examined this fourth principle.

In sum, the first two principles are widely accepted and supported by social psychological research, the third principle accumulated much less empirical evidence and received less emphasis in the literature, and the fourth principle has not been examined so far in empirical research. Förster, Liberman, and Higgins (under review) aimed to close this empirical gap by testing all four principles in a single series of studies.

In a series of studies conducted by Förster et al. (under review), participants looked through a series of pictures with the goal of finding a picture of glasses that was followed by a picture of scissors in order to report it to the experimenter. They were told that there was one and only one such combination in the entire set of stimuli. Participants in the control, no-goal condition looked through the same pictures without being instructed to find a target. Specifically, glasses and scissors were mentioned to them as examples of stimuli that they might see, but they did not receive any special instructions about these stimuli. Participants in both groups looked through four blocks of pictures. Pictures of glasses and pictures of scissors appeared a number of times among the stimuli but the target combination appeared only once, in the third block. Thus, Blocks 1 and 2 constituted the prefulfillment stage, and Blocks 3 and 4 constituted the postfulfillment stage.

After viewing each block of pictures, participants performed a lexical decision task in which they had to indicate as quickly and as accurately as they could whether a string of letters was a word or a nonword. Faster lexical decisions on semantic associates of a construct indicated higher accessibility of the construct (Neely, 1991). Words related to glasses, words unrelated to glasses, and nonwords were presented randomly. In this way, we examined the accessibility of goal-related and goal-unrelated constructs, both before and after goal fulfillment, and compared those to the accessibility of the same constructs in a control, no-goal condition. We computed a measure of the relative advantage of goal-related constructs as the difference in mean reaction times between goal-unrelated words and goal-related words. A higher score on that measure indicates a greater advantage of goal-related words relative to goal-unrelated words.

The results showed that, as predicted, in the goal condition, accessibility of goal-related words was enhanced prior to goal fulfillment. Furthermore, it increased from Block 1 to Block 2. Inhibition of goal-related constructs was evident immediately after fulfillment, in Block 3. Notably, postfulfillment inhibition was evident both in comparing the postfulfillment stage to the prefulfillment stage and in comparing the goal condition to the control, no-goal condition. It is interesting to note that postfulfillment inhibition was partially released later, in Block 4.

Subsequent studies manipulated the expectancy of fulfilling the goal, the payment associated with achieving the goal (i.e., the value of the goal), and a combination of expectancy and value. For example, in one study, participants in the high-expectancy condition were told that the target combination of glasses and scissors was present in 90% of the cases, whereas participants in the low-expectancy condition were told that the target would be there in only 5% of the cases. The no-goal, control group was identical to that in the previous study. The relative advantage of goal-related words was defined as before, and was examined as a function of experimental condition and block.

As predicted, accessibility of goal-related words prior to fulfillment and inhibition after fulfillment were found in the high-expectancy condition but not in the low-expectancy condition. Thus, as suggested by our fourth principle of motivation-related accessibility, both goal-related activation and postfulfillment inhibition were proportional to the strength of the motivation, which was manipulated here by the goal's expectancy.

Another study manipulated the goal's value. Participants in the high-value condition were told that they would receive €1 if they found the target combination of glasses and scissors, whereas participants in the low-value condition were told that they would get only €0.05 for finding the target. Similar to the previous studies, participants in the control, no-goal condition, were not given a goal. The results were quite similar to those of the expectancy study: Enhanced accessibility of goal-related words prior to fulfillment and inhibition after fulfillment were found in the high-value condition but not in the low-value condition. Here too, then, both goal-related accessibility and postfulfillment inhibition were found to be proportional to the motivation to achieve the goal.

In a fourth study, both expectancy and value were manipulated in an orthogonal way, and it was found that goal-related accessibility and post-fulfillment inhibition occurred when both expectancy and value were high but not when either of them was low. Thus, the effect of expectancy and value on goal-related accessibility and on postfulfillment inhibition was interactive (i.e., multiplicative) and thus similar to the effect of expectancy and value on motivation. This pattern lends further support to the notion that both goal-related activation and postfulfillment inhibition are proportional to the strength of the motivation to achieve the goal.

A FUNCTIONAL VIEW OF MOTIVATION-RELATED ACCESSIBILITY

In the previous section we proposed and reviewed some extant and novel evidence for four principles of accessibility from motivational sources: (a) motivation enhances the accessibility of goal-related constructs; (b) accessibility persists until the motivation is fulfilled or becomes irrelevant; (c) fulfillment inhibits the accessibility of motivation-related constructs; (d) accessibility of motivation-related constructs and postfulfillment inhibition are proportional to the strength of the motivation. Given the relative weight of empirical evidence for the four accessibility principles, the next obvious question is: What is the theoretical rationale behind these effects?

We believe that the proposed principles of accessibility from motivational sources are consistent with a functional view of the interface between motivation and cognition. Specifically, we propose that all these principles are conducive to efficient self-regulation.

Similar to many theories of motivation and volition, we assume that a heightened accessibility of goal-related constructs helps to detect environmental stimuli that are instrumental for efficient goal pursuit and thus contributes to the likelihood of goal-achievement (see Ach, 1935; Gollwitzer, 1999; Kuhl, 1983). For example, while searching for something (e.g., glasses), it would be useful to activate concepts that are related to the target of search, such as its typical or likely locations (e.g., case, bag, bedroom) or typical activities for which the target is used (reading, watching TV), because the target of search is likely to be in proximity to the associated object or the activity (e.g., the glasses are likely to be near the TV). For that same reason, it is functional to retain a state of heightened activation until the goal is fulfilled.

Also in line with other theories, we think that upon goal fulfillment, the accessibility of goal-related constructs loses its functionality and could potentially interfere with other tasks that the individual faces. In cybernetic models of goal hierarchies (Carver & Scheier, 1999; Vallacher & Wegner, 1987), for example, goal attainment (e.g., buying groceries) is followed by a reinstatement of a higher-order superordinate goal (e.g., cooking dinner), which constituted the reason for pursuing the original (i.e., subordinated) goal. In this view, constructs that are related to the fulfilled goal (e.g., money, supermarket) are clearly irrelevant and could potentially interfere with successful performance of the next task at hand. "Clearing up" the mental system from such constructs could be highly instrumental (see also Gollwitzer, 1999; Kuhl, 1983; Mayr & Keele, 2000). In the preceding example, both *supermarket* and *cook* could be strong associates of *food*, and thus could interfere with each other's retrieval from long-term memory (Anderson & Spellman, 1995). Thus, inhibiting *supermarket* after successfully completing the shopping could be instrumental for performing the next task, which is cooking.

We believe that the fourth principle – proportionality of goal-related accessibility and postfulfillment inhibition to the strength of the motivation – is also consistent with the functional view. Specifically, we suggest that a strong motivation to fulfill a goal means that the individual is ready to invest a lot of energy in goal pursuit and probably gives it a high priority over other goals. Enhancing the accessibility of goal-related constructs could help to achieve the focal goal, but at the same time, it could interfere with achieving other goals (Shah, Friedman, & Kruglanski, 2002). For example, enhanced accessibility of *glasses* and its associates could help to find glasses, but it would probably detract the ability from to pursue other goals (preexisting or newly introduced) that require simultaneous attention (e.g., engaging in a conversation). Thus, because of its potential costs, enhanced accessibility of goal-related constructs should be proportional to the emphasis one is ready to assign to the pursuit of this particular goal (i.e., to the motivation to pursue the goal). To consider another example, suppose that a person sets a goal to oppose the next sexist remark by a colleague. To pursue that goal efficiently, that person needs to be sensitive to sexist issues, which can effectively be achieved if the accessibility of constructs related to sexism is heightened, because the higher this accessibility, the easier it becomes to detect such content (see Gollwitzer, 1999; Goschke & Kuhl, 1993). Such enhanced accessibility, however, would detract from the person's ability to engage in other simultaneous tasks (e.g., impression management) and thus should be employed only when there is a strong motivation to oppose sexist remarks.

Thus, accessibility of goal-related constructs should be proportional to the goal's importance. But why would the extent of postfulfillment inhibition be proportional to the strength of the motivation to achieve the goal? Why would more inhibition follow the fulfillment of more motivating goals? Possibly, achievement of highly motivating goals is more salient and therefore inhibition is more likely to follow fulfillment of such goals than fulfillment of less motivating goals. We propose that a similar prediction follows also from the functional reasoning we introduced before. Specifically, it is reasonable to assume that highly motivating goals are more likely than slightly motivating goals to suppress (or put on hold) even important alternative goals. For example, a high motivation to respond to sexist remarks may suppress the important goal of self-presentation, but a weak motivation would not suffice to produce such suppression. Therefore, as a rule, the goal one turns to after completion of a previous goal is likely to be more important if the previously fulfilled goal was highly motivating. Turning next to this important goal is facilitated by strong inhibition of the constructs related to the previous goal. Thus, the more motivating the initial goal, the more functional it is to inhibit its related constructs after goal fulfillment in order to turn back to the important alternative goal that was suppressed.

ACCESSIBILITY FROM MOTIVATION AND ACCESSIBILITY FROM CONSTRUCT USE

Although the evidence for motivation-related priming seems compelling, we need to consider how this kind of priming differs from typical semantic priming effects. We mentioned earlier that some properties of motivation-induced accessibility distinguish it from the accessibility that is produced, for example, by recent semantic priming. Specifically, the relative endurance of accessibility of motivation-related constructs is distinct from the relatively rapid decay of primed constructs. Also, postfulfillment inhibition is inconsistent with the principle that additional processing of a construct necessarily increases its accessibility, inasmuch as fulfilling a goal involves processing of goal-related constructs. Our finding about the moderation of goal-related accessibility and postfulfillment inhibition by goal value and goal expectancy provide further evidence for the dissociation of accessibility from goals and accessibility from recent semantic priming. We think that these differences warrant treatment of accessibility of motivation as distinct from accessibility from simple construct use (see Higgins, 1996, for a related discussion of the distinction between stimuli as stimulants and stimuli as targets).

It would be interesting to examine the functionality of accessibility and decay from recent construct use. It has been suggested that enhanced accessibility after using a construct functions to facilitate perception of related constructs, which would be beneficial if redundancy is expected (Neely, 1991). For example, it is functional that processing the word *nurse* would enhance the accessibility of the construct *doctor* because in many contexts these two stimuli tend to co-occur. If so, one could predict that if the expectation of co-occurrence is altered, accessibility due to construct use would change correspondingly. This could be done, for example, by changing the situation between the presentation of the two targets or by experimentally embedding a negative correlation between semantically related stimuli. Possibly, and consistent with the functional view of accessibility, inhibition would obtain in the latter case.

FULFILLMENT OF DIFFERENT TYPES OF GOALS

There is always the possibility that certain substantive effects are mere artifacts of a particular paradigmatic approach. As such, two important properties of the paradigm applied in our studies should be noted. First and foremost, the fact that participants knew that there was one and only one target in the entire set of pictures designated finding the target as a clear and final case of goal fulfillment. Inhibition after fulfillment in this case was particularly strategically advantageous, because once the target was found, no additional targets were to be sought, and information related to it could not be useful anymore. Second, in our paradigm, the target of search was a combination of pictures (a picture of glasses followed by a picture of scissors) rather than a single picture; in addition, the first picture of the compound appeared a number of times throughout the set of pictures (but, of course, was followed by the second target picture only once). Possibly, this aspect of the paradigm helped to create an especially strong activation of the first construct of the compound, because each time participants encountered the first picture (glasses), they had to keep it in mind until they saw the following picture in order to decide whether this was or was not the target combination. We think that this aspect of the paradigm mimics real-life situations in which a number of attempts to achieve a goal are made before successful completion.

More generally, it is possible that different types of goals would be associated with different patterns of activation and inhibition of goal-related constructs. In particular, standards could be thought of as a subtype of goals that can be instantiated but cannot be entirely fulfilled. For example, a standard of being an egalitarian person is instantiated or met but not fulfilled by admitting a minority candidate. In contrast, a goal of showing a token of egalitarian behavior may be fulfilled by the same behavior. According to the functional view of goal-related accessibility, one should

expect less inhibition after an instantiation of standards than after fulfillment of a goal. It would be interesting to examine the possibility that some
goals, because they cannot be fulfilled but only instantiated, would not
produce postfulfillment inhibition.

An interesting situation would occur if the same behavior fulfills a goal
for some individuals but instantiates a standard for others. For example,
admitting a minority candidate may fulfill the goal of showing a token of
egalitarian behavior and instantiate the standard of being egalitarian. We
would expect that in the former case, but not in the latter case, postfulfillment inhibition would ensue. As a result, a person whose goal is to show a
token of egalitarian behavior would show a *rebound effect*: He or she would
experience a decreased accessibility of constructs related to egalitarianism
after admitting a minority candidate. In contrast, a person who operates
under the standard of being egalitarian would not show the same effect.

IMPLICATIONS FOR PERSON PERCEPTION

Our focus up to now has been on the cognitive processes involved in goal
accessibility, but our findings do have a variety of implications for social
psychological research and theorizing, especially in areas such as person
perception. Social psychological literature has particular interest in the effects of construct accessibility on person perception (e.g., Devine, 1989;
Higgins, Rholes, & Jones, 1977; Srull & Wyer, 1979). What exactly are the
implications of our findings for that domain? The principles of goal-related
activation and postfulfillment inhibition, for example, predict a perception
of an ambiguous social target in goal-related terms (an assimilation effect)
before goal fulfillment and a perception in opposite terms (a contrast effect) after goal fulfillment. For example, suppose that Sarah has a goal to
aggress against Susan. We would predict that compared to a situation in
which no goals related to aggression are activated, Sarah would perceive an
ambiguously aggressive behavior as more aggressive before fulfilling the
goal to aggress, and would perceive the same behavior as less aggressive
after fulfilling the goal to aggress.

It is interesting to relate this prediction to the findings on the effects
of completed versus interrupted priming tasks, because it is possible to
conceptualize task completion as goal attainment and task interruption as
a state of an active goal, in line with Lewin's classic field theory and the
Zeigarnik (1927) effect. If so, then we would predict enhanced accessibility
after an interrupted priming task and inhibition after a completed priming
task. Consistent with this prediction, Martin (1986; see also Higgins, Bargh,
& Lombardi, 1985) demonstrated that a completed priming task created
contrast in subsequent perceptions of ambiguous social targets, whereas
an interrupted priming task produced assimilation.

To explain these results, Martin (1986) suggested that after completing a task, people *reset* their mental states and refrain from using the accessible construct in subsequent judgments (see also Martin & Achee, 1992). Specifically, set-reset theory proposes that an interrupted task leaves the cognitive system in the "set of the interrupted task, and causes an enhanced accessibility of the activated construct during formation of the target impression" (p. 502). That is, an interrupted priming task causes an assimilation of the target to the constructs activated by the prime. In contrast, a completed task is theorized to cause the cognitive system to reset the previously activated construct. According to Martin (1986), "Reset refers to the suppressed use of a contextually primed concept and the encoding of the stimulus in terms of an independently activated one. Resetting may be most likely to occur when use of the initially primed concept would appear to bias an independent judgment or the target . . . or when there are demands to exclude from consideration information that has activated a concept" (p. 502).

Notably, our notion of postfulfillment inhibition is different from Martin's notion of resetting because postfulfillment inhibition involves a reduction in accessibility (inhibition) after task completion (or goal fulfillment). It takes place regardless of whether a new target is encountered. Resetting, on the other hand, occurs upon encountering a new target and involves refraining from using an accessible construct (suppression). Based on this distinction between inhibition and suppression (resetting), Liberman, Förster, and Higgins (under review) reasoned that postfulfillment inhibition but not resetting would happen with an implicit task. We reasoned that measuring accessibility with a lexical decision task would reflect accessibility that is unaffected by suppression attempts (i.e., resetting) because participants would not be aware when performing this task of the potential relevance of the primes for their decisions. They would therefore not suppress accessible constructs. In fact, in a lexical decision task, accessibility has the desirable effect of enhancing the speed and efficiency of one's performance, and there would be no strategic reason to engage in suppression.

To examine these differential predictions, we replicated Martin's (1986) study but added a lexical decision task before the impression formation task. Consistent with the notion of postfulfillment inhibition but not with the idea of resetting, the implicit accessibility measure indicated increased accessibility of the primed construct after an interrupted priming task but not after a completed priming task.

IMPLICATIONS FOR POSTSUPPRESSIONAL REBOUND

Our findings may also have important implications for another interesting and topical research area in social psychology: thought suppression. In a seminal work, Wegner, Schneider, Carter, and White (1987) demonstrated

that trying not to think of white bears was not only difficult, but also produced a paradoxical aftereffect: White bears became even more accessible
than with no prior suppression attempts. The postsuppressional rebound
effect has been replicated with a wide variety of constructs, including white
bears (Förster & Liberman, 2001; Wegner, Schneider, Knutson, & McMahon,
1991; Wenzlaff, Wegner, & Klein, 1991), green rabbits (Clark, Ball, & Pape,
1991; Clark, Winton, & Thynn, 1993), thoughts about a film showing a fire
in an office building (Davies & Clark, 1998), thoughts about one's own
former romantic relationships (Wegner & Gold, 1995), and mood (Wegner,
Erber, & Zanakos, 1993). It has also been shown that suppressing stereotypes in describing a member of a stereotyped group resulted in more
stereotypic descriptions and in enhanced accessibility of stereotype-related
concepts compared with no suppression (Macrae, Bodenhausen, & Milne,
1998; Macrae, Bodenhausen, Milne, & Jetten, 1994). Suppressing thoughts
about one's undesirable traits enhanced the tendency to use these traits in
interpreting others' behavior (Newman, Duff, & Baumeister, 1997).

   We (Liberman & Förster, 2000) attempted to explain postsuppressional
rebound within a motivation-related accessibility framework. Specifically,
we suggested that suppressing a construct enhances the motivation to use
it, thereby also enhancing its accessibility. For example, writing an essay
about a day in the life of an African American person while suppressing
stereotypes of African Americans may be experienced as difficult. Participants may interpret this difficulty as indicating a motivation on their part
to use the stereotype (i.e., they might think "If it is so difficult for me not
to use the stereotype, then it must be the case that I really need to use it").
The inferred motivation, in turn, would increase the accessibility of the
stereotype.

   We further reasoned, based on the principle of postfulfillment inhibition,
that expressing a construct after suppressing it would fulfill the motivation
to use the construct and reduce its accessibility. For example, using stereotypes of African Americans after suppressing them would decrease the
accessibility of the stereotypes. This prediction allowed us to distinguish
motivation-related accessibility from accessibility that is produced by construct use (i.e., priming), because the latter could increase only after further
construct use. For example, using stereotypes of African Americans without prior suppression would increase rather than decrease the accessibility
of the stereotypes.

   Five studies tested this prediction with suppression of color words in
describing a colorful abstract painting and with suppression of stereotypes
of women and African Americans. In all five studies, participants first either suppressed or did not suppress a construct and then either expressed
or did not express the construct. Accessibility of the relevant construct
was then measured. In all five studies, the postsuppressional rebound was
replicated (i.e., suppression enhanced the accessibility of the suppressed

construct) and the knowledge activation (priming) effect was obtained (i.e., expressing a construct enhanced its accessibility). Most important, in all five studies, when expression followed suppression, accessibility was reduced relative to both the suppression-alone condition and the expression-alone condition.

IMPLICATIONS FOR CATHARSIS OF AGGRESSION

Interestingly, the idea of postfulfillment inhibition is akin to that of catharsis: Fulfilling a motivation results in an inhibition of goal-related constructs in the same way (and, we believe, for the same reasons) that fulfilling a motivation reduces the wish to invest further effort in pursuing it. It is thus interesting to examine the implications of our model for the notion of catharsis. In social psychology, the notion of catharsis has been widely discussed in the context of aggressive behavior. Specifically, a question has been raised about whether watching aggressive stimuli (e.g., violent TV programs) or performing aggressive acts (e.g., engaging in aggressive sports) reduces aggressive behavior, as would be predicted by the notion of catharsis (Dollard, Dobb, Miller, Mowrer, & Sears, 1939). An opposite prediction is made by the stimulation principle, according to which watching aggression or performing aggressive acts increases aggression via disinhibition, social learning (Bandura, 1973), or priming (Berkowitz & LePage, 1967). Note that this latter prediction that aggression is increased by activation of aggression via observing or performing aggressive acts is akin to the principle of activation from construct use.

Reviews of the literature tend to conclude that the notion of catharsis, despite its popularity (Russel, Arms, & Bibby, 1995), has received little empirical support (Geen & Quanty, 1977), a conclusion that is echoed in many textbooks in the field (e.g., Brehm, Kassin, & Fein, 1998). Likewise, the conclusion that watching TV violence increases rather than decreases aggression is now widely accepted (Huesman & Eron, 1986; Huesman & Miller, 1994).

Our model of accessibility from motivation may provide more specific predictions as to when catharsis is supposed to obtain. Specifically, we predict that when an action fulfills an aggressive goal, it would be followed by an inhibition of aggressive constructs (motivational theories would also predict a reduced tendency to perform further aggressive acts toward the same goal). An observation of our effects as well as the logic of our model does not predict this effect to be a long-term one. In our results, postfulfillment inhibition was evident directly after the combination of scissors and glasses was found (in Block 3) but was released either partially or fully some minutes afterward (in Block 4). Thus, our model does not contradict the findings about an aggregate, long-term effect of increased aggression as a result of performing or observing aggressive acts.

Another interesting aspect of our model's predictions regarding catharsis is that postfulfillment inhibition is expected only if a motivated act of
aggression fulfills an aggressive motivation. For example, if Dan wanted to
humiliate a colleague, then publicly insulting him would fulfill a goal and
would be followed by an inhibition of aggressive constructs. Inhibition
should not follow a goal-directed aggressive act that failed to achieve its
goal. In this example, if Dan managed to cause only what he perceived
to be a slight embarrassment to his colleague, then he might feel that his
goal of insulting the colleague was not fulfilled and thus would experience
no postfulfillment inhibition. As discussed before, it could be the case that
some types of motivation, such as generalized, profound hatred, disgust,
and hostility toward one's colleagues, would rarely produce a sense of fulfillment, and consequently would rarely produce a state of postfulfillment
inhibition. Nor would inhibition follow performance of aggressive acts
that are not directed toward fulfilling an aggressive goal. Thus, according
to our model, watching TV or engaging in aggressive sports should not
produce postfulfillment inhibition.

Notably, the function of the aggressive act as fulfilling a goal, but not
the type or intensity of the act, is crucial for catharsis. Thus, to produce
catharsis, aggressive acts do not have to be physical, intense, or overt,
nor should they have the opposite characteristics. The type or intensity
of the aggressive act are not important for catharsis. The intensity of the
original goal, however, is important. Specifically, our findings suggest that
fulfilling an important goal produces a more intense inhibition. Applied
to the notion of catharsis in aggression, this would suggest that fulfilling
an important goal to aggress would produce more catharsis, irrespective
of the intensity of the action that constituted fulfillment.

To provide an initial test of our predictions on catharsis of aggression, we
(Förster & Liberman, 2003) made male and female participants read about
and take the perspective of a person who returns home and finds his or her
romantic partner making love to his or her best friend. In the second stage,
participants in the successful revenge group were instructed to imagine a
detailed scene in which they take revenge on the friend, whereas participants in the failed revenge group were instructed to imagine planning to
take revenge and having their plans thwarted. Participants in the control
group read a happy scenario about a birthday party in both stages. Speed
of lexical decision on words related to aggression and on words unrelated
to aggression was examined both after the first stage and after the second
stage.

Consistent with the notion of goal activation, we found that reading
the first scenario increased the accessibility of aggression-related words
in the experimental groups relative to the control group. We also found,
consistent with the catharsis hypothesis, that imagining revenge reduced
the accessibility of aggression-related words to the baseline level obtained

in the control group. Imagining a failed revenge, on the other hand, further increased the accessibility of aggression-related words. We believe that this was the case because in this condition an aggressive motivation continued to exist.

CONSCIOUS OR UNCONSCIOUS? AWARENESS OF GOAL ACTIVATION AND FULFILLMENT

Schooler and Schreiber's (this volume) summary of the chapters raises the question of whether awareness of a goal is needed in order for inhibition after goal fulfillment to occur. This issue is important because in some everyday situations goal fulfillment might be consciously represented (a person thinks: "Great, I eventually brought the letter to the mail room"), whereas in other cases, proceduralization of daily activities might lead to less awareness of goal fulfillment (the secretary going to the mail room twice a day; e.g., a habit; see Wood & Quinn, this volume). At present, we do not have data to address this question. However, that goals may be automatically activated and fulfilled is widely documented in the literature (e.g., for reviews, see Bargh, 1997; Gollwitzer, 1999). The logic of our functional explanation applies to unconscious goals, and thus predicts that activation and inhibition would follow setting and fulfillment of such goals. It would be interesting to examine whether awareness enhances the effects of activation and inhibition. Aarts and Hassin's (this volume) work on unconscious goal activation via contagion provides an interesting paradigm in which to examine the effects of unconscious goals. Caution is needed, however, to ensure that consciousness does not affect strength of motivation. For example, it is possible that consciousness would be more likely with more important goals, or that people would be more aware of fulfilling difficult goals than easy goals. Our research might open a new field of research on unconscious goal attainment and fulfillment.

CONCLUSION

We presented four principles that we believe characterize accessibility from motivational sources: (a) Motivation enhances the accessibility of motivation-related constructs; (b) accessibility from motivational sources persists until the motivation is fulfilled or becomes irrelevant; (c) fulfillment of the motivation inhibits the accessibility of motivation-related constructs; (d) accessibility of motivation-related constructs and postfulfillment inhibition are proportional to the strength of the motivation. Whereas the first two principles are widely accepted and extensively demonstrated in the social psychological literature, the third and fourth principles have received much less attention and emphasis. The fourth principle, in particular, has been tested systematically in our series of studies for the first time.

We discussed these principles within a general theoretical approach, emphasizing their functionality for effective goal pursuit.

We then discussed the implications of our model for person perception, postsuppressional rebound, and catharsis of aggression. Finally, we discussed awareness of goal fulfillment as a precondition for postfulfillment inhibition. In all these domains, we presented evidence for the usefulness of the concept of motivation-related accessibility for explaining existing phenomena and generating novel and interesting predictions.

References

Aarts, H., Hassin, R., & Gollwitzer, P. (under review). *Goal contagion: Perceiving is for pursuing.* Manuscript.

Ach, N. (1935). Analyse des Willens. In E. Abderhalden (Ed.), *Handbuch der biologischen Arbeitsmethoden, Bd. IV* (pp. 000–000). Berlin: Urban & Schwarzenberg.

Anderson, J. R. (1983). *The architecture of cognition.* Cambridge, MA: Harvard University Press.

Anderson, M. C., & Spellman, B. A. (1995). On the status of inhibitory mechanisms in cognition: Memory retrieval as a model case. *Psychological Review, 102,* 68–100.

Atkinson, J. W. (1964). *An introduction to motivation.* Princeton, NJ: D. Van Nostrand.

Bandura, A. (1973). *Aggression: A social learning analysis.* Englewood Cliffs, NJ: Prentice-Hall.

Bargh, J. A. (1997). The automaticity of everyday life. In R. S. Wyer & T. K. Srull (Eds.), *Handbook of social cognition* (Vol. 10, pp. 1–61). Hillsdale, NJ: Erlbaum.

Bargh, J. A., & Barndollar, K. (1996). Automaticity in action: The unconscious as repository of chronic goals and motives. In P. M. Gollwitzer & J. A. Bargh (Eds.), *The psychology of action: Linking cognition and motivation to behavior* (pp. 457–481). New York: Guilford Press.

Berkowitz, L., & LePage, A. (1967). Weapons and aggression eliciting stimuli. *Journal of Personality and Social Psychology, 7,* 202–207.

Brehm, S. S., Kassin, S. M., & Fein, S. (1998). *Social psychology.* Boston: Houghton Mifflin.

Bruner, J. S. (1957). Going beyond the information given. In H. E. Gruber, K. H. Hammond, & R. Jessor (Eds.), *Contemporary approaches to cognition* (pp. 41–69). Cambridge, MA: Harvard University Press.

Butterfield, E. C. (1964). The interruption of tasks: Methodological, factual and theoretical issues. *Psychological Bulletin, 62,* 309–322.

Carver, C. S., & Scheier, M. F. (1999). Themes and issues in the self-regulation of behavior. In Robert S. Wyer, Jr. (Ed.), *Advances in social cognition* (Vol. 12, pp. 1–106). Hillsdale, NJ: Erlbaum.

Clark, D. M., Ball, S., & Pape, D. (1991). An experimental investigation of thought suppression. *Behaviour Research and Therapy, 29,* 253–257.

Clark, D. M., Winton, E., & Thynn, L. (1993). A further experimental investigation of thought suppression. *Behaviour Research and Therapy, 31,* 207–210.

Davies, M. I., & Clark, D. M. (1998). Thought suppression produces rebound effect with analogue post-traumatic intentions. *Behaviour Research and Therapy, 36,* 571–582.

Devine, P. G. (1989). Stereotypes and prejudice: Their automatic and controlled components. *Journal of Personality and Social Psychology, 56,* 5–18.

Dollard, J., Dobb, L. W., Miller, N. E., Mowrer, O. H., & Sears, R. R. (1939). *Frustration and aggression.* New Haven, CT: Yale University Press.

Fishbein, M., & Ajzen, I. (1974). Attitudes toward objects as predictors of single and multiple behavioral criteria. *Psychological Review, 81,* 59–74.

Förster, J., & Liberman, N. (2001). The role of attribution of motivation in producing post-suppressional rebound. *Journal of Personality and Social Psychology, 81,* 377–390.

Förster, J., & Liberman, N. (2003). *Aggression as goal fulfillment.* Unpublished data.

Förster, J., Liberman, N., & Higgins, E. T. (under review). *Accessibility from goals.* Manuscript.

Geen, R. G., & Quanty, M. B. (1977). The catharsis of aggression: An evaluation of a hypothesis. In L. Berkowitz (Ed.)., *Advances in experimental social psychology* (Vol. 10, pp. 10–37). New York: Academic Press.

Gollwitzer, P. M. (1996). The volitional benefits of planning. In P. M. Gollwitzer & J. A. Bargh (Eds.), *The psychology of action* (pp. 287–312). New York: Guilford Press.

Gollwitzer, P. M. (1999). Implementation intentions: Strong effects of simple plans. *American Psychologist, 54,* 493–503.

Gollwitzer, P. M., & Moskowitz, G. B. (1996). Goal effects on action and cognition. In E. T. Higgins & A. W. Kruglanski (Eds.), *Social psychology: Handbook of basic principles* (pp. 361–399). New York: Guilford Press.

Goschke, T., & Kuhl, J. (1993). Representation of intentions: Persisting activation in memory. *Journal of Experimental Psychology: Learning, Memory, and Cognition, 19,* 1211–1226.

Heckhausen, H. (1991). *Motivation and action.* Berlin: Springer-Verlag.

Higgins, E. T. (1996). Knowledge activation: Accessibility, applicability and salience. In E. T. Higgins & A. W. Kruglanski (Eds.), *Social psychology: Handbook of basic principles* (pp. 133–168). New York: Guilford Press.

Higgins, E. T., Bargh, J. A., & Lombardi, W. (1985). The nature of priming effects on categorization. *Journal of Experimental Psychology: Learning, Memory and Cognition, 11,* 59–69.

Higgins, E. T., & King, G. A. (1981). Accessibility of social constructs: Information-processing consequences of individual and contextual variability. In N. Cantor & J. Kihlstrom (Eds.), *Personality, cognition and social interaction* (pp. 69–122). Hillsdale: NJ: Erlbaum.

Higgins, E. T., Rholes, W. S., & Jones, C. R. (1977). Category accessibility and impression formation. *Journal of Experimental Social Psychology, 13,* 141–154.

Huesmann, L. R., & Eron, L. D. (Eds.). (1986). *Television and the aggressive child: A cross-national comparison.* Hillsdale, NJ: Erlbaum.

Huesmann, L. R., & Miller, L. S. (1994). Long term effects of repeated exposure to media violence in childhood, In L. R. Huesmann (Ed.), *Aggressive behavior: Current perspectives* (pp. 153–186). New York: Plenum Press.

Klinger, E. (1977). *Meaning and void.* Minneapolis: University of Minnesota Press.

Klinger, E. (1987). Current concerns and disengagement from incentives. In F. Halisch & J. Kuhl (Eds.), *Motivation, intention, and volition* (pp. 337–347). New York: Springer.

Klinger, E. (1996). Emotional influences on cognitive processing, with implications for theories of both. In P. M. Gollwitzer & J. A. Bargh (Eds.), *The psychology of action: Linking cognition and motivation to behavior* (pp. 197–218). New York: Guilford Press.

Kuhl, J. (1983). *Motivation, Konflikt und Handlungskontrolle.* New York: Springer.

Kuhl, J. (1987). Action control: The maintenance of motivational states. In F. Halisch & J. Kuhl (Eds.), *Motivation, intention, and volition* (pp. 279–291). New York: Springer.

Kuhl, J., & Kazén-Saad, M. (1988). A motivational approach to volition: Activation and deactivation of memory representations related to unfulfilled intentions. In V. Hamilton, G. H. Bower, & N. H. Frijda (Eds.), *Cognitive perspectives on emotion and motivation* (pp. 63–85). Dordrecht, the Netherlands: Martinus Nijhoff.

Lewin, K. (1951). *Field theory in social science.* New York: Harper.

Liberman, N., & Förster, J. (2000). Expression after suppression: A motivational explanation of postsuppressional rebound. *Journal of Personality and Social Psychology, 79,* 190–203.

Liberman, N., Förster, J., & Higgins, E. T. (under review). *Accessibility and completed vs. interrupted priming: The role of post-fulfillment inhibition.* Manuscript.

Macrae, C. M., Bodenhausen, G. V., & Milne, A. B. (1998). Saying no to unwanted thoughts: Self-focus and the regulation of mental life. *Journal of Personality and Social Psychology, 72,* 578–589.

Macrae, C. M., Bodenhausen, G. V., Milne, A. B., & Jetten, J. (1994). Out of mind but back in sight: Stereotypes on the rebound. *Journal of Personality and Social Psychology, 67,* 808–817.

Marsh, R. L., Hicks, J. L., & Bink, M. L. (1998). Activation of completed, uncompleted and partially completed intentions. *Journal of Experimental Psychology: Learning, Memory and Cognition, 24,* 350–361.

Marsh, R. L., Hicks, J. L., & Bryan, E. S. (1999). The activation of unrelated and canceled intentions. *Memory and Cognition, 27,* 320–327.

Martin, L. L. (1986). Set/reset: Use and disuse of concepts in impression formation. *Journal of Personality and Social Psychology, 51,* 493–504.

Martin, L. L., & Achee, J. W. (1992). Beyond accessibility: The role of processing objectives in judgment. In L. L. Martin & A. Tesser (Eds.), *The construction of social judgments* (pp. 195–216). Hillsdale, NJ: Erlbaum.

Martin, L. L., & Tesser, A. (1996). Some ruminative thoughts. In R. S. Wyer, Jr. (Ed.), *Advances in social cognition* (Vol. 9, pp. 1–47). Hillsdale, NJ: Erlbaum.

Mayr, U., & Keele, S. W. (2000). Changing internal constraints on action in the role of backward inhibition. *Journal of Experimental Psychology: General, 129,* 4–26.

Neely, J. H. (1991). Semantic priming effects in visual word recognition: A selective review of current findings and theories. In D. Besner & G. W. Humphreys (Eds.), *Basic processes in reading: Visual word recognition* (pp. 264–336). Hillsdale, NJ: Erlbaum.

Newman, L. S., Duff., K. L., & Baumeister, R. F. (1997). A new look at defensive projection: Thought suppression, accessibility, and biased person perception. *Journal of Personality and Social Psychology, 72,* 980–1001.

Russel, G. W., Arms, R. L., & Bibby, R. W. (1995). Canadians' belief in catharsis. *Social Behavior and Personality, 23,* 223–228.

Shah, J. Y., Friedman, R., & Kruglanski, A. W. (2002). Forgetting all else: On the antecedents and consequences of goal shielding. *Journal of Personality and Social Psychology, 86*, 1261–1280.

Srull, T. K., & Wyer, R. S. (1979). The role of category accessibility in the interpretation of information about persons: Some determinants and implications. *Journal of Personality and Social Psychology, 37*, 1660–1672.

Tulving, E., & Patterson, R. D. (1968). Functional units and retrieval processes in free recall. *Journal of Experimental Psychology, 77*, 239–248.

Vallacher, R. R., & Wegner, D. M. (1987). What do people think they're doing? Action identification and human behavior. *Psychological Review, 94*, 3–15.

Wegner, D. M., Erber, R., & Zanakos, S. (1993). Ironic processes in the mental control of mood and mood related thought. *Journal of Personality and Social Psychology, 65*, 1093–1104.

Wegner, D. M., & Gold, D. G. (1995). Fanning old flames: Emotional and cognitive effects of suppressing thought of past relationship. *Journal of Personality and Social Psychology, 68*, 782–792.

Wegner, D. M., Schneider, D. J., Carter, S., & White, L. (1987). Paradoxical effects of thought suppression. *Journal of Personality and Social Psychology, 53*, 5–13.

Wegner, D. M., Schneider, D. J., Knutson, B., & McMahon, S. (1991). Polluting the stream of consciousness: The influence of thought suppression on the mind's environment. *Cognitive Therapy and Research, 15*, 141–152.

Wenzlaff, R. M., Wegner, D. M., & Klein, S. B. (1991). The role of thought suppression in the association of thought and mood. *Journal of Personality and Social Psychology, 60*, 500–508.

Wicklund, R. A., & Gollwitzer, P. M. (1982). *Symbolic self-completion.* Hillsdale, NJ: Erlbaum.

Wyer, R. S., & Srull, T. K. (1986). Human cognition in its social context. *Psychological Review, 93*, 322–359.

Wyer, R. S., & Srull, T. K. (1989). *Memory and cognition in its social context.* Hillsdale, NJ: Erlbaum.

Zeigarnik, B. (1927). Das Behalten erledigter und unerledigter Handlungen [The memory of completed and uncompleted actions]. *Psychologische Forschung, 9*, 1–85.

PART III

CONSCIOUS AND UNCONSCIOUS SOCIAL MOTIVATION

Some Consequences and Applications

14

Self-Regulatory Processes in Interracial Interactions

The Role of Internal and External Motivation to Respond without Prejudice

Patricia G. Devine, Amanda B. Brodish,
and Stephanie L. Vance

INTRODUCTION

In recent years, students of intergroup relations have shown increased interest in exploring and understanding the challenges involved in intergroup interactions. Several researchers have noted, for example, the importance of considering the types of interpersonal concerns people bring to intergroup interactions that may affect their expectations, perceptions, feelings, and behavior in such settings (Devine, Evett, & Vasquez, 1996; Plant & Devine, 2003a, 2003b; Shelton, 2003; Vorauer & Kumhyr, 2001; Vorauer, Main, & O'Connell, 1998). For majority group members, most often these concerns are framed in terms of the possibility of appearing prejudiced in such interactions and the potential to be evaluated negatively should one be viewed as prejudiced. Against a backdrop of contemporary social norms discouraging overt expressions of prejudice, sensitivity to the possibility of appearing prejudiced in intergroup interactions is likely to be heightened.

Indeed, recent research suggests that majority group members expect to viewed as prejudiced by outgroup members and that this expectation is easily activated in situations in which the potential for evaluation by an outgroup member is likely (Vorauer, Hunter, Main, & Roy, 2000; Vorauer & Kumhyr, 2001; Vorauer et al., 1998). Vorauer and colleagues speculated that these expectations may play a role in the unfolding dynamics of intergroup interactions, affecting, for example, people's strategies for interaction and how people feel about intergroup interactions. In her work on the dynamic nature of intergroup interactions, Shelton (2003) echoed the importance of majority group members' evaluative concerns in intergroup interactions when she suggested that many majority group members are "concerned with the debilitating fear of appearing prejudiced" (p. 173).

Address correspondence to Patricia Devine at e-mail: pgdevine@wisc.edu.

Fears about appearing prejudiced in intergroup interactions have been implicated in the experience of intergroup anxiety – feelings of tension and distress experienced in intergroup settings. Specifically, intergroup anxiety arises when people's concerns about appearing prejudiced motivate them to present a nonprejudiced image to their interaction partner but they doubt that they will succeed in their efforts (i.e., they expect to be viewed as prejudiced) (see Britt, Boniecki, Vescio, Biernat, & Brown, 1996; Plant & Devine, 2003a; Stephan & Stephan, 1985, 1989). This type of anxiety has been shown to be a disruptive force in intergroup interactions. For example, those who report anxiety in intergroup settings expect such interactions to be difficult (Britt et al., 1996) and, when possible, they avoid such interactions altogether (Plant & Devine, 2003a). Although there is clear evidence that many people are concerned about appearing prejudiced, and that such concerns can have adverse implications for intergroup interactions, to date the motive to make a nonprejudiced impression has generally been treated as though it were monolithic in nature. That is, the extant research has not considered the possibility that people may be motivated to present a nonprejudiced identity for different reasons. The core argument to be developed in this chapter is that to understand the nature of interpersonal concerns and the experience of intergroup anxiety in intergroup interactions, it is not sufficient to simply know that a person *is* motivated to make a nonprejudiced impression; it is also important to know *why* he or she is motivated.

Although not explored in depth, some scholars have noted that people may be motivated to present a nonprejudiced impression and experience anxiety in intergroup settings for different reasons. For example, Britt et al. (1996) speculated that due to pervasive social norms discouraging the expression of prejudice, the "dominant tendency may be for individuals to avoid making a bad impression (e.g., appearing prejudiced), rather than creating a desired impression" (p. 1185). From this perspective, not being sure how to avoid making a prejudiced impression leads to anxiety. Alternatively, they suggested that for others, intergroup anxiety may reflect uncertainty about how to translate their nonprejudiced personal attitudes into behavior consistent with those attitudes. Echoing these alternative motivational orientations, Fazio and colleagues (1995) suggested that concern with making a nonprejudiced impression may "vary from a sincere distaste for the negative reaction . . . to a more strategic self-presentation dictated by perceptions of the social norms" (p. 1025). Together, these observations suggest that, indeed, people may be motivated to make a nonprejudiced impression to achieve distinct self-presentational goals. Specifically, whereas for some people the goal of presenting a nonprejudiced identity in intergroup interactions reflects an effort to reveal one's personally accepted nonprejudiced identity, for others this goal reflects strategic efforts to conceal one's personally accepted prejudice from others.

The first step in exploring these issues is to identify those individuals who are likely to pursue these alternative goals in intergroup interactions. Plant and Devine (1998) showed that there are meaningful individual differences in the extent to which people are motivated to respond without prejudice for personal (i.e., internal) and for normative (i.e., external) reasons and that these differences are consequential for the regulation of prejudice. We argue that knowing *why* people are motivated to respond without prejudice may shed light on the extent to which efforts to reveal a nonprejudiced impression in intergroup interactions reflect the sincere distaste for prejudiced responses versus strategic self-presentational efforts to conceal prejudice in order to meet social norms. Harackiewicz et al. (this volume) and Lewicki (this volume) also provide analyses of how social behavior can be motivated in response to internal (intrinsic) and external (extrinsic) forces. In the present context, the goals people pursue as a function of their motivation to respond without prejudice are likely to involve the reflective system described by Strack and Deutsch (this volume), though, as will become clear, the more automatic processes may pose particular challenges for some persons more than others.

Further, we suggest that to fully understand the implications of these distinct self-presentational goals in intergroup interactions requires their discussion in terms of the specific self-regulatory challenges involved in intergroup contact settings. To this end, we offer a model of the self-regulatory processes involved in interracial interactions, in which we argue that intergroup anxiety arises in response to people's concerns that they will fail to meet specific self-presentational goals. Specifically, the model addresses the origins of the alternative self-presentational goals adopted in intergroup interactions, the qualitatively distinct pathways to anxiety in such interactions, the strategies pursued in regulating one's behavior to achieve the distinct goals, and the implications of these processes for behavior and outcomes in interracial settings.

Before proceeding, is important to note that in the work to be reviewed and in our model of the self-regulatory processes in interracial interactions, we focus on interracial interactions between Blacks and Whites. Several interrelated factors contribute to this emphasis. First, intergroup tension in the interracial context has long been recognized as a significant social problem. Second, a majority of the previous theory and research on prejudice and stereotyping has examined Whites' prejudice toward Blacks (see Devine, Plant, & Blair, 2001; Jones, 1997). As well, a great deal of intergroup anxiety research has been done in the context of White–Black interactions (e.g., Britt et al., 1996; Plant & Devine, 2003a). Third, the measures of the alternative sources of motivation to respond without prejudice, which are central to our reasoning, were designed specifically to address motivation(s) to respond without prejudice toward Blacks (e.g., Amodio, Harmon-Jones, & Devine, 2003; Devine, Plant, Amodio, Harmon-Jones, & Vance, 2002; Plant & Devine, 1998, 2001, 2003b; Plant, Devine, & Brazy, 2003). The emphasis on interracial interactions is not meant to imply that interactions with other groups (e.g., Latinos, gays) are not important or worthy of study. However, our previous work and the existing intergroup anxiety research position us best to address White–Black interactions.

INTERNAL AND EXTERNAL MOTIVATION TO RESPOND WITHOUT PREJUDICE

In a series of studies, Plant and Devine (1998) developed and validated separate scales of internal motivation to respond without prejudice (IMS) and external motivation to respond without prejudice (EMS) toward Blacks. The crucial difference between internal and external motivation is the evaluative audience who imposes the standards proscribing prejudice (i.e., self versus others, respectively). Internal motivation arises from internalized, personally important nonprejudiced beliefs. Sample IMS items include "I attempt to act in nonprejudiced ways because it is personally important to me" and "Being nonprejudiced toward Black people is important to my self-concept." In contrast, external motivation arises from a desire to avoid negative reactions from others. Sample EMS items include "I attempt to appear nonprejudiced toward Black people in order to avoid disapproval from others" and "I try to act nonprejudiced toward Blacks because of pressure from others."

Plant and Devine (1998) demonstrated that the IMS and EMS are reliable and provided evidence regarding the scales' convergent, discriminant, and predictive validity. The IMS, for example, is highly correlated with self-report measures of prejudice including the Attitudes Towards Blacks scale (Brigham, 1993) and the Modern Racism Scale (McConahay, Hardee, & Batts, 1981) such that high IMS scores are associated with lower prejudice scores. The EMS, in contrast, is only modestly correlated with traditional prejudice measures, such that high EMS scores are associated with higher prejudice scores. In addition, the EMS is only slightly correlated with measures of general social evaluation, including the Interaction Anxiousness Scale (Leary, 1983), the Social Desirability Scale (Crowne & Marlow, 1960), the Self-Monitoring Scale (Snyder & Gangested, 1986), and the Fear of Negative Evaluation Scale (Watson & Friend, 1969). These rather small correlations suggest that the EMS assesses something distinct from generalized fear and anxiety in social situations. Across many samples, the IMS and EMS are largely independent (average $r = -.09$). Thus, individuals can be motivated to respond without prejudice primarily for internal reasons, primarily for external reasons, for both reasons, or they may not be motivated for either reason.

SELF-REGULATORY SIGNIFICANCE OF IMS AND EMS

In this section, we review evidence from published research and preliminary studies suggesting that internal and external motivation to respond without prejudice have implications for the regulation of prejudice generally and specifically in the context of interracial interactions. In classic self-regulation models (e.g., Carver & Scheier, 1981, 1998), self-regulation is a continuous process in which one's current behavior or performance is compared to a standard or reference value (see also Liberman & Förster, this volume). According to Carver and Scheier (1998), human behavior is produced by self-regulatory systems consisting of negative and positive feedback loops. These feedback loops function at all levels of behavior, regulating the pursuit of higher-order goals (e.g., being a thoughtful person) as well as the pursuit of specific strategies that will help to achieve the goals (e.g., opening the door for someone carrying groceries).

Research has demonstrated that the standards that get activated and serve as reference values are a function of the circumstances in which people find themselves. For example, because of the public nature of interracial interactions, an individual's self-focus increases, which results in attention being drawn to standards of behavior that are relevant for the situation (Duval & Wicklund, 1972). As attention is drawn to standards, people tend to compare themselves against these standards. To the extent that a discrepancy exists between standards and people's actual responses, adjustments in behavior are initiated to bring behavior in line with the standards (Aronson, 1968; Bandura, 1986; Duval & Wicklund, 1972; Festinger, 1957; Pyszczynski & Greenberg, 1986, 1987; Wicklund, 1975). In a negative, or discrepancy-reducing, feedback loop, behavior is initiated to reduce any discrepancy detected between the behavior and a desired reference value. In contrast, in a positive, or discrepancy-enhancing, feedback loop, behavior is initiated to increase the discrepancy between the behavior and an undesired reference value.

Our goal is to explore self-regulatory processes in the context of interracial interactions. In what follows, we review evidence from Plant, Devine, and colleagues' unfolding program of research addressing the alternative sources of motivation to respond without prejudice, which, we argue, has direct implications for a variety of issues concerning self-regulation and anxiety in interracial interactions, including (a) the standards or reference values against which behavior is regulated; (b) the likelihood of meeting the standards to respond without prejudice (i.e., discrepancies from standards); (c) outcome expectancies in interracial interactions; (d) who is most likely to experience anxiety in interracial interactions; and (e) the approach and avoidance goals set and strategies pursued in interracial interactions. By considering the cumulative implications of this program of research, we are able to pinpoint who is likely to have concerns about appearing prejudiced in interracial interactions, and the distinct self-presentational goals set for interracial interactions, as well as the strategies pursued to regulate behavior toward these goals.

Regulatory Significance of Self- versus Other-Imposed Standards Proscribing Prejudice

Plant and Devine (1998) reasoned that possessing internal and external motivation to respond without prejudice would make particular evaluative audiences salient and that these audiences would define the standards against which individuals would evaluate their behavior. They further reasoned that to the extent that these standards were important self-regulatory reference values, violations of them would lead to distinct patterns of affective distress (e.g., Higgins, 1987). Higgins's (1987) self-discrepancy theory, for example, posits that when people's actual self-characteristics are discrepant from ought (should) standards, agitation-related emotions result, the specific form of which depends on whether the standard violated is one's own (i.e., internal) or imposed on one by others (i.e., external). According to the theory, discrepancies between people's actual responses and their *personal standards* for whom they think they *should* be (i.e., ought–own discrepancies) lead to feelings of guilt, uneasiness, and self-contempt (i.e., the feelings associated with self-punishment that result from violating a personally accepted moral standard). When others *prescribe the should standard* against which the appropriateness of responses is evaluated, however, discrepancies (i.e., ought–other discrepancies) are associated with feeling fearful and threatened (i.e., the feelings associated with impending punishments from others).

To explore these issues, Plant and Devine adapted the method developed by Devine and her colleagues (e.g., Devine, Monteith, Zuwerink, & Elliot, 1991) to assess the affective consequences of discrepancies between how one *should* respond and how one reports one actually *would* respond across a variety of interracial scenarios. Specifically, Plant and Devine measured participants' self-imposed (personal) standards for how they should treat Blacks and, in a separate sample, measured participants' perceptions of other-imposed (normative) standards for how they should treat Blacks. Whereas participants' self-imposed standards were linearly related to their level of IMS, such that high-IMS participants' standards proscribed prejudice and low-IMS participants' standards permitted much higher levels of prejudice, all participants indicated that the other-imposed (University of Wisconsin–Madison campus) standards proscribed prejudice. Plant and Devine also measured how participants reported they actually would respond in the interpersonal setting as an indicator of their current performance. To illustrate the significance of these self- and other-imposed standards, Plant and Devine examined the affective consequences of violating the standards (i.e., responding with more prejudice than the standards permitted) as a function of participants' level of IMS and EMS.

Consistent with expectations, Plant and Devine (1998) found that the quality of participants' affective distress was determined jointly by the source of their motivation to respond without prejudice and whether their responses violated a self-imposed or other-imposed standard. Specifically, violations of self-imposed standards were associated with guilt and self-criticism, particularly for high-IMS people, suggesting that self-imposed standards serve as important reference values for these people. Violations of other-imposed nonprejudiced standards, however, were associated with threatened affect, particularly for high-EMS people, suggesting that other-imposed standards serve as important reference values for these people.

There was an additional important finding in this study: When violations were assessed against other-imposed standards, high-EMS people who also reported being personally motivated to respond without prejudice (i.e., high IMS) felt not only threat-related affect but also guilt and self-criticism. Plant and Devine (1998) argued that for those high in both IMS and EMS, thinking about other-imposed standards also brings to mind their self-imposed standards. That is, violating other-imposed standards also reflects the violation of a self-imposed standard for individuals high in both EMS and IMS. Providing convergent evidence for this reasoning in a recent preliminary study, participants who scored high in EMS provided open-ended responses to the question "How would you feel if you violated your external standards to respond without prejudice?" These responses were coded for the presence/absence of negative self-directed affect words (e.g., *guilty*, *ashamed*, *disappointed in self*) and threat-related affect (e.g., *afraid*, *fearful*). Although all participants were equally likely to report threat-related affect, consistent with Plant and Devine's reasoning, high-IMS participants were more likely to report guilt-related affect than their low-IMS counterparts, further bolstering the evidence that violating other-imposed standards also reflects a violation of self-imposed standards for high-IMS, high-EMS individuals. In sum, it appears that when other-imposed standards are activated, participants who are high in both EMS and IMS also activate their personal, self-imposed standards. Taken together, these findings suggest that in interracial interactions, such self- and other-imposed standards are likely to be activated and serve as the reference value(s) against which people are likely evaluate their behavior.

Likelihood of Meeting the Standards

Whether the standards proscribing prejudice are self- or other-imposed, some people are more likely than others to violate these standards. For example, in a recent series of studies assessing the magnitude of implicit race bias, Devine et al. (2002) showed that some people are more vulnerable to responding in ways that violate these standards than others. Implicit responses are likely to be particularly problematic in interracial interactions because they occur without intention and are difficult to control (see Son Hing et al., this volume, for an analysis in terms of aversive racism and Spencer et al., this volume, and Wood & Quinn, this volume, for a discussion of when habitual or immediate responses conflict with intentional responses). As a result, they may create the need to engage self-regulatory processes to mitigate their effects for those whose standards (whether self- or other-imposed) proscribe prejudice. Using two different measures of implicit bias [i.e., the sequential priming measure (Fazio et al., 1995) and the Implicit Association Test, (Greenwald, McGhee, & Schwartz, 1998)] across three studies, Devine et al. found that the likelihood of responding with implicit race bias varied as a function of IMS and EMS. Specifically, high-IMS/low-EMS participants reported much lower levels of implicit bias than participants with all other combinations of IMS and EMS – and the level of implicit bias was equally high for these latter participants. These findings were replicated conceptually using another difficult-to-control psychophysiological measure of race bias [i.e., the startle eyeblink measure (Amodio et al., 2003)].

We reasoned that the presence of implicit race bias is likely to have implications for people's outcome expectancies (i.e., expectancies concerning whether one will create a nonprejudiced impression in interracial interactions). Specifically, those who manifest evidence of these difficult-to-control forms of race bias may be specifically concerned that such bias will be detected in interracial interactions. This issue is important because, although Britt et al. (1996) and Plant and Devine (2003a) showed that negative outcome expectancies in interracial interactions were related to negative outcomes (i.e., anxiety and avoidance) for such interactions, they did not identify who among their research participants was most likely to report negative, compared with more positive, outcome expectancies.

Outcome Expectancies in Interracial Interactions

To explore this issue, in a recent study, using measures developed by Plant and Devine (2003a), we examined participants' outcome expectancies for an interracial interaction as a function of IMS and EMS. Data were collected in a mass testing session. In addition to the IMS and EMS, participants completed a questionnaire assessing their outcome expectancies for an interaction with a Black student. Items assessing outcome expectancies reflected concerns about the likelihood that the Black student would view the participant as prejudiced (e.g., "When interacting with a Black person, he or she would see me as prejudiced no matter what I do"; "Even if we hadn't met before, a Black person would expect me to be prejudiced"; "If I were interacting with a Black person, regardless of my behavior he or she would see me as prejudiced"). Participants indicated their agreement with the statements, and their responses were averaged to create an outcome expectancy index. The key finding from this study was an IMS × EMS interaction. The form of this interaction suggests that whereas high-IMS, low-EMS participants reported positive outcome expectancies, all other participants reported fairly negative outcome expectancies. These data are consistent with the implicit race bias findings reported earlier and suggest that outcome expectancies are systematically associated with the source of people's motivation to respond without prejudice. We next reasoned that for those who are likely to be concerned about responding with prejudice in interracial interactions (e.g., those high in IMS and/or EMS), possessing negative outcome expectancies may make them vulnerable to intergroup anxiety (Britt et al., 1996; Plant & Devine, 2003a).

Anxiety in Interracial Interactions

To explore this possibility, in an additional study we tested the hypothesis that if people were motivated to respond without prejudice for any reason and had negative outcome expectancies (the two high EMS groups), they should experience anxiety in the context of an interracial interaction. None of the low-EMS participants were expected to report elevated anxiety prior to the intergroup interaction. That is, high-IMS/low-EMS individuals have positive outcome expectancies and low-IMS/low-EMS individuals are not motivated to respond without prejudice; as such, each low-EMS group lacks one of the necessary ingredients to experience intergroup anxiety (i.e., negative outcome expectancies and motivation to respond without prejudice, respectively). In this study, White participants were led to believe that they would interact with a Black student about a topic relevant to student life on campus. At that point, their interaction partner, a Black confederate, entered the room. Before the interaction, participants reported their affect about the upcoming interaction. Embedded in the affect questionnaire were items designed to assess intergroup anxiety (e.g., anxious, tense, nervous, uneasy). As expected, high-EMS participants reported higher levels of anxiety in anticipation of the interracial interaction than their low-EMS counterparts. Although the amount of intergroup anxiety reported among high-EMS participants did not vary as a function of their level of IMS, we will argue in developing our model that their anxiety followed from concerns about failing to reach distinct self-presentational goals. Before developing this logic, we consider what the existing research suggests about the goals set and strategies pursued by such individuals in interracial interactions.

Goals and Strategies for Interracial Interactions

Any analysis of self-regulation would be incomplete without an understanding of the types of goals people set for behavior and the strategies they pursue to meet these goals. Building on classic motivation and self-regulation models, which distinguish between self-regulation that focuses on approaching a desired end-state and self-regulation that focuses on avoiding an undesired end-state (Atkinsin, 1964; Carver & Scheier, 1981, 1990, 1998; Higgins, 1997; Higgins, Roney, Crowe, & Hymes, 1994), Plant and Devine (2003b) proposed a conceptual framework exploring the relation between the alternative sources of motivation to respond without prejudice and people's goals and strategies in interracial interactions.

Briefly, the distinction between the motive to achieve success (a desired end-state) and the motive to avoid failure (an undesired end-state) features prominently in both classic and contemporary achievement motivation work (e.g., Atkinson, 1964; Atkinson & Litwin, 1960; Elliot & Church, 1997; Elliot & Harackiewicz, 1996; Feather, 1967; Hembree, 1988; Mahone, 1960). In this work, for example, the motivation to achieve success leads to active pursuit of the end-state, whereas the motivation to avoid failure results in the tendency to avoid performing actions that are expected to produce the undesired end-state. Similarly, Carver and Scheier (1981, 1990, 1998), in their cybernetic theory of self-regulation, also distinguished between two types of motivational systems, those that focus on approaching desired end-states and those that focus on avoiding undesired end-states. In systems focused on approaching a desired end-state, current behavior is compared to a positive (i.e., desired) reference value. If a discrepancy is detected between the current behavior and the desired end-state, behavior is adjusted in order to diminish the discrepancy (i.e., to approach the desired end-state). In contrast, discrepancy-amplifying systems compare current behavior to a negative (i.e., undesired) reference value. If current behavior is too close to the reference value, behavior is adjusted in order to amplify the discrepancy (i.e., avoid the undesired end-state).

Plant and Devine (2003b) reasoned that the distinction between self-regulation focused on approaching desired end-states and self-regulation focused on avoiding undesired end-states, when considered in conjunction with the alternative sources of motivation to respond without prejudice, would shed light on the regulatory goals and strategies pursued in interracial interactions. They argued that, in attempting to regulate prejudice, some people are likely to be concerned with approaching the desired end-state of egalitarianism, whereas others are concerned with avoiding the undesired end-state of overt bias. Whether one is primarily concerned with approaching a desired end-state of egalitarianism or avoiding an undesired end-state of overt bias depends on the source of one's motivation to respond without prejudice. Plant and Devine argued that highly internally motivated people wish to respond consistently with their internalized non-prejudiced standards and that their primary goal is to approach a desired end-state of egalitarian responding. Supporting this reasoning, Monteith and colleagues (Devine & Monteith, 1993; Monteith, 1993; Monteith,

Ashburn-Nardo, Voils, & Czopp, 2002) found that guilt resulting from violations of personal nonprejudiced standards activates a self-regulatory cycle that facilitates bringing responses closer to egalitarian, nonprejudiced standards (i.e., a desired end-state). Highly externally motivated people, Plant and Devine suggested, want to respond without prejudice in order to avoid social disapproval; hence their primary goal is to avoid an undesired end-state of responding with overt bias that would make them vulnerable to threat-related affect and negative reactions from others. Unlike guilt, threat-related affect motivates people to move responses away from the unwanted outcome (i.e., overt bias resulting in social disapproval) (Carver, 2001). They argued that strategies in interracial interactions would be pursued to the extent that they facilitated goal pursuit. In a series of four studies, Plant and Devine obtained strong support for their framework.

In one study designed to explore the link between the source of people's motivation to respond without prejudice and their self-reported goals in interracial interactions, participants were asked to generate their goals for an upcoming interaction in an open-ended format. Participants' responses were coded for approach goals (e.g., "Be friendly," "Treat the person like I would anyone else," "Act normal") and avoidance goals (e.g., "Avoid acting prejudiced," "Don't make racial jokes [or ethnic slurs]," "Try not to think about the stereotype"). High-IMS participants were more likely than low-IMS participants to generate goals that focused on approaching egalitarian responding. In contrast, high-EMS participants were more likely than low-EMS participants to generate goals that focused on avoiding biased responding. Further, the high-IMS/high-EMS participants reported both types of goals. These findings suggest that high-IMS/high-EMS individuals are concerned with approaching the desired end-state of egalitarianism, but ever mindful of their potential failures in interracial interactions (i.e., negative outcome expectancies, implicit forms of bias), they are also concerned with avoiding the undesired end-state of biased responding.

In a second study, participants anticipating an interaction with a Black student were asked to indicate their goals for the upcoming interaction (Plant and Devine, 2003b). Embedded in the list were items assessing the extent to which they endorsed a goal of approaching egalitarianism (e.g., to be open, friendly, and unbiased) or a goal of avoiding overt bias (e.g., avoid using stereotypes, avoid coming across as prejudiced, keep the interaction short) during the interaction. The pattern of goal endorsement replicated the self-reported goals. That is, as expected, high-IMS participants were more likely to endorse a goal of approaching egalitarianism compared to low-IMS participants. In addition, high-EMS participants were more likely to endorse a goal of avoiding overt bias in the interaction than their low-EMS counterparts.

In two additional studies, Plant and Devine (2003b) examined the consequences of the "approach egalitarianism" and "avoid overt bias" goals for people's pursuit of a regulatory strategy that would facilitate goal attainment. They reasoned that any given strategy should be pursued only to the extent that it facilitates effective goal pursuit. In considering the pursuit of strategies to eliminate bias, Plant and Devine argued that it is important to take into account both whether one believes that a biased response is likely in interracial interactions and whether one cares about responding with bias. That is, regulatory strategies to reduce bias should be of interest only to the extent that people anticipate that they are likely to respond with bias in interracial situations and would be concerned if they responded with such bias. As noted previously, the extant literature examining the implications of the source of people's motivation to respond without prejudice indicates that only people highly internally motivated who are also low in external motivation individuals do not anticipate responding with bias in interracial interactions and have been found to respond with less bias than others on a variety of measures (Amodio et al., 2003; Devine et al., 2002; Plant & Devine, 2001; Plant et al., 2003). Therefore, these participants may not be interested in pursuing any bias-reducing strategies. Further, participants who are neither internally nor externally motivated are not particularly concerned with responding without bias. Thus, they should not be very interested in pursuing strategies to reduce bias.

In contrast, highly externally motivated people, whether they are high or low in internal motivation, believe they are likely to respond with bias and are concerned about responding with bias. Thus, they are likely to be interested in pursuing bias reduction strategies; however, their interest is likely to vary as a function of how they believe the strategy will help them. People who are high in external motivation but low in internal motivation are concerned with concealing bias from others in order to avoid social disapproval, but they are not personally motivated to overcome prejudice. For these people, strategies that enable one to avoid observable forms of bias should be especially appealing; in contrast, overcoming subtle bias that is not detectable by others would not facilitate their goal pursuit and should be of little interest. Plant and Devine reasoned that for people high in both internal and external motivation, any strategy that facilitates egalitarian responding should be appealing (i.e., whether or not the bias is observable to others).

In one study designed to explore these issues, participants with varying levels of IMS and EMS were led to believe that they would be interacting with a Black person. Prior to the interaction, they were provided with the opportunity to complete a computer program framed as a strategy that would facilitate approaching egalitarianism or avoiding overt bias. Plant and Devine developed these strategies specifically to address the regulatory concerns generated and endorsed by participants in the previous two studies. Half of the participants were told that the program would help them to approach true egalitarian responding by reducing subtle bias that *is not detectable* in interracial interactions. The other half of the participants were told that the program would help them to avoid overt bias by reducing bias that *is detectable* in interracial interactions. The amount of time that participants spent on the program was viewed as an indicator of their interest in pursuing the bias reduction strategy.

Results indicated that participants' pursuit of the alternative strategies was determined jointly by the source of their motivation to respond without prejudice and how the strategy was framed. As expected, low-EMS participants spent relatively little time on the program in either condition, presumably because the program was not viewed as needed (i.e., for high-IMS/low-EMS participants who do not expect to respond with prejudice) or useful (i.e., for low-IMS, low-EMS participants who lack motivation to respond without prejudice). The findings for high-EMS participants were also consistent with expectations. Specifically, when the program facilitated approaching egalitarianism but had no positive benefits for the upcoming interaction, high-IMS/high-EMS participants spent more time on the program than did all other participants. When the program facilitated avoiding overt bias in the upcoming interaction, high-EMS participants, regardless of their level of IMS, spent more time on the program than low-EMS participants.

MODEL OF SELF-REGULATORY PROCESSES IN INTERRACIAL INTERACTIONS

The preceding review reveals that internal and external motivation to respond without prejudice is systematically associated with important components of self-regulation in interracial interactions. However, we suggest that synthesizing Plant and Devine's work on the sources of motivation to respond without prejudice with the extant literature addressing intergroup anxiety and interpersonal concerns in interracial interactions leads to a more complete model of self-regulatory processes in interracial interactions. That is, we suggest that each of these literatures provides some key insights, but that their integration will lead to novel predictions about the nature of the self-regulatory challenges and the specific self-presentational goals pursued in interracial interactions. For example, the intergroup anxiety literature has not addressed individual differences in vulnerability to anxiety in interracial interactions or the specific self-presentational goals pursued in such interactions (e.g., Britt et al., 1996; Plant & Devine, 2003a). In addition, Plant and Devine's (2003b) work, although addressing general goals and strategies in interracial interactions, has not addressed intergroup anxiety. The additional preliminary research examining the relation between Plant and Devine's IMS and EMS and outcome expectancies, as well as the experience of intergroup anxiety, suggests that synthesizing these literatures may prove fruitful in the context of developing a model of the self-regulatory processes specifically involved in interracial interactions. Before providing a description of the model, we review key findings from the research that are central to our analysis.

Although the findings for individuals with all combinations of IMS and EMS are interesting and informative, we suggest that the findings for the high-EMS individuals are most central to addressing issues in intergroup anxiety and exploring the processes involved in self-regulation in interracial interactions. As such, the proposed model focuses on high-EMS individuals. We will draw on the similarities and differences among high-EMS individuals as they vary in their level of IMS to provide the basis for arguing that these individuals have different interpersonal concerns in interracial interactions that lead them to adopt distinct and specific self-presentational goals. Consider first some of the similarities. Regardless of their level of IMS, high-EMS individuals both have reason to be and are concerned about appearing prejudiced in interracial interactions. That is, high-EMS individuals show high levels of implicit bias, a type of response that is both hard to control and would violate nonprejudiced standards. In addition, high-EMS individuals report negative outcome expectancies (i.e., expect to be seen as prejudiced) and high levels of anxiety in interracial interactions. Although they are similar on the dimensions described, we suggest that considering their differences will highlight the specific self-regulatory challenges experienced by high-EMS individuals as they vary in their level of IMS.

A major difference concerns the standards against which they evaluate their behavior in interracial settings. Whereas all high-EMS individuals report being sensitive to other-imposed standards proscribing prejudice, those high in IMS also possess self-imposed standards prohibiting prejudice. Thus, in settings where one's responses are observable to others, such as interracial interactions, high-EMS/low-IMS individuals need only be concerned about violating other-imposed standards and the sanctions such failures may elicit. In contrast, high-EMS/high-IMS individuals are at risk for violating both other- and self-imposed standards and hence are at risk for the possibility of failing to meet two significant standards. We reviewed evidence indicating that, when thinking about the failure to meet other-imposed standards, all high-EMS individuals report threat-related affect, as would be expected following violations of other-imposed standards, but only high-IMS/high-EMS individuals reported that such failures would lead to guilt and self-criticism, the type of affect associated with violations of self-imposed standards. Thus, even when responses were evaluated against other-imposed standards, high-EMS/high-IMS people brought to mind their self-imposed evaluative standards.

An additional meaningful difference between high-EMS people as they vary in IMS focuses on the strategies they will pursue to regulate prejudice in interracial interactions. For example, high-EMS/low-IMS individuals were highly strategic in their decision about whether or not to exert effort to reduce prejudice. When the effort would only help them to approach personal levels of low prejudice, they eschewed the opportunity; however, when their efforts would enable them to conceal prejudice from the other person, they exerted high levels of effort (see also Plant & Devine, 1998; Plant et al., 2003). High-EMS/high-IMS individuals, in contrast, were motivated to take advantage of any opportunity to overcome prejudice – that is, whether or not the effort would help them to respond without prejudice in the upcoming interaction. Our interpretation is that high-EMS/high-IMS individuals are striving to overcome prejudice in all of its forms. Taken together, the pattern of differences reviewed suggests that the specific self-presentational goals adopted by high-EMS individuals in interracial interactions vary as a function of their level of IMS. Specifically, we suggest, whereas high-EMS/low-IMS individuals adopt the goal of concealing their personally accepted prejudice from others, their high-IMS counterparts adopt the goal of striving to respond consistently with their personally accepted values in order to reveal their personally accepted nonprejudiced identity to others.

Building on the evidence reviewed, we offer a model of the self-regulatory processes involved in interracial interactions. The model addresses the self-regulatory processes of those most likely to report being concerned about appearing prejudiced in interracial interactions and who, as a result, need to regulate their responses in such interactions. As such, the model focuses on high-EMS individuals, arguing that the core self-regulatory challenges (i.e., goals and strategies) differ for those who are low, compared to high, in IMS. For example, high-EMS/low-IMS individuals seem to be primarily concerned with strategically concealing prejudice from others as the way to meet their other-imposed standard proscribing prejudice; we refer to these individuals as *Strategics*. In contrast, high-EMS/high-IMS individuals appear to be striving to overcome prejudice in any form as the way to meet both their other-imposed and self-imposed nonprejudiced standards; as such, we refer to these individuals as *Strivers*.[1] We offer one additional observation before describing the model: Low-EMS individuals are not of concern in this model because they either lack motivation to respond without prejudice (i.e., low-EMS/low-IMS) or lack concern over appearing prejudiced in interracial interactions because they have positive outcome expectancies (i.e., low-EMS/high-IMS).[2]

We begin with two basic assumptions. First, we contend that in order to develop a better understanding of the nature of intergroup relations,

---

[1] Although we recognize that EMS and IMS are assessed on continua and we have not done the necessary work to develop typologies (see Waller & Meehl, 1998), we believe these labels capture these individuals' core self-regulatory challenges in interracial interactions and will facilitate the presentation of our model and its assumptions.

[2] Our research has led us to identify high-IMS, low-EMS people as *Accomplished* and low-IMS/low-EMS people as *Indifferent*.

one must consider that contact between groups occurs in an interpersonal setting. That is, it takes the form of interpersonal interactions between two or more members of different social groups (e.g., different ethnicities). Second, consistent with cybernetic models (e.g., Carver & Scheier, 1998), we suggest that behavior in this interpersonal context is goal-directed and feedback-controlled. Thus, in what follows, we present an analysis of the self-regulatory processes involved specifically in interracial interactions. In our analysis, we place strong emphasis on the prejudice-relevant concerns and expectations that individuals chronically possess, as well as the unique role of the interpersonal setting in activating these concerns and expectations. Finally, we suggest that the specific goals and strategies that individuals adopt in order to regulate their behavior in interracial interactions are dependent upon the nature of these chronic concerns and expectations.

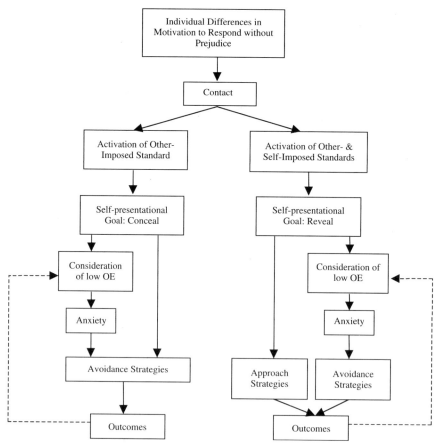

FIGURE 14.1 Model of self-regulatory processes in interracial interactions. OE refers to outcome expectancies.

First, according to the model (see Figure 14.1), there are individual differences in the extent to which people are chronically motivated to respond without prejudice for internal or external reasons. Second, when people enter interracial contact situations, self-focus increases and the relevant standards against which behavior will be evaluated are activated. However, the relevant standards vary for Strategics compared with Strivers. For Strategics, other-imposed standards are activated. For Strivers, both other-imposed and self-imposed standards are activated. It is these standards against which Strivers and Strategics will monitor their performance in the interaction. Third, the activation of relevant standards is linked to distinct self-presentational goals in interracial interactions. The self-presentational goal activated for Strategics focuses on the need to conceal their self-accepted prejudice from others (e.g., the interaction partner or other observers). In contrast, the self-presentational goal activated for Strivers focuses on their desire to accurately communicate or reveal their personally accepted nonprejudiced identity in the interaction. It is at this point that people consider the likelihood of achieving their self-presentational goal (i.e., consider their outcome expectancies). As previously noted, both Strategics and Strivers report negative outcome expectancies. We suggest, however, that rather than these outcome expectancies being general (i.e., general concern over appearing prejudiced), as is argued in the intergroup anxiety literature, participants' negative outcome expectancies are specific to their concern over the likely failure to meet their distinct conceal or reveal self-presentational goals. Fourth, the combination of their specific self-presentational goal and their negative outcome expectancies results in both Strategics and Strivers experiencing anxiety in the intergroup setting.

Fifth, the strategies pursued in the interaction follow from both the specific self-presentational goal and intergroup anxiety. Specifically, whereas Strategics' conceal goal leads to the activation and pursuit of avoidance-related strategies, Strivers' reveal goal leads to the activation and pursuit of approach-related strategies. For both Strivers and Strategics, intergroup anxiety is associated with activation and pursuit of avoidance strategies. This reasoning is consistent with, but more specific than, Plant and Devine's (2003b) analysis of goal pursuit in interracial interactions and is broader in that it incorporates a role for intergroup anxiety. Sixth, the various strategies pursued will lead to outcomes that can be evaluated against one's standards and goals to determine the extent to which adjustments in behavior are needed to bring behavior in line with the standards and goals. Seventh, the model is dynamic in that outcomes or feedback about one's performance in the interaction can influence one's affective reactions as well as one's outcome expectancies (e.g., success can lead to the development of more positive outcome expectancies). According to the model, altering outcome expectancies will affect actual performance in interracial interactions.

Preliminary Evidence in Support of the Model

We derived the core assumptions of our model of the self-regulatory processes involved in intergroup interactions based on our synthesis of existing work addressing intergroup anxiety, interpersonal concerns in intergroup interactions, and alternative sources of motivation to respond without prejudice. Whereas the empirical studies reviewed previously provide indirect support for the model's assumptions, directly testing these assumptions is part of a larger program of research currently underway. Suggesting the promise of the model, we recently obtained encouraging preliminary evidence in direct support of the model's core assumption – that Strivers and Strategics adopt distinct self-presentational goals in interracial interactions. In two studies, using both self-report and behavioral measures, we demonstrated that Strivers are more likely to report adopting and pursuing the goal of revealing their self-accepted nonprejudiced identity, whereas Strategics are more likely to report and pursue the goal of concealing their prejudice in interracial interactions. We briefly review this evidence.

Self-Reported Goals for Interracial Interactions. The goal of this study was to examine Strivers' and Strategics' self-reported goals for an imagined interaction with a Black student. To this end, in a mass testing session, we asked White participants a series of questions concerning an imagined interaction with a Black student. Embedded in this questionnaire were items designed to assess the conceal and reveal goals (e.g., "My goal for the interaction would be to hide my personal attitudes toward Blacks"; "My goal for the interaction would be for the Black person to see the real me," respectively). The conceal and reveal goal items were rated on a scale from 1 (*not at all*) to 7 (*very much*) and were averaged separately to form a conceal index ($\alpha = .91$) and a reveal index ($\alpha = .80$). Participants also completed the IMS ($\alpha = .79$) and EMS ($\alpha = .79$) during the same mass testing session.

Although our primary interest centers on Strategics and Strivers (i.e., high-EMS participants), we present data from all participants. Thus we examined if participants' responses on the conceal and reveal indices varied as a function of IMS and EMS. On the conceal index, this analysis revealed main effects for both IMS and EMS. However, these main effects were qualified by a significant IMS × EMS interaction, the form of which indicates that high-EMS, low-IMS participants (Strategics) reported the greatest endorsement of the conceal goal relative to all other participants. On the reveal index, this analysis only revealed a main effect for IMS, such that high-IMS participants reported greater endorsement of the reveal goal relative to low-IMS participants.

Pursuit of Strategies to Meet Specific Self-Presentational Goals. The goal of this study was to obtain behavioral evidence that Strivers and Strategics were interested in pursuing specific and distinct self-presentational goals for interracial interactions. To this end, high-EMS participants (i.e., Strivers and Strategics) were led to believe that they were going to interact with a same-sex Black student. Before the interaction began, participants were provided with the opportunity to complete a computer task that ostensibly would improve the course of the upcoming interaction. Participants were led to believe that the computer task would either help them to conceal any feelings that they might have about their partner in the upcoming interaction (conceal framing) or would help them to reveal any feelings that they might have about their partner (reveal framing). Our key dependent measure in this study was the amount of time participants spent on the computer task, which we examined as a function of group (Striver versus Strategic) and framing condition (conceal versus reveal). This analysis revealed only an interaction between group and framing condition. Whereas Strivers spent more time on the program in the reveal framing condition, Strategics spent more time on the program in the conceal framing condition. These data provide compelling preliminary evidence that Strivers and Strategics pursue distinct self-presentational goals for interracial interactions. As such, these findings provide encouraging direct support for one of the model's core assumptions and suggest that the model holds promise for understanding the distinct self-regulatory challenges involved in interracial interactions.

SUMMARY AND CONCLUSIONS

The goal of this chapter and of our current program of research is to develop an analysis of the self-regulatory processes involved in intergroup interactions. To that end, we reviewed literature suggesting that many majority group members have concerns about appearing prejudiced in intergroup interactions and are anxious in such settings. The extant work, however, was largely silent on both the specific nature of these concerns and on identifying who is particularly vulnerable to experiencing intergroup anxiety. We believe that both issues are critically important in developing an analysis of the dynamic processes of intergroup interactions as they unfold in the context of ongoing interactions. That is, the reason one may be concerned about appearing prejudiced is likely to affect one's goals for the interaction, the strategies pursued to attain the goals, and ultimately the outcomes of the interaction. We presented a model of the self-regulatory processes involved in interracial interactions for individuals who have such concerns. Of central importance to this model is the contention that being concerned with appearing prejudiced takes on a qualitatively distinct form and has distinct consequences, depending on people's chronically held sources of motivation to respond without prejudice. Specifically, the model addresses the origins of the alternative self-presentational goals adopted in intergroup interactions (e.g., to reveal one's nonprejudiced self versus to conceal one's prejudiced self), the qualitatively distinct pathways to anxiety in such interactions, the strategies pursued in regulating one's behavior toward the distinct goals, and the implications of these processes for behavior and outcomes in intergroup contact settings. With its focus on the importance of considering multiple determinants of motivation, our work shares a core theme with many of the chapter in this book (by Aarts & Hassin, Lewicki, Harackiewicz et al., Schooler, Spencer et al., Strack & Deutsch, and Wood & Quinn).

We believe that this model effectively integrates extant work addressing the interpersonal aspects of intergroup contact and leads to novel insights into the challenges involved in intergroup interactions not anticipated by consideration of any of the other literatures alone. Whereas the previous literature treated the motive to respond without prejudice as monolithic in nature, we suggest that the joint consideration of internal and external sources of motivation helps to pinpoint who is most likely to be concerned about appearing prejudiced in intergroup interactions, the specific nature of such concerns, and the distinct self-presentational goals pursued during intergroup interactions. That is, our work and model underscore that it is not enough to know if a person is motivated to respond without prejudice; one must also know the reasons motivating the person. Consider, for example, that, if instead of assessing the source of people's motivation to respond without prejudice, the current studies had only assessed the degree to which people were motivated to respond without prejudice (i.e., the amount of motivation; see Dunton & Fazio, 1997). This strategy would have clouded the distinction between Strivers' and Strategics' reveal versus conceal self-presentational goals, a distinction that may ultimately affect the quality of the interaction for both majority and minority group members.

For example, consider the role of anxiety in our model. Anxiety, according to our analysis, arises in response to concerns over the likelihood of failing to achieve distinct self-presentational goals (e.g., reveal versus conceal) and is directly linked to the pursuit of avoidance strategies. If Strivers were provided with feedback that they are good at revealing their personal racial attitudes in intergroup encounters, their anxiety should abate. In contrast, the same feedback for Strategics would, if anything, be likely to heighten their anxiety. In addition, if anxiety could be eliminated (i.e., through misattribution of arousal or through changes in outcome expectancies), avoidance strategies would no longer follow from anxiety. Instead, the strategies pursued by Strivers and Strategics would follow only from their goals and thus would differ. Whereas Strivers would show approach strategies derived from their reveal goal, Strategics would still pursue avoidance strategies derived from their conceal goal. Hence, in this situation, Strivers and Strategics might behave differently and such differences would likely be noticeable to their interaction partners. Thus, by considering the source of people's motivation to respond without prejudice, our analysis provides a more nuanced understanding of the nature of intergroup interactions.

Our framing of interracial interactions in the context of goal-driven self-regulatory processes provides a point of departure for taking on the challenges of studying ongoing, dynamic processes involved in interracial interactions. The detailed study of ongoing interracial interactions has received comparatively little attention but is critical for understanding interracial tensions and barriers to interracial harmony (e.g., Devine et al., 1996). In future work, it will be important to examine the implications of these distinct regulatory concerns and their concomitant goals and strategies for actual interracial interactions. The cybernetic nature of the model lends itself well to an examination of how people may respond to feedback from their partner or others that they either succeeded or failed to convey the desired impression during the interaction and how these outcomes may also affect the salience of self- or other-imposed standards to be monitored during such interactions. Will failures lead to new efforts to respond without prejudice or, alternatively to a desire to avoid intergroup interactions? Does the outcome depend on whether one is striving to overcome prejudice versus conceal prejudice? Will successes affect outcome expectancies or one's sense of efficacy in such interactions and, therefore, mitigate intergroup anxiety?

Consider as well that the current model assumes that Strivers and Strategics will always engage in self-regulation in interracial interactions situations. However, self-regulation is a costly enterprise. That is, research has shown that engaging in self-regulatory efforts expends a limited, consumable resource, and as such, self-control efforts degrade over time (e.g., Muraven & Baumeister, 2000). Richeson and Shelton (2003) showed, for example, that self-regulatory efforts in an interracial interaction depleted White participants' cognitive resources, hampering executive functioning and performance on a subsequent self-regulation task. Determining whether such self-regulation efforts are more demanding for Strivers or Strategics may shed light on these individuals' overall willingness to pursue efforts to regulate prejudice in interracial interactions as well as the ultimate effectiveness of such efforts. Plant and Devine (2001) showed that the participants we characterize as Strategics in this chapter (i.e., low IMS, high EMS) resent being "required" to respond without prejudice and may be more likely than Strivers to withdraw from or otherwise avoid interracial interactions. This may be especially true when interactions are ongoing and dynamic and thus hold the potential for one to be evaluated constantly for signs of failure to respond without prejudice. Given that, for Strategics, responding without prejudice is not a personally accepted goal, efforts to regulate their behavior may be viewed as extremely costly and efforts to escape such situations may be especially appealing.

Although we believe that our model holds promise for improving the understanding of majority group members' experiences in interracial interactions, no analysis of these interactions would be complete without consideration of the minority group perspective and the complex interplay between majority group and minority group members as interactions unfold in real time (Devine et al., 1996). Minority group individuals are likely to bring their own interpersonal concerns, goals, and strategies to interracial interactions. We strongly suspect that, just as we have found with majority group members, the concerns and goals of minority group members may be similarly nuanced and complex. They too are likely to be guided by personal (internal) and normative (external) concerns that will affect the extent to which they are trusting or suspicious of majority group members' intentions and attitudes (Devine et al., 1996; Vorauer et al., 1998, 2000). Some minority group members may actually expect majority group members to be prejudiced, whereas others may be less inclined to have such expectations. And, external pressures (i.e., not to be viewed as too sensitive; e.g., Kaiser & Miller, 2001) may affect their interaction strategies as well. Bringing these issues into focus only serves to highlight the complexities of studying intergroup interactions. We believe, however, that our efforts to do so, and to promote positive and harmonious interactions, will be facilitated by developing a clear analysis of the distinct interpersonal concerns people bring to interracial interactions and the self-regulatory challenges involved in such interactions.

References

Amodio, D. M., Harmon-Jones, E., & Devine, P. G. (2003). Individual differences in the activation and control of affective race bias as assessed by startle eyeblink responses and self-report. *Journal of Personality and Social Psychology, 84,* 738–753.

Aronson, E. (1968). The theory of cognitive dissonance: A current perspective. In L. Berkowitz (Ed.), *Advances in experimental social psychology* (Vol. 4, pp. 1–34). San Diego, CA: Academic Press.

Atkinson, J. W. (1964). *An introduction to achievement motivation.* Princeton, NJ: Van Nostrand.

Atkinson, J. W., & Litwin, G. H., (1960). Achievement motive and test anxiety conceived as motive to approach success and motive to avoid failure. *Journal of Abnormal and Social Psychology, 60,* 52–63.

Bandura, A. (1986). *Social foundations of thought and action: A social cognitive theory.* Englewood Cliffs, NJ: Prentice-Hall.

Brigham, J. C. (1993). College students' racial attitudes. *Journal of Applied and Social Psychology, 23,* 1933–1967.

Britt, T. W., Boniecki, K. A., Vescio, T. K., Biernat, M., & Brown, L. M. (1996). Intergroup anxiety: A person X situation approach. *Personality and Social Psychology Bulletin, 22,* 1177–1188.

Carver, C. S. (2001). Affect and functional bases of behavior: On the dimensional structure of affective experience. *Personality and Social Psychology Review, 5,* 345–356.

Carver, C. S., & Scheier, M. F. (1981). *Attention and self-regulation: A control theory approach to behavior.* New York: Springer-Verlag.

Carver, C. S., & Scheier, M. F. (1990). Principles of self-regulation: Action and emotion. In E. T. Higgins & R. M. Sorrentino (Eds.), *Handbook of motivation and cognition: Foundations of social behavior* (Vol. 2, pp. 3–53). New York: Guilford Press.

Carver, C. S., & Scheier, M. F. (1998). *On the self-regulation of behavior.* Cambridge: Cambridge University Press.

Crowne, D. P., & Marlowe, D. (1960). A new scale of social desirability independent of psychopathology. *Journal of Consulting Psychology, 24,* 349–354.

Devine, P. G., Evett, S. R., & Vasquez-Suson, K. A. (1996). Exploring the interpersonal dynamics of intergroup context. In R. M. Sorrentino & E. T. Higgins (Eds.), *Handbook of motivation and cognition: The interpersonal context* (Vol. 3, pp. 423–464). New York: Guilford Press.

Devine, P. G., & Monteith, M. J. (1993). The role of discrepancy-associated affect in prejudice reduction. In D. M. Mackie & D. L. Hamilton (Eds.), *Affect, cognition, and stereotyping: Interactive processes in group perception* (pp. 317–344). San Diego, CA: Academic Press.

Devine, P. G., Monteith, M. J., Zuwerink, J. R., & Elliot, A. J. (1991). Prejudice with and without compunction. *Journal of Personality and Social Psychology, 60,* 817–830.

Devine, P. G., Plant, E. A., Amodio, D. M., Harmon-Jones, E., & Vance, S. L. (2002). Exploring the relationship between implicit and explicit prejudice: The role of motivations to respond without prejudice. *Journal of Personality and Social Psychology, 82,* 835–848.

Devine, P. G., Plant, E. A., & Blair, I. V. (2001). Classic and contemporary analyses of racial prejudice. In R. Brown & S. Gaertner (Eds.), *Blackwell handbook of social psychology: Intergroup processes* (pp. 198–217) Malden, MA: Blackwell.

Dovidio, J. F., Kawakami, K., Johnson, C., Johnson, B., & Howard, A. (1997). On the nature of prejudice: Automatic and controlled processes. *Journal of Experimental Social Psychology, 33,* 510–540.

Dunton, B. C., & Fazio, R. H. (1997). An individual difference measure of motivation to control prejudiced reactions. *Personality and Social Psychology Bulletin, 23,* 316–326.

Duval, S., & Wicklund, R. A. (1972). *A theory of objective self-awareness.* New York: Academic Press.

Elliot, A. J., & Church, M. A. (1997). A hierarchical model of approach and avoidance achievement motivation. *Journal of Personality and Social Psychology, 72,* 218–232.

Elliot, A. J., & Harackiewicz, J. M. (1996). Approach and avoidance achievement goals and intrinsic motivation: A mediational analysis. *Journal of Personality and Social Psychology, 70,* 461–475.

Fazio, R. H., Jackson, J. R., Dunton, B. C., & Williams, C. J. (1995). Variability in automatic activation as an unobtrusive measure of racial attitudes: A bona fide pipeline? *Journal of Personality and Social Psychology, 69,* 1013–1027.

Feather, N. T. (1967). Level of aspiration and performance variability. *Journal of Personality and Social Psychology, 6,* 37–46.

Festinger, L. (1957). *A cognitive theory of dissonance.* Stanford, CA: Stanford University Press.

Greenwald, A., McGhee, D., & Schwartz, J. (1998). Measuring individual differences in implicit cognition: The Implicit Association Test. *Journal of Personality and Social Psychology, 74,* 1464–1480.

Hembree, R. (1988). Correlates, causes, effects, and treatment of test anxiety. *Review of Educational Research, 58,* 47–77.

Higgins, E. T. (1987). Self-discrepancy: A theory relating self and affect. *Psychological Review, 94,* 319–340.

Higgins, E. T. (1997). Beyond pleasure and pain. *American Psychologist, 52,* 1280–1300.

Higgins, E. T., Roney, C. R., Crowe, E., & Hymes, C. (1994). Ideal versus ought predilections for approach and avoidance: Distinct self-regulatory systems. *Journal of Personality and Social Psychology, 66,* 276–286.

Jones, J. M. (1997). *Prejudice and racism* (2nd ed.). New York: McGraw-Hill.

Kaiser, C. R., & Miller, C. T. (2001). Stop complaining! The social costs of making attributions to discrimination. *Personality and Social Psychology Bulletin, 27,* 254–263.

Leary, M. R. (1983). Social anxiousness: The construct and its measurement. *Journal of Personality Assessment, 47,* 66–75.

Leary, M. R., & Kowalski, R. M. (1995). *Social anxiety.* New York: Guilford Press.

Mahone, C. H. (1960). Fear of failure and unrealistic vocational aspiration. *Journal of Abnormal and Social Psychology, 60,* 253–261.

McConahay, J. B., Hardee, B. B., & Batts, V. (1981). Has racism declined? It depends on who's asking and what is asked. *Journal of Conflict Resolution, 25,* 563–579.

Monteith, M. J. (1993). Self-regulation of prejudiced responses: Implications for progress in prejudice-reduction efforts. *Journal of Personality and Social Psychology, 65,* 469–485.

Monteith, M. J., Ashburn-Nardo, L., Voils, C. I., & Czopp, A. (2002). Putting the brakes on prejudice: On the development and operation of cues for control. *Journal of Personality and Social Psychology, 83,* 1029–1050.

Muraven, M., & Baumeister, R. F. (2000). Self-regulation and depletion of limited resources: Does self-control resemble a muscle? *Psychological Bulletin, 126,* 247–259.

Plant, E. A., & Devine, P. G. (1998). Internal and external motivation to respond without prejudice. *Journal of Personality and Social Psychology, 75,* 811–832.

Plant, E. A., & Devine, P. G. (2001). Beyond compliance with nonprejudiced social pressure: Acceptance or backlash? *Journal of Experimental Social Psychology, 37,* 486–501.

Plant, E. A., & Devine, P. G. (2003a). The antecedents and implications of interracial anxiety. *Personality and Social Psychology Bulletin, 29,* 790–801.

Plant, E. A., & Devine, P. G. (2003b). Regulatory concerns in interracial interactions: Approaching egalitarianism and avoiding over bias. Unpublished manuscript, University of Wisconsin.

Plant, E. A., Devine, P. G., & Brazy, P. C. (2003). The bogus pipeline and motivations to respond without prejudice: Revisiting the fading and faking of racial prejudice. *Group Processes and Intergroup Relations, 6,* 187–200.

Pyszczynski, T., & Greenberg, J. (1986). Persistent high self-focus after failure and low self-focus after success: The depressive self-focusing style. *Journal of Personality and Social Psychology, 50,* 1039–1044.

Pyszczynski, T., & Greenberg, J. (1987). Self-regulatory preservation and that depressive self-focusing style: A self-awareness theory of reactive depression. *Psychological Bulletin, 102,* 122–138.

Richeson, J. A., & Shelton, J. N. (2003). When prejudice doesn't pay: Effects of interracial contact on executive function. *Psychological Science, 13,* 287–290.

Shelton, J. N. (2003). Interpersonal concerns in social encounters between majority and minority group members. *Group Processes and Intergroup Relations, 6,* 171–185.

Snyder, M., & Gangestad, S. (1986). On the nature of self-monitoring: Matters of assessment, matters of validity. *Journal of Personality and Social Psychology, 51,* 125–139.

Stephan, W. G., & Stephan, C. W. (1985). Intergroup anxiety. *Journal of Social Issues, 41,* 157–175.

Stephan, W. G., & Stephan, C. W. (1989). Antecedents of intergroup anxiety in Asian-Americans and Hispanic Americans. *International Journal of Intercultural Relations, 13,* 203–219.

Vorauer, J. D., Hunter, A. J., Main, K. J., & Roy, S. A. (2000). Meta-stereotype activation: Evidence from indirect measures for specific evaluation concerns experienced by members of dominant groups in intergroup interactions. *Journal of Personality and Social Psychology, 78,* 690–707.

Vorauer, J. D., & Kumhyr. S. M. (2001). Is this about you or me? Self- versus other-directed judgments and feelings in response to intergroup interactions. *Personality and Social Psychology Bulletin, 27,* 706–709.

Vorauer, J. D., Main, K. J., & O'Connell, G. B. (1998). How do individuals expect to be viewed by members of lower status groups? Content and implications of meta-stereotypes. *Journal of Personality and Social Psychology, 75,* 917–937.

Waller, N. G., & Meehl, P. E. (1998). *Multivariate taxometric procedures: Distinguishing types from continua.* Thousand Oaks, CA: Sage.

Watson, D., & Friend, R. (1969). Measurement of social-evaluative anxiety. *Journal of Consulting and Clinical Psychology, 33,* 448–457.

Wicklund, R. A. (1975). Objective self-awareness. In L. Berkowitz (Ed.), *Advances in experimental social psychology* (Vol. 8, pp. 233–275). New York: Academic Press.

15

Exploring the Discrepancy Between Implicit and Explicit Prejudice

A Test of Aversive Racism Theory

Leanne S. Son Hing, Greg A. Chung-Yan, Robert
Grunfeld, Lori K. Robichaud, and Mark P. Zanna

INTRODUCTION

Many have argued that over recent decades the nature of prejudice has
become more subtle, less negative, and less hateful (Gaertner & Dovidio,
1986; Katz & Hass, 1988; McConahay, 1986). It is therefore difficult to rec-
oncile such reports of lessened prejudice with the racial discrimination
found in laboratory and field studies, as well as labor statistics (Human
Resources Development Canada, 2001; Landau, 1995; Rudman & Glick,
1999; Sackett & DuBois, 1991; Sinclair & Kunda, 1999). One possible reason for the inconsistency between lessened prejudice, on the one hand,
and continuing discrimination, on the other hand, is that the apparent
decline in prejudice is illusory. It is possible that as societal norms have
become more egalitarian, people report less prejudiced attitudes due to
internal or external motivations (Crandall, O'Brien, & Eshleman, 2002;
Devine, Brodish, & Vance, this volume; Plant & Devine, 1998). A second

This project was funded by Social Sciences and Humanities Research Council of Canada
(SSHRC) research grants awarded to the first and last authors. We thank Serge Desmarais,
Jack Dovidio, Joe Forgas, Sam Gaertner, and Gordon Hodson for their comments on an
earlier draft of this chapter. We also thank the research assistants involved in this project:
Diane Abreu, Christina Bandomir, Jeff Bennett, Rick Byers, Stephanie Gee, Maxine McBride,
Amanda Moorhead, Amanda Ono, Katie Orazietti, Amy Thomson, and Wendy Wood. Study
1 was presented by the first author at the biennial meeting of the Society for the Psychological
Study of Social Issues, June 2002, Toronto, Ontario, Canada. A more detailed account of Study
1 can be found in the *Journal of Experimental Social Psychology* by Son Hing, Li, and Zanna (2002).
Study 3 was presented by the second author at the annual meeting of the Society for Industrial
and Organizational Psychology, April 2003, Orlando, Florida, USA. A summary of this chapter
was presented by the first author at the Sixth Annual Sydney Social Psychology Symposium
on Social Motivation: Conscious and Unconscious Processes, March 2003, Sydney, Australia.

Correspondence concerning this chapter should be addressed to Leanne S. Son Hing, Department of Psychology, University of Guelph, Guelph, Ontario, Canada N1G 2W1; e-mail:
sonhing@psy.uoguelph.ca.

possible reason for the apparent inconsistency is that discrimination is due to prejudices that people are unaware they hold. If individuals are not consciously aware of their racism, they will honestly report low-prejudiced attitudes. Yet, such unconscious prejudice may result in discriminatory behavior.

The theory of aversive racism (Gaertner & Dovidio, 1986) deals specifically with individuals who are presumed to be consciously egalitarian yet unconsciously prejudiced. In this chapter, we review research in which we reconceptualize aversive racists as those with a discrepancy between their relatively low-prejudiced attitudes at the explicit (i.e., conscious and controlled) level and their relatively high-prejudiced attitudes at the implicit (i.e., unconscious and automatic) level. In three studies, we compare the discriminatory behavior of participants identified as truly low-prejudiced with those identified as aversive racists to test the theory of aversive racism.

AVERSIVE RACISM

According to Gaertner and Dovidio (1986), aversive racism is a subtle, unintentional form of bias that is presumed to characterize a substantial proportion of White liberals. Aversive racists are motivated to be, and consciously experience themselves to be, nonprejudiced. However, they unconsciously have unavoidable negative thoughts and feelings (e.g., discomfort) about outgroup members, feelings about which they are typically unaware. In other words, aversive racists are those individuals who are consciously nonprejudiced and yet unconsciously prejudiced. Such discrepant attitudes are presumed to derive from two competing forces: (a) the internalization of societal egalitarian values and (b) normal functioning (e.g., ingroup bias) that leads to prejudice (Dovidio, Kawakami, & Gaertner, 2000).

The discrepancy between aversive racists' conscious and unconscious attitudes leads to some interesting predictions for their behavior toward outgroup members (Gaertner & Dovidio, 1986). Because aversive racists are motivated to uphold their egalitarian self-image, they should not discriminate in situations where there are clear guidelines for appropriate, nonprejudiced responses. However, aversive racists should discriminate in situations where guidelines for nonprejudiced responses are ambiguous, such as when a non-race-related justification or excuse for behavior exists. We refer to the contingency of aversive racists' discriminatory behavior on situational cues as the *aversive racism effect*. Gaertner and Dovidio (1986) provide one additional prediction for the discriminatory behavior of aversive racists: Although aversive racists are typically unaware of their prejudice, if the negative portion of their attitudes is made salient, in order to restore their egalitarian self-image they should bend over backward to avoid discriminating.

There is good empirical support for aversive racism theory. In a classic study, Gaertner and Dovidio (1977, as cited in Gaertner & Dovidio, 1986) capitalized on the bystander intervention effect (Darley & Latané, 1968) to manipulate justification or excuse to avoid helping a Black confederate. As predicted, when clear guidelines for behavior existed (i.e., participants were alone with the confederate who needed help), participants did not discriminate against the Black confederate. In contrast, and consistent with the theory of aversive racism, when a non-race-related excuse for behavior was present (i.e., participants believed that others were present), participants were much less likely to help the Black than the White confederate.

The aversive racism effect has been found in more recent research on discrimination in university admissions (Hodson, Dovidio, & Gaertner, 2002) and in personnel selection (Dovidio & Gaertner, 2000). In unambiguous situations (i.e., when the target's qualifications were very strong or when they were very weak), White and Black candidates were recommended equally for university admission or for a job. In contrast, when the situation was ambiguous (i.e., when the candidate's qualifications were mixed), the White candidate was recommended more strongly than the matched Black candidate.

Previous research indicates that a large proportion of participants behave in a manner consistent with aversive racism theory (Dovidio & Gaertner, 2000; Gaertner & Dovidio, 1977, 1986; Hodson et al., 2002). However, it is not clear that the aversive racism effect is in fact driven by individuals who are aversive racists. Aversive racists were not identified in previous research because no individual difference measure of aversive racism existed. Presumably, people do not have access to their unconscious attitudes; therefore, self-report measures could not be used to tap unconscious prejudice.

IDENTIFYING AVERSIVE RACISTS: CAPITALIZING ON THE DUALITY OF IMPLICIT AND EXPLICIT PREJUDICE

The goal of our research program is to test aversive racism theory by identifying aversive racists and comparing their behavior to that of truly low-prejudiced people. Influenced by recent work on automatic and controlled processes and on implicit and explicit attitudes (e.g., Fazio, 1990; Greenwald & Banaji, 1995; see also Strack & Deutsch's Reflexive Impulsive Model, this volume), we reconceptualized aversive racists as individuals with a discrepancy between their prejudicial attitudes at the implicit versus explicit level (see also Dovidio 2001; Wilson, Lindsey, & Schooler, 2000). Whereas explicit prejudice is a consciously endorsed attitude that influences deliberate or controllable expressions of prejudice, implicit prejudice is a more automatic evaluation of outgroups that influences unintentional or uncontrollable expressions of prejudice (Fazio, 1990; Wilson et al., 2000). Explicit attitudes are typically assessed using self-report questionnaires, as they tap conscious attitudes. Implicit attitudes are typically assessed using response latency measures that tap automatic responses that are presumed to reflect unconscious attitudes (Fazio & Olson, 2003).

We believe that aversive racists should be identified as those low in explicit prejudice because at a conscious level they reject prejudice; however, they should be identified as high in implicit prejudice because at an unconscious level they have negative reactions to outgroup members. An initial wave of research on implicit prejudice revealed that it is possible for people to hold either consistent or inconsistent attitudes at the implicit and explicit levels (Wilson et al., 2000) because measures of implicit and explicit prejudice are only weakly related (Dovidio, Kawakami, & Gaertner, 2002; Dovidio, Kawakami, Johnson, Johnson, & Howard, 1997; Fazio, Jackson, Dunton, & Williams, 1995; Florak, Scarabis, & Bless, 2001; Greenwald, McGee, & Schwartz, 1998; cf. McConnell & Leibold, 2001; Wittenbrink, Judd, & Park, 1997). A second wave of research on implicit prejudice revealed that implicit and explicit measures of prejudice are distinct constructs that tend to predict different types of behavior. For the most part, the evidence reveals that explicit prejudice predicts deliberate or controlled behavior such as verbal friendliness, whereas implicit prejudice predicts unintentional or uncontrollable behavior such as nonverbal friendliness (Dovidio et al., 1997, 2002; Fazio, 1990; McConnell & Leibold, 2001; Wilson et al., 2000).

TESTING AVERSIVE RACISM THEORY: A NEW WAVE
OF RESEARCH ON IMPLICIT ATTITUDES

Our work on aversive racism represents a third wave of research on implicit and explicit prejudice in that we examine the interaction between the two. More specifically, we focus on the discrepancy between those holding low-prejudiced attitudes at the explicit level and high-prejudiced attitudes at the implicit level to examine the discriminatory behavior of aversive racists: a group hypothesized to be consciously nonprejudiced and unconsciously prejudiced but that has yet to be identified a priori (Gaertner & Dovidio, 1986).

In this chapter, we review an initial study (Son Hing, Li, & Zanna, 2002) in which we tested and found that aversive racists bend over backward to avoid discriminatory behavior if they are made aware of the negative portion of their attitudes. In the second and third studies, we turned to the aversive racism effect. In both an academic context (Study 2) and an employment context (Study 3), we found support for the hypothesis that aversive racists will discriminate only when a non-race-related justification exists. Although aversive racism theory originated to explain Whites' attitudes toward Blacks, it has since been generalized to other groups (e.g., Latinos in Dovidio, Gaertner, Anastasio, & Sanitioso, 1992). We chose to study aversive racism against East and Southeast Asians because they constitute 48% of Canada's visible minority population and 36% of new Canadian immigrants (Statistics Canada, 1996a, 1996b).

Study 1

In the first study (for more details see Son Hing et al., 2002), we sought to identify aversive racists and test whether they reduce their discriminatory behavior when reminded of the negative portion of their attitudes, as predicted by aversive racism theory (Gaertner & Dovidio, 1986). We created such awareness among aversive racists by using a hypocrisy induction procedure. Hypocrisy occurs when people espouse one, usually socially desirable, position while being aware of times when they have violated these principles. In order to induce the experience of hypocrisy and subsequent behavior change, people must initially advocate an attitude-consistent position and later be reminded of times when they failed to live up to this standard (Aronson, 1999; Stone, Aronson, Crain, Winslow, & Fried, 1994). Aversive racists are motivated to be egalitarian and believe themselves to be nonprejudiced; therefore, they should be able to advocate nonprejudice publicly. In addition, aversive racists are theorized to (a) sometimes discriminate and (b) sometimes have insight into their negative attitudes (Gaertner & Dovidio, 1986); therefore they should also be able to recall past prejudicial slip-ups.

We compared the effects of being assigned to a hypocrisy versus a control condition among participants identified as aversive racists (i.e., low in explicit but high in implicit prejudice) or as truly low-prejudiced (i.e., low in explicit and implicit prejudice). Among aversive racists, the hypocrisy induction procedure was expected to result in feelings of guilt and discomfort because it made salient the discrepancy between their "should" versus actual reactions toward Asians (Devine, Monteith, Zuwerink, & Elliot, 1991; Monteith, 1996). In addition, the experience of hypocrisy was expected to motivate aversive racists to bend over backward to avoid discriminatory behavior because, when made aware of the negative portion of their attitudes, aversive racists are theorized to "overreact and amplify their positive behavior in ways that would reaffirm their egalitarian convictions and their apparently nonracist attitudes" (Gaertner & Dovidio, 1986, p. 62). In contrast, we did not expect a hypocrisy induction to influence the affective responses or the discriminatory behavior of people who are truly low-prejudiced. Considering our design from a different perspective, because we designed discriminatory behavior to be ambiguous, we expected aversive racists to discriminate more against Asians than truly low-prejudiced participants in the control condition. However, because aversive racists in the hypocrisy condition should be motivated to amplify or reaffirm their egalitarian self-image, they were expected to discriminate less against Asians than truly low-prejudiced participants.

Participants were 47 undergraduate students who had been identified as non-Asian and low in explicit prejudice in an early phase of the research. More specifically, they scored below the median on an Asian Racism Scale (median $= -0.89$). A sample item is "There are too many Asian students being allowed to attend university in Canada" ($-4 = very strongly disagree$ to $4 = very strongly agree$). Students were recruited to participate in two ostensibly unrelated studies.

Upon arriving at the lab, participants were met by an Asian experimenter. We adjusted Gilbert and Hixon's (1991) measure of stereotype activation to assess implicit prejudice, and the experimenter operated as the Asian prime for all participants. The number of negative and positive stereotypic completions that participants made on a word fragment completion task (e.g., NIP or NAP, SMART or START) was recorded. We computed the number of negative stereotypic completions minus the number of positive stereotypic completions that participants made to measure implicit prejudice. In other words, implicit prejudice was operationalized as the degree to which negative, but not positive, aspects of the Asian stereotype were activated by the prime (i.e., the Asian experimenter). Implicit prejudice scores ranged from -2 to 2.[1] A median split (median $=$ 0.00) was conducted on implicit prejudice to classify participants either as truly low-prejudiced (low in both explicit and implicit prejudice) or as aversive racists (low in explicit but high in implicit prejudice). Because all participants were low in explicit prejudice, consistent with our reconceptualization of aversive racism, we interpret individual differences in implicit prejudice as synonymous with individual differences in aversive racism.[2]

Participants were led to the next study, run by a White experimenter, in which they were randomly assigned to the control or hypocrisy condition. Participants were informed that their university was initiating a Racial Equality Forum as part of first-year orientation.[3] The goal of the

[1] Implicit and explicit prejudice were not correlated in any of our three studies.

[2] In future research, the independent and interactive effects of implicit and explicit prejudice should be tested for the full range of these variables (i.e., low explicit/low implicit, low explicit/high implicit, high explicit/low implicit, high explicit/high implicit).

[3] The Racial Equality Forum materials were lent to us by Vance and Devine (1999) and altered for the current study.

forum was to educate incoming students about prejudice (e.g., racism, sexism, homophobia) at the university. All participants were "randomly" assigned to write essays on the importance of treating Asian students fairly. It was explained that excerpts from the essays might be used for a brochure advertising the forum. After completing their essays, participants in the hypocrisy condition were asked to "briefly write about two situations in which you reacted more negatively to an Asian person than you thought you should or treated an Asian person in a prejudiced manner" for the forum's focus group discussions. Thus, all participants publicly advocated a nonprejudiced stance, but only those in the hypocrisy condition were then reminded of their own prejudicial slip-ups.

Participants completed an affect measure (Monteith, Devine, & Zuwerink, 1993) either when they completed their essays (control condition) or when they completed their essays and their personal examples (hypocrisy condition) so that we could assess their feelings of guilt and discomfort (e.g., guilty, uncomfortable; Cronbach's alpha .94). Participants were then informed that the study was complete; however, they were asked to complete a ballot for the university's student government on how funding cuts should be allocated to various campus groups. Ostensibly a 20% cut in funding was needed for the budget of 10 campus groups – one of which was the Asian Students' Association (ASA). We consider cuts to the ASA to be a subtle measure of discriminatory behavior.

Preliminary analyses confirmed that there were no differences between aversive racists and truly low-prejudiced participants in terms of (a) the degree to which they expressed antiprejudiced ideals in their essays and (b) the degree to which they recalled prejudicial slip-ups that revealed negative thoughts and feelings. However, as expected, participants tended to have different affective reactions to the hypocrisy condition, depending on their level of aversive racism ($p = .08$). Simple effects tests revealed that truly low-prejudiced participants experienced equally low levels of guilt and discomfort in the control ($M = 2.51$) and the hypocrisy conditions ($M = 2.80$, *ns*). In contrast, aversive racists in the hypocrisy condition ($M = 3.71$) experienced greater guilt and discomfort than those in the control condition ($M = 2.09$, $p = .003$). Thus, the hypocrisy induction led to feelings of guilt and discomfort for aversive racists but not for truly low-prejudiced participants, perhaps because truly low-prejudiced participants recognized that an occasional negative thought or feeling is normal and need not reflect prejudice.

Is it the case that when reminded of their past negative reactions, aversive racists bent over backward to reaffirm their egalitarian self-image by reducing cuts to the ASA? As predicted, a Condition × Aversive Racism interaction was found ($p = .004$) (see Figure 15.1). The discriminatory

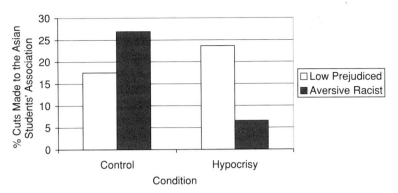

FIGURE 15.1 Study 1: Discriminatory behavior as a function of hypocrisy condition.

behavior of truly low-prejudiced participants was not affected by the hypocrisy manipulation (*ns*). However, consistent with aversive racism theory, the hypocrisy manipulation led aversive racists to substantially reduce their discriminatory behavior ($p = .001$). Thus, reminders of past prejudicial slip-ups led aversive racists, but not truly low-prejudiced participants, to make fewer cuts to the ASA.

Looking at the interaction from a different perspective, in the control condition aversive racists tended to make greater cuts to the ASA than truly low-prejudiced participants ($p = .09$). Indeed, significantly more aversive racists (54%) than truly low-prejudiced participants (18%) cut more than the requisite 20% of the ASA's budget, $\chi^2(1, N = 24) = 3.23, p = .04$ (one-tailed test). Thus, when a justification existed (i.e., cuts needed to be made), aversive racists tended to discriminate more than did low-prejudiced participants. In contrast, in the hypocrisy condition, aversive racists cut less than did the truly low-prejudiced ($p = .009$). Thus, when aversive racists were made aware of their prejudicial tendencies, they overcompensated in their attempts to be nonprejudicial.

To summarize, we found that inducing hypocrisy in aversive racists led them to feel more guilty and uncomfortable and to overcorrect their discriminatory behavior. Furthermore, we found that aversive racists in the control condition discriminated more against the ASA on the budget reduction ballot than did truly low-prejudiced participants. That is, less than 5 minutes after writing an essay stating that students at their university shouldn't discriminate against Asians – an essay that participants believed might be used for incoming students – aversive racists essentially voted to dispossess Asian students on campus by disproportionately cutting the budget of their student association. These results strongly support the notion that those low in explicit but high in implicit prejudice behave exactly as we would expect aversive racists to act: When their behavior is subtle and justified, they "lower the boom" on the outgroup.

Study 2

Our goal for Study 2 was to test the discriminatory behavior of aversive racists by employing the classic aversive racism paradigm in which the presence of a non-race-related justification for discrimination is manipulated. According to the theory of aversive racism (Gaertner & Dovidio, 1986), aversive racists should discriminate against an outgroup member when an excuse for discrimination exists, and they should behave in an egalitarian fashion in the absence of an excuse. The current research is the first, to our knowledge, that tests the aversive racism effect for participants who are identified as aversive racists or as truly low-prejudiced. In Study 2, we also changed our measure of implicit prejudice to the more conventional and well-validated Implicit Association Test (IAT) (Greenwald et al., 1998; Rudman, Greenwald, Mellott, & Schwartz, 1999). We modified the IAT to measure implicit attitudes toward Whites and Asians by using last names that pilot testing revealed as clearly of Asian or Caucasian origin and equal in familiarity (e.g., Wong and Chan vs. Swanson and Landry).

In Study 2, we had a 2 (ethnicity condition: White vs. Asian) × 2 (excuse condition: no-excuse-to-discriminate vs. excuse-to-discriminate) × 2 (aversive racism: truly low-prejudiced vs. aversive racist) design. A White target condition was included to ensure that the aversive racism effect was indeed due to racism. Participants evaluated a fictitious Asian or White student whom they read about in a detailed vignette. The vignette described how the Asian or White target was approached for last-minute help from a struggling and irresponsible fellow student. In the no-excuse-to-discriminate condition, the target politely offered his assistance. In the excuse-to-discriminate condition, he exhibited reluctance and only grudgingly assisted the student in need.

We hypothesized that the most negative evaluations of the target would occur when aversive racists evaluated the Asian student in the excuse-to-discriminate condition. In other words, we expected discrimination to be greater for one cell of the study design than for the other seven cells. In addition, we had three specific hypotheses concerning the Asian/excuse/aversive racist condition. First, we expected aversive racists in the excuse condition to evaluate the Asian target more negatively than the matched White target. Second, we expected aversive racists to evaluate the Asian target more negatively in the excuse-to-discriminate condition than their counterparts in the no-excuse-to-discriminate condition. Third, we expected that aversive racists would evaluate the Asian target in the excuse condition more negatively than the truly low-prejudiced participants. In contrast, truly low-prejudiced participants in the Asian/excuse condition were not expected to differ in their evaluations compared with truly low-prejudiced participants in the other three conditions.

Participants were 77 non-Asian undergraduates who were identified as low in explicit prejudice in mass testing. Participants were recruited to participate in two supposedly unrelated studies that were conducted approximately 2 weeks apart. The first study ostensibly investigated participants' reactions to student probation. Participants read about a struggling student, Alexander, who is on academic probation and will be kicked out of school if he fails any course. During the last class, Alexander asks a more studious classmate named Brian Chang (Asian condition)/Brian McKay (White condition) to lend him his notes. In the no-excuse-to-discriminate condition, Brian responds:

"I don't know how much they will help you at this stage of the game, but I hope that it's enough."

In the excuse-to-discriminate condition, Brian responds:

"Well, I don't really see how much the notes are going to help you if you haven't come to class all term but fine, take them.... Really, you put yourself in this situation. You shouldn't expect other people to help you out."

After reading the vignette, participants rated Alexander's and Brian's likability and compassion (e.g., "I like Brian", "Brian is sympathetic"; Cronbach's alpha. 83). Approximately 2 weeks later, a different experimenter assessed participants' implicit prejudice with the Asian and White IAT. As in Study 1, a median split on implicit prejudice was used to determine truly low-prejudiced versus aversive racist participants.

When testing participants' evaluations of the target, we conducted a planned comparison test in which seven cells of the design were compared against one (i.e., 1, 1, 1, 1, 1, 1, 1, -7; Rosenthal, Rosnow &, Rubin, 2000).[4] In support of our central hypothesis, we found that the target was evaluated significantly worse by aversive racists evaluating an Asian student in the excuse condition compared with participants in the other seven conditions ($p = .03$) (see Figure 15.2). Planned comparison analyses were conducted to test our other predictions. First, as expected, aversive racists in the excuse condition evaluated the Asian target more negatively than the matched White target ($p < .001$). Second, aversive racists evaluated the Asian target more negatively in the excuse condition compared with their

---

[4] Although there is little need for omnibus testing if specific, focused questions and comparisons are investigated (Rosenthal et al., 2000), we did conduct an Ethnicity Condition (Asian vs. White) × Excuse Condition (no excuse vs. excuse) × Aversive Racism (truly low-prejudiced vs. aversive racist) analysis of variance for the interested reader. A significant three-way interaction was found ($p = .02$).

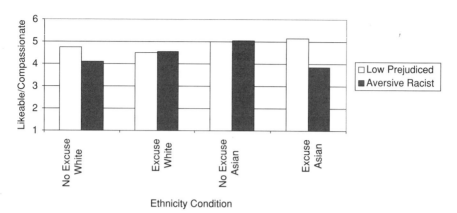

FIGURE 15.2 Study 2: Target evaluation as a function of excuse and target ethnicity.

counterparts in the no-excuse condition ($p = .009$). Third, as expected, aversive racists evaluated the Asian target in the excuse condition more negatively, than did truly low-prejudiced participants ($p = .005$). In contrast, truly low-prejudiced participants in the Asian/excuse condition did not differ in their evaluations of the target compared with their counterparts in the other conditions (*ns*).

In conclusion, in Study 2, we found strong evidence that aversive racists, but not truly low-prejudiced participants, demonstrate the aversive racism effect. First, we found that when an excuse exists, aversive racists discriminate on the basis of ethnicity. Specifically, when the target was reluctant and resentful when asked for help, aversive racists evaluated him more negatively when he was Asian than when he was White. Second, and consistent with the theory of aversive racism, aversive racists discriminated more when there was an excuse, compared with when there was no excuse to negatively evaluate the Asian target. Third, individual differences in aversive racism predicted discrimination against an Asian target in the excuse condition such that aversive racists evaluated him more negatively than did truly low-prejudiced participants. In contrast, truly low-prejudiced participants' evaluations of the target were consistent regardless of the excuse or ethnicity condition.

Study 3

To test the aversive racism effect under conditions of higher experimental realism, in Study 3 (Chung-Yan, Son Hing, & Zanna, submitted for publication) we led participants to believe that their judgments had real-world consequences. Participants were told that their evaluations of job candidates would be used to assess the effectiveness of a new interviewing tool for a consulting company. We also attempted to investigate how aversive racists might justify, post hoc, their discriminatory evaluations.

Study 3 had a 2 (ethnicity condition: White vs. Asian) × 2 (excuse condition: no-excuse-to-discriminate vs. excuse-to-discriminate) × 2 (aversive racism: truly low-prejudiced vs. aversive racist) design. We manipulated-non-race-related excuse to discriminate by varying the degree to which the requirements of a job matched the candidate's qualifications. The candidate was always described as having strong intellectual skills and work ethic but weaker social and communication skills. In the no-excuse condition, the candidate was evaluated for a data analyst position for which he was clearly qualified – because of his strong intellectual skills. In the excuse condition, the candidate was evaluated for an employee relations specialist position for which he was only somewhat qualified because of his mediocre social skills.

Our hypotheses for Study 3 paralleled those for Study 2. We hypothesized that the target should be discriminated against most when aversive racists evaluate an Asian job candidate in the excuse-to-discriminate condition (i.e., for the employee relations specialist job). In addition, we predicted that (a) aversive racists in the excuse condition should be less likely to recommend the Asian job candidate for employment, compared with the matched White candidate, (b) aversive racists should be less likely to recommend the Asian job candidate for employment in the excuse-to-discriminate condition compared with their counterparts in the no-excuse-to-discriminate condition, and (c) in the excuse condition, aversive racists should be less likely to recommend the Asian job candidate for employment, compared with truly low-prejudiced participants. In contrast, truly low-prejudiced participants were not expected to differ in their recommendations, depending on their condition.

The justification to discriminate involved the strong social skills that the employee relations specialist job required and the candidate's merely satisfactory performance in this area. Therefore, we were particularly interested in participants' perceptions and memories of the candidate's interpersonal and communication skills (i.e., his social skills). We assessed participants' initial perceptions of the target while reading the interview summary. Thus, we could test whether, when performance indicators were clear, the candidate was seen as less socially skilled when he was an Asian evaluated by aversive racists.

In addition, we assessed participants' recollections of the target *after* they had provided their hiring recommendations. We predicted that aversive racist should be motivated to remember the Asian target as having very poor social skills after evaluating him for the employee relations specialist position because they might retrieve job-relevant information in a biased manner to excuse their discriminatory behavior. Furthermore, the more aversive racists discriminated against the Asian job candidate in the excuse condition, the more they should subsequently justify this behavior by recalling his interpersonal and communication skills as particularly poor.

We selected non-Asian participants, who were identified as low in explicit prejudice, to participate in two supposedly unrelated studies. To assess their implicit prejudice against Asians, we had 139 participants complete the Asian and White IAT. Participants were then led to the second study, run by a different experimenter, who was unaware of participants' level of implicit prejudice.

Ostensibly, an organizational consulting firm was testing the utility of a new tool that summarized information gathered during the interview into competency statements (i.e., descriptions of the candidate's critical thinking, interpersonal, communication, learning/work ethic, and organizational skills). The candidate was described as strong in critical thinking and learning skills/work ethic competencies but only satisfactory in communication and interpersonal skills.[5] For instance, under critical thinking he was described as "very familiar with well-established methods of problem solving," and under interpersonal skills he was described as "moderately successful at understanding the concerns and feelings of others." The candidate was identified as Gary Chang (the Asian condition) or Gary Walsh (the White condition). While being able to refer to the interview summary, participants evaluated the candidate on each competency (e.g., "This candidate has exceptional interpersonal skills").

Participants were then randomly assigned to either the excuse-to-discriminate condition or the no-excuse-to-discriminate condition. In the no-excuse condition, participants read a job description for a data analyst position. The job included duties such as analyzing and interpreting statistics to make conclusions. In the excuse condition, participants read a job description for an employee relations specialist that that involved counseling employees regarding work or personal problems. Without being able to refer to the interview summary, participants responded to the dependent measures: "I recommend that Gary Chang (Walsh) be hired as a data analyst (or employee relations specialist)" and "Gary Chang (Walsh) is well-suited for the data analyst job (or employee relations specialist job)." The two items were highly correlated, $r(136) = .76, p < .001$, and therefore aggregated.

Finally, participants were asked to recall the gist of the interview summary. Three judges who were unaware of the experimental condition independently rated the degree to which the statements recalled by participants positively reflected each of the competencies ($1 = negative$ to $5 = positive$). There was high interrater agreement for all five competencies (Cronbach's alphas range from .84 to .90).

---

[5] We did not intentionally design the candidate's organizational skills to be either strong or merely satisfactory. Therefore, we do not analyze any effects for this competency.

Preliminary analyses revealed that there was a strong correlation between participants' initial ratings of the candidate's interpersonal and communication skills, $r(137) = .70, p < .001$, so they were aggregated into a social skills competency measure. As intended, the candidate was perceived to be stronger on critical thinking skills ($M = 5.07$) and on learning skills/work ethic ($M = 5.59$) than on the social skills competencies ($M = 4.61$), both $ps < .001$.

We investigated whether initial perceptions of the candidates' competencies varied, depending on the participants' level of aversive racism and the target's ethnicity. Job condition was not included as a factor in these analyses because participants had not yet read the job descriptions when making their competency ratings. No effects were found for aversive racism or ethnicity condition (*ns*). Thus, when participants were able to refer to the interview summary, they rated the target's competencies as similar regardless of his race or their level of aversive racism.

To test our central hypothesis – that discrimination should be greatest when aversive racists evaluated the Asian target for the employee relations specialist position – we conducted a planned comparison test in which seven cells of the design were compared against one (Rosenthal et al., 2000).[6] The target was significantly less likely to be recommended for hire by aversive racists evaluating an Asian candidate in the excuse condition ($p = .002$), compared with participants in the other seven conditions (see Figure 15.3). Planned comparison tests were conducted to test our specific hypotheses. As predicted, aversive racists in the excuse condition were less likely to recommend that the Asian job candidate be hired than the matched White candidate ($p < .001$). In addition, aversive racists were less likely to recommend that the Asian job candidate be hired in the excuse condition compared with their counterparts in the no-excuse condition ($p = .02$). Finally, aversive racists were less likely to recommend that the Asian job candidate in the excuse condition be hired than truly low-prejudiced participants ($p = .05$). In contrast, truly low-prejudiced participants did not differ in their recommendations, regardless of condition (*ns*).

Participants' memories for the target's competencies were then examined. The interrater agreement for the judges' ratings of the participants' recollections was very high, and the positivity of the statements recalled for interpersonal skills and for communication skills were strongly correlated, $r(137) = .64, p < .001$. Thus, analyses were conducted on the degree to which participants recalled the candidate's social (i.e., interpersonal and

---

[6] When an Ethnicity Condition × Excuse Condition × Aversive Racism analysis of variance is conducted, the three-way interaction was not significant ($p = .11$), but a significant Ethnicity Condition × Aversive Racism interaction was found, $F(1, 131) = 4.64, p = .03$. The Ethnicity Condition × Aversive Racism interaction was significant in the excuse condition ($p = .02$) but not in the no-excuse condition (*ns*).

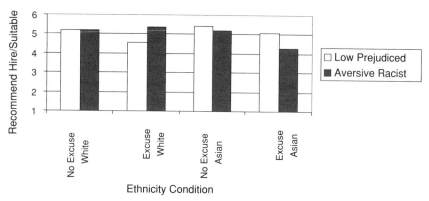

FIGURE 15.3 Study 3: Recommendation for employment as a function of excuse and target ethnicity.

Note. $^*p = .05$ $^{**}p <= .01$ $^{***}p <= .001$

FIGURE 15.4 Study 3: Mediation of memories of the target's social skills by recommendation for hire.

communication) skills as strong. These responses were judged by three raters.

We hypothesized that aversive racists who discriminated most against the Asian candidate for the employee relations specialist position subsequently should have the least positive memories of the target's social skills among all participants. Therefore, we tested whether hiring recommendations mediated participants' later memories of the target's social skills by conducting regression analyses, as suggested by Baron and Kenny (1986). As shown in Figure 15.4, the contrast test significantly predicted the proposed mediator: hiring recommendations. The contrast test also predicted participants' memories of the target's social skills. The target was remembered as having worse social skills when he was an Asian candidate evaluated by aversive racists in the excuse condition compared with the other seven conditions. In addition, when controlling for the contrast test, the stronger the participants' hiring recommendations, the more positive their memories of the job candidate's social skills were. Importantly, the relation between the contrast test and memories of the target's social skills

($\beta = .17, p = .05$) dropped to zero ($\beta = .04$, *ns*) once participants' hiring recommendations were controlled, $z = 2.77, p = .006$ (Goodman, 1960). Thus, mediation analyses are consistent with the notion that what led aversive racists to remember the Asian job candidate as having poor social skills was the degree to which they recommended that he not be hired for the employee relations specialist position.

In summary, we found strong evidence for the aversive racism effect in Study 3. Aversive racists evaluating the Asian candidate in the excuse condition were least likely to recommend that the target be hired compared with all other study participants. More specifically, (a) when an excuse existed, aversive racists were less likely to recommend that the Asian be hired compared with the White candidate; (b) the presence versus absence of a non-race-related excuse to discriminate affected the discriminatory behavior of aversive racists toward an Asian job candidate; and (c) when the situation was ambiguous, because it was not clear whether the candidate had the strong social skills demanded by the job (i.e., the employee relations specialist position), aversive racists were significantly less likely to recommend that the Asian target be hired compared with truly low-prejudiced participants.

Although no differences emerged based on participants' ethnicity condition or level of aversive racism when the candidate's social skills were first evaluated, a race bias emerges among aversive racists after they had provided their evaluations of the job candidate when asked to recall their memories of the job candidate's social skills. Furthermore, we discovered that the more aversive racists discriminated against the Asian candidate for the employee relations specialist position, the more they subsequently recalled his social competencies as weak. In other words, discrimination in hiring recommendations mediated the tendency for participants to recall the candidate as socially unskilled. This intriguing finding is consistent with the notion that once aversive racists failed to recommend that Gary Chang be hired for the employee relations specialist position, they engaged in a motivated, biased retrieval process that served to amplify the target's shortcomings – thus rationalizing their decision.

GENERAL DISCUSSION

To date, the evidence for aversive racism theory has been based only on general patterns: Race-based discrimination occurs in the presence of a non-race-related excuse, and discrimination does not occur in the absence of an excuse. The present work, by using the discrepancy between participants' prejudiced attitudes at the explicit and implicit levels, allows us to identify aversive racists and provides greater precision in predicting discriminatory behavior. Using a word fragment completion task in Study 1 and the IAT in Studies 2 and 3, participants identified as high in implicit prejudice but low in explicit prejudice behaved in a manner totally consistent with aversive racism theory (Gaertner & Dovidio, 1986). The aversive racism effect was found when participants' level of implicit prejudice was assessed both before the discrimination measure (Study 3) and after the discrimination measure (Study 2). Furthermore, the pattern of discrimination found among aversive racists was the same regardless of whether the excuse to discriminate was stereotype inconsistent (i.e., an assertive response in Study 2) or stereotype consistent (i.e., mediocre social skills in Study 3). In Studies 2 and 3, when norms for interracial behavior were ambiguous because there was an excuse for discrimination, aversive racists negatively evaluated an Asian target. That is, in Study 2, when Brian Chang became indignant when asked for help, aversive racists particularly disliked him and saw him as uncompassionate. And in Study 3, when Gary Chang, who had satisfactory but not exceptional social skills, was evaluated for the employee relations specialist position, he was less likely to be recommended for hire by aversive racists.

Lest one think that aversive racists are simply more prejudiced, we have evidence that situational cues can be used to motivate aversive racists to reduce their discriminatory behavior. In Study 1, when reminded of their past prejudicial slip-ups through a hypocrisy induction procedure, aversive racists felt more guilty and discriminated less than truly low-prejudiced participants when assigning cuts to the ASA's budget. These findings further demonstrate the importance of implicit attitudes for understanding intergroup behavior.

We have advanced previous research by identifying those who are and those who are not aversive racists and by comparing their responses when situational cues vary in the degree to which they justify discriminatory behavior or motivate nondiscriminatory behavior. Our findings further reveal how aversive racists discriminate and yet manage to keep their prejudices outside the realm of consciousness. Aversive racists appear to discriminate only when there is a non-race-related excuse or justification for their behavior. Furthermore, once aversive racists have engaged in discriminatory behavior, they appear to retrieve memories in a motivated fashion so as to derogate the target. Thus, aversive racists are able to discriminate without acknowledging their prejudice because they excuse or justify their behavior on "reasonable" grounds.

On the one hand, our findings suggest that due to aversive racists' memory retrieval biases, it may be difficult for them to change their discriminatory ways. On the other hand, our findings indicate that there are many situations in which aversive racists do not discriminate. Aversive racists do not discriminate in the absence of a non-race-related excuse to discriminate, nor do they differentiate between an Asian and a White target when they can examine detailed information and therefore be completely "data driven." Thus, aversive racists should be encouraged to base their judgments on specific, detailed information rather than general impressions. We also found that when aversive racists are made aware of their negative responses, they actually overcorrect to avoid discriminatory behavior. The duality of aversive racists' implicit and explicit attitudes should be brought to their attention. Once aversive racists become consciously aware of their negative implicit biases, they should be motivated to avoid discriminating on the basis of them.

References

Aronson, E. (1999). Dissonance, hypocrisy, and the self concept. In E. Harmon-Jones & J. Mills (Eds.), *Cognitive dissonance: Progress on a pivotal theory in social psychology* (pp. 103–126). Washington, DC: American Psychological Association.

Baron, R. M., & Kenny, D. A. (1986). The moderator–mediator variable distinction in social psychological research: Conceptual, strategic, and statistical consideration. *Journal of Personality and Social Psychology, 51*, 1173–1182.

Chung-Yan, G. A., Son Hing, L. S., & Zanna, M. P. (submitted for publication). *The role of aversive racism in discriminatory selection decisions*. Manuscript.

Crandall, C. S., O'Brien, L. T., & Eshleman, A. (2002). Adapting the self to local group norms: Internalizing the suppression of prejudice. In J. P. Forgas & K. D. Williams (Eds.), *The social self: Cognitive, interpersonal, and intergroup perspectives* (pp. 293–308). New York: Psychology Press.

Darley, J. M., & Latané, B. (1968). Bystander intervention in emergencies: Diffusion of responsibility. *Journal of Personality and Social Psychology, 8*, 377–383.

Devine, P. G., Monteith, M. J., Zuwerink, J. R., & Elliot, A. J. (1991). Prejudice with and without compunction. *Journal of Personality and Social Psychology, 60*, 817–830.

Dovidio, J. F. (2001). On the nature of contemporary prejudice: The third wave. *Journal of Social Issues, 57*, 829–849.

Dovidio, J. F., & Gaertner, S. L. (2000). Aversive racism and selection decisions: 1989 and 1999. *Psychological Science, 11*, 315–319.

Dovidio, J. F., Gaertner, S. L., Anastasio, P. A., & Sanitioso, R. (1992). Cognitive and motivational bases of bias: The implications of aversive racism for attitudes toward Hispanics. In S. Knouse, P. Rosenfeld, & A. Culbertson (Eds.), *Hispanics in the workplace* (pp. 75–106). Newbury Park, CA: Sage.

Dovidio, J. F., Kawakami, K., & Gaertner, S. L. (2000). Reducing contemporary prejudice: Combating explicit and implicit bias at the individual and intergroup level. In S. Oskamp (Ed.), *The Claremont symposium on applied social psychology: Reducing prejudice and discrimination* (pp. 137–163). Mahwah, NJ: Erlbaum.

Dovidio, J. F., Kawakami, K., & Gaertner, S. L. (2002). Implicit and explicit prejudice and interracial interactions. *Journal of Personality and Social Psychology, 82*, 62–68.

Dovidio, J. F., Kawakami, K., Johnson, C., Johnson, B., & Howard, A. (1997). On the nature of prejudice: Automatic and controlled processes. *Journal of Experimental Social Psychology, 33*, 510–540.

Fazio, R. H. (1990). Multiple processes by which attitudes guide behavior: The MODE model as an integrative framework. In M. P. Zanna (Ed.), *Advances in experimental social psychology* (Vol. 23, pp. 75–109). San Diego, CA: Academic Press.

Fazio, R. H., Jackson, J. R., Dunton, B. C., & Williams, C. J. (1995). Variability in automatic activation as an unobtrusive measure of racial attitudes: A bona fide pipeline? *Journal of Personality and Social Psychology, 69*, 1013–1027.

Fazio, R. H., & Olson, M. A. (2003). Implicit measures in social cognition research: Their meaning and use. *Annual Review of Psychology, 54*, 297–327.

Florak, A., Scarabis, M., & Bless, H. (2001). When do associations matter?: The use of implicit associations toward ethnic groups in person judgments. *Journal of Experimental Social Psychology, 37*, 518–524.

Gaertner, S. L., & Dovidio, J. F. (1986). The aversive form of racism. In J. F. Dovidio & S. L. Gaertner (Eds.), *Prejudice, discrimination, and racism* (pp. 61–86). Orlando, FL: Academic Press.

Gilbert, D. T., & Hixon, G. H. (1991). The trouble of thinking: Activation and application of stereotypic beliefs. *Journal of Personality and Social Psychology, 60*, 509–517.

Goodman, L. A. (1960). On the exact variance of products. *Journal of the American Statistical Association, 55*, 708–713.

Greenwald, A. G., & Banaji, M. R. (1995). Implicit social cognition: Attitudes, self-esteem, and stereotypes. *Psychological Review, 102*, 4–27.

Greenwald, A. G., McGee, D. E., & Schwartz, J. L. K. (1998). Measuring individual differences in implicit cognition: The implicit association test. *Journal of Personality and Social Psychology, 74*, 1464–1480.

Hodson, G., Dovidio, J. F., & Gaertner, S. L. (2002). Processes in racial discrimination: Differential weighing of conflicting information. *Personality and Social Psychology Bulletin, 28*, 460–471.

Human Resources Development Canada. (2001). 2001 Employment equity annual report, members of visible minorities. Retrieved January 14, 2003, from http://info.load-otea.hrdc-drhc.gc.ca/workplace_equity/leep/annual/2001/annualreport2001alt.shtml

Katz, I., & Hass, R. G. (1988). Racial ambivalence and American value conflict: Correlational and priming studies of dual cognitive structures. *Journal of Personality and Social Psychology, 55*, 893–905.

Landau, J. (1995). The relationship of race and gender to managers' ratings of promotion potential. *Journal of Organizational Behavior, 16*, 391–400.

McConahay, J. B. (1986). Modern racism, ambivalence, and the modern racism scale. In J. F. Dovidio & S. L. Gaertner (Eds.), *Prejudice, discrimination, and racism* (pp. 91–125). Orlando, FL: Academic Press.

McConnell, A. R., & Leibold, J. M. (2001). Relations between the Implicit Association Test, explicit racial attitudes, and discriminatory behavior. *Journal of Experimental Social Psychology, 37*, 435–442.

Monteith, M. J. (1996). Affective reactions to prejudice-related discrepant responses: The impact of standard salience. *Personality and Social Psychology Bulletin, 22*, 48–59.

Monteith, M. J., Devine, P. G., & Zuwerink, J. R. (1993). Self-directed versus other-directed affect as a consequence of prejudice-related discrepancies. *Journal of Personality and Social Psychology, 64*, 198–210.

Plant, E. A., & Devine, P. G. (1998). Internal and external motivation to respond without prejudice. *Journal of Personality and Social Psychology, 75*, 811–832.

Rosenthal, R., Rosnow, R. L., & Rubin, D. B. (2000). *Contrasts and effect sizes in behavioral research: A correlational approach.* New York: Cambridge University Press.

Rudman, L. A., & Glick, P. (1999). Feminized management and backlash toward agentic women: The hidden costs to women of a kinder, gentler image of middle managers. *Journal of Personality and Social Psychology, 77*, 1004–1010.

Rudman, L. A., Greenwald, A. G., Mellott, D. S., & Schwartz, J. L. K. (1999). Measuring the automatic components of prejudice: Flexibility and generality of the Implicit Association Test. *Social Cognition, 17*, 437–465.

Sackett, P. R., & DuBois, C. L. Z. (1991). Rater-ratee effects on performance evaluation: Challenging meta-analytic conclusions. *Journal of Applied Psychology, 76*, 873–877.

Sinclair, L., & Kunda, Z. (1999). Reactions to a Black professional: Motivated inhibition and activation of conflicting stereotypes. *Journal of Personality and Social Psychology, 77*, 885–904.

Son Hing, L. S., Li, W., & Zanna, M. P. (2002). Inducing hypocrisy to reduce prejudicial responses among aversive racists. *Journal of Experimental Social Psychology, 38*, 71–78.

Stone, J., Aronson, E., Crain, A. L., Winslow, M. P., & Fried, C. B. (1994). Inducing hypocrisy as a means of encouraging young adults to use condoms. *Personality and Social Psychology Bulletin, 20*, 116–128.

Vance, K. M., & Devine, P. G. (1999, May). *How self-affirmations influence the motivation and behaviors associated with prejudice reduction.* Paper presented at the annual meeting of the Midwestern Psychological Association, Chicago.

Wilson, T. D., Lindsey, S., & Schooler, T. Y. (2000). A model of dual attitudes. *Psychological Review, 107*, 101–126.

Wittenbrink, B., Judd, C. M., & Park, B. (1997). Evidence for racial prejudice at the implicit level and its relationship with questionnaire measures. *Journal of Personality and Social Psychology, 72*, 262–274.

16

Ostracism

When Competing Motivations Collide

Wayne A. Warburton and Kipling D. Williams

INTRODUCTION

In a recent investigation into the causes of 15 school shootings in the United States, Leary, Kowalski, Smith, and Phillips (2003) found that acute or chronic rejection in the form of ostracism, bullying, or romantic rejection was a significant factor in all but two cases, and concluded that these rejection experiences had motivated many of the shooters to behave violently, either as a way of achieving retribution against the rejecting group or gaining social respect. Laboratory research has also shown that in certain circumstances, individuals who experience social exclusion are more likely to exhibit aggressive behaviors than those who are included (Twenge, Baumeister, Tice, & Stucke, 2001; Twenge & Campbell, 2003). As a rather extreme example (hopefully), a recent newspaper article ("Put to the Sword" in *The Australian*, June 23, 2003) reported on a Thai woman who killed her husband before slicing off his penis, boiling it, and then hanging herself. In her suicide note, she indicated that she was saddened by the fact that her husband had ignored her. Clearly, the act of excluding or rejecting another can have profound motivational consequences for the target, and these motivations may lead to antisocial and even aggressive behaviors.

Conversely, many individuals experience social ostracism on a daily basis without showing any signs that they are being driven by aggressive or antisocial motives (Williams, 2001). Indeed, experiments have demonstrated that ostracized individuals exhibit the sorts of prosocial behaviors that would indicate a strong motivation to be reincluded in the group, such as social compensation (Williams & Sommer, 1997), conformity (Williams,

This research was funded by an Australian Research Council grant to the second author. We thank Trevor Case for his input in earlier drafts of this chapter. Please address all correspondence to Kipling D. Williams, Department of Psychology, Macquarie University, Sydney, NSW 2109; e-mail: kip@psy.mq.edu.au.

Cheung, & Choi, 2000b), paying greater attention to socially relevant information (Gardner, Pickett, & Brewer, 2000), or being more attracted to other individuals or groups (Wheaton, 2001).

It is possible that this dichotomy in research findings reflects fundamental differences between the concepts of ostracism, rejection, and social exclusion, and that the different streams of research are tapping into different phenomena. *Ostracism* refers to ignoring or excluding one or more individuals (Williams, 2001), *rejection* usually refers to expelling a person from a group accompanied by derogation (Leary, 2001), and *social exclusion* refers to exclusion but does not usually extend to ignoring (Twenge, et al., 2001). Different operationalizations of exclusion, rejection, and ostracism also exist between these streams, and it is possible that these procedural differences elicit different reactions. For instance, ostracism research tends to immerse the participant in a prolonged experience of being ignored and excluded in the physical or imagined presence of the ostracizers, whereas exclusion and rejection research tends to deliver a message to the participant that others have rejected or will reject him or her. Nevertheless, there are certainly strong overlapping themes of exclusion across all three research domains, and until future research uncovers crucial distinctions between these phenomena, we will consider them similarly and, for our purposes, refer to them as ostracism.

SOCIAL MOTIVES ACTIVATED BY OSTRACISM

Many researchers emphasize a single motivational force in ostracism – the powerful motivation to belong (see Baumeister & Leary, 1995; Baumeister, Twenge, & Nuss, 2002; Gardner et al., 2000; Twenge et al., 2001; Twenge & Campbell, 2003; Twenge, Catanese, & Baumeister, 2002). In this chapter, we will argue that along with belonging motives, at least three other social motives play a significant role in ostracism: control motives (that also include related motives of efficacy and power), self-esteem-related motives, and motives related to maintaining the belief that one's life is meaningful within the broader social context.

Sometimes these motives seem to work in parallel without clashing, but at other times they may compete. To the extent that the motives are similarly affected in a parallel fashion, they would appear to be indistinguishable, and it could be argued that it is not parsimonious to propose four separate motives. In fact, several studies indicate that compared to included individuals, ostracized individuals report lower levels of all four needs. On the other hand, there are instances in which we would predict that the motives may not work in parallel. Sometimes, because of the nature of the ostracism, certain motives may be more affected. At other times, the motives may actually elicit opposing behaviors. In this chapter, we will consider how ostracism may elicit either prosocial or antisocial behaviors.

We propose that both types of response are possible because in different instances different motives will dominate, activating more strongly the cognitions and action tendencies linked to those motives and producing either pro- or antisocial behaviors, depending on the nature of those links (see Harackiewicz, Durik, & Barron, this volume, on complementary motivations and multiple goals). Accordingly, we will examine several factors that might influence which motives will prevail in different circumstances, and discuss ways in which these factors may influence one well-demonstrated effect: aggressive responding to ostracism.

It is quite possible that all four motives are separable at psychological and behavioral levels, and depending upon which motive dominates, four different paths of responses could emerge. At this point, however, our analysis suggests that we can separate the four motives into two general classes: those motives related primarily to social evaluation (belonging and self-esteem) and those motives related to efficacy and existence (control and meaningful existence). We will now examine motives from these two streams, before discussing ways in which these motives may work in parallel or collide, and the antecedent conditions and outcomes that seem to be associated with different motivational pairings.

MOTIVES RELATED TO SOCIAL EVALUATION

Belonging

It is not surprising that so much of the ostracism literature focuses on belonging motives, because these are argued to be both powerful and universal and, in evolutionary terms, may play an important role in human adaptation. Repeatedly, studies have shown that people are motivated strongly to maintain stable and ongoing positive connections with others (Baumeister & Leary, 1995). Baumeister and Leary conclude that the loss of such connections through ostracism, the death of a loved one, or any other event that directly threatens the basic need to belong may lead to a range of ill effects. For example, those who do not enjoy a network of close social connections are at a higher risk of developing physical diseases and psychopathology, and may even be more inclined to engage in antisocial or criminal behavior than those with rich social connections. In addition, they suggest that the motivation for belonging serves an important evolutionary function. Our propensity to seek out others for social interaction and to exist in groups provides an adaptive advantage, in that it increases the chance that we will obtain food, find a mate, and we and our offspring will survive predatory attacks. In short, the belonging motive has both survival and reproductive benefits (see also Neuberg, Kenrick, Maner, & Schaller, this volume, on the relative strength of motives related to self-protection and mating).

Because humans are motivated to belong, they use many strategies to minimize the chance of being socially excluded. These usually take the form of a number of prosocial behaviors, such as demonstrating a willingness to contribute to group efforts or to behave in other socially desirable ways (Baumeister & Tice, 1990). Such strategies are found repeatedly in the laboratory: Compared to included individuals, ostracized individuals are more likely to conform to group standards (Williams et al., 2000b), be open to the overtures of others (Wheaton, 2001), process socially relevant information (Gardner et al., 2000), and socially compensate or engage in face-saving behaviors such as projecting a confident, positive self-image (Williams & Sommer, 1997; see also Ezrakhovich et al., 1998).

Self-Esteem

There are consistent findings indicating that a substantial drop in self-esteem occurs after ostracism (see Williams, 2001, for a review), and analysis of more than 50 interviews suggests that this may result partly from being rejected as unworthy of the ostracizer's attention (Zadro, Williams, & Richardson, 2003). In addition, the ambiguous nature of most instances of ostracism may prompt the target to explore any number of self-deprecating justifications for this rejection (Williams, 2001). Although those with low initial self-esteem might be particularly sensitive to and affected by ostracism in the first place (Nezlek, Kowalski, Leary, Blevins, & Holgate, 1997; Sommer & Baumeister, 2002), there is also evidence that those who respond to ostracism with apparently self-confident behaviors may be masking an underlying loss of self-esteem (Williams & Sommer, 1997).

Temporary threats to self-esteem result in a corresponding motivation to restore self-esteem, and given the importance of adequate self-esteem for maintaining psychological well-being (Steele, 1988; Tesser, 1988), such a motivation would appear to be adaptive. Many observed postostracism behaviors may be relevant to the restoration of self-esteem. These include attempts to appear confident, attractive, and powerful, to be noticed by others, and to be effective in the social and physical worlds, as well as the prosocial behaviors of conformity, attention to social information, attraction to others, and social compensation.

MOTIVES RELATED TO EFFICACY AND EXISTENCE

In all of these studies, however, ostracized individuals face social evaluation, either from the ostracizing individuals or at the very least from the experimenter. In situations in which the ostracized individual faces social evaluation, it seems clear that motives of belonging are primary and strong. But what motives operate when ostracized individuals can behave without social evaluations or repercussions? We argue that other social motives coexist with belonging and esteem when an individual is ostracized, and that these motives, although less obvious and less well researched, also determine behavior, especially when the target of ostracism can behave without being scrutinized by others.

Control

The need for control has long been identified as a fundamental motivation in the psychological literature (e.g., deCharms, 1968; White, 1959). It may stem from many sources, such as the need to have effective physical or social control over an individual's environment (Thompson, 1981), the desire for a sense of self-efficacy (Bandura, 1997; see also Wood & Quinn, this volume, on habits and efficacy), the wish to have adequate choices (Langer & Rodin, 1975), or the need for personal power as opposed to helplessness (Alloy & Abramson, 1982). Threats to control may be eliminated by actions that restore specific lost freedoms (c.f. reactance: Wortman & Brehm, 1975) *or* provide a control gain in *another* area (Pittman & D'Agostino, 1989). In other words, control motivation may generalize from one area to another (Pittman & Pittman, 1980).

The motivation to predict, understand, and control our environment offers considerable adaptive value for day-to-day survival. Furthermore, heightened perceptions of control have positive consequences for physical and psychological well-being (Taylor & Brown, 1988), whereas prolonged perceptions of undermined control are associated with negative consequences and depression (Abramson, Seligman, & Teasdale, 1978).

Ostracism threatens perceptions of control, because the act of ignoring and excluding is *imposed* upon the target. Additionally, the target is left helpless to effect his or her own reinclusion or subsequent interactions. Because ostracism threatens other motives (belonging, self-esteem, and meaningful existence), ostracism increases further control motivation, because individuals need some control over the environment in order to affect any of the changes needed to restore those needs or reduce threats to goals.

Ostracism-elicited control motivation has been found using various types of self-report and behavioral measures. For example, Lawson Williams and Williams (1998) ostracized or included participants in an apparently spontaneous game of ball toss, and had the confederates pose either as friends with each other or as strangers (in all cases, the confederates were strangers to the participant). They found that targets of ostracism who were ostracized by two individuals who appeared to be friends with each other were more likely to indicate greater need for control on a state form of the Desire for Control scale (Burger, 1992) than included participants. In a second study for which the cover story was an investigation of nonverbal leakage, Lawson Williams and Williams set ostracized and included participants the task of identifying a concealed card at which another participant (a third confederate) was gazing. Participants were also told that each side of a person's face revealed different types of nonverbal cues, and that in order to determine the identity of the concealed card, they could request that the card gazer turn his head as often as they wanted him to until they felt they had adequate information from his face. Thus, individuals had an opportunity to exert social control over another person (who had nothing to do with the ostracism) by directing that individual to turn his head as often as the participant wished. Only those individuals who were ostracized by two people appearing to be friends with each other requested more head turns than did included participants. Both of these studies suggest that the more ostracism deprives individuals of social control, the more they desire control and will reassert it when the opportunity occurs.

In addition, in more than a dozen studies in our laboratory, we have used three-item self-report scales to assess the impact on control, and have consistently found that ostracised individuals report having less control than included participants (Williams, 2001). A recent exception occurred when we compared face-to-face social ostracism in a conversation paradigm to chat room ostracism on the Intranet. We found that ostracized chat room participants were engaging in provocative verbal and nonverbal behaviors that seemed to satisfy their control needs (Williams et al., 2002).

Meaningful Existence

Another fundamental motivation that Williams (1997, 2001) proposes is affected by ostracism is the motive to feel that one's existence is meaningful. A large body of literature attests to the idea that people have a basic fear of facing the inevitability of their own death and the meaninglessness of their existence (Greenberg, Solomon, & Pyszczynski, 1997). Furthermore, socially constructed worldviews (e.g., belief in an afterlife) buffer against the paralyzing terror associated with confronting an inherently meaningless existence and the reality of mortality; so, when meaningful existence is threatened, individuals bolster their commitment to those worldviews. According to Williams (1997, 2001), ostracism is a powerful metaphor for social death (see also Case & Williams, in press). Targets of ostracism become socially invisible when excluded from interaction, and in this sense they cease to exist. Indeed, many targets of both long- and short-term ostracism spontaneously report questioning their own existence (Sommer, Williams, Ciarocco, & Baumeister, 2001; Williams, Shore, & Grahe, 1998). In one experiment, a participant was observed pinching himself while being ostracized, possibly to test his senses to make sure he was actually there. As such, ostracism may have similar effects to being confronted with reminders of physical death.

In the laboratory, there is clear evidence that ostracized individuals feel that their existence is less meaningful than included participants (Twenge, Catanese, & Baumeister, in press; Williams, 2001). Twenge and her colleagues theorize that this is part of an almost demotivated malaise in which socially excluded individuals respond to consequent emotional and cognitive overload by shutting down into the type of deconstructed state also reported by those who are presuicidal. In contrast, Williams (1997, 2001) notes that ostracism often seems to elicit a highly motivated state in which individuals try to offset the feeling of being invisible or nonexistent by trying very hard to be noticed. For example, in their Scarlet Letter study, Williams, Bernieri, Faulkner, Grahe, and Gada-Jain (2000a) found that when each of the authors took his or her turn to be ostracized by colleagues for just one day, most felt motivated to behave in unusual and even aggressive ways in order to draw attention to themselves. For example, Mr. Blue (a pseudonym) wanted to smack Ms. Yellow on the head to get her attention; Dr. Black beeped his car horn at Dr. Brown and stuck a red *O* on his forehead in order to be noticed. In his diary, Mr. Blue wrote that "he felt like a ghost" (p. 54) and consequently wanted to be noticed. He also wrote, "I'm seeing my goal today as trying to get people to recognise my existence, with good or bad evaluation – it doesn't matter" (p. 54). We propose that the easiest and surest way of gaining immediate and wide recognition is through antisocial action. Consider an individual who is consumed with the desire to be recognized and seen as having an effect on others. What could such an individual do at that very moment to achieve such an outcome? A troubling (and perhaps accurate) revelation may be that violent acts are more certain to achieve immediate recognition and social impact than executing any prosocial act. What single prosocial act could bring the individual instant and global fame more than going on a shooting rampage? To gain global recognition for doing something positive, like inventing a cure for cancer, would require much more time and talent. Unfortunately, little time or talent is necessary to shoot people.

Nevertheless, both research streams present credible experimental evidence regarding ostracism and existence threats, and it may be that behavioral outcomes will differ, depending on the context of the ostracism episodes and the other motives that co-occur with it.

In sum, ostracism appears to elicit a substantial control motivation, as well as the motivation to gather reassurance that one's existence has meaning and is recognized by others. Whereas control motives may gain ascendance out of the public glare or guide behavior at a more implicit level, existence motivations may lead to behaviors that attract an explicitly negative social evaluation. Motives related to efficacy and/or existence may account for many of the antisocial responses to ostracism that have been found recently (e.g., Tice, Twenge, & Schmeichel, 2002; Twenge et al., 2001; Twenge & Campbell, 2003; Williams, 2001). Before addressing aggressive responding to ostracism, however, it seems pertinent to examine first which of the ostracism-elicited motives may work in harmony and why these pairings produce primarily prosocial behaviors.

MOTIVES THAT WORK IN PARALLEL

Because being socially attractive to others is an important factor for inclusion (Baumeister & Leary, 1995), belonging motives often drive individuals to present their most appealing self-image. Leary, Tambor, Terdal, and Downs (1995) extend this idea with their *sociometer theory*, which suggests that because high personal self-esteem serves to project an image that increases an individual's attractiveness, and hence inclusiveness to others, motivations related to maintaining or increasing self-esteem are also in the service of enhancing one's level of belonging. According to this theory, individuals use the current status of their self-esteem beliefs as an indicator (or sociometer) of their fluctuating inclusionary status. It seems reasonable to assume, then, that belonging and self-esteem, which are both related to positive social evaluation and acceptance, may work in parallel and without conflict to drive many of the ostracism-elicited prosocial behaviors demonstrated in the laboratory.

For example, Williams and Sommer (1997) either excluded or included participants in the ball-tossing task already described. Participants were then set the task of generating as many uses for an object as possible. They performed this task either collectively (in which only the group performance was recorded) or coactively (in which individual performances were compared within the group). For women, ostracism resulted in the rarely observed phenomenon of social compensation, or greater performance when the task was collective than when it was coactive. Williams and Sommer inferred that ostracized women worked harder and contributed more to the collective total in order to appease the others who had just rejected them. In another study, Williams et al. (2000b) used an Internet version of the ball-tossing paradigm to induce ostracism, and found that ostracism (compared to inclusion) increased conformity on a perceptual conformity task. It is noteworthy that participants in this study were led to believe that they were completing the conformity task with a new group of participants, demonstrating that targets did not confine their prosocial attempts as a means for reinclusion to a group who previously ostracized them.

Such prosocial responses to ostracism may reflect an underlying propensity to focus on social information. This is consistent with the findings of Gardner et al. (2000), who reported that participants who had been previously excluded in a computer chat room interaction demonstrated greater memory for social events presented in a diary than those who were included. The authors suggested that enhanced social memory resulted from a desire to quench the need for belonging. These and other similar findings (for reviews see Williams, 2001; Williams & Zadro, 2001) demonstrate that targets of ostracism often behave prosocially. These behaviors presumably are rooted in the motivations to belong and maintain high self-esteem.

Self-esteem motivations can also appear to work in parallel with motivations related to meaningful existence. According to terror management theory (see Greenberg et al., 1997, for a review; see also Pyszczynski et al., this volume), "people need self-esteem because it is the central psychological mechanism for protecting individuals from the anxiety that awareness of their vulnerability and mortality would otherwise create" (Greenberg et al., 1992, p. 913). It seems reasonable to suggest, then, that when a person experiences being ignored or treated as if nonexistent, self-esteem motivation would be aroused alongside motivations to restore a sense of purpose and meaning.

Unlike the self-esteem and belonging motivational combination, however, it seems plausible that the consequences of the motivational combination of self-esteem and meaningful existence could be either prosocial or antisocial in nature, depending on the strategies the individual uses to increase self-esteem and thus buffer against any mortality fears aroused (see Case & Williams, in press). These may encompass the prosocial strategies to increase acceptance already discussed, or may involve attempts to be noticed at any social cost, as Williams et al. (2000a) found in their Scarlet Letter study. Perhaps such outcomes depend on which of the two motivations is more strongly activated. If self-esteem motives are more threatened or more salient, prosocial behaviors may be more likely, but if existence needs dominate, efforts to be noticed may lead to antisocial behaviors.

Control motivation should also work in parallel with the other three motives. After all, if individuals are motivated to restore various threatened needs, they will need some level of control over their physical and social environments to do so. For this reason alone, it is not surprising that control motivation seems to co-occur consistently with other ostracism-related motivations (see Williams, 2001; Williams & Zadro, 2001).

MOTIVES THAT COLLIDE

Perhaps the newest area of ostracism research involves exploring those factors that guide behavior when opposing motivations compete for behavioral outcomes. Research into the competing motives that may be aroused by ostracism currently focuses primarily on explaining the apparently contradictory findings that ostracism may lead to aggression (e.g., Tice et al., 2002; Twenge et al., 2001; Twenge & Campbell, 2003) or to the variety of prosocial behaviors already detailed.

Williams, Case, and Govan (2003) theorized that this dichotomy might be explained by two factors. Firstly, explicit motives may differ from implicit motives, and behavioral outcomes may depend on which level of motivation is guiding behavior at the time or on which level is being assessed (see also Son Hing, Chung-Yan, Grunfeld, Robichaud, & Zanna, this volume; Spencer, Fein, Strahan, & Zanna, this volume; Wood and Quinn, this volume, on the relative effects of implicit and explicit motives). Secondly, outcomes may depend on which type of motive has been most threatened by ostracism. If belonging and esteem motives are most threatened, responses are more likely to involve an attempt to facilitate reinclusion, whereas if control and meaningful existence needs are most threatened, behaviors are more likely to involve an attempt to facilitate restored control or being noticed, even if the strategies used are antisocial or aggressive.

Consistent with this notion of dual reactions to ostracism, Williams et al. (2003) induced ostracism by either including or excluding individuals in a computerized version of a ball-tossing game (Cyberball) in which participants believed they were interacting with two other participants. After this, they were given an implicit association test (Greenwald, McGhee, & Schwartz, 1998) specifically designed to assess attitudes toward aboriginal and European names. Finally, participants completed an explicit measure of prejudice against aboriginal people (Pedersen & Walker, 1997). Ostracized targets showed more prejudice against aboriginal people on the implicit measure of attitudes than did included targets. However, there were no differences between ostracized and included targets when an explicit measure of racism was used. When explicit measures of prejudice were used, everyone's responses reflected low levels of prejudice.

Both the implicit-explicit explanation and the most threatened need explanation are consistent with the notion that ostracism-related behavioral outcomes will depend on which of two or more opposing motivational forces come to guide the ostracized individual's actions. Simply put, ostracism may produce explicit motivations related to social evaluation – a drive to belong and to look good in the eyes of others – but may also produce implicit motivations related to regaining control or being noticed. The implicit motivations may lead to conscious or nonconscious goals to restore those needs, and aggressive or antisocial behaviors may be one outcome if such goals are pursued. Thus, if the ostracized individual is subject to social evaluation, powerful and explicit motivations related to belonging and self-esteem may lead to actions explicitly intended to increase interpersonal attractiveness, whereas the simultaneously aroused control and meaningful existence – related motivations will be submerged (along with a variety of negative sentiments), limiting subsequent responses to implicit reactions. If the individual is not subject to social evaluation, he or she may feel less constrained to inhibit antisocial responses, and implicit motivations may be more likely to guide behavior.

In this way, aggressive responding to ostracism may reflect implicit attempts to regain control or meaningful existence (e.g., by bolstering one's worldview at the expense of others or by controlling another through causing hurt), whereas prosocial reactions to ostracism may reflect explicit attempts to reconnect and restore a sense of belonging and self-esteem.

This explanation fits with a variety of existing findings. For example, it seems that in all of the experiments in which Twenge and her colleagues found aggressive responding to ostracism, aggressive options were presented in a way that allowed participants to feel that they would not face any social consequences for their actions, and in which aggressive responses were socially approved and justifiable. In contrast, many of the prosocial responses reported by Williams and others occurred when participants could have realistically expected to be reunited with the group that ostracized them, a new group, or were under the evaluative eye of the experimenter. In these instances, participants may have anticipated negative evaluations by other participants or the experimenter if they behaved in a less than socially desirable manner.

In addition, control motivation may have been a significant factor in the findings of Twenge et al. (2001). In their first three experiments, excluded participants would have experienced a highly aversive and salient loss of control, because they had been told that psychological tests had revealed that their current friendships would dissolve over time, leaving them isolated and alone later in life. By implication, this would occur regardless of any efforts to stave off such an outcome. Given the almost primal human need to belong (Baumeister & Leary, 1995), such news should have elicited far greater emotional and motivational responses than the news given in either the belonging condition (in which rich friendships were predicted) or the misfortune control condition (in which they were told that they would become more accident-prone later in life). It seems reasonable to assume, then, that although the misfortune group may have experienced some threat to control needs by facing the prospect of future accidents, the scope of this control motivation would pale beside the sheer power of the motivation elicited by the prospect of lifelong isolation. The life-alone groups were by far the most aggressive in their first two experiments. However, when their excluded participants were given positive feedback about an essay they had written (and thus enjoyed a restoration of either self-efficacy, self-esteem, or both), they were no more aggressive than participants from any other groups (Experiment 3). In their Experiments 4 and 5, participants either experienced a loss of social control, by being told that members of a group in which they had just interacted had *not* nominated them for further inclusion, or experienced having social control by being nominated for future group inclusion. Again, the groups with the least control were most aggressive in all cases. Overall, it seems reasonable to suggest that the aggressive responses found by Twenge et al. may have co-occurred with variations in control motivation.

Perhaps, then, in situations where ostracized individuals are not subject to social evaluation, and where explicit affiliation and self-esteem motivations are consequently less strong, implicit motivations related to control and meaningful existence are more likely to guide behavior and to result in aggressive or antisocial actions. It would make particular sense that control motivation could be a primary factor in findings where ostracism elicits aggression, because control motivation and aggression have many well-documented links.

For a start, control motivation has been linked to anger and hostility (Brehm, 1966; Depret & Fiske, 1993), and some motivational theorists, such as McClelland (1985), have found that implicit power motivations (including the implicit motivation to impact on people and the world that we theorize is elicited by ostracism) seem to have an integral and specific link to anger (see also Forgas & Laham, this volume, on mood and motivation). Although anger does not necessarily cause aggression (cf. Berkowitz, 1983), it is often thought of as an intervening condition that instigates and then guides aggressive behavior (Geen, 1990). The highly influential cognitive neo-association theory of aggression (Berkowitz, 1993) suggests that this sort of negative emotional arousal would automatically stimulate various thoughts, attributions, memories, expressive motor reactions, and physiological responses associated with fight or flight tendencies and raise the preparedness to aggress of the angry person (see Strack & Deutsch, this volume, on impulsive-aggressive versus reflective-prosocial determinants of behavior). Thus, control motivation may be linked intrinsically to an increased preparedness to aggress, although other factors, such as attributions and elaborated thinking, and impulsiveness versus reflectivity, may determine whether the behavioral outcomes are aggressive or not.

Control motivation also seems to have direct links with aggressive behaviors per se. Anderson and Bushman (2002) note that aggression helps people to feel in control, and suggest that need-threats may thus elicit control motivation and aggression as a means to refortify threatened needs. Mueller (1983) theorized that a loss of personal control could lead to aggression, either as a reactant attempt to restore a lost freedom or as an angry response to frustration. In their social interaction theory of aggression, Tedeschi and Felson (1994) portray aggressive acts as a coercive tool that may be used to control the behavior of others. Other theorists suggest that individuals may directly aggress against others as a way of restoring a generalized sense of personal power or control over others (see Depret & Fiske, 1993; Frieze & Boneva, 2001), and this should be especially true if this has been a successful strategy in the past (Pittman & D'Agostino,

1989) or where such strategies have been successfully modeled by others (e.g., Bandura, 1983).

There are also links between control and aggression in the media and thus in popular consciousness. The modern media environment in Western countries are producing an ever-increasing amount of material promoting the idea that aggressive acts can restore social control (Smith & Donnerstein, 1998). For example, Anderson, Carnagey, and Eubanks (2003) examined the effects of aggressive song lyrics on thoughts and feelings. Some of the lyrics they used as stimuli contained the clear message that aggressive acts can provide power over another (e.g., "I should play God and shoot you myself" from the song "Jerk-Off" by Tool, 1992). They found across five experiments that aggressive lyrics consistently primed aggressive thoughts and hostile feelings. It is somewhat frightening to speculate what thoughts and feelings might be primed in response to songs like "Stan," by Eminem (2000), in which a fan kills himself and his pregnant girlfriend in response to being ignored by his idol.

When beliefs and scripts that have been obtained in popular culture are activated, people often behave in accordance with these scripts in everyday life (Huesmann, 1986). Given that repeatedly activated scripts may also produce automatic, nonconscious goals Bargh (1997), an explicit threat to control or power (such as ostracism) could automatically produce an implicit goal to aggress in some people (see Bargh & Alvarez, 2001; Todorov & Bargh, 2002). In such a case, it seems conceivable that the individual might behave aggressively in response to ostracism, but may not be cognizant of the reasons for choosing to be aggressive. Implicit control motives may also direct some instances of indirect aggression (Williams & Warburton, 2003).

To test directly whether control motivation would moderate aggressive responses to ostracism, Warburton (2002) excluded or included participants in a game of toss, and then exposed them to an aversive noise over which they either had control or had no control. Aggression was then measured as the amount of hot sauce participants gave to a stranger knowing that the sauce was hot and that the stranger, who was known to dislike hot foods, would have to eat all of the hot sauce that they allocated. Ostracized participants who had no control over the noise allocated more than four times as much hot sauce as ostracized participants who were given subsequent control over the noise, suggesting that aggressive responding to ostracism can be moderated by altering levels of control motivation.

Recently, in a real-world analogue of parts of this experiment, a very similar scenario was played out on the reality television show "Big Brother" (Australia). Participants in the show live totally secluded from any outside influences in a house where dozens of cameras record their every activity. In the relevant episode, housemates were divided into two groups – the haves and have-nots. The have-nots were expected to serve the haves, to eat tasteless food, and to sleep in a closet. In a sense, the have nots were excluded from their former life, and frequently reported feeling rejected by the others. This appeared to create some level of hostility, but because a central imperative of the show is that housemates need to appear attractive to the television audience (who choose one member to be voted out each week), affiliation and acceptance motivations appeared to override any outright expressions of hostility or acts of aggression. One have-not, however, mentioned to the other have-nots that they might make that night's curry a little bit hotter than usual for the haves, and the other have-nots readily agreed to help (see Aarts & Hassin, this volume, on automatically making someone else's goal your own). As a result, the have-nots poured so much hot sauce into the evening meal that the haves suffered through the evening meal with tears running from their eyes and burning throats. Although this action was sufficiently ambiguous to be explained as a culinary mistake, and although housemates may even have justified the action to themselves as a prank, this behavior could be considered aggressive, because it was carried out with the immediate goal (implicit or explicit) of harming another (Anderson & Bushman, 2002; Bargh & Alvarez, 2001). Although this action may be explained as simple revenge for social rejection (as, indeed, some have explained the school shootings), it also demonstrates what may happen when rejected individuals experience both antisocial motivations and a powerful motivation for positive social evaluation: Affiliation motivations dominate at an explicit level and in the short term, but the other motivations remain implicitly active until an opportunity to satisfy them arises and may be a more predictive determinant of long-term outcomes.

In sum, there is some evidence that ostracism produces a strong control motivation, and that this may, in turn, increase the target's preparedness to aggress. However, in situations where the individual is subject to social evaluation, the powerful affiliation motivation will probably determine the nature of the ostracism target's explicit responses, overriding aggressive impulses and driving the individual toward more prosocial behaviors. In this circumstance, implicit control motivation should remain active, and may lead to *later* aggression, if control cannot be restored in some sphere.

Whereas belonging motives seem to override control motives in public domains, this may not be true of motives related to meaningful existence. One outcome that is probably more aversive than the loss of social ties is the fear of not existing at all. It is not surprising, then, that there are so many instances in which people behave in highly antisocial ways in order to be noticed, and to increase their feeling that their existence has some effect and meaning in the world. Many of the school shooters who had been ostracized by their schoolmates reported being motivated to gain respect and be noticed (Leary et al., 2003; Twenge & Campbell, 2003). For example,

Eric Harris and Dylan Klebold, who killed 13 people at Columbine High School in Littleton, Colorado, in 1999, talked of being respected because of their actions, of making other people believe anything they wanted them to believe about their exploits, and boasted that Hollywood directors would fight over their story (Twenge & Campbell, 2003). Andrew Golden, a school shooter at Jonesboro, Arizona, in 1998, appeared to be trying to gain the respect and attention of others when he told friends that "he had a lot of killing to do," and Michael Carneal, who killed three students at his school in Paducah, Kentucky, in 1997, was reported as saying afterward that "people respect me now" (Leary et al., 2003, p. 206).

Such behaviors seem consistent with a powerful social motivation to boost the importance and meaningfulness of one's own existence through being noticed, gaining social respect, or appearing powerful and resonate with predictions from Williams's (2001) model of ostracism, which argues that threats to meaningful existence may result in desperate attempts to seize attention and recognition, thus restoring the target's visibility. In addition, Williams maintains that restoring meaningful existence needs also involves maintaining cultural buffers, which is achieved in part by derogating those who violate the individual's worldview (Case & Williams, in press; Greenberg et al., 1997). Accordingly, in an attempt to validate their existence, targets of ostracism may behave provocatively, antisocially, and even aggressively.

It is important to note here that meaningful existence–related motivations also seem to have a significant control component – a need to feel or be seen as effective, powerful, and capable of independent action. We would argue, however, that control motivation alone might not be sufficient to elicit public antisocial responses to ostracism. Rather, it may be necessary for that individual to also feel that the meaning of his or her very existence is threatened. It is this fear (or even terror) that may provide the motivational impetus to behave in ways that will result in being noticed and recognized, and may swamp the motivation to belong with its power.

Although it seems that existence motivations may thus override belonging motivations at times, and may consequently drive an individual toward antisocial or aggressive behaviors, this outcome is not always observed. One example already noted is the contrasting data from Twenge et al. (in press) that suggests that ostracism-elicited existence threats may lead to a demotivated, deconstructed state. One explanation for this dichotomy in findings may be that social evaluation is the differentiating factor. In Williams's laboratory, participants may have become motivated to display social energy in the face of peer and experimenter evaluation, whereas in the experiments of Twenge et al., where participants did not face further group evaluation, participants may have felt able to withdraw into a demotivated, lethargic state.

All in all, it appears that when social motivations clash in targets of ostracism, the determinants of thoughts and behavior involve the immediacy of social evaluation, the cognitive level of the motivation (implicit versus explicit), and the relative strength of each motivation experienced within the social situation.

SUMMARY

Ostracism appears to elicit a variety of strong social motivations. Those that are related to social evaluation, such as belonging motivation and motives related to personal esteem, seem to work in parallel and without conflict to elicit explicit and generally prosocial behaviors. At times, however, these may collide with strong motivations related to control and existence. Specifically, ostracism also produces control motivation and motives related to the meaningfulness of an individual's existence, and these may produce implicit goals to aggress or behave antisocially. When evaluation-based motives conflict with control-existence motives in a public arena (where social evaluation is likely), conscious, prosocial goals are likely to direct behavior and drive conflicting motivations and goals to an implicit level, where they may influence later, less public behaviors. If an ostracized individual is able to act in a nonpublic environment, implicit efficacy and existence motives may direct that individual to behave aggressively or antisocially in order to restore a sense of personal power and control. Although there is no question that current ostracism theorists are correct in asserting that belonging motives play a vital role in determining ostracized individuals' behaviors, a case can be made that such motivations work in tandem with, or conflict with, other equally important motives, and that in certain circumstances, control and existence motives may be stronger determinants of behavior.

References

Abramson, L. Y., Seligman, M. E., & Teasdale, J. D. (1978). Learned helplessness in humans: Critique and reformulation. *Journal of Abnormal Psychology, 83*, 49–74.

Alloy, L. B., & Abramson, L. Y. (1982). Learned helplessness, depression, and the illusion of control. *Journal of Personality and Social Psychology, 42*, 1114–1126.

Anderson, C. A., & Bushman, B. J. (2002). Human aggression. *Annual Review of Psychology, 53*, 27–51.

Anderson, C. A., Carnagey, N. L., & Eubanks, J. (2003). Exposure to violent media: The effects of songs with violent lyrics on aggressive thoughts and feelings. *Journal of Personality and Social Psychology, 84*, 960–973.

Bandura, A. (1983). Psychological mechanisms of aggression. In R. G. Geen & E. Donnerstein (Eds.), *Aggression: Theoretical and empirical reviews* (pp. 1–11). New York: Academic Press.

Bandura, A. (1997). *Self-efficacy: The exercise of control.* New York: W. H. Freeman.

Bargh, J. A. (1997). The automaticity of everyday life. In R. S. Wyer, Jr. (Ed.), *The automaticity of everyday life: Advances in social cognition* (Vol. 11, pp. 1–61). Mahwah, NJ: Erlbaum.

Bargh, J. A., & Alvarez, J. (2001). The road to hell: Good intentions in the face of nonconscious tendencies to use power. In A. Y. Lee-Chai & J. A. Bargh (Eds.), *The use and abuse of power* (pp. 41–56). Philadelphia: Psychology Press.

Baumeister, R. F., & Leary, M. R. (1995). The need to belong: Desire for interpersonal attachments as a fundamental human motivation. *Psychological Bulletin, 117,* 497–529.

Baumeister, R. F., & Tice, D. M. (1990). Anxiety and social exclusion. *Journal of Social and Clinical Psychology, 9,* 165–195.

Baumeister, R. F., Twenge, J. M., & Nuss, C. K. (2002). Effects of social exclusion on cognitive processes: Anticipated aloneness reduces intelligent thought. *Journal of Personality and Social Psychology, 83,* 817–827.

Berkowitz, L. (1983). The experience of anger as a parallel process in the display of impulsive angry aggression. In R. G. Geen & E. Donnerstein (Eds.), *Aggression: Theoretical and empirical reviews, Vol. 1: Theoretical and methodological issues* (pp. 103–133). New York: Academic Press.

Berkowitz, L. (1993). Pain and aggression: Some findings and implications. *Motivation and Emotion, 17,* 277–293.

Brehm, J. W. (1966). *A theory of psychological reactance.* New York: Academic Press.

Burger, J. M. (1992). *Desire for control: Personality, social and clinical perspectives.* New York: Plenum Press.

Case, T. I., & Williams, K. D. (in press). Ostracism: A metaphor for death. In J. Greenberg, S. L. Koole, & T. Pyszczynski (Eds.), *A handbook of experimental existential psychology.* New York: Guilford Press.

deCharms, R. (1968). *Personal causation: The internal affective determinants of behavior.* New York: Academic Press.

Depret, E., & Fiske, S. T. (1993). Social cognition and power: Some cognitive consequences of social structure as a source of control deprivation. In G. Weary, F. Gleicher, & K. L. Marsh (Eds.), *Control motivation and social cognition* (pp. 176–202). New York: Springer-Verlag.

Eminem. (2000). Stan. *The Marshall Mathers LP* [CD]. Santa Monica, CA: Aftermath/Interscope.

Ezrakhovich, A., Kerr, A., Cheung, S., Elliot, K., Jerrems, A., & Williams, K. D. (1998, April). *Effects of causal clarity of ostracism on individual performance in groups.* Presented in the symposium on "Social Psychology on the Web" of the Society for Australasian Social Psychology, Christchurch, NZ.

Frieze, I. H., & Boneva, B. S. (2001). Power motivation and motivation to help others. In A. Y. Lee-Chai & J. A. Bargh (Eds.), *The use and abuse of power* (pp. 75–89). Philadelphia: Psychology Press.

Gardner, W. L., Pickett, C. L., & Brewer, M. B. (2000). Social exclusion and selective memory: How the need to belong influences memory for social events. *Personality and Social Psychology Bulletin, 26,* 486–496.

Geen, R. G. (1990). *Human aggression.* Pacific Grove CA: Brooks/Cole.

Greenberg, J., Solomon, S., & Pyszczynski, T. (1997). Terror management theory of self-esteem and cultural worldviews: Empirical assessments and conceptual refinements. In L. Berkowitz (Ed.), *Advances in Experimental Social Psychology, 29*, 61–139.

Greenberg, J., Solomon, S., Pyszczynski, T., Rosenblatt, A., Burling, J., Lyon, D., Simon, L., & Pinel, E. (1992). Why do people need self-esteem?: Converging evidence that self-esteem serves an anxiety-buffering function. *Journal of Personality and Social Psychology, 63*, 913–922.

Greenwald, A. G., McGhee, D. E., & Schwartz, J. L. K. (1998). Measuring individual differences in implicit cognition: The implicit association test. *Journal of Personality and Social Psychology, 74*, 1022–1038.

Huesmann, L. R. (1986). Psychological processes promoting the relation between exposure to media violence and aggressive behavior by the viewer. *Journal of Social Issues, 42*, 125–140.

Langer, E. J., & Rodin, J. (1975). The effects of choice and enhanced personal responsibility: A field experiment in an institutional setting. *Journal of Personality and Social Psychology, 34*, 191–198.

Lawson-Williams, H., & Williams, K. D. (1998, April). *Effects of social ostracism on desire for control.* Paper presented at the meeting of the Society for Australasian Social Psychology, Christchurch, New Zealand.

Leary, M. (Ed.). (2001). *Interpersonal rejection.* New York: Oxford University Press.

Leary, M., Kowalski, R. M., Smith, L., & Phillips, S. (2003). Teasing, rejection and violence: Case studies of the school shootings. *Aggressive Behavior, 29*, 202–214.

Leary, M. R., Tambor, E. S., Terdal, S. K., & Downs, D. L. (1995). Self-esteem as an interpersonal monitor: The sociometer hypothesis. *Journal of Personality and Social Psychology, 68*, 518–530.

McClelland, D. C. (1985). *Human motivation.* New York: Cambridge University Press.

Mueller, C. W. (1983). Environmental stressors and aggressive behavior. In R. G. Geen & E. I. Donnerstein (Eds.), *Aggression: Theoretical and empirical reviews, Vol. 2: Issues in research* (pp. 51–76). New York: Academic Press.

Murray, H. A. (1938). *Explorations in personality.* New York: Oxford University Press.

Nezlek, J., Kowalski, R., Leary, M., Blevins, T., & Holgate, S. (1997). Personality moderators of reactions to interpersonal rejection: Depression and trait self-esteem. *Personality and Social Psychology Bulletin, 23*, 1235–1244.

Pedersen, A., & Walker, I. (1997). Prejudice against Australian aborigines: Old-fashioned and modern forms. *European Journal of Social Psychology, 27*, 561–587.

Pittman, T. S., & D'Agostino, P. R. (1989). Motivation and cognition: Control deprivation and the nature of subsequent information processing. *Journal of Experimental Social Psychology, 25*, 465–480.

Pittman, T. S., & Pittman, N. L. (1980). Deprivation of control and the attribution process. *Journal of Personality and Social Psychology, 39*, 377–389.

Smith, S. L., & Donnerstein, E. (1998). Harmful effects of exposure to media violence: Learning of aggression, emotional desensitization, and fear. In R. G. Geen & E. Donnerstein (Eds.), *Human aggression: Theories, research and implications for social policy* (pp. 168–204). San Diego CA: Academic Press.

Sommer, K. L., & Baumeister, R. F. (2002). Self-evaluation, persistence, and performance following implicit rejection: The role of trait self-esteem. *Personality and Social Psychology Bulletin, 28*, 926–938.

Sommer, K. L., Williams, K. D., Ciarocco, N. J., & Baumeister, R. F. (2001). When silence speaks louder than words: Explorations into the intrapsychic and interpersonal consequences of social ostracism. *Basic and Applied Social Psychology, 23,* 225–243.

Steele, C. M. (1988). The psychology of self-affirmation: Sustaining the integrity of the self. In L. Berkowitz (Ed.), *Advances in experimental social psychology* (Vol. 21, pp. 261–302). San Diego, CA: Academic Press.

Taylor, S. E., & Brown, J. D. (1988). Illusion and well-being: A social psychological perspective on mental health. *Psychological Bulletin, 103,* 193–210.

Tedeschi, J. T., & Felson, R. B. (1994). *Violence, aggression and coercive actions.* Washington, DC: American Psychological Association.

Tesser, A. (1988). Toward a self-evaluation maintenance model of social behavior. In L. Berkowitz (Ed.), *Advances in experimental social psychology* (Vol. 21, pp. 181–227). San Diego, CA: Academic Press.

Thompson, S. C. (1981). Will it hurt less if I can control it? A complex answer to a simple question. *Psychological Bulletin, 90,* 89–101.

Tice, D. M., Twenge, J. M., & Schmeichel, B. (2002). Threatened selves: The effects of social exclusion on prosocial and anti-social behavior. In J. P. Forgas & K. D. Williams (Eds.), *The social self: Cognitive, interpersonal and intergroup perspectives* (pp. 175–188). New York: Psychology Press.

Todorov, A., & Bargh, J. A. (2002). Automatic sources of aggression. *Aggression and Violent Behavior, 7,* 53–68.

Tool. (1992). Jerk-off. On *Opiate* [CD]. New York: BMG Music.

Twenge, J. M., Baumeister, R. F., Tice, D. M., & Stucke, T. S. (2001). If you can't join them, beat them: Effects of social exclusion on aggressive behavior. *Journal of Personality and Social Psychology, 81,* 1058–1069.

Twenge, J. M., & Campbell, W. K. (2003). "Isn't it fun to get the respect we're going to deserve?" Narcissism, social rejection, and aggression. *Personality and Social Psychology Bulletin, 29,* 261–272.

Twenge, J. M., Catanese, K. R., & Baumeister, R. F. (2002). Social exclusion causes self-defeating behavior. *Journal of Personality and Social Psychology, 83,* 606–615.

Twenge, J. M., Catanese, K. R., & Baumeister, R. F. (in press). Social exclusion and the deconstructed state: Time perception, meaninglessness, lethargy, lack of emotion and self-awareness. *Journal of Personality and Social Psychology.*

Warburton, W. A. (2002). *Aggressive responding to ostracism: The moderating roles of control motivation and narcissistic vulnerability, and the mediating role of negative affect.* Unpublished honours thesis, Macquarie University, Sydney, Australia.

Wheaton, A. (2001). *Ostracism and susceptibility to the overtures of socially deviant groups and individuals.* Unpublished honours thesis, Macquarie University, Sydney, Australia.

White, R. W. (1959). Motivation reconsidered: The concept of competence. *Psychological Review, 66,* 297–333.

Williams, K. D. (1997). Social ostracism. In R. M. Kowalski (Ed.), *Aversive interpersonal behaviors: The Plenum series in social/clinical psychology* (pp. 133–170). New York: Plenum Press.

Williams, K. D. (2001). *Ostracism: The power of silence.* New York: Guilford Press.

Williams, K. D., Bernieri, F., Faulkner, S., Grahe, J., & Gada-Jain, N. (2000a). The Scarlet Letter Study: Five days of social ostracism. *Journal of Personal and Interpersonal Loss, 5,* 19–63.

Williams, K. D., Case, T. I., & Govan, C. L. (2003). Impact of ostracism on social judgments and decisions. In J. P. Forgas, K. D. Williams, & W. von Hippel (Eds.), *Social judgments: Implicit and explicit processes* (pp. 325–342). London: Cambridge University Press.

Williams, K. D., Cheung, C. K. T., & Choi, W. (2000b). Cyberostracism: Effects of being ignored over the Internet. *Journal of Personality and Social Psychology, 79,* 748–762.

Williams, K. D., Govan, C. L., Croker, V., Tynan, D., Cruickshank, M., & Lam, A. (2002). Investigations into differences between social and cyber ostracism. *Group Dynamics: Theory, Research, and Practice, 6,* 65–77.

Williams, K. D., Shore, W. J., & Grahe, J. E. (1998). The silent treatment: Perceptions of its behaviors and associated feelings. *Group Processes and Intergroup Relations, 1,* 117–141.

Williams, K. D., & Sommer, K. L. (1997). Social ostracism by coworkers: Does rejection lead to loafing or compensation? *Personality and Social Psychology Bulletin, 23,* 693–706.

Williams, K. D., & Warburton, W. A. (2003). Ostracism: A form of indirect aggression that can result in aggression. *International Review of Social Psychology, 16,* 101–126.

Williams, K. D., & Zadro, L. (2001). Ostracism: On being ignored, excluded, and rejected. In M. R. Leary (Ed.), *Interpersonal rejection* (pp. 21–53). New York: Oxford University Press.

Wortman, C. B., & Brehm, J. W. (1975). Responses to uncontrollable outcomes: An integration of reactance theory and the learned helplessness model. In L. Berkowitz (Ed.). *Advances in experimental social psychology* (Vol. 8, pp. 277–336). New York: Academic Press.

Zadro, L., Williams, K. D., & Richardson, R. (2003, April). *Interviews with long-term sources and targets of the silent treatment.* Presented at the 32nd annual meeting of the Society of Australasian Social Psychologists, Bondi Beach, Australia.

17

Attentional and Regulatory Mechanisms of Momentary Work Motivation and Performance

Howard M. Weiss, Neal M. Ashkanasy,
and Daniel J. Beal

INTRODUCTION

The study of affect in work settings, and particularly the study of the performance implications of affective states, has a long but especially disappointing history. We say disappointing for a number of reasons. First, even the smallest amount of reflection will convince anyone that organizations are settings of emotional intensity. If emotions are generated by appraisals of the reaching or impeding of important personal goals or values, then where is this more likely to play out than in work settings? Each day at work, our needs, desires, and identities are challenged and affirmed. So, one would think that the study of emotions at work would be a core topic of organizational research. It is not. Second, performance has been *the* criterion of interest for organizational researchers. So, one would think that the relationship between emotional states and work performance would receive great attention. It has not.

Third, research on the performance implications of true affective states took place at the beginning of work psychology. Hersey (1932) examined daily moods states (he didn't call them that, but he used what today would be considered a mood checklist) among blue-collar workers. He tracked those mood states with daily performance measures. He showed that on negative mood days performance deteriorated quite a bit, but on positive mood days there was little enhancement of performance. Yet, this promising beginning was lost in a paradigm shift that substituted the attitude construct of job satisfaction for affect constructs like moods and emotions (Weiss & Brief, 2001). For almost 60 years, the study of affect was pushed aside for the study of job satisfaction and the correlation of job satisfaction and performance. One of the most ubiquitous findings in this arena

Send correspondence to: Howard M. Weiss, Dept. of Psychological Sciences, Purdue University, West Lafayette, IN 47907; e-mail: weiss@psych.purdue.edu.

is the negligible relationship between job satisfaction and performance (Iaffaldano & Muchinsky, 1985). Many, confusing satisfaction with affect, took this as an indication that the performance implications of affect were not worth studying.

The 1980s and 1990s saw a rebirth of interest in affect research and with that a rebirth of interest in the performance implications of affective states. Weiss and Cropanzano (1996) developed an overarching framework for studying affect at work that has spawned a good deal of research on the topic (e.g., Ashkanasy, Härtel, & Daus, 2002; Fisher, 2000; Weiss, Nicholas, & Daus, 1999). With regard to performance, Weiss and Cropanzano (1996) argued that affect–performance relationships required better process models that focused on the consequences of true affective experiences and studied those relationships in an episodic time structure.

We think progress in this area can now be made by paying close attention to advances in the basic literature on the motivational and cognitive effects of affective states (e.g., Forgas & Laham, this volume). Organizations may be unique social settings, but behavior at work still conforms to the same psychological processes that exist everywhere. In this chapter, we will describe our own attempts to integrate some of these findings, many of which are discussed in papers presented at the Sydney Symposium, of Social Psychology (2003), into a general model of episodic work motivation and performance. Our discussion will focus particularly on using this model to explore the work performance consequences of affective states.

AFFECT AND PERFORMANCE: THE TRADITIONAL PARADIGM AND ITS LIMITATIONS

That organizational psychology is an applied field generally means that few phenomena of work life are studied without considering their performance implications. Certainly, this is true for the study of affect at work. Unfortunately, for decades it has been impossible to develop any true understanding of the relationship between affective experiences and performance because of the confusion between the constructs of job satisfaction and affect.

Since the 1930s, organizational psychologists have believed that they have been studying work-related affect when they studied job satisfaction. Operationally, job satisfaction is assessed as an attitude one has about one's job. Rigorous and ad hoc attitude scales were developed and used to measure evaluative judgments about jobs or elements of job experience (pay, coworkers, etc.). Theoretically, these operations had been thought to capture "emotions about one's job" (see Locke, 1976, for example) and so for most organizational researchers, the construct of job satisfaction was synonymous with the construct of emotion. When these researchers studied job satisfaction, they thought they were studying affect or emotions.

Numerous reviews and meta-analyses have consistently shown that job satisfaction shows negligible relations with job performance, heroic efforts to save the construct through statistical corrections notwithstanding (Judge, Thoreson, Bono, & Patton, 2001). Consequently, organizational psychologists were hard pressed to acknowledge that affect had much to do with performance. Thorough process models need not be entertained to explain relationships that do not exist. Instead, it was believed that performance could best be explained by models of workers deciding among courses of action with different payoffs.

As research on emotions heated up across the fields of psychology, organizational psychologists began to realize that the satisfaction paradigm was too narrow (see Weiss & Brief, 2001, for a history of research on affect in organizations). Emotional experiences – the fear of losing one's job, the anger at being passed over for promotion, the elation from being noticed by higher management – are not captured by the attitudinal framework of job satisfaction. Nor are the day-to-day rhythms of moods. Moods and emotions offered richer phenomena to study; moreover, the basic research on these phenomena has described consequences of clear relevance to organizational motivation and performance (see Forgas & Laham, this volume).

Throughout the 1990s, organizational research on emotions blossomed and numerous studies of affect and performance were conducted. By and large, these studies described affect in terms closer to its real meaning and followed the directions pointed out by the basic research. So, for example, organizational studies have shown that positive mood states enhance workers' creative problem solving (Estrada, Isen, & Young, 1997), encourage prosocial behavior (helping) among individual workers and work teams (George, 1990, 1991), and facilitate cooperation in negotiations (Forgas, 1998).

Limitations

It is fair to say that more recent research on affect and performance has been substantially more sophisticated than prior research on satisfaction and performance. Much of this new research has been well grounded in basic theory and findings, particularly research about the behavioral and judgmental consequences of mood states. This is a good thing. It is also fair to say, however, that this new research remains overly narrow in its perspectives, and that this narrowness owes much to the domination of applied thinking and the vestiges of the satisfaction paradigm.

One illustration of this narrowness is the overwhelming emphasis on the effects of mood states at the expense of studying the consequences of discrete emotions. Certainly, moods vary throughout the course of a day, and these variations have performance implications. However, so do discrete emotions. People respond to the events of the workday with various emotional reactions. Happiness, guilt, pride, fear, and anger comprise an important part of affective life, and organizational researchers have been slower to study these states than to focus on mood states. Why is this so? The applied nature of the field encourages us to look for easy and direct connections to performance. Organizational research is still too often driven by particular criteria. Researchers list important performance criteria, search the basic literature for affect predictors, and then demonstrate the relationship in organizational settings. In the affect area, so far, mood effects have been easier to connect to criteria (mood biases judgments, mood affects helping, etc.) than have discrete emotions. The consequences of emotional states have generally not been studied in so direct a fashion (see Neuberg et al., this volume, for an exception). We will have more to say about this later.

Another limitation comes from the satisfaction tradition itself. That tradition examined the effects of between-person differences in attitudes on between-person differences in performance. The classic question is whether more satisfied workers are more productive workers. Much of the newer affect literature follows this between-persons paradigm. So, for example, researchers ask whether people who report typically being in positive states are more likely to do X or Y. Even when purportedly assessing *affect states*, researchers use between-person assessments that strain the concept of state. George (1991), for example, looked at "mood states" by asking people to report their general affect levels over a week's time. Apart from whether people can make such judgments accurately, such between-person assessments of aggregated affect states ignore one of the most important aspects of affective experience: their momentary and transient nature (see Robinson & Clore, 2002, for a discussion of episodic versus semantic memory for emotional experiences).

The between-person model is severely limiting for the study of affect–performance relationships. Yet, although troublesome, the dominance of this paradigm in organizational research is not surprising. Indeed, the prevailing model of organizational research looks at the associations among various characteristics of organizationally relevant entities. This approach assumes that organizational phenomena are best modeled as relationships among features or characteristics that vary across entities. In most cases the entities are people, but in other cases the entities are teams or even organizations as a whole. So, for example, organizational researchers study whether individual properties such as intelligence or conscientiousness predict performance, with performance taken as a relatively stable feature of the person (i.e., what kind of performer is he?). One consequence of this prevailing approach is the almost exclusive use of between-persons designs to study organizational processes, comparing people (or teams or organizations) with different levels of the characteristic of interest. Given the fundamental acceptance of this approach, it is easy to see why satisfaction was, for a very long time, the accepted way to study affect. With satisfaction, affect could be studied as a property of individual workers, and the association of that property with properties of tasks or jobs could be examined.

Unfortunately, the associated properties paradigm is inappropriate for studying affect–performance relationships for several reasons. One reason is that affect itself is not well conceptualized as a property of individuals (Ekman & Davidson, 1994; Larsen, 1987). Affective experiences, whether they are moods or discrete emotions, are transient states. Happiness, sadness, pride, and anger are not characteristics of people. They are experiential states that vary meaningfully over time within individuals. As a consequence, studying them as properties is inherently limiting.

Of course, a counterargument is that there is stability to these states when they are aggregated over time. That is, although it is true that individuals vary over time in their own levels of affect, there also are individual differences in characteristic levels of affective states that can be understood and studied as properties. Although there is meaningful between-person variance in affect, this between-person variance generally is lower than the within-person variance on the same constructs (Fleeson, 2001; Larsen, 1987). Further – and this point will be emphasized later – treating affect as disposition tends to obscure affective processes in organizational settings (Weiss et al., 1999).

Another reason the associated properties paradigm is inappropriate for studying affect–performance relations is that performance is not a stable construct. Although the transient nature of affective states is easy to accept, the meaningfulness of within-person variance in performance is too often dismissed. Organizational researchers have understood for quite a long time that performance varies within persons (e.g., Kane & Lawler, 1979). Many organizational researchers, however, have generally considered this within-person variability to be an error in the context of the associated properties paradigm. However, recent work has documented how much variance in performance is ignored by dismissing the within-person component and has started to model this component of the total variance in performance. So, for example, Fisher and Noble (2004) measured momentary performance five times a day over a 2-week period. They found that 78% of the total (i.e., the sum of the within- and between-persons) variance in performance was within-persons variance. Other researchers conducting variance components analyses of performance have often found nearly 50% or more of the variance to be due to within-person fluctuations (e.g., Deadrick, Bennett, & Russell, 1997; Miner, 2001). Further, this within-person variance is not simply error, as it is systematically related to other variables measured in the same time frame.

Although it is clear that the percentage of total variance accounted for by within- and between-persons factors will vary across people, jobs, and measurement procedures, the lesson will still be the same. Performance varies across time; that variance is systematic, not error; and between-persons analyses cannot capture the processes that account for these changes.

WITHIN-PERSON ANALYSES OF AFFECT AND
WORK PERFORMANCE

Affective states show meaningful changes over time. Performance shows meaningful changes over time. Emotion research tells us that the consequences of emotions are likely to have performance implications. Taken together, the conclusion drawn from these findings is obvious. Meaningful examinations of the relationships between affect and work performance must model the momentary relationship between changes in affective states and changes in episodic performance. In the remaining sections of this chapter, we will lay out some thoughts about the momentary processes that describe these relationships.

Two Categories of Affect–Performance Processes

Weiss and Cropanzano (1996) made the distinction between *affect*-driven and *judgment*-driven work behaviors. Affect-driven behaviors are those behaviors, decisions, and judgments that have (relatively) immediate consequences of being in particular affective states. Affective states are the proximal causes of these behaviors and, as such, they are temporally co-incident with those states and consequently time bound. So, for example, people may display more creative problem solving or more helping behavior when in a positive mood. When that mood disappears, so do the consequences for creativity and helping. Judgment-driven behaviors are those behaviors, decisions, or judgments that are driven by more enduring attitudes about the job or organization. Evaluative judgments, or attitudes, are the proximal causes of these behaviors, although affective experiences may influence those attitudes as well. Generally, these behaviors are determined by more considered decision-making processes. So, for example, job satisfaction and organizational commitment predict turnover. Presumably they do so by entering into a decision process in which attitude toward the job is one factor being considered. Immediate affective states may play a smaller proximal role and some distal role, but they do not drive the behavior in the same immediate and time-bound manner that is seen with affect-driven behaviors.

Weiss and Cropanzano (1996) made this distinction to call attention to the differences between satisfaction as attitude and true affect and to show why satisfaction/attitude historically has shown weak associations with job performance. True affective experiences do, in fact, have important performance implications, but they are relatively immediate, transient, and variable within persons over time. Weiss and Cropanzano further argued that productive analyses of affect and performance would require that assessment of true affective experiences (moods and emotions) replace measures of job satisfaction, that such research be done using within-persons analyses, and that better process models based upon the burgeoning literature on the consequences of affective states be developed.

We think we are now in a position to accomplish this research agenda. The field of organizational psychology has (grudgingly) accepted the idea that job satisfaction is a very poor way to operationalize affective experiences at work. Newer data collection [Ecological Momentary Assessment (EMA)] and analytic (multilevel modeling) techniques allow for rigorous within-person research. The basic research on moods and emotions has made real progress in understanding the consequences of affective states, and there is now a genuine opportunity to start using that basic research to understand how these states impact job performance.

For heuristic purposes, we have organized our thoughts about affect–performance processes into two broad categories. Some behaviors and cognitive processes are the natural consequences of the affective state itself. So, for example, positive moods appear to enhance creativity. For want of a better term, we will refer to these as *direct effects*. Other behaviors and cognitive processes are the general (non-emotion-specific) consequences of either the interfering elements of the emotional state or the attempts to regulate affective states. To contrast these processes with the more direct processes we might call these *indirect* processes, although *nonspecific* might be more descriptive.

Our primary interest is in these latter processes, and we will spend some time talking about them. However, we would be remiss if we did not at least acknowledge the more direct effects. Research on the effects of moods and emotions on behaviors, judgments, creativity, and so on is extensive (see Weiss, 2002, for a review.). For example, research indicates that moods and emotions bias ratings and judgments in the direction of the state. People evaluate all manner of things (reports, other people) throughout the workday, and these evaluations tend to be more positive when they are in a positive affective state and more negative when they are in a negative affective state (Bower, 1981, 1991; Weiss, 2002). Research also indicates that being in a positive mood seems to lead to a more heuristic processing style with more reliance on existing knowledge structures. In addition, perhaps the most widely supported finding regarding positive moods is that they enhance innovation and creative problem solving (Isen, 1999, 2000).

In contrast, negative moods foster a more systematic information processing style that relies on a detailed examination of the available information (Fiedler, 2001; Schwarz, 2000). People in negative moods have been found to rely less on stereotypes (Park & Banaji, 2000) and to be less persuaded by weak arguments than those in positive moods (Bless, Mackie, & Schwarz, 1992). In addition, affective states influence various social behaviors. Isen and Baron (1991) review the evidence demonstrating that positive mood promotes helping behavior. Furthermore, positive mood seems to promote cooperation during negotiations (Baron, 1990; Forgas, 1998). Isen (2000) asserts that positive mood, in general, leads to better interactions with others.

When moods and emotions occur at work, they are likely to have direct effects on performance. At least for the duration of the affective state, certain behavioral styles are favored over others. Whether a particular affective state contributes to or hinders a performance episode depends on the match between the performance requirements of the situation and the particular consequences of the specific affective state (Weiss & Cropanzano, 1996).

Finally, although we have followed the literature and focused primarily on the behavioral and cognitive effects of mood states, we should point out that discrete emotions also have direct effects that are consequential for work performance. However, discrete emotions clearly have behavioral consequences specific to particular emotions (anger and aggression or shame and withdrawal, for example; see Neuberg et al., this volume). Further, research now shows that discrete emotions have unique cognitive processing outcomes as well (DeSteno, Petty, Wegener, & Rucker, 2000; Keltner, Elsworth, & Edwards, 1993). As with moods, the performance implications of the consequences of these emotions depend upon the job requirements.

In this section, we have discussed the numerous ways in which affect can have a direct effect upon a variety of performance-related processes such as creativity, organizational citizenship, retaliatory behavior, and systematic processing of relevant work stimuli. As we go through the workday, fluctuations in our moods color how we perform a variety of tasks and may help explain some portion of the within-person variability in performance. These affective processing styles influence performance directly (e.g., Estrada et al., 1997; Forgas, 1998; Isen, 2000). The next section turns to the second category of explanatory processes, those more nonspecific consequences of attentional and regulatory processes.

COGNITIVE AND REGULATORY DETERMINANTS OF WITHIN-PERSON PERFORMANCE

Aside from the direct effects of affect on processing style, what role do emotions play in determining how well someone performs at any given moment in time? Broadly, we focus on two intermediate processes. First, we discuss the amount of attention or cognitive resources devoted to the current task as a primary determinant of performance. Second, we examine the regulation of these cognitive resources toward or away from the focal task. The role of self-regulation is more complex, as it includes both the motivation and the ability to regulate attention. Moreover, the effects of self-regulation are temporally prior to those of attention in determining performance during a particular episode. As such, a detailed causal analysis of these processes is necessarily more elaborate. Throughout our discussion of the processes that link affect with performance, we will also identify potential moderators of these effects that are particularly relevant to performance in an organizational setting.

Affect, Cognitive Resources, and Performance

Central to the link between affect and performance is the simple notion that greater attention to the task will lead to higher levels of performance, all else being equal. The within-person perspective is particularly important here. We do not suggest that, across people, attention to the task is the best predictor of performance. When considering fluctuations within a single person's performance, however, the amount of attention paid to the task is perhaps the best and most proximal predictor of how well the person will perform at any given occasion (Kahneman, 1973; Nissen & Bullemer, 1987). Thus, our theorizing on the indirect effects of affect on performance focuses on how emotional experiences can take attention away from the current task, thereby resulting in lower performance.

We should mention that most of the indirect effects we discuss involve actual emotion episodes as opposed to more diffuse moods. As such, these affective experiences involve some sense of agency for their causes. That is, one of the key differences between emotions and moods is that there are attributable reasons or targets for emotions (Frijda, 1993): Someone angers you; you feel pride in discernible accomplishments; and you are elated in response to a particular occurrence. Because emotions have perceivable causes, when an emotion is experienced at work, the cause of that emotion represents an additional element to consider in the work environment. That is, tasks compete with external concerns for attention. Assuming that the emotion episode is not directly related to the task at hand, any attention paid to the cause of the emotion will, by definition, detract from attention that could be devoted to that task. If the task requires a high level of attention, then one's performance on the task will most likely suffer as a result of the emotional event.

Implicit in this logic is the notion that the cognitive resource requirements of the task will moderate emotion–performance relations. If the task does not require significant cognitive resources, then one can focus these resources on the emotion-eliciting target without noticeable decrements in the level of performance. If, however, the task is highly complex, requiring more than trivial amounts of attention, then the presence of an emotion-eliciting target will frequently draw attention away from the task, resulting in lower levels of performance (Posner & Snyder, 1975; Schneider & Fisk, 1982).

Recently, Weiss, Beal, and Groves (2003) tested this hypothesis in a laboratory study examining the performance implications of an emotional event. Participants were brought into the lab and told that we would be examining the effects of rewards on task performance. Participants also were told that they might or might not be participating in a psychology department questionnaire to evaluate experiences during experimental participation. Whether or not they participated in this second part would be decided later at random. At this point, all participants worked on an anagram task and were told that if they scored above average, they would be allowed to draw for potential monetary prizes. The purpose of this design was to manipulate various forms of injustice because being treated unfairly (particularly with negative outcomes) is often experienced as an emotional event.

At this point, the outcomes of the anagram tasks were manipulated so that some people scored above average (did get to draw) and some people scored below average (did not get to draw). The drawing was rigged so that everyone drawing received a $30 prize. Subsequently, however, the experimenter informed participants in the unfair condition that they could not keep the money because they had been chosen to take part in the psychology department evaluation, and that incentives could not be given prior to this evaluation because it would bias the results. Thus, participants who had just drawn a $30 prize had the prize unfairly taken away from them. Participants in the fair condition were not told this and assumed that they could keep the money (in actuality, no prizes were given, but all participants were given equal chances at a drawing for a larger prize to be held later).

All participants next completed the "psychology department evaluation," which consisted of an affect questionnaire and suitable filler items. Finally, participants completed a second task (paper-folding puzzles) for an even larger potential reward. Two versions of this task existed: a fairly simple version and a complex version (in pilot testing, performance on the simple version was fairly resistant to cognitive load effects, whereas performance on the complex version declined with the introduction of cognitive load). Time to completion on this task served as the dependent measure of performance.

First of all, the manipulation of affective reactions was effective. Participants in the unfair condition had significantly higher levels of anger in comparison to all other conditions. More important, however, the justice by task complexity interaction was significant for puzzle task performance.

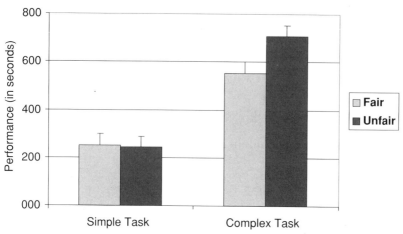

FIGURE 17.1 Effects of procedural justice and task complexity on performance.

As can be seen in Figure 17.1, for the simple task it did not matter whether the participants were treated fairly or unfairly. For participants in the complex task, however, those who were treated unfairly performed worse than those who were treated fairly. Thus, the cognitive demands of the task moderated the expected emotion–performance relation.

It is likely that participants were not simply distracted by the presence of the person who treated them unfairly. That is, attending to the emotion-eliciting stimulus is not the only reason we think about our emotions instead of the current task. Most people can attest to the fact that their thoughts continue to dwell on emotional experiences well after the cause of the emotion is gone. Generally, this concept is referred to as *rumination*, and recently it has been examined from several different perspectives, including the nature and causes of ruminative thought (Martin & Tesser, 1996). Martin and Tesser have defined rumination as "a class of conscious thoughts that revolve around a common instrumental theme and that recur in the absence of immediate environmental demands requiring the thoughts" (p. 7).

When does rumination occur? Martin and Tesser discuss one main precursor of rumination: discrepancies in goal progress. When people realize that they are not making progress toward a goal, they are more likely to engage in rumination relevant to the goal and the causes of the goal blockage, perhaps because of enhanced accessibility of the goal (see Liberman & Förster, this volume). Furthermore, because goals are contained within a hierarchy of importance, it is probable that blockage of more important goals will cause greater rumination than blockage of less important goals. Goal blockage can also precede an emotional response such as frustration, anger, or anxiety (Averill, 1983; Berkowitz, 1989). Indeed, many psychologists have suggested that emotional reactions can serve to inform people that progress toward a goal has been halted (e.g., Carver & Scheier, 1998), resulting in increased ruminative thought (Martin & Tesser, 1996). The exact causal dynamics of the emotion–rumination link, however, are less clear (but see Forgas & Laham, this volume). For example, rumination can occur in the absence of negative or any emotional experience (Martin & Stoner, 1996), and people do not always ruminate about their emotions. It appears obvious, however, that emotions play an important role in the initiation and persistence of ruminative thought.

Affect, Self-Regulation, and Performance

We have just discussed several ways in which experiencing an emotion can affect performance, either by directly stealing attention from a task or by encouraging off-task ruminative thought, which also steals attention. Obviously, we require cognitive resources to perform many work tasks. Sometimes, however, we can prevent emotions from affecting our performance on a given task simply by refusing to succumb to their distracting or ruminative effects. That is, occasionally we can self-regulate our thoughts and emotions so that the attention-grabbing and ruminative potentials of an emotion are kept at bay. Such regulation allows us to refocus our cognitive resources on the task at hand, minimizing the impact of emotions on performance. Whether workers are successful at this type of self-regulation is determined mainly by two factors: their motivation to attend to the task, and their ability to regulate attention in line with their goals.

Emotion Regulation in a Work Environment

Attentional Pull. When considering the reasons people are willing to regulate their attention toward the task at hand, we obviously consider the motivating aspects of the task itself. Many of the aspects that draw attention to work parallel the broad research literature on work motivation. We do not wish to canvass this voluminous area; instead, we offer several examples that make the comparison clear. First, the attentional pull of the task itself brings to mind research on intrinsic motivation (Harackiewicz et al., this volume; Pintrich & de Groot, 1990). That is, if the task itself generates significant interest among employees, then it should be far easier for these employees to regulate their attention to the task as opposed to other potential distractions, including interfering emotional events. To the extent that tasks are intrinsically motivating, they should have a relative advantage over less intrinsically motivating tasks in terms of cognitive interference from emotions.

The work environment can also affect our willingness to regulate attention to the task. In particular, goal-setting theory (Locke & Latham, 1990) discusses how difficult specific goals, in comparison to other types of goals, cause people to focus their attention on the task. Although there is little empirical work on this tenet of goal-setting theory, the implication is that difficult specific goals may serve as a buffer to the attention-grabbing elements of emotional events, making effective attention regulation easier. Undoubtedly, other elements of the work environment apart from particular goal-setting strategies (e.g., job enrichment, perceived organizational support) can also impact on the attentional pull of the task at hand.

Self-Regulatory Ability. In contrast to our willingness to regulate attention to work is the additional factor of our ability to regulate attention to the task as opposed to focusing on the events surrounding emotional experiences or the emotions themselves. First, we must consider the attentional allure of the off-task concern. For example, it is easy to understand how people are capable of maintaining their focus on work instead of on a relatively minor and common event such as getting a bad parking spot. At the moment of the occurrence it may have held some emotional significance, but most people do not ruminate on such occurrences throughout the day. In contrast, getting into an accident in the parking lot may present a greater challenge to the attentional pull of the task. Thus, all emotional events do not have equal ruminative potential, and as such, they can present a greater challenge to our ability to regulate task-focused attention.

Aside from the relative ruminative potential of emotional events, there is another key factor that helps to determine whether we are able to marshal our attention to performance. Muraven and Baumeister (2000) posit that our self-regulatory resources are finite in capacity and that they drain with continued use. In fact, they use the analogy of a muscle to describe the workings of our self-regulatory abilities. At its peak, we are most able to engage in self-regulation successfully, but with each additional regulatory burden (e.g., maintaining a diet, regulating emotions, staying focused on a task) this limited ability is lessened. Without a chance to replenish our self-regulatory resources (i.e., allow the muscle time to regain its strength), a failure to regulate successfully is inevitable. Interestingly, the same resource is affected irrespective of the particular type of self-regulation (Muraven, Tice, & Baumeister, 1998) or whether the regulation is conscious or unconscious (Vohs, 2003). So, whether we are working toward implicit achievement goals or trying not to think about the recent auto accident or the feeling of anxiety we have concerning it, we are depleting the same resource. Undoubtedly some self-regulatory efforts are greater resource drains than others, but because they all affect our general capacity to regulate, all efforts at self-regulation play a part in our ability to stay focused on a given task.

Emotions, Regulation, Attention, and Performance

Now that we have laid out what we see as the relevant processes linking emotions and performance, we will summarize how they fit together and influence the performances of a single person performing across time. We begin with the experience of an emotional event that has implications for the workplace. For example, upon arrival at work we get into a small auto accident in the parking lot. Once the event itself has passed and cannot directly occupy our attention, there are many aspects of the event, such as financial and time burdens, that could potentially block goals and set in motion the tendency to ruminate. Obviously, such rumination would serve to interfere with the tasks on our "to do" list, but all is not yet lost: Being aware of the ruminative potential of the accident and its potentially negative effects on work, we attempt to suppress our thoughts concerning the accident and focus instead on our list.

At this point, our notions concerning self-regulation come into play. If the task is one with substantial pull (e.g., high intrinsic or extrinsic interest, a well-defined and difficult objective) or there is a high degree of motivation to perform, it may be quite easy to put aside our concerns over the accident and focus our attention on the task. If, however, there is little performance motivation, it may be quite difficult to stay on task. In such cases, the burden on our regulatory resources will be comparably greater. Given that it is the beginning of the day, we can assume (for the sake of the example) that our regulatory resources are near their peak and that the immediate regulation of our attention to the task is successful. Such a regulatory effort, however, comes at a price, for it has depleted significant amounts of our regulatory resources, making future efforts at self-regulation more difficult. The consequences of this depletion may be observed later in the day, when it becomes difficult to focus our attention on much of anything except every passing fancy.

CONCLUSIONS

We have said that the traditional approach to examining links between affect and work performance has produced disappointing results. That disappointment has been a direct result of the failure to distinguish between job satisfaction and true affective states. The treatment of satisfaction as equivalent to emotion has led to a long history of comparing performance differences among people who differ in job satisfaction and assuming that these (mostly insignificant) associations were informing us about the role of affect.

The recent focus on true affective experiences in work settings has opened up new ways of thinking about the performance consequences of affective states. Specifically, it has forced recognition of the time-bound nature of those associations and the need for within-persons designs and models for appropriate study. Further, the productive research on the cognitive and behavioral consequences of affective states has provided more directions for developing process discussions of the relationship between affect and work performance. In this chapter, we have offered some thoughts on a general approach for studying this relationship that, we hope, will lead to a newer appreciation of the performance implications of affective experiences at work.

References

Ashkanasy, N. M., Härtel, C. E. J., & Daus, C. S. (2002). Advances in organizational behavior: Diversity and emotions. *Journal of Management, 28*, 307–338.

Averill, J. R. (1983). Studies on anger and aggression: Implications for theories of emotion. *American Psychologist, 38*, 1145–1160.

Baron, R. A. (1990). Environmentally induced positive affect: Its impact on self-efficacy, task performance, negotiation, and conflict. *Journal of Applied Social Psychology, 20*, 368–384.

Berkowitz, L. (1989). Frustration-aggression hypothesis: Examination and reformulation. *Psychological Bulletin, 106*, 59–73.

Bless, H., Mackie, D. M., & Schwarz, N. (1992). Mood effects on attitude judgments: Independent effects of mood before and after message elaboration. *Journal of Personality and Social Psychology, 63*, 585–595.

Bower, G. H. (1981). Mood and memory. *American Psychologist, 36*, 129–148.

Bower, G. H. (1991). Mood congruity of social judgments. In J. P. Forgas (Ed.), *Affect and social judgments* (pp. 31–53). Oxford: Pergamon.

Brief, A. P., & Weiss, H. M. (2002). Organizational behavior: Affect at work. *Annual Review of Psychology, 53*, 279–307.

Carver, C. S., & Scheier, M. F. (1998). The self-regulation of behavior. In R. Wyer & T. Srull (Eds.), *Advances in social cognition* (Vol. 12, pp. 1–105). Mahwah, NJ: Erlbaum.

Deadrick, D. L., Bennett, N., & Russell, C. J. (1997). Using hierarchical linear modeling to examine dynamic performance criteria over time. *Journal of Management, 23*, 745–757.

DeSteno, D., Petty, R. E., Wegener, D. T., & Rucker, D. D. (2000). Beyond valence in the perception of likelihood: The role of emotion specificity. *Journal of Personality and Social Psychology, 78*, 397–416.

Ekman, P., & Davidson, R. J. (1994). *The nature of emotion.* New York: Oxford University Press.

Estrada, C. A., Isen, A. M., & Young, M. J. (1997). Positive affect facilitates integration of information and decreases anchoring in reasoning among physicians. *Organizational Behavior and Human Decision Processes, 72*, 117–135.

Fiedler, K. (2001). Affective influences on social information processing. In J. P. Forgas (Ed.), *Handbook of affect and social cognition* (pp. 163–185). Mahwah, NJ: Erlbaum.

Fisher, C. D. (2000). Mood and emotions while working: Missing pieces of job satisfaction? *Journal of Organizational Behavior, 21*, 185–202.

Fisher, C. D., & Noble, C. S. (2004). A within-person examination of correlates of performance and emotions while working. *Human Performance, 17*, 145–168.

Fleeson, W. (2001). Toward a structure- and process-integrated view of personality: Traits as density distributions of states. *Journal of Personality and Social Psychology, 80*, 1011–1027.

Forgas, J. P. (1998). On feeling good and getting your way: Mood effects on negotiator cognition and bargaining strategies. *Journal of Personality and Social Psychology, 74*, 565–577.

Frijda, N. H. (1993). Moods, emotion episodes, and emotions. In M. Lewis & J. M. Haviland (Eds.), *Handbook of emotions* (pp. 381–404). New York: Guilford Press.

George, J. M. (1990). Personality, affect, and behavior in groups. *Journal of Applied Psychology, 75*, 107–116.

George, J. M. (1991). State or trait: Effects of positive mood on prosocial behaviors at work. *Journal of Applied Psychology, 76*, 299–307.

Hersey, R. B. (1932). *Workers' emotions in shop and home: A study of individual workers from the psychological and physiological standpoint.* Philadelphia: University of Pennsylvania Press.

Iaffaldano, M. T., & Muchinsky, P. M. (1985). Job satisfaction and job performance: A meta-analysis. *Psychological Bulletin, 97*, 251–273.

Isen, A. M. (1999). Positive affect. In T. Dalgleish & M. Power (Eds.), *Handbook of cognition and emotion* (pp. 521–540). Chichester, England: Wiley.

Isen, A. M. (2000). Positive affect and decision making. In M. Lewis & J. M. Haviland-Jones (Eds.), *Handbook of emotions* (2nd ed., pp. 417–435). New York: Guilford Press.

Isen, A., & Baron, R. (1991). Positive affect as a factor in organizational behavior. In L. L. Cummings & B. M. Staw (Eds.), *Research in organizational behavior* (Vol. 13, pp. 1–54). Greenwich, CT: JAI Press.

Judge, T. A., Thoresen, C. J., Bono, J. E., & Patton, G. K. (2001). The job satisfaction–job performance relationship: A qualitative and quantitative review. *Psychological Bulletin, 127*, 376–407.

Kahneman, D. (1973). *Attention and effort.* Englewood Cliffs, NJ: Prentice-Hall.

Kane, J. S., & Lawler, E. E. (1979). Performance appraisal effectiveness: Its assessment and determinants. In B. Staw (Ed.), *Research in organizational behavior* (Vol. 1, pp. 425–478). Greenwich, CT: JAI Press.

Keltner, D., Ellsworth, P. C., & Edwards, K. (1993). Beyond simple pessimism: Effects of sadness and anger on social perception. *Journal of Personality and Social Psychology, 64*, 740–752.

Larsen, R. J. (1987). The stability of mood variability: A spectral analytic approach to daily mood assessments. *Journal of Personality and Social Psychology, 52*, 1195–1204.

Locke, E. A. (1976). The nature and causes of job satisfaction. In M. Dunnette (Ed.), *Handbook of industrial and organizational psychology* (pp. 1297–1350). Chicago: Rand McNally.

Locke, E. A., & Latham, G. P. (1990). *A theory of goal setting and task performance.* Englewood Cliffs, NJ: Prentice-Hall.

Martin, L. L., & Stoner, P. (1996). Mood as input: What we think about how we feel determines how we think. In L. L. Martin & A. Tesser (Eds.), *Striving and feeling: Interactions among goals, affect, and self-regulation* (pp. 279–301). Hillsdale, NJ: Erlbaum.

Martin, L. L., & Tesser, A. (1996). Some ruminative thoughts. In R. S. Wyer, Jr. (Ed.), *Advances in social cognition* (Vol. 9, pp. 1–47). Mahwah, NJ: Erlbaum.

Miner, A. G. (2001). *Experience sampling events, moods, behaviors, and performance at work.* Unpublished doctoral dissertation, University of Illinois, Urbana-Champaign.

Muraven, M., & Baumeister, R. F. (2000). Self-regulation and depletion of limited resources: Does self-control resemble a muscle? *Psychological Bulletin, 126,* 247–259.

Muraven, M., Tice, D. M., & Baumeister, R. F. (1998). Self-control as a limited resource: Regulatory depletion patterns. *Journal of Personality and Social Psychology, 74,* 774–789.

Nissen, M. J., & Bullemer, P. (1987). Attentional requirements of learning: Evidence from performance measures. *Cognitive Psychology, 19,* 1–32.

Park, J., & Banaji, M. R. (2000). Mood and heuristics: The influence of happy and sad states on sensitivity and bias in stereotyping. *Journal of Personality and Social Psychology, 78,* 1005–1023.

Pintrich, P. R., & de Groot, E. V. (1990). Motivational and self-regulated learning components of classroom academic performance. *Journal of Educational Psychology, 82,* 33–40.

Posner, M. I., & Snyder, C. R. R. (1975). Attention and cognitive control. In R. L. Solso (Ed.), *Information processing and cognition* (pp. 55–85). Hillsdale, NJ: Erlbaum.

Robinson, M. D., & Clore, G. L. (2002). Belief and feeling: Evidence for an accessibility model of emotional self-report. *Psychological Bulletin, 128,* 934–960.

Schneider, W., & Fisk, A. D. (1982). Dual task automatic and control processing: Can it be done without cost? *Journal of Experimental Psychology: Learning, Memory, and Cognition, 8,* 261–278.

Schwarz, N. (2000). Emotion, cognition, and decision making. *Cognition and Emotion, 14,* 433–440.

Vohs, K. D. (2003, February). *Nonconscious self-regulation and the limited resource model.* Poster presented at the fourth annual meeting of the Society for Personality and Social Psychology, Los Angeles.

Weiss, H. M. (2002). Conceptual and empirical foundations for the study of affect at work. In R. G. Lord, R. J. Klimoski, & R. Kanfer (Eds.), *Emotions in the workplace: Understanding the structure and role of emotions in organizational behavior* (pp. 20–63). San Francisco: Jossey-Bass.

Weiss, H. M., Beal, D. J., & Groves, M. S. (2003, April). *Injustice affects performance through anger and cognitive interference.* Paper presented at the 18th annual conference of the Society for Industrial and Organizational Psychology, Orlando, FL.

Weiss, H. M., & Brief, A. P. (2001). Affect at work: An historical perspective. In R. L. Payne & C. L. Cooper (Eds.), *Emotions at work: Theory, research, and application in management* (pp. 133–173). Chichester, England: Wiley.

Weiss, H. M., & Cropanzano, R. (1996). Affective events theory: A theoretical discussion of the structure, causes and consequences of affective experiences at work.

In B. M. Staw & L. L. Cummings (Eds.), *Research in organizational behavior* (Vol. 18, pp. 1–74). Greenwich, CT: Jai Press.

Weiss, H. M., Nicholas, J. P., & Daus, C. (1999). An examination of the joint effects of affective experiences and job beliefs on job satisfaction and variations in affective experiences over time. *Organizational Behavior and Human Decision Processes, 78,* 1–24.

18

Social Motivation and Object Relations

Narcissism and Interpersonal Self-Esteem Regulation

Frederick Rhodewalt

INTRODUCTION

The construct of narcissism has enjoyed a long but controversial history in clinical psychology (Akhtar & Thompson, 1982; Cooper, 1959; Rhodewalt & Sorrow, 2002). In this literature, narcissism is viewed as a rich and complex personality disorder organized around the core characteristic of pathological self-love. Paradoxically, narcissistic self-love does not exist in an intrapsychic vacuum but rather is played out within the individual's interpersonal relationships. Thus, for the narcissist, social motivation involves interacting with others for the purpose of self-esteem maintenance or enhancement. The narcissist's dependence on others for a sense of self-worth and validation is the focus of this chapter.

The issue of social motivation has long been at the heart of psychoanalytic models of narcissism. Despite the fact that there has been considerable debate about causes and manifestations of the disorder, the major psychodynamic theorists appear to agree that adult narcissism results from a childhood history of problematic interpersonal relationships. As adults, narcissists possess grandiose self-concepts that incorporate a conflicted psychological dependence on others. For example, Kohut (1971) proposed that normal development of the self occurs through interactions with others who provide the child with opportunities to gain approval and enhancement and simultaneously allow the child to identify with positive or perfect models. When significant others (parents) fail to provide these opportunities or are unempathetic, children undergo developmental arrest in which they childishly view the social world as being there to fulfill their needs. Although they appear grandiose and invulnerable on the outside, narcissists are, according to Kohut, empty and isolated on the inside and, thus, are overly dependent on others to maintain self-esteem through

Address correspondence to Frederick Rhodewalt at e-mail: fred.rhodewalt@psych.utah.edu.

mirroring and association. In contrast, Kernberg (1976) views narcissism as a defense against cold and rejecting parents. The child focuses on some aspect of the self that the parents did value, develops a grandiose self-concept around these core aspects, and "splits" off or denies perceived weakness. In Kernberg's view, narcissism is a fixation in which the individual is unable to differentiate actual self-representations, ideal self-representations, and ideal significant other representations. It is a lack of clear self-knowledge that causes the narcissist to depend so heavily on others for a sense of self. In a similar vein, Annie Reich (1960) describes the narcissistic defect as the inability of a mature ego to test reality and develop an accurate sense of self. In her view, the narcissist engages in a pathological form of self-esteem regulation involving chronic compensatory self-inflation in order to support a megalomanic self-image.

In summary, there appears to be a consensus among clinical theorists that narcissism is energized by concerns about self-esteem maintenance and enhancement. Moreover, and most important, narcissists' self-esteem concerns are played out and satisfied or frustrated through their social interactions. Narcissistic social motivation, the desire to interact with others, is largely for the purpose of self-esteem regulation.

Why are other people's evaluations so important to the self-esteem of narcissists? Current interpersonal theories of self-esteem suggest at least two interpersonal motives: social acceptance and dominance (Leary, 2002; see also Warburton & Williams, this volume). Sociometer theory (Leary, 1999; Leary & Baumeister, 2000; Leary & Downs, 1995) contends that self-esteem serves as an internal gauge that indicates one's level of social acceptance or inclusion. Diminishing self-esteem cues the individual that his or her social value is declining. The prime social motive, according to sociometer theory, is to maintain and enhance relational value because doing so is adaptive. According to this view, people are not motivated to increase their self-esteem per se.

Similar to sociometer theory, Barkow's (1975) dominance theory assumes that self-esteem is an indicator of a person's relation to the social environment. However, rather than signaling social inclusion, self-esteem monitors social dominance. The self-esteem system monitors one's social standing and motivates responses that increase standing or dominance. Leary (2002) contends that although social acceptance and dominance are inherently confounded in the real world, survey data indicate that both account for unique variance in self-esteem.

The question, then, is, do narcissists seek positive regard from others because they want to be accepted or because they want to be admired? I will attempt to address this question in the following pages. Specifically, the goals of this chapter are to present briefly our evolving social cognitive self-regulatory processing model of narcissism (Morf & Rhodewalt, 2001a, 2001b; Rhodewalt, 2001; Rhodewalt & Sorrow, 2002) and to focus on self-esteem regulation and social motivation. It will present new data and attempt to integrate our work on narcissistic social motivation with contemporary interpersonal approaches to self-esteem (Leary, 2002). The chapter will conclude by extending the lessons from the study of narcissism to the issue of social motivation and people in general.

NARCISSISM AS PERSONALITY PROCESS: A DYNAMIC SELF-REGULATION PERSPECTIVE

Narcissism embodies a diverse set of cognitive, affective, and behavioral characteristics. The *Statistical Manual of Mental Disorders* (*DSM-IV-TR*) (American Psychiatric Association, 2000) lists the following characteristics as defining the syndrome: (a) a pervasive pattern of grandiosity, self-importance, and perceived uniqueness; (b) a preoccupation with fantasies of unlimited success, wealth, beauty, and power; (c) exhibitionism and attention seeking, and (d) emotional lability, particularly in response to criticism or threat to self-esteem, with feelings of rage, shame, or humiliation. According to the *DSM-IV-TR*, narcissists are also prone to interpersonal difficulties. Not surprisingly, these difficulties most likely arise from their own doing. Narcissists display entitlement and expect special treatment from others without the need to reciprocate or show empathy. In fact, they exploit others for their own needs. With regard to self-esteem, the *DSM-IV-TR* specifies that "self-esteem is almost invariably very fragile; the person may be preoccupied with how well he or she is doing and how well he or she is regarded by others. . . . In response to criticism, he or she may react with rage, shame, or humiliation" (p. 350).[1]

The overarching question guiding our research asks if narcissism might be fruitfully cast in social-cognitive personality process terms rather

---

[1] Another benefit of the publication of the DSM diagnostic criteria is the development of a number of "face valid" narcissism scales. Among these scales, the Narcissistic Personality Inventory (NPI; Raskin & Hall, 1979; see Emmons, 1987; Raskin & Terry, 1988; Rhodewalt & Morf, 1995) has received the most research attention and is the one used almost exclusively in our research. Raskin and Hall (1979) based the NPI on DSM criteria for narcissistic personality disorder. Factor analyses of the NPI (Emmons, 1984, 1987) indicate that it consists of four moderately correlated factors: Leadership/Authority, Self-Absorption/Self-Admiration, Superiority/Arrogance, and Exploitiveness/Entitlement. Prifitera and Ryan (1984) reported that narcissistic and nonnarcissistic psychiatric patients could be distinguished on the basis of their NPI scores, suggesting that the scale does indeed capture pathological narcissism. NPI scores in the less extreme range are thought to reflect narcissism as a personality trait, albeit a multifaceted one.

The NPI is associated with egocentrism and self-focus (Emmons, 1987), hostility (Rhodewalt & Morf, 1995), aggression, dominance, exhibitionism, and self-centeredness (Raskin & Terry, 1988), all of which are characteristics of pathological narcissism. However, while it is plausible to assume that the model described in this chapter characterizes both trait and pathological narcissism, the empirical support comes primarily from individuals best described as exhibiting the narcissistic personality type.

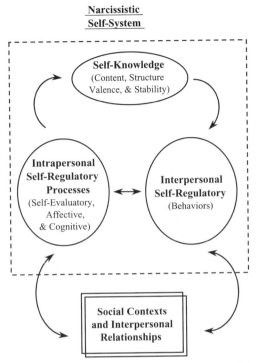

FIGURE 18.1 Self-regulatory processing model of narcissism. (From Rhodewalt & Sorrow, 2002)

than as a static individual difference or syndrome (Morf & Rhodewalt, 2001a; Rhodewalt, 2001; Rhodewalt & Sorrow, 2002). Embedded in this question is our attempt to bring coherence to the diverse and often contradictory components of narcissism (Morf & Rhodewalt, 2001a, 2001b). For example, how does one account simultaneously for narcissists' grandiose sense of self and their hypersensitivity to threat? How is it that narcissists are so invested in obtaining positive regard from others and yet so neglectful and often abusive of their social relationships? The model depicted in Figure 18.1 represents the current status of our efforts to address these questions by advancing a self-regulatory processing view of narcissism (see also Morf & Rhodewalt, 2001a).

Our model is very specifically a model of *self*-regulation. That is, in our view, it is the narcissist's self-concept that is being regulated through a set of intra- and interpersonal strategies. Narcissists are seen as individuals who possess transient, overblown, and fragile self-images that can only be sustained through social validation. Thus, narcissists are critically reliant on others for their sense of self-worth. The model is a dynamic and recursive one in that it characterizes narcissistic self-esteem regulation as shaped and guided by ongoing and changing self-concerns and social contexts. Narcissists' concerns about self-definition and worth guide their interpersonal behaviors that shape the social context. The social context, in turn, makes salient, intensifies, or rechannels current self-concerns. In fact, it can be argued that the narcissist's self is context bound and that transitions from one social context to another increase the fragility and vulnerability of their self-views.

The narcissistic self-system depicted in Figure 18.1 is composed of three interacting units: the self-concept, interpersonal strategies, and intrapersonal processes. The system incorporates both the content and the process of self-esteem regulation and in this regard is similar in conception to the social intelligence model of personality proposed by Cantor and Kihlstrom (1987; Cantor, 1990). The narcissistic self-concept incorporates both the cognitive and affective or evaluative components of the self. It contains what is known about the self, the Jamesian "me." This *cognitive self* component (Linville & Carlston, 1994) is the mental repository of autobiographical information, reflected appraisals, self-ascribed traits and competencies, and self-schemata including possible selves, self-with-others, and undesired selves. It also contains the attendant evaluations of what is known about the self or, collectively, self-esteem. The model addresses both the valence and the stability of self-esteem.

The narcissistic self-concept interconnects with the social environment through a set of self-regulatory units that include both intra- and interpersonal strategies enacted to protect or enhance positive self-views. Narcissists are active manipulators of social feedback both at the point of its generation (interpersonal regulation) and at the point of its interpretation (intrapersonal regulation). Intrapersonal strategies include distorted interpretations of outcomes and selective recall of past events. Interpersonal regulation covers a multitude of self-presentational gambits and social manipulations also in the service of engineering positive feedback or blunting negative feedback about the self. We have found that the model has heuristic value in terms of focusing questions and guiding research. However, it should be evident that the elements are neither discrete nor static entities but, rather, personality process units that intertwine and interact with one another. Finally, the model depicted in Figure 18.1 includes both uni- and bidirectional influences. The unidirectional relations are meant to suggest that the preponderance of influence is in one direction or another. Bidirectional relations indicate a more equally reciprocal and recursive set of transaction between components.

NARCISSISM AND SELF-ESTEEM REGULATION

If narcissism is characterized by pathological self-love, then narcissists' self-views and self-esteem should be positive and inflated. They are. Across a number of studies, narcissism, as defined by the Narcissistic Personality Inventory (NPI), is associated with high self-esteem (Emmons, 1984, 1987; Kernis & Sun, 1994; Morf & Rhodewalt, 1993; Raskin, Novacek, & Hogan, 1991; Raskin & Terry, 1988; Rhodewalt & Eddings, 2002; Rhodewalt, Madrian, & Cheney, 1998; Rhodewalt & Morf, 1995, 1998; Watson, Taylor, & Morris, 1987). In a collection of questionnaire studies, Rhodewalt and Morf (1995) measured the association between the NPI and various indicators of self-esteem. The NPI was positively and significantly associated with self-esteem as measured by Janis and Field's Feelings of Inadequacy Scale, Pelham and Swann's Self-Attributes Questionnaire, and Helmreich and Stapp's Texas Social Behavior Inventory. Narcissism has also been positively related to Rosenberg's measure of self-esteem and to McFarland and Ross' Resultant Self-Esteem Scale (Rhodewalt et al., 1998). Narcissists also report lower actual/ideal self-discrepancies than do less narcissistic people (Rhodewalt & Morf, 1995).

In a study that is directly relevant to the issue of social motivation, Raskin et al. (1991) assessed the relations between narcissism and what they termed *true self-esteem* and *defensive self-enhancement*. Defensive self-enhancement was subdivided further into grandiosity, or the need to be admired, and social desirability, or the need to be liked. The NPI correlated positively with true self-esteem and grandiosity but was uncorrelated with social desirability. In other words, narcissists need to be admired but not necessarily liked.

On the surface, narcissistic self-esteem appears to be high, but is this the whole story? In an excellent review of the clinical features of narcissism, Akhtar and Thompson (1982) characterize the narcissistic self-concept as overtly grandiose but covertly fragile, with feelings of inferiority and worthlessness. This observation raises two additional questions. First, are narcissistic self-evaluations merely positive but accurate or are they inflated? Second, are narcissistic self-evaluations covertly fragile and/or negative? With regard to the former question, evidence indicates that narcissists' self-evaluations are inflated compared to objective reality. Gabriel, Critelli, and Ee (1994) asked individuals to rate their intelligence and physical attractiveness. Compared to less narcissistic individuals, narcissists overestimated their intelligence and attractiveness compared to objective standards (IQ test scores, raters' evaluations of attractiveness). A more "online" demonstration of narcissistic self-aggrandizement comes from a study by Rhodewalt and Eddings (2002). High- and low-NPI men interacted with a woman over the telephone for the ostensible purpose of making a future date. The men were unaware that the woman's responses were completely scripted so that each interaction was identical with regard to social feedback. Nonetheless, narcissistic men concluded that the woman was more attracted to them and viewed them more positively than did less narcissistic men.

It has been more difficult to determine if narcissistic grandiosity is a veneer over a core of self-doubt and low self-esteem, as suggested by Kernberg (1976) and Akhtar and Thompson (1982). There is considerable evidence that narcissists are hyperresponsive to threats to the self, reacting with anger and reductions in self-esteem (Rhodewalt & Morf, 1998). These reactions betray the fact that their positive self-views are confidently held but do not provide conclusive evidence of the fact. Recent developments in the assessment of implicit cognition may offer an alternative way of exploring this issue. Already there are some suggestive findings. For example, Jordan, Spencer, Zanna, Hoshino-Browne, and Correll (2003) administered the NPI to a group of individuals categorized as possessing high or low explicit self-esteem and high or low implicit self-esteem. They report that high explicit/low implicit self-esteem individual were the most narcissistic, as indicated by their NPI scores (submitted). Consistent with this finding, Abend, Kernis, and Hampton (submitted for publication) found that high explicit/low implicit individuals were more self-aggrandizing than were people who were high on both measures of self-esteem. Many questions remain to be answered about the assessment and meaning of implicit self-esteem (see Fazio & Olson, 2003), but work in this area may provide important insights into the social motivations of narcissistic individuals.

Vulnerability may be revealed in other ways. Kohut (1971, p. 17) noted that "a pervasive hypochondriacal brooding ... may suddenly disappear and (usually as a consequence of having received external praise or having had the benefit of interest from the environment) the patient suddenly feels alive and happy, and for a while at least, shows initiative and has a sense of deep and lively participation in the world. These upward swings, however, are generally short-lived." Translating Kohut's observation into contemporary terms suggests that narcissists should display emotional lability, especially with regard to affect about the self. In fact, NPI-defined narcissism has been linked to emotional lability (Emmons, 1987). More to the point, we have provided evidence that this emotional instability is most pronounced and systematic in the area of feelings of self-worth. For example, Rhodewalt and Morf (1998) provided participants with success and failure feedback on successive tests of intelligence. The impact of this feedback produced greater changes in the self-esteem of high-NPI participants than it did among low-NPI participants. We have also tested this issue in four separate daily diary studies in which participants reported events of the day and their mood and self-esteem each evening for 5 to 7 consecutive days (Rhodewalt et al., 1998; Rhodewalt, Tragakis, & Finley, 2002; Rhodewalt, Tragakis, & Hunh, in prep.). In three of the four studies, NPI-defined narcissism was significantly related to instability of self-esteem. Paradoxically, we have observed narcissistic self-esteem instability using the Rosenberg Self-Esteem Scale (Rhodewalt et al., 1998) and the McFarland and Ross Resultant Self-Esteem Scale (RSES) (Rhodewalt et al., 1998, 2000) but not when using the Heatherton and Polivy State Self-Esteem Scale (Rhodewalt et al., 2002) to assess daily self-esteem. One would expect an explicit state measure to be most sensitive to instability, but it was not in this study.[2]

Evidence of high but unstable self-esteem among narcissists links our self-regulatory model to the impressive body of research on self-esteem instability conducted by Michael Kernis (1993, 2003; Kernis & Goldman, this volume). We have discussed elsewhere the parallels between narcissism and high but unstable self-esteem individuals (Kernis, 2003; Rhodewalt, 2001; Rhodewalt & Sorrow, 2002). Particularly relevant to the present discussion is that Kernis (1993) argues that high but unstable self-esteem is associated with enhanced sensitivity to evaluative events, increased concern about one's self-image, and overreliance on social sources of evaluation. Moreover, the goal of people with high, unstable self-esteem, according to Kernis, is to build more stable self-views and to enhance positive self-feelings. Thus, they are especially sensitive to both positive and negative social feedback, reacting to both with more extreme affective responses than do stable self-esteem individuals (Kernis, Cornell, Sun, Berry, & Harlow, 1993). Research also indicates that unstable, high self-esteem individuals are more hostile and angry (Kernis, Grannemann, & Barclay, 1989). This portrait is very similar to both clinical descriptions of narcissism, construct validity data produced with the NPI, and the self-regulatory model of narcissism.

Like unstable, high self-esteem individuals, narcissists are also more likely to display antagonism toward and a cynical mistrust of others (Bushman & Baumeister, 1998; Rhodewalt & Morf, 1995; Ruiz, Smith, & Rhodewalt, 2001). They react to self-esteem threats by derogating the source of that threat (Morf & Rhodewalt, 1993) and devaluing the negative feedback (Kernis & Sun, 1994), while viewing positive feedback as more valid and the evaluator as more competent than do less narcissistic individuals (Kernis & Sun, 1994; Rhodewalt & Eddings, 2002).

NARCISSISM, SOCIAL MOTIVATION, AND SOCIAL INTERACTION

Given that there is fairly consistent evidence that narcissists display greater fluctuations in their feelings of self-worth than do less narcissistic

---

[2] In both studies reported by Rhodewalt et al. (1998), there were interactions between level of narcissism and level of evaluative integration on self-esteem instability in addition to the main effects for narcissism. These interactions reflected the fact that narcissists who were highly compartmentalized in the distribution of positive and negative information about the self were the ones who displayed the most unstable self-esteem. Evaluative integration was not assessed in either the Rhodewalt et al. (2000) or the Rhodewalt et al. (2002) study.

individuals, we have considered why this might be the case. Kernis proposes that unstable self-esteem develops in individuals whose self-esteem is highly dependent upon self-evaluative information from the social context. Self-esteem will be unstable to the extent that it is contingent on social feedback and to the extent that feedback varies in its evaluative implications. Narcissism is characterized by disturbances in interpersonal relations. If one's relationships wax and wane from the positive to the conflicted, then self-evaluative social feedback should also be highly varied and inconsistent. Theories of narcissism also point to difficulties with interpersonal sources of evaluation and inconsistencies in the coherence of narcissists' self-concepts. Although their emphases are different, the theories of Kernberg (1976) and Kohut (1971) both argue that deficiencies in self-evaluative aspects of parent–child interactions (insufficient feedback) lay the foundation for adult narcissism. Thus, narcissism and self-esteem instability may both have their origins in inconsistent or neglectful reinforcement histories that impede the development of confidently held, stable self-conceptions and require constant vigilance for self-defining information. Kernis (2003) concludes that narcissism and unstable high self-esteem are two partially independent forms of fragile self-esteem.

Our daily diary studies have attempted to investigate linkages between narcissists' feelings of self-worth and qualities of their social interactions. Our main question takes the following form: If narcissistic self-esteem is unstable and unusually sensitive to social feedback, what are the attributes of their social interactions to which their self-esteem is entrained, if indeed it is entrained? In a first crude attempt to address this question, we asked our daily diary respondents to complete each day, in addition to a measure of self-esteem, a schedule of hassles and uplifts they encountered that day (Rhodewalt et al., 1998, Study 1). We categorized hassles and uplifts into those that were interpersonal (your spouse, your boss) and those that were impersonal (exercise, homework). Narcissism was associated with the increased reporting of hassles and uplifts, both interpersonal and impersonal. Across the reporting period, narcissists compared to less narcissistic individuals displayed the greatest self-esteem instability if they also reported a large number of interpersonal hassles. There was a nonsignificant tendency for narcissists to display stable self-esteem if they also reported a large number of interpersonal uplifts. There was no similar moderating relation between narcissism and self-esteem instability and impersonal events.

These results suggest that narcissists have unstable self-esteem, particularly if they experience a large number of negative interactions. The findings do not speak to the issue of whethers their self-esteem is contingent on social feedback. In our second study (Rhodewalt et al., 1998, Study 2), we employed an adapted version of the Rochester Interaction Record (RIR; Nezlek, Wheeler, & Reis, 1983) to chart respondents' daily social interactions. The RIR requires respondents to describe each significant interaction that transpired during a specified period. Respondents evaluated the interactions along dimensions such as intimacy, amount of disclosure, the extent to which they felt socially integrated, and the quality of the interaction. They also completed daily reports of self-esteem. Again, narcissism predicted self-esteem instability. With regard to social interactions, although narcissism was not related to the number of interactions reported, it was related to the quality of social exchanges. Narcissists reported on average that 25% of their interactions were negative compared to 16% for less narcissistic individuals, supporting the claim that narcissism is characterized by difficult interpersonal relationships.

Was the overall positivity of their daily social encounters related to their daily feelings of self-worth? This entrainment question was addressed in the following way: The proportion of the day's interactions that were negative was calculated for each day for each participant. Then, using a multilevel analysis strategy (Kenny, Kashy, & Bolger, 1997), we regressed daily self-esteem on the daily proportion of negative interactions for each participant, producing a within-subject regression slope that then became the dependent variable in a second regression analysis that included level of narcissism. The results indicated that daily interactions, specifically the extent to which they are cumulatively negative or problematic, were related to self-esteem for all participants. However, level of narcissism predicted the magnitude of the relationship (high NPI ß $= -.52$; low NPI ß $= -.19$). As the percentage of negative interactions increased on any given day, self-esteem decreased; this relationship was particularly descriptive of narcissists.

For narcissists, online variations in feelings of self-worth are more closely contingent on variations in the quality of social interactions than is the self-esteem of less narcissistic people. Are there specific qualities of these interactions to which narcissistic self-esteem is entrained? We sought to answer this question via another daily diary study in which we asked respondents to provide a more refined analysis of their transactions with other people (Rhodewalt et al., in prep.). The RIR was adapted to provide a more fine-grained analysis of the psychological qualities of social interactions. Participants evaluated each interaction for the extent to which they felt like their true selves in the interaction and the degree of social inclusion, influence, and conflict they experienced in the interaction. Participants who were preselected for extreme scores on the NPI completed the adapted RIR and the RSES each evening for 5 consecutive days. As in our earlier diary studies, narcissists displayed high self-esteem and greater self-esteem instability than did less narcissistic participants.

Scores were computed from the daily RIRs so that we could examine, on average, the qualities of the participants' interactions for each day. That is, these scores reflected how much the person was satisfied, felt included, experienced conflict, and so forth in his or her interactions on average for each day of the assessment period. We then conducted a series of hier-archical linear regressions (HLM) in which daily self-esteem and average qualities of the daily interactions were entered as level 1 within-participant variables, and level of narcissism and sex of participant were entered as level 2 between-participant variables.

The level 1 findings are important because they reveal the extent to which daily self-esteem covaries or is entrained with one's social inter-actions for people in general. Participants evaluated their interactions on nine dimensions. Fluctuations on six of the dimensions were significantly related to fluctuations in self-esteem. For all individuals, self-esteem rose and fell with the extent to which their interactions supported their self-concepts, made them feel included and engendered a sense of intimacy, were satisfying and positive, and were free of conflict. Who initiated and influenced the interaction was not related to daily self-esteem for the sam-ple in general.

The level 2 results revealed that these relationships were significantly different for high and low narcissists on two dimensions and marginally significant on a third. The relation between fluctuations in the extent to which one felt socially included in their social interactions was significantly stronger for narcissists than it was for less narcissistic individuals. This was also true for who initiated the interaction and marginally so ($p < .08$) for the extent to which the interactions supported their senses of self. Figure 18.2 displays the average within-participant regression slopes between daily

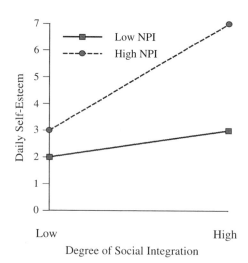

FIGURE 18.2 Day-to-day fluctuations in self-esteem and fluctuations in social inte-gration by level of narcissism.

feelings of social inclusion and daily self-esteem separately for high and low narcissists.

Our model of narcissistic interpersonal self-esteem regulation anticipated the result that narcissists' self-esteem was more closely related to the extent to which their interactions affected their feelings about themselves. However, we were surprised that narcissists' daily self-esteem was also strongly influenced by how much they felt included and accepted by their interaction partners. Although sociometer theory (Leary, 2002) predicts the general association between self-esteem and social integration, our model of narcissism suggests, if anything, that this relationship is stronger for low narcissists than for high narcissists. That is, social inclusion is thought to reflect the extent to which the individual is liked and accepted by the group. Given that narcissistic self-esteem appears to be based more on the degree to which others admire them than on the degree to which others approve of them (Raskin et al., 1991), one might expect that social inclusion, if it is merely an index of approval and acceptance, would have less impact on narcissists' self-esteem than it would for others.

However, it is possible that social inclusion or integration means something different to narcissists than it does to others. Social inclusion can mean approval based on acceptance, but it might also indicate admiration-based acceptance. That is, narcissists may feel more included in a group or relationship to the extent that the group or partner validates their self-concept or admires them. In order to explore this possibility, we designed a questionnaire to assess the layperson's understanding of what it means to feel socially included (Rhodewalt, Tragakis, Eddings, & Sorrow, 2001). We began by identifying as many ways as possible that people can feel connected to and included in their social relationships. Face valid items were generated that we believed reflected each category. The list of categories and sample items are found in Table 18.1. As one can see, our six categories went beyond social acceptance and included the possibilities that people felt more a part of the group or interaction if it made them feel admired or influential, if it validated and respected their opinions, if it made them feel influential or helpful, or if it directly bolstered their self-esteem. We attempted to distinguish between social approval (i.e., acceptance) and self-esteem support (i.e., the provision of positive self-evaluations). A questionnaire was created in which respondents were instructed to indicate the extent to which each of 56 items made them feel part of a group. Each item completed the sentence stem "I feel more included in a group or relationship when that group or partner..." for example "sees my side of things." Respondents indicated how much the statement applied to them on a 7-point scale ranging from 1 (*not at all*) to 7 (extremely).

The questionnaire was administered to a sample of 110 participants (who also completed the NPI measure of narcissism), and an exploratory

TABLE 18.1 *Social Inclusion Survey Categories and Sample Items*

"I feel more included in a group or relationship when that group or partner ..."
Admiration ($\alpha = .77$)
   Looks up to me
   Shows a little envy of me
Benefits others ($\alpha = .83$)
   Let's be help them
   Feels happier after interacting with me
Influence ($\alpha = .85$)
   Conforms to my beliefs
   Takes my advice
Social approval ($\alpha = .82$)
   Makes me feel like I belong
   Accepts me for who I am
Self-esteem ($\alpha = .85$)
   Makes me feel good about myself
   Provides me with feelings of worth
Validate ($\alpha = .76$)
   Sees my side of things
   Agrees with me about who I am

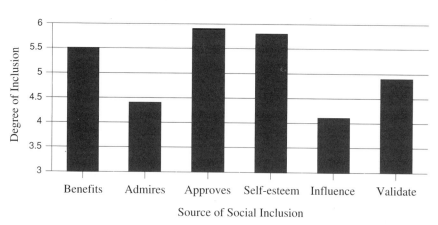

FIGURE 18.3 Sources of social inclusion.

principal components factor analysis was conducted. Items were dropped or reassigned to other categories based on their factor loadings. Internal consistency reliabilities and item-total correlations were computed for each factor, and additional items were excluded based on these analyses. Figure 18.3 displays the mean endorsements for each category. A repeated measures analysis of variance (ANOVA) on these factors indicated that there were significant differences among categories in the extent to which they promoted a sense of inclusion and acceptance from their social

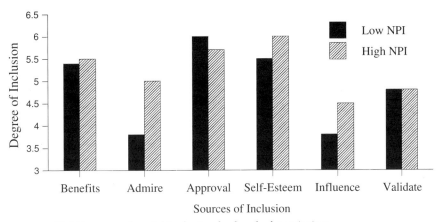

FIGURE 18.4 Sources of social inclusion by level of narcissism.

interactions, $F(5, 104) = 136.58, p < .001$. Pairwise Bonferroni comparisons indicated that respondents reported that social approval and self-esteem support were associated with the highest feelings of inclusion. Benefitting others and validation resulted in significantly lower experienced social inclusion than approval and esteem support, and admiration and influence resulted in significantly lower experienced social inclusion than the other four.

These analyses also produced a significant repeated measure by level of narcissism effect, $F(5, 104) = 6.74, p < .001$, which was followed up with univariate ANOVAs the means of which are displayed in Figure 18.4. Narcissists, compared to less narcissistic individuals, reported that they felt significantly more included and accepted by the group or interaction partner when they were admired, had their self-esteem supported, and felt influential. It is noteworthy and consistent with past research that narcissists reported that social approval was less a source of feelings of inclusion and acceptance than did less narcissistic respondents.[3] These findings were then replicated in an independent sample of 90 participants who also completed the NPI and the RSES (Rhodewalt et al., 2002). Again, social inclusion was most strongly indicated by social approval and social support, significantly less so by benefiting others and validation, and even significantly less so by admiration and influence. More important, the previously reported narcissism effects were again replicated. Narcissists felt more included than less narcissistic individuals if they felt admired and

---

[3] These analyses also produced three interactions between level of narcissism and sex of participant. For example, narcissistic women reported feeling more included to the extent that they could benefit others compared to less narcissistic women and high and low narcissism men. Likewise, narcissistic women reported that validation led to greater feelings of inclusion than did the other three groups. Finally, with regard to social approval, it was least important to narcissistic men.

influential and had their self-esteem supported. These relationships were independent of trait self-esteem.

Thus far, our findings indicate that narcissists' self-esteem varies closely with the extent to which they feel socially included and accepted in their daily social interactions. And, for narcissists, social inclusion means that they have influence, are admired, and have their (high) self-esteem supported. We (Rhodewalt et al., 2002) conducted another daily diary study in which we asked participants to report on their interactions at the end of each day for 7 consecutive days. The RIR was again modified so that in addition to ratings of intimacy, feelings about the self and interaction partners, social integration, influence, and conflict, participants also indicated how much they benefited others (not at all to a great deal) and how admired by others they were (not at all to a great deal) in each interaction. They also completed a state measure of self-esteem at the end of each day (Heatherton & Polivy, 1991).

We first examined narcissists' perceived social worlds by computing averages for each evaluative dimension of their interactions for each reporting day. A weekly average was then computed from the daily averages and entered into regression analyses with the NPI, trait self-esteem, sex of the participant, and his or her interactions as predictors. Narcissism was significantly and positively related to experiencing one's interactions as positive, making one feel good about oneself, and feeling admired. Narcissists were also more likely to believe that they were more integrated into the group and that others benefited from interacting with them. Paradoxically but not surprisingly, given past research, they also reported that their interactions on average contained more conflict. Again, it is important to note that these relationships are independent of level of trait self-esteem.

As noted previously, this study failed to find an effect for level of narcissism on self-esteem variability.[4] Nonetheless, HLM analyses were conducted in which level 1 data were daily state self-esteem and qualities of the daily interactions and level 2 data were level of narcissism, trait self-esteem, and sex. Consistent with our previous research, we found that overall daily self-esteem fluctuated significantly and predictably with fluctuations in the qualities of people's social interactions. Specifically, day-to-day variation in the experience of intimacy, feelings about the self, social integration, benefiting others, admiration, influence, and conflict was significantly related to day-to-day fluctuations in state self-esteem. Finally, and as expected,

---

[4] This study differed from our previous diary studies in several important ways that may have contributed to this outcome. First, it used a state measure of self-esteem instead of a trait measure. It may be that it is only on trait self-esteem that greater instability is observed among narcissists. Second, the Rhodewalt, Tragakis, and Hunh (2000) study preselected for extreme groups on level of narcissism, whereas the present study did not.

fluctuations in the overall positivity of daily interactions was significantly associated with fluctuations in daily self-esteem.

Because this study differed from our earlier diary studies in that it used an explicit state measure of self-esteem, we examined the relationship between qualities of the last interaction of the day and state self-esteem. Fluctuations in these interactions and fluctuations in self-esteem were significantly related for feelings about the self, social integration, admiration, influence, and conflict. These particular interactions had a greater impact on the daily self-esteem of narcissists than on the daily self-esteem of less narcissistic participants through their most immediate interaction dimensions of feelings about the self and admiration. That is, the extent to which narcissists felt admired by others in their most recent interaction significantly predicted their state self-esteem to a greater extent than recent admiration predicted the state self-esteem of less narcissistic people.

CONCLUSION: SELF-ESTEEM AND SOCIAL MOTIVATION REVISITED

Interpersonal models of self-esteem specify that moment-to-moment feelings of self-worth are influenced, in part, by people's perceived relation to their social worlds. For example, sociometer theory proposes that self-esteem is an indicator of one's relational value or social inclusion (Leary, 2002). The findings reported in this chapter provided compelling naturalistic support for this proposition. Across studies, participants' self-esteem covaried online with their social interactions. In particular and most relevant to sociometer theory, day-to-day fluctuations in self-esteem were reliably related to day-to-day fluctuations in the extent to which people felt included and integrated in their social interactions. However, the relations between the self and one's social world appear to be broader than those specified by sociometer theory. How the interaction made one feel about oneself, the overall positivity of the interaction, the opportunity to help or benefit others, the absence of conflict, and the receipt of admiration (in one study) all covaried online with one's self-esteem.

It may be that all of these dimensions of social interaction are derivatives of social inclusion. I agree, but only if one adopts a broader understanding of what it means to feel socially included. Our findings show that people understand social inclusion to mean more than mere acceptance by interaction partners or groups. It also means that interaction partners and groups are "buying" the self that one is "selling." In addition, it means that the group respects and validates the individual's views and is influenced by the individual, a finding that is consistent with the social dominance view of self-esteem (Barkow, 1975).

It was our attempt to understand narcissism in terms of interpersonal self-esteem regulation that led us to uncover these general relationships between social interaction and self-esteem. This research also indicates that people differ in the extent to which their feelings of self-worth are linked to their social relations. As clinical theory suggests, narcissists' self-esteem is more entrained to the extent to which they feel positively regarded by others. Whereas most people seek acceptance, narcissists seek self-enhancement and dominance. In an earlier work (Rhodewalt, 2001), it was suggested that narcissism served as an individual difference marker of ego involvement and reactivity to social feedback. As such, it served as a vehicle by which researchers might explore the general processes of social construction and maintenance of the self. The studies of narcissism and social entrainment of self-esteem are vivid illustrations of this claim.

References

Abend, T., Kernis, M. H., & Hampton, C. (submitted for publication). Discrepancies between explicit and implicit self-esteem and self-serving responses. Manuscript, University of Georgia.

Akhtar, S., & Thompson, J. A. (1982). Overview: Narcissistic personality disorder. *American Journal of Psychiatry, 139,* 12–20.

American Psychiatric Association (1980/1987, 1994, 2000). *Diagnostic and statistical manual of mental disorders* (DSM-III /III-R/IV/IV-TR). Washington, DC: Author.

Barkow, J. H. (1975). Prestige and culture: A biosocial interpretation. *Current Anthropology, 16,* 553–562.

Bushman, B., & Baumeister, R. F. (1998). Threatened egotism, narcissism, self-esteem and, direct and displaced aggression: Does self-love or self-hate lead to violence? *Journal of Personality and Social Psychology, 75,* 219–229.

Cantor, N. (1990). From thought to behavior: "Having" and "doing" in the study of personality and cognition. *American Psychologist, 45,* 735–750.

Cantor, N., & Kihlstrom, J. F. (1987). *Personality and social intelligence.* Englewood Cliffs, NJ: Prentice-Hall.

Cooper, A. (1959). Narcissism. In S. Arieti (Ed.), *American handbook of psychiatry* (pp. 297–316). New York: Basic Books.

Emmons, R. A. (1984). Factor analysis and construct validity of the Narcissistic Personality Inventory. *Journal of Personality and Social Psychology, 48,* 291–300.

Emmons, R. A., (1987). Narcissism: Theory and measurement. *Journal of Personality and Social Psychology, 52,* 11–17.

Fazio, R. H., & Olsen, M. A. (2003). Implicit measures in social cognitive research: Their meaning and use. *Annual Review of Psychology, 54,* 297–327.

Gabriel, M. T., Critelli, J. W., & Ee, J. S. (1994). Narcissistic illusions in self-evaluations of intelligence and attractiveness. *Journal of Personality, 62,* 143–155.

Heatherton, T. F., & Polivy, J. (1991). Development and validation of a scale for measuring state self-esteem. *Journal of Personality and Social Psychology, 60,* 895–910.

Jordan, C. H., Spencer, S. J., Zanna, M. P., Hoshino-Brown, E., & Correll, J. (2003). Secure and defensive high self-esteem. *Journal of Personality and Social Psychology, 85,* 969–979.

Kenny, D. A., Kashy, D. A., & Bolger, N. (1997). Data analysis in social psychology. In D. Gilbert, S. T. Fiske, & G. Lindzey (Eds.), *Handbook of social psychology* (4th ed., pp. 233–265). New York: Academic Press.

Kernberg, O. F. (1976). *Borderline conditions and pathological narcissism*. New York: Jason Aronson.

Kernis, M. H. (1993). The roles of stability and level of self-esteem in psychological functioning. In R. Baumeister (Ed.), *Self-esteem: The puzzle of low self-regard* (pp. 167–182). New York: Plenum Press.

Kernis, M. H. (2003). Toward a conceptualization of optimal self-esteem. *Psychological Inquiry, 14*, 1–26.

Kernis, M. H., Cornell, D. P., Sun, C. R., Berry, A. J., & Harlow, T. (1993). There's more to self-esteem than whether it is high or low: The importance of stability of self-esteem. *Journal of Personality and Social Psychology, 65*, 1190–1204.

Kernis, M. H., & Sun, C.-R. (1994). Narcissism and reactions to interpersonal feedback. *Journal of Research in Personality, 28*, 4–13.

Leary, M. R. (1999). The social and psychological importance of self-esteem. In R. M. Kowolski & M. R. Leary, (Eds.), *The social psychology of emotional and behavioral problems: Interfaces of social and clinical psychology* (pp. 197–121). Washington, DC: American Psychological Association.

Leary, M. R. (2002). The interpersonal basis of self-esteem: Death, devaluations, and deference. In J. P. Forgas and K. D. Williams (Eds.), *The social self: Cognitive, interpersonal, and intergroup perspectives* (pp. 143–160). New York: Psychology Press.

Leary, M. R., & Baumeister, R. F. (2000). The nature and function of self-esteem: Sociometer theory. In M. P. Zanna (Ed.), *Advances in experimental social psychology* (Vol. 32, pp. 1–62). New York: Academic Press.

Leary, M. R., & Downs, D. L. (1995). Interpersonal functions of the self-esteem motive: The self-esteem system as a sociometer. In M. Kernis (Ed.), *Efficacy, agency, and self-esteem* (pp. 123–144). New York: Plenum Press.

Linville, P. W., & Carlston, D. (1994). Social cognition and the self. In P. Devine, D. L. Hamilton, & T. Ostrom (Eds.), *Social cognition: Its impact on social psychology* (pp. 143–193). San Diego, Academic Press.

Morf, C. C., & Rhodewalt, F. (1993). Narcissism and self-evaluation maintenance: Explorations in object relations. *Personality and Social Psychology Bulletin, 19*, 668–676.

Morf, C. C., & Rhodewalt, F. (2001a). Unraveling the paradoxes of narcissism: A dynamic self-regulatory processing model. *Psychological Inquiry, 12*, 177–196.

Morf, C. C., & Rhodewalt, F. (2001b). Expanding the dynamic self-regulatory processing model of narcissism. *Psychological Inquiry, 12*, 243–251.

Nezlek, J., Wheeler, L., & Reis, H. T. (1983). Studies of social participation. *New Directions for Methodology of Social and Behavioral Sciences, 15*, 57–73.

Prifitera, A., & Ryan, J. J. (1984). Validity of the Narcissistic Personality Inventory in a psychiatric sample. *Journal of Clinical Psychology, 40*, 140–142.

Raskin, R., & Hall, C. S. (1979). A narcissistic personality inventory. *Psychological Reports, 45*, 590.

Raskin, R., Novacek, J., & Hogan, R. (1991). Narcissism, self-esteem, and defensive self-enhancement. *Journal of Personality, 59*, 20–38.

Raskin, R., & Terry, H. (1988). A principal-components analysis of the Narcissistic Personality Inventory and further evidence of its construct validity. *Journal of Personality and Social Psychology, 54,* 890–902.

Reich, A. (1960). Pathologic forms of self-esteem regulation. *Psychoanalytic Study of the Child, 18,* 218–238.

Rhodewalt, F. (2001). The social mind of the narcissist: Cognitive and motivational aspects of interpersonal self-construction. In J. P. Forgas, K. Williams, & L. Wheeler (Eds.), *The social mind: Cognitive and motivational aspects of interpersonal behavior* (pp. 177–197). New York: Cambridge University Press.

Rhodewalt, F., & Eddings, S. (2002). Narcissus reflects: Memory distortion in response to ego relevant feedback in high and low narcissistic men. *Journal of Research in Personality, 36,* 97–116.

Rhodewalt, F., Madrian, J. C., & Cheney, S. (1998). Narcissism, self-knowledge organization, and emotional reactivity: The effect of daily experiences on self-esteem and affect. *Personality and Social Psychology Bulletin, 24,* 75–87.

Rhodewalt, F., & Morf, C. C. (1995). Self and interpersonal correlates of the Narcissistic Personality Inventory: A review and new findings. *Journal of Research in Personality, 29,* 1–23.

Rhodewalt, F., & Morf, C. C. (1998). On self-aggrandizement and anger: A temporal analysis of narcissism and affective reactions to success and failure. *Journal of Personality and Social Psycholgy, 74,* 672–685.

Rhodewalt, F., & Sorrow, D. (2002). Interpersonal self-regualtion: Lessons from the study of narcissism. In M. Leary & J. P. Tangney (Eds.), *Handbook of self and identity* (pp. 519–535). New York: Guilford Press.

Rhodewalt, F., Tragakis, M. Eddings, S., & Sorrow, D. (2001). Unpublished data, University of Utah.

Rhodewalt, F., Tragakis, M., & Finley, E. (2002). *Narcissism, social interaction, and self-esteem II: The meaning of social inclusion.* Unpublished data, University of Utah.

Rhodewalt, F., Tragakis, M., & Hunh, S. (in preparation). *Narcissism, social interaction, and self-esteem.* Manuscript.

Ruiz, J., Smith, T. W., & Rhodewalt, F. (2001). Distinguishing narcissism from hostility: Similarities and differences in interpersonal circumplex and five-factor correlates. *Journal of Personality Assessment, 76,* 537–555.

Watson, P. J., Taylor, D., & Morris, R. J. (1987). Narcissism, sex roles, and self-functioning. *Sex Roles, 16,* 335–350.

19

To Know or Not to Know

Consciousness, Meta-consciousness, and Motivation

Jonathan W. Schooler and Charles A. Schreiber

INTRODUCTION

Consciousness is invariably a slippery construct, but especially so when it comes to considering its relationship to motivation. To take an everyday example, consider the case of scratching an insect bite. When bitten by a mosquito, one knows that scratching will ultimately just increase the itching. Sometimes one simply gives in to the urge and deliberately scratches the darn thing, knowing full well the subsequent price that will be paid. In this case, it is clear that the motivation to scratch was fully conscious. But what about the case in which one suddenly catches oneself scratching the forbidden itch? There is this moment of realization to the effect, "Ahh, that feels good, but oh, I didn't want to do that." In one sense, such actions lack conscious awareness, as the action that one is engaged in is precisely counter to one's goals. Moreover, there is the sense in which one has "caught" oneself "absentmindedly" engaging in the forbidden behavior. In another sense, however, the action and its concomitant motivation are conscious. That is, after one catches oneself, there is an appreciation of the pleasure that the scratching afforded as it temporarily relieved the itch. In short, when one catches oneself scratching an itch, there is a distinct sense that both the motivation to scratch (the itch) and the action itself (scratching) have been consciously experienced. One simply has temporarily failed to take stock of what one was doing and thus has not realized that the actions were counter to one's explicit goal of not scratching.

A central problem in considering the relationship between consciousness and motivation is the simple fact that the term *consciousness* has more than one meaning. Among the five different definitions of consciousness considered in Webster's dictionary are "the state of being characterized

Address correspondence to Jonathan Schooler at e-mail: schooler+@pitt.edu.

by sensation, emotion, volition, and thought" and "the quality or state of being aware especially of something within oneself." When it comes to conceptualizing motivations, these two definitions are really quite different. As the example of scratching an itch illustrates, one can exist in a motivational state (e.g., itching) without explicitly reflecting on the fact that one is in that state. Indeed, one can even carry out and *enjoy* the desired goal (i.e., scratching) without explicitly realizing that that is what one is doing. Thus, the example of absentminded scratching illustrates how one can experience a motivational state (fulfilling the first of the listed definitions of consciousness) while failing to be explicitly aware of that state within oneself (thereby failing to fulfill the second definition). Such discrepancies have led the first author (Schooler, 2001, 2002; Schooler, Ariely, & Loewenstein, 2003) to argue for the value of explicitly distinguishing between these two usages of the term consciousness, with the term *experiential consciousness* (or simply *consciousness*) used to describe ongoing experience (e.g., itching) and *meta-consciousness* (or *meta-awareness*) used to refer to the explicit awareness of the contents of consciousness (e.g., noticing that one is scratching an itch).

In this chapter, we review the logic and evidence underlying the distinction between consciousness and meta-consciousness, briefly describing a rudimentary model characterizing their relationship and empirical evidence for two types of dissociations between them: *temporal dissociations*, in which consciousness occurs in the absence of meta-consciousness, and *translation dissociations*, in which meta-consciousness misrepresents the contents of consciousness. We then illustrate the value of this distinction by considering how it may apply to the various chapters in this volume. As we hope to illustrate, surprising new insights and alternative accounts for a variety of motivational phenomena can be gained simply by considering the manner in which they relate to the distinction between consciousness and meta-consciousness.

A RUDIMENTARY MODEL OF THE RELATIONSHIP BETWEEN NONCONSCIOUS, CONSCIOUS, AND META-CONSCIOUS PROCESSES

People are inherently homeostatic systems (Carver & Scheier, 1990). In addition to maintaining bodily functions, elaborate monitoring processes appear to be involved in modulating the complex set of cognitions and behaviors necessary to regulate emotion and social behaviors. A central tenet of our approach, as well as others described both here (e.g., Forgas & Laham; Strack & Deutsch, this volume) and elsewhere (e.g., Bargh, 1997; Wegner, 1994), is that much of these regulatory monitoring processes go on outside of awareness. For example, Bargh and colleagues present considerable evidence indicating that individuals can activate and accomplish goals without realizing that they are doing so. Such goal achievement indicates some type of tacit monitoring process that at a minimum is sensitive to conditions under which the goal is appropriate and, potentially further, tracks its success. Similarly, Wegner's "ironic" processing model of thought control postulates a conscious control process that attempts to think about things other than the unwanted thought and an automatic monitoring processes that monitors for the unwanted thought. A key assumption of Wegner's model is that this monitoring process is nonconscious, which is why cognitive load impairs the conscious control process but not the monitoring process, thereby causing the hyperaccessibility of the unwanted thought.

Although it seems clear that many monitoring processes can go on at a nonconscious level, there are some types of regulation that require explicit attention. A good example is the case of mind-wandering (or *zoning out*) while reading. Although we hope that readers have managed to keep their minds on this chapter while reading it, we are confident that all readers have had the experience of suddenly realizing that, despite their best intentions and despite the fact that their eyes have continued to move across the page, they had no idea what they were reading. When the mind wanders, it is clear that the tacit monitoring systems are not always capable of catching the mind's drifting, and instead require a higher-level explicit monitoring process to take stock of the specific contents of thought and alert one to the fact that one has completely wandered off task. Once this meta-level of awareness takes effect, one takes note of their state and realizes that one's mind has wandered off track.

This explicit monitoring level (meta-consciousness) acts in effect like the pilot of an airplane. Although the autopilot system can handle mild adjustments due to normal shifts in wind and other conditions, when anything major occurs, the pilot is still needed to handle the situation. This second level of regulation has many more resources available to it, but because it draws on conscious processing, it is resource-demanding and, as will be argued, can even interfere with carrying out concurrent tasks. Thus, it is important to activate it only when needed, as often the most effective performance may occur when individuals can operate smoothly without having to reflect deliberately on what they are doing.

In sum, then, our model simply assumes that at any given moment during waking consciousness, individuals maintain both a continuous stream of consciousness (experiential consciousness) and various tacit monitoring processes that help to maintain homeostasis and make routine adjustments. Periodically, however, the mind encounters situations (e.g., wandering off task) that cannot be adequately corrected by the tacit system and require a more resource-dependent conscious monitoring process. Such conscious monitoring processes may simply be thought of as consciousness turned back to itself. In this sense, meta-consciousness simply involves a re-representation of one's ongoing conscious experience to oneself. In effect, it occurs anytime one explicitly attempts to answer the question "What am I thinking or feeling?" Given that this answer represents a description of one's state rather than the state itself, it offers individuals the opportunity to step out of the situation, which may be critical for many of the innovative behaviors that individuals are capable of. However, it also raises the possibility that in the redescription process individuals might get it wrong.

Two types of dissociation follow from the claim that meta-consciousness involves the intermittent re-representation of the contents of consciousness. Temporal dissociations occur when meta-consciousness is directed toward an experience that previously occurred in the absence of explicit awareness. The case of catching your mind wandering during reading illustrates a temporal dissociation. Once meta-consciousness is triggered, translation dissociations may occur if the re-representation process misrepresents the original experience. Such dissociations are particularly likely when one verbally reflects on nonverbal experiences or attempts to take stock of ambiguous experiences.

Temporal Dissociations

Temporal dissociations between consciousness and meta-consciousness are illustrated by cases in which the induction of meta-consciousness causes one to assess aspects of experience that had previously eluded explicit appraisal.

Mind Wandering. Although considerable research has examined mind wandering (see Giambra, 1995, for a review), surprisingly little research has focused on its occurrence with demanding tasks for which mind wandering is antithetical to success. The occurrence of mind wandering during attentionally demanding tasks is particularly informative because it is incompatible with carrying out such tasks, successfully, and thus suggests that individuals have lost meta-awareness of what they are currently thinking about. Recently, Schooler, Reichle, and Halpern (in press) developed a paradigm to specifically identify temporal lapses of meta-consciousness during the attentionally demanding task of reading. In this research, participants read passages of text and indicated every time they caught their minds wandering (zoning out). They were then asked whether they had been aware that they had been zoning out prior to reporting it. In a second condition, participants were additionally probed intermittently and asked to indicate whether they had been zoning out at that moment. The results revealed that participants: (a) frequently caught themselves zoning out during reading, (b) were still often caught zoning out by the probes, and (c) frequently reported that they had been unaware that they had been zoning out, particularly when they were caught by the probes. These findings demonstrate that individuals frequently lack meta-consciousness of the fact that they are daydreaming, even when they are in a study where they are specifically instructed to be vigilant for such lapses.

Emotional Awareness. The experience of moods, emotions, and general well-being represents another domain in which temporal dissociations between experience and the awareness of the experience are apt to happen. For example, we often fail to notice explicitly our own emotional states (e.g., sullenness, cheerfulness) until someone points them out to us. If we commonly lack meta-consciousness of affective states, then it follows that inducing continuous meta-consciousness of affect may alter that experience. To explore this issue, Schooler et al. (2003) examined the effects of requiring participants to report online happiness while listening to hedonically ambiguous music (by Stravinsky). Hedonically ambiguous music was selected because it was hypothesized to be more challenging to assess and, therefore, particularly susceptible to the effects of monitoring (see the subsequent section on "Ambiguous Experiences"). Schooler et al. found that continuous hedonic monitoring significantly reduced individuals' postmusic happiness ratings relative to a condition in which participants listened to music without monitoring. These findings suggest that continuous hedonic monitoring can alter experience, implying that in the absence of monitoring instructions, individuals are, at most, only intermittently meta-conscious of their affective state.

Automaticity. Automatic behaviors are often assumed to be nonconscious (Bargh, 1997; Jacoby, Yonelinas, & Jennings, 1997). However, there is a peculiarity to this designation. Consider a person driving automatically while engaging in some secondary task (e.g., talking). Although such driving is compromised, the driver still experiences the road at some level. Thus, a more appropriate characterization of the consciousness of automatic behaviors may be that they are experienced but lack meta-consciousness, the latter taking hold only when individuals run into difficulty.

Unwanted Thoughts. As noted earlier, Wegner (1994) has proposed a compelling theory suggesting that individuals possess a tacit monitoring system that tracks unwanted thoughts in order to veer away from them. However, one critical issue involves what exactly the tacit monitoring system is monitoring. Wegner suggests that it is monitoring the contents of preconsciousness (i.e., thoughts that are near, but not yet past, the threshold of consciousness). Although this is certainly possible, the distinction between consciousness and meta-consciousness raises the additional possibility that the tacit monitoring system may actually be monitoring the contents of consciousness itself. In short, it may be possible that individuals can think about a white bear without realizing that they are doing so. In this case, the implicit monitor may catch the unwanted thought and raise it to the level of meta-awareness, in effect offering the message "There you go again, thinking about that unwanted thought."

Translation Dissociations

If meta-consciousness requires re-representing the contents of consciousness, then it follows that some information may become lost or distorted in the translation, as with any recoding process. The likelihood of noise entering the translation process may be particularly great when individuals (a) verbally reflect on inherently nonverbal experiences, (b) assess ambiguous or subtle visceral signals, (c) are motivated to misrepresent their experience, or (d) possess a lay theory that is inconsistent with their actual experience.

The Effects of Verbal Reflection. There are some experiences that are inherently difficult to put into words: the appearance of a face, the taste of a wine, the intuitions leading to insights. If individuals attempt to translate these inherently nonverbal experiences into words, then the resulting re-representations may fail to do justice to the original experience. Schooler and Engstler-Schooler (1990) examined the effects of describing a form of cognition (memory for faces) that is notoriously difficult to commit to words. Participants viewed a face and subsequently either described it in detail or engaged in an unrelated verbal activity. When given a recognition test that included a different photograph of the target face, along with verbally similar distractors, verbalization participants performed substantially worse than controls. This effect of verbalization, termed *verbal overshadowing*, has been replicated in numerous labs (Meissner & Brigham, 2001) and generalized to a variety of other domains of visual memory (Schooler, Fiore, & Brandimonte, 1997), including colors (Schooler & Engstler-Schooler, 1990), shapes (Brandimonte, Schooler, & Gabbino, 1997), and cars (Brown & Lloyd-Jones, 2003), as well as other modalities such as audition (Schooler et al., 1997) and taste (Melcher & Schooler, 1996). Similar disruptions resulting from verbal reflection have also been observed in various other domains hypothesized to rely on nonverbal cognition. Thinking aloud during problem solving can disrupt the intuitive processes associated with insight problem solving while having no effect on the logical processes associated with analytical problem solving (Schooler, Ohlsson, & Brooks, 1993). Verbally reflecting on the basis of affective judgments can reduce the quality of affective decision making, as assessed both by the opinions of experts (Wilson & Schooler, 1991) and by postchoice satisfaction (Wilson et al., 1993). Verbally articulating the basis of the match between analogical stories can reduce people's sensitivity to meaningful deep-structure relationships while increasing their emphasis on superficial surface–structure relationships (Sieck, Quinn, & Schooler, 1999).

Although verbal re-representation can qualitatively alter conscious experience, in many cases verbal analysis can be more benign. Verbal reflection does not hamper performance when individuals describe experiences that are readily translated into words, due either to the nature of the task (e.g., logical problem solving; Schooler et al., 1993) or to individuals' unique verbal expertise (e.g., wine experts; Melcher & Schooler, 1996). Moreover, even in the case of difficult-to-describe holistic or ambiguous experiences, verbal descriptions often have little effect if they are relatively modest (Meissner & Brigham, 2001; Meissner, Brigham, & Kelley, 2001). In short, verbal reflection does not inevitably distort experience. However, extensive verbal reflection about nonverbalizable experiences often, although certainly not always, can cause individuals to become meta-aware of the individual pieces of their experience and how they are trying to fit those pieces together. When the task requires one to break down and carefully analyze an experience, as in logical problem solving, the re-representational processes associated with verbalization can be benign or even helpful. However, when individuals have holistic experiences, verbalization can produce a translation dissociation in which the individual elements emerging from verbal reflection inadequately represent the gestalt experience from which those elements were extracted.

Ambiguous Experiences. Many experiences are hedonically unambiguous: A superb meal is clearly pleasurable, and the sight of a corpse is unquestionably upsetting. However, other experiences, perhaps even the majority, are less straightforward. When faced with the need to decipher one's hedonic state, one may fail to notice subtle signals that, though coloring experience, are insufficiently strong to be explicitly noticed. Several strands of evidence indicate that meta-consciousness can be insensitive to subtle or ambiguous aspects of experience. For example, in the happiness monitoring study (Schooler et al., 2003) mentioned earlier, the pleasure of listening to the complex tonalities of Stravinsky may be too difficult at any given moment to be recognized. When asked to monitor their experience, continuously, individuals may, failing to appreciate their subtle pleasure, conclude that they are not having a good time. In contrast, in the absence of explicit monitoring, the modest pleasure associated with this experience may gradually accumulate, ultimately leading individuals to report greater happiness.

Motivation. There are some situations in which individuals may be explicitly motivated to misrepresent their experiences to themselves. For example, individuals who are homophobic would clearly not want to recognize that they were actually aroused by viewing graphic depictions of homosexual acts. Nevertheless, Adams, Wright, and Lohr (1996) found exactly that: When homophobes were shown explicit movies of individuals engaging in homosexual acts, their degree of sexual arousal, as measured by penile tumescence, was significantly greater than that of controls. As Baumeister, Dale, and Sommer (1998) note, this finding raises the paradoxical question "[How] does someone manage to feel sexually turned off when his or her body is exhibiting a strong positive arousal?" However, the distinction between experiential consciousness and meta-consciousness may offer a potential answer. Specifically, individuals may experience the arousal but, because of their strong motivation to ignore it, fail to become meta-aware of that experience. A similar account may help to explain why individuals labeled as *repressors* can show substantial physiological (galvanic skin response) markers of experiencing stress when shown stressful videos but report no stress (Asendorpf & Scherer, 1983). Because they are highly motivated to deny their stress, they simply do not allow themselves to acknowledge it. In these situations, such individuals do show facial expressions associated with stress, which is notable since facial expressions can be controlled (Ekman, 1992). Repressors' failure to control their expressions suggests that their failure to report stress is due to a lack of insight into their experience and not simply to an unwillingness to acknowledge their stress to the experimenter. The notion that motivation can prevent individuals from taking stock of experienced emotions also suggests a somewhat different way of conceptualizing the notion of repression. Freud argued that repression prevents unwanted thoughts and feelings from coming to consciousness. However, from the current vantage point, repression may also, or alternatively, prevent such experiences from reaching meta-awareness (Schooler, 2002). Individuals may have the thoughts and feelings, but they may simply fail to take stock of this fact.

Faulty Theories. A final potential source of translation dissociation stems from individuals' beliefs about what they would ordinarily experience in a given circumstance. If individuals have a particularly strong theory about what they would feel in a particular situation, this may color their appraisal of their actual experience. A compelling recent example of this comes from people's reports of their experience of catching a ball (McLeod, Reed, & Dienes, 2003). Most people believe that as they watch a ball, their eyes first rise and then fall, following the trajectory of the ball. This is indeed the case when one watches someone else catch a ball. However, when people catch a ball themselves, they actually maintain the ball at precisely the same visual angle. Indeed, it is apparently this simple heuristic that enables individuals to avoid the complex computations that would otherwise be required for catching. Nevertheless, when people who just caught a ball are asked what they experienced, they rely on their theory of experience rather than on what they actually did.

APPLYING THE CONSCIOUS–META-CONSCIOUS DISTINCTION TO THE CHAPTERS IN THIS VOLUME

A critical test of the value of a new distinction is the degree to which it can offer fresh insights into existing findings. Evidence of the novelty of this distinction comes from the fact that although virtually all of the chapters in this volume grapple with how individuals' findings relate to consciousness, none of the authors distinguish explicitly between consciousness in the sense of experience and consciousness in the sense of awareness of experience (i.e., meta-consciousness). As will be seen, when we introduce this very basic distinction and its corollary implications regarding multiple types of monitoring, temporal and translation dissociations, a variety of new interpretations and perspectives become apparent.

In reviewing the various chapters in this volume, we find that there are a number of overlapping strands that could be used to organize them. Here, however, we will focus on three basic questions that seem to particularly unite certain chapters: (a) What is the relationship between conscious and nonconscious motivation? (b) How does self-regulation mediate motivation? (c) What is the role of evolutionarily basic goals in mediating motivation? We will consider each of these questions (and the chapters that address them) in turn, with a particular eye toward illustrating how the distinction between consciousness and meta-consciousness can help to illuminate both the individual chapters and the more general questions that they address.

The Relationship Between Conscious and Nonconscious Motivational Processes

Consistent with the title of this volume, many of the chapters take as their central question the relationship between consciousness and nonconscious motivational processes. However, as noted, these chapters do not clearly differentiate between consciousness in the sense of what we are referring to as *experiential consciousness*, on the one hand, and consciousness in the sense of meta-awareness, on the other. Thus, in many cases, what researchers argue are nonconscious processes might, we suggest, more reasonably be characterized as conscious but not meta-conscious.

Aversive Racism. Son Hing et al. introduce the notion of *aversive racists*, defined as individuals who reveal evidence of implicit racism but are not conscious of their racist tendencies. Thus, their chapter speaks directly to the disparities that can emerge when discrepant motivations exist at different levels of consciousness. Aversive racists are identified empirically as being those individuals who score high on racism when gauged with implicit measures (i.e., the Implicit Association Test) but low when gauged with explicit measures. Evidence for the importance of this distinction comes from the examination of aversive racists' evaluations of stories depicting other-race target individuals who vary on the degree to which low liking ratings can be attributed to something other than race. When aversive racists have no excuse for holding negative attitudes toward other-race individuals (e.g., when the target person is characterized as acting politely), they behave very much like individuals with no racist tendencies. However, when there is an opportunity to justify their discriminatory behavior in a manner that does not necessarily invoke the label of racist (e.g., when the target individual behaves in slightly unfriendly manner), these individuals do act like racists. Son Hing et al. suggest that aversive racists behave in this fashion because they hold nonconscious racist views that are inconsistent with their conscious views and can rely on their racist tendencies only when they can avoid construing them as such. However, with the distinction between consciousness and meta-consciousness, there is another possibility: namely, that when individuals experience racist tendencies, they simply do not recognize this experience due to motivation not to take stock of racist tendencies. Accordingly, when confronted with the behaviors of an individual toward whom they have racist attitudes, aversive racists experience negative affect. If a justification for this affect exists that is consistent with their view of themselves (i.e., that the individual behaved somewhat rudely), then they embrace this affect. However, when no such outlet is available, they ignore it. Critical to this account, however, is the notion that they are actually experiencing the affect; it is simply a matter of whether or not they are prepared to allow themselves to take stock of it. Thus, a reasonable alternative way to characterize aversive racists is to suggest that they experience racism but lack explicit awareness of this experience, or, in the terms of meta-consciousness theory, that they exhibit translation dissociations due to a motivation to not acknowledge their racists tendencies.

Ostracism. Warburton and Williams's discussion of the nature of individuals' responses to ostracism also highlights differences between individuals' conscious versus nonconscious motivations. They find, for example, that when ostracized by members of an outgroup (aboriginal people), individuals show no more explicit racism then nonostracized individuals; however, they do show more implicit racism (as measured by the IAT). Moreover, in at least some conditions, ostracized individuals also show greater aggressive tendencies in an apparent effort to regain control, though they report feeling no greater hostility. Warburton and Williams suggest that this aggressive tendency to regain control is likely to occurr at the implicit level, noting that "motivation may have remained active at an implicit level leading to aggressive responses in order to satisfy this motive to regain control, but without conscious awareness of this motivation." In fact, this account is generally consistent with a meta-consciousness interpretation, with the exception that because of the vagaries of common usages of the terms *implicit* and *conscious awareness*, it is not clear whether Warburton and Williams are speculating that the motivations are being experienced but simply failing to be recognized as such, or whether they are occurring entirely outside of the realm of conscious experience. Within the context of meta-consciousness, we propose that one reasonable account is that ostracized individuals experience aversive affect and aggressive tendencies corresponding to the loss of control resulting from ostracism, but they simply fail to become meta-conscious of this fact.

Terror Management. In their chapter on the impact of mortality salience on individuals' tendency to manage the existential angst associated with death, Pyszczynski et al. also explicitly grapple with differences between conscious and nonconscious motivational states. They observe, for example, that whereas highly salient references to mortality cause individuals to engage in explicit rationalizations for coping with death (e.g., a bias to reduce perceived vulnerability to a short life expectancy), the more subtle responses characterized by the terror management literature (e.g., worldview defenses such as increased patriotism) occur only with less salient manipulations. Pyszczynski et al. interpret such findings as suggesting that subtle mortality salience manipulations activate individuals' "potential for affect" rather than "the actual experience of affect." As evidence for this conjecture, they note that giving people a placebo of calming tea reduced worldview defenses, even though placebos are known to augment the experience of emotion rather than ameliorate it (Cooper, Zanna, & Taves, 1978). Although their account is certainly possible, the distinction between consciousness and meta-consciousness suggests a rather straightforward alternative: namely, that mortality salience manipulations produce an anxiety about death that is experienced but for which individuals lack meta-awareness. Accordingly, when mortality manipulations are sufficiently salient, individuals recognize their angst and engage in deliberate rationalization processes in order to minimize their sense of risk. However, when the mortality manipulations are subtler, participants experience the angst but fail to recognize it. This inchoate state of insecurity induces the more basic associations with fundamental sources of security, such as home and country. Pyszczynski et al. suggest that the effectiveness of the placebo manipulation argues against the possibility that individuals may actually be experiencing the stress. However, it is important to note that the finding that placebos enhance rather than reduce the impact of emotion is not consistently observed (Bond, 1981). Indeed, one possible account for the variability of this finding may be due to individuals' varying degree of meta-awareness of their affective state. When individuals are meta-aware of experiencing stress, the presence of a supposedly ameliorating placebo may exacerbate this experience. People may reason, "I am experiencing stress, and I just took this pill that should relax me, so I must be really stressed." However, when individuals are not meta-aware of their affect, this counteractive reasoning process may not take place, enabling them to enjoy the standard placating effects of the placebo. This indeed may have happened in Pyszczynski et al.'s study, as evidenced by the reduction in worldview defenses following use of the placebo. Thus, it seems quite plausible that the affect associated with terror may in fact be experienced but in the absence of meta-awareness.

Habitual versus Intentional Systems. In their discussion of the differences between intentional and habitual behaviors, Wood and Quinn also address the question of the differences between conscious and nonconscious motivation. Habitual responses, defined as behavioral tendencies to repeat well-practiced acts, are characterized as occurring largely outside of people's awareness. In contrast, intentional responses, involving reasoned actions identified in order to yield desirable outcomes, are characterized as relatively more conscious. Evidence for this distinction comes from differences in the circumstances in which the two types of systems are invoked and differences in people's ability to predict their behaviors under these conditions. Intentional behaviors are hypothesized to occur in uncommon, unstable situations, whereas habits are hypothesized to occur in common, stable situations. Wood and Quinn fluctuate in their discussion of the consciousness associated with habits, at one point suggesting that "habits are part of the *wise unconscious,*" while at other times suggesting that "habits are guided by minimal or sporadic cognitive monitoring rather than a complete absence of thought." Again, a reasonable account of the consciousness associated with habitual behaviors is that habitual behaviors are experienced but often without meta-awareness. Like the itch that is mindlessly scratched or the absorbing mind-wandering episode that nevertheless temporarily goes uncaught, the activities associated with habitual behavior are experienced, but without reflection.

Authenticity. According to Kernis and Goldman, critical elements of the trait of *authenticity* are an awareness of, and trust in, one's motives, feelings, desires, and self-relevant cognitions. Thus, whether or not individuals are authentic depends on the degree to which they are conscious of their motivations. Once again, however, meta-consciousness is arguably the operative term, as what Kernis and Goldman are really proposing is that individuals can vary in the degree to which they are meta-conscious of their feelings and motives. Such variation critically influences the degree to which they can behave authentically. Although we are sympathetic to their view, the observation that meta-consciousness can misrepresent experience also raises some questions about the findings on which Kernis and

Goldman base their conclusion. Specifically, all of the data that they report regarding differences in individuals' awareness of their motivations involve self-report measures. However, just because individuals think they are accurately aware of their feelings and emotions does not mean that they necessarily are. Indeed, given the ways in which self-reflection has been found to hamper individuals' access to their own feelings (e.g., Wilson & Schooler, 1991), it seems plausible that individuals who are chronically reflecting on their motives and feelings might actually behave in ways that are antithetical to their true motives and feelings. Thus, although authenticity may be associated with chronic meta-awareness of one's feelings, the existence of translation dissociations raises genuine concerns about relying exclusively on self-reports to substantiate this hypothesis.

How Do Self-Regulation Strategies Mediate Motivation?

A second central issue that is addressed by a number of the chapters in this volume is the role of self-regulation strategies in mediating motivational states. As noted at the outset, one of the central premises of our account of meta-consciousness is that all self-regulation strategies are not alike. Some occur outside of consciousness, working in effect behind the scenes. Others are much more explicit and demand more resources. As will be seen, this delineation may provide new insights for understanding the role of self-regulation in mediating motivation.

Mastery versus Performance. Harackiewicz, Durik, and Barron focus on the self-regulatory goals that individuals use in approaching their studies. It is often suggested that mastery goals (i.e., individuals' motivation to develop competence in an area) are best suited for maximum performance (e.g., Dweck, 1999). However, Harackiewicz et al. provide compelling evidence that whereas mastery goals are the best predictors of individuals' interest in a topic, performance goals (i.e., the motive to demonstrate competence relative to others) are be the best predictor of actual academic performance. One outstanding question, however, is precisely why performance goals exceed mastery goals despite the well-known importance of intrinsic interest in learning. One possible answer to this question involves the types of self-regulation strategies that mastery and performance goals may invoke. Individuals who hold mastery goals may rely more on nonconscious regulation processes. While reading, they may particularly seek out *flow states* in which they entirely avoid meta-awareness, as in the case of being "lost in a novel." In contrast, individuals with performance goals may be much more likely to rely on explicit meta-conscious self-regulation strategies, regularly "checking in" to make sure they that are on task and understand what they are reading. Although this latter strategy may disrupt the flow, it may have the advantage of ensuring that individuals know when they are learning and when they need to review.

Regulation of Racism. Although racism may be a deeply entrenched response to members of outgroups, Devine et al. provide compelling evidence that people work very hard to regulate their expression of racism. However, their motivations for this self-regulation differ considerably. Some individuals are intrinsically motivated not to be racists so that they can maintain their egalitarian view of themselves. Other individuals are extrinsically motivated to avoid appearing racist to others. With respect to meta-consciousness, the difference in the acceptability of racism to intrinsically motivated versus extrinsically motivated individuals should be substantial. Intrinsically motivated individuals should lack meta-awareness of their racism due to the fact that it is antithetical to their self-view. In contrast, extrinsically motivated individuals may not mind perceiving themselves as racist as long as this view is not transmitted to others.

Goal Accessibility. A central component of self-regulation is to maintain the current goal. Liberman and Förster suggest that one critical aspect of maintaining the current goal is to reduce the accessibility of a prior goal. In support of this claim, they find that prior to the attainment of a goal, individuals show positive priming for the goal item. However, following attainment of the goal, individuals actually show negative priming. Given the postulation of both explicit and implicit self-regulation processes, an intriguing question arises regarding which system these findings address. Do individuals necessarily need to be explicitly aware of the goal in order for this effect to be observed? What, for example, would happen if the goal were activated in a nonconscious manner, such as done by Bargh (1997). Furthermore, do people need to be meta-aware of the successful attainment of the goal in order for an item's accessibility to be reduced? Although we can only speculate, it seems quite plausible that fluctuations in accessibility may represent one of the many automatic self-regulation processes carried out by the tacit monitoring system.

Effort and Goal Attainment. A critical element in the self-regulation of goals is determining how much effort must be exerted in order reach one's goals. Gendolla and Wright demonstrate that individuals work harder (as indicated by cardiovascular response) when confronted with moderately difficult goals than when confronted with either an extremely difficult task or an easy one. In keeping with Brehms's original theorizing, they suggest that this occurs because individuals appraise the situation and exert maximal effort only when they believe it will result in success. Consistent with this account, they find that low-ability participants actually exert more effort than high-ability subjects, but only when they view success as possible and worthwhile. As with the other studies, Gendolla and Wright do not explicitly consider the level of awareness associated with this type of affective regulation. We suspect that whereas the fluctuations in goal accessibility mentioned in the prior section may be mediated by a tacit self-regulation system, judgments of the amount of effort expended relative to the likelihood of success may be mediated by the explicit system. That is, such contingencies may depend critically on individuals deliberately reflecting on how likely they are to succeed at the task and how hard they will have to work in order to do so, then calculating the appropriate effort accordingly. This predicts, of course, that goals that are activated through nonconscious channels should not exhibit this pattern.

Self-Regulation of Work Performance. Many of the goals that individuals pursue are related to work. Thus, it stands to reason that the workplace would provide an excellent domain in which to explore self-regulatory processes. Using a variety of self-report measures, Weiss, Ashkanasy and Beal show that individuals' work performance is powerfully regulated by momentary perceptions of uplifts and hassles. Although this work provides useful insights into the self-regulatory conditions of which individuals are aware, the notion that performance may be modulated in part by tacit regulatory processes raises the important need to complement this research with tacit measures to gauge the potentially critical role that tacit regulation may play in the workplace.

Narcissism. Although self-regulation is clearly critical to achieving one's goals, it seems possible that there could be too much of a good thing. In this vein, Rhodewalt provides compelling evidence that the behavior of narcissists can be understood as resulting from their constant need to engage in self-regulation strategies associated with protecting and bolstering their self-esteem. The apparent reason for this need is that narcissists appear to have high explicit self-esteem but low implicit self-esteem. The shaky foundation upon which their explicit self-esteem rests requires them to protect it vigilantly. The present approach suggests a number of potentially important insights about narcissists. First, in keeping with the preceding discussion, it seems quite plausible that narcissists, like homophobes, aversive racists, and repressors, may be subject to motivational translation dissociations. Narcissists may experience the insecurity associated with their low implicit self-esteem but, for motivational reasons, fail to acknowledge this experience. Nevertheless, this continuous unrecognized experience of insecurity may motivate them to remain constantly on the lookout for slights that might further exacerbate this insecurity. As a result, narcissists may keep their explicit self-regulation system continuously on high alert. In short, they may be continuously appraising the situation (explaining their hypersensitivity to social feedback) meta-consciously in order to protect and bolster their fragile self-esteem.

Affect and Self-Regulation. Forgas and Laham provide an extensive review of the evidence indicating that the modulation of affective states plays a key role in the self-regulation of goals and behavior. Forgas and Laham argue that social situations that require monitoring of ambiguous or indeterminate information typically invoke constructive processing in which individuals generate novel strategies that can be highly influenced by affect. In contrast, when individuals are in more routine situations, they are more likely to engage in motivated processing that draws on preexisting behavior patterns and are relatively immune to affect infusion, thereby helping to modulate affect. Forgas and Laham further speculate that individuals may "alternate between [these] two complimentary processing strategies . . . in order to achieve an automatic, homeostatic, system of mood management." Accordingly, indeterminate situations may produce affect infusion and the accentuation of existing affective states, whereas routine situations may produce motivated processing that resulted in incongruent outcomes by inhibiting affect. The self-regulatory system proposed by Forgas and Laham has much in common with the view described here and by Schooler (2002). Both posit multiple regulatory systems that work in concert to maintain homeostasis. Both assume that regulation processes can go on automatically without explicit reflection. Indeed, Forgas and Laham's model suggests that non-meta-aware affective processes may be most likely to occur when individuals are deeply engaged in resource-demanding processing. Given that controlled tasks require more resources, it makes great sense that individuals would be less meta-aware of their affective states and therefore potentially more vulnerable to affect infusion (see Berkokwitz, Jaffee, Jo, & Troccoli, 2000).

Reflection and Impulsiveness. Like Forgas and Laham, Strack and Deutsch present a dual system model of self-regulation that shares important similarities with the meta-consciousness account presented here. Strack and Deutsch suggest that self-regulation, and social behavior more generally, are carried out by two systems: a reflective system that relies on knowledge about facts and values, and an impulsive system that is based on associative links and motivational orientations. The differential information base upon which the two systems rely critically determines the types of responses that they engender. The reflective system, drawing on propositions about the world, behaves in a relatively more rational, logical, and deliberative manner. In contrast, the impulsive system, drawing on low-level associations, instincts, and affect, leads to nonreasoned actions. Although also related to the meta-conscious approach described here, considering together the models both of Strack and Deutsch and of

Forgas and Laham illustrates their important difference in emphasis. As Forgas and Laham's model suggests, affect infusion (which is likely to be often associated with an absence of awareness of the affect per se) is particularly likely to occur when individuals are engaged in generative, nonstereotyped (and therefore reflective) processing. Reflection on one's situation does not necessarily imply reflection on one's state. Indeed, generative activities that may be particularly likely to induce reflections about one's situation at times frequently may prevent reflection about one's own state. Thus, the distinction between reflecting and not reflecting on one's situation should not be confused with the distinction between reflecting and not reflecting on one's state.

What Is the Role of Evolutionarily Basic Goals in Mediating Motivation?

A final issue addressed by several of the chapters in this volume is the attempt to expound the potential importance of evolutionarily basic goals in understanding motivation. From an evolutionary perspective, it seems quite likely that meta-consciousness was pretty late on the scene. Presumably, human brains were dealing with evolutionarily basic goals long before they had meta-consciousness to take stock of such goals. Meta-consciousness may not be required, therefore, when it comes to evolutionarily basic goals. Indeed, this is precisely what several chapters suggest.

Thirst. Spencer et al. present compelling evidence that the activation of an evolutionarily relevant need state (e.g., thirst) can make individuals uniquely susceptible to activating goals associated with that need state. For example, when individuals were water deprived, they drank more when presented subliminally with the word *thirst*. In contrast, when they were not in a need state, such subliminal primes had no effect. Interestingly, although it affected their drinking, the subliminal primes had no effect on people's reported thirst, suggesting that the mechanisms mediating the operation of evolutionarily basic drives can occur without meta-awareness. At the same time, given that they influence behavior, it seems quite plausible that these goal states nevertheless influence individuals' actual experience (Schooler, 2002).

Sex. Aarts and Hassin provide evidence suggesting that the goal of having sex also can be activated entirely without individuals' meta-awareness. Male subjects read a text that alluded to casual sex and were then given the opportunity to help either a male or a female student by providing feedback on a task that the fictitious student had allegedly developed. Having read the allusion to casual sex increased the helping behavior of male subjects (as measured by time and words used in the feedback) but only when the student was described as female. Given that men recognize that helping behavior can be instrumental in getting sex, this finding is consistent with the hypothesis that the allusion to sex activated behaviors aimed at getting sex. However, given the subtlety of the manipulation and the fact that students had no realistic reason to think that their helping would lead to sex (as there was no prospect of ever meeting the women they were helping), it seems that here again they may have lacked meta-awareness of the fact that the goal had been activated. Nevertheless, the story may have stirred sexual feelings that lingered outside of meta-awareness.

Threat. Neuberg et al. (see also the chapter by Spencer et al.) similarly demonstrate the manner in which the evolutionarily basic goal of pro-tecting the self from danger can be tacitly activated. Men viewed video clips that sometimes depicted threatening situations (*The Silence of the Lambs*) and then judged the emotions of African Americans. When previously ex-posed to the threat-inducing clips, men were significantly more likely to perceive African American faces as expressing anger – an interpretation that would prepare them for engaging in defensive behavior (i.e., fighting). Interestingly, women did not show this pattern, further suggesting a very basic evolutionary basis for the result. Again, although consciousness of the motivation was not measured directly, it seems highly unlikely that in-dividuals would have explicitly perceived themselves to be in any danger from a photograph, suggesting that this motivation was likely not directly reflected on. Nevertheless, as in Aarts and Hassin's study, the manipu-lation may have left a mild but lingering feeling (in this case, a sense of threat), which, though outside of meta-awareness, nevertheless influenced their experience and thereby influenced their judgment.

CONCLUSIONS

As we hope this chapter has illustrated, new perspectives on a variety of motivational findings and theories can be gained by considering the pos-sibility that phenomena typically referred to as implicit or nonconscious may actually be experienced but simply may be lacking in meta-awareness. In many of the situations reviewed here, we have proposed the possibil-ity that the critical line is between consciousness and meta-consciousness rather than between consciousness and nonconsciousness. At the same time, however, we in no way mean to discount the existence of truly non-conscious processes and, indeed, speculate that such processes (e.g., those associated with the nonconscious regulatory system that we postulate) are quite likely as critical as they are ubiquitous. Thus, we are not propos-ing an alternative to the conscious–nonconscious distinction but merely a supplement to it.

A critical question thus arises: How can we distinguish empirically between processes that are experienced without meta-awareness and processes that are genuinely nonconscious? It should be emphasized that simply recognizing that there are two reasonable options is an important and often overlooked point. Having said that, however, we must concede that distinguishing between these two accounts requires finesse. A failure of verbal report is often the signature of both an absence of meta-awareness and an absence of experience. Nevertheless, there are several promising research approaches for making this distinction.

Self-Caught versus Probe-Caught States

If individuals have conscious experiences in the absence of meta-awareness, they should fail to report them online using self-report measures. Nevertheless, it should be possible to catch them in the state with an experience-sampling procedure. This is the strategy that we (Schooler et al., in press) have used successfully with catching zoning out in order to demonstrate the striking frequency with which individuals lack meta-awareness of their drifting thoughts. In principle, similar strategies could be used in other paradigms. For example, in Wood et al.'s research on habits, it seems quite likely that individuals would fail to report engaging in habitual motivations but would easily be caught experiencing them if probed at the right time, illustrating that these motivations are experienced without meta-awareness.

Reactivity of Monitoring

If individuals routinely lack meta-awareness of a state, then forcing them to engage in chronic monitoring should have an effect. This is the logic underlying the investigation of the impact of monitoring on happiness (Schooler et al., 2003), and it also may be relevant to some of the paradigms described here. For example, if affect infusions require an absence of meta-awareness, then continual monitoring of affect may reduce its impact.

Discrepancies Between Self-Report and All Other Measures

If a variety of indirect measures (e.g., behavioral, physiological) are consistent with the contention that individuals are having a particular experience but are simply failing to report it, then eventually it seems that we can become increasingly confident that they are indeed, having the experience that they are failing to report. Of course, in such cases it is always possible that the problem is one of unwillingness to disclose. However, there are also indirect ways of assessing this, such as giving people rewards for accurate calibration between self-report and other measures, including social desirability measures. Though tricky, applying such approaches to examining the fluctuations in calibration between self-report measures and other indirect measures of motivational states can begin to give insights into when people lack experience and when they simply lack reflective awareness of the experience.

Retrospective Memory

Finally, if individuals are experiencing something without meta-awareness at the time, then in principle it may be possible to give people a new perspective on their old state (e.g., through biofeedback, mindfulness training, or the provision of some additional source of self-insight), which may enable them to recall motivational states that they failed to notice at the time. For example, individuals going through the breakup of a romantic relationship may retrospectively recognize past experiences of anger states that had previously escaped meta-awareness. Similarly, if individuals were alerted to the nature of the experience associated with the state invoked by mortality salience, they might be able to retrospectively recognize being in that state, even if they failed to notice it at the time. Such retrospective recall may provide a useful tool for establishing experiences in the absence of meta-awareness.

In closing, although our suggestion that people may lack meta-awareness of their own experiences has often been lost on the field, we note that it is in fact a central element of the lay vernacular for talking about feelings. Although perhaps less so than in the heyday of the 1960s, people routinely talk about getting "in touch" with their feelings, and everyone knows the famous refrain "If you are happy *and you know it*, clap your hands." Indeed, it seems that basic emotions may well be thought of as experiential states corresponding to fundamental goals of reward, avoidance, protection, reproduction, and so forth. In many situations, individuals' meta-awareness of those experiential states may be unnecessary, and in some cases it may even undermine individuals' ability to act. In the latter circumstance, as Shakespeare noted long ago, "If ignorance is bliss, 'tis folly to be wise."

References

Adams, H. E., Wright, L. W., & Lohr, B. A. (1996). Is homophobia associated with homosexual arousal? *Journal of Abnormal Psychology, 105*(3), 440–445.

Asendorph, J. B., & Scherer, K. R. (1983). The discrepant repressor: Differentiation between low anxiety, high anxiety, and repression of anxiety by autonomic-facial-verbal patterns of behavior. *Journal of Personality and Social Psychology, 45*, 1334–1346.

Bargh, J. A. (1997). Advances in social cognition. In R. S. Wyer, Jr. (Ed.), *The automaticity of everyday life* (pp. 1–61). Mahwah, NJ: Erlbaum.

Baumeister, R. F., Dale, K., & Sommer, K. L. (1998). Freudian defense mechanisms and empirical findings in modern social psychology: Reaction formation, projection, displacement, undoing, isolation, sublimation, and denial. *Journal of Personality, 66*(6), 1081–1124.

Berkowitz, L., Jaffee, S., Jo, E., & Troccoli, B. T. (2000). On the correction of feeling-induced judgmental biases. In J. P. Forgas (Ed.), *Feeling and thinking: The role of affect in social cognition* (pp. 131–152). New York: Cambridge University Press.

Bond, C. F. (1981). Dissonance and the pill: An interpersonal simulation. *Personality and Social Psychology Bulletin, 7*(3), 398–403.

Brandimonte, M. A., Schooler, J. W., & Gabbino, P. (1997). Attentuating verbal overshadowing through visual retrieval cues. *Journal of Experimental Psychology: Learning, Memory, and Cognition, 23*, 915–931.

Brown, C., & Lloyd-Jones, T. J. (2003). Verbal overshadowing of multiple face and car recognition: Effects of within versus across-category verbal descriptions. *Applied Cognitive Psychology, 17*, 183–201.

Carver, C. S., & Scheier, M. S. (1990) Origins and functions of positive and negative affect: A control-process view. *Psychological Review, 197*, 19–35.

Cooper, J., Zanna, M. P., & Taves, P. A. (1978). Arousal as a necessary condition for attitude change following induced compliance. *Journal of Personality and Social Psychology, 36*(10), 1101–1106.

Dweck, C. S. (1999). *Self-theories: Their role in motivation, personality, and development.* Philadelphia: Psychology Press.

Ekman, P. (1992). *Telling lies: Clues to deceit in the marketplace, politics, and marriage.* New York: W. W. Norton.

Giambra, L. M. (1995). A laboratory method for investigating influences on switching attention to task-unrelated imagery and thought. *Consciousness and Cognition, 4*, 1–21.

Jacoby, L. L., Yonelinas, A. P., & Jennings, J. M. (1997). The relation between conscious and unconscious (automatic) influences: A declaration of independence. In J. C. Cohen & J. W. Schooler (Eds.), *Scientific approaches to consciousness* (pp. 13–48). Mahwah, NJ: Erlbaum.

McLeod, P., Reed, N., & Dienes, Z. (2003, July). *What implicit knowledge and motor skill: People do not know about how they catch a ball.* Paper presented at the annual meeting of the European Society of Philosophy and Psychology Congress, Turin, Italy.

Meissner, C. A., & Brigham, J. C. (2001) A meta-analysis of the verbal overshadowing effect in face identification. *Applied Cognitive Psychology, 15*, 603–616.

Meissner, C. A., Brigham, J. C., & Kelley, C. M. (2001). The influence of retrieval processes in verbal overshadowing. *Memory and Cognition, 29*(1), 176–186.

Melcher, J., & Schooler, J. W. (1996). The misremembrance of wines past: Verbal and perceptual expertise differentially mediate verbal overshadowing of taste. *Journal of Memory and Language, 35*, 231–245.

Schooler, J. W. (2001). Discovering memories in the light of meta-consciousness. *Journal of Aggression, Maltreatment and Trauma, 4*, 105–136

Schooler, J. W. (2002) Re-representing consciousness: Dissociations between consciousness and meta-consciousness. *Trends in Cognitive Science, 6*, 339–344.

Schooler, J. W., Ariely, D., & Loewenstein, G. (2003). The pursuit and assessment of happiness may be self-defeating. In J. Carrillo & I. Brocas (Eds.), *Psychology and economics* (pp. 41–70). Oxford: Oxford University Press.

Schooler, J. W., & Engstler-Schooler, T. Y. (1990). Verbal overshadowing of visual memories: Some things are better left unsaid. *Cognitive Psychology, 17,* 36–71.

Schooler, J. W., Fiore, S. M., & Brandimonte, M. A. (1997). At a loss from words: Verbal overshadowing of perceptual memories. In D. L. Medin (Ed.), *The psychology of learning and motivation* (pp. 293–334). San Diego: Academic Press.

Schooler, J. W., Ohlsson, S., & Brooks, K. (1993). Thoughts beyond words: When language overshadows insight. *Journal of Experimental Psychology: General, 122,* 166–183.

Schooler, J. W., Reichle, E. D., & Halpern, D. V. (in press). Zoning out during reading: Evidence for dissociations between experience and meta-consciousness. In D. T. Levin (Ed.), *Thinking and seeing: Visual metacognition in adults and children.* Cambridge, MA: MIT Press.

Sieck, W. R., Quinn, C. N., & Schooler, J. W. (1999). Justification effects on the judgment of analogy. *Memory and Cognition, 27,* 844–855.

Wegner, D. M. (1994). Ironic processes of mental control. *Psychological Review, 101,* 34–52.

Wilson, T. D., Lisle, D. J., Schooler, J. W., Hodges, S. D., Klaaren, K. J., & LaFleur, S. J. (1993). Introspecting about reasons can reduce post-choice satisfaction. *Personality and Social Psychology Bulletin, 19,* 331–339.

Wilson, T. D., & Schooler, J. W. (1991). Thinking too much: Introspection can reduce the quality of preferences and decisions. *Journal of Personality and Social Psychology, 60,* 181–192.

Author Index

Note: Page numbers in italics refer to citations in references.

Aarts, H., 2, 8, 11, 22, 32, 58, 60, 61, 62, *67, 70,*
  86, 87, 91, 92, 95, 98, *107, 112,* 135, *148,*
  153, 154, 155, 156, 158, 160, 161, 183, 184,
  185, 186, 187, 188, 229, 241, *242,* 268, 307,
  367, 367
Abbey, A., 145, *148*
Abelson, R.P., 63, *67*
Abend, T., 338, *348*
Abramson, L.Y., 298, *309*
Ach, N., 72, *87,* 91, *109,* 228, 232, *242*
Adams, H.E., 358, *370*
Adolphs, R., 168, *189*
Ajzen, I., 56, 58, 67, *68,* 91, 96, *109,* 154, *164,*
  230, *243*
Akhtar, S., 332, 337, 338, *348*
Albarracin, D., 60, *67*
Albrecht, J.E., 161, *164*
Allen, J., 47, *51, 149*
Alloy, L.B., 298, *309*
Allport, G.W., 3, *15*
Altemeyer, B., 138, *148*
Alvarez, J., 306, 307, *310*
Ames, C., 24, 28, *36, 38*
Ames, R., *36*
Amodio, D.M., 252, 256, 260, *270, 271*
Anastasio, P.A., 278, *291*
Archer, J., 24, 28, 29, *36*
Arms, R.L., 239, *244*
Arndt, J., 41, 42, 43, 46, 47, 49, *51, 52, 53, 54*
Aronson, E., *15,* 253, *270,* 278, *291, 293*
Ascalon, E., 205, *208*
Ashburn-Nardo, L., 259, *272*
Atash, M.N., 200, *208*

Atkinson, J.W., 25, *36,* 87, 104, *111,* 154, *164,*
  230, *242,* 258, *270*
Austin, J.T., *67*

Bagozzi, R.P., *67*
Baird, W., 35, *38*
Baldwin, M., 77, *89*
Balleine, B., 154, *165*
Banaji, M.R., *53,* 194, *208, 276, 292,* 320, *330*
Bandura, A., 22, *36,* 71, *88,* 91, 96, *109,* 154,
  165, 239, 247, 253, *270,* 298, 306, *309, 310*
Bargh, J.A., 3, 8, *15, 16,* 45, *51,* 55, 58, 63, *67
  68,* 93, 97, 103, 106, *109, 110, 111,* 113, 114,
  128, 134, 135, 147, *148,* 155, 156, 163, *165,
  166,* 229, 236, 241, *242, 243, 244,* 306, 307,
  310, 312, 352, 355, 364, *370*
Barndollar, K., 58, 59, *67,* 155, *165,* 229, *241*
Barnett, B., *68,* 216, *227*
Baron, R., 134, 135, *151, 189,* 288, *291,* 321,
  328, 329
Barron, K.E., 2, 7, 21, 24, 27, 28, 29, 31, 33, *36,
  37,* 154, 169, 296, 363
Barsalou, L.W., 94, *109*
Batson, C.D., 77, *88*
Batts, V., 252, *272*
Baumeister, R.F., 5, *25,* 36, *52, 54,* 60, *68,* 81,
  88, 186, 187, 188, *189,* 238, *244,* 269, *272,*
  294, 295, 296, 297, 299, 300, 301, 304, *310,
  311, 312,* 326, *330,* 333, *348, 349,* 358, *371*
Bechara, A., 105, *109*
Becker, D.V., 43, *51*
Beckmann, J., 61, *69*
Bekkering, H., 160, *165*

Bem, D.J., 4, *15*, 99, 100, 105, *109*
Berkowitz, L., 170, 184, 186, *189*, 239, *242*, 305, *310*, 325, *328*, *371*
Bibby, P.A., 60, *68*
Bibby, R.M., 239, *244*
Biernat, M., 250, *270*
Bindra, D., 2, *16*, 154, *165*
Bink, M.L., 163, *166*
Biro, S., 157, *166*
Bizot, E., 197, *209*
Blair, I.V., 59, 251, *271*
Blascovich, J., 85, 86, *88*, 168, 169, *189*
Bless, H., 8, *16*, 104, *109*, 174, *189*, 277, 292, 321, *328*
Bobo, L., 145, *152*
Bodenhausen, G.V., 238, *244*
Boneva, B.S., 305, *311*
Boniecki, K.A., 250, *270*
Boss, A., 196, *218*
Bower, G.H., 169, 170, 171, 172, 173, *189*, *190*, *191*, 320, *328*
Boyd, C., 134, *151*
Bradley, M.M., 103, *111*
Bratslavsky, E., 60, *68*
Braverman, D.L., 189, *192*
Brazy, P.C., 252, *272*
Brehm, J.W., 10, 71, 72, 73, 75, 76, 84, 87, *88*, *89*, 239, *242*, 298, 305, *310*, *313*
Breus, M., 42, *53*
Brewer, M.B., 58, 59, *68*, 295, *320*
Brigham, J.C., 252, *270*
Britt, T.W., 250, 251, 256, 257, 261, *270*
Brown, C., 201, *208*
Brown, J.D., 186, *190*, 299, 300, *312*
Brown, L.M., 250, *270*
Brown, R., 139, *151*
Bruner, J.S., 95, 98, *109*, 114, *128*, 135, *148*, 228, *242*
Brunstein, J., 219, *226*
Buehler, R., 182, *192*
Bugental, D.B., 135, *148*
Burger, J.M., 298, *310*
Burrows, L., 63, *67*
Bushman, B.J., 78, *88*
Buss, D.M., 5, *16*, 136, 138, 140, 142, 144, 145, *148*, *150*, 162, 165, 168, *190*, *192*
Butner, J., 136, *150*
Byrne, R.W., 157, *165*

Cabanac, M., 154, *165*
Cacioppo, J.T., 98, 101, 102, *109*, 147, *151*
Campbell, J.D., 215, *226*

Canary, D.J., 162, *165*
Cantor, N., 197, *208*
Capitman, J.A., 163, *167*
Carducci, D., 211, *226*
Carpenter, C., 145, *149*
Carpenter, K.M., 104, *110*
Carter, S.M., 28, *37*
Carver, C.S., 5, 7, *16*, 26, *36*, 56, 64, 65, *68*, 106, *109*, 169, *190*, 233, *242*, 253, 258, 259, 263, *271*, 325, *328*, 352, *371*
Case, T.I., 299, 302, 303, 308, *310*, *313*
Centerbar, D.B., 182, *193*
Chaiken, S., 93, *109*, 160, *165*
Chambers, W., 106, *109*
Chartrand, T.L., 8, *16*, 58, 63, *67*, *68*, 92, *109*, 113, *128*, 135, *148*, 155, *165*
Chen, M., 63, *67*, 93, 103, 106, *109*, 160, *165*
Cheney, D., 145, *149*
Cheung, S., 295, *310*, *313*
Christenson, A.J., 77, *89*
Chung-Yan, G.A., 2, 13, 113, 274, 284, *291*, 303
Church, M.A., 31, *36*, *37*, 258, *271*
Cialdini, R.B., 104, *110*
Ciarocco, N.J., 299, *312*
Ciarrochi, J.V., 169, 171, 172, 183, 184, 185, 186, 188, *190*, *191*
Clark, M.S., 134, 142, *151*, 163, 173, 182, 184, *190*, 238, 242
Clore, G.L., 82, *90*, 105, *112*, 170, 171, 172, 173, 184, *190*, 317, *330*
Collins, A.M., 94, *109*
Combs, D., 196, *208*
Connell, J.P., 212, *227*
Contrada, R.J., 76, *89*
Cooke, R., 155, *167*
Cooper, J., 49, *54*
Cosmides, L., 136, *149*
Crain, E.L., 278, *293*
Crandall, C.S., 274, *291*
Crowe, E., 258, *272*
Crowne, D.P., 200, 252, *271*
Csibra, G., 157, *166*
Cummins, D.D., 136, *149*
Custers, R., 155, *165*
Cuthbert, B.N., 103, *111*
Czopp, A., 259, *272*
Czyzewska, M., 196, 197, *208*

Daly, M., 145, *149*, *152*
Damasio, A.R., 105, *109*, 154, 165, 168, 170, *189*, *190*

Damhave, K.W., 162, *165*
Darley, J.M., 276, *291*
Darwin, C.R., 2, *16*, 99, *109*, 142, *149*
Davidson, R.J., 92, 99, *111, 112*, 318, *328*
Davies, P.G., 116, *129*
De Grada, E., 200, *208*
De Haan, E., 144, *152*
De Sousa, R.D., 170, *190*
De Vries, P., 98, 108, 135, *148*, 155, *164*
Dechesne, M., 42, 43, *53*
Deci, E.L., 21, *36*, 154, *165*, 211, 216, 217, 218, *226, 227*
DeCoster, J., 59, *69*
Delton, A.W., 133, *150*
Depret, E., 305, *310*
Desaulniers, J., 50, *54*
Deutsch, R., 2, 8, 10, 32, 58, 59, 86, 91, 93, 106, 107, *110, 112*, 113, 251, 268, 276, 305, 352, 366
Devine, P.G., 2, 6, 13, 32, 116, *129*, 236, *243*, 249, 250, 251, 252, 253, 254, 255, 256, 257, 258, 259, 260, 261, 263, 265, 269, 270, *271, 272*, 274, 278, 280, *291, 292, 293*, 364
Dewey, J., 35, *37*, 86, *87*
Di Lollo, V., 135, *149*
Dickinson, A., 154, *165*
Diener, E., 219, *226*
Dijksterhuis, A., 56, 58, 61, 62, 63, *67, 68*, 86, *87*, 95, 96, 106, *108, 110*, 135, 155, *164*
Dill, J.C., 76, 78, 84, *89, 90*
Dimberg, U., 102, *110*
Dobb, L.W., 239, *243*
Dolby, R., 216, *227*
Dollard, J., 239, *243*
Donnerstein, E., 306, *330*
Dovidio, J.F., 106, *111*, 116, *128*, 274, 275, 276, 277, 278, 290, *291, 292*
Downey, J.L., 162, *165*
Downs, D.L., 301, *311*
Drake, C.A., 189, *192*
Drambarean, N.C., 98, *112*
DuBois, C.L.Z., 274, *293*
Duff, K.L., 238, *244*
Dunn, M., 114, *129*
Dunton, B.C., 268, *271*, 277, *292*
Durik, A.M., 2, 8, 21, 33, 34, *37*, 154, 169, 296, 363
Duval, S., 253, *271*
Dweck, C.S., 24, *37*, 81, *88*, 363, *371*

East, R., 198, *208*
Eccles, J.S., 33, 34, *37, 39*, 56, *68*

Eisenberger, R., 71, *88*
Eisenstadt, D., 48, *52*
Ekman, P., 144, *149*, 318, *328*
Elliot, A.J., 24, 25, 26, 27, 28, 29, 31, *36, 37*, 102, *108*, 212, 254, 258, *271*, 278, *291*
Ellis, H.D., 142, *152*
Emmers-Sommer, T.M., 162, *165*
Emmons, R., 219, *226*
Epley, N., 106, *110*
Epstein, S., 47, *52*, 113, *128*
Erber, M., 169, 184, *190*
Erber, R., 120, 128, 169, 184, *190*, 238, *245*
Eron, L.D., 239, *243*
Eshleman, A., 274, *291*
Esteves, F., 138, *151*
Evans, T.W., 189, *192*
Evett, S.R., 249, *271*

Faulkner, J., 136, *151*
Fazio, R.H., 60, 65, *68*, 250, 256, 268, *271*, 276, 277, *291, 292*, 338
Feather, N.T., 91, *110*, 258, *271*
Fein, S., 2, 10, 98, 113, 114, 116, *128, 129*, 135, 239, *242*, 303
Feingold, A., 142, 144, *149*
Felson, R.B., 305, *312*
Ferguson, M., 3, 8, *15*, 60, *68*, 156, *166*, 187, *193*
Festinger, L., 3, 4, 5, *16*, 253, *272*
Fiedler, K., 7, *16*, 170, 171, 172, 173, 179, 184, 189, *190, 191*, 320, *328*
Fishbein, M., 56, *68*
Fishkin, S., 189, *192*
Fiske, S.T., 134, 135, 147, *149, 151, 152*, 305, *310*
Florak, A., 277, *292*
Florian, V., 42, 43, *53, 54*
Fong, C., 114, *129*
Forgas, J.P., 1, 2, 3, 7, 8, 9, *10*, 82, *88*, 104, *109*, 168, 169, 170, 171, 172, 173, 174, 175, 176, 177, 178, 179, 180, 181, 182, 183, 184, 185, 186, 187, 188, 189, *190, 191*, 198, *208*, 305, 315, 316, 321, 325, *329*, 352, 366, 367
Förster, J., 2, 8, 13, 22, 92, 98, 100, 101, 103, *110*, 113, 135, 155, 163, 169, 228, 230, 237, 238, 240, *243, 244*, 253, 324, 364
Foster, J.D., 212, 221, *226*
Fowles, D.C., 71, *88*
Frak, V., 106, *110*
Franklin, J.H., 74, *89*
Freud, S., 2, *16*, 358
Freund, T., 135, *150*

Fried, C.B., 278, *293*
Friedman, R., 113, *129*, 233, *245*
Friend, R., 96, 252, *273*
Friesen, C.K., 134, *149*
Frijda, N.H., 64, *68*, 174, *192*, 322, *329*
Froming, W.J., 106, *109*
Funder, D.C., 134, *150*

Gaertner, S.L., 126, *128*, 274, 276, 277, 278,
    282, 290, *291*, *292*
Ganellen, R.J., 106, *109*
Gangestad, S.W., 138, 139, 142, 145, *149*, *152*
Gardner, W.L., 295, 297, 301, *310*
Gattis, M., 160, *165*
Gaunt, R., 57, *69*
Gawronski, B., 106, *110*
Geen, R.G., 78, *88*
Gendolla, G.H.E., 2, 10, 26, 71, 74, 75, 79, 81,
    82, 83, 84, 86, *88*, 364, 365
Gergely, G., 157, *166*
Gibson, J.J., 147, *149*
Gigerenzer, G., 134, 136, *152*
Gilbert, D.T., 1, *17*, 57, *69*, 114, *129*, 156, *166*,
    182, *193*, 279, *292*
Gill, T., 196, 200, 201, 203, *208*
Gilovich, T., 106, *110*
Gleason, C.A., 93, *111*
Glick, P., 274, *293*
Goethals, G.R., 215, *227*
Gold, D.G., 238, *245*
Goldenberg, J.L., 42, 43, 47, *51*, *52*, *53*
Goldman, B.M., 2, 6, 12, 32, 41, 195, 212, 214,
    217, 218, 221, *226*, 339, 362, 363
Goldsmith, R., 197, *209*
Goldstone, R.L., 57, *69*
Gollwitzer, P.M., 8, *12*, 55, 63, *67*, *68*, 92, 97,
    110, 113, 119, *129*, 154, 155, 161, *164*, *165*,
    166, 228, 229, 230, 232, 233, 241, *242*, *243*,
    245
Goodall, J., 145, *149*
Goodenough, D.R., 200, *209*
Goodman, C.C., 135, *148*
Gray, J.A., 92, 99, *110*
Greenberg, J., 2, 9, *16*, 40, 41, 42, 43, 44, 45,
    46, 47, 48, 50, *51*, *52*, *53*, *54*, 113, 253, *273*,
    299, 302, 308, *310*, *311*
Greenwald, A.G., 45, 48, *53*, 196, *208*, 256,
    272, 276, 277, 282, *292*, *293*, 303, *311*
Gregory, W.L., 104, *110*
Grolnick, W.S., 211, *227*
Groth, G., 142, *150*
Grubb, M., 196, 202, *209*

Grunedal, S., 102, *110*
Guerrero-Witt, M., 64, *68*
Gutierres, S.E., 136, 142, *149*

Hansen, C.H., 138, 144, *150*
Hansen, R.D., 138, 144, *150*
Harackiewicz, J.M., 2, 6, 8, 9, 21, 23, 24, 25,
    26, 27, 28, 29, 30, 31, 32, 33, 34, 35, *36*, *37*,
    38, *39*, 81, *88*, 169, 251, 258, 268, *271*, 296,
    325, 363
Hardee, B.B., 252, *272*
Harlow, T., 339, *349*
Harmon-Jones, E., 41, *53*, 252, *270*, *271*, *292*
Harter, S., 216, *226*
Haselton, M., 140, 144, 145, *150*, 166, *192*
Hass, R.G., 274, *292*
Hassebrauck, M., 142, *150*
Hassin, R.R., 2, 8, 11, 22, 32, 86, 91, 113, 153,
    156, 157, 158, 159, 161, *164*, *166*, 229, *242*,
    268, 307, 367
Hatfield, E., 142, *149*
Hauser, M.D., 157, *166*
Hawkins, C., 135, *152*
Hay, J.F., 61, *68*
Heatherton, T.F., 339, 346, *348*
Heckhausen, H., 61, *69*, 230, *243*
Hefferline, R.F., 214, *227*
Heider, F., 3, 4, 6, *16*, 157, *166*
Hembree, R., 258, *272*
Herabadi, A., 59, *70*
Hermann, A., 212, *226*
Hersey, R.B., 314, *329*
Hess, M., 102, *111*
Hicks, J.L., 163, *166*, *244*
Hidi, S., 24, 31, 32, 35, *38*
Higgins, E.T., 5, *16*, *17*, 51, 56, *69*, 91, 104,
    109, *110*, 113, *128*, *129*, 162, 163, *166*, 173,
    174, *192*, 197, *208*, 228, 229, 230, 234, 236,
    237, *243*, *244*, 245, 258, *271*, *272*
Hilgard, E.R., 188, *192*
Hill, T., 196, 197, 204, *208*, *209*
Hirschberger, G., 43, *53*
Hirst, W., 94, *110*
Hixon, J.G., 114, *129*
Hodson, G., 274, 276, *292*
Hoffman, H., 197, *209*
Hogan, R., 337, *349*
Holmes, J.G., 44, *53*
Horowitz, L.M., 186, *192*, 224, *226*
Hoshino-Brown, E., 116, *129*, 338, *348*
Howard, A., 277, *291*
Huesmann, L.R., 239

Hull, C.L., 3, 55, *69*, 92, *110*
Hunh, S., 338, *350*
Hunter, A.J., 249, *273*
Hunter, S.B., 85, *88*
Hymes, C., 258, *272*

Ilardi, B., 213, *227*
Isbell, L.M., 82, *90*
Isen, A.M., 173, 182, 184, *190*, 316, 320, 321, *328, 329*

Jackson, D.N., 25, *38*
Jackson, J.R., 277, *292*
Jacoby, L.L., 61, 68, *69*, 355, *371*
Jaffee, S., 170, *189*, 366, *371*
James, W., 2, *16*, 97, *110*, 147, *150*
Jeannerod, M., 106, *110, 112*
Jennings, J.M., 355, *371*
Jetten, J., 238, *244*
Jo, E., 170, *189*, 266, *371*
John, O.P., 138, *151*
Johnson, B., 277, *291*
Johnson, B.T., 60, *67*
Johnson, C., 277, *291*
Johnson, M.K., 94, *110*
Johnson, R., 183, *191*
Jonas, E., 42, 48, 50, *52, 53*
Jones, C.R., 77, *89*, 230, *247*
Jones, J.M., 251, *272*
Jordan, C.H., 338, *348*
Judge, T.A., 316, *329*

Kahneman, D., 105, *112*, 134, *149, 150*, 322, *329*
Kane, J.S., 318, *329*
Kaplan, A., 31, *38*
Kashy, D.A., 57, *70*, 86, *89*, 341, *349*
Katz, I.M., 274, *292*
Kawahara, J., 135, *149*
Kawakami, K., 106, *111*, 116, *128*, 275, 277, *291*
Kazén-Saad, M., 228, *244*
Keefe, R.C., 136, *150*
Keele, S.W., 233, *244*
Kelley, C.M., 61, *69*, 357, *371*
Kelley, H., 105, *111*
Keltner, D., 321, *329*
Kenny, D.A., 288, *291*, 341, *349*
Kenrick, D.T., 2, 11, 104, 113, 133, 136, 138, 142, 144, *148, 149, 150*, 163, 182, *190*, 248
Kernberg, O.F., 333, 340, 348, *349*

Kernis, M.H., 2, 6, 12, 32, 41, 194, 210, 212, 213, 214, 217, 218, 219, 220, 221, 222, 223, 224, *226*, 337, 338, 339, *349*, 362
Kihlstrom, J.F., 113, *129*, 194, *208*, 336, *348*
Killebrew, K., 78, *89*
Kim, J.I., 135, *152*
King, G.A., 197, *208*, 228, *243*
King, K., 211, *227*
Kingstone, A., 134, *149*
Kirby, L.D., 75, 85, 86, *89*
Kite, M.E., 145, 149
Klein, G.S., 80, *88*
Klein, S.B., 238, *245*
Klinger, E., 229, *243, 244*
Knutson, B., 238, *245*
Koestner, R., 211, *226*
Koriat, A., 95, *111*
Krantz, S., 172, *191*
Krapp, A., 32, *38*
Krones, J.M., 136, *150*
Kuhl, J., 163, *166*, 228, 229, 230, 232, 233, *243, 244*
Kukla, A., 73, *89*
Kumhyr, S.M., 249, *273*
Kumkale, G.T., 60, *67*
Kunda, Z., 7, *16*, 116, 119, *129*, 134, 147, *150*, 274, *293*
Kurzban, R., 140, *150*

Laham, S.M., 1, 2, 7, 12, 82, 104, 168, 198, 305, 315, 316, 325, 352, 366, *367*
Laird, J.D., 100, *111*
Landau, M.J., 42, 43, 44, *52, 53*
Lang, P.J., 92, 99, 103, *111*
Langer, E.J., 298, *311*
Larsen, R.J., 219, *247*, 318, *329*
Latham, G.P., 22, *38*, 154, *166*, 326, *329*
Lawler, E.E., 318, *329*
Lawrence, J.W., 26, *36*
Lazarus, R.S., 106, *111*
Leary, M.R., 5, *15*, 140, *150*, 189, *226*, 252, *272*, 284, 295, 296, 297, 301, 304, 307, 309, *310, 311, 313*, 333, 334, 343, 347, *349, 350*
LeeChai, A., 155, *165*
Leggett, E.L., 24, *37*
Lehto, A.T., 28, *37*
Leibold, J.M., 277, *292*
Lengfelder, A., 63, *68*
Lerma, M., 139, *152*
Lewicki, P., 2, 12, 194, 196, 197, 201, *208, 209*, 251, 268
Lewin, K., 3, 4, 92, *111*, 229, 230, *244*

Li, N.P., 136, *150*
Li, W., 277, *293*
Liberman, N., 2, 8, 13, 22, 65, 92, 98, 113, 135, 155, 163, 169, 228, 230, 237, 238, 240, *243, 245*, 253, 324, 364
Libet, B., 93, *111*
Lickel, B., 85, *88*
Lieberman, M.D., 57, 58, 59, 66, *69*
Lindsey, S., 92, *112*, 276, *293*
Linnenbrink, L., 34, *37*
Linville, P.W., 336, *349*
Lippa, Y., 57, *69*
Little, B.R., 214, 221, *227*
Litwin, G.H., 258, *270*
Lloyd-Jones, T.J., 356, *371*
Locke, E.A., 22, *38*, 87, *89*, 154, *166*, 315, 326, *330*
Locke, K.D., 186, *192*
Loewenstein, G., 352, *372*
Logan, G.D., 108, *111*
Lohr, B.A., 358, *370*
Lombardi, W., 229, 236, *243*
Losier, G.F., 211, *226*
Lucas, D., 61, *69*
Lundqvist, D., 138, *151*
Lynch, J.H., 211, *227*
Lyon, D., 42, *52, 53, 54*

Mackie, D.M., 321, *328*
Macrae, C.M., 238, *244*
Madrian, J.C., 337, *350*
Maehr, M.L., 23, 24, 29, *38*
Mahone, C.H., 258, *272*
Main, K.J., 249, *273*
Maner, J.K., 2, 11, 104, 113, 133, 142, 144, *150*, 163, 297
Mankowski, T.A., 186, *190*
Mannetti, L., 200, *208*
Markus, H., 211, *226*
Marsh, R.L., 163, *166*, 230, *244*
Martens, A., 42, 48, 50, *52, 53*
Martin, L.L., 100, *112*, 229, 236, 237, *244*, 324, 325, *329, 330*
Martindale, C., 137, *150*
Maslow, A.H., 211, *227*
Mason, R.A., 161, *164*
Mayer, J.D., 189, *192*
Mayr, U., 233, *244*
McArthur, L.Z., 134, *151*
McClelland, D.C., 94, 104, *111*, 305, *311*
McClelland, J.L., 25, 57, *69*
McClure, J.L., 158, *166*

McConahay, J.B., 252, *272*, 274, *292*
McConnell, A.R., 277, *292*
McCoy, S.K., 42, 43, *52*
McDougall, W., 2, *16*
McGhee, D.E., 48, *53*, 256, *272, 303, 311*
McGinnies, E., 114, *128*
McGregor, H., 42, 44, *53*
McGregor, H.A., 31, *37*
McGregor, I., 214, 221, *227*
McKoon, G., 156, 159, *166*
McLeod, P., 358, *371*
McNaughton, B.L., 94, *111*
Mead, G.H., 6, *16*
Meehl, P.E., 263, *273*
Meissner, C.A., 356, 357, *371*
Melcher, J., 356, 357, *371*
Mellott, D.S., 282, *293*
Meltzoff, A.N., 160, *165, 166*
Mendes, W.B., 85, *88*, 168, *189*
Metcalfe, J., 93, 106, 107, 108, *111*
Michotte, A., 157, *166*
Middleton, M.J., 28, 31, *38*
Midgley, C., 28, 31, *38*
Mikulincer, M., 42, 43, 44, *53, 54*
Miller, C.T., 270, *272*
Miller, N.E., 239, *243*
Milne, A.B., 238, *244*
Mineka, S., 136, 138, 141, 142, 144, *151*
Miner, A.G., 318, *330*
Mitchell, M., 35, *38*
Monteith, M.J., 116, *129*, 254, 258, *271, 272*, 278, 280, *291, 292*
Moonen, A., 60, *70*
Morf, C.C., 333, 334, 335, 337, 338, 339, *349, 350*
Morris, R.J., 337, *350*
Moskowitz, D.S., 50, *54*, 92, *110*, 113, 119, *129*, 134, *151*, 154, 156, *166, 167*, 228, *243*
Mowrer, O.H., 239, *243*
Moylan, S.J., 189, *192*
Muchinsky, P.M., 315, *329*
Mueller, A., 136, *151*
Mueller, C.W., 305, *311*
Mullen, B., 139, *151*
Muraven, M., 47, *54*, 60, *68*, 269, *272*, 326, *330*
Mussweiler, T., 105, *111, 112*
Myers, J.L., 161, *164*

Nadasdy, Z., 157, *166*
Narayan, S., 135, *152*
Neely, J.H., 231, 235, *244*

Neubauer, R.M., 196, *208*
Neuberg, S.L., 2, 7, 11, 104, 113, 133, 134, 135, 136, 147, *149, 150, 151,* 163, 169, 298, 317, 321, 368
Neumann, R., 101, 102, 103, *111*
Newman, L.S., 156, *167,* 238, *244*
Newsom, J.T., 134, *151*
Nezlek, J., 297, *311,* 340, *349*
Nicholas, J.P., 315, *331*
Nicholls, J.G., 23, *38,* 81, *89*
Nisbett, R., 4, *16*
Nissen, M.J., 322, *330*
Noble, C.S., 318, *329*
Norman, D.A., 96, *101,* 134, *151*
Norrander, B., 50, *54*
Novacek, J., 337, *349*
Nurius, P., 211, *226*
Nuss, C.K., 295, *310*
Nuttin, J., 154, *166*

Obrist, P.A., 71, 76, *89*
Ohlsson, S., 356, *372*
Öhman, A., 136, 138, 141, 142, 144, *151*
Olson, M.A., 60, 65, *68, 277, 292,* 338
Osicki, M.A., 207, *209*

Papillo, J.F., 76, *89*
Paradise, A.W., 213, 218, 219, 223, *226*
Park, B., 136, 139, *150,* 277, *293*
Park, J., 320, *330*
Parrott, W.G., 170, *192*
Partch, J., 136, *149*
Patane, M.J., 76, *89*
Patterson, R.D., 230, *245*
Patton, G.K., 316, *329*
Pearl, D.K., 93, *111*
Perls, F., 214, 215, *227*
Pervin, L.A., 154, *167*
Petty, R.E., 101, 103, *112,* 147, *151,* 185, 187, 192, 321, *328*
Phillips, S., 203, 294, *311*
Piasecki, R., 212, 221, *226*
Pickett, C.L., 295, *310*
Pierro, A., 200, *208*
Pimpalapure, D., 78, *89*
Pintrich, P.R., 24, 28, 31, *31, 38, 39,* 325, *330*
Pittman, T.S., 6, *16,* 29, 305, *311*
Plant, E.A., 249, 250, 251, 252, 253, 254, 255, 256, 257, 258, 259, 260, 261, 263, 265, 269, *271, 272,* 274, *293*
Plutchik, R., 135, 136, *151, 152*
Polivy, J., 346, *348*

Posner, M.I., 56, *69,* 197, *209,* 323, *330*
Postman, L., 114, *128*
Pratto, F., 138, 145, *151, 152*
Prifitera, A., 334, *349*
Pyszczynski, T., 2, 5, 9, *16,* 40, 42, 43, 44, 45, 46, 47, 48, 49, 50, *51, 52, 53, 54,* 113, 253, *273,* 299, 302, *310, 311,* 361, 362

Quanty, M.B., 239, *243*
Quillian, M.R., 94, *109*
Quinn, J.M., 2, 3, 8, 9, 10, 11, 32, 55, 57, 66, *69, 70,* 86, *89,* 92, 96, 113, 241, 256, 268, 298, 303, 357, 362, 383

Radloff, C.E., 215, *227*
Raskin, R., 334, 337, 343, *349, 350*
Ratcliff, R., 156, 159, *166*
Reason, J., 61, *69*
Reed, N., 358, *371*
Reed, S.K., 197, *209*
Reich, A., 333, *350*
Reichle, E.D., 354, *372*
Reis, H.T., 340, *349*
Renninger, K.A., 32, *38*
Rensink, R.A., 134, *151*
Rhodewalt, F., 2, 14, 194, 211, 217, 332, 333, 334, 335, 336, 337, 338, 339, 340, 341, 342, 343, 344, 345, 346, 347, 348, *349, 350,* 365
Rholes, W.S., 236, *243*
Richardson, R., 297, *313*
Richeson, J.A., 269, *273*
Richter, M., 79, 81, *88*
Rigby, S., 211, *227*
Rivis, A.J., 155, *167*
Rizzolatti, G., 106, *112*
Robinson, M.D., 317, *330*
Rodin, G.C., 211, *227*
Rodin, J., 298, *311*
Rogers, C.R., 211, *227*
Roney, C.R., 258, *272*
Rosenberg, M., *227,* 338
Rosenblatt, A., 42, *52, 53, 54*
Rosenthal, R., 283, 287, *293*
Rosnow, R.L., 283, *293*
Ross, L., 4, *16*
Ross, M., 182, *192*
Roth, M., 106, *112*
Rothgerber, H., 139, *151*
Roy, S.A., 249, *273*
Rubin, D.B., 283, *293*
Rucker, D.D., 231, *328*
Rudman, L.A., 274, 282, *293*

Ruiz, J., 339, *350*
Russell, C.J., 318, *328*
Russon, A.E., 157, *165*
Rusting, C., 176, 182, 186, *192*
Ryan, R.M., 21, *36*, 154, *165*, 211, 212, 213, 216, 217, 218, *226*, *227*, 334, *349*
Ryff, C., 213, 223, *227*

Sackett, P.R., 274, *293*
Sadalla, E.K., 136, 142, *150*
Sailor, S., 202, 203, *209*
Salovey, P., 189, *192*
Sande, G.N., 215, *227*
Sanitioso, R., 278, *291*
Sansone, C., 21, 23, 25, 32, *38*
Sasaki, I., 196, *209*
Schaal, B., 119, *129*
Schacter, S., 186, *192*
Schaller, M., 2, 11, 104, 113, 133, 134, 136, 139, *151*, 163, 296
Schechter, D., 160, *165*
Scheier, M.F., 5, 7, *16*, 26, *36*, 56, 65, *68*, 233, *242*, 253, 258, 263, *271*, 325, *328*, 352, *371*
Scherer, K.R., 144, *152*, 358, *370*
Schiefele, U., 32, *39*
Schimel, J., 42, 43, 47, *51*, *52*, *53*, *54*
Schmeichel, B., 300, *312*
Schmitt, D.P., 142, *148*
Schneider, D.J., 237, *245*
Schneider, W., 323, *330*
Schoenfeld, N., 80, *88*
Schooler, J.W., 2, 15, 21, 32, 59, 67, *69*, 92, 127, 241, 268, 352, 354, 355, 356, 357, 358, 359, 360, 361, 362, 363, 364, 365, 366, 367, 368, 369, 370, *371*
Schooler, T.Y., 95, *112*, 276, *293*
Schuller, G., 196, *208*
Schwartz, J.L.K., 48, *53*, 256, 272, 277, 282, *292*, *293*, 303, *311*
Schwarz, N., 105, *112*, 170, 173, *190*, *192*, 320, 321, *328*, *330*
Scott, J.P., 135, 136, *152*
Sears, R.R., 239, *243*
Sedikides, C., 170, 171, 173, 184, 185, 187, 189, *192*
Seligman, M.E., 298, *309*
Senko, C.M., 26, *39*
Seta, C.E., 79, *89*
Seta, J.J., 79, *89*
Shackelford, T.K., 142, *152*
Shah, J.Y., 64, *69*, 113, *129*, 155, *166*, *167*, 233, 245

Shallice, T., 96, *111*
Shapiro, D., 76, *89*
Shaw, L.L., 77, *89*
Sheeran, P., 155, *167*
Sheldon, K.M., 211, 212, 213, 215, 216, 227
Shelton, J.N., 249, 269, *273*
Shepard, J.W., 142, *152*
Shoda, Y., 215, *227*
Shore, W.J., 299, *313*
Sidanius, J., 145, *152*
Sieck, W.R., 357, *372*
Simmel, M., 157, *166*
Simon, L., 42, 46, 47, *51*, *52*, *53*, *54*
Simpson, J.A., 138, 139, 142, 145, *149*, *152*
Sinclair, L., 119, *129*, 274, *293*
Singer, R.D., 171, *190*
Sloman, S.A., 61, *69*, 93, 108, *112*
Smith, C., 139, *151*
Smith, E.R., 59, *69*, 94, 108, *112*
Smith, L., 296, 306, *311*
Smith, S.M., 185, 187, *192*
Smith, T.W., 77, 86, *89*, 339, *350*
Smolensky, P., 57, *70*
Snyder, C.R.R., 56, *69*, 323, *330*
Snyder, M., 252, *294*
Solarz, A.K., 103, *112*
Solomon, S., 2, 9, *16*, 40, 42, 43, 44, 45, 46, 47, 48, *51*, *52*, *53*, *54*, 113, 299, *310*, *311*
Sommer, K.L., 294, 297, 299, 301, *311*, *312*, *313*, 358, *371*
Son Hing, L.S., 2, 13, 14, 113, 256, 274, 277, 278, 284, *291*, *293*, 303, 359, 360
Sorrentino, R.M., 5, *16*, *17*
Sorrow, D., 332, 333, 335, 339, 343, *350*
Spencer, S.J., 2, 10, 11, 32, 44, *53*, 98, 104, 113, 114, 116, 119, *128*, *129*, 135, 161, 229, 256, 268, 303, 338, *348*, 367, 368
Srull, T.K., 228, 229, 236, *242*, *245*
Stadler, M., 201, *209*
Stam, H., 144, *152*
Stamov-Rossnagel, C., 196, 201, *209*
Steele, C.M., 6, *16*, 297, *312*
Stephan, C.W., 250, *273*
Stephan, W.G., 250, *273*
Stepper, S., 100, *112*
Stevens, L.E., 135, *152*
Stewart, J., 2, *16*
Stiller, J., 211, *227*
Stone, J., 278, *293*
Stoner, P., 235, *329*
Strack, F., 2, 8, 10, *11*, 22, 32, 58, 59, 86, 91, 92, 93, 100, 101, 102, 103, 105, 106, *110*, *111*, *112*, 113, 251, 268, 276, 305, 352, 366

Stretton, M., 189, *192*
Stucke, T.S., 294, *312*
Suh, E., 50, *54*
Sun, C.R., 337, 339, *349*
Sutton, S.K., 92, 99, *112*

Tambor, E.S., 301, *311*
Tannock, R., 108, *111*
Taubman Ben-Ari, O., 42, *54*
Tauer, J.M., 25, 28, 34, *37, 38, 39*
Taves, P.A., 361, *371*
Taylor, D., 337, *350*
Taylor, S.E., 134, *149*, 298, *312*
Teasdale, J.D., 298, *309*
Tedeschi, J.T., 305, *312*
Terdal, S.K., 301, *311*
Terry, H., 334, 337, *350*
Tesser, A., 6, 7, 229, *244*, 297, *312*, 324, 325, *330*
Tetlock, P.E., 135, *152*
Therriault, N., 120, *128*
Thompson, J.A., 332, 337, 338, *348*
Thompson, S.C., 298, *312*
Thorndike, E.L., 55, *70*
Thrash, T.M., 24, *37*
Thunberg, M., 102, *110*
Tice, D.M., 60, *68*, 294, 297, 300, 302, *310, 312*, 326, *330*
Tipper, S.P., 136, *152*
Tison, J., 44, *51*
Todd, P.M., 134, 136, *152*
Todorov, A., 156, *167*, 306, *312*
Tolman, E.C., 3, 154, *167*
Tomaka, J., 169, *189*
Tooby, J., 136, *149*
Tragakis, M., 338, 342, 343, *350*
Tranel, D., 105, *109*
Troccoli, B.T., 170, *189*, 266, *371*
Trope, Y., 4, *17*, 57, *69*, 93, *109*, 187, *193*
Trost, M.R., 142, *150*
Tuiten, A., 144, *152*
Tulving, E., 230, *245*
Tversky, A., 105, *112*
Twenge, J.M., 294, 295, 300, 301, 304, 305, 307, 308, *310, 312*

Uleman, J.S., 156, 159, *166, 167*, 307, 308, *310, 312*
Uller, C., 157, *168*

Vaillant, G., 216, *227*
Vallacher, R.R., 58, *70*, 233, *245*
Vallerand, R.J., 211, *226*

van den Bos, K., 44, *54*
Van Honk, J., 144, *152*
Van Knippenberg, A., 60, *70*, 155, *164*
Vance, K.M., 2, 13, 116, 249, 252, *271*
Vance, S.L., 274, *293*
Velten, E., 186, *193*
Vequist, D., 196, *209*
Verplanken, B., 60, 62, *70*, 92, *112*, 155, *164*
Vescio, T.K., 250, *270*
Visser, T.A.W., 135, *149*
Vohs, K.D., 326, *330*
Voils, C.I., 159, *167*, 259, *272*
von Hippel, W., 135, *152*
Vorauer, J.D., 249, *270, 273*

Walker, I., 303, *311*
Wallbott, H.G., 144, *152*
Waller, N.G., 263, *273*
Warburton, W.A., 2, 5, 14, 48, 87, 294, 306, *312, 313*, 333, 360
Wasel, W., 119, *129*
Waters, B., 216, *227*
Watson, D., 252, *273*
Watson, P.J., 337, *350*
Webb, T.L., 155, *167*
Webster, D.M., 144, *150*
Wegner, D.M., 1, *17*, 47, *43*, 58, *70*, 93, *112*, 120, *128*, 233, 237, 238, *245*, 352, 353, 355, *372*
Weiss, H.M., 2, 7, 14, 169, 314, 315, 318, 319, 320, 321, 323, *328, 330, 331*, 365
Wells, G.L., 102, *112*
Welton, K.E., Jr., 197, *209*
Westen, D., 113, *129*
Wheatman, S., 213, *226*
Wheaton, A., 295, 297, *312*
Wheeler, L., 340, *349*
Whitaker, D., 213, *226*
Wicklund, R.A., 230, *245*
Wigfield, A., 33, 35, *39*, 56, 58, *68*
Wilbur, C., 133, *150*
Williams, K.D., 1, 2, 14, 41, 48, *68*, 76, 87, *90*, 211, *227*, 277, *291*, 294, 295, 297, 298, 299, 300, 301, 302, 303, 304, 308, *310, 311, 312, 313*, 333, *349*, 360, 361
Wilson, M., 145, *149*
Wilson, T.D., 92, *112*, 182, 184, *193*, 276, 277, *293*, 356, 363, *372*
Winslow, M.P., 278, *293*
Winter, L., 156, *167*
Witkin, H.A., 200, *209*
Wolfe, C., 114, *129*
Wolters, C.A., 28, *39*

Wood, W., 2, 3, 8, 9, 10, 21, 32, 55, 56, 57, 60, 64, 65, 66, 67, *68, 69, 70,* 86, *89,* 92, 96, *109,* 113, 241, 256, 268, 303, 362
Wortman, C.B., 298, *313*
Wrangham, R., 145, *149, 152*
Wright, E.W., 93, *111*
Wright, R.A., 2, 10, 71, 74, 75, 76, 77, 78, 79, 80, 84, 85, 86, *89, 90*
Wyer, R.S., 228, 229, 236, *242, 245*
Wynne, L.C., 48, *54*

Yohannes, J., 134, *151*
Yonelinas, A.P., 355, *371*
Young, H., 45, 106, *111*

Young, M.J., 316, *328*
Yu, S.L., 28, *39*

Zadro, L., 297, 302, *313*
Zajonc, R.B., 7, *17,* 169, *193*
Zanakos, S., 238, *245*
Zanna, M.P., 2, 10, 13, 44, 49, *53, 54,* 98, 113, *129,* 135, 229, 274, 277, 284, *291, 293,* 303, 338, *348, 371*
Zarate, M.A., 159, *167*
Zeigarnik, B., 230, 236, *245*
Zierk, K.L., 136, *150*
Zuwerink, J.R., 254, *271,* 278, 280, *291, 292*

Subject Index

ability, 73–76, 82, 84–85, 87
acceptance, 301–302, 307
accessibility, 229, 324
  and cultural worldview 49–50
  and death-related thought 46–47
achievement motivation, 23–26, 28
  mediators of, 26–28
  moderators of, 25–26
affect, 41–43
  and conditioning, 171
  control, 182–186
  and information processing, 171–174
  infusion, 170–172
  and goals, 169
  and motivation, 103–104
  and performance, 315–319
  and psychodynamic theory, 171
  as a resource, 187–188
  and self-regulation, 325–327
  and social motivation, 7, 168–169, 171
  and terror management, 47–49
  See also emotions; mood
Affect Infusion Model, 172–173
affective influences
  on negotiation, 174–176
  on requesting, 178–182
  on self-disclosure, 176–177
affiliation goals, 295–298, 301–304, 305,
  307–309
aggression, 239–242, 294, 296, 300, 302–309
anchoring bias, 105
antisocial behaviors, 294–296, 300, 302–305,
  307–309
anxiety-buffer hypothesis, 45–46
appraisals, 73–75
approach/avoidance, 91–93, 98–99, 101–103,
  106–108

associative processing, 57–58
attention, 133, 134, 138, 139, 140, 142–144,
  321–323, 325–327
attitudes, 277–291
authenticity, 12, 362–363
  and awareness, 214–215, 217–218,
  220–225
  behavioral, 214, 216, 218, 220–221, 223,
  225
  and unbiased processing, 215–218, 220,
  223, 225
automaticity, 92, 210–225
  and causal inferences, 156
  and goal inferences, 157
  and goal pursuit, 155
aversive racism, 13, 275–291, 359–360
  and implicit attitudes, 277–289

behavioral schemata, 94–98, 100, 105–108

cardiovascular responses, 76, 85
catharsis, 239–241
cognitive resources, 321–325
competence valuation, 26–27
conformity, 294, 297, 301
conscious attitudes, 275
conscious goal pursuit, 154
conscious vs. unconscious threat, 45–47
consciousness, 351–370
  and non-conscious processes, 359–363
construct accessibility, 228–242
  and catharsis of aggression, 239–241
  and motivation, 232–242
  and person perception, 236–237
  and postsuppressional rebound,
  237–239
control, 295–296, 298–300, 302–309

delay of gratification, 107–108
depression, 204
Dual Component Model of Defense, 45–46

ecological psychology, 133, 135–137, 139, 147
effort, 71–79, 82–84, 86–87. *See also* motivation; social motivation
ego depletion, 326–327
ego involvement, 79–81
emotion regulation, 325–327
emotions, 64–65, 314–328
    mood and perception, 144–147
    See also affect
empathy, 77–79
encoding, 138–140, 144–147
encoding style, 87
    and children, 201
    and culture, 202
    internal vs. external, 194, 198
Encoding Style Questionnaire (ESQ), 199
evolutionary psychology, 135–138, 142–145, 147–148
explicit prejudice, 276
eye movements, 143–144

facial expressions
    and anger, 138, 140–141, 144–147
    and sexual arousal, 145–146
fairness, 323–324
fear, 138, 141, 145–148
frequency estimation, 143–144

gender, 134, 136, 138, 140, 142–146
goal contagion, 11, 160
    and approach responses, 162
    and earning money, 161
    and helping, 162
    and imitation, 160
    and motivation, 161
    and persistent activation, 163
    and perspective taking, 161
goal inhibition, 137, 140–141
goal priming, 13
goal pursuit, 11, 155–156, 213–214, 221–222, 224
goals, 153–164, 229, 324–327
    and achievement, 23–25
    automatic pursuit of, 155–156
    contagion of, 160–161
    evolutionary, 367–368
    and mastery, 9, 24–26, 28–34, 363–364
    and mating, 133, 136–146, 148

and meaningful existence, 295, 296, 298–300, 302–305, 307–309
    multiple, 28–31
    and performance, 9, 24–26, 28–31
    and self-protection, 133, 136–141, 144–148
    and social cognition, 134, 135
    thirst, 367
    See also motivation; social motivation; habit
goal-setting theory, 326

habit, 9, 56–67, 92, 95
    and associative processing, 56–58
    and automaticity, 62–63
    and the self, 63–67
homeostatic dysregulations, 96, 98

identity, 79–81
implicit affect, 48
Implicit Association Test, 282
implicit biases, 291 implicit cognition, 195
implicit prejudice, 13, 277
implicit vs. explicit, 300, 303–307, 309
impulsivity, 94–95, 97–98, 104–105
inhibition, 230
intentions, 58–62, 97, 105, 107
    and symbolic processing, 58–60
    See also habit; motivation; social motivation
interest, 29, 32
    continuing, 33–36
    and enjoyment, 32
    individual, 32
    situational, 32
interracial relations, 256–270
    and anxiety, 257
    and outcome expectancies, 256–257
    and self-regulation, 261–269

job satisfaction, 314–316, 319–320, 327
justice, 323–324

life satisfaction, 212–213, 218–220, 223

mastery, 28–31
matching hypothesis, 25, 30–31
mating goals, 138–139
mediator variables, 22–23, 26–27
memory, 138–142, 144
meta-awareness, 351–370
meta-consciousness, 351–370
    temporal dissociations of, 354–356
    translation dissociations of, 356–360

mind wandering, 354–355, 369
mood, 82–84, 314, 316–322
  and cardiovascular response, 82–84
  See also affect; emotions
mood-behavior model, 82
mortality salience, 41–43
motivation, 2–5, 294–309
  and accessibility, 229–232
  and adjustment, 210–225
  and affiliation/belonging, 295–298,
    301–304, 305, 307–309
  and conflict, 302–309
  conscious vs. unconscious, 91–108,
    113–126, 127
  and control, 295–296, 298–300, 302–309
  difficulty law of, 72, 81
  intensity, 72–73
  intrinsic, 21–22, 325
  and meaningful existence, 295–296,
    298–300, 302–305, 307–309
  potential, 72, 75, 78
  and prejudice, 249–270
  and self-esteem, 295–298, 301–305, 336
  and work, 315, 325
motivational intensity theory, 72–73
motivational orientation, 92, 96–99, 101–104,
  106, 108
  and affect, 103–104

narcissism, 14, 334–336, 365
  dynamic self-regulation model of, 334
  and self-esteem regulation, 336–339
  and social interaction, 339–342
need for structure, 134–135, 147
need to belong, 14. *See also* affiliation goals
neuroticism, 204

ostracism, 87, 294–309, 360–361
  and aggression, 294, 296, 300, 302–309
  and belonging, 296–297
  and control, 298–299
  and evolution, 296
  and meaningful existence, 299–301
  and psychopathy, 296
  and self-esteem, 297
  and well-being, 296–298
  Williams's needs-threat model of, 308
outgroups
  and ethnicity, 134, 136, 138–140, 144–147

performance, 314–328
performance goals, 28–31

person perception, 236–237
personal identity, 79, 81
personality, 334–348
personnel selection, 276
physical attractiveness, 133–134, 136,
  138–146
physical threat, 136, 138–141, 144–148
postsuppressional rebound, 237
power, 295, 297–298, 305–306, 308–309
prejudice, 274–291, 303
  and internal vs. external motivations,
    252–256
  nonconscious, 275
  See also racism
priming, 63
propositional representation, 96, 104, 106
prosocial behaviors, 294–295, 297, 300–302,
  304–305, 307, 309

race, 133, 146
racism, 257–261, 359–360, 364
Reflective Impulsive Model (RIM), 10,
  93–108
relational orientation, 214, 218, 220, 223–225
requests, 178–180
risk taking, 42
rumination, 324–327

schemata, 197
school shootings, 294, 300, 306–308
scripts, 62–63
self-concept, 65–66, 211, 215
self-control, 107
self-determination, 211–213, 221, 223
self-disclosure, 176–178
self-efficacy, 298, 304
self-esteem, 212, 214, 216, 218–221, 223–224
  and dominance theory, 333
  implicit, 338
  and instability, 339
  optimal, 221, 223–224
  and regulation, 336
  and sociometer theory, 333
self-regulation, 62, 63–64, 322, 325–327,
  363–367
sex, 367–368
sexual restrictedness, 143–145
social attraction, 295, 297, 300–301, 303, 307
social cognition, 134–135
social compensation, 294, 297, 301
social evaluation, 77–78, 84
social exclusion, 294–295. *See also* ostracism

social interaction, 339–347
social motivation, 5–6
    and affect, 7, 11
    conscious vs. unconscious, 8–9, 13
    history of, 2–3
    intrinsic vs. extrinsic, 21–22
    and ostracism, 295–296
    and work, 314–328
    See also motivation
sociometer theory, 301
stereotype activation, 114–116, 279
stereotype application, 122
stereotype inhibition, 116–119
subliminal perception, 201
subliminal priming, 119–121
    and persuasion, 123–125

task complexity, 323–324
task involvement, 26–27

Terror Management Theory, 9, 41–45, 302, 361–362
    and affect, 47–49
    and attachment, 43–44
    and the body, 43
    gender differences, 51–52
    and ingroup bias, 42
    and health-related behavior, 45–46
thought suppression, 46–47, 237
threat, 45–46
true-self, 212–213

verbal overshadowing, 356–357

well-being, 212–214, 216, 218, 220, 223–224
worldview defense, 49–50

Zeigarnik effect, 230
zoning-out, 354–355, 369

Continued from page iii

SSSP 3. SOCIAL INFLUENCE: DIRECT AND INDIRECT PROCESSES (Edited by Joseph P. Forgas and Kipling D. Williams). Contributors: Robert Cialdini (*Arizona*), Eric Knowles et al. (*Arkansas*), Bibb Latane (*Florida Atlantic*), Marty Bourgeois (*Wyoming*), Mark Schaller (*UBC*), Ap Dijksterhuis (*Nijmegen*), James Tedeschi (*SUNY*), Richard Petty (*Ohio State*), Joseph P. Forgas (*UNSW*), Herbert Bless (*Mannheim*), Fritz Strack (*Wurzburg*), Sik Hung Ng (*Hong Kong*), Thomas Mussweiler (*Wurzburg*), Kip Williams (*Macquarie*), Chuck Stangor and Gretchen Sechrist (*Maryland*), John Jost (*Stanford*), Debbie Terry and Michael Hogg (*Queensland*), Stephen Harkins (*Northeastern*), Barbara David and John Turner (*Australian National*), Robin Martin (*Queensland*), Miles Hewstone (*Cardiff*), Russell Spears and Tom Postmes (*Amsterdam*), Martin Lea (*Manchester*), Susan Watt (*Amsterdam*). Psychology Press, New York, 2002; ISBN 1-84169-038-4 (hardback), 1-84169-039-2 (paperback).

SSSP 4. THE SOCIAL SELF: COGNITIVE, INTERPERSONAL AND INTERGROUP PERSPECTIVES (Edited by Joseph P. Forgas, Kipling D. Williams, and William von Hippel). Contributors: Herbert Bless (*Mannheim*), Marilynn Brewer (*OSU*), Tanya Chartrand (*OSU*), Klaus Fiedler (*Heidelberg*), Joseph P. Forgas (*UNSW*), David C. Funder (*UC Riverside*), Adam Galinsky (*Utah*), Martie G. Haselton (*UCLA*), David Buss (*Texas*), Lucy Johnston (*Canterbury, NZ*), Arie Kruglanski (*Maryland*), Matt Lieberman (*UCLA*), Phil Shaver (*UC Davis*), Mario Mikulincer (*Bar-Ilan*), Diederik Stapel (*Groningen*), Jerry Suls (*Iowa*), Bill von Hippel (*UNSW*), Kip Williams (*Macquarie*), Michael Zárate (*Texas*). Psychology Press, New York, 2002; ISBN 1-84169-062-7 (hardback).

SSSP 5. SOCIAL JUDGMENTS: IMPLICIT AND EXPLICIT PROCESSES (Edited by Joseph P. Forgas, Kipling D. Williams, and William von Hippel). Contributors: Joseph P. Forgas (*UNSW*), Kipling D. Williams (*Macquarie*), William von Hippel (*UNSW*), Martie G. Haselton (*UCLA*), David M. Buss (*Texas*), Matthew D. Lieberman (*UCLA*), Michael A. Zárate (*Texas*), Colby J. Stoever (*Texas*), Phillip R. Shaver (*UC Davis*), Mario Mikulincer (*Bar-Ilan*), David C. Funder (*UC Riverside*), Arie W. Kruglanski (*Maryland*), Woo Young Chun (*Maryland*), Hans Peter Erb (*Halle*), Antonio Pierro (*Rome*), Lucia Mannetti (*Rome*), Scott Spiegel (*Columbia*), Klaus Fiedler (*Heidelberg*), Peter Freytag (*Heidelberg*), Herbert Bless (*Mannheim*), Norbert Schwarz (*Michigan*), Michaela Wänke (*Basel*), Rebekah East (*UNSW*), Diederik A. Stapel (*Groningen*), Patrick Vargas (*Illinois*), Denise Sekaquaptewa (*Michigan*), Jerry Suls (*Iowa*), Réne Martin (*Iowa*), Ladd Wheeler (*Macquarie*), Tanya Chartrand (*Ohio State*), Valerie E. Jefferis (*Ohio State*), John L. McClure (*Wellington*), Robbie M. Sutton (*Keele*), Denis J. Hilton (*Toulouse*), Trevor I. Case (*Macquarie*), Cassandra L. Govan (*Macquarie*), Adam D. Galinsky (*Northwestern*), Paul V. Martorana (*Northwestern*), Gillian Ku (*Northwestern*), Lucy Johnston (*Canterbury*), Lynden Miles (*Canterbury*), Marilynn B. Brewer (*Ohio State*). Cambridge University Press, New York, 2003; ISBN 0-521-82248-3 (hardback).